CAPETIAN FRANCE
987–1328

Capetian France
987–1328

ELIZABETH M. HALLAM

LONGMAN
London and New York

Longman Group Limited
Longman House
Burnt Mill, Harlow, Essex, UK

*Published in the United States of America
by Longman Inc., New York*

© Longman Group Limited 1980

First published 1980

British Library Cataloguing in Publication Data

Hallam, Elizabeth M
Capetian France, 987–1328.
1. France – History – Capetians, 987–1328
I. Title
944'.021   DC82   80–41087
ISBN 0-582-48909-1

Set in 11/12pt V-I-P Garamond No. 3
Printed and bound in Great Britain by
William Clowes (Beccles) Limited
Beccles and London

To my parents

Contents

List of maps, figures and tables x
Preface xii
Acknowledgements xiii
List of abbreviations xiv

CHAPTER ONE
French Society in the Early Capetian Period

1.1 Introduction 1
  1.1.1 The origins of West Francia.
1.2 The French Economy and Society 6
  1.2.1 A stagnant economy? 1.2.2 Nobles and knights. 1.2.3 Lords and peasants.
1.3 The Structure of Power 13
  1.3.1 The fragmentation of central authority: the principalities, counties and castellanies. 1.3.2 The bonds of society: vassalage and the fief and bannal lordship. 1.3.3 Church and society.
1.4 Political Developments of the Tenth Century 20
  1.4.1 987: the beginning of a new era?
Notes and further reading 24

CHAPTER TWO
Politics and Society: A Regional View

2.1 Introduction 27
  2.1.1 Local societies in the French kingdom. 2.1.2 The princes in eleventh- and twelfth-century France.
2.2 Politics and Society: Some Case Studies 30
  2.2.1 The disintegration of the duchy of Burgundy. 2.2.2 A local society in disintegration: the Mâconnais. 2.2.3 The duchy of Normandy. 2.2.4 The lands of Blois-Champagne: a problem for the Capetians.

2.3 Principalities in Northern and Western France: An Outline 50
  2.3.1 Flanders, Picardy, Brittany. 2.3.2 Greater Anjou and the duchy of Aquitaine.
2.4 The South 54
  2.4.1 Southern society. 2.4.2 Gascony, Toulouse and Barcelona.
Notes and further reading 62

CHAPTER THREE
The Early Capetians, 987–1108

3.1 Introduction 64
  3.1.1 The early Capetians: mere territorial princes?
3.2 The Kings and their Reigns 67
  3.2.1 Hugh Capet, 987–996. 3.2.2 Robert II 'the Pious', 996–1031. 3.2.3 Henry I, 1031–60. 3.2.4 Philip I, 1060–1108.
3.3 The Basis of Royal Power 78
  3.3.1 The royal domain. 3.3.2 The ecclesiastical domain. 3.3.3 The royal principality. 3.3.4 Royal government and the royal entourage. 3.3.5 The king and the territorial princes. 3.3.6 Royal defence.
3.4 The Kings and the Church 99
  3.4.1 The kings, the episcopate and the Cluniacs, 987–1049. 3.4.2 The monarchy and the papal reforms 1049–1108.
Notes and further reading 108

CHAPTER FOUR
The Revival of Royal Power, 1108–1226

4.1 Introduction 111
  4.1.1 The Capetian revival: an inevitable development?
4.2 The Kings and their Reigns 114
  4.2.1 Louis VI, 1108–37. 4.2.2 Louis VII, 1137–80. 4.2.3 Philip II 'Augustus', 1180–1223. 4.2.4 Louis VIII, 1223–26.
4.3 French Society, 1108–1226 137
  4.3.1 Social and economic changes. 4.3.2 Urban and rural communities: the growth of Paris. 4.3.3 Orthodox and heretical religious movements. 4.3.4 Learning, literature and the schools in France.
4.4 The Rise of the French Monarchy, 1108–1226 156
  4.4.1 The consolidation of Capetian power: the royal principality and the domain to c. 1200. 4.4.2 The royal household and royal administration. 4.4.3 Communal privileges and royal defence. 4.4.4 Royal resources. 4.4.5 The king in the kingdom. 4.4.6 The image of monarchy. 4.4.7 The Plantagenet lands, 1150–99. 4.4.8 The conquest of Normandy, Anjou and Poitou. 4.4.9 The Capetians and the Languedoc.
4.5 The Kings and the Church 190
  4.5.1 Louis VI, Louis VII and the church. 4.5.2 Philip Augustus, Louis VIII and the church.
Notes and further reading 200

CHAPTER FIVE
Louis IX: The Consolidation of Royal Power, 1226–70

5.1 Introduction 204
    5.1.1 Louis IX: holy kingship and political power.
5.2 The Reign of Louis IX 207
    5.2.1 Blanche of Castile and the early years of Louis's reign, 1226–44.
    5.2.2 Louis IX, the crusader king, 1244–70.
5.3 French Society in the Thirteenth Century 224
    5.3.1 French society, 1226–70: the example of Paris and the Ile de France.
    5.3.2 Religion and learning: the friars, the universities and the inquisition.
5.4 Louis IX and the Church 230
    5.4.1 The piety of Louis IX. 5.4.2 Louis IX, the French church and the papacy.
5.5 The Consolidation of Royal Power 239
    5.5.1 Royal government and administration. 5.5.2 The royal domain and the apanages to 1328. 5.5.3 Royal power in Normandy and the Languedoc. 5.5.4 Louis IX and Alfonso of Poitiers. 5.5.5 The image of monarchy and changing views of the kingdom. 5.5.6 Criticisms of the king. 5.5.7 The king and the principalities: the problem of Gascony. 5.5.8 The achievements of Louis IX.
Notes and further reading 270

CHAPTER SIX
The Last Capetians, 1270–1328: The Apogee of Royal Power

6.1 Introduction 273
    6.1.1 Royal power under the last Capetians.
6.2 The Kings and their Reigns 275
    6.2.1 Philip III, 1270–85. 6.2.2 Philip IV 'the Fair', 1285–1314. 6.2.3 Louis X (1314–16), Philip V (1316–22) and Charles IV (1322–28).
6.3 The French Economy and Society 285
    6.3.1 Economic and social conditions: the first signs of crisis. 6.3.2 The population of France in 1328: a problem in quantitative history. 6.3.3 Rural life. A village community: Montaillou. 6.3.4 The king and the social order.
6.4 The Nature of Royal Power 291
    6.4.1 Royal government and administration. 6.4.2 Factions and policy changes: the royal entourage. 6.4.3 Land and rights: the extension of royal power. 6.4.4 General and regional assemblies. 6.4.5 The crisis of 1314 and the charters of 1315. 6.4.6 Kingdom and principalities in fourteenth-century France. 6.4.7 The image of monarchy and the reality of royal power.
6.5 The Kings and the Church 310
    6.5.1 The kings and the French church, 1270–1328. 6.5.2 The canonisation and the cult of Louis IX. 6.5.3 Philip IV and Boniface VIII – a crisis in church–state relationships. 6.5.4 The suppression of the Templars. 6.5.5 The Avignon papacy.
Notes and further reading 321

CONTENTS

CHAPTER SEVEN
Conclusion

7.1 The succession and the Hundred Years War 325
7.2 The rise of the Capetians: some general perspectives 326
7.3 The French kingdom and European society 328

Appendix I: Why the 'Capetians'? 330
Appendix II: A note on the sources for Capetian history 332
Appendix III: Select bibliography 334

Index 342

List of maps, figures and tables

Chapter 1

Map 1.1 Ecclesiastical provinces in medieval France 2
    1.2 The Frankish expansion, 356–795 3
    1.3 The Carolingian Empire 4
    1.4 France in the mid-eleventh century 5

Chapter 2

Map 2.1 The duchy of Burgundy in the mid-eleventh century 31
    2.2 Normandy in the eleventh and twelfth centuries 35
    2.3 The lands of Blois-Champagne in the later twelfth century 44
    2.4 The principalities of the south in the mid-eleventh century 55
    2.5 The Toulouse principality in the eleventh century 60
Fig. 2.1 Outline genealogy of the Anglo-Norman royal house 41
    2.2 Outline genealogy of the counts of Champagne 46

Chapter 3

Map 3.1 The royal principality in the mid-eleventh century 79
    3.2 Henry I's secular domain 80
    3.3 Henry I's ecclesiastical domain 81

Chapter 4

Map 4.1 The lands of Henry II and Louis VII in the 1170s 124
    4.2 The royal lands in 1223 134
    4.3 Paris in the reign of Philip Augustus 144
Fig. 4.1 Outline genealogy of the Capetian kings, 987–1226 113

Chapter 5

Map 5.1 Louis IX's first crusade, 1249–50 217
    5.2 France in 1259 220
    5.3 Legal customs in northern France in the thirteenth century 265

Fig. 5.1 Outline genealogy of the Capetian kings, 1226–1328 249

Table 5.1 The almsgiving of Louis IX, 2 June–15 August, 1256 .. 233

5.2 Summary of the receipts and expenses of Louis VIII and Louis IX, 1226 and 1238 241

5.3 Estimated receipts from the *bailliages* and *prévôtés*, 1238 and 1248 242

Chapter 6

Map 6.1 France in 1328 274

Table 6.1 Summary of royal receipts and expenses, 1286–93 292

6.2 Household expenses of the king, 1286–92 293

6.3 Royal expenses, 1296–1301 293

6.4 Royal receipts and expenses, 1322–29 293

Preface

Professor Robert Fawtier's book, *The Capetian Kings of France, Monarchy and Nation, 987–1328,* has been the standard text on its period since the 1940s. It is in many ways a valuable work, the product of a career devoted to research and teaching. Since it was written, however, many of the matters it discussed have been the subject of detailed research, and new problems and new perspectives have emerged. For this reason alone, a fresh account of the period is needed. Moreover the arrangement of Fawtier's book in terms of general themes, while producing many valuable insights, disguises the changes in French politics and society which took place in the period 987–1328. This account of the Capetians and their kingdom is by contrast divided into chronological periods, with divisions in 1108, 1226 and 1270. Within these still broad sweeps of time a thematic approach has been adopted; a brief introductory section is followed by a discussion of each king and a narrative of political events, and in the later chapters a brief analysis of social and economic conditions. Against this background is set the central part of each chapter, a discussion of royal authority, government and administration and of the relationship of the kings and the church. A whole chapter is devoted to the French principalities, whose importance in the history of France in this period is sometimes underestimated. Nevertheless the monarchy remains at the centre of the story. It has not been possible to treat all the themes and problems with an equal degree of detail; and the chapter on the last Capetians is not quite as full as some of the others, largely because there is already far more in English on France from 1270 to 1328 than on earlier periods. It is hoped that this account will stimulate general interest in Capetian France, and will also encourage further detailed research into the many areas which still remain to be investigated.

Acknowledgements

A number of generous friends have offered advice on earlier drafts of this book. I am particularly indebted to Professor Christopher Brooke, whose comments have been invaluable. Dr David Bates and Dr David Carpenter have also made many useful and helpful suggestions. The text has been typed by Mrs Margaret Hamblin, who has devoted much time and trouble to it.

Writing a book of this scope in my 'spare' time has – predictably – not proved a very restful activity, but my family and friends have shown a commendable patience and tolerance. I would like to thank a number of my colleagues at the Public Record Office, and particularly Dr Roy Hunnisett and Mrs Alexandra Nicol, for their encouragement. My husband, Terence Smith, has borne the brunt of my literary efforts and I am very grateful to him. My interest in medieval France was first awakened by my parents, and the dedication of this book to them is in thanks for this, and for all their subsequent help and support.

List of abbreviations

Bibl. E C = *Bibliothèque de l'École des Chartes.*
F[awtier], *Capetian Kings* = R. Fawtier, *The Capetian Kings of France, Monarchy and Nation, 987–1328*, trans. L. Butler and R. J. Adams (London, 1960).
JMH = *Journal of Medieval History.*
HIFr. = ed. R. Fawtier, F. Lot *et. al.*, *Histoire des Institutions Françaises au Moyen Age*, 3 vols (Paris, 1957–62).
RHF = *Recueil des historiens des Gaulles et de la France*, 24 vols (Paris, 1737–1904).
RS = *Rolls Series*, 245 vols (London, 1858–91).
PL = ed. J.-P. Migne, *Patrologiae Latinae . . . Cursus Completus*, 221 vols (Paris, 1844–55).

CHAPTER ONE

French Society in the Early Capetian Period

1.1 INTRODUCTION

1.1.1 The origins of West Francia

From the later Middle Ages onwards the idea that France had 'natural limits' was a widely held one. The identification of the French kingdom with Roman Gaul, with its boundaries formed by the Alps, the Rhine and the Pyrenees, was used to justify the aggressive expansionist policies of French rulers. Yet this view had almost no foundations. The kingdom of France, far from developing as a natural political and geographical unit, evolved gradually during the early Middle Ages from the decaying Roman empire and the Frankish kingdoms which arose in its place and reached their apogee in the Carolingian empire. The lands which were to make up France showed a great diversity in their languages, races and cultures, a series of contrasts which have continued to influence French history, and which are further emphasised by its great geographical diversity. The northern and central regions of France are in a temperate zone, while the south enjoys a mediterranean climate, but there are further variations of climate and vegetation connected with the existence of the great central mountainous region, the Massif Central, the Alps and the Pyrenees. The valleys of the great rivers, the Loire, the Seine, the Rhône are fertile and provide good channels of communication. They were settled early, but the settlements were separated by great tracts of forest, marsh and heath.

Before the Romans came these lands were inhabited by the Gauls, living in villages organised into tribal groups; these the Romans described as *pagi*, and their larger groupings still, as *civitates*. Mediterranean Gaul had a well-developed city life and was a prosperous region, and it was conquered by the Romans as early as 121 B.C. As the province of Narbonne it became an important part of the Roman empire. Expansion into northern Gaul came rather later; Caesar conquered it in 58–51 B.C and it was divided between the provinces of Aquitaine, Lyon, and Belgica. Existing *pagi* and *civitates* were often taken over by the Romans as the basis of their local government system, and Gallic and then Roman cities remained as regional centres and capitals into the Middle Ages and

1

beyond. One important reason for this continuity of settlement was the adoption of these cities as centres of bishoprics by the Christian church, and although some were lost and others gained in succeeding centuries, the ecclesiastical provinces which eventually emerged in the tenth century and lasted virtually unchanged

Map 1.1   Ecclesiastical provinces in medieval France

until the French Revolution bore a very close correspondence with the divisions of Gaul into *civitates*, and the Roman administrative organisation.

Gallic and Roman settlements had been denser in the south, and thus more archiepiscopal and episcopal sees were found there. The more isolated seats of bishops in the north often shrank greatly in size and were heavily fortified; some became the centres of important lordships. The ecclesiastical geography of France remained to some extent at variance with its political geography, and tensions sometimes arose as a result (e.g. compare Maps 1.1 and 1.4).

The barbarian invasions of the Roman empire brought a number of peoples

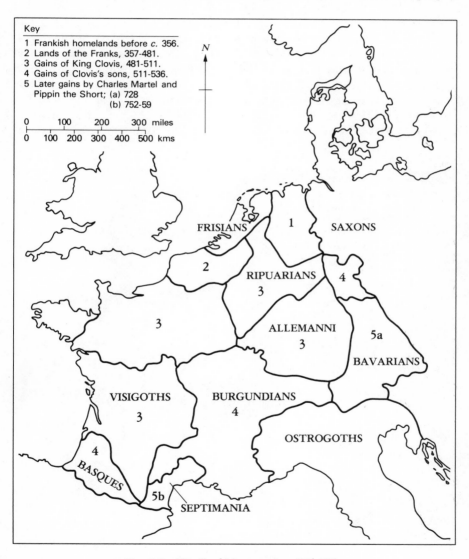

Key

1 Frankish homelands before *c.* 356.
2 Lands of the Franks, 357-481.
3 Gains of King Clovis, 481-511.
4 Gains of Clovis's sons, 511-536.
5 Later gains by Charles Martel and
  Pippin the Short; (a) 728
                    (b) 752-59

Map 1.2 The Frankish expansion, 356–795

into Gaul who superimposed their own racial stocks, languages and cultures upon the existing inhabitants in varying degrees. The Celtic-speaking Bretons moved into Brittany from western Britain; the Burgundians settled in south-eastern Gaul, the Visigoths in its south-west, although leaving room for a Basque expansion in this region as well. Most striking of all was the expansion of the Franks who, after leaving their homeland near Mainz in the middle of the fourth century, first settled in the low countries and then, under King Clovis and his sons, overran the whole of Gaul.

The western parts of the possessions of these Merovingian kings were known as Neustria. The Carolingian kings who succeeded the Merovingians expanded Francia, the lands of the Franks, to their maximum extent (Map 1.3), but in accordance with custom the successors of the Emperor Charlemagne (died 814) made several attempts to partition it. The one which prefigured future political developments most closely was effected by the Treaty of Verdun in 843, which produced three broad divisions, east Francia, west Francia and the Middle Kingdom or Lotharingia, which soon disintegrated into a series of smaller states. East Francia, which broadly coincided with the lands which the Roman writer Tacitus called Germania, was to develop into the kingdom later known as

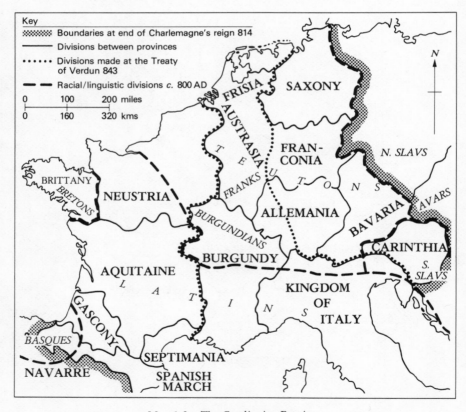

Map 1.3 The Carolingian Empire

Germany, its inhabitants speaking the German language, although the name Germania did not have any very precise meaning in the ninth and tenth centuries. Indeed the name of Francia, Franconia, was used to describe one of its constituent duchies. In most of west Francia the common language was a Romance tongue based on low Latin, which was to develop into the French language.

There were regional differences in this tongue of which the most striking was the divide between the language of the south, the *Langue d'oc*, which was quite

Map 1.4   France in the mid-eleventh century

close to Catalan and was later known as Provençal, and the language of the north, the *Langue d'oil* which had a stronger German influence on it and which developed into modern French. The distinguishing '*oc*' and '*oil*' were the words used for 'yes' in the two parts of France, and the names Languedoil and Languedoc were later used for the northern and southern lands. Indeed, there were other considerable differences between them which emerged clearly as in the tenth and eleventh centuries west Francia disintegrated into a series of principalities. The southern lands used Roman law, which was written down; the northern lands followed customs which developed gradually and were not codified until the thirteenth century. Society in the north had a considerable 'feudal' element in it; vassalage and the fief were almost unknown in the south (2.4.1). There were other more local contrasts too, and some stemmed from the different peoples found within the west Frankish kingdom, such as the Basques, the Bretons and later the Normans. The common language of the church, and hence of administration, remained Latin, and it was a vitally important medium of contact in the political life of western Europe as the Carolingian Empire came apart.

What did the name Francia mean in the tenth and eleventh centuries? It still retained a wide general use; both Byzantine and western writers at the time of the crusades described the western forces as Franks. But it was also taking on more specific meanings. From 911 onwards the west Frankish king was known as the *Rex Francorum* – king of the Franks, and the name Francia could be used to describe his kingdom, as it was also used for the east Frankish, or German kingdom. In its 'French' context, as the area where the king could assert his authority shrank, the name Francia was also used to describe one of the three divisions of the kingdom (Francia, Aquitania, Burgundia). The Robertines, forerunners of the Capetians, were *duces francorum*, dukes of the Franks, and their 'duchy' covered in theory most of northern France. Then as royal power contracted further, leaving the early Capetians (Appendix I) only a small bloc of lands round Paris and Orléans (Map 1.4), the term Francia was used for this region (3.3.3). In the eleventh century the name could thus mean one of several things, and this is symptomatic of the political decentralisation of the west Frankish – or French – kingdom in this period.

1.2 THE FRENCH ECONOMY AND SOCIETY

1.2.1 *A stagnant economy?*

To understand the political milieu of the early Capetian kings it is essential to examine the economic and social forces which shaped events. For many years the ninth and tenth centuries were considered an era of stagnation in the economy of northern and western Europe. The ideas of Henri Pirenne were very influential in shaping this view.[1] He suggested that the Germanic invasions of the fifth century which brought to an end the Imperial Roman government in the west and established the Merovingian kingdoms, still allowed the existing patterns of trade, centring on Constantinople, and economic life to continue. It was the rise of Islam in the seventh century which caused the true break with antiquity; the empire of Charlemagne, blocked off from the Byzantine world, was focused northwards. The economy of the Carolingian empire he considered extremely weak, static, agricultural and localised, despite Charlemagne's attempts to revive it; symbolic of this was the disappearance of gold coinage in the eighth century, not to reappear until the thirteenth. Further disruption was caused by the Vikings and other invaders in the eighth and ninth centuries, and signs of economic recovery, particularly an expansion in towns and commerce, were not to appear until the eleventh.

Ever since these ideas were put forward, historians have argued about them, and recently they have been considerably revised. Professor Robert Latouche, for example, suggests that the Merovingian economy was already weak and that the Islamic advances did very little damage to it.[2] Charlemagne attempted to put it on a new footing, but the beginnings of a new growth were in many areas nipped in the bud by the invasions of the eighth and ninth centuries. He demonstrates that for the ninth century there are still signs of markets selling both local produce and goods from further afield such as salt, slaves and luxuries – silk, spices and ivory. Urban life was beginning to revive, but all this was on a small scale for the late Carolingian economy was undeniably agrarian-based. Professor Grierson demonstrates that apart from rare gold coins with a ritual function, such as those struck for Louis the Pious, Carolingian coinage, which was fixed and controlled by the emperor until the late ninth century was entirely silver.[3] In another recent account Professor Georges Duby stresses that the late eighth and ninth centuries were a time of slow economic expansion, particularly in areas where little disruption was experienced; agricultural yields were improving, and the population was growing slowly.[4] Trade was expanding on the peripheries of the Carolingian states in particular. Our sources for this period, primarily ecclesiastical, appear to demonstrate that some expansion was taking place.

The effects on this slowly expanding economy of the new wave of invasions which gathered strength in the ninth century have also provoked considerable historical debate. These incursions came from several directions – the Vikings from the north, the Muslims from the south, the Hungarians from the east. The Saracen pirates set up a base at Fraxinetum in Provence, controlling the Alpine passes, terrorising the coast and causing considerable disruption in the area, both to life and trade. The Hungarian horsemen swept in from Pannonia, raiding frequently in northern Italy and Germany, and at times in France as well; in 937, for example, they reached Orléans. Their looting and pillaging produced major problems in lands east of France, and some localised hardship in France itself.

Far more significant for France were the activities of the Vikings. Our sources for their expeditions in the ninth century, as seen from the Frankish side, tend to present a picture of unmitigated gloom. In his celebrated mid-ninth-century account of the wanderings of the monks of Noirmoutier who fled from their island on the west coast of France eventually to settle at Saint-Philibert at Tournus, the monk Ermentarius writes:

The number of ships grows larger and larger, the great host of Northmen continually increases; on every hand the Christians are the victims of massacres, looting, incendiarism, clear proof of which will remain as long as the world itself endures; they capture every city they pass through, and none can withstand them; they take the cities of Bordeaux, Périgueux, Limoges, Angoulême and Toulouse. Angers and Tours, as well as Orléans, are wiped out; the ashes of many a saint are carried away.[5]

To monastic chronicles such as Ermentarius the hordes of savage heathen raiders seemed to be a manifestation of the wrath of God. Accounts such as theirs, though coloured by the outlook of the cloister should not, however, be swept aside merely as hysterical imaginings. In France as in England, the earlier raids, with their plundering and burning, clearly caused much hardship, damage and misery on a local level in the monasteries, castles and towns attacked, although the Noirmoutier monks probably travelled further than most others. The long-term impact of the raids is harder to assess, for the destruction they wreaked clearly varied from region to region. The Paris basin, though often a target for raids, emerged fairly rapidly and relatively unscathed. It is quite probable that western France, stretching from the coast to the Limousin, was experiencing a period of expansion in the ninth century before the destruction of growing towns such as Bordeaux, and the disruptions and sense of danger which seem to have caused whole communities of peasants and monks to migrate. From this psychological as well as physical insecurity these areas probably took several centuries to recover.

Burgundy, by contrast, an area almost entirely unaffected by invasion, became a refuge for fleeing ecclesiastics, and a flourishing monasticism grew up there. Furthermore, the raiding activities of the Vikings gradually mixed with and then gave way to trading; eventually settlements resulted. The Scandinavian settlement on the banks of the Seine, recognised in 911 by Charles the Simple and later to develop into the Duchy of Normandy, was to play a vital role in trade and in seafaring, as well as in the political life of northern France (2.2.3).

From the tenth century there are clear signs of economic expansion in western Europe; the cessation of the invasions and the stimulation of trade by the settlers may have been in part responsible for this. The Rhine valley, linking up with Flanders, Brabant and England, became a flourishing trade route; over a longer distance, the volume of trade with Venice and Byzantium began to expand. Later in the eleventh century the Norman conquests in southern Italy, Sicily and England followed by the first crusade, were to give a further boost to the longer trade routes. On the northern coast of France and Flanders new ports began to appear in the eleventh century, at Ghent, at Harfleur. The dukes of Normandy and the counts of Flanders encouraged and often founded them, and they also created new towns, such as Caen and Lille, in areas of expansion. The townspeople, who, though they clearly had links with the surrounding countryside, developed an entirely different outlook, were often granted privileges, special franchises giving both freedom from taxation and personal liberty. These were later extended to commercial and judicial privileges. In the late eleventh century the communes, personal associations formed to govern the towns, began to develop. Some were recognised by charters from the duke or count in the twelfth century allowing self-government in return for an often substantial payment to their lord (4.3.2).

Normandy and Flanders appear to have been precocious in their development along these lines; towns and trade in other areas of France evolved more slowly. In the tenth century urban life in most of France tended to be centred on the great monastic houses rather than the merchant communities such as were found in the Rhineland towns. Commerce grew up here more slowly during the eleventh century. Local markets in France also began to expand from the tenth century, and the use of silver currency became widespread. Like other public powers, the right of striking coins devolved to the princes and in many cases to local counts. But more important, agricultural expansion also took place at an increasing rate. There was, it seems, a general increase in population, an improvement in farming techniques, and perhaps most significant, a great movement of land clearance. This was probably spontaneous at first, but in the eleventh and twelfth centuries was under the surveillance of the nobility, who created new privileged communities. Here France seems to have been in general considerably in advance of Germany; again, however, there was great local and regional variation in the rate at which development took place (4.3.1).

Raoul Glaber, writing in the earlier eleventh century, commented upon some of the signs of a new expansion, which he saw as much in spiritual as in economic terms. There were, he said, an ever increasing number of pilgrims on the roads, and

as the third year following the millenium was drawing nigh, you could see church basilicas being renovated over almost the entire face of the earth, but especially in Italy and Gaul. Although most of these had no need of it, being of sound construction, rivalry would drive each Christian community to have one more sumptuous than its neighbours.[6]

One of the earliest areas to develop was the Paris basin, the Ile de France, where the Capetian kings' domain was centred. Although their political powers were limited, their own resources, the basis for future expansion, were becoming increasingly valuable.

In the south and the west of France the incursions of the Saracens and the Vikings brought considerable economic setbacks between the ninth and the eleventh centuries. This was not the case for many other areas. Towns with groups of merchants had emerged on the northern coast by the tenth century, long distance trade continued and began to expand in the eleventh, as did local markets. There was an agricultural expansion which although slow and tentative in the ninth century, hampered by anarchical conditions in many areas, gradually and then rapidly gathered momentum in the tenth and the eleventh. In the 980s economic life in France was largely localised but by no means stagnant; in the 1120s it was still localised to a considerable degree, but growing rapidly.

1.2.2 Nobles and knights

Medieval writers frequently make the distinction between the *oratores*, the *laboratores* and the *bellatores*, those who pray, those who work and those who fight.

Such a clearcut division is valid in one sense, but it also presents society as largely static. Although a man in France from the ninth century to the early twelfth would normally have fallen into one of these three categories – or into that of the growing number of merchants and townsfolk – within each his status might have varied very considerably. The higher clergy and monks were almost all drawn from the *bellatores*, although the monastic revival which began in the eleventh century was increasingly to bring in the townsfolk, and later, in the twelfth century, the peasantry in the form of lay brothers. But between the great archbishop and the parish priest was a gulf as great as or greater than that which divided the great territorial prince and the lesser knight. Between the free peasant with considerable allodial holdings and the poorest wage labourer, too, there was a great social difference.

In his important work, *Feudal Society*,[7] Professor Marc Bloch suggested that in the anarchical conditions of the ninth and tenth centuries the Carolingian nobility largely disappeared, to be replaced by a new group, whose functions as leaders of society and warriors made them 'noble'. This new noble-knightly group did not become a fixed aristocratic caste until the later twelfth century. These views were subsequently developed by a considerable number of historians – although there were dissenters. Professor Duby in his study of the Mâconnais also generally echoed this theory (2.2.2). He stressed that although some of the ancient nobility survived, an important element in this new aristocracy was the knights, the creation of the church; he in his turn was echoing views of such historians as Professor Guilhiermoz who early in this century proposed that it was the knights of the eleventh and twelfth centuries who were the ancestors of the nobility of the *ancien régime*.

More recently many scholars, Professor Duby amongst them, have swung away from this interpretation. The origins of the nobility of the *ancien régime* have in many cases been traced back in far greater numbers to the Carolingian nobility. A group of German historians, most notably Professor K. F. Werner, have demonstrated that many of the high and middle aristocracy of the tenth and eleventh centuries were descended directly from earlier Carolingian counts and palace officials, and remained a closed noble caste well into the twelfth century.[8] The male and female lines were equally important in this. Werner gives as examples the houses of Vermandois and Anjou, and the last has been accepted by Guillot in his study of Anjou in the eleventh century. Similar conclusions have been reached for the Namur area of the middle kingdom by Professor Génicot, for the Chartrain by M. Chédeville, for the Loire area by Professor Boussard, for Poitou and Aquitaine by Dr Martindale.[9] Thus in many parts of France the lines of the Carolingian nobility continued into the tenth century and onwards and the territorial princes were their descendants, as were likewise the great counts. The lesser counts and castellans, too, were often though not invariably offshoots of cadet branches. Normandy was of course an exception where ducal blood was important in conferring nobility. Awareness of Carolingian origins has also been seen as an important cohesive force among the higher nobility, though less so among the lesser nobles. This was not always allied with a man's function in society, but nevertheless was clearly recognised in the tenth and eleventh centuries.

An interesting illustration of this idea is given by the monastic chronicler Adhémar of Chabannes. In 1018, he says, William, duke of Aquitaine halted the fighting in a battle against the Normans, for the sake of those taken prisoner, for they were *ex nobilioribus*, from the nobler of his men. The importance of noble rank is emphasised by Adhémar in this extract, and so too is by implication, the gulf between the ranks within the *bellatores*. This Professor J. R. Strayer characterises as the 'two levels of feudalism'.[10]

Until about 1000 the knights formed a lowly group, the descendants of the Carolingian retainers, described as vassals. Their holdings were limited in size, often being little larger than those of the wealthier peasants. While the nobles, from king to castellan tended to build castles, the knights had none. By the twelfth century, however, in most areas of France the knightly and noble classes were beginning to come together.[11] In the eleventh century, the church had begun to glorify the institution of Christian knighthood in an attempt to curb anarchy and in connection with the peace and truce of God. The knight had been given a code of conduct to follow which would make salvation a possibility through the pursuit of knightly ideals as an alternative to entering the cloister. The knight's social position began to improve; he began to receive land in return for services and he was described as *miles* rather than as *vassus*. As many noble estates split up and castellanies formed, patterns of landholding became confused in many areas. Knightly benefices or fiefs now increased in numbers and size. Knightly ideals also began to permeate upwards through society, the nobles tended to accept the chivalrous ethos, to be dubbed as knights. It seems clear that by about 1200 the two elements, noble and knightly, had in much of France joined to become a new wider aristocracy of blood, which became ever more closed. Some knights began to live in fortified houses, and although often eclipsed in wealth by rich peasants and merchants were still part of a group set apart by its ideals, although these developments may not have had much economic and social significance. Nevertheless the *bellatores* had become in some senses more of an order in the thirteenth century than they had been in the tenth.

1.2.3 Lords and peasants

French society from the ninth to the twelfth century was predominantly rural, but it underwent a profound series of transformations. In the ninth century agrarian life was based primarily on the *villae*, the great landed estates such as those described in the *polyptiques* or surveys of great landholders like Irminon, abbot of Saint-Germain-des-Prés. These *villae* were often very extensive, and centred on the lord's domain, worked by the peasantry who in their turn had estates of sizes and statuses varying between free and unfree. The peasants likewise varied in status between free *coloni* and serfs, but the status of their holding and of their person did not always coincide. From unfree tenements the lord could demand rents, but his principal interest was in labour services. For the farming of his lands he often supplemented these by taking on wage-earners. Such organisations as these were common in the areas between the Loire and the Rhine, but land was by no means invariably farmed in this way. There is evidence, for example, for the medium-sized estate in Picardy, and for small free peasant holdings or allods (estates held without acknowledgement to a superior) in many areas, particularly in the south where the use of Roman law favoured the survival of free holdings.

By the eleventh century the classical *villa* was beginning to break down, and our sources indicate highly diverse patterns of landholding in France. In the Seine, Oise and Somme areas large units still prevailed; in north-east France, Normandy and Anjou they were normally of a medium size, in Brittany very small. In Maine, Poitou, Anjou and Saintonge independent holdings or *bordages* were grouped together to form larger economic units – found also at times in Normandy and Brittany. In the disintegration of the larger units land was often usurped, divided amongst heirs or granted to the church. The lord's domain lands shrank, often being taken over by stewards or bailiffs, or granted out in farms to the peasants. In Normandy servitude disappeared altogether; in other areas labour services were lightened. Much of this stemmed from new economic factors: the reclamation of land at an increasing rate which produced the class of *hôtes*, relatively free colonisers, the improvement in agricultural techniques allowing better food production and some sale of surpluses, the growth of exchange and the use of silver coinage were all part of a general expansion (4.3.1).

The breakdown in earlier patterns of land holding, allied with often anarchical conditions, brought with them new kinds of manorial organisations. In the ninth century the lord had exercised certain seigneurial rights over his men: he demanded labour services and rents from them and held judicial powers comprising what came later to be called low justice, involving the maintenance of law and order on the estate. But as political authority and the public power fragmented, lords in many areas came to exercise a greatly increased control over their men, based on rights granted by or taken from king, prince, count or even lesser noble. These were in part judicial, involving high justice, rights over life and limb. They also had financial aspects. New dues were levied and by the twelfth century and later were seen as customary dues or *coutûmes*, an inherent part of the power of the lord. They were originally derived from the public authority, but this was often lost sight of quite early on in their development. Thus the lord held monopolies over mining, banking and wine pressing; he controlled tolls, markets and fairs. He could levy the *taille* or head tax, demand military service, and later attempt to impose heavier labour dues. These powers extended to cover men who would not have come under his jurisdiction in the ninth century: the free tenants within his estate and also the holders of precarial lands outside its boundaries, whose ancestors had commended themselves to him for protection. In many parts of the Paris basin, Burgundy, Maine, Poitou and other northern areas, this kind of domination, the bannal lordship, was common, and a symbol of the disintegration of the public authority. But in these areas, too, the general increase in prosperity was, it appears, benefiting the peasantry considerably.

1.3 THE STRUCTURE OF POWER

1.3.1 The fragmentation of central authority: the principalities, counties and castellanies

In the ninth century royal power in the west Frankish kingdom began to be divided. Royal administrators entrusted with the government and defence of the various provinces or sub-kingdoms became increasingly powerful as they were delegated many royal powers within their lands by the Carolingian monarchs; by the early tenth century they were known as dukes (duces) or princes (principes). These sub-kings ruled in the provinces of Aquitaine and Burgundy; the border states of Gascony, the Spanish March (Barcelona) and Septimania (Toulouse) also split away from the kingdom and became semi-autonomous. Royal power was concentrated in the north of the kingdom, in Neustria, and royal weakness (1.4.1) undoubtedly helped these princes to consolidate their authority; but as Werner has demonstrated, in the early stages of fragmentation the principalities were legitimate creations.[12] The importance of the princely office is exemplified in the struggles between the counts of Toulouse, Poitou and Auvergne to gain the title of duke of Aquitaine.

During the tenth century royal authority over princely and comital dynasties declined, and the great duchies began to fragment in their turn into their constituent counties.[13] In the north of France the Norman settlers were given their own lands, and a number of other political units appeared: Brittany (with a strong ethnic basis), Anjou, Maine, Blois, Flanders. Many were created by local counts who amassed a number of counties and consolidated them into a principality. Some of their rulers were styled as princes, and used the titles of duke or count. The royal lands contracted as the Robertine house, dukes of Francia built up its power in the Paris and Orléans area, and its members, later the Capetians, eventually replaced the Carolingians as kings. By 987 when what turned out to be the final Carolingian reign ended many of the principalities, areas where the king had no practical powers except with the consent of the ruler, had become well established (Ch. 2, passim).

Some remained well established, and almost all remained as recognised principalities, but equally all were affected in some degree by the rise of the bannal lordships,[14] for in many parts of France the counties and the pagi, their constituent units, disappeared, as the idea of public authority was lost, and they were replaced by these new political units. In a bannal lordship the local seigneur, whether a castellan or a monastery, wielded a powerful and independent economic, judicial and fiscal authority over his men. This was not in northern France based on public powers, for they had been transformed into customary powers (coutûmes). So although initially a castellan might have been delegated various rights with the custody of his castle for his lord, his family might in many cases have succeeded in making the lordship and the rights hereditary, and he was often able to prevent his overlord from repossessing the castle itself. In many cases, too, new castles sprang up without the permission of the local count and their holders took customary powers over the local inhabitants. Usually these new families were offshoots of existing castellan houses of the area. In areas such as

Picardy, Berry, parts of Burgundy, these lords were the rulers. In other principalities such as Blois and Anjou they gained a great deal of power, and in the royal principality in the eleventh century they posed a considerable problem to the kings. In Normandy, where ducal power was for its time remarkably strong, they began to appear at times of relative ducal weakness.

The later eleventh and twelfth centuries were the time when various princely dynasties, and the royal house, fought their way back to power against such lords, many of whom had built up major local baronies. The king and the princes had to reassert the right to occupy their castles, and to affirm a real feudal dominance over them, with its obligations of military service, aid and obedience. They had to restrict private wars and to build up their own administrative and judicial systems. In many cases this was achieved only with great difficulty, for the castellans, like the princes, had a major place in French society at the time of the early Capetians.

Society in the early Capetian period was characterised by great local variations in the structure of power, the frequent isolation of small local communities, great confusion over lands and rights, and constant fighting for the domination of blocs of territory. This raises the question of how society was organised and what was the nature of the links between the knights, the lesser and greater nobles and the king.

1.3.2 The bonds of society: vassalage and the fief and the bannal lordship

Of the various elements which 'feudal society' is considered by many historians to encompass, we have already dealt briefly with the fragmented nature of political authority, with the classes of knights and nobles, and with the infrastructure — the rural manors where the great bulk of the population lived and worked. Whereas the social arrangement of the peasantry was geared towards agricultural production, those members of the knightly and noble ranks in society who were not in the church organised themselves to rule and to conduct warfare. This last, in the eleventh century, they indulged in with a startling frequency and vigour. The institutions of vassalage and the fief have for many years been considered as having been the principal means of providing the nobility with the resources to fight and to have formed the basis of a social organisation which was, in theory at least, hierarchical. The detailed research carried out since the last war on the social structure of certain areas of France in the eleventh and the twelfth century have cast many doubts on this general thesis, particularly for the early period.

In order to see this questioning in context, it is necessary briefly to rehearse and examine the 'classical' interpretation of this so-called 'feudal' order. The work of Professor Ganshof on the origins and development of vassalage and the fief, concentrating strongly on their juridical aspects is still of great importance, while Professor Bloch's classic, *Feudal Society*, examines these phenomena in a wider context.[15] Broadly similar lines to theirs have been followed by many other historians, but this is not the place to examine the differences between their studies; it is more profitable to trace in general outline the emergence of vassalage and the fief in their footsteps, and then to assess their importance in social

14

organisation. The discussion which follows relates mainly to northern and central France; conditions were different in the Midi (2.4.1).

The bond of vassalage was an ancient and personal one. One man commended himself to another, paid homage by ceremonially placing his hands between those of his lord, and from Carolingian times took an oath of fidelity to him. The oath was often sworn on relics, and this gave the ceremony a religious character. For both parties obligations were involved: the lord would afford his man protection and sustenance, the vassal would in return give him loyalty and service. In Merovingian and early Carolingian times this could involve little more than a noble keeping armed retainers in his household, and this practice continued throughout the Middle Ages. Increasingly, however, the sustenance of a vassal involved the granting of a benefice which came normally to be described as a fief from the eleventh century onwards, though its origins were several centuries earlier. This reverted to the lord on the death of the vassal, in theory at least. But the Carolingian kings began to take on as vassals men of an increasingly high social standing, frequently men of noble rank who held great allodial estates as well. Often they were granted benefices for holding public offices as counts or markgraves, and increasingly during the ninth century, they put down local roots, made their benefices hereditary and attempted if possible to convert them into allodial holdings, involving no ties of dependency. This was often done with considerable success. Also, where earlier benefices had frequently been granted to men who were not vassals, and vassals had not always been given benefices, later vassalage and benefices became more closely associated. Royal control was undermined, and as commendation and grants of benefices spread down rapidly from the princes to the counts and then to vicars or to viscounts, so here too the rights of the lord could be and were taken over. Princely and comital authority often decayed in the wake of royal power (1.3.1).

By the eleventh century, then, the bonds of vassalage had spread down through society, the grant of the fief had become a fairly frequent concomitant of commendation, and fiefs were becoming hereditary on a wide scale. The mutual obligations and safeguards surrounding them had also been clarified. The fief would revert to the lord's control when there was no heir, when the heir was a woman or a minor, or as the penalty for the withdrawal of faith by a vassal. Nor in theory could fiefs be dismembered or sold without the lord's permission. The vassal's obligations from the ninth century onwards were recognised as *auxilium* — military or monetary aid — and *consilium*, counsel, attendance at the lord's court and the giving of advice, sitting in judgement or being judged.

The bonds of vassalage, the grant of a fief and the paying of homage appeared widely in various parts of France in the eleventh and twelfth centuries, as many sources testify. A noted letter of Bishop Fulbert of Chartres gives a clear and full definition of the mutual obligations of the lord and the vassal. In offering advice to Duke William of Aquitaine over a rebellious vassal in about 1020, Fulbert says that:

He who swears fidelity to his lord should always keep these six terms in mind: safe and sound, secure, honest, useful, easy, possible. Safe and sound, that is, not to cause his lord any harm as to his body. Secure, that is, not to endanger him by betraying his secrets or the fortresses which make it possible for him to be secure. Honest, that is, not to do anything that would detract from his lord's rights of justice or the other prerogatives which have to do with his honour. Useful, not to cause him any loss as regards his possessions. Easy and possible, not to make it difficult for his lord to do something that would be of value to him and that he could otherwise do with ease, or to render it impossible for him to do what was otherwise possible. That the vassal should avoid injuring his lord in any of these ways is only right, but this does not entitle him to a fief; for it is not enough for him to abstain from evil, it is also necessary to do good. So it remains for him to give his lord faithful counsel and aid as regards these six points if he wishes to be considered worthy of his benefice and secure as to the fidelity he has sworn. The lord, in his turn, should be faithful to his vassal in these matters.[16]

This is to some extent an idealised picture, as is shown by the various double dealings which actually took place between the duke and his vassal, Hugh of Lusignan, but it is nevertheless a valuable statement about the ideals of the feudal relationship.

An interesting account of the rendering of homage is given by Galbert of Bruges in his work on the murder of Charles the Good, count of Flanders, and the election in his stead of William Clito; this dates from the early twelfth century. The nobility of Flanders came before the new count in April 1127.

First they did homage in this way. The count asked each one if he wished to become wholly his man, and the latter replied 'I so wish', and his hands clasped and enclosed by the count, they were bound together with a kiss. Secondly he who had done homage pledged his faith to the count's spokesman in these words: 'I promise on my faith that I will henceforth be faithful to Count William and that I will maintain my homage towards him completely against everyone, in good faith and without guile,' and in the third place he swore an oath to this effect on sacred relics. Then the count, with a wand which he held in his hand, gave investiture to all those who by this compact had promised loyalty and done homage and likewise taken an oath.[17]

Such an organisation should in ideal circumstances have produced a neatly ordered and structured society, with the king at the top and below him orders of nobles bound to one another by mutual obligations. In theory, for example, the knight would do homage to a castellan, who would do homage to a count, who would do homage to a duke, who would do homage to the king. In Normandy and England the king-dukes had the power to insist that the vassals of their vassals owed ultimate allegiance to them; elsewhere direct authority tended to be recognised only on the rung of the ladder directly below a lord. Thus in the eleventh century the king had feudal powers only over the princes, not their men.

How hierarchical was French society in the eleventh century? The church played an important role in promoting the idea, and the layered organisation developed by the Cluniac congregation of monasteries may have later provided the notion of a pattern for a lay social order. The chronicler Raoul Glaber frequently refers to hierarchy in a social sense, distinguishing loosely between the *maximi*, the *mediocres* and the *minimi* – those of the greater, the middling and the lesser sorts, although the precise composition of those in the middle is not easy to discern. In Abbot Suger's *Life of King Louis VI the Fat*, again a twelfth-century work, the duke of Aquitaine is portrayed as declaring that the count of Auvergne holds his county from him, and he holds his duchy from the king. This was written when the reality of the hierarchy was beginning to emerge and is an example of an account which sought to foster it. It was further helped by the development of the money fief, which was used by the king and the nobility from the twelfth century onwards to buy homage. Clearly in the eleventh century as well as in the twelfth both the concepts and the institutions of vassalage and the fief, and also the idea of a hierarchical society, were widespread in France.

Yet from the tenth century to the twelfth it was only in kingdoms where such an organisation was spread from above, as in Norman England or the Latin crusader states, that there was any actual clear and general hierarchical order in society, and even here the gap between theory and reality was considerable. France in the eleventh century was at the opposite end of the spectrum from these states, its political organisation variable and at times highly confused. Vassalage and the fief had existed since Merovingian times and continued to do so, especially in northern France. In areas such as Normandy and Flanders and to a lesser extent in Anjou they were a strong weapon in the maintenance of ducal or comital control. In many other parts of France during the late tenth and eleventh centuries, though, they only formed part of the picture. It was inevitable that there would be problems in an organisation where control at the top was weak. Vassals could and frequently did commend themselves to two or more lords, diluting the significance of fealty and often making their military obligations exceedingly difficult to honour. As a result feudal bonds became crossed and tangled, and lost much of their importance. In response to this problem, the concept of liege homage was evolved in the twelfth century. Here the vassal's obligations to one lord, often the most powerful, outweighed all others. This too, however, rapidly became debased. As Professor Lemarignier has it: 'vassalage and feudal practices always carried within themselves the yeast of anarchy and a threat of disorder for society'.[18] It is striking that in cases of multiple commendation by a vassal the king's rights were recognised above those of all other lords. But another problem was that a noble might not be sufficiently strong to intervene within the fief of an erring vassal, to punish him for his misdeeds or to prevent him from usurping rights such as those of justice and taxation.

In many areas of France, the social structure was very far from being based on vassalage and the fief. The important studies of two politically decentralised societies, the Mâconnais in Burgundy by Professor Georges Duby, and Picardy by Professor Robert Fossier (Ch. 2), have shown that in these areas fiefs were not common until the late twelfth century, and that in the eleventh and earlier twelfth centuries lands were normally held as allods. Homage and fidelity certainly existed, but they were regarded as much as political agreements or treaties as a means of control. This was often because such contracts did not involve land. A pyramidal social structure did not emerge in any form in either area, or in other similar regions, until the thirteenth century. In other more southern areas of France, too, such as Gascony and the county of Toulouse, allods existed in large numbers into the later Middle Ages, contracts of vassalage were virtually unknown, and the independence of the castellans proved a considerable problem to those who tried to dominate them (Ch. 2, *passim*).

In the tenth and eleventh centuries, then, the ties of vassalage and the fief, although existing widely and holding an important place in the social organisation of many areas of France, by no means always provided a structure for society. Throughout the early Capetian period they were viewed primarily as marking a personal relationship rather than a contract of landholding and service. In many areas they did not exist as a means of control until the twelfth or thirteenth century or even later, and then often their growth coincided with the spread of royal influence. The important local unit of power in many regions of France in the eleventh century was the castellany, almost autonomous and centred on the castle, its lords possessing many aspects of the public authority which had devolved to them, gradually being transformed into customary powers.

1.3.3 Church and society

Another vitally important power in tenth and eleventh-century French society was the church. During the Carolingian era the great cathedrals and abbeys had frequently had their extensive estates used to support the secular hierarchy, especially by kings and also by lay advocates; they were a source of revenues and extra power, a reservoir of lands to be drawn on for benefices for loyal followers, and also in many cases providers of military contingents. Such practices they had tried to resist, and the general reform of the church which began in the eleventh century sought to stamp out such abuses altogether. This 'exploitation' from the church's point of view, was symptomatic of the realities of local political geography. The ecclesiastical estates were closely connected with their local communities; indeed by the eleventh century they had often profited from the disintegration of political authority and held the powers of the bannal lordship. But as the centralised structure of power broke down the king's authority over many – although by no means all – bishoprics and abbeys fell into the hands of the territorial princes, counts and castellans who often exploited rather than protected them. In many areas the king was too weak to render practical assistance and they turned to the episcopate and to the papacy for help. The church was able to find various practical solutions, providing some degree of protection, stability and structure both for ecclesiastics and for the populace in general.

The abbey of Cluny (3.4.1) set an important example, The mother-house of a great congregation, it first gained exemption from episcopal authority for a few houses and then extended it to all. By c. 1027 it was dependent on the papacy alone. Various early eleventh-century popes granted Cluny and its daughter-houses freedom from the exactions of temporal lords (this was not easy to enforce) and exemption from episcopal surveillance. All these factors probably stimulated the organisation of Cluny's daughter-houses into a hierarchical structure. This may also be seen as a reaction against the generally anarchical conditions prevailing in many parts of France, and it presented an ordered pattern in an age not noted for centralised administration. How did the lay powers react to this?

The French kings interested themselves mainly in Cluniac houses whic[h] royal or in the royal principality. Philip I granted Saint-Martin-des-Cha[mps] the order but as far as possible resisted any encroachment of papal aut[hority]. Henry I, his father, had tended to favour monasteries of canons regular which were dependent on the local episcopate, rather than the great Benedictine religious houses which were building up a considerable measure of autonomy. In other parts of France lay reaction varied. Some important monastic patrons and benefactors granted their houses to this increasingly prestigious order. Duke William of Aquitaine gave Saint-Eutrope at Saintes to Cluny in 1081, and placed great emphasis on its connections with the papacy, which had begun somewhat before this. Often however it was papal rather than royal or noble initiative which extended Cluniac influence and while the Cluniacs did not directly promulgate the papal reforms of the eleventh century, they represented a pattern of an exempt group of religious, and they often helped to disseminate general ideas of renewal and of the independence of ecclesiastical lands and communities from the laity.

The church also resisted anarchical conditions in society by promulgating the peace of God and the truce of God. These originated in the troubled areas of Burgundy and Aquitaine in the late tenth century. Both here and further south in the Languedoc where Roman law, with its emphasis on public peace, still persisted, these movements were of fundamental importance in introducing the notion of a general terrestrial law and order reflecting an ideal heavenly harmony. This the political institutions of society were patently unable to provide. The movements may have gained an additional impetus through popular fears associated with the millennium, which have perhaps been underestimated in some recent accounts.

There are a number of contemporary references to the millennium in the chronicle sources of the period, and their writers indicate that in a general climate of fear and insecurity the years 1000 and 1033, a thousand years after Christ's death and resurrection, stood out. A remedy for an anarchical society was clearly needed. The peace of God placed under ecclesiastical protection both ecclesiastics and church property and buildings, together with the poor and their goods. Oaths of peace parallel with those of fidelity were also given. Similar protection had been granted by the Carolingian kings but now the initiative passed to secular church councils headed by the episcopate and often including great lay magnates. The first clear examples of these were at Le Puy in 975 and Charroux in 989–90 where canons were issued in defence of the poor and the church; these were followed rapidly by other councils in southern France such as Narbonne, Limoges, Poitiers, Verdun-sur-le-Doubs. The movement spread rapidly to other parts of France including the royal domain.

A vivid portrayal of the peace council at Limoges in 994, is given by Adhémar of Chabannes. He describes the climate of unrest, exacerbated by widespread disease which he saw as a punishment by God for mens' sins. All this came to an end when the relics of Saint Martial, of whom the author was a fervent admirer, were brought out, and the duke of Aquitaine and his leading men concluded a pact of peace. The truce of God followed on from the peace.[19] This attempted to ban acts of violence at particular times, initially between Saturday evenings and

Monday mornings. It first appeared at the council of Toulonges in Roussillon, and in the 1030s and 1040s spread widely, both in the geographical area covered and in the number of prohibited days. Perhaps the culmination of the whole movement was the ecclesiastical council of Narbonne in 1054 where it was declared that no Christian should kill another; later it lost impetus. But it opened up the ground for the preaching of the first crusade which called for an internally peaceful Christian society joining together and waging war against the infidel. Furthermore in areas such as Normandy and Flanders where the church was firmly under ducal or comital control, the peace and truce of God were promulgated by the secular leaders and eventually became associated with the idea of ducal or public peace. Later too it became associated with the idea of royal peace. Thus as with lay institutions the organisation of the church varied from area to area in France according to the state of political power and as a reaction to local conditions. In the regions where political power was most fragmented it began to provide leadership and to create some kind of structure for society.

1.4 POLITICAL DEVELOPMENTS OF THE TENTH CENTURY

1.4.1 987: the beginning of a new era?

In 985 Gerbert of Aurillac wrote from Reims to two secret correspondents in Germany: 'Lothar is king of France in name only; Hugh not in name, but in deed and in fact.'[20] Within two years Hugh Capet duke of the Franks had become king of France in name as well, in succession to Lothar's shortlived heir, Louis V, the last Carolingian king of France. The historian is easily beguiled into endowing this event with a particular significance. In 987 a dynasty began to rule under which the fragmented west Frankish society of the late tenth century (1.3.1) developed into what was, for its time, a centralised, powerful and intensely governed state. This was a family which produced as its leaders, as well as a fair share of kings of only moderate talent and courage, able warriors, capable administrators, calculating and successful politicians, and a saint, and under whom the authority and prestige of France reached heights unsurpassed by any other western European kingdom.

From a dynastic point of view there is a perfect validity in discussing and analysing developments in France between 987 and 1328, but it is arguable that the political and military occurrences of 1124, 1204 and 1337 are of far greater general historical importance in medieval French history than the times of dynastic break. While in an account revolving largely round the monarchy, the years 987 and 1328 provide us with a convenient timespan, the relative lack of importance given to these events by contemporaries must not be forgotten.

Looked at in the context of the previous century of the history of France the election of Hugh Capet was altogether lacking in drama. The Carolingian house, it is true, had been accepted as the ruling dynasty in normal circumstances, but where the heir was clearly too young or too weak to carry out his kingly duties the throne passed into the hands of nobles with the power, wealth and influence to rule, and with the ability to hold the throne against the shifting and turbulent coalitions of other nobles and ecclesiastics which struggled against them. These men were all of the same noble family, known as the Robertines, which was later to produce Hugh Capet.

In 888 Odo, the first of them, was elected king in preference to the young Carolingian, Charles the Simple. He ruled the march of Neustria, which comprised most of northern France, and he wielded great influence in the kingdom in general, so that he appeared the only suitable leader against the invading Northmen. After his death in 898 the Carolingian Charles the Simple became king, but his ineffectual rule aroused the opposition of a group of nobles who had Robert, brother of Odo, crowned in 922. After Robert's death in 923 his son-in-law Raoul was crowned in his place, and after the death of Charles the Simple in 929 he managed to hold on to the throne until his own demise in 936. The title of king then reverted to the young Carolingian Louis IV *'d'Outremer'*, although Hugh the Great, son of King Robert, was undoubtedly the most powerful noble in the kingdom. Duke of the Franks, he was the heir to the overlordship of Neustria, count of Paris, and lay abbot of several important monasteries. He also held Burgundy from 943. He nevertheless supported the election of Louis IV, and at first tried to dominate him. As the reign progressed, however, it was marked by constantly shifting alliances between the king, Hugh the Great, Emperor Otto I of Germany and powerful nobles including Herbert of Vermandois, Theobald count of Blois and Richard duke of Normandy. Hugh overpowered Louis; in 945 he imprisoned him and took Laon from him, but was excommunicated in 948 by Pope Agapitus II and eventually submitted to the king in 950.

Although the Carolingian lands were very limited, and appeared dwarfed by the estates of the *dux Francorum*, when Louis died in 954 he was replaced as king by his eldest son Lothar. Hugh the Great died in 956 and his lands were divided; his eldest son Hugh, later known as 'Capet' (App. I), took the northern French lands, and his second son took Burgundy. The pattern of shifting alliances of the previous reign continued. King Lothar, clearly realising the weakness of his position, tried to remedy matters by overrunning Upper Lorraine, part of the middle kingdom in dispute with the holy Roman emperors. This resulted in a conflict with Otto II, who with the help of Hugh Capet reconquered the lost land and overran parts of France. In 983 Otto died, leaving as his heir the infant Otto III, with Henry duke of Bavaria as a rival for the German throne. Henry promised Lothar Upper Lorraine in return for his support, and the king, taking advantage of this offer, moved into Lorraine and besieged and took Verdun.

Opposition to Lothar was meanwhile mounting within France. Adalbero, the powerful archbishop of the important see of Reims and a native of Lorraine, was the brother of the count of Verdun. Self-interest and local sympathy made him a supporter of the Ottonians; furthermore several of his relatives were captured by Lothar at Verdun. Adalbero had re-established the school at Reims with the help of the noted scholar Gerbert of Aurillac, who was later to become Pope Sylvester II. Gerbert too was sympathetic towards the Ottonians who had given him considerable assistance. In 980 Otto II had made him abbot of the wealthy monastery of Bobbio. Gerbert and Adalbero gave full support to the young Otto III and his mother the Empress Theophano, and they also managed to involve Hugh Capet (whose mother was the sister of Otto I) and other nobles against Lothar and Henry of Bavaria. Lothar, realising the gravity of the threat summoned Adalbero, who was at the centre of the intrigue, to appear before an assembly at Compiègne in 985. This was broken up by Hugh Capet. Henry of Bavaria then relinquished his claims, and in 986 Lothar died.

Lothar's son Louis, already crowned during his father's lifetime in 979, succeeded to both the kingdom and his father's policies. He summoned the incorrigible Adalbero before another assembly at Compiègne, but died suddenly in 987 just before it met. The assembly proved something of a shambles. The question which loomed was that of who the next king should be. The nearest Carolingian claimant to the throne was Charles, Lothar's brother, duke of Lower Lorraine. As with many of his relatives and contemporaries his career had been punctuated with shifts of allegiance. He had supported Otto II against his brother Lothar, when the latter tried to seize Upper Lorraine, but had then moved over to support Lothar against the infant Otto III. This made him a highly undesirable candidate to Adalbero, who saw Hugh Capet as the more suitable successor to Louis V; Adalbero was probably instrumental in engineering Hugh's election at an assembly at Senlis, and Hugh was then crowned in July 987. He was the fourth of his family to occupy the French throne. Like Lothar he had his son Robert crowned in his own lifetime, and like Lothar and Louis V he had to contend with a powerful rival. It was not until 991 that he contrived to have Charles of Lorraine captured (2.2.1). Events seemed to be continuing in predictable patterns at the beginning of Hugh Capet's reign, and Hugh's election does not seem an epoch-making event; indeed viewed from a long-term perspective it is perhaps rather less striking than the choice of Odo as king in 888.

What do contemporary and near-contemporary writers have to say about all this? Raoul Glaber, a Cluniac monk, wrote in the 1040s:

After the deaths of King Lothar and King Louis, the government of France fell upon Hugh, son of Hugh the Great, duke of Paris . . . and brother of the illustrious Henry, duke of Burgundy. The great men of the whole realm gathered for the crowning of Hugh as king. He was, as we have seen, a blood relation of the kings of Germany through Otto I, whose mother was the sister of Hugh the Great.[21] Having taken on the government of the French kingdom, Hugh soon found his authority ignored by men who had shortly before all submitted to him; but thanks to his vigour of body and spirit he at length put down all the rebels.[22]

Richer, a monk of Saint-Rémi at Reims writing in the 990s, gives almost a blow-by-blow account of the assembly at Senlis which decided for Hugh. Into the mouth of Adalbero he puts a speech clearly modelled on Sallust's style of writing. He makes Adalbero condemn the next Carolingian claimant, Charles of Lorraine, his accusations being a lack of honour, of being more loyal to German than French interests, and of contracting a *mésalliance* by marrying the daughter of a mere vassal. The throne should not necessarily pass to the next blood relation of the late king, but should pass to a man of nobility and vigour: 'Choose blessings rather than calamities for the state. If you wish it ill, create Charles king; if you desire good fortune, have Hugh, the illustrious duke, crowned.'

Adalbero carried the assembly, and Hugh was elected and crowned, and recognised as king by the Gauls, Bretons, Normans, Aquitanians, Goths, Spanish and Gascons. He is portrayed as issuing decrees and legislating according to royal custom, surrounded by the great men of the realm.[23] The value of Richer's work as a source is dubious. While he may well have witnessed some of the events, and was certainly contemporary to them, he was very strongly biased by his admiration of Gerbert of Aurillac, who when Richer wrote was the archbishop of Reims, and his associates. The speech of Adalbero has all the hallmarks of fiction and is clearly intended for dramatic effect. Yet the influence the man himself wielded, and some of the arguments he used, may not be far from the truth. His role as an intriguer-extraordinary is revealed in the letters which he and Gerbert wrote to the German court in the 980s; nor did he stop after Hugh's election, as a letter written by Gerbert on his behalf to Charles of Lorraine reveals. Adalbero's excuses for Hugh's election are presented:

for who was I that I alone should set a king over the French? These affairs are public matters, not private. You think I hate the royal family [i.e. the Carolingians]; I call my redeemer to witness that I do not hate it.[24]

In their attempts to hedge their bets, do Adalbero and Gerbert protest too much?

These sources, limited though they may be in one sense, are nevertheless enlightening on the considerations borne in mind at the election of a French king. In many ways the same factors that were important in 888 were still so in 987; blood ties with the Carolingians had great status, but apart from Charles of Lorraine the line had failed. Hugh Capet's connections with the Ottonians through his mother, pointed out incorrectly by Glaber, may have helped him to some extent. But what was set above blood in 987 was what Glaber called vigour of body and spirit, and Richer, speaking via Adalbero, nobility and vigour. Adalbero and Gerbert, from within their web of intrigue, would probably have seen this quality more as acceptability, though power also had much to do with it. Odo had been elected king to lead armies against the Viking invaders, and Robert and Raoul because of the weakness of Charles the Simple. At the same time, the intrigues of the lay and ecclesiastical magnates surrounding them played an important part; but interests beyond those of northern France may have been taken into account, even though royal influence in these areas was already shrinking.

With Hugh Capet's election the question of interests and connections became much clearer. Hugh was elected because he was more acceptable to the northern French magnates than Charles of Lorraine, whose preoccupations appeared to lie principally outside the French kingdom, but who also seemed to threaten the interests and designs of a group of powerful nobles and ecclesiastics headed by Adalbero. In other words, the candidate chosen as king in the immediate circumstances of 987 was the one most favoured by the weighty and influential coalition whose continuing support he needed in order to consolidate his position. The sources, then, highlight this localised intrigue, which was symptomatic of the decline of central authority in France, and of the changed attitude of both the kings and magnates to the royal power.

Hugh was recognised as king by the Gauls, Bretons, Normans and the others, but like his immediate predecessors his real powers in the outer fringes of France were minimal, showing a marked decline from the already shrinking ones of a century before – a trend which was to continue into the eleventh century. Areas such as Aquitaine and Gascony continued to recognise that they formed part of the *regnum Francorum*, the kingdom of the Franks, and indeed, never denied royal overlordship. This was later to prove a great advantage to the monarchy when it was imposing royal authority in outlying areas. But who was king was of relatively little moment in areas where the royal authority of the early Capetians was not felt. In the areas centred on the Paris basin, the middle reaches of the Seine and Loire and into Picardy, often described by contemporaties as Francia, royal authority was more immediate. But here too, as in the great counties and duchies, centrifugal forces appeared to be at work, and power was becoming increasingly fragmented. Although Hugh Capet held far more lands here in person than had the last Carolingians, the sum total of these was far less than those which his ancestors the Robertines had controlled. Kingship, as well as power, was becoming localised.

Was 987 the beginning of a new era? Dynastically it proved to be; but because of the prevailing social fragmentation and the limited field of effective action of the monarchy, the change of dynasty was of very little importance in large portions of France. When the events of 888–987 are considered, with the alternation of the Carolingians and the Robertines, the accession of another member of the latter family, the fifth to occupy the throne, seems less remarkable. That he and his direct descendants rapidly established an exclusive claim to royal office and succeeded in retaining it is perhaps more striking. Otherwise little had changed apart from the royal dynasty. The Capetian king enjoyed the same sacral powers as his Carolingian predecessors, he had the same alliance with the clergy and the same shifting pattern of wars and truces with the great nobles. He held very slightly increased domain lands in the same area, Francia, centred on Orléans and the Paris basin. But the decline of royal influence and the fragmentation of political authority, well under way in 987, continued inexorably into the eleventh century.

NOTES AND FURTHER READING

Asterisked titles are recommended for further reading, and additional titles are suggested below. Place of publication London unless otherwise indicated.

Notes

1. H. Pirenne, *Mohammed and Charlemagne*, trans. B. Miall (1939) and *Medieval Cities, Their Origin and the Revival of Trade,* trans. F. D. Halsey (repr. Princeton, 1969).

2. R. Latouche, *The Birth of the Western Economy*, trans. E. M. Wilkinson, 2nd edn (1967).
3. P. Grierson, *Monnaies du Moyen Age* (Fribourg, 1976).
4. G. Duby, **The Early Growth of the European Economy*, trans. H. B. Clarke (Princeton, 1974).
5. R. Latouche, *Textes d'histoire médiévale* (Paris, 1951) 132–3.
6. Duby, *op. cit.*, 159–60.
7. M. Bloch, **Feudal Society*, trans. L. A. Manyon, 2nd edn (1962).
8. K. F. Werner, **'*Untersüchungen zur Frühzeit des Französischen Fürstentums', *Die Welt als Geshichte*, xviii (1958), 256–89, xix (1959), 146–93, xx (1960), 87–119.
9. See notes and further reading to Chapter 2, 62–3.
10. J. R. Strayer, 'The two levels of feudalism', in G. Post, ed., *Medieval Statecraft and the Perspectives of History, Essays by J. R. Strayer* (Princeton, 1971), 63–76.
11. These matters are well summarised in J. Martindale, **'*The French aristocracy in the early Middle Ages: a re-appraisal', *Past and Present*, lxxv (1977), 5–45.
12. K. F. Werner, **'*Kingdom and principality in twelfth-century France', in T. Reuter, ed. and trans., *The Medieval Nobility* (Amsterdam/New York/Oxford, 1979), 243–90, esp. 243–54.
13. J. Dhondt, **Études sur la naissance des principautés territoriales en France, IXe–Xe siècle* (Bruges, 1948), suggested that all the principalities were created by the usurpation of power.
14. Here I think that Werner in his 'Kingdom and principality', underestimates the importance of this secondary disintegration.
15. Bloch, *op. cit.*, and F. Ganshof, *Feudalism,* trans. P. Grierson, 3rd edn (1964).
16. F. Behrends, ed. and trans., *The Letters and Poems of Fulbert of Chartres* (Oxford, 1976), 91–2.
17. Quoted from Galbert of Bruges, *The Murder of Charles the Good, Count of Flanders*, trans. J. B. Ross (New York, 1960), 206–7.
18. J. F. Lemarignier, **'*Political and monastic structures in France at the end of the tenth and the beginning of the eleventh century', in F. L. Cheyette, ed., *Lordship and Community in Medieval Europe* (New York, 1968), 100–27 esp. 108.
19. H. E. J. Cowdrey, **'*The peace and truce of God in the eleventh century', *Past and Present*, xliii (1970), 42–62.
20. H. P. Lattin, trans., *The Letters of Gerbert of Aurillac with his Papal Privileges as Sylvester II* (New York, 1961), 95.
21. Glaber is incorrect here: Hugh was related to the Ottonians, but through his mother, Hadewig, sister of Otto I and wife of Hugh the Great.
22. M. Prou, ed., *Raoul Glaber, les cinq livres de ses histoires; 900–1044* (Paris, 1886), 26.
23. Richer, *Histoire de France*, ed. R. Latouche, ii (Paris, 1937), 159–67.
24. Lattin, *op. cit.*, 161–2.

Additional titles for further reading

E. A. R. Brown, 'The tyranny of a construct: feudalism and historians of medieval Europe', *American Historical Review*, lxxix (1974), 1063–88.

G. Duby, *The Chivalrous Society*, ed. and trans. C. Postan (1977).

G. Fourquin, *Lordship and Feudalism in the Middle Ages*, trans. I. and A. Lytton-Sells (1976).

J. F. Lemarignier, 'La dislocation du *"pagus"* et le problème des *"consuetudines"* ', in *Mélanges d'histoire du moyen-âge dédiés à la mémoire de Louis Halphen* (Paris, 1951), 401–10.

See also Notes and further reading for Chapters 2 and 3.

CHAPTER TWO

Politics and Society: A Regional View

2.1 INTRODUCTION

2.1.1 Local societies in the French kingdom

The numerous regional and local studies of French society and politics in the Middle Ages produced since the 1950s have done much to change our perspectives and perceptions of medieval France. French society in the early Capetian period no longer appears as a clearly defined feudal hierarchy on the lines put forward by Fulbert of Chartres and other ecclesiastics of the time and by innumerable historians since. It is now clear that although in northern France vassalage and the fief appeared quite often they were not often the basis on which societies functioned. In many areas the tie of vassalage was used as little more than a treaty to be broken at will, and this was true equally of the castellans' relationship with the territorial princes and of the princes with the king. In many areas effective political power was held by the semi-autonomous castellan whose ties with his overlord were tenuous. In two principalities, Normandy and Flanders, however, the reality of hierarchy was kept alive to a large extent, and in the late eleventh and twelfth centuries it was gradually imposed in other principalities by belligerence against the nobles on the part of the princes helped by the development of administrative institutions, and the declining economic position of many bannal lords (4.3.1). Homage, and particularly liege homage, assumed greater importance and gradually feudal hierarchies formed. These developments were greatly to help the Capetians when they began to reassert royal authority.

Nor is French society now so often depicted only from a central viewpoint. It may instead be seen as a number of regions and localities containing a diversity of social structures, varying according to the way in which power was transmitted and the extent disintegration had reached. At one end of the spectrum is Berry, where by the tenth century public authority had disappeared almost completely. Clearly the isolation of this area may have been an important factor here, but in Picardy, where society remained equally fragmented until the later twelfth century, the very proximity of the monarchy produced similar conditions to

Berry. At the other extreme are Normandy and Flanders, where public powers and political authority rested for the most part at the level of the territorial prince. But this was not maintained without a strenuous effort on the part of the ruling dynasties. Personalities and power of leadership as well as propitious political circumstances all played their part here. The rulers of these two states generally managed to resist the forces of disintegration at times of crisis, to maintain authority over most of the castles, counts and castellans in their lands and to use vassalage and the fief to reinforce their authority.

Even here, however, centrifugal forces were at work and immediately showed during times of weakness at the centre. In Maine, Anjou and Poitou-Aquitaine political crises in the eleventh century went far enough to allow the widespread abuse of 'feudal' institutions which became a force for anarchy. In the south public power remained strong in theory, but in reality the territorial princes preserved some degree of authority only by making *convenientiae*, alliances with the lesser nobles, and relying on the peace of God and a rigid social structure to keep them in a predominant position. Castles appeared in great numbers in this region as well as in many others, and it is clear that the emergence of fortifications without princely licence is a sign of weak central authority. Conversely the power to occupy or confiscate the castle of a rebellious vassal is a sign of strength. To control its strong places was to dominate an area, and the wars of the princes against the nobles in their lands were intended to rebuild this power as the basis of a revived authority.

2.1.2 *The princes in eleventh- and twelfth-century France*

Local studies have also emphasised the political and social significance of many of the princes, and have highlighted the importance of character and ability in the holding of power. The successful prince possessed great importance, the prince who had lost his power was relatively obscure. Aggrandisement could be achieved by the kind of man who had the ability to marry well, to fight ruthlessly and to conclude effective alliances in a politically confused society. Fulk Nerra of Anjou, Odo II of Blois and William the Conqueror of Normandy were all of this character; against them the Capetians appeared weak and ineffectual. But the grand schemes of the princes were generally formed within the preconceptions and rules of their own society. They would frequently divide their lands between their sons, bowing to custom or political necessity. In particular they tended to grant their patrimony to their eldest son and acquisitions to cadets. While this could be done in *parage*, and lands often reverted to or were seized by the senior line, it does not argue for a conscious empire-building policy on the part of the princes. Rather it suggests a wish to consolidate their own position and to build up the power and prestige of the whole family, to follow accepted customs rather than resisting them. Authority, wealth, aggrandisement they wanted, but this was gained with family interests at heart and within the framework of the French kingdom.

The princes fought against the king, perhaps, as in 1031, on behalf of a rival claimant to the throne, but they never tried to dispute the existence of his royal office. By the eleventh century the Capetians were firmly on the throne, and no other family managed to dominate them as they had done the Carolingians. The counts of Blois-Champagne attempted to do so; hence perhaps Odo II's frequently repeated assertion that he did not want to be king, just always the king's master. But Blois-Champagne was not strong enough, and other princes came to the aid of the king, as in 1031, as they would to the aid of one another. The king was in practical terms in the mid-eleventh century very much one of the princes despite his high office, acting alternatively as their opponent or ally. They rendered him military service and homage or fidelity not on a regular basis, but as expediency dictated and as a sign of alliance. But even when ignoring the king they did not deny his theoretical powers (3.1.1).

It is striking, indeed, that the princes tended to imitate the king in many different ways, taking the ceremonial and vocabulary of royal powers along with their reality. Since ducal authority carried a greater status than comital power, and was closely associated with royal power (after all, the dukes of the ninth century had been sub-kings), the more powerful counts, such as the rulers of Brittany and Normandy, aimed for ducal rank. They were described in their charters as princes ruling by the grace of God, as the Capetians were kings by the grace of God; they had their fiscs and their forests, the bishops and monasteries over which they exercised regalian rights. As lords of their lands they had the duties of defending and protecting them, the right to levy service and the obligation to keep the peace. Like the Capetians they designated their heirs in their own lifetimes – indeed this was probably a noble rather than a royal custom in origin. They were invested as princes, and each had his own household, entourage and administrators. The only real difference was the royal title conferred by crowning and unction, giving the royal office a sacral and special feudal dimension, and this the princes did not have. But royal power was so ineffective for much of the eleventh century that although widely recognised it was often ignored.

In the twelfth century administrations began to develop in the principalities and the king's suzerainty became more fully effective. But in practice expediency still governed the links between the king and the princes, who continued to render homage and service, if more frequently, still as a mark of alliance (4.4.5). The real shift in the balance did not take place until the reign of Philip Augustus, and stemmed largely from his defeat of King John of England, a territorial prince in France on the grand scale. And the principalities, even when brought under a closer royal control in the thirteenth century, retained their own customs, laws and traditions. All this emphasises the continuing divisions within the French kingdom, divisions which were most visible in the eleventh century but which continued throughout the Middle Ages and beyond.

The following discussion is centred on case studies selected to show the range of political and social developments which took place in different principalities from the ninth to the twelfth century. Burgundy and the Mâconnais are examples of a principality and a county in disintegration; Normandy of a duchy held together by the power and authority of its rulers, eclipsing the French monarchy in its political importance. The lands of Blois-Champagne come somewhere between the two; their princes wielded effective power, but their possessions lacked political or territorial coherence. Other regions and principalities – Flanders, Picardy, Brittany, Greater Anjou and Aquitaine – are given a more cursory treatment, which covers only their general development and political importance, but the society of the south, and the two important states of Toulouse and Barcelona are again looked at in more detail as a contrast with the north.

2.2 POLITICS AND SOCIETY: SOME CASE STUDIES

2.2.1 The disintegration of the duchy of Burgundy

The duchy of Burgundy evolved straight from a part of one of the sub-kingdoms of the Carolingian empire to a territorial principality. It then followed the classic pattern of internal political disintegration during the eleventh century, and the gradual rebuilding of ducal power during the twelfth and thirteenth centuries, which makes it a useful case study. Duke Richard the Justiciar who was delegated with royal powers in the region at the end of the ninth century did not exercise them over the whole of the earlier sub-kingdom. A substantial portion of it became a kingdom in its own right, owing allegiance to the holy Roman empire; and the county of Burgundy, also known later as Franche Comté, was likewise detached from the duchy. Richard the Justiciar ruled the lands around Autun, Sens, Nevers and Auxerre, all in west Francia (Map 2. 1), a region which became a quite strong territorial principality at a time of general political disruption. During the tenth century, however, his successors lost a certain amount of the authority he had built up, not helping themselves by a marriage alliance with the Robertines which involved them in intrigues over the French throne. The counties on the edge of their duchy, such as Dijon, Mâcon and Langres, moved out of their direct sphere of influence.

When Duke Henry I died in 1002 he left no direct heirs. He designated as his successor Odo-William, count of Mâcon, son of Gerberga his wife and of King Adalbert of Lombardy. Odo-William had a considerable following among the nobility of the region, but King Robert the Pious claimed Burgundy for himself as Henry's nephew, and backed this up with violent action. He invaded the duchy, taking Auxerre and Avallon, and in 1005 Odo-William and his son-in-law, Landri count of Nevers, submitted to the king. But Bishop Lietri of Langres and certain nobles continued to oppose the king until 1015–16 when Robert took Sens and Dijon. He now gave Burgundy to his son Henry, who held it until forced to relinquish the duchy to his brother Robert in 1032 – probably a price of Robert's acceptance that Henry was king (3.2.3).

The succession of wars had done much to weaken the practical authority of both the duke and the counts, and the late tenth century and the early years of the Capetian dukes, 1002–78, marked the decline of Burgundy as a principality. The extent of the lands controlled directly by the dukes were, although in theory

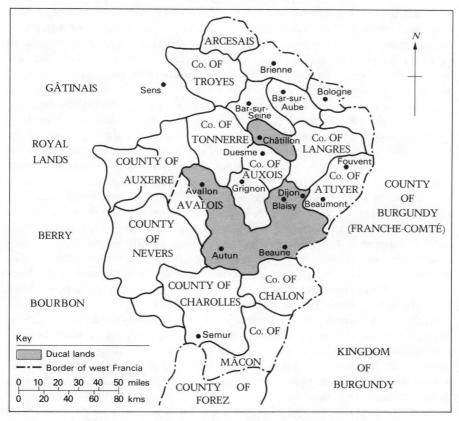

Map 2.1   The duchy of Burgundy in the mid-eleventh century

covering the *pagi* delegated to counts and vicars, in practice very limited indeed, even though the dukes made considerable efforts to conserve and extend them. Robert I held lands round Avallon, Autun, Beaune, Blaisy and Châtillon. He lost control of Auxerre altogether, although he took part of the Dijonnais. He emerges from the sources as a violent man, a pillager of churches, and a murderer of his relatives. The later years of his rule were beset with difficulties, as were also those of his grandson and successor, Hugh I.

While the ducal institutions, the courts, the administrators, the idea of the delegated public power, survived in some areas, their importance diminished rapidly, so that by the 1070s ducal authority was theoretical in most of French Burgundy. The ring of nobles whose lands surrounded the ducal holdings, such as the counts of Troyes, Chalon and Mâcon (Map 2.1), were in practice independent from him, but many had lost their own authority in their counties to viscounts, *vicarii* and castellans. As they were in theory the duke's vassals, they owed homage to him, but this was often done on the borders, with the implications of a peace treaty rather than an agreement of obedience. The great

31

ecclesiastical estates, previously a mainstay of ducal power, were also beginning to go their own way. The bishops of Autun built up an important lordship, and as the ecclesiastical reform movement gathered impetus many monastic lands slipped away from the dukes. Furthermore the lands of monasteries of the new orders such as the Cistercians (4.3.3) were held in free alms and had wide judicial privileges, giving them an autonomous status.

In the wake of the disintegration of ducal power, comital power also began to suffer from the growth of bannal lordships. Independent castles, their centres, began to spring up in the late tenth and eleventh centuries. Certain of the castellans were granted or took over comital and vicarial titles, but in some areas these patterns of landholding broke down altogether and the castellanies were based on entirely new centres. For example the tenth century county of Atuyer was divided in the eleventh century between the self-styled counts of Beaumont and Fouvent. Later these titles were lost, and these castellans were known as the lords of Beaumont and Fouvent. Such men, of whom there were a considerable number, appear to have rendered homage spasmodically to the dukes, major counts and one another, but there was no resulting hierarchy of power; first, because of the crisscross pattern of the ties, and secondly because of the large number of allodial holdings which gave many nobles an independent power base. Thus there were many ties of vassalage but few fiefs.

In the twelfth century ducal power began to revive slowly. The dukes had from the eleventh maintained ties with the Capetian kings, rendering them homage and military service on occasions. As with the king in the kingdom, the duke's authority in Burgundy continued to be recognised in theory, however few his powers were in practice. More practically, the dukes tried to adapt the system of local castellan rule to their own ends. During the twelfth century they managed to strengthen or rebuild the obligations of vassalage of the castellans towards them, using the idea of liege homage to create a centralised system and to allow the dukes access to the seigneurial castles – much of this backed up with violent campaigns. They were helped in their efforts because although most of the lords had important allodial holdings, the castles themselves were often built on lands held as fiefs.

When such conditions did not exist, they attempted to draw the castellans into their dependence by granting them new fiefs. The peace and truce of God had helped to keep alive the idea of public order in the eleventh century, and the dukes, while they had lost control over much church land, were still patrons and advocates of some important abbeys in the region. As patrons of Cluny, for example, they were connected with one of the most influential spiritual forces of their time. During the twelfth century, too, local ducal administrators again began to appear, and gradually taking over some of the powers of the castellans they began slowly to reduce the latters' local authority and independence. Nevertheless, warfare was perhaps the most crucial aspect of the slow climb of the dukes back to power, and many of the changes outlined above were imposed only after successful military campaigns.

Meanwhile the dukes were building up their own lands in the duchy as a power base. In the later eleventh century parts of Auxois and Duesmois were annexed to the ducal holdings. Odo II (1143–62) concentrated mainly on dominating the ecclesiastical estates, bringing the disruptive bishop of Langres to heel. His successor Hugh III gained by marriage the nearby county of Albon in the empire; this gave him a powerful position as the vassal of both French and German kings, and he appeared to be taking an independent political line. King Philip Augustus, alarmed by this, invaded the duchy in 1186 in defence of the lord of Vergy, who feeling himself victimised by the duke's wish to seize his lands, had conveniently commended himself directly to the king (4.2.3). Hugh III was defeated and the duchy came more closely under royal influence.

2.2.2 *A local society in disintegration: the Mâconnais*

Professor Duby's study of the Mâconnais region of Burgundy[1] has proved a seminal work in French local history studies, and his methods and approach have been widely followed. This is a county for which plentiful sources (mainly ecclesiastical cartularies) are extant for the eleventh and twelfth centuries and Duby traces in some depth the series of changes which first transformed a ninth-century Carolingian county into a series of castellanies, and then led to the revival of comital power in the later twelfth century. By the year 980, he suggests, the influence of the duke of Burgundy in this area had waned, although the debris of the authority of the count of Mâcon still existed. The count retained a hold on the estates of the cathedral of Saint-Vincent at Mâcon and on some lands belonging to the abbey of Cluny. His public powers were delegated to *vicarii* who attended his councils and courts. In the early eleventh century, however, his authority diminished rapidly so that by about 1030 the great churches and castellans had become in effect independent. Cluny was increasingly prestigious, and with Tournus abbey and Saint-Vincent at Mâcon profited from grants of immunity from secular authority. Pursuing this to the full, they set up their own courts, forming bannal lordships. The peace and truce of God organised by the church in this area, only served further to diminish the count's moral and judicial authority.

Gradually the nobles ceased to behave as the count's officials and acted in a private capacity, taking certain formerly public powers and making them customary. They no longer attended the count's court, nor did they render him military service regularly; he in his turn did little to resist these trends. By the mid-eleventh century a network of private franchises had emerged in the Mâconnais, strengthened by the large numbers of allodial holdings here. Cohesion between the castellanies was loose, based only on ties of vassalage, which in the early eleventh century were very much like private contracts or treaties of alliance. Later they came to be connected with the holding of land, and by 1070 were almost invariably associated with it. Homage could, however, be sworn to several lords by one individual. The counts tried to gain the support and obedience of a number of castellans by granting them fiefs, but succeeded in dominating very few, and merely alienated their own land.

On the whole, vassalage was for the upper ranks of society, where central control had entirely disappeared and bonds were inextricably crisscrossed, an instrument of independence, the way towards anarchy. On the next level of society it was more effective, since the castellans probably exercised some degree of authority over their own clientèles of lesser nobles and knights. Here too, however, the plurality of ties and the many allodial holdings still gave the knights, a separate group but closely linked to the nobility, considerable independence.

The years 1110–60 marked a period of increasing social stability in the Mâconnais, when a more hierarchical pattern of relationships emerged based on the castellany, which reached its apogee. The fragmentation of power had stopped, and the great bannal lords, lay and ecclesiastic, had established a firm control over their localities, over the middling nobles and the rising group of knights and the peasantry. Operating on the same level as the count of Mâcon, these men, such as the lords of Beaujeu, had wideranging and important connections and indulged in politics outside Burgundy. Meanwhile a commercial revival was taking place, manifesting itself in the appearance of groups of wealthy burgesses, a wider monetary circulation and an increasing taste for luxury goods. This seems to have contributed in its turn to an upheaval in society which began in the late twelfth century, with a resulting impoverishment of many of the great lay families and monasteries, but the enrichment of a few at the top. The distinction between fiefs and allods began to break down, as homage began to be sold, often to wealthy burgesses and peasants. A relatively clear hierarchy of vassals was now established, but economic factors modified the way in which land was held, bringing many non-noble and non-military landholders into the pyramid. The old nobility and knights were regarded as an aristocracy of lineage rather than wealth, and these changed conditions allowed comital, ducal and royal power gradually to increase.

2.2.3 The duchy of Normandy

As befits the most dynamic and powerful French principality of the eleventh and early twelfth centuries, Normandy's history and development have been widely discussed, and its strong connections with England have given it an extra appeal. Normandy was based on a Viking settlement in the lower Seine region, whose rulers expanded their powers by conquest and colonisation. The nascent state was given recognition by the west Frankish kings when in 911 Charles the Simple invested Rollo the Viking leader with upper Normandy at Saint-Clair-sur-Epte; and in 924 lands which probably consisted of the Bessin and the Hiémois were handed over on behalf of King Raoul. In 933 the same king ceded the Avranchin and Cotentin. Links with their homelands were maintained by the Normans well into the eleventh century, but Normandy also developed strong similarities with the neighbouring French states. By the end of William the Conqueror's rule in 1087 it had become a strong and for its time a well-controlled principality with a clear territorial definition in comparison with its neighbours. How far can this relative unity and centralisation be traced back, and does it mark a continuing Frankish structure of government in the province of Neustria, or is it a creation of the Vikings?

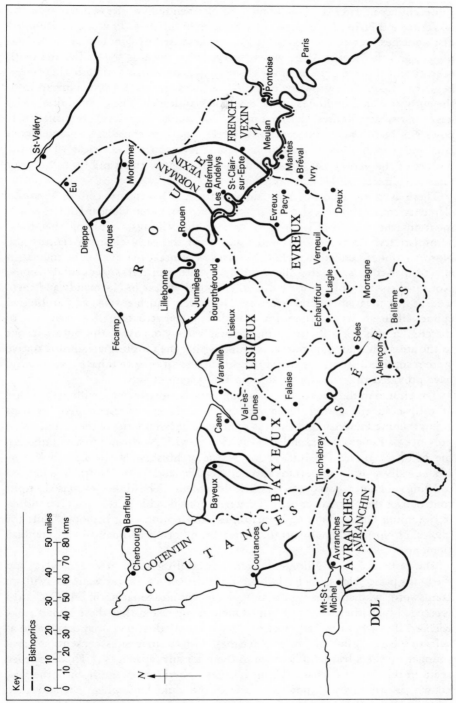

Map 2.2   Normandy in the eleventh and twelfth centuries

Recent accounts of the development of Normandy have stressed the mingling of Viking and Frankish elements in the making of the state. Professor Le Patourel[2] distinguishes between a 'Viking' stage, characterised by conquest, plunder and piracy, and the 'feudal' stage which succeeded it towards the end of the tenth century and at the beginning of the eleventh, when the institutions of the 'duchy' begin to emerge. The growing 'ducal' power, he suggests, stemmed in part from the authority and attributes of the Scandinavian leader. The early 'dukes', who were charismatic figures, defeated other rival bands of settlers, exercising their powers of banishment and gaining and retaining very considerable amounts of land and wealth. But they also inherited or revived (it is not clear which) the powers of the earlier Carolingian counts which gave them public rights over forests, coinage, castles and taxation.

There is some evidence that during the tenth century certain Frankish elements continued to exist within the Norman state; Flodoard for example mentions the cession of a group of *pagi* to the Vikings, implying that these administrative units still survived,[3] and until the early eleventh century the Norman 'dukes' tended to style themselves as princes, marquesses or counts, in effect super-counts, holding the entire duchy rather than its *pagi* or subdivisions. Not until the eleventh century did other counts appear in Normandy and these were at first invariably ducal relatives. This is very much a style of a Carolingian count, albeit an atypical one, but was there a real structure of government to match? There is not sufficient evidence conclusively to answer this question, but in the areas devastated by war, it is unlikely that the Carolingian administrative system survived. In other parts of the principality it may well have done so, and have provided the basis for rebuilding the system of *pagi*.

The church in the duchy, like its administrative institutions, suffered a period of eclipse in the earlier tenth century, but later on re-emerged, perhaps strengthening Frankish traditions as it did so. The boundaries of the ecclesiastical province of Rouen corresponded fairly closely with Normandy itself, although the inclusion under the jurisdiction of the archbishop of the French Vexin, strategically a vitally important area between the lands of the Norman dukes and the kings of France, was to cause political problems. The 'dukes' exercised a tight control over the Norman church. They took considerable initiative in rebuilding it, founding and refounding monasteries, and nominating bishops. Thus the 'dukes' of Normandy built up their state from both Scandinavian and Frankish elements.

The early 'dukes' of Normandy were powerful men and great achievers, and they also passed down their lands undivided. Rollo's estates went to William Longsword, who augmented them, and after his assassination in 942 Richard I succeeded his father. Dudo of Saint-Quentin suggested that these 'dukes', like Richard II of whom he had more first-hand knowledge, had been designated as heirs to the duchy in their father's lifetimes, with the magnates' consent, and that younger brothers had paid homage to them for any 'apanages'.[4] This happened again in the case of Richard III; his brother Robert 'the Magnificent' otherwise known as 'the Devil', however, seized the dukedom when Richard died mysteriously in 1027, and sent Richard's son Nicholas to a monastery. On his own death in 1035 William, his bastard son and designated heir, was to succeed him.

The Norman state, styled in some *acta* as a duchy from the early eleventh century, and as a *regnum* from the late 1020s, was treated as indivisible, and it was also deemed by a strong Norman tradition to be an allod, entirely independent from the French king. Norman chroniclers from Dudo of Saint-Quentin to Robert of Torigny (early eleventh century to mid-twelfth century) emphasised that the grant of 911 had not implied any subordination of the duke. The French kings' view was that the Norman rulers were, like the rest of the territorial princes, royal vassals, and they also refused officially to recognise their ducal status up to 1204, referring to them in royal *acta* as counts. But in practice the Normans had a privileged position; until 1060 any homage rendered was done on the borders of 'France' and Normandy, suggesting a treaty of peace rather than an oath of submission. After the 1060s the dukes, now kings of England, do not seem to have done homage at all. This is probably explained in part by the theory that no king could do homage, as well as by traditions of Norman independence, but it does not seem to imply that Normandy and England were seen by William as an indivisible unit, for at the same time as he failed to pay homage to the French king for the duchy, William rendered him military service: this was done spasmodically, but it fits in well with the behaviour of the other princes (3.3.5).

Norman traditions of relative feudal independence continued until 1151 when Henry Plantagenet paid homage for the duchy to Louis VII in Paris, and in 1156 when he repeated the homage as king. But an admission of the theoretical supremacy of the French king began to emerge much earlier. As well as the continuation of spasmodic military service by the dukes, they allowed two successive designated heirs to the duchy, William Aetheling son of Henry I, and Eustace son of Stephen, neither of whom in the event succeeded, to do homage for it in 1120 and 1137 respectively. In 1109 Henry I had been joined by the dukes of Burgundy and Aquitaine in openly refusing homage to Louis VI, but the defiant position of the Norman kings of England was gradually weakened by the growing legal and political significance of the feudal bond between the king and the princes (4.4.5).

Normandy in the early eleventh century[5] was in relative terms a well-controlled principality, but it is a mistake to exaggerate the power of the dukes and to ignore the clear signs of political problems similar to those which affected the other princes. There were signs of the decay of ducal authority under Robert the Magnificent, who alienated a considerable amount of land and was unable to curb many of his vassals. In the minority of William the Conqueror, Robert's illegitimate son, who succeeded in 1035, disruptive forces began to manifest themselves even more strongly. In many areas, because of weakness at the centre, *pagi* began to break down and power devolved to nobles such as the viscounts of the Bessin and the Cotentin. Private castles began to appear, bringing with them problems of law and order. On the borders the lordship of Bellême, an independent and troublesome state, was consolidated; so too were Laigle and Echauffour. Private wars broke out, and the possibility of an almost complete collapse of ducal power was not avoided until 1047 when King Henry I of France helped William to defeat and crush the most dangerous insurgents. But after this battle William's position was still far from secure. He married Matilda, daughter of Baldwin V count of Flanders, in 1051–52 and gained a valuable ally, but he also faced papal censure as he and Matilda were apparently related within the prohibited degrees. Moreover King Henry I now turned against William in alliance with the powerful Geoffrey Martel of Anjou. In 1054 they staged an invasion of Normandy in support of the count of Arques and other nobles who were hostile to William. The duke defeated one army at Mortemer in 1054, and in 1058 cut off and massacred the rearguard of a royal force at Varaville, but little was decided until 1060 when both the king and Geoffrey of Anjou died.

William's rise to power from 1060 was spectacular and rapid. He seems to have used external aggression as a means of uniting the Norman nobility, for certainly internal consolidation of ducal power went closely with external conquests. First he invaded and conquered Maine, long dominated by Anjou, in 1063, obtaining the overlordship for a time. This was done on the grounds of the betrothal of his son Robert to Margaret, infant sister of count Herbert of Maine, who had died in 1062 promising William the succession. The count of Ponthieu was also forced to pay the duke homage; and the Vexin, held by Count Walter but claimed by William, was harried by him. Then in 1064 William invaded Brittany, building up a powerful opposition within it to Count Conan II and a following for himself. The death of Conan in December 1066 was to remove another important rival of William, but in the meantime the duke of Normandy had invaded England.[6]

William arrived in England in the autumn of 1066 with a great host of Norman, Flemish and Breton nobles and knights, although probably without papal approval. His defeat of Harold at Hastings owed a great deal to good fortune, but in his subjugation of England he left little to chance, using and adapting the existing sophisticated and centralised administrative system of the kingdom to back up a power initially well established by force. The vast majority of the Anglo-Saxon nobles were dispossessed and their lands were granted to William's followers, the majority of whom were Normans. Thus many important cross-channel estates were built up and close links of family, tenure and patronage joined the kingdom and the duchy. The Norman church provided many bishops and abbots for England and Norman monasteries built up valuable lands in the kingdom. The two states continued to share their ruler apart from during the years 1087–96, 1100–06 and 1144–54 and some of the ties between them survived by many years the capture of the duchy by the French king in 1204 (4.4.8).

The conquest of England can be seen as part of a far wider movement which took soldiers and settlers from the duchy into southern Europe and the Middle East. A Norman tradition held that in about 1018 a group of Norman pilgrims on the way home from Palestine went to the shrine of Saint Michael at Monte Gargano in Italy, and by playing off the Lombards and Greeks, they had by the middle of the eleventh century succeeded in establishing strong power bases at Aversa and Melfi. They were soon drawn into the complex politics of the area, an involvement which they turned to their own advantage, and used to build up states in Apulia and Calabria under the leadership of the Hauteville family and Richard of Aversa. By the late 1090s Roger I the Great Count, a Hauteville, dominated Apulia, Calabria and Sicily; and he laid the foundations of the Norman kingdom of Sicily. Meanwhile his relative Bohémond had taken a leading role in the first crusade and in 1100, having founded a new Christian state in the east, was invested as prince of Antioch. He was described graphically by the Byzantine princess Anna Comnena, as a man of cunning and arrogance, with a certain charm but considerable savageness and greed, and above all emanating strength and power: 'even his laugh sounded like a threat to others'.[7] Other Norman nobles were somewhat less ruthless politically, but equally enthusiastic crusaders. Robert Curthose, duke of Normandy, pledged his duchy to his brother William Rufus to enable him to go to the East and eventually, despite his military prowess, lost it to him altogether.

As a result of their conquests, the Normans played an important role in the secular and ecclesiastical politics of western Europe and its relations with the Byzantine empire and the Muslims. They were closely allied with the papacy; they promoted an increasing intransigence in the western church towards the Greek church as well as towards Islam, the latter stemming from their enthusiasm for the idea of holy war. Their achievements can easily be overrated and overstated, for like most of their contemporaries they were struggling for wealth and power, but they were often successful in getting them. Certainly in comparison with many contemporary nobles they had administrative and political skills, effective military techniques, and a flourishing and tightly controlled church. Their architectural style was strong and innovative, and appears in their castles, such as the White Tower in London, and in their churches, from Durham cathedral to Bari. These are the visual reminders of the interchange of ideas between the different areas under Norman domination.

In Normandy itself William gradually reimposed law and order and rebuilt on the institutions of his predecessors. Some of this he achieved before 1060, but the process seems to have been greatly speeded up after this date. He had introduced the peace of God probably in 1047, and this proved a highly effective way of reinforcing ducal peace; later private wars were forbidden by Norman custom. Although vassalage and the fief were found in Normandy before the 1060s, they were not within the kind of relatively ordered and relatively hierarchical structure which was to grow up in England after 1066 and also to spread in post-conquest Normandy. It was to evolve with the growth of ducal authority which was manifested in a number of ways. The dukes maintained the right to confiscate the lands and rights of the nobility, although only when they rebelled, for their estates seem to have been regarded as hereditary. Following the rebellion of William, count of Arques, for example, the lands of one of his associates, Roger of Mortemer, were forfeit. The castle at Mortemer and valuable estates were granted to William of Warenne by the duke. Furthermore the duke insisted on receiving the homage of the vassals of his vassals, maintaining a position as liege lord. In 1080 at the council of Lillebonne he required the great nobles and ecclesiastics to recognise that they were obliged to bring their disputes to the ducal court. Military service was also levied effectively by the duke, the greater nobles and the ecclesiastical estates gradually becoming liable for a fixed number of knights in the later part of William's rule. High justice was either kept by the duke or granted out to the great nobles under ducal surveillance. And William exercised considerable authority over the Norman church, introducing many of the disciplinary aspects of the papal reforms without relinquishing any of his own powers. He also encouraged the growth of the Norman towns, founding *bourgs* and stimulating trade.

William's power in his French principality was greater by far than that of any his contemporaries in France. He was violent and charismatic; as the Anglo-Saxon chronicler put it, he was

a very wise man, and very powerful and more worshipful and stronger than any predecessor of his had been. He was gentle to the good men who loved God, and stern beyond all measure to those people who resisted his will.[8]

The Norman chroniclers William of Jumièges and William of Poitiers give far more partisan accounts. The first, writing in the early 1070s describes the duke as the wisest and most gracious king, a keeper of peace and dispenser of justice. The second, a ducal chaplain, produced an account at about the same time which is at once a panegyric and a well-informed and useful source. But both these writers, like the Bayeux tapestry, the celebrated embroidered narrative of the conquest of England, stress the personal power and strength of William. Once he had died in 1087 and his lands were disputed between Robert Curthose and William Rufus much of the authority he had built up in the ducal office was dissipated. In Normandy private castles multiplied and confused political conditions developed.

This breakdown of central authority illustrates and highlights one major problem confronting the successful territorial prince of the eleventh and twelfth centuries, that of succession. William, despite the attempts of Philip I of France to stir his sons to rebellion and perhaps even to separate England and Normandy, had succeeded in holding together his lands. In many ways he might have preferred that England and Normandy should be inherited by one son – perhaps William Rufus since Robert Curthose the eldest, was, it is said, disliked by and consistently disloyal to his father. Because of the cross-channel estates and the interests built up by the Norman nobility and church this would have been a popular course. Many historians have suggested that this was originally intended by William but that events eventually forced a compromise on him, whereby Robert would inherit Normandy, the patrimony, and William, England, the acquisition. The question of whether the division was forced on William is not readily resolved, but it has been suggested that the partition which in the end resulted was quite in keeping with Norman noble inheritance customs and also with those in much of northern France.[9] Be this as it may, William's eldest son Robert was ousted as duke of Normandy by both his brothers, first by William Rufus and then by Henry I, both of whom were also kings of England.

When William Rufus took possession of England he met with considerable opposition from much of the Anglo-Norman baronage; Robert, anxious to take England, attempted to invade but had the tables turned on him by William, who managed both to hold down his kingdom and to establish himself in the duchy. He then helped Robert to rebuild his power in Normandy and Maine and the

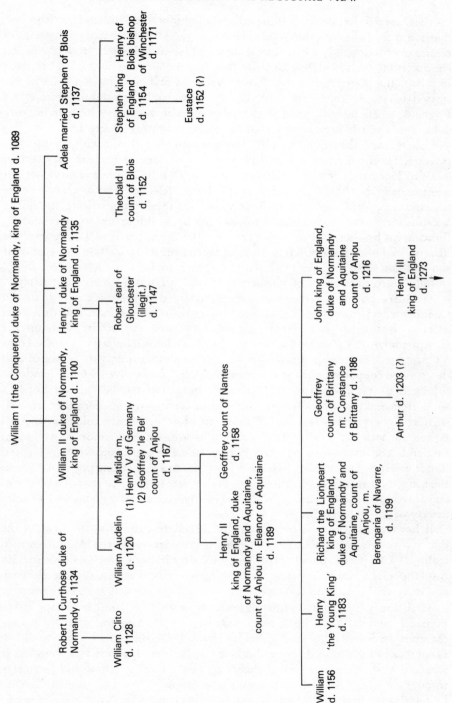

Fig. 2.1 Outline genealogy of the Anglo-Norman royal house

brothers agreed that if one died the other should inherit all his lands; neither was married at the time. But they soon fell out again and Rufus seemed on the verge of taking over Normandy when Robert departed on crusade in 1096, and pawned the duchy for 10,000 marks. William therefore remained as duke until his death in 1100, but shortly after this Robert returned and took his lands back. He missed having to repay his debt, but he was unable to establish himself in England, where he in fact had considerable support, because of his own dilatory behaviour and the determination of his younger brother Henry I.

Robert invaded England in 1101 but was easily bought off with the lure of a pension. He furthermore released Henry from homage he had done for certain lands in Normandy if he gave them all up save Domfront – but Henry does not seem to have abandoned his claims to the duchy. It is not clear whether he gave his lands in Normandy back to Robert, but his intention of taking the duchy became increasingly apparent. This he did by building up support and by fighting his brother, whom he defeated in 1106 at the battle of Tinchebray. He dispossessed both Robert, whom he held captive until his death in 1134, and his son William Clito, born in 1102. This prince was to die in battle in 1128, trying to hold on to the county of Flanders with which Louis VI had invested him.

The succession arrangements originally envisaged for the lands of William the Conqueror, whether they had in fact involved partition or not, had thus been utterly overturned, and Henry, the youngest son, cut off by William the Conqueror with a substantial sum of money, had taken all his father's lands. Louis VI protested and campaigned against Henry, but against this powerful and determined opponent he was almost entirely ineffective. Henry, indeed, managed to reimpose order in Normandy quite rapidly; he crushed Robert's supporters and those nobles who might have been dangerous for other reasons, such as Robert of Bellême and William of Mortain. Henry ruled 'with royal power' in both parts of his lands, acting as king in Normandy as well as in England. The royal title which gave him considerable status and which prevented him from rendering homage to Louis VI put him in a very strong position *vis-à-vis* the king. Normandy's position within France was in practice that of a powerful and autonomous principality, its links with the monarchy tenuous and its ruler utterly overshadowing his French suzerain.

It has recently been fashionable for historians to emphasise the links of the duchy with England to such an extent that the two are seen as the 'Anglo-Norman realm'.[10] This is a convenient term, but what does it mean, and does it tie in with contemporary usage? Certainly the term *regnum* was often used in the eleventh and early twelfth centuries to apply to principalities as well as to kingdoms. It was frequently applied to Normandy both before and after 1066; it was applied to England, and it could be applied loosely to both England and Normandy together, to describe the lands ruled by Henry I. On the other hand it would be dangerous to infer from this that England and Normandy formed one *kingdom*. It is true that the two were linked closely by ties of family, tenure and patronage throughout their long if interrupted association. Then the title of king of England was often used in the formal acts of Henry I for Normandy either to replace or in conjunction with the title of duke, and the Hyde chronicler went so far as to describe Henry as *rex Norman-Anglorum*. But he is a rare and literary exception, and it is clear that the inconsistency of the terminology used in 'official' documents shows the lack of a clear distinction between ducal and royal authority and also a total lack of any defined idea of an Anglo-Norman kingship.

Professor C. W. Hollister argues that as Henry I had been crowned in England in 1100 he did not need and thus did not get investiture in Normandy after its capture, yet Professor Le Patourel points out, the ceremonies he held in the duchy in 1107 may have included a form of investiture, and Stephen was to be both crowned in England and invested in Normandy. Then there is the problem of homage to the French king. It is true that no duke-cum-king of England and Normandy seems to have recognised the overlordship of the Capetians in person from about 1060 until 1156, but this does not imply that Normandy was seen as attached to England rather than France, as Hollister suggests. For the designated heirs both of Henry I and of Stephen paid border homage to the French kings for Normandy, an important gesture. In short, despite the ambiguities surrounding the use of the royal and ducal titles, despite the strong ties between the kingdom and the duchy, the Anglo-Norman realm as a kingdom exists far more clearly in the minds of modern historians than it did in the consciousness of contemporaries: Henry I ruled with kingly powers in both but he was not king of both. Normandy remained a French principality, albeit the strongest and most independent, but it still had links with the French king and these were to strengthen later in the twelfth century (4.4.2).

Henry I proved a strong and able ruler of Normandy who really set its administration on a sound footing, and a dangerous adversary for the Capetian Louis VI, but he too suffered from the problem of finding a suitable heir. His only legitimate son William, to whom he intended to leave both the kingdom and the duchy, died in a tragic shipwreck in 1120. This left the English king with only one direct legitimate descendant, the Empress Matilda, wife then widow of Henry V of Germany. Henry, rather than pass his lands to William Clito, son of Robert Curthose, or to Theobald or Stephen of Blois, also his nephews and the latter a favourite of his, designated his daughter his heiress in 1126–27, made his magnates swear to recognise her and married her to Geoffrey, count of Anjou. But when Henry died in 1135 Stephen seized the English throne and ousted both Theobald (2.2.4) and Matilda. The Empress and her husband fought back. After a period of civil war in England and Normandy, Geoffrey overran the duchy in 1144, and began to impose order again, a task continued by his son Henry II who dominated the English kingdom along with half of France.

2.2.4 The lands of Blois-Champagne: a problem for the Capetians

The lands of the counts of Blois and Troyes almost encircled the royal principality, and the power of this family was a considerable problem for the Capetians. Nevertheless the counts were not able to carve out a clear and well defined principality until the late eleventh century, and this was due in considerable measure to the influence of the kings, who tried as far as possible to contain their dangerous rivals using neighbouring princes to help them. In his

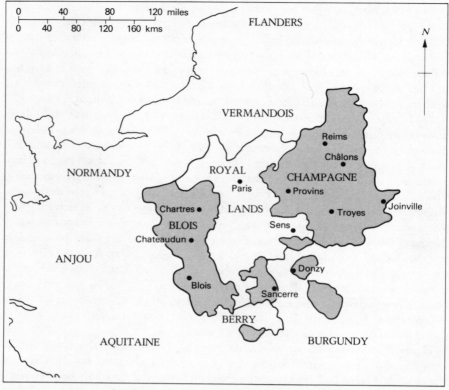

Map 2.3   The lands of Blois-Champagne in the later twelfth century

study of Champagne, M. Bur questions whether the counts were really territorial princes at all, for their lands lacked a set of local customs, territorial definition and historical traditions, and their family had no genealogies devoted to them, no monastic burial house and little of the other panoply of the other eleventh-century princes. But he concludes that despite these important missing features, in practical terms the counts exercised the same kind of power as the other princes, with their peace-keeping functions, with their own domains, with a group of counties in their feudal *mouvance* or dependence, with their clientèles of lesser nobles and knights, and their wars and negotiations with neighbouring magnates and the king.[11]

The lack of any chronicles and contemporary genealogies relating to the counts means that on the whole they remain shadowy figures; charter evidence is the keystone of research into the counties of Blois and Troyes. The latter, together with areas to its south, came increasingly to be described as Champagne from the eleventh century onwards, although the designation was unofficial until the thirteenth century. The dual principality began to form in the ninth century as the central areas of the duchy of Francia (3.3.3) disintegrated politically; the only firm boundary remaining was that of the archbishopric of Reims.

In the tenth century Herbert II count of Vermandois, descended from the

Carolingians, and his son Herbert 'the Old' began to collect lands together, but after Herbert the Old's death in 980–4 his lands were divided. His nephews Herbert 'the Young' and Odo I took the most important lands and rights; Herbert, already count of Meaux and Troyes, received Epernay and the Perthois, and Odo the county of Omois together with control of the county of Reims and the abbey of Saint-Médard at Soissons. He was already count of Blois, Tours, Chateaudun and Chartres, which he had inherited from his father Theobald the Trickster. The area round Saint-Quentin went to Albert, count of Vermandois, Herbert's brother. Meanwhile on the fringes of these shifting blocs of domination independent castellanies were springing up around important fortresses. Examples from the diocese of Reims are Porcien, Rethel, Roucy and Oulchy.

In the eleventh century the fortunes of the house of Blois-Troyes began to rise. Their history illustrates both the problems and the advantages of the state builders of the period. Allied by blood and marriage to almost all the important families of northern France, they inherited a number of important lands and often held on to them, if necessary by battle. But they also suffered from their proximity to the Capetians, who were anxious not to be crushed between the two parts of the holding and were liable to approve or even demand their partition between heirs, which does seem to have become customary. On the other hand the connections of the various parts seem to have been maintained, so that when one branch of the family failed the other inherited its lands. But their lands also lacked a strong territorial base, a city or a county as their centre and this continued to be the case for much of the eleventh century. Nevertheless the counts were able to wield a considerable degree of power and influence in this period, based on their domain and their followers.

Odo II the Great, count of Blois, helped by the strong if intermittent attachment of King Robert the Pious to his mother, Bertha (3.2.2), began to assemble a conglomeration of lands. He seems to have been a remarkable but also a rash and reckless man, with his sights set, in his later years, on the kingdom of Burgundy. In 1004 he added the Champagne possessions around Reims and Provins to Blois, Tours, Chartres and Vendôme. Then as claims to other lands emerged he used them to the full.

His first wife Matilda, sister of Duke Richard II of Normandy, had brought as a dowry part of the town of Dreux and the surrounding area. After her death her brother claimed it back and defeated Odo in battle. Yet the king gave Richard Tillières and allowed Odo to retain Dreux. But this was just a beginning. In *c.* 1022 Stephen count of Troyes died without heirs. Odo was clearly in the running for his lands as a relative, and had the division of 943 made by Herbert II been in *parage*, as Professor Lot suggested was the case, Odo's claim would have been greatly strengthened. The evidence is by no means clear. Raoul Glaber seems to imply that there was a *parage* arrangement, but recently M. Bur has suggested that Herbert II made a straightforward division.[12] In any case the king was a rival claimant. Odo settled the matter by invading the counties of Troyes and Meaux, and the king reluctantly invested him with these lands. But Odo soon caused further trouble by attacking the lands of his new neighbour, the duke of Lorraine. This angered the Emperor Henry II, and when he met Robert the Pious at

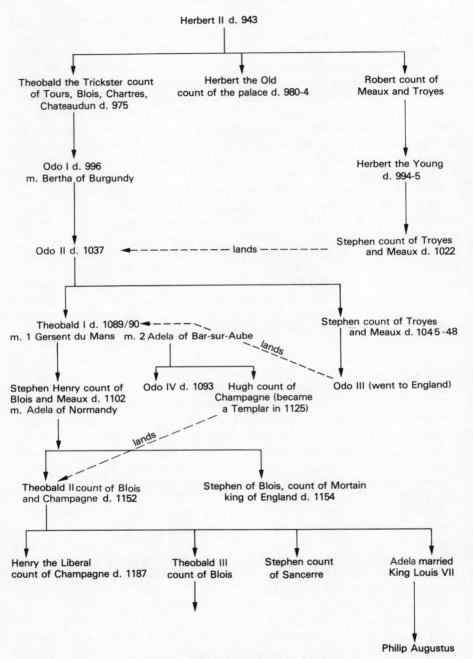

Fig. 2.2   Outline genealogy of the counts of Champagne

Mouzon in 1023 they together formally condemned Odo. His lands may have been judged forfeit; certainly Odo thought they had been for he took up arms against the king. He refused to go before the royal court and had written on his behalf a celebrated letter.[13] Professor Fawtier quoted from it to show that the great nobles never pursued a vendetta against the king since even when quarrelling with him, they recognised his as the ultimate authority. But the later part of this letter which best illustrates this point may also be viewed as a normal attempt of a vassal to make peace with his lord, in this case the king, a point Professor Halphen emphasised.[14]

For it is very painful for me to quarrel with you, my lord. From the man who is at loggerheads with you are withheld the blessings kingships bestows, justice and peace. Wherefore I implore you to show me that clemency which is a well-spring within you, and which only evil council can cause to be dried up. And I pray you to cease persecuting me, and let me be reconciled with you.

The tone of this last section, indeed, contrasts strikingly with an earlier passage where Odo boldly states his claims to the lands:

I am astounded that without having heard me in my own defence, you should hasten to pronounce me unworthy of the fief I hold of you. For consider my ancestry: by dint of it I am, thank God, entitled to succeed to the counties of Meaux and Troyes. Consider the fief you have bestowed on me [i.e. Blois]: it was not granted out of your royal fisc, but is part of the lands which have come down to me by hereditary right and of your royal grace.

The contemporary chronicler Wipo alleges that Odo frequently declared 'I don't want to be king, just always the king's master.'[15] This might be an ironic statement, for Odo's ambitions stretched to kingdoms beyond the west Frankish border, and there was nothing to prevent him from coveting the French kingdom too. Or was it the utterance of a territorial prince aware of the realities of political power and more concerned with these than with the royal title? Certainly by the 1030s Odo, palatine count like many of his line, seemed to be in a good position to overshadow Henry I as Henry's ancestors had the Carolingians. For in 1023 he succeeded in retaining Troyes and Meaux, and he then moved on to wider schemes. He claimed the kingdom of Burgundy through his mother Bertha of Burgundy, and he even allied briefly with Robert the Pious and with Duke William of Aquitaine against Conrad II, the new emperor, in pursuit of it. But this coalition was unable to agree on concerted action and Odo was soon at war with the king again.

In 1031 when Robert the Pious died he supported Queen Constance and her second surviving son, Robert, against Henry I, his father's designated heir. Odo received a considerable sum of money and half the town of Sens as the price of his aid; and the early 1030s saw the apogee of his power in France. The coalition was defeated by Henry I with the help of Robert the Magnificent, duke of Normandy, but Odo had meanwhile managed to build up a substantial clientèle of castellans from within the royal principality, which undermined the king's power there. Then in 1033 he took up arms again in favour of the king's brother Odo, but also still in pursuit of his claim to the kingdom of Burgundy. This had been strengthened when in 1032 King Rudolph, his mother's brother, had died. The Emperor Conrad II and Henry I of France both stepped in to prevent this claim from being made good, and in 1034 Odo made peace. But when he died in 1037, this was during yet another campaign in Lorraine.

Despite Odo's aggression, the control he exercised over his own diverse lands was not deeply based. Indeed he was unable to form a cohesive principality in the eastern parts of his possessions. Reims and Châlons were royal bishoprics and Meaux strongly under royal influence. There were many independent lordships in the area and Troyes was the only town where comital power was strong. And when in 1037 Odo died his eldest son, Theobald I, took the paternal lands of Blois, and his second son , Stephen I, became count of Troyes and Meaux. The latter died between 1045 and 1048 and these lands returned temporarily to the care of Theobald I until the young Odo III came of age. Meanwhile Theobald had lost the Touraine and Vendôme to Geoffrey count of Anjou who had the backing of the king. Furthermore in the period 1047–65 new independent castles were appearing in considerable numbers on the borders of Champagne, posing a further problem to the counts. In the 1050s Theobald was in alliance with the king, and his power began to build up again. He began to expand southwards from the Troyes lands, and when in 1058–60 his nephew Odo III came of age, he paid Theobald homage for them. Thus when he went to live in England in the late 1060s Theobald was able to take back these counties.

A rival to the count of Blois emerged in the 1060s in the shape of Raoul IV of Valois (2.3.1). But when his son Simon became a monk in 1077 some of the estates of this family, Bar and Vitry, passed to Theobald through his wife, further enhancing his power. Theobald was, indeed, in a commanding position by the end of his rule, and he had also begun to consolidate his power within his dual-sided principality, exerting a growing authority over many of the castellans in the county of Blois in particular. He was count of the palace to Philip I, and linked to the king by ties of vassalage, but he nevertheless supported both the order of Cluny and the papal reformers against the royal interest.

A measure of his power seems to be that the king insisted that the customary division of his lands should take place in 1089–90 when he died. One of his sons, Odo IV, inherited the county of Troyes, but Stephen Henry, his brother, was given the county of Meaux to the east of Paris, as well as Blois and Chartres. In 1093 Odo IV died and was succeeded by another brother Hugh, who began to push the county of Champagne yet further to the south, basing his authority on Troyes, Épernay, Saint-Florentin and Provins. He married Constance, daughter of King Philip I, and this brought him Attigny, but he also managed to dominate Argonne. He had some difficulty in controlling castellans such as the Dampierre, Chappes and ·Trainel families in the county of Troyes, but eventually he succeeded in imposing some degree of authority in the region. Although Hugh's power had by this time a firm base, he suffered several unhappy marriages and in 1125 became a Templar. Champagne now passed back to the counts of Blois.

Meanwhile, Stephen Henry, count of Blois and Meaux, appears, like his possessions, to have been governed by his wife Adela, daughter of William the Conqueror. When he went on crusade in 1096 she was officially made his regent, and although he returned from the east with extreme rapidity she soon sent him back again. He died in Outremer in 1102. Theobald II, his young son, became the next count. His power had, like that of his uncle the count of Champagne, an increasingly strong base, and the feudal links of the castellans with the counts were growing. The Broyes and the Roucy were powerful and independent, but they were as much a problem for the French king as the count of Blois.

Theobald II was described by the chronicler of Morigny as being second only to the king in the kingdom. He wielded great political power and during his long rule as count of Blois and Champagne the eastern parts of his lands in particular became very prosperous. Theobald, like his contemporaries Thierry and Philip counts of Flanders, gave direct encouragement to the growth of trade in his lands. By grants of privileges and safeguards he diverted merchants travelling between Flanders and the Languedoc away from the episcopal cities of Reims and Orléans to towns under his own control or where he could profit directly. Troyes, Provins, Meaux, Lagny and Bar-sur-Aube all gained custom at the expense of Reims, but also of Paris. Hence Louis VI and Louis VII tried to fix a monopoly on Parisian water traffic, while Reims joined a trading league with other northern French towns such as Arras, Cambrai and Saint-Quentin. Largely as a result of its prosperity, Champagne rather than Blois now became the centre of the comital holdings. The authority of the counts, however, seems to have remained a feudal one, in the earlier twelfth century not backed up with a developing administration as was the case in Normandy.

Theobald II's resources were considerable. He controlled the profits of valuable trade, he held about two-thirds of the castles in Champagne, together with domain lands and rights: Troyes, the Perthois and Epernay regions, Meaux, Coulommiers and Bar-sur-Aube. He was lay advocate of a number of important abbeys and feudal overlord of most of the castellans. Indeed the build-up of his feudal authority was helped by changing patterns of landholding, for where before 1075 one out of every two parcels of land was allodial, after this date there was a dwindling in the ratio, one allod being outnumbered by six fiefs. More landed knights also began to appear. The count was the vassal of the French kings, the emperors and the dukes of Burgundy for various lands, but his successors did not acknowledge the French king as suzerain for all their holdings until 1198. Theobald II thus enjoyed a considerable degree of independence, and he was an important figure in the politics of the French court.

In the early part of his reign he posed something of a threat to Louis VI, fighting him in the Brie area in 1111–19 and again from 1128 to 1135. Then Henry I, king of England, his uncle, died. Theobald seemed a strong contender for the English throne, for Henry's only direct heir was the Empress Matilda. But he was pre-empted by his brothers Stephen, and Henry, bishop of Winchester, Stephen taking the crown with Henry's support. Theobald gave Stephen some help in his fight against Matilda and her husband Geoffrey of Anjou, but from now on his preoccupations seem to have been more with the economy of Champagne than with politics. Nevertheless in 1142–43 he was involved in hostilities with Louis VII, emerging unscathed. Abbot Suger, Louis's principal adviser, favoured détente with Blois-Champagne rather than warfare, however, and Theobald's later relations with Louis VII tended to be more peaceful.

In 1152 Theobald II died and his lands were divided. His eldest son, Henry the Liberal, took Champagne, but one cadet, Theobald, was given Blois and Chartres and another, Stephen, Sancerre. Henry however, remained as suzerain of all the lands, and this M. Bur suggests, marks a change from earlier divisions.[16] Henry was, like his father, an important figure in French politics. He managed to steer a middle course between Louis VII and the Emperor Frederick Barbarossa over the papal schism in the 1160s, although he generally supported Louis against Henry II of England. He married Marie de France, daughter of Louis VII and Eleanor of Aquitaine, while Louis VII took as his second wife Adela, Henry's sister. Within Champagne Henry now built up a comital administration in the form of *prévôts* and later *baillis* set over the castellanies on the model of the royal lands, and seems to have enforced his military and fiscal rights as well. He organised and regulated commerce and granted franchises to urban and rural communities. He also went on crusade at the end of his life. In 1181 he was succeeded by Count Henry II, another enthusiastic crusader, and from 1197 to 1201 Henry's younger brother, Theobald III, was count. His wife, Blanche of Navarre, acted as regent for the infant Theobald IV, born after his father's death, and he became king of Navarre in 1234. It was now that suzerainty over Blois was relinquished to the French king (5.2.1). In 1284 Joan of Navarre, heiress to Champagne, married the future King Philip IV, and the independent existence of Champagne was soon to come to an end.

2.3 PRINCIPALITIES IN NORTHERN AND WESTERN FRANCE: AN OUTLINE

2.3.1 *Flanders, Picardy, Brittany*

Flanders was the only French principality, apart from Normandy, where the disintegration of princely power to below the level of the prince only occurred in a limited way and was reversed quite easily. Unlike Normandy it was not a stable geographical unit, but well into the fourteenth century contained the changing lands dominated by its counts. Flanders began as an independent principality when in 862 Baldwin I abducted Judith, daughter of Charles the Bald, and Charles, although initially somewhat reluctant to favour him, later granted him the *pagus* of Flanders. For most of the tenth century this was an important state in northern France, and after a temporary setback to comital power at the end of the tenth century during Baldwin IV's minority, the counts began to expand into German lands and south into Hainault. Baldwin V (1035–67) married Adela, daughter of King Robert the Pious of France, and from 1060 to 1067 he acted as guardian to his young nephew, Philip I of France.

In 1070, however, problems emerged when Baldwin VI died and his brother Robert the Frisian tried to seize his lands from his legitimate heirs and their mother the Countess Richilda. Both sides called on King Philip I for support and Richilda was initially successful in gaining it. Philip I defeated Robert the Frisian at the battle of Cassel in 1071, but Arnulf, the legitimate heir to Flanders was killed, and Robert was given the county. Richilda presented her own lands of

Hainault to her next son Baldwin. Robert the Frisian's two successors were generally allies of the king and both died fighting for him. Another crisis erupted in 1127 when Count Charles the Good (1119–27) was murdered while at mass in Bruges by a group of disaffected nobles. Louis VI immediately went to Flanders and in his presence William Clito, son of the imprisoned Robert Curthose, duke of Normandy, but grandson, too, of Matilda of Flanders, was elected as the next count of Flanders. A violent civil war ensued, which was graphically described by the chronicler Galbert of Bruges. A group of towns rejected William Clito as count and chose Thierry of Alsace instead. William was defeated and killed in battle and Louis VI had to recognise his rival.

Thierry and his successor Philip of Alsace (1128–91) managed to tame the urban communities by imposing law and order on them, but also by encouraging their economic growth by making grants of valuable privileges. They brought the castellans to heel, carrying out what amounted to a purge in the north of the county; they strengthened their feudal powers and they developed a sophisticated administration. The *Gros Brief* of 1187, an account roll of the count's domain, reveals an effective financial machine and also highlights the wealth of the Flemish counts in the twelfth century.

In Picardy, lying to the west of Flanders, political power devolved straight to the castellans, and despite attempts by various nobles to form principalities in the region, these always foundered on the opposition of the kings whose lands lay directly to the south. The nearest approximation to a principality which emerged here was in the lands built up by Raoul of Crépy, from 1055 onwards. His family, descended from the Carolingians, was firmly implanted in the area at the end of the tenth century. Raoul was already count of Bar-sur-Aube by marriage when in 1063 he added Amiens and the Vexin by inheritance. He also held the lordship of Montdidier. These were key areas in the domination of northern France. Simon, his heir, saw the Vexin overrun by Philip I of France, and in 1077 became a monk, leaving sisters to inherit. His estates were divided between his relatives, and the shortlived proto-principality was no longer a problem either to the kings, or the counts of Blois.

Professor Fossier shows that the crown played a very important role in the region, helping to organise its society in the thirteenth century but also preventing political power from cohering in the eleventh. Picardy was, he says, with the Ile de France

the only part of the kingdom from which the king was never absent from the age of the invasions to the modern period. The permanence of his control over the clergy and the aristocracy, the visits or the campaigns he made, the ties of family or of interest established with the counts of Ponthieu, Vermandois, Soissons and many other lords, did more to maintain his presence than his castle at Montreuil or his rights over Corbie and Saint-Riquier. It has to be conceded that the development of an important territorial principality in Picardy was prevented mainly by the king's fear of a threat to his possessions on the Oise or the Aisne.[17]

In this the development of Picardy was unique. Although there are many similarities between this area and the Mâconnais, the evolution of their social structures took place under different circumstances. In the Mâconnais there was a power vacuum; in Picardy royal power was strong enough to prevent a principality from forming, and consequently allowed the development of castellanies. The Capetians did not become strong enough to bring Picardy under their direct domination until the late twelfth century.

Brittany was a region with strong traditions of independence, with a racial identity, a language and culture of its own. Nominoé and Erispoé who transformed it from a Carolingian march to a principality in the mid-ninth century built up such authority that its rulers called themselves kings. In the tenth and eleventh centuries, however, they styled themselves as counts, and their power had been much diminished by Viking attacks, by power struggles amongst the nobility and by adulterine castellanies. The dukes of Normandy claimed overlordship of Brittany and Robert the Magnificent and William the Conqueror both realised it. Lands in England given to the Breton counts after the Norman conquest were during the twelfth century consolidated into the earldom of Richmond, giving the Bretons important links with the English kingdom. Further connections were built up when in 1166 Constance, heiress to Brittany was married to Geoffrey, son of Henry II. He began to revive central power in Brittany, now styled a duchy. In the thirteenth century this work was continued not by his son Arthur, probably murdered by King John in 1203, but by Peter Mauclerc, a Capetian prince. He was the husband of Alice, heiress of Brittany, the daughter of Constance and her third husband Guy of Thouars.

2.3.2 Greater Anjou and the duchy of Aquitaine

Until 1060 Anjou was, like Normandy and Flanders, a powerful principality strongly dominated by its ruling house. It had formed in the tenth century during the second stage of disintegration, when counts Fulk the Good and Geoffrey Greymantle consolidated their power over the *pagus* of Angers and surrounding areas. Fulk Nerra (987–1040) and Geoffrey Martel (1040–60) managed, as Sir Richard Southern has demonstrated, to extend their power by a mixture of belligerence and good marriages, taking over Touraine, Vendôme and Saintonge.[18] Their political importance in France and Europe became considerable. The exploits of Fulk, who switched dramatically from war to prayer, are legendary; Geoffrey was a calculating politician who switched more subtly from ally to ally. In 1060 he died, leaving no direct heirs, and a political crisis followed, triggered off by the weakness and political maladroitness of the next count, Geoffrey the Bearded. Fulk Réchin his brother ousted him with the support of the papacy, which was gained as result of Geoffrey's dispute with the archbishop of Tours. It took a long while before the resulting breakdown of comital authority could be reversed and independent lordships such as Amboise and Craon brought back under the count's control.

In the twelfth century the lands of the Angevins began to increase rapidly and dramatically. Count Fulk V gained Maine by marriage and later became king of Jerusalem. His son Geoffrey 'le Bel' (1128–51) fought long and hard against the castellans, and made a splendid match when he married the Empress Matilda, designated in 1128 as heiress to England and Normandy. Despite the disputed succession and the reign of Stephen of Blois in England (1135–54), Henry II, son of Geoffrey and Matilda, succeeded in gaining control of England, Normandy and Greater Anjou, and took Aquitaine by marriage. He continued his father's struggles against the castellans in Anjou, reduced them to feudal obedience, and developed an administration for the ducal domains.

The duchy of Aquitaine was a large and diverse collection of counties and lordships, stretching down the whole west coast of France south of Brittany, inland to the heart of the Massif Central and south to the Pyrenees. There was a hiatus between the Carolingian duchy and its successor which was assembled by counts of Poitou in the early tenth century. By the time of William the Great who died in 1030, the dukes, as well as controlling Poitou, exercised a varying degree of authority in the counties of Limoges, Berry, Saintonge, Auvergne, Périgord and La Marche. In some they were overlords in name only, although in the last two they could intervene quite successfully. William the Great was regarded as a powerful ruler and a dangerous military adversary by his contemporaries, although he seems to have lost some of the authority of his predecessors.[19] Under his sons, ducal power diminished further, independent castellanies began to appear in considerable numbers even in Poitou, and Aquitaine came strongly under the influence of Anjou.

The fourth and last son to succeed William the Great, William VIII or Guy-Geoffrey (1058–86) managed to regain a considerable amount of ground. He recaptured the Saintonge from Anjou in 1062, and in the next year he added Gascony to the ducal holdings. This was claimed through Brisca, one of William the Great's several wives, but it was a difficult area to control, as it contained many independent lordships (2.4.2). Guy-Geoffrey and his successors William IX the Young (1086–1126) and William X the Toulousain (1126–37) were heavily preoccupied with their southern lands. William IX married Philippa of Toulouse in 1094, giving their descendants a claim to this neighbouring principality, which they were never able fully to realise despite long and continuing efforts. These dukes were patrons of the troubadours – William IX was one himself – and enthusiastic crusaders. As a result of their southern outlook they paid less attention to Poitou than they might have done. They waged sporadic campaigns against castellans such as the lords of Parthenay and Lusignan, but they never really succeeded in dominating them in the way that the French kings and the counts of Anjou were doing in their lands. Nevertheless they were wealthy and powerful rulers with wide and important connections.

In 1137 William X died, leaving his daughter Eleanor and his duchy to the French crown, a gain of major importance to the Capetians. Eleanor bore Louis VII two daughters, but their marriage broke down and was dissolved by the pope on the grounds of consanguinity (4.2.2). In 1152 she married Henry of Anjou, later king of England, bringing Aquitaine into his vast assemblage of lands, and passing it to their sons Richard I and John (4.4.7). The attempts of Richard to dominate the turbulent nobles proved not entirely successful, and the lords of the Limousin, Angoulême and La Marche were to play a crucial role in the destinies of not only of the duchy, but of all the Angevin dominions. Richard I was to meet his death fighting them,[20] and John's lands were declared forfeit by Philip

Augustus for his mishandling of them. The English kings managed to retain Gascony into the thirteenth century and beyond (5.4.5), and the regional lords of Thouars, Parthenay, Mauléon and Lusignan dominated Poitou until the 1240s, when their power was broken by Louis's brother, Alfonso of Poitiers (5.5.4).

2.4 THE SOUTH

2.4.1 Southern society

The south of France, Languedoc and the Spanish march and Gascony, showed marked contrasts with northern and central France in its language, social structure and customs (1.1.1). From the tenth to the early thirteenth century the connections of the Midi with the pope were far stronger than its ties to the French king. This was only to change after the Albigensian crusade, when certain patterns of landholding and methods of administration were to be introduced from the north in the wake of the royal conquests. But this was not the first occasion on which an army from the north had brought with it major social and political modifications in the region. In the eighth and early ninth centuries the Carolingian kings had fought their way down into the south, at the expense of the Islamic people who occupied the Iberian peninsula and much of the Mediterranean coast of France. Gascony and Catalonia were constituted as marcher states, and the Carolingian administrative system was also introduced into Languedoc, Provence and Aquitaine. Power was held by counts or markgraves, the majority Frankish, others Gascons or Goths.

During the course of the ninth century royal authority weakened in this region and by 900 a number of territorial principalities had emerged: the duchy of Gascony, the counties of Toulouse, Carcassonne, Ampurias-Roussillon and the kingdom of Provence. The last became part of the larger kingdom of Burgundy although its links with the lands to the west remained strong. The great families of the area, the descendants of the earlier Carolingian officials, were unable fully to retain their powers, and in many areas lesser counts and viscounts began to enjoy public powers as though they were private. The prevalence of the allod, private land, and the rarity of benefices in the south helped this, but on the other hand the idea that the delegated powers of administration and justice were public survived in the Languedoc, and so too did the rendability of castles to the count, enabling him to repossess them at will.

Customs did not take the place of public authority as in much of the north. Yet many of the nobles, while acknowledging the count of Toulouse's rights, often took little heed of them in real terms. The region was in the tenth century a politically confused one. Although the threat of external invasion decreased, castles proliferated, and they seem to have been a symbol of local domination and aggression against the immediate neighbours of their holders. In the Toulouse principality in the late tenth and early eleventh century there were few great nobles. The counts of Toulouse and Carcassonne were the two leading families;

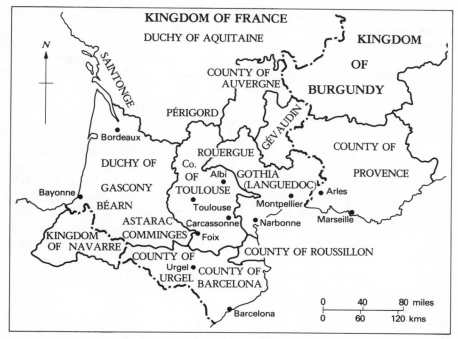

Map 2.4   The principalities of the south in the mid-eleventh century

and the former retained the sole right to the comital title in their lands and managed to control many of the lesser nobles such as the viscounts of Rouergue, Narbonne, Béziers, Lodève, Nîmes and Toulouse, who were related to the counts of Toulouse and based their social standing on this. During the eleventh century, however, a considerable threat to comital control emerged in the shape of a new group of nobles. Many were the newly enriched advocates of ecclesiastical establishments or *viguiers*; others were castellans who managed to make hereditary the lands they were responsible for. Castles were multiplying further in the region in this period. These new nobles represented a problem for the great families, but they were to some extent kept in check by agreements of *convenientiae* or alliance, and a great gulf still separated them from their social superiors. Although the count's judicial institutions were decaying noticeably in this period, and the church had taken over the guardianship of order, justice and peace, still the counts managed to reserve many of the major causes for themselves and their direct agents. The idea of the public power, if not always its reality, remained strong in the Midi, perhaps because of the prevalence of Roman law.

The lordships of southern France differed from their northern counterparts in a number of ways because of the distinctive social and political conditions here. The frequent appearance of the allod or free holding at all levels of society gave some lords a considerable degree of independence, but other officials who made their lands and offices private still found small allodialists within their lands. Meanwhile a new social group, the knights, were emerging around 1000 A.D. and might act as retainers in the private castles. This group formed during the eleventh century into two parts, the lesser knights, or retainers, and the greater, the landholders. By 1100 a split had emerged in the peasantry too, the richer peasants, officials and townsfolk forming a group between the knights and the lesser peasants, whose position appears to have deteriorated, as some were brought into a more servile status. But the wide use of coinage on a local level encouraged the levying of rents rather than labour services by lords, and the burdens imposed on the peasantry generally tended to be lighter than those in the north.

Grants of lands or rights as fiefs were almost unknown in the south. Land tended to be given in exchange for rents rather than services, and for a limited period, such as a lifetime, rather than becoming a hereditary holding. Grants of *precaria* of this kind were made most frequently by ecclesiastical landholders, but similar contracts were also occasionally made by lay lords. Benefices, then, were normally granted conditionally and for a limited period; and although occasionally military service was involved as well as rents this did not automatically involve an oath of fidelity and never brought homage with it. Castles were often held as allods but could be granted in part to another family in a form of *parage* or shared lordship. Military aid was acquired by the making of *convenientiae*, treaties of mutual assistance between nobles involving castle-guard, aid and sometimes pensions. There were also other kinds of land grants. Land colonisation was encouraged by the *medium plantum* grant which gave the settler full rights until he had reclaimed the land. It was then divided between him and the allodial holder. The contrasts between northern and southern France in the three centuries before the Albigensian crusade, then, are striking. As Mme Magnou-Nortier has it, in the south

we are in a land where vassalage was unknown, and with it homage, where fidelity, by contrast, did not cease to inspire contracts of *convenientia*, source of the authority of the great men; these were, like oaths of fidelity themselves, promises of security between equals.[21]

The importance of the church in the tenth and eleventh centuries was considerable. In the Midi the *Eigenkirche*, the lay possession of churches as private property, was entirely unknown. The lay advocate was responsible for defending his church's properties and for disposing of some of its revenues, but the bishop and abbot, the patron saint and God were viewed as its proprietors. This prevented the great ecclesiastical lordships from losing substantial amounts of land to their advocates. Indeed in the tenth century the religious houses, such as Saint-Gilles, Lézat and Psalmodi which had major aristocratic families as patrons, were more prosperous than the others. Those monasteries which lacked potent defenders relied on the peace of God and on papal bulls of protection. Before the middle of the eleventh century very few were directly dependent on the papacy; they tended rather to be subject to the local bishops. The church was a cohesive community in the Languedoc and greatly respected for its peace-keeping activities.

The ecclesiastical reform movement brought a number of changes in its wake, however. The church councils of the Midi were now concerned less with the peace of God and more with ecclesiastical reform. The direct authority of the papacy became strikingly greater in the later eleventh century. Pope Gregory VII intervened in two elections to the archbishopric of Narbonne, and the bishop of Albi and Nîmes was excommunicated for simony. The members of a number of cathedral chapters including Toulouse and Albi became canons regular (3.4.2) following papal intervention, and abbeys with strong papal connections built up congregations in the area; Moissac, a Cluniac house, was one, and Saint-Pons-de-Thomières another. Lay patrons of abbeys lost control of altar dues and tithes to some degree, and were almost entirely excluded from elections to abbacies and bishoprics. The church in the Midi seems to have lost much of its coherence and vitality as laymen and the ecclesiastical hierarchy became increasingly estranged; their only major area of cooperation was the crusades.

In the eleventh century communes began to play an important part in the political life of the south. They spread rapidly both in the towns and in the countryside, and unlike their northern counterparts (4.3.2) they frequently included members of the local nobility. Toulouse was the centre of a strong political movement against the authority of the count. The citizens, led by the rich merchants and powerful urban knights, achieved a great measure of independence by the end of the twelfth century. Montpellier was a merchant commune, Carcassonne was more militarily orientated, and Lézat a rural commune. Throughout the south both towns and village communities tried to gain judicial, financial and military privileges. In this they frequently succeeded and violence occurred less often than in the north. These movements were supported by the increasing wealth of the Languedoc, and in particular on reviving trade, both local and long-distance. Toulouse, for example, thrived on the profits of markets of wine, oil, grain, leather and metalware. It had links with England, Flanders and Champagne to the north, and the Levant and Italy to the south. Other towns too, Arles, Avignon, Barcelona, Montpellier, Narbonne, Saint-Gilles became wealthy and prosperous. At the same time the rural economy was expanding, particularly in the river valleys and on the coastal plains. Land colonisation increased and lay and ecclesiastical lords founded towns and villages.

The south of France was also the home of a thriving culture. The school at Montpellier was important for the study of medicine and Roman law. Superb Romanesque churches with fine sculptures were constructed at Moissac, Conques and Toulouse (Saint-Sernin), where they may still be seen. In this area, too, troubadour poetry flourished, a vernacular literature which had probably originated in Aquitaine in the late eleventh century and which was supported with enthusiasm by the nobility of the Languedoc. Duke William the Young of Aquitaine, Raymond VI count of Toulouse and Richard the Lionheart were all patrons and practitioners of the poetry.

One of its central preoccupations was the cult of 'courtly love', in which a lady is worshipped from afar by a lover who seeks to win her favour by displaying the chivalrous virtues of patience, constancy and prowess. Debates about its meaning and significance have been endless; one recent account concludes that it was at once 'a literary movement, an ideology, an ethical system, a style of life, an expression of the play element in culture, which arose in an aristocratic Christian environment exposed to Hispano-Arabic influences'.[22] Certainly it proved widely popular and spread to northern France during the twelfth century. But there were other strands in this troubadour poetry as well, one of which exalted the married state and exhorted young girls to remain pure and chaste in preparation. There were also far more earthy elements in certain lyrics produced by the southern poets. This was a cultured and affluent society for its time, and one which found the hopes of adventure, gain and salvation held out by the crusades a highly alluring prospect. The princes of Aquitaine, Toulouse and Barcelona and many of the nobility devoted much enthusiasm and effort to adventures in the east.

In the earlier twelfth century there was some interest in the heretical preaching of Peter of Bruis and Henry of Lausanne in the Languedoc (4.3.3), and in the later years of the century the Cathar and Waldensian heresies spread rapidly here, and gained a powerful foothold. The reasons often given for this are the opportunities for the interchange of ideas in this relatively urbanised, relatively tolerant and wealthy society, and the contrasts which the austere practices of Catharism and the Waldensian apostolic life (4.3.3) presented with the often ill-disciplined and worldly hierarchy of the Catholic church. The church was, it is clear, not outstandingly fervent, and several of its most important ministers were clearly unsuited to their tasks. Archbishop Berengar of Narbonne (1190–1212), related to the royal house of Aragon, was accused by Pope Innocent III of loving only one god, money, and by 1213 he and eight other prelates had been deposed or suspended for failing to do their pastoral duties. But on much of the rest of the Catholic church in the Midi the records are silent and it is probable that the contrasts between it and the church in other parts of France and Europe are often exaggerated. Matthew, bishop of Toul (1198–1210) and Hugh, bishop of Auxerre (1183–1206) were as bad, if not worse than their Languedocian contemporaries, although the latter helped his reputation considerably by his keen pursuit of heretics.

At the council of Lombers, called in 1165 to examine early Cathar preachers in the region, one archbishop, five bishops, six abbots and other important ecclesiastics attended. This was not a formal church council, and as Dr Moore has shown, its condemnation of the heretics was given without the support of the nobility of the region, many of whom were present.[23] This was probably an important factor in the spread of the heresy. Some nobles actively supported it, as did too the knights, and from the counts of Toulouse downwards there was no consistent and active opposition to heretics, as was found in other parts of France.

In 1177 Count Raymond called on the pope and the Cistercians for help against the Cathars, but his motives were not solely religious. The heretics were closely connected with the consuls, a group of citizens of Toulouse at that time trying to win self-government, and the church helped him to crush them. His successors, Raymond VI and Raymond VII, were not to be wholehearted supporters of the extirpation of heresy (4.4.9; 5.5.3). And where any of the greater nobles did try to impose a policy of persecution on their men, they were unable to make any noticeable impact because of the social conditions of the region, the fragmentation of political authority. The wealth and secular interests of the church, its general slackness in discipline, and its spiritual apathy, did not help, but this was probably only one factor amongst several, albeit an important one, in the growth and spread of Catharism and Waldensianism. The austerity and asceticism of the heretics clearly won them many adherents, and the adoption of a similar pattern of life by the Cistercians and the Dominicans who mounted preaching campaigns against the heretics did not prove effective enough. It was to take the violence of the Albigensian crusade and the severity of the inquisition to drive heresy from the Languedoc (4.4.9; 5.3.2).

2.4.2 Gascony, Toulouse and Barcelona

The great county of Gascony, stretching from Bordeaux to the Pyrenees, showed far more similarities in its political and social structures to Toulouse than to most of the rest of the duchy of Aquitaine, to whose ruler it belonged from the mid-eleventh century. Much of it was uncultivated and was held as allods rather than as benefices – indeed the whole duchy was later considered an allod (6.4.3). Central political power was weak and society remarkably lacking in hierarchy. It had been constituted a Carolingian march, and was then ruled by an independent comital family from Bordeaux until its transfer to the dukes of Aquitaine, who did nothing to strengthen central authority. In the rich river valleys of the Garonne and the Adour and in other settled areas were to be found important castellanies, such as Lesparre, Castillon, Albret. In the south the viscounts of Dax were constant and valuable allies of the dukes, although they expended much energy in fighting the independent principality of Béarn. Growing towns such as Bayonne and Mont-de-Marsan helped to increase the wealth of their lords, but in many parts of Gascony the castellans were virtually ungovernable. Dukes William IX and William X made some headway, and later so too did Richard the Lionheart, but they were only partly successful. In this fragmentation of power, Gascony resembled its southern neighbours, the principalities of Toulouse and Barcelona.

For most of the tenth century the politics of the south were complex. The counts of Toulouse and the counts of Carcassonne were unable to build up strong principalities and the church took the lead in trying to maintain law and order. However, following the Gregorian reform in the area the greater nobles again began to build up their powers in the region, and two major principalities emerged, the county of Toulouse and the county of Barcelona, formerly the Spanish March. The two princes fought to dominate the area from the river Ebro, stretching over the Pyrenees and over as far as the river Rhône. Their aims and intentions have been variously interpreted. M. Higounet thought that the counts of Barcelona wanted to create a great empire in the region, but Señor d'Abadal i de Vinyals suggested that Count Raymond-Berengar I, who began the expansion of Barcelona, was seeking to enrich younger sons rather than to increase his patrimony.[24] Whatever their intentions, by 1100 the rivalry of the two houses had become intense.

The county of Toulouse originally formed in the tenth century. In 924 Raymond III had annexed Gothia, the area stretching from Narbonne to Nîmes,

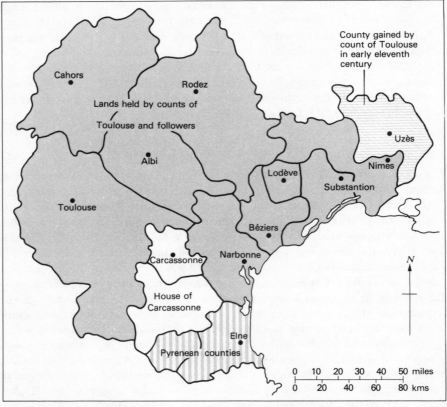

Map 2.5   The Toulouse principality in the eleventh century

and in 990 the marriage of count William Tailefer to Emma of Provence brought Tarascon and Argence to the county. In the eleventh century the lands were dismembered, but in 1093 Raymond IV of Saint-Gilles (a family name) succeeded his brother William as count and began to gather them together again. Raymond achieved great renown in the first crusade, and was succeeded by Bertrand and Alfonso Jordan, an able administrator and fighter.

Despite their relatively limited domains, the problems posed by independent nobles such as the Trencavel and the viscounts of Narbonne who frequently allied with their enemies, and the independence and power of the ecclesiastical lordships, they managed to retain some degree of authority, although their frequent departures to the Holy Land and the periodical invasions of the dukes of Aquitaine made concerted efforts at centralisation and consolidation of power rather difficult. Their authority was based on *convenientiae* rather than the direct application of public powers, their domains were scattered, but they were beginning to develop an administration and to attempt to tap the fast growing commerce of Toulouse and other towns. Anarchy was kept in check by the continuing idea of public powers, by the rigidity of the social hierarchy, by the binding force of the contracts of alliance, and by the peace of God.

In Catalonia the counts of Barcelona built up considerable power in the early tenth century, but their authority gradually contracted after this and in the 1040s and 1050s was strongly challenged by a wealthy and aggressive aristocracy. Raymond-Berengar I (1035-76) overcame these problems by fighting the castellans and buying their support, and he reorganised the military and judicial institutions of the county, and supported the peace of God and the ecclesiastical reform movement. In 1067 he took Carcassonne and in 1071 Razès, which gave him a valuable foothold north of the Pyrenees. He attempted to leave all his lands in *parage* to his sons Raymond-Berengar II and Berengar-Raymond II but his plan foundered on internecine strife and provoked the intervention of Pope Gregory VII. But after a period Raymond-Berengar III succeeded, and he was a worthy rival of Alfonso Jordan of Toulouse. A contemporary chronicler described him as 'a most pleasant and generous man, very skilled in arms'.[25] Under him his lands south of the Pyrenees acquired a stronger political organisation and a name, Catalonia, symbolising their growing sense of identity. He built up many allies from amongst the smaller nobles to the north of the Pyrenees, while in 1113 he married Douce, heiress to Provence, and took this area, claimed by the counts of Toulouse since 1094 from another marriage alliance. Alfonso Jordan of Toulouse rallied the citizens of Carcassonne, the count of Comminges and the king of Aragon against Raymond-Berengar III and his allies, the viscount of Narbonne and Duke William of Aquitaine. After one war they divided Provence in 1125, but more hostilities followed and then peace again in 1134. Meanwhile Raymond-Berengar III had died. His eldest son Raymond-Berengar IV took Barcelona, and Provence went to his brother Berengar-Raymond.

M. Poly[26] shows that in Provence the counts of Barcelona imposed a strong degree of control over the castellans in the twelfth century, taxing them and demanding services and oaths of fidelity, though rarely getting homage. In their other lands the counts also wielded a relatively potent and coherent power based on force, monetary grants and personal success.[27] Like most of the other territorial princes, they were unable to extend this throughout their lands, but they had the resources to build up a great deal of authority in northern Spain and the French Midi, for in 1137 Raymond-Berengar IV became the heir to the king of Aragon by marrying his daughter Petronilla. This gave him the expectation of a great bloc of land to the south of the Pyrenees as well as authority over the client states of Béarn and Bigorre to the north. In 1159 he allied with Henry II Plantagenet, who wished to make good the claims of Aquitaine over Toulouse. Together they attacked the city, but the young count, Raymond V, was saved by the intervention of King Louis VII. Yet the house of Barcelona continued to become increasingly powerful in the Languedoc and was involved in politics on the European scale. Raymond-Berengar of Provence, nephew of Raymond-Berengar IV, married the niece of the Emperor Frederick Barbarossa.

The next generation, Alfonso II of Aragon and Barcelona and Raymond V count of Toulouse, spent a substantial part of their reigns fighting one another although they were still quite unable to dominate many of the lands nominally under their authority. By the 1190s the king of Aragon seemed to control the south of France. His brothers held Millau and Gevaudan, he was allied with the

Trencavels, the viscounts of Narbonne and the counts of Foix. He overshadowed the county of Toulouse and only the independent county of Comminges under Bernard IV escaped. At the end of the twelfth century, however, Aragonese power in the Midi diminished considerably. In 1196 Alfonso II died and his lands were divided. Peter, his eldest son, took Aragon and Barcelona – the latter was finally to be released from its feudal dependence by the French king in 1258 (5.2.2) – and Alfonso took Millau, Gevaudan and Provence. But Peter II and Raymond VI of Toulouse entirely reversed the pattern of the previous century. When threatened by the crusaders from the north they stood together (4.4.9).

NOTES AND FURTHER READING

Asterisked titles in the notes are recommended for further reading, and additional titles are suggested below. Place of publication London unless otherwise indicated.

Notes

1. His work is summarised in G. Duby, * 'The nobility in eleventh- and twelfth-century Mâconnais', in F. L. Cheyette, ed., *Lordship and Community in Medieval Europe* (New York, 1968), 137–55.
2. J. le Patourel, *The Norman Empire* (1976), *passim.*
3. P. Lauer, ed., *Les Annales de Flodoard* (Paris, 1906), 55.
4. H. Prentout, *Étude critique sur Dudon de Saint-Quentin* (Caen, 1915), 13–15.
5. See the forthcoming study of eleventh-century Normandy by Dr David Bates (to be published by Longman).
6. On this see D. C. Douglas, *William the Conqueror* (1964), 175–8.
7. E. R. A. Sewter, ed. and trans., *The Alexiad of Anna Comnena* (Penguin, 1969), 422–3.
8. D. C. Douglas and D. W. Greenaway, eds, *English Historical Documents*, ii (1953), 163.
9. J. C. Holt, 'Politics and property in medieval England', *Past and Present*, lvii (1972), 3–53.
10. C. W. Hollister, *'Normandy, France and the Anglo-Norman *regnum*', *Speculum*, li (1976), 202–42; le Patourel, *op. cit., passim.*
11. M. Bur, *La formation du comté de Champagne, v. 950–v. 1150* (Nancy, 1977).
12. *Ibid*, 125–6; F. Lot, *Études sur le règne de Hugues Capet et la fin du Xe siècle* (Paris, 1903), 397–413; M. Prou, ed., *Raoul Glaber, Les cinq livres de ses histoires, 900–1044* (Paris, 1886), 85–6.
13. Quoted in F., *Capetian Kings*, 65–6; text in *RHF*, x, 501–2.
14. L. Halphen, *A Travers l'histoire du moyen âge* (Paris, 1950), 241–50.
15. *RHF*, xi, 4.
16. Bur, *op. cit.*, 475.
17. R. Fossier, *La Terre et les hommes en Picardie jusqu'à la fin du XIIIe siècle* (Paris/Louvain, 1965), 732–3.
18. R. W. Southern, *The Making of the Middle Ages* (1953), 80–9.
19. B. S. Bachrach, *'Towards a re-appraisal of William the Great, duke of Aquitaine (995–1030)', *JMH*, v (1979), 11–21.

20. J. Gillingham, *Richard the Lionheart* (1978), 9–23 *et passim*, and 'The unromantic death of Richard I', *Speculum*, liv (1979), 18–41.
21. E. Magnou-Nortier, *La Société laïque et l'église dans la province ecclésiastique de Narbonne*. . . (Toulouse, 1974), 647.
22. Quoted from R. Boase, *The Origin and Meaning of Courtly Love* . . . (Manchester, 1977), 129–30.
23. R. I. Moore, *The Origins of European Dissent* (1977), 200–3, 232–7; see also W. L. Wakefield, *Heresy, Crusade and Inquisition in Southern France, 1100–1250* (1974), 65–6.
24. C. Hignounet, 'Un grand chapitre de l'histoire de XIIe siècle: la rivalité des maisons de Toulouse et de Barcelone pour la prépondérance méridionale', *Mélanges . . . Louis Halphen* (Paris, 1951), 313–22. R. d'Abadal i de Vinyals, 'A propos de la domination de la maison comtale de Barcelone sur le midi Français', *Annales du Midi*, lxxvi (1964), 315–45.
25. *RHF*, xii, 377.
26. J. P. Poly, *la Provence et la société féodale (879–1166)* . . . (Paris, 1976).
27. P. Bonnassie, *La Catalogne du milieu du Xe à la fin du XIe siècle* . . . , 2 vols (Toulouse, 1975–76).

Additional titles for further reading

G. T. Beech, *A Rural Society in Medieval France: the Gâtine of Poitou in the eleventh and twelfth centuries* (Baltimore, 1964).
T. N. Bisson, 'The problem of feudal monarchy: Aragon, Catalonia and France', *Speculum,* liii (1978), 460–78.
C. L. H. Coulson, 'Rendability and castellation in medieval France' *Château Gaillard, Études de Castellologie Médiévale, vi (Venlo, 1972)* (Caen, 1973), 59–67.
G. Duby, *La société aux XIe et XIIe siècles dans la région Mâconnaise*, 2nd edn (Paris, 1971).
Galbert of Bruges, *The Murder of Charles the Good, Count of Flanders*, ed. and trans. J. B. Ross (New York, 1960).
E. M. Hallam, 'The king and the princes in eleventh century France', *Bulletin of the Institute of Historical Research*, liii (1980).
A. R. Lewis, *The Development of Southern French and Catalan Society, 718–1058* (University of Texas, 1965).
J. Martindale, 'Conventum inter Guillelmum Aquitanorum comes et Hugonem Chiliarchum', *English Historical Review*, lxxxiv (1969), 528–48.
S. Painter, 'Castellans of the plain of Poitou in the eleventh and twelfth centuries', and 'The lords of Lusignan in the eleventh and twelfth centuries', *Feudalism and Liberty, Articles and Addresses of Sydney Painter*, ed. Fred. A. Cazel Jnr (Baltimore, 1961), 17–72.
K. F. Werner, 'Kingdom and principality in twelfth-century France', ed. and trans. T. Reuter, *The Medieval Nobility* (Amsterdam/New York/Oxford, 1979), 243–90.
J. Yver, 'Les châteaux-forts en Normandie jusqu'au milieu du XIIe siècle', *Bulletin de la Société des Antiquaires de la Normandie*, liii (1955–56), 28–115.

CHAPTER THREE

The Early Capetians, 987–1108

3.1 INTRODUCTION

3.1.1 The early Capetians: mere territorial princes?

The king and the princes in eleventh-century France were similar in many different ways (2.1.2): in their outlook, in the nature of their power, in the ceremonial they used. The eleventh century was in many senses the apogee of princely power, for royal authority was weak, the dukes or counts of the more centralised states such as Normandy and Flanders could enjoy what amounted to sovereign authority almost undisturbed by their nominal rulers, and these rulers were in practice virtually one of their number. The Robertines, ancestors of the Capetians and very powerful princes in the tenth century, had eventually dislodged the Carolingians from the throne (1.4.1) and continued to hold their own principality to which they added some Carolingian lands and rights. But during the late tenth and eleventh centuries royal power both in the principality and in the kingdom declined, putting the Capetians on the level of a not very powerful territorial prince. And they behaved as such too, fighting and jockeying for land and power at the expense of their neighbours, treating the princes as allies or enemies and not as subordinates. In the mid-eleventh century the king was very close to being a mere territorial prince.

Despite the limitations of royal power the king's sacral and judicial attributes and his role as overlord still continued to be recognised and even on some occasions to be observed. Many of his powers were claimed by the princes as well, a sign that France was far from being demonarchised. Nevertheless the recognition of royal attributes, both secular and ecclesiastical, even at their most theoretical, while quite widely stressed under Hugh Capet and Robert the Pious, became increasingly rare in the middle of the eleventh century when royal power had reached a low ebb. By the end of the 1050s there was some slight recovery in the secular power of the king, perhaps as a result of social changes which were beginning to make society more hierarchical. This increased a little more under Philip I, and under Louis VI the importance of the king's sacral power revived as well, as Abbot Suger of Saint-Denis gave him a resplendent image (4.4.6), which went beyond even the veneration shown for Robert the Pious early in the eleventh century. But this is far from constituting a continuing and strong ecclesiastical tradition, just as on the secular side royal overlordship did not remain a potent force throughout the eleventh century. In the first part of the reign of Henry I the Capetians came nearest to becoming mere territorial princes.

Hugh Capet and Robert the Pious inherited many of the sacral attributes of their Carolingian predecessors along with the crown. A clear example of this appears in the collections of canons of Abbo, Abbot of Fleury, written in the 990s. The king, he says, is by God's grace responsible for regulating the affairs of the whole of his kingdom. His is the sole and overriding authority, founded on many sacred texts.[1] Much of this is clearly based on earlier writings, and in particular on those of Jonas, Bishop of Orléans, who drew together contemporary theories of kingship in the early ninth century. These embodied strong theocratic elements. The king was seen as the head of church and state, avenger of wrongs but yet maker of peace, the last idea being reinforced by the notion that Charlemagne's empire marked the revival of the Roman empire with its emphasis on public order. Fulbert of Chartres emphasised in the early eleventh century that the king was the fountain-head of justice, with the power to punish wrongdoers for the good of the state, even though he was not always able effectively to fulfil this charge.[2]

The traditions of sacral kingship, the creation of the Carolingian episcopacy, were transferred by the bishops of northern France to the new ruling house in 987, along with their political loyalty. The accepted patterns of king-making were followed on this occasion with the coronation and the anointing of the king, a solemn and serious rite, as their centrepiece. It was this ceremony which set the king apart from his people.

The process of king-making began when a ruler designated his eldest surviving son to succeed him. All the Capetians until Philip Augustus did this, and all apart from Philip I had their heirs crowned in their own lifetimes. It has often been said that they used anticipatory association of the heir as a system to perpetuate the dynasty's claims to the throne and as a reaction to its insecurity, but recently it has been suggested that this interpretation only really makes sense for Hugh Capet's association of Robert the Pious. Later the device was used for a number of reasons; in Robert the Pious's case, to decide which son should succeed, in Louis VII's to provide himself with a coadjutor because he was unable to rule through sickness. The greater nobility also associated heirs with their fathers, and stopped using the device at about the same time as the Capetians.[3] Although this designation secured the throne for the heir, he still had to be chosen by his people at a solemn assembly. In the eleventh century these were attended by nobles, knights and clerics from a limited area of the French kingdom, but their significance was recognised by those who did not participate. William duke of Aquitaine did not bother to travel to court for Henry I's election in 1031, but he was well aware it was taking place.[4] The assembled gathering would 'elect' the king, and although there is no evidence that any western European *electio* involved a majority vote, at least until the later twelfth century, the princes, bishops and other magnates in giving the new king their assent and acknowledgement were recognising him and offering him their support. The election was thus a prelude to homage-giving.

Once the king had been chosen by his people he was consecrated by the church. In another solemn ceremony he was blessed by the bishops, and he then promised in his coronation oath to uphold justice and to fight God's enemies. He was next anointed with the holy chrism, which set him apart from his people and put him on a par with the bishops and archbishops. The earliest recorded anointing in France is that of Pippin in 751, although legend had it that the chrism had been brought from heaven by a dove for Clovis's coronation at Reims. This was the traditional coronation church of the Carolingians, and Hugh Capet's coronation here rather than at Sens, where the Robertines had been crowned was the sign of his acceptance (3.4.1). The anointing was followed by the investiture of the king with his regalia, the symbols of his office, the sword, ring, sceptre and rod, given by the bishops. He was next crowned, normally by the archbishop of Reims, and enthroned. The order of service (*ordo*) used in the early Capetian period was the Frankish one drawn together by Hincmar of Reims in the late ninth century. For Louis VI's coronation, held at Sens, however, an English *ordo* was used, containing references in the prayers to the Anglo-Saxon kingdoms. Though later coronations were again at Reims, this same *ordo* continued to be used, doubtless sanctified by tradition, until the end of the Capetian period.[5]

The coronations of the early Capetians were important events, which gave them a claim to exercise holy kingship. But while the sacral attributes of Hugh Capet and Robert the Pious were emphasised by the royalist bishops and were widely reflected in contemporary writings, during the reigns of Henry I and Philip I who succeeded them, far less emphasis was placed on holy kingship. Philip, indeed, was said to have lost the healing touch of his father. Nor did either king inspire much interest from ecclesiastical writers; though many of the princes found biographers and apologists, the kings do not play a central role even in general narratives of the period. The Capetians also lacked the heroic attributes which their Carolingian predecessors enjoyed throughout this period; though they became their legitimate successors to the throne they lost much of their *kudos*. This was no longer the case at the highest level in the twelfth century when Charlemagne's cult was canalised for Capetian use and when the sacral role of the king was regenerated as royal authority revived, but in the later eleventh century the lack of interest in Henry I and Philip I is a sad reflection of the limited nature of their real powers.

Yet the sacral attributes of the royal office were never completely forgotten, nor was the king's role as lawgiver and keeper of the peace, even though in much of the kingdom this duty was actually carried out by the church. The king was also recognised as the overlord of the whole kingdom, to whom the great men of the kingdom, as his vassals, owed service and counsel, as Abbo of Fleury affirmed.[6] His position at the summit of a hierarchy was widely acknowledged, even though actually he was not the focus of political power, because there was no one focus, just as most of the French regional and local societies were far from being neatly organised in descending order. But the king's theoretical place as overlord to whom homage was due from the princes and to whom military service was to be rendered was clear, and the latter obligation was sometimes fulfilled, particularly in the late eleventh century. And although most of the territorial princes did not pay homage or attend the royal court with any regularity during the eleventh century, and the king's entourage was composed of increasingly humble men, the idea that the great of the realm owed him ultimate fidelity was never entirely lost sight of. When articulated by Abbot Suger in the twelfth century and backed up with royal action in the thirteenth, it was generally accepted in practice. The example of the emperors and of the Anglo-Norman kings was perhaps to be of some value here.

Thus all these notions about kingship continued to be understood during the eleventh century, even though they were generally lost sight of in the 1030s and 1040s. At the highest level of ecclesiastical writing the kings were not viewed as mere territorial princes, and the princes themselves imitated royal powers and recognised the role the king should play in their society. Sometimes too, they observed this in practice, although this was rarer. Thus a clear distinction should be drawn between political theory and practice. In the realms of theory the kings retained their powers, although in the middle of the eleventh century even here reality was beginning to show through. There was some revival from the late 1050s, but in the period before, at the level of practical politics there was very little difference between the king and the princes. An understanding of this dichotomy is fundamental in an analysis of the events of the early Capetian period.

3.2 THE KINGS AND THEIR REIGNS

3.2.1 Hugh Capet, 987–996

Hugh Capet's reign seems to have marked little significant change in the powers and policies of the French kings (1.4.1). The first Capetian king is, indeed, a rather ill-documented figure. Raoul Glaber described him as active in body and mind, but this stereotyped phrase is not very revealing. Like Richer, Glaber chronicles the events of the reign but gives very little insight into Hugh as a person. It is suggested by these writers that his tastes were simple, and Helgaud of Fleury emphasised his interest in monasticism. The events of Hugh's reign suggest that he relied on diplomacy rather than war where possible; the royal *acta* point up the strength of his alliance with the higher clergy. Of the dozen or so of his extant charters which can be accepted as genuine almost all went to important prelates and to monasteries, and most of these in the north of the kingdom. It is striking, however, that for Hugh's contemporary, Emperor Otto III of Germany, more than three hundred genuine charters survive. Professor Lot in his study of the reign[7] suggests that this reflects a difference in the level of production of French royal *acta* as much as a lower survival rate. Many of the great monastic houses, realising how limited royal power was becoming stopped asking the king for charters.

The support of the important churchmen had been vital in Hugh's election and he continued to rely on them against the challenge of the Carolingian claimant to the throne, Charles of Lorraine. Hugh had his own son crowned so as to ensure his future succession, and he gave the town of Verdun, in dispute with the empire, to the young Otto III as a peace offering. Then, early in the reign, an appeal for support against the Muslims in the south came from Borel, count of Barcelona. Hugh, it seems, intended to help him, but was prevented from doing so by an attack launched in northern France by Charles of Lorraine, and Borel and the other southern princes began to look elsewhere for political support, for the king was occupied with his Carolingian rivals.

Charles, supported by Arnulf, an illegitimate son of the Carolingian king Lothar who died in 986, seized the strongly fortified city of Laon and defied and challenged the king. Hugh's response was twofold. He called an ecclesiastical council which excommunicated Charles and he also tried to recapture Laon. The latter scheme failed; but Hugh, not deterred, tried to win over Arnulf by making him archbishop of Reims in succession to Adalbero, who had just died. This was not in the event a wise move. At first Charles merely continued to dominate the Laonnais, while the attempts to mediate by the Empress Theophano, regent for Otto III, met with no success. Then in 989 Arnulf handed over the Reims area to Charles as well. Charles also won the support of Conrad, king of Burgundy, and Odo I, count of Blois. Even the influential ecclesiastic Gerbert of Aurillac appeared to be moving towards the Carolingian camp, although this was shortlived, for Gerbert not long afterwards wrote to Pope John XV on Hugh's behalf, asking that Arnulf be condemned for his depredations. But Hugh was forced to act by the strength of the opposition, and in 990 he gathered together an army against his adversaries. When Charles of Lorraine offered battle he retreated, however, and turned to diplomacy again. This time he was more fortunate, for he succeeded in conciliating Odo of Blois, and then the really decisive blow was struck for him. In 991 Adalbero, bishop of Laon, entered this town under the pretext of negotiating with Charles and Arnulf, and managed to take both of them prisoner. Charles was kept in captivity and appears to have died in about 993. He left sons but, perhaps curiously, they aroused little discontent.

Led by the bishops, the northern French nobility were soon reconciled to the new arrangement whereby the Capetians became the one ruling dynasty, as the Robertines, their ancestors, had not been. This was achieved with the backing of the church, and with the playing up of what was in fact a rather commonplace blood link, very much like that of the other princes, with the Carolingians. This, carefully presented by ecclesiastical writers such as André of Fleury and Odoran of Sens, gave them a mantle of respectable legitimacy.

Meanwhile the treacherous Arnulf, archbishop of Reims, still remained a problem for the king, and in 991 at the council of Saint-Basle Hugh had him tried for treason. Abbo, abbot of Fleury, upheld the right of the papacy to conduct this process, but Arnulf, bishop of Orléans, dismissing the pontiffs as weak and corrupt placemen, held that this was a matter for the French church and not the papacy. Hugh and his bishops tried, condemned and dethroned Arnulf of Reims, and Gerbert of Aurillac was elected in his stead. This infuriated both the pope and the emperor. Papal legates were sent to France to try to discipline the French bishops, but they meanwhile held further councils antagonistic to any such idea. The synod of Chelles in 993, for example, declared that if the pope put forward an opinion which ran counter to the scriptures it was invalid, and that no one should dare rashly to attack the findings of a provincial synod. All this was indicative of a strong anti-papal sentiment in the late tenth-century French church, and an impasse was reached which was only broken after Hugh's death in 996. Then Robert the Pious made peace with the pope; Gerbert fled to Germany and then to Italy and became first archbishop of Ravenna and then pope at the behest of Otto III. Arnulf was reinstated as archbishop of Reims.

The shifting of allegiance by Archbishop Arnulf between the king and his rivals was paralleled by the double dealing of Odo I, count of Blois. Hugh granted him the town of Dreux in 991 in return for the promise of his help against Charles of Lorraine. Odo rendered the king no assistance, and he also seized the town of Melun; Hugh was forced to lay siege to it in order to retrieve it. With the perfidious Adalbero, bishop of Laon, Odo then plotted against Hugh. It was known to contemporaries that he hoped to hand France over to the Emperor Otto III and to become duke of the Franks himself. This scheme came to nothing, and Odo was now threatened in his turn by Fulk Nerra, count of Anjou, who was trying to capture the Touraine. So the count of Blois aligned himself with Richard, duke of Normandy, William, duke of Aquitaine, and Baldwin, count of Flanders, while Fulk Nerra allied with the king against this powerful coalition. The king's enemies, however, were unable to devise a concerted plan of action, and little was achieved by them. Odo offered the king peace in 994 and Hugh accepted this. When the count of Blois died in 996 he left only children, Odo II and Theobald, to succeed him, and the threat to the Capetians from this quarter diminished for a while. Throughout Hugh's last year of life, however, he had to contend with the repercussions of the young king, Robert's relationship with Bertha of Blois, wife, then widow of Odo I. As they were cousins in the third degree, the liaison was greatly frowned on by the church.[8]

Little was achieved by Hugh in political terms beyond mere survival as king. In his diplomacy and alliances he continued to behave as the territorial prince he had been before his accession. In practical political terms he was weaker by far than Fulk Nerra, count of Anjou, and he was opposed directly first by Charles of Lorraine and then by Odo I of Blois. He owed his eventual ascendancy over them to his own good fortune and the incompetence of his rivals rather than to military prowess; he escaped open defeat by rarely taking to the field and by negotiating with his opponents. In this he probably gained by the prestige which the royal office brought with it, as well as by the backing of much of the church in France. Despite these advantages the first Capetian king emerges as an unimposing figure.

3.2.2 Robert II 'the Pious', 996–1031

Many of our perceptions of King Robert the Pious emanate from his biography, written by his chaplain Helgaud, monk of Fleury. This is a naïve and enthusiastic work, semi-hagiographical in content. Robert is portrayed as the perfect king, a lover of the poor and weak, a dispenser of charity, a humble man of pronounced piety, constantly at prayer and frequently founding and building religious houses and churches. 'For in him', says Helgaud, 'priests, abbots and monks found an example of virtue not only worthy of imitation but also of admiration.' Yet Helgaud is not entirely misleading, for some of our other sources confirm Robert's piety in the later part of his reign in a rather less hyperbolic way. Adhémar of Chabannes saw him as 'a man of clear virtue and great piety' and Raoul Glaber as 'striking in piety'. Richer portrays him taking part in church synods with the French bishops, discussing and regulating ecclesiastical affairs. Furthermore, he was the first king who was attributed with the power of touching for scrofula.[9] His surviving charters suggest that, like his father, he relied heavily on ecclesiastical support, and that he was generous to the church. He granted a number of monasteries protection and privileges, and to others, such as Saint-Denis, Saint-Corneille at Compiègne and the college of canons at Poissy, he gave valuable rights. He introduced the Cluniacs into Saint-Denis and Saint-Germain-des-Prés in order to reform these houses (3.4.1). Helgaud said that Robert might have been taken for a monk and Adalbero of Laon suggested less flatteringly that Abbot Odilo of Cluny rather than Robert was king.

This paragon had another side. On one occasion the monastery of Saint-Germain at Auxerre stood in the way of a military campaign and he burned it down; this happened in 1003 during his invasion of Burgundy. He also gave his natural brother Gauzlin the abbacy of Saint-Benoit-sur-Loire (Fleury) in 1004, and in 1012 he made him archbishop of Bourges as well. On both occasions this provoked much opposition from the communities involved, according to Adhémar of Chabannes; for Gauzlin was illegitimate, although in the event he proved an able administrator and builder at Fleury, which flourished under his rule. Robert also defied much of the French church and the papacy for several years by living openly with Bertha of Blois, who was not regarded as his lawful wife. This episode is carefully glossed over by Helgaud, who suggests that although the liaison was considered by some as illicit, the king more than made up for it in time in his pious reconciliation with the church. Later in his reign Robert seems to have done more to deserve the epithet of 'pious'.

The king is said by Helgaud and by Adalbero of Laon to have been tall and thickset with a fair complexion. He was educated at the cathedral school at Reims under the tutelage of Gerbert of Aurillac and continued as something of a scholar later in life. Glaber judged him 'prudent and erudite in the study of arts and letters',[10] and Richer said that he knew a great deal of canon law and applied himself well to liberal studies. The same writer also described him as an energetic man who loved waging war. Yet Robert, while showing drive and vigour throughout his reign, achieved relatively little for his efforts, perhaps because he lacked the perseverance to carry through the projects he conceived with such enthusiasm.

In the early years of his rule there was considerable tension between Robert and much of the French church. Initially Hugh Capet had hoped that his son could marry a daughter of the Byzantine Emperor Constantine. This plan had failed, and instead Robert married Rozala or Suzanne, daughter of Berengar, former king of Italy, and widow of Arnulf II, count of Flanders. But Robert took a strong dislike to her and in 991 he repudiated her, although he was careful to retain Montreuil in Ponthieu which had come as her dowry. This infuriated her son Baldwin IV, count of Flanders.

When Robert became king in 996 he was already much attracted by Bertha countess of Blois, a Carolingian, and a daughter of Conrad II, king of Burgundy. The timely death of her husband Odo I had enabled him to contemplate a second marriage. In 997 this ceremony was performed for him by Archambaud, archbishop of Tours, but the ceremony was clearly in breach of canon law. Not only were Robert and Bertha related in the third degree but Robert was the godfather of one of Bertha's children, giving them spiritual affinity as well. The second alone was normally enough to prevent a marriage from taking place. Pope Gregory V, although in a precarious position in Italy, having been driven out of Rome by Crescentius, nevertheless summoned the synod of Pavia and condemned the union. This was with the encouragement of the Emperor Otto III who was anxious to prevent a claim to the kingdom of Burgundy being created for the French kings; and for the pope it was a blow against the independence of the French bishops.[11] The ruling had no effect and in 998 a general council of the church was called. This pronounced an anathema against Robert and severely rebuked those French bishops who had supported the king. Again there was little reaction, and when in 999 Gerbert of Aurillac became pope, pressure was taken off Robert. His connections with Bertha had meanwhile brought him into alliance with the house of Blois and hostility towards the enemy of Blois, Anjou. Bertha's young sons, Odo II and Theobald II were given a considerable degree of protection.

In about 1004 Robert put aside Bertha, perhaps through rather tardy religious scruples, or perhaps because she had given him no children, and he then married Constance, daughter of William I, count of Arles, and of Adela of Anjou, and thus first cousin to Fulk Nerra. An imperious and unscrupulous woman, she introduced what Glaber saw as scandalous habits from the south into the court. But worse, she polarised the court into two factions, one favouring herself and the Angevin interest, the other, Bertha and her sons. The king tired rapidly of Constance and began to turn back towards Bertha and her family. On one, Hugh count of Beauvais, he heaped honours and titles, including that of count palatine. The Angevins struck back in sinister fashion. In 1008 Fulk Nerra had Hugh assassinated while he was out hunting with the king, and then, ignoring a summons to appear before the royal court he set off on a pilgrimage to the Holy Land. In a letter written at about this time, Fulbert of Chartres comments that the king 'whose position makes him the fountain-head of justice, is so beset by wickedness that at present he is unable to avenge himself or aid us as he should'.[12] In 1010 the king tried to divorce Constance but was dissuaded from this by Pope Sergius IV. The couple remained married and continued to quarrel for the rest of Robert's life. Hugh, their eldest son, was crowned in 1017 but died in 1025. The next son, Henry, was now his father's choice of successor, but Constance favoured their third son Robert and fomented rebellions in his favour. On her husband's death she was to attempt a *coup d'état* on his behalf (3.2.3).

Although Robert's vigorous military campaigns did not always meet with much success, one enterprise did bring great rewards. In 1002 Henry, duke of Burgundy and brother of Hugh Capet, died without leaving a direct heir. The king, as his nephew, decided to claim the duchy for himself. He was opposed by Otto-William, count of Mâcon, son of Gerberga, who had married Henry, duke of Burgundy, *c.* 974; Odo-William had been adopted by him and designated his heir. The Burgundian nobility seemed to favour his candidature and he was able to resist the king strongly for a while. In the face of a violent ravaging of the duchy by a royal army first he, and then his own son-in-law Landri, count of Nevers, submitted. The king held Auxerre and Avallon but it took another decade of sporadic campaigning before he reduced Sens and Dijon and his victory was recognised by the nobles. His son Henry was invested as duke but after the king's death and the war between his sons, Burgundy was to go to Robert, the kingdom to Henry, repeating the pattern of Hugh Capet's reign, but weakening royal resources (2.2.1).

In the 1020s Robert, emboldened by his eventual success in Burgundy, turned to more grandiose schemes. He first made an alliance with Odo II, count of Blois, and William the Great, duke of Aquitaine, whereby various claims were to be made good – his own to Lorraine, Odo's to the kingdom of Burgundy and William's to the crown of Lombardy, which Robert had been offered but had turned down. These schemes directed against the emperor amounted to very little in practice, and had to be abandoned because the parties could not agree. They also left the way open for Conrad II to invade Lombardy. Nevertheless they are a measure of a somewhat revived prestige of the king in France, also reflected in his dealings with other princes. Although he attacked Flanders twice (1006 and 1019) in alliance with the emperor, he managed at other times to remain on moderately good terms with its counts. His daughter Adela married Baldwin son of Baldwin IV, count of Flanders. The king oscillated between alliances with Anjou and Blois, and that they did not together turn on the king is perhaps an indication of the depths of their rivalry. Indeed in all his dealings Robert the Pious achieved little in terms of longlasting gain, but his neo-Carolingian horizons (3.3.4), his negotiations and military campaigns which ranged more widely within the kingdom than those of his father Hugh Capet or of his son Henry I, seem to have revived a wider awareness of the monarchy for a few years at least.[13]

3.2.3 Henry I, 1031–60

Of Henry I's character we know very little indeed. His reign is not very well covered by contemporary sources and until recently it has attracted relatively little attention from historians. Professors Dhondt and Lemarignier have done much to remedy this, but the former admits that 'Henry I remains a phantom to the historian'.[14] This king, married in 1043 to Matilda, niece of the Emperor Henry III, who died in 1044, and in 1051 to Anne, daughter of Jaroslav grand duke of the powerful state of Kiev, appears to have been unexceptionable in his private life. He attracted little critical comment apart from Hariulf of Saint-Riquier, who described him as covetous, probably because he took a village away from his abbey. Glaber describes Henry as lively in mind and active in body, but this is a formula much favoured by this writer. The monastic author of the *Life of Saint Lietbert*, Ralph, said he was 'a man vigorous in arms and worthy of the realm he held'.[15] A monastic writer described him as a most active knight. His surviving *acta* show that he was conventionally generous to the church, and in about 1060 he founded the monastery of Saint-Martin-des-Champs for regular canons and showed much interest in this new group of religious, in part for political reasons (3.4.2).

The Fleury chronicle describes how, soon after the death of Robert the Pious in 1031, his widow Constance seized on behalf of her son and favourite Robert the towns or castles of Senlis, Sens, Béthisy, Dammartin, Le Puiset, Melun and Poissy. She bought the support of Odo II of Blois by handing over half of Sens to him. Henry, the designated and crowned heir of his father, fled to Robert the Magnificent, duke of Normandy, and asked for his help. Robert gave him generous support; so too did Fulk Nerra of Anjou and perhaps Baldwin of Flanders as well. With their help Henry regained Poissy and Le Puiset, and Constance surrendered to him. Robert his brother was granted the duchy of Burgundy, at the time held by the king himself. Had Henry retained it, it would have been a valuable addition to royal resources, but the grant was quite in keeping with contemporary inheritance patterns. Robert the Pious's intentions for Burgundy are not clear, however, and we do not know whether in handing over the duchy to his brother, Henry I was fulfilling Robert's own wishes, or paying his brother off – or both. The new king may also have granted away the French Vexin to the Norman duke as a reward for his support. These were considerable losses to a king whose position was already weakened by warfare. A difficult political crisis had been resolved, but royal power in France and the royal principality had suffered considerably.

The events of Henry's reign seem to fall into two main phases. Until about 1044 he was preoccupied with Odo II of Blois, who was trying to make good his own claim to the kingdom of Burgundy, and the nobles of the Ile de France, many of whom were acting in concert with him. In 1033 Henry concluded an alliance with the Emperor Conrad II but the count of Blois took the part of Odo, the king's youngest brother, who had been left landless. They rallied a coalition of nobles in opposition to Henry. In 1034 after savage fighting Odo of Blois submitted, but war broke out again soon afterwards.

In 1037 Odo of Blois died while fighting in Lorraine and his lands were divided between his sons, Theobald I who took Blois and Stephen who was given Troyes and Meaux. The war with the king continued, as Stephen and Theobald now took the part of Odo the king's brother, a focus for discontent. The king was victorious: Odo was captured, Stephen defeated and his ally, the count of Vermandois, imprisoned. Their supporters from the castellans of the royal principality were brought to heel for a time. The king took control of Sens together with the abbeys of Saint-Père at Châlons and Saint-Médard at Soissons, and later in 1055 when the count of Sens died, Henry was able to take over his office and powers. In 1044 Geoffrey Martel of Anjou, acting on the sanction given by a royal investiture a few years previously, captured the Touraine and Vendôme from Theobald I of Blois. These were grave setbacks for the house of Blois, and Theobald now became rather more closely aligned with the king. The immediate threat to the principality had been overcome, and Henry was now able to consolidate his power here and to fight the princes of northern France on more equal terms.

In the later part of his reign Henry I fought first against Geoffrey Martel of Anjou and then against William of Normandy, playing off one against the other and involving himself in their growing rivalry. By 1040 Geoffrey's power in France was considerable, and he was emerging as a dangerous rival to the king. He had gained as an ally the future Emperor Henry III, who married his wife's daughter, Agnes, in 1043. Later Pope Leo IX, hostile to royal power over the French church, also supported Geoffrey, as did William Aigret, duke of Aquitaine, whose mother, Agnes, Geoffrey married. After the count's capture of Tours in 1044 the king turned against him and against the Emperor Henry III. Godfrey of Upper Lorraine was also fighting the emperor because he had not been allowed to inherit Lower Lorraine from his father and became the ally of the king and of Baldwin of Flanders. They hoped to invade Lorraine in 1047, but in 1048 the king concluded a treaty of peace with Henry III and abandoned Godfrey. Henry had meanwhile gained another ally in William of Normandy, who now wished to defend himself against Angevin aggression; but as the illegitimate son of Robert the Magnificent, William, who had succeeded to Normandy in 1035 when still a minor, was in a precarious position inside the duchy. In 1047 a powerful coalition of nobles massed against him. He sought royal support and was rescued by the king, who defeated the rebels at the battle of Val-ès-Dunes. Then from 1048 until 1052 Henry and William together made war on Anjou. In 1048 they captured Mouliherne and in 1049 William went into Maine while the king went into the Touraine.

By the early 1050s William began to seem a greater threat to the king than Geoffrey Martel, and in 1052 another royal volte-face took place as the king switched his alliance from Normandy to Anjou. Geoffrey Martel had repudiated his wife Agnes, descended from Odo-William of Burgundy and former wife of William the Great of Aquitaine, and with her had alienated her daughter, the Emperor Henry III's wife. This isolated Geoffrey from the emperor, and he sought Henry I's friendship; and he and the king found a common enemy in William of Normandy. Henry I supported the rebellion of the count of Arques against the Norman duke in 1053, and in 1054 he and Geoffrey moved into Normandy, together with the king's brother Odo. The latter was soundly beaten by William at Mortemer and the king and Geoffrey retreated. William went on the offensive and moved into Maine, but his gains were shortlived. In 1058 the king and Geoffrey Martel again invaded Normandy but part of their army was cut off and massacred at Varaville. In 1060 when both of them died little had been decided, but their disappearance from the political scene gave William of Normandy ample opportunities for territorial expansion. These he used to considerable effect.

The king was less closely involved in other political rivalries of the time. In the early 1050s William Aigret, duke of Aquitaine, had declared war on Anjou, but in 1053 peace was re-established by the duke. Another short but inconclusive war was waged between Theobald of Blois and Geoffrey of Anjou in the mid 1050s, in which the king took little part. Nor did he intervene in the war between Germany and Flanders, though the emperor offered him part of Lorraine in return for his neutrality; he was too occupied with Normandy to do anything about it. In 1056 the king fell out with the emperor, but Henry died soon afterwards. Very little emerged from all these shifting coalitions. Although Henry I had made half hearted attempts to regain influence in Lorraine, he achieved nothing to this end.

Henry I's reign is often seen as a time when royal power, although initially weak, rallied somewhat.[16] As a territorial prince in the limited sphere of northern France Henry was not entirely unsuccessful. He managed effectively to contain the threat of Blois-Champagne and to profit from the involvement of Normandy and Anjou against one another. He consolidated his power within the royal principality from the mid-1040s (3.3.3), and although he did not manage effectively to dominate it, here, at least, he contained the most dangerous opposition and put royal power back on the map. His wider schemes, particularly for regaining Lorraine were far less successful, and in this kind of enterprise Geoffrey Martel's effectiveness appears to have been far greater than the king's. The sphere of his politics and warfare was more limited than that of his father, as was the distribution of his *acta* (3.3.4). Professors Dhondt and Lemarignier both suggest that Henry I was a realist who recognised the reduced importance of the monarchy, and who consolidated what he had. The second is a fair point, for Henry did manage effectively to hold and strengthen his powers in the Ile de France. The reduced royal horizons and range of royal activities, however, while a natural consequence of the weakness of Henry's power surely served only to narrow further the influence of the French king in a wider France. Perhaps Henry I was through force of circumstance too much a territorial prince, too little a king.

3.2.4 Philip I, 1060–1108

Philip I enjoyed an almost uniformly bad press from his contemporaries. In part this is explained by his hostility towards the reforming elements in the church. But Robert his grandfather had shown an almost equal antipathy to ecclesiastical claims, and had burned down a monastery, and yet was dubbed 'the Pious'. Philip probably went rather further than Robert in personal turpitude, and in the age of papal reform his many actions opposed to the ecclesiastical programme were highlighted in the eyes of the more militant reforming clergy. He was 'a man most mercenary in what belonged to God' according to Guibert of Nogent, who also asserted that he had lost the healing touch of many of his line.[17] Certainly ignoring all ecclesiastical sanctions he lived openly with Bertrada of Montfort, wife of Fulk Réchin of Anjou, in what was considered an incestuous, and by some a bigamous union. He seems to have sold church offices, and to have aroused widespread hostility from the French episcopate. He also plundered religious houses. He was often moderately though not conspicuously openhanded to the monastic orders; although he refounded his father's house of Saint-Martin-des-Champs as a Cluniac priory he was not outstandingly generous towards Saint-Benoit-sur-Loire or Fleury, where he was eventually buried (3.4.2); the latter may reflect a shift of political emphasis towards the south of the royal principality as much as a wish for personalised intercession. In his youth Philip is said by Raoul Tortaire, one of the Saint-Benoit-sur-Loire chroniclers, to have been an active man. Another writer described him as a man of prudence and intelligence. More of an opportunist than a warrior, he rapidly became obese and inactive, spending most of his time, again according to Tortaire, in gluttony and sleep. Orderic Vitalis wrote: 'King Philip was indolent, fat and unfit for war'.[18] The fourth Capetian king emerges as a somewhat distasteful figure.

From 1060 until 1067 France was under the regency of Baldwin V count of Flanders. The Fleury chronicle praises him as a prudent administrator who dominated the nobility of the realm by wise counsel as well as by force, maintaining peace in France. Philip, once he had come of age, was soon to break it. Normandy was now a very powerful rival to the crown; with the conquest of England in 1066, William's prestige was immense. Baldwin V's daughter, Matilda of Flanders, was married to William; Baldwin, as regent, had allowed Norman expansion to proceed. Philip clearly saw this as a derogation of royal power, and during the first part of his reign he tried to block further Norman expansion in all possible ways.

In 1070–71 Philip intervened in the war of succession in Flanders (2.3.1), an action closely linked with his hostility to Normandy. He initially backed the widow and son of Baldwin VI who were defeated at the battle of Cassel, and he had to accept the victorious Robert the Frisian as count, but he married Robert's step-daughter Bertha, securing his alliance against Normandy, and he also gained Corbie from the transaction. In 1076 he went to the relief of Dol with an army, and prevented William from overrunning Brittany. He also had to hold the French Vexin against him. In Henry I's reign the overlordship of this band of territory to the north of Paris, of vital strategic importance, had been granted to Normandy, but in 1075–76 Philip overran it during the minority of Simon of Crépy, count of Valois and the Vexin. William demanded it back, arguing that he was its overlord and not Philip, and in 1087 he invaded it. Having burned Mantes he fell ill and shortly afterwards died.

Meanwhile Philip had been encouraging the divisions in his family, lending spasmodic and opportunist support to Robert Curthose in his rebellions against his father. This was to become a favoured ploy of the French kings against their Anglo-Norman rivals. Robert continued to receive Philip's support against William Rufus after the Conqueror's death; the king extracted from him in return the town of Gisors and substantial sums of money. Philip had backed the wrong horse, as William Rufus eventually took over Normandy. Although the king drove him out of the Vexin in the 1090s, he did not take the offensive in 1099 when Rufus was heavily preoccupied with problems in Maine. Nor did he help Robert Curthose against Rufus's successor, Henry I of England. In 1106 the battle of Tinchebray, where Robert was defeated by Henry, restored the latter to the strong position held by his father and the domination of both England and Normandy.

In the latter part of his reign Philip's preoccupations moved away from politics and warfare. These he left to the son of his first marriage to Bertha of Holland, the future Louis VI of France. Bertha he had tired of and put aside; and in 1092 he carried off Bertrada of Montfort, wife of Fulk of Anjou. Almost all the French bishops supported his proposed marriage to her, but the important canonist, Ivo of Chartres was amongst a group of ecclesiastics who were strongly against it. Ivo wrote to the king

I should neither wish nor would be able to assist at the nuptials to which you call me, unless I knew that you and your wife were divorced by virtue of a decision of a general council, and that you could contract a legitimate marriage with the woman you have chosen. . . . This does not go against the fidelity I owe you, but is in virtue of the highest fidelity of all, for I am convinced that such a union would endanger both your soul and your crown.[19]

The marriage, he thought, would also constitute incest. Ivo was to be imprisoned for his opposition to the king, and the nuptials were celebrated. Philip was already in disfavour with the papacy since he opposed the ecclesiastical reforms, which would if fully implemented deprive him of the control of the temporalities of some great ecclesiastical estates, of great importance to his power, as well as preventing him from selling offices. Pope Gregory VII had quarrelled with him on the issue of elections in particular (3.4.2). Now Urban II took stronger action over the king's personal life. In 1095 the council of Clermont in France excommunicated Philip. Urban and his successor Paschal II continued to hurl anathemas in Philip's direction, but with very little-effect, for many French bishops remained behind the king, including Bertrada's brother, the new bishop of Paris.

The disputes raised by Philip's marriage to Bertrada illustrate the clash between the ideas of the high-born laity about marriage and the firm stance taken by the reforming church on the issues of divorce, bigamy and incest. Ivo of Chartres was in the front line, and helped to inflate the problem. The resulting scandal left Philip with the reputation of a greedy, lecherous adulterer and seducer; in fact his actions would have seemed quite acceptable to many of his lay contemporaries, and a sensible move to produce more heirs and safeguard the succession.[20] By 1100 the resolve of the church was beginning to weaken, and moves towards a reconciliation were made. The king promised to compromise over the bishopric of Beauvais, at that time in dispute between a royal and papal candidate, and to put aside Bertrada. In 1104 after further mediation by Ivo of Chartres, he agreed at the council of Beaugency to repudiate her. Even though he continued to live with her after this, his relationship with the papacy from now on was far more friendly. In general, indeed, the disputes of the English kings and the emperors with the holy see were far more acrimonious than those in France, where personal affairs seem to have loomed as large as investitures to bishoprics as issues of contention. Perhaps this is a measure of the relative insignificance of French royal power, but certainly it paved the way for later cooperation between the Capetians and the papacy.

Philip's authority within his royal lands was not particularly strong. In 1080, for example, he was defeated by the castellan Hugh, lord of Le Puiset, and his army routed. Later in his reign his son Louis began to fight the castellans in the royal principality, and he was beginning to increase his authority by his father's death in 1108. Philip had added parts of the Gâtinais to the royal lands in 1067 and Corbie ten years later; he managed to assert a closer control of the Vexin, and in 1101 regained the viscounty of Bourges. His horizons were still little wider than his father's. He intervened in Normandy which directly threatened his lands to the north, but his only other major involvement was his struggle with the reforming church, which was increasingly influential and powerful in France, the result of his own personal attitudes and activities to which the church objected, rather than positive aggression on his part. Philip certainly felt little interest in the crusading movement or in ecclesiastical reform. Despite his largely negative qualities, royal power began to show signs of revival during his reign, as some important castellans in the royal principality began to hold high office in the royal court, and others could no longer afford to ignore royal power altogether, largely through the efforts of Prince Louis to dominate the more rebellious among them (3.3.4; 4.2.1).

Robert the Pious was the only early Capetian king whose ambitions went much beyond the Seine and the Loire valleys. Although he revived his influence to some extent outside the north of France, little of this proved durable. Indeed, his european schemes were more the product of ambition and enthusiasm than of realism. The horizons of his son Henry I and his grandson Philip I were focused closely on the north of France, their activities largely concerned with their immediate neighbours. In practical terms their royal power was predominately a local affair.

3.3 THE BASIS OF ROYAL POWER

3.3.1 *The royal domain*

What was the nature of early Capetian power? The foregoing narrative of the events and politics of the reigns of Hugh Capet and his successors has traced the decline of royal authority and the early signs of revival under Philip I, but to understand these events more fully it is necessary to examine the nature of royal authority in this period. This requires a careful analysis, for royal power had a number of different components. The king was attributed with sacral and feudal powers (3.1.1) but more practically he was actually supported by his domain, his collection of secular and ecclesiastical rights and the lands he held directly. Then he had his principality, the area he dominated, which had a wider, more territorial identity than the domain, though the domain was its centre. Beyond this he had a larger and a more theoretical authority in the kingdom, and operating on all these levels, he had his rather undeveloped and primitive machinery of government, based on his household and important ecclesiastical establishments, which issued charters in his name.

78

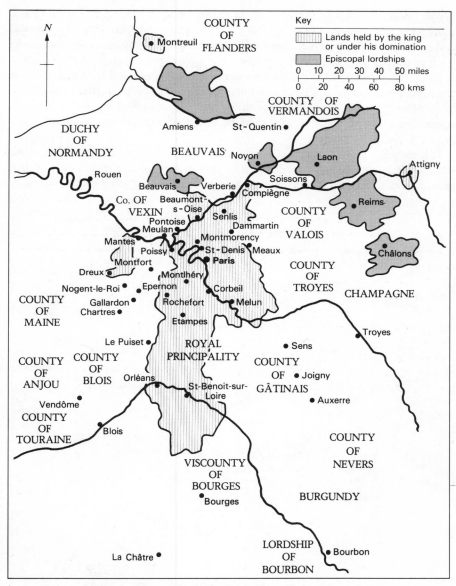

Map 3.1 The royal principality in the mid-eleventh century

What was the royal domain? This is a question which has long vexed historians of Capetian France. There has been a consensus on its general implications – those of lands or rights directly under royal control – but many different interpretations within this wide definition. In Professor Longnon's historical atlas of France there is a map depicting France in 1032. A large area of land around Orléans, Melun, Paris, Rochefort, Poissy, Senlis and Dreux is shaded pink, and described in the key as the royal domain. Other maps of France in 1154, 1200, 1223, 1241 and 1254 show the expansion of this domain. This is essentially a territorial approach, and it is one that has a considerable value; indeed the geographical extent of direct royal authority may usefully be looked at as a royal principality in the eleventh and twelfth centuries (3.3.3). Nevertheless there are some problems in depicting the royal principality as a clearly defined area, as when it is shaded in on a map (e.g. Map 3.1), for in practice the king was only as effective as the lands he controlled in person and as the men he could dominate, so fragmented was political authority (3.3.2).

It is only the lands and rights held directly by the king and from which profit was derived, to which many historians now apply the term domain for this period, and clearly their known extent is going to be far narrower – especially

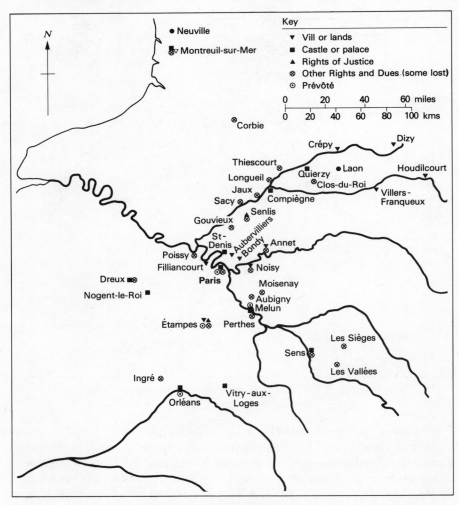

Map 3.2   Henry I's secular domain

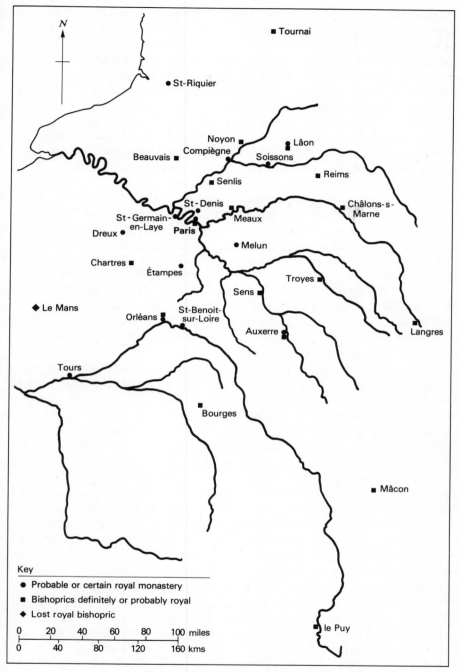

Map 3.3   Henry I's ecclesiastical domain

during periods of sparse documentation – than the territorial blocs depicted by Longnon.[21] These powers over castles, villages and estates, forests, towns, religious houses and bishoprics, and rights of justice, tolls and taxes appear on a map as a network, more concentrated in some areas than in others, rather than as a unit of land (Map 3.2. and Map 3.3). This approach was first applied to the royal domain by Professor Newman and has also been used for the domains of a number of great nobles. M. Bur, for example, applies it to Champagne. But the royal domain in this sense differs strikingly from that of the princes in one way, for whereas the most powerful noble could expect to control only a few bishoprics and monasteries, the king dominated a more substantial proportion of the French bishoprics and a considerable number of ancient and important religious houses. His ecclesiastical domain was far wider geographically than the lands and rights he controlled, and this at times gave him a certain advantage (3.3.2).

What did this collection amount to in practice, and where was it located in the eleventh century? As Professor Newman showed, our surviving sources suggest that the secular domain of the king in this period was centred in three related areas. One stretched from the north of the Loire to Paris, another fell between Dreux, Mantes, Saint-Denis and Paris, and a third was round Senlis and Compiègne, stretching up to Soissons and Laon. There were lesser centres at Montreuil, Beauvais, Chaumont-en-Vexin, Sens and Tours (Map 3.2). Not until the twelfth century was there a marked increase in the geographical extent of the secular domain, and not until the thirteenth did it grow dramatically.

The lands, customs and rights which made up the domain had come to the king in a number of different ways. Some were royal in origin, though by the eleventh century the great majority were also enjoyed by princes, nobles and castellans, as for example forest rights and rights of minting. Others, still public in origin, the king had inherited from lesser officials, such as the secular official known as the *viguier* or vicar. A third group were seigneurial: the manorial rights enjoyed by all lords. And this variegated collection was held by the Capetians in a number of different guises, as king, count, viscount or vicar; it was the sum total of the domains of a number of many different lands (3.3.3). These were both granted out and added to by the kings during the eleventh century. Robert the Pious gained the counties of Paris, Dreux and Melun, and arranged for the reversion of part of the town and the county of Sens to the crown after Count Renaud's death; this happened in 1055. Henry I granted Burgundy to his brother Robert and the French Vexin to the duke of Normandy, and he gave the lordship of Corbie to the count of Flanders as the dowry of his sister Adela. Philip I acquired parts of the Gâtinais in c. 1068, took back the French Vexin in the 1070s, and probably regained Corbie from his first marriage to Bertha of Holland. Between 1097 and 1102 he purchased the viscounty of Bourges from its holder, Odo Arpin, who needed funds to go on crusade, while in 1108 Guy of Montlhéry ceded his lands to the future Louis VI. In all these cases, the king was involved as 'count' or lord, and he gained or gave away in effect the domainial rights going with the title, not the entire county or lordship.

Land however was a very important element in the secular domain, and the king was in his own right a great landed proprietor. He held many manors which were cultivated directly for him, some parts of which were in domain, others worked by the peasants for themselves, their labour services acting as rents. These services were known as the *corvée*, and included the tilling of the land by the peasants and their animals, and the transportation of the produce. Money rents later replaced some of these services. Other land was rented out to tenants directly, for which the *champart*, a proportion of the harvest, or the *cens*, a money rent, was paid. The king had the standard seigneurial monopolies over mills for grinding corn and ovens for baking bread, and other miscellaneous powers. An example is *forage*, a domainial right over wine which finds occasional mention in charters. Peasants from the royal domain paid normal, standard dues to the king, but enjoyed certain judicial privileges as royal serfs. The products of the land under direct royal exploitation were gathered in royal *granges* as at Gonesse and Mantes and *celliers* as at Orléans and Argenteuil for use by the royal household or for resale. All these rights were the kind enjoyed by the nobility and were tied up with the system of cultivation used in northern France.

Through his foresters the king controlled the great areas of forest land, and this was a royal right in origin, though it had been much divided amongst the nobility. In forests such as Rouvray, Halatte, Chantilly-Hermenonville, in the Bois-de-Boulogne and the Bois-de-Vincennes the king enjoyed exclusive hunting rights which made the forests a valuable source of meat. Royal flocks and herds were pastured there and honey and wood gathered. Dues had to be paid by others who used the forests in this way. But these areas were also a valuable source of uncleared and uncultivated land and the king offered privileges to colonisers or *hôtes*, including judicial rights and exemption from military service, *taille* and *corvée*. He would in turn later benefit from part of the profits.

Many palaces and castles were held by the king directly; indeed the rights of castle building, like those over city walls, had originally been exclusively royal. This idea survived throughout the early Capetian period, although often in practice other lords took over these powers (3.3.6). Castles were of value for defence and for the local administration of royal rights, and like royal palaces provided locations – for example, in Paris, Senlis, Poissy, Etampes, Orléans – for the king and his household to stay in the course of their almost constant travels. Many towns were also directly under royal control. Some, the new towns or *villeneuves*, were newly founded settlements of royal creation, often intended to open up an area for land colonisation, and given special privileges. Other older settlements began to thrive on an increasing trade and to contain a growing number of burgesses who profited from it. Many such communities were in the twelfth century to seek the semi-autonomy of a self-governing commune. Some were granted this in return for a large annual rent, but Paris and Orléans, invaluable strategically, were exceptions here (4.3.2).

Some of the rights and revenues belonging to the king had, like the lands he controlled, originated from royal powers; others came from seigneurial authority. One in the first category was the right of the king and his entourage to hospitality in castles and monasteries controlled either by him or sometimes by a local noble. This could at times be a heavy imposition. By exempting the monastery of Saint-Rémi at Sens, Henry I was clearly giving it a valuable privilege, but the price of avoiding the *gîte* was often high, running at times to the granting of land or to a fixed annual payment. An allied right was the *droit de prise*, which enabled food to be purloined for the royal household and the king's horses and hounds either very cheaply or free of charge.

The king had many mints with the monopoly of striking money in a given area, again a right once exclusively royal but in the early Capetian period shared by many lords. He also controlled many roads where tolls or *péage* for safe-conducts could be levied. Philip I, for example, allowed the profits of a road near the monastery of Saint-Martin-des-Champs to be used to help to support the hospital of the religious house. *Rouage* was levied on wheeled vehicles and *transit* paid on passage by road or by water. Such rights could be held *in toto* or a proportion of them could be granted out as a concession. The king also often controlled fairs or markets. Philip I for example gave to the city of Orléans half the profits of the fair held there on 1 November. He could regulate the price of sale of various merchandise, for example wine, and also levied another tax, the *hauban*, on all those carrying out a trade or profession. Furthermore, since he was seen as the protector of various Jewish communities, he was able to levy valuable dues from them. Philip I gave revenues extracted from the Jews at Tours to his wife Bertrada.

The profits of a number of other dues and taxes were also raised by the king. Tithes paid to the parish priest by his parishioners, a tenth of their produce intended for his support, had often fallen into lay hands by the eleventh century. Like other lords, the king levied part or all of the tithes of numerous churches. Rents, the *cens*, were furthermore payable to the king on rights as well as on land, as for example, on tolls or on *prévôtés*, the administrative offices of the domain. The king might at times pay the cens himself on lands or rights leased from other lords. From the later eleventh century the Capetians began to levy tallage, a personal tax, a forced payment in origin of which the yields were considerable, demanded from free men and serfs alike. Over his serfs the king had a number of other seigneurial rights, including *mainmorte*, which enabled him to seize movables on the death of a peasant, together with immovables if there was no heir. *Chevage* was a tax of four pennies paid by all unfree persons each year.

In the ninth century justice over all free men had belonged to the king, but like other rights it had fragmented subsequently, and become largely private in character. It was not always allied with landholding, for an estate could be granted out with or without judicial rights, or with the reservation of some men but not of others. The precise sense in which the word itself, *justitia*, is used in royal charters, is sometimes hard to discern. At times it appears to signify justice in an abstract sense, and at others, the dues culled from it. The interchangeability of the two, however, reflects the widely accepted view that justice could at times be a profitable affair.

In the ninth century there had been a clear distinction between major and minor causes; the Carolingian count heard on behalf of the emperor major criminal cases carrying the death penalty or the reduction to servile status of the guilty party, lawsuits concerning allods and cases to determine servile or free status. The other minor cases were heard locally by the count's delegate, the *viguier* or vicar. In the early eleventh century, in Burgundy at least, the public courts of these officials gradually lost their authority and disappeared, to be transformed into or replaced by the private jurisdictions of the castellans and lesser nobles. Gradually a hierarchy of such courts was built up; the castellans and great ecclesiastical establishments heard capital cases including murder, treason, theft, rape and arson, later included in high justice; minor offences were tried in local manorial courts. In this part of France there seems to be no evidence of continuity between Carolingian major causes and later high justice; the latter may be linked with the emergence of the peace and truce of God and the obligations they imposed on the greater nobles and ecclesiastics.[22] All over northern France, however, the pattern was not a simple one and developments were not clearcut, and although later on, high justice passed to the king, princes, counts and castellans and low justice to the manorial lords, the eleventh century saw many overlapping judicial institutions, decaying or emerging.

The royal court at times sat as a court of law, acting in both a royal and a domainial capacity according to the cases which came before it, without making any distinction between them. To be subject to the royal ban as opposed to seigneurial justice was clearly considered a great privilege; in 1046 for example, Henry I granted it to the favoured house of canons at Etampes (3.4.2). Royal justice was often delegated to *prévôts* or mayors in given localities as part of their administrative duties, although in certain areas it was kept directly in the king's hands. In 1008 Robert the Pious reserved judicial rights in Saint-Denis and its locality for himself, but generally such royal enclaves were limited in size. Although royal justice sometimes overrode the basic rule of thumb that free men should be judged by their peers and vassals by their overlord, equally, at times the king's free vassals were not always judged in the royal court. In some areas the king held the *vicaria*, which involved administrative as well as judicial functions. Carolingian in origin, but in many regions losing its effectiveness in the early Capetian period, its holder the vicar was the peace-keeping authority in a given district. In practice the king's powers were probably much the same whether he held a *vicaria* or the ban (judicial rights) in a particular place, but the variations in terminology underline the diversity in judicial rights and practices, which stemmed in part from their varying origins – royal, feudal, manorial or vicarial; the pattern was not to stabilise until much later.

Clearly the collection of lands and rights which made up the domain needed organising so that they could be exploited to the advantage of the king and retained for his use. One method of doing this was the direct one; the king and his entourage travelled between royal castles and manors, consuming their produce, supervising their administration and holding courts. Royal power was also delegated to local officials. There are references to viscounts and to *viguiers* in many early Capetian charters, but it seems that these were often found only because the scribes were copying from much earlier models; in many areas these officials were fast disappearing, to be replaced by new agents of royal power, the provosts or *prévôts*, first found in the mid-eleventh century. By Louis VI's reign most of the royal lands had been divided into a number of *prévôtés*, the areas which they controlled. Their functions were wideranging, both financial and judicial, and they were able to extend both royal rights and the profits they made from them. Occasionally one of their number opposed the king, and like some of the earlier castellan families whose powers had originally been derived from public offices, they could pose a considerable threat to law and order in the Ile de France. The loyal *prévôts* by contrast proved zealous in the extension of royal power in the districts they controlled.

3.3.2. *The ecclesiastical domain*

As well as having a network of secular rights and lands under his control the king exercised valuable and important powers over the church. These were far more wideranging geographically than his secular domain, for often, even though the fisc had been alienated in a given area, the crown had retained control over all or some of the bishops and monasteries there. Charlemagne and Louis the Pious had been the effective masters of the church in west Francia, and while their Capetian successors no longer exercised the same overall control, their ecclesiastical domain was still much wider than that of any territorial prince. Even at their weakest, the early Capetians still controlled more bishoprics and key monasteries than any other great lord in France.

Over these establishments the king exercised regalian rights, the power to hold their estates during vacancies resulting from the death of the bishop or abbot and to administer the lands for his own profit. Prebends and other offices falling vacant at this time would have their new holders nominated by the king. This made them a valuable source of patronage to be given to deserving royal servants. Often too, in the case of bishoprics, the king could dispose of the chattels of the defunct incumbent. Then he would 'elect' the new bishop, sometimes selling the office to the highest bidder, and invest him with the ring and staff, symbol of his lands and dignity. Both theses practices were condemned by the ecclesiastical reformers of the later eleventh century (3.4.2). They formed one area of opposition to royal rights over bishoprics and abbeys, and another came from rival lords with their own candidates. The king nevertheless managed to maintain his ecclesiastical domain relatively unscathed into the twelfth century.

There was some fluctuation in the number of bishoprics controlled by the early Capetians but broadly speaking Hugh Capet appears to have held the bishoprics of Le Mans, Chartres, Orléans, Paris, Meaux, Beauvais, Senlis, Soissons, Noyon-Tournai, Laon, Langres and Le Puy, and the archbishoprics of Sens and Reims. Robert the Pious probably gained Troyes, Auxerre, Mâcon, Châlons-sur-Marne and the archbishopric of Bourges, and Henry I lost Le Mans. Philip I added Thérouanne, Amiens, Chalon-sur-Saône and the archbishopric of Tours. The monasteries are less well documented but many, such as Saint-Benoit-sur-Loire, Saint-Aignan at Orléans and Saint-Riquier remained in royal hands continuously between 987 and 1108. There is evidence that between forty and fifty were at some time royal during this period. As the map (3.3) indicates, Henry I's ecclesiastical domain stretched into Burgundy, Berry, the Loire Valley and Picardy, a far wider area than that in which his secular rights were concentrated.

A royal bishopric was one where the king retained or gained the power to appoint and to administer in a vacancy. The royal abbey has been rather less easy to describe. Professor Lot and M. Pfister considered as royal houses all monasteries to which confirmation charters and safeguards had been granted.[23] But the first group of such grants often merely backed up the foundation or donation of another patron, and although they could be given to royal monasteries, clearly not all the houses to which they were issued were necessarily royal [The second group of grants, the safeguards, were of varying significance. Sometimes they amounted to the promise of protection only for a small outlying parcel of monastic land, perhaps one situated near to an area of strong royal influence. At other times they could involve complete royal protection promised for the house and all its lands. In this case the monastery involved would almost always have been under royal domination-plus-protection anyway, and this is the criterion for a monastery in the ecclesiastical domain of the king offered by Professor Newman.[24] Grants of protection to monasteries aimed to extend the royal domain were not common; charters promising some royal protection would give the king an influence and an importance with the monastery without necessarily giving him control of its resources. Again, he might arrange for its reform, but this would not automatically make him its lord.

To be the lord of a monastery the king had to combine the functions of founder and patron. The early Capetians controlled a considerable number of monasteries in this way for a number of reasons. Hugh Capet had held one group before he became king, and they fell naturally to his successors. Another group of houses formerly under the domination of the Carolingian kings passed to the new royal dynasty. These included Fleury (Saint-Benoît-sur-Loire) and Saint-Corneille at Compiègne. A third group consisted of the foundations or refoundations of the Capetians themselves, such as Saint-Martin-des-Champs; sometimes too the foundations of other lords could be given a substantial donation and then be brought under royal control by the annexation of the office of founder to the crown. In other cases the king became founder and patron by bringing the monastery under royal protection, with no donation involved; this was not a common occurrence.

It is not always clear in what sense the king was acting as a protector of certain monasteries. In the ninth century he had had a *tuitio*, a guardianship over all monastic houses, but by the eleventh many had found other protectors, their *avoués* or advocates. This office had grown out of that held by a low-ranking lay servant who had protected the monasteries in the ninth and tenth centuries. Local nobles had often taken it over and used it as a way of dominating the religious house and its valuable estates. The king was sometimes called in by such communities to defend them against their advocates. In England and Normandy the advocacy was almost always subsumed into the office of patron and founder; in France the two did not always coincide. The king could be either or he could be both, but only when he was patron and founder can the house properly be said to form part of the royal domain. Even so, the extent of this domain was considerable under the first Capetians. Royal monasteries enjoyed a number of privileges. They were subject to royal justice alone, but enjoyed judicial privileges in their own lands. They were free from the authority of the local bishop. The king in his spiritual role was their direct controller, and this gave him in practice regalian rights, as in the case of the bishoprics.

The early Capetians are sometimes portrayed as saintly protectors of the monasteries. Certainly they defended a number of religious houses, but others they exploited ruthlessly. An example of the latter is the abbey of Saint-Germain-des-Prés, in the Middle Ages just outside the walls of Paris. Founded in the Merovingian period, by the ninth century its lands were very considerable and scattered throughout France, as the *polyptique* of Abbot Irminon shows. From the late ninth century however, it gradually lost most of these lands. The first blow was the Norman invasions, when the mother house was destroyed and had to be rebuilt, and many of its estates were devastated. The next fell more gradually, under the lay abbacy of Duke Hugh the Great. He granted out a number of parcels of fisc, including Combs, Nogent, Villemeux and Palaiseau to his vassals. Robert the Pious further dissipated the abbey's estates, using some, including Beynes and Maule, for the construction of castles then granted to vassals, intended to protect Paris from Odo II of Blois. New centres of the alienated fiscs grew up to replace the old, and new patterns of landholding replaced those represented in the *polyptique*.

In about 1025 William of Volpiano was called in by the king to refound and reform the monastery, and from this time onwards some of the former lands and churches of the house, albeit generally those in the Ile de France, were restored to Saint-Germain. Henry I was unable to give back whole *villae*, and contented himself with the grant of the church of Saint-Martin at Dreux. The recovery of the abbey's estates was slow, and the whole process reveals the extent to which ecclesiastical estates could be exploited and regranted by the king and the nobles in the tenth and eleventh centuries.[25] Saint-Germain was nevertheless an important cultural centre in the eleventh century, with a *scriptorium* which produced fine and delicately coloured illuminated manuscripts. The rebuilding of its church was begun, and the tower and the nave with its fine capitals, which still survive, are an indication of the quality of the craftsmanship in the Paris area in this period.

3.3.3 *The royal principality*

The material side of royal power was based on the royal domain, the sum total of the king's lands and rights, but there was a political and territorial side to royal authority in the Ile de France and Orléans regions as well. The king was recognised as having power in the geographical area which surrounded and included the domain and this may, because of its political and social similarities to other French principalities of the eleventh century, conveniently be termed the royal principality. It was centred on the counties and viscounties held directly by the king, the Parisis, Orléanais, Etampais, Châtrais, Pincerais and Melunais which had been the core of the Robertine lands, and the débris of the Carolingian domain, including the royal palaces of Attigny (Ardennes), Compiègne and Verberie. Then there were the important episcopal counties such as Laon, Reims and Châlons, dominated by the king, together with other episcopal and monastic estates in the ecclesiastical domain. Around these lands were another group of counties and lordships in the king's feudal *mouvance*, held directly from him. These included the Vendômois, Corbonnais (Mortagne and Bellême), Gâtinais, Melunais, Arcésis (Arcis-sur-Aube and Ramerupt), Valois (including Crépy), Soissonais, the French Vexin, Beaumont-sur-Oise, Beauvaisis, Breteuil, Amiénois, Vermandois, Ponthieu and Vimeu, Sens and Joigny, the viscounty of Bourges and possibly the lordship of Bourbon (Map 3.1).

Though some of the lands were scattered, they were centred on the Paris and Orléans areas, and here the king was recognised as the major power, even though in practice he was unable effectively to dominate all these regions. Fawtier comments that 'to regard (the early Capetians) as *"petits seigneurs"* of the Ile de France is to perpetuate a myth',[26] but although the kings were far from being small lords they did not control and dominate their own principality as effectively as William the Conqueror did Normandy. In the eleventh century the castellans not the Capetians wielded effective political power in areas which surrounded and interspersed with those of the king and his loyal vassals — they were often, indeed, his disloyal vassals — and local wars and violence flourished. This was not confined to the royal lands, it was the pattern which prevailed in the Mâconnais, Maine, Anjou and Poitou as well as much of the south, and it is a clear symptom of weak central authority.

The Robertines, ancestors of the Capetians, had built up a considerable collection of lands in northern France in the ninth and tenth centuries. Robert 'the Strong' had been granted lands between the Seine, the Loire and the Mayenne. Odo had added estates around Paris, Orléans, Etampes, Melun and La Châtre. Although he was rivalled by Normandy to the north and Anjou to the west, Hugh the Great managed to consolidate his lands by playing off his rivals, and this his Capetian descendants were to continue to do. In 943 Hugh was granted the title of *dux Francorum*, duke of the Franks, which implied an overall authority in Francia. This area, which included Normandy, Anjou and Maine, was one of the three principal divisions of the kingdom in the mid-tenth century; Flodoard said that when in 954 Lothar was crowned this was done with the consent of the great men of the realm from Burgundy, Aquitaine and Francia.[27]

The *dux francorum* had no real authority over the outlying areas which were themselves forming as principalities, such as Normandy and Anjou, and the idea of the duchy in its widest geographical extent began to disappear. In 987 its duke became king, and by about 1000 the two offices seem to have fused. The name 'Francia' used in its narrower sense was by now normally applied only to the central area of the former duchy, where the lands of the king and of the counts of Blois lay, and by the twelfth century it was to be used to describe only the royal principality. During the eleventh century the counts of Blois held the title of count palatine, but they never managed to overshadow the Capetians as the Robertines had done the Carolingians.

In the tenth century most of the Robertine lands had been in the regions round the Ile de France, yet despite their considerable extent they did not form a coherent political unit like Normandy or Flanders. Until 987 the Carolingians still held land here and the Robertines and the house of Vermandois, later the counts of Blois, were vying against one another. Within the Robertine lands there were a number of important nobles. Most notable amongst these was Bouchard the Venerable, count of Vendôme, whose life was written fifty years after his death by Odo of Saint-Maur. He held the counties of Melun and Paris as well as Vendôme, and obtained the castle and lordship of Corbeil by marriage. In 1006, an aged man, he retired to the monastery of Saint-Maur-des-Fossés, and his lands were divided up, the king resuming the county of Paris. The Robertines were not able fully to consolidate and dominate their lands, and unlike Bouchard, many of the counts and viscounts of the area escaped from their direct control and in the early eleventh century in many parts of the principality independent castellans with bannal lordships began to appear. Indeed, some of the old centres of power in the *pagi* were replaced with new ones as the *pagi* broke down; some of their lords assumed comital titles, as when the earlier counts of Chambly were replaced by the counts of Beaumont-sur-Oise. Other new counts in the early eleventh century were Manasses of Dammartin, Robert of Rochefort-en-Yvelines and Galeran, count of Meulan.

Though the centres of power were new, their holders normally were not, for most, it seems, were descendants of the earlier comital families of the area, who because of the weakness of royal control were able to consolidate an increased and private authority based around their own castles and customs. Many such castellans, like the 'sires' of Montlhéry, did not take the comital title at all. This family carved out a lordship from the lands of the bishopric of Paris, while the Montmorency and Montfort families held lands formerly belonging to the king. As in many areas of France, these estates originated in quite legitimate grants of lands as fiefs – for landholding in the area was centred on the fief, and allods were rare – but these vassals became increasingly independent from their lords and were able to consolidate their own holdings at their lords' expense. Although some ecclesiastical lands in the area, like the royal estates, suffered from this process, many religious establishments in the Ile de France also managed to extend privileges of immunity to their lands and to consolidate bannal lordships within the patchwork of estates which was forming.[28]

The process began slowly. In the reign of Hugh Capet the Meulan lordship appeared, and then Montmorency around the year 1000, followed by Gallardon, Nogent-le-Roi, Montfort-l'Amaury and Epernon. At this time too a large collection of lands was built up by Gendouin de Breteuil in the Vexin, Beauvaisis and other areas between the Seine and Somme, but this never became a permanent holding. Robert the Pious was obliged to fight the castellans of the Beauce, but these independent nobles did not become an acute problem until Henry I's reign, when lesser castellanies multiplied. Adulterine castles seemed to proliferate, and the whole group of castellan families, as they intermarried, spawned further cadet offshoots. The succession dispute of 1031–32 greatly weakened royal power in the region, and the ambitious Odo II of Blois drew many of these families into dependence on him and posed a considerable threat to the king. Henry managed to defeat him, and by 1040 the crisis was over.

Nevertheless for the rest of the eleventh century royal power remained relatively circumscribed and much of the principality was dominated by powerful and established castellan families, such as the Montlhéry and Montmorency, and those who rose from knightly origins such as the Garlande. Many castellans continued to ignore or defy the king. In 1080 Hugh of Le Puiset defeated the royal army in the field, and Philip I also had considerable problems with the Montlhéry. He managed eventually to acquire the castle there by marrying his son by Bertrada de Montfort to the daughter and heiress of Guy Troussel, lord of Montlhéry. Abbot Suger reports that Philip said to Louis VI when on his deathbed: 'Look, son, make sure you never let the tower of Montlhéry out of your keeping. It has caused me untold trouble. Frankly, that tower has made me old before my time.'[29]

Nevertheless by the end of Philip I's reign there were signs of future royal recovery in the principality. The royal entourage was composed mainly of lesser men from the area, but the major offices in the royal household were now held by leading castellans of the Ile de France. As a result they tended to dominate the king, but this at least gave him a following from a higher social stratum (3.3.5). Prince Louis's wars against some of the more independent castellans had begun to re-establish law and order, to revive royal prestige and widen effective royal justice, though as King Louis VI he still had a long way to go (4.2.1). By 1108, however, royal power was beginning very slowly to make a comeback in the royal principality.

3.3.4 Royal government and the royal entourage

Royal power shrank continuously during the first century or so of Capetian rule in France, and only began to make a slow recovery at the end of Philip I's reign. This pattern emerges in an examination of the politics of the reigns, in an analysis of the developments in the domain and the principality, and in a look at the relationship of the king and the territorial princes. It shows up most strikingly of all in the survey of royal government by Professor Lemarignier, based largely on the acts issued by the king's chancery or in some cases drawn up by ecclesiastical establishments when they were the recipients.[30]

The form, style, and content of royal charters, our principal evidence, are all of considerable interest. Dr Marjorie Chibnall has recently stressed the similarities of many of the chronicles and charters produced in northern France in the eleventh century; charters drawn up in monasteries often contain valuable background information, and can also reflect royal pretensions just as much as those produced by the royal chancery. The king's charters also often had multiple witness lists, and the content of these is of interest, for they catalogue the royal entourage, the king's following, on the day the act was drawn up. Individuals who can be identified within the lists can, taken collectively, give an idea of the area and of the social group from which the entourage was drawn. An analysis of the beneficiaries likewise shows the areas where nobles and churches turned to the king for land grants, confirmations and safeguards, and is one way of measuring the geographical extent of royal influence.

Between 987 and the middle of the eleventh century the form taken by royal charters underwent a change. Carolingian *acta* had been witnessed by the king and by the chancellor, and so too were most early Capetian charters. But a noble style of charter, with a multiple witness list at the end, also began to appear amongst royal acts, and this seems to symbolise a new view of monarchy. First in 988, then in 1005, a whole string of names appears at the end of a royal charter. The Carolingian style royal diploma continued to be used extensively, but the multiple witness charter gradually gained ground, so that for the whole period 995 to 1025 it comprised a third of all royal acts. This includes the charters of nobles witnessed by the king, again a new development.

Such signs of the decline of royal power must be set against certain features of a Carolingian style of royal authority which continued into the eleventh century. Some of the charters in the older format contained mentions of the king's *fideles*, his faithful men, with whose consent they were said to be given, and this is an earlier form of words, although under Robert the Pious mentions of *fideles* decline in numbers. Again important events, such as the siege of Avallon, the synod of Chelles which condemned the murder of Hugh of Beauvais, or the consecration of the future Henry I were marked by gatherings of the greater nobility, lay and ecclesiastical. These are in a sense the continuation of the Carolingian *placita*, the royal councils where the king presided over his leading subjects who ratified his decisions. Professor Lemarignier suggests that this impression is not wholly misleading, for the royal government under Robert the Pious still seemed largely dominated by the aristocracy, and especially by the episcopate, as it had been a century before. By the 1020s this was becoming a façade.

Between about 1028 and 1031, when the throne was disputed between Robert's sons, royal power lost ground dramatically. The charters with multiple witness lists increased rapidly and the Carolingian style diploma was gradually eclipsed. Bishops and counts still appeared as witnesses but their names were intermingled with, and sometimes overwhelmed by, those of the castellans and knights from the Ile de France. The few greater nobles appeared as *fideles*, but the lesser men witnessed the *acta*, it seems, more in recognition of their local power than as a sign of their obedience to the king. Charters were validated by the powerful men of a given area rather than the vassals of the king. The traditional role of the archbishops of Reims as archchancellors of France gradually fell into disuse after the death of Archbishop Adalbero. The chancellor was now appearing as only one amongst a plethora of other witnesses. Another important development was that customs, *consuetudines*, are frequently referred to in the place of the royal or public power. In general there was little apart from his title to distinguish the king in his charters from a great noble or even a castellan.

There was a further slow decline in royal authority as shown in royal charters during the reign of Henry I and the early years of Philip I. Henry managed to consolidate his power in the royal principality to some extent, but his field of action was limited. He was a king with the outlook of a territorial prince (3.2.3) and his localised influence is reflected in the more limited areas from which the beneficiaries of royal charters came. Whereas under Robert the Pious the majority had been granted in the regions bounded by Tours, Montreuil and Châlons, with some few in outlying areas, under his successors fewer went to the regions of the lower Loire and Burgundy, Normandy and Flanders, and their concentration upon Orléans and even more upon Paris, became closer. The gradual disappearance of the Carolingian style diploma also continued. By the early years of Philip I's reign about seven-eighths of surviving charters with royal connections were either issued by the king, ending with a multiple witness list, or involved the king as one witness of a private act.

Bishops and counts continue to appear among these witnesses, and on some few occasions they are the only group from which the witnesses are drawn. One example is in 1048 when a charter of protection to Saint-Médard at Soissons was validated by two archbishops, ten bishops and eleven great nobles. This, it seems, marked a general alliance against the Emperor Henry III. In 1077 the grant of the monastery of Saint-Symphorien at Autun to Saint-Benoit-sur-Loire was witnessed by a similarly large and noble concourse, and this probably shows an alliance against William of Normandy. Generally, if bishops, princes and lesser counts are still appearing fairly frequently as witnesses, castellans and knights show up more and more often as lists grow in length. The area from which they come gradually shrinks to the Ile de France and its surrounding regions (the royal principality) and if a charter affects a particular locality, often the local men appear as its witnesses. By Philip I's reign, castellans of small lordships often benefited from royal *acta*, and they also often appear as witnesses. So too do knights, frequently lords of only one village, and the overwhelming impression of the royal entourage during this period is that it consisted of local men. These are described as *testes*, witnesses, rather than the *fideles* of the king.

After about 1077 this pattern, which had remained broadly stable for fifty years or so, began to change somewhat. In the wake of the papal reforms the bishops appeared as witnesses markedly less often. The greater nobility, too, almost disappeared. Burgesses begin to be found as witnesses alongside the castellans and knights – perhaps a sign of expanding urban economies. In this sense the composition of the entourage has fallen to a striking degree of localisation and social mediocrity. Philip I's itinerary[31] is also much more limited in extent than that of Robert the Pious. Where Robert had travelled extensively in Burgundy, Aquitaine and Flanders, and went on pilgrimage to Rome twice and through the Languedoc and the Massif Central once, Philip, apart from one spell in Poitou, remained in the Paris region.

There are also signs of the future recovery of royal power. The Capetian kings first seem to have had their own constable and butler in the 1040s, and the other household officials, the seneschal and the chamberlain appeared soon afterwards. By the 1080s they had become prominent in the entourage, and often witnessed charters in company with only a few, or no other witnesses, and this trend was to continue and to increase. Whereas originally they had come from the lesser nobility, now they were leading castellans of the principality, descended from lines such as the Montlhéry-Rochefort and the Riche, or from newly risen but powerful families such as the Garlande. Their domination was to be a problem for Louis VI, but under Philip I their growing importance marked the emergence of a following for the king from a higher social stratum. The king, it seems, was beginning to govern with the counsel of his great household officials. The charters themselves were also written in a more consistent form and style.

On a local level, too, royal power appeared to be increasing slowly. The royal *prévôts*, whose offices may have had a public rather than a feudal character, begin to show up as the witnesses of some local *acta*, and then after about 1082 they start to receive *mandements*, terse instructions from the king for action in their administrative area; these acts were probably influenced by the procedures of the Anglo-Saxon and Norman kings in England and by the papal chancery. At the end of Philip I's reign these acts become quite frequent, and they are a clear sign of a reviving royal power in the Ile de France. Royal justice was also becoming more effective, so that by the end of Philip's reign his son, Prince Louis, was able to pass judgement on many nobles in the area and to use force to back it up. In the early years of the twelfth century the king's power was still weak, and his principality was still dominated in many areas by the castellans. There were however clear signs that royal power was beginning slowly to revive, both in the principality, and in a wider area in the north of the kingdom.

3.3.5 The king and the territorial princes

Early in the eleventh century Abbo, abbot of Fleury, went to visit the abbey of La Réole in Gascony, and declared to his companions: 'Here I am more powerful than the king of France, for no one in this region fears his domination.'[32] The links of Gascony with the French monarchy were in any case not strong, but this comment would have been equally applicable for the Spanish March and the Languedoc. In the eleventh century the papacy was more powerful in the south of France than the king, and the church, not the crown, had taken on the role of keeper of the peace. Very few charters of Hugh Capet and Robert the Pious found their way to the south, and the territorial princes of the region never appeared as witnesses of royal acts. Likewise the count of Brittany was not in evidence as a royal follower, and the duke of Aquitaine and the counts of Auvergne and La Marche only rarely so. In much of northern and central France, however, the king's presence was more strongly felt, and he was closely involved in the changing patterns of alliances which involved the dukes of Normandy, the counts of Anjou and of Blois-Champagne. What was the nature of the king's connections with these territorial princes?

Professor Fawtier wrote:

The six great feudatories who at the beginning of the thirteenth century became the six lay peers of the realm, had been in the juridical sense strictly bound to the king for the previous two hundred years and more, and had been his vassals, his 'men', however remarkable in other respects had been their independence of the monarchy.[33]

This directly echoed the views of Professor Lot who held that the ties and the duties of the princes towards the king were unchanged from the tenth to the twelfth century. According to this interpretation, their connections were to a great extent theoretical during the eleventh century, but revived during the twelfth – indeed Fawtier held that 'with almost unfailing consistency and success the Capetians insisted on these juridical ties and the rights they conferred on the crown',[34] even in the eleventh century. Now it is clear that throughout the eleventh century the king's place as suzerain was widely recognised (3.1.1) and that the princes sometimes paid him homage or intermittently swore him fidelity. But what did these actions really imply?

Although the vocabulary used to describe feudal bonds remained broadly unchanged during the early Capetian period, it has recently become very clear that the real implications of homage and fealty in 1200 were something rather different from in 1000. Considerable changes had taken place by 1100. In the early eleventh century homage was paid, it seems, quite regularly in many parts of northern France, but it did not create a social hierarchy (1.3.2). In the Mâconnais the castellans did homage to one another as a sign of alliance, not of subordination.[35] Peace homage was frequently performed, its name emphasising its use to form a pact. In some cases homage was done on the borders of the lands of the lord and the vassal, perhaps a matter of convenience in part, but also emphasising the relative equality of the two contracting parties, as with the dukes of Normandy and the kings of France before about 1060.[36] Chains of vassals were rare, but multiple vassalage was common, weakening any links as they were created. 'Vassalage was thought of, above all, in terms of personal devotion. The economic consideration, the grant of a benefice, implied no chain linking these benefices amongst themselves.'[37] The king and the princes seem in practice to have differed very little in their use of homage and fealty from the castellans and lesser nobles. Homage and service were given by the princes when they were in alliance with the king, but forgotten when they were not.

In the later eleventh century changes began to take place in French society, and both the idea and the reality of social hierarchy began to appear, fostered by the church.[38] This was reflected in changes in the meaning of homage and fealty. Homage attached to the holding of land began increasingly to involve all, not just some of them. Chains of vassals began to form as the lord's position was strengthened by the use of liege homage, which put him above the other lords of any individual. This also strengthened the obligation of the vassal to give aid and counsel, where simple homage had been more of a personal bond. These developments strengthened the king's position at the summit of the hierarchy, which was emphasised in royalist writings such as those of Abbot Suger (4.4.6). The growth of the monarchy's feudal power was also closely connected with a new aggressive attitude on the part of Louis VI in the royal lands, and with his increasing reputation outside them for kingly activities, such as dispensing justice and protecting churches (4.2.1). It began noticeably to revive in Philip I's reign, however, with some foretaste of this at the end of Henry I's rule, and where the princes had treated the kings as equals up to about 1050 they began more fully to acknowledge, if not always to carry out, their obligations to Philip I and Louis VI.

The changing attitudes of the princes to homage and military service are two useful indicators of the revival of royal feudal power. The latter appears to have revived before the former. Odo II of Blois, in his letter to the king of 1023 (2.2.4)[39] emphasises he has regularly paid service to Robert, thus fully recognising his obligations. In fact this was only done when he was in alliance with the king and ignored when he was neutral or hostile. The dukes of Normandy also paid service in 1005–06, 1031 and 1048, but again as a mark of alliance. In the later eleventh century the princes began to give service on a more regular basis, even when they had not done homage to the king and had not been to court. In 1071 the Norman duke, William the Conqueror sent a small force to Flanders in support of Philip I, even though he was not his vassal; although self-interest was clearly involved in maintaining his wife's more well-disposed relatives in power in this neighbouring state. More significant, perhaps is the reaction of the princes to King Henry I's call to arms in 1051–52 described by William of Poitiers.[40] Henry took contingents to Normandy from Burgundy, Auvergne and Gascony, but the counts of Blois and Anjou and the duke of Aquitaine, who did not go, found it intolerable that they should have to join the royal army wherever it was summoned.

Military service was becoming an important issue, and the obligation actually to perform it more widely recognised by this date.[41] The next step was the giving of service even when this was not in the interests of the prince, and in 1101, Robert count of Flanders made an agreement with Henry I of England, his ally, that if Philip I, his lord, called on him to serve in England, he would do so. This would be only with the minimum of followers to ensure that he did not forfeit his fief of Flanders. During the twelfth century such obligations were widely recognised, and ignored only by the most hostile of princes.

The paying of homage by the princes to the king seems to have taken place more intermittently than the rendering of service, which was not dependent on it. In tracing the frequency with which it happened, we are hampered in many cases by the reticence of our sources, which might describe a meeting and a pact of friendship between the king and a territorial prince, but do not mention homage as such. Nevertheless it is probable that a peace homage did often take place at such meetings, as when in 1060 the young Philip I met William the Conqueror at Dreux, and concluded a 'firm peace and serene friendship'[42] and the princes were at times described as the king's faithful men or vassals, which implies homage may have been sworn. Odo II of Blois was given these labels but, as with his successors, this tie did not prevent him from taking to the field against the king with considerable frequency (2.2.4). There is no evidence that Baldwin V of Flanders paid homage to Henry I or Philip I at all, even though he married the king's sister and was Philip I's guardian. His successors, Counts Robert I and Robert II, however, seem to have done so. The counts of Anjou were known as the king's *fideles* when they were in alliance with him, and this, though it may involve royal overlordship for small parcels of land rather than the whole county, may also reflect the swearing of peace homages.

Before 1060 the Norman dukes paid border homage to the French king on occasions, as in 1013–14; after 1060 it seems they refused to pay homage altogether until well into the twelfth century. This autonomous line stemmed partly from long traditions of Norman independence, partly from the position of the dukes as kings of England, and no king could do homage (2.2.3). But they did render service, and their reluctance to pay homage in the later eleventh century seems to show an awareness of its reviving significance in France. For this revival, indeed, they may have been responsible in part, since William the Conqueror emphasised the importance of feudal ties in both Normandy and

England. This does not seem to have affected the paying of homage by the other princes to the king until the second part of Philip I's reign. For much of the eleventh century the king and the princes used homage as a sign of alliance rather than a mark of subordination, and this serves to underline their equality in practical terms.

3.3.6 Royal defence

The king, like the territorial princes, was responsible for the defence of his principality, and for this purpose he was able to summon a force of vassals and footsoldiers from the *prévôtés* and towns. As king he was also responsible for the defence of the realm, and was owed service by the territorial princes (3.3.5). Throughout the eleventh century he was involved in warfare with the princes very much on their level, however, and in such a context military service to the overlord could take on an ambiguous role. When the king and the count of Anjou were in league against the count of Blois, the military support of the Angevins would appear as much an act of alliance (like *hommage en marche*) as of service. But the obligation was recognised, if it was also at times resented, and in 1124, when there was a genuine external threat to 'France' from the emperor, the response of the nobility to the call to arms was excellent (4.2.1).

Royal armies had in the Carolingian era consisted of heavy cavalry in conjunction with footsoldiers, and were based on levies raised from the *pagi* on the principle that all free men were liable for military service. This theory continued to be accepted in the tenth and eleventh centuries, but in the changed political and military conditions the reality was somewhat different. During the tenth century warfare came to be focused more and more around the castle and the mounted knight, less around the foot soldier. The *miles* or knight came into his own as the core of the fighting force, and his status in society began to change from that of a retainer-vassal to that of a landed man. Castles, both the strongholds under royal or princely control, and the private constructions of some castellans, all with political as well as military implications, proliferated during this period, and their earlier layout, a palace or hall in a fairly spacious compound, was replaced with the compact motte and bailey, which was easier to defend. As power fragmented in many areas warfare became more localised, and this the peace and truce of God movements attempted to curb. During the eleventh century there were further developments in castle building – the wooden towers which surmounted the motte and baileys often being replaced by a stone tower or *donjon* – and armies probably increased in size, but the basic patterns of warfare appear to have remained the same.

There was still a place for the levy and the footsoldier in this system, albeit a changed and rather reduced one. Trained footsoldiers, *servientes*, were very often used as part of a fighting force; in 1016 in the battle between Odo II of Blois and Fulk Nerra of Anjou both knights and footsoldiers took part. There was a similar composition in William the Conqueror's army at Hastings in 1066. *Servientes* were also needed for castle guard and patrols. They appear to have been recruited by *prévôtés* and castellanies, and increasingly from the towns. In 988 when Hugh

Capet was beseiging Laon, the urban militia there fell on his knights during their siesta,[43] but particularly from the twelfth century the kings were also to use such troops, levied by hearths, to their own advantage. The peace associations which preceded the development of urban and rural communes had the aim of maintaining themselves against local oppressors, and hence their interests often coincided with those of the Capetians; indeed, parochial and diocesan militia were used by the kings to assist in the enforcement of the peace and truce of God. In Philip I's reign the inhabitants of the town of Corbie, led by the abbot, participated in several wars of the king in the Ile de France, strengthening the royal army.

The core of the royal and noble armies in this period was the knight. These specialised heavy cavalrymen had originally been supported as retainers in the households of the powerful, but many knights came to hold benefices or fiefs in return for which they rendered service to their lords. Their status in society was thereby improving, a contributory and linked factor being the growth in the cult of chivalry. They owed their lord service, and he owed service to his overlord, in the form of a contingent of knights to perform castle guard or to go on campaign. The *ost*, a full-scale military campaign, was clearly distinguished from the *chevauchée*, a brief expedition or escort duty. In Normandy the quotas due were fairly firmly fixed; in other areas of France they were more negotiable in the eleventh century, but the obligation was widely recognised. The system remained flexible, with many landless knights prepared to accept money payments for fighting, who were able to augment the 'feudal' contingents. The pyramid was in this period very incomplete, but even when it was only partially effective, the king would benefit from it, for he was in theory owed service by his own knights, by the nobles of the Ile de France, and also by the other territorial princes, supposedly his vassals. Even though in practice many withdrew their fidelity, and many never paid homage at all, the princes of northern and central France rendered the king service on occasions (3.3.5).

Contingents of vassals did not always provide a sufficient fighting strength and they were often supplemented with mercenaries, paid troops; Fulk Nerra of Anjou used them in 991 and Odo II of Blois in 994–95, according to Richer. William the Conqueror hired stipendiary knights for the conquest of England. Indeed, with the subinfeudation of noble estates taking place only gradually, and in some areas in a very limited way, it is a mistake to draw too great a distinction between the landed knight and the paid knight; socially they were often on equal terms. A real gulf between the then more numerous enfeoffed knights and the landless adventurers does not seem to have developed until the twelfth century.

The rendering of military service was one aspect of a wide recognition of the king's feudal overlordship, but he had another important military power which was public in origin: his right to control the castles of his own men. In the earlier Carolingian era this had been exercised effectively, and although the later Carolingians and early Capetians accepted, indeed probably condoned, the widespread spontaneous fortification which was taking place, the notion that the king, duke or count had the right to license all these new castles, and that these castles were public survived. In practice of course this power had been divided out with other public powers, and its application varied from a formal assurance that the castellan would not use the castle in any way prejudicial to his lord's interests, to full rendability, where the lord could take possession of the castle for a certain length of time.[44] This latter power was widespread in the south of France in the eleventh century, but was not to be widely used in the north until the later twelfth and thirteenth centuries. William the Conqueror was able to exercise this right in his duchy, and even in the Ile de France, where it was far from being generally observed, its existence was not forgotten. It was often invoked for and linked with the protection of churches, another royal duty.

The royal power to license the building of castles was more widely acknowledged. Bouchard of Montmorency built himself a castle only with the permission of Robert the Pious, and the same king had had destroyed the castle of Gallardon, built by Geoffrey, viscount of Châteaudun, which threatened the canons of Chartres. In 1092 Philip I granted the canons of Saint-Corneille at Compiègne the royal right to oppose the building of any fortifications around Compiègne. In the eleventh century there were a considerable number of 'illegal' castles in the royal principality, and these are a sign of royal weakness, but the existence of royal rights of licence and rendability were to help the king in his fight to dominate the independent nobles of the area in the twelfth century.

3.4 THE KINGS AND THE CHURCH

3.4.1 The kings, the episcopate and the Cluniacs, 987–1049

In the early ninth century the Frankish emperors had controlled all the bishoprics in their lands. They had chosen the bishops and kept a firm control over their activities and their lands. The church continued to play an important role in royal government, but as power fragmented, the west Frankish kings lost control over many outlying bishoprics to the territorial princes. Those they retained were of some value to the maintenance of their power in the kingdom, and most important of these were the group of sees in northern France, including Reims, Laon, Châlons and Beauvais, where the bishops held counties as part of their lands as well as exercising spiritual powers. This group of bishops played a crucial part in the transference of power to the Capetians, and at the centre was Arnulf archbishop of Reims.[45] He had wide spiritual authority in northern France, stretching into the empire and the office of archchancellor of France, which went with his office, as well as important political connections and a personal *kudos* from reforming his cathedral chapter and refounding the schools at Reims.

Furthermore, although the kings chose the archbishops of Reims, they also had the privilege of making the king, since all the later Carolingian kings had been crowned by Adalbero and his predecessors. The Robertines had this service performed by the archbishops of Sens, primates of France, and the willingness of Adalbero of Reims to crown both Hugh Capet and his son Robert as his heir immediately afterwards, was of great significance. It symbolised the transference of the loyalties of the northern French episcopate to the new ruling house, and although some, such as Adalbero's successor at Reims, Arnulf, and Adalbero of Laon, did not prove faithful allies of Hugh, he gained enough ecclesiastical as well as lay support finally to defeat Charles of Lorraine.

Arnulf, bishop of Orléans, close counsellor of Hugh Capet, is a leading example of the royalist bishop. Intent on upholding the rights of the episcopate against the flourishing monastic houses, particularly those of the Cluniac order, he was equally firm on the issue of papal interference with the French church, which he condemned. He was one of the leaders of the synod which overthrew Arnulf, archbishop of Reims and replaced him with Gerbert of Aurillac, thereby incurring considerable papal displeasure. But a substantial group of the French bishops stood behind the king, and continued to do so in the face of spasmodic papal threats in the 990s. These were largely ineffective in practice, since the papacy was in a weak position politically and spiritually, and control of the office of pope was in dispute between the emperors and the counts of Tusculum.

Hugh Capet's influence over the northern French church was based as much on alliance as on the bowing of ecclesiastics to royal authority, but was nevertheless effective. The deposition of Arnulf of Reims reaffirmed the Carolingian principle that a king could remove a disloyal prelate, but his right to nominate all the bishops in France had slipped away in the early tenth century. The Robertines had controlled many bishoprics in the provinces of Reims, Tours and Sens, and some of these they added to the débris of the Carolingian ecclesiastical rights in 987. Royal authority over the episcopate under the Capetians was much diminished in comparison with the situation a century before. Hugh's surviving charters suggest that a similar geographical shrinking had taken place in royal grants of protection to monasteries. But although a royal safeguard was not as widely valued as earlier, the king still controlled a number of important monasteries as founder and patron. Some, such as Saint-Germain-des-Prés and Saint-Denis, had been under Robertine control; others such as Fleury were inherited from the Carolingians (3.3.2).

The abbey of Cluny and its dependent houses were an increasingly powerful force in France in the tenth and early eleventh centuries. Their way of life was based on customs worked out during the Carolingian era, but the organisation of the order and the degree of liberty it enjoyed were entirely new. In 817 at the synod of Aachen, Saint Benedict of Aniane and a group of abbots had promulgated a series of capitularies regulating the monastic life, building on the sixth century *Rule of Saint Benedict*. These had diminished the original emphasis on manual labour and had added considerably to the prescribed daily liturgical round. These 'reforms' and the support of Charlemagne and his son Louis the Pious had helped to make the Benedictine rule the preeminent monastic custom in western Europe. Despite the disruptions of the ninth century this style of monastic observance was to continue into the tenth and eleventh centuries.

The abbey of Cluny and its dependencies were the first group of monasteries to provide a structure of government for themselves, built up in the mid-eleventh century in default of adequate lay protection. This they were able to do because of the favoured and independent position the Cluniacs enjoyed. The mother house was founded in 909 by Berno of Baume, in the duchy of Burgundy. It began as a small, struggling house, but its foundation charter which was given by Duke William of Aquitaine, contained provisions which were to be a milestone in the relationship between monastic houses, the episcopate and the papacy. William declared that the monks were to be free to elect their own abbot on Berno's death:

following the rule promulgated by Saint Benedict – in such a wise that neither by intervention of our own or of any power they may be impeded from making a purely canonical election. Every five years, moreover, the aforesaid monks shall pay to the church of the apostles ten shillings to supply them with lights; and they shall have the protection of those same apostles and the defence of the Roman pontiff. . . . And, through God and all his saints, and by the awful day of judgement, I warn and abjure that no one of the secular princes, no count, no bishop whatever, not the pontiff of the aforesaid Roman see, shall invade the property of these servants of God, or alienate it, or diminish it, or give it as a benefice to anyone.[46]

The new house, then, was to enjoy free abbatial elections, to be directly subject to and under the protection of the pope, and, William hoped, to be free from outside interference. Cluny and some of her satellites achieved this, and in their freedom from secular control they contrasted with Gorze and Brogne, monasteries at the centre of similar revivals, but under the patronage of the German king and the princes.[47]

Progress with building the abbey of Cluny was slow. A royal charter of confirmation was not obtained until 927 and a papal one not until 931; the second allowed monks from Cluniac houses to reform other monasteries where discipline had become slack. Such a privilege was rare and was greatly to increase Cluniac influence. Under Abbot Odo its importance began to grow in France. The great abbey of Saint-Benoit-sur-Loire fell under its influence. Under Odo's successors, Aymard, Maiolus and Odilo – who played a leading part in the peace of God movement – Cluniac customs spread widely as Cluniac monks were called into reform other monasteries in many parts of France. Under the long abbacy of Saint Hugh (1049–1109) an administrative system was evolved for the mother house and its dependents as they were gradually organised into a hierarchy, and arguably reached the apogee of their reputation and influence.

The Cluniac way of life had many attractions in a turbulent age. It was ordered, focused to a large extent on an elaborate round of liturgical ceremony and prayer, spent in personal poverty but in the setting of finely decorated and ornamented cloisters and churches. Surviving buildings of houses under Cluniac influence, as at Vézelay and Saint-Benoit-sur-Loire, give a vivid visual illustration of this magnificence. Much of the time of some monks had also to be devoted to the administration of the very considerable estates amassed by the major houses. These, and the spiritual force of the order, gave it a pre-eminent place, both in local societies and also in a wider political context.

The exemption from the authority of the episcopate which the developing order managed to consolidate during the tenth century led to many deep rifts between bishops and the Cluniac houses in their dioceses, symptomatic of a deeper rivalry. The abbots of Saint-Benoit-sur-Loire and the bishops of Orléans were bitter adversaries in the eleventh century. Robert the Pious's natural brother, Gauzlin, abbot of Fleury from 1004, engaged in the conflict with the bishop with some enthusiasm. In 1008 he refused obedience to Fulk, and when the bishop attempted to make a visitation of the house he was driven out. The king was subsequently ordered by Pope John XVIII to defend Saint-Benoit against Fulk, for he said, the monastery had been placed under the custody of Saint Peter.

Robert the Pious may not have required any such exhortation, for his interest in the Cluniacs was considerable. In his satirical poem to King Robert, Adalbero of Laon dwelt on the power that Abbot Odilo of Cluny exercised over this king. Although it gives a highly exaggerated picture, coloured by the rivalry of the secular clergy and the Cluniacs, it also reveals the extent to which some bishops, at least, identified the king with Cluny. Indeed Robert was generous to many houses under Cluniac influence, including Saint-Denis and to some limited extent Saint-Germain-des-Prés (although compare 3.3.2) – both royal houses reformed by the Cluniacs – and to Marmoutiers and Saint-Benoit-sur-Loire. Abbot Odilo and his fellow monks found considerable favour with Robert, and despite a rupture after 1005 when Robert, invading Burgundy, burned the monastery of Saint-Germain at Auxerre, Odilo appears to have forgiven him later on. In 1016 the king was in Rome when Pope Benedict VIII fulminated against the depredators of Cluny's lands and goods; indeed this papal bull may have been drawn up at his request. In 1027 Odilo assisted at the crowning of the future Henry I.

However, other monasteries besides those of the Cluniacs found favour with Robert the Pious. His charters indicate that he gave substantially to the abbey of Saint-Aignan at Orléans (although here he held the lay abbacy himself) and to the colleges of secular canons at Etampes, Melun and Poissy, to which he granted important lands and rights. Abbeys such as Saint-Serge at Angers and Fécamp in Normandy also benefited from his generosity, and this was a neo-Carolingian pattern of donations. But, as Professor Lemarignier points out, he made no real attempt to gather together dissipated lands of royal abbeys such as Saint-Germain-des-Prés.[48] Instead he confirmed foundations such as the small college of secular canons at Coulombs in the Beauce. This house was built on the former fisc of Saint-Germain-des-Prés at Villemeux, lost a century before. Robert's confirmation to Coulombs was given at the end of his reign, at the same time as a noticeable shift in the witnesses of royal charters from abbots of great monasteries to the heads of small collegiate churches was taking place. This is symptomatic of the dwindling status of the churchmen, like the laymen, in the king's entourage.

Nevertheless the episcopate of Robert's reign still had an important part to play in royal affairs. The letters of Fulbert of Chartres contain many interesting insights into the relationship of the crown and the bishops. One element which Fulbert is at pains to stress is the sacral nature of the office of king. In 1015 he supported Robert's actions against the suspected heretic count of Sens:

May you know, brothers, that king [Robert] acts rightly when he aids Christians and harms heretics; and all his vassals (*fideles*), myself included, should strengthen and aid him in doing this, for it is his office, and through it he must work out his salvation.[49]

He is willing to give the king support in his choice of Franco for the bishopric of Paris: 'if the clerk is well educated and can speak with ease,' he will be a suitable choice.[50] But his letters also show something of the profoundly disturbed state of much of northern French society at the time. In 1021–2 Fulbert wrote to the king:

I am still keeping most of those who live in the area of Chartres from breaking out and injuring you, but as for Herbert and Geoffrey [not identified by the editor], enjoin them as I will, I have not been able to restrain them. Some of your servants who have been injured by these evil-doers . . . are venting their wrath against the land of our most holy Lady, plundering our crops and other possessions in the neighbourhood . . . To these troubles is added the burning of our church.[51]

Small wonder, perhaps, that Robert the Pious was an enthusiastic supporter of the peace of God, and had plans to give it a wider footing than merely within his own lands, where it emerged in about 1020. In 1023, while negotiating with the Emperor Henry II he discussed with him the possibility of adopting it throughout both their kingdoms.

In Henry I's reign the role of the episcopate seems somewhat to have dwindled, as the royal entourage was increasingly composed of lesser nobles and lesser ecclesiastics from the Capetian principality. The Cluniacs under the abbacies of Odilo and Hugh were reaching the apogee of their power and prestige. Henry was not, however, the enthusiastic patron of Cluny that his father had been. He preferred to favour the Carolingian style of abbey, powerful locally but independent from other religious houses. In 1048 he brought Saint-Médard at Soissons directly under royal protection, and on this occasion an unusually large group of bishops and nobles witnessed the charter effecting this act. Henry also, as Robert had done, confirmed a considerable number of small noble monastic foundations.

3.4.2 *The monarchy and the papal reforms 1049–1108*

The late 1040s marked the beginning of the papal reform programme, a new era in the history of the western church, which was greatly to modify the attitudes of lay rulers to various elements in the church: the papacy, the episcopate and the monastic orders. For the previous century the papal office had been the object of faction fights between Roman families, with periodic imperial intervention to complicate matters further. Respect in western Christendom for Rome itself, the see of Saint Peter and an important centre of pilgrimage, remained in general undiminished, even though the moral authority of its pontiff was greatly eroded. Some popes, such as the imperial nominee Sylvester II (formerly Gerbert of Aurillac), had clearly been worthy of their office, but others had manifested a striking degree of turpitude.

A tide of dissatisfaction with the church was growing, but needed direction, and this was provided by the Emperor Henry III. In 1046 he came to Rome for his coronation. Being a man strongly interested in church reform, and finding three rival candidates vying for the papal office, he dismissed them all and installed as pope his own nominee, Clement II. This pope, and the next, Damasus II, both died suspiciously quickly, but Henry's third candidate, Bruno bishop of Toul, who became Pope Leo IX, and was a relative of the emperor, began to implement a sweeping reform programme. He appointed reforming clergy from France and Germany as well as from Italy as cardinals, and he gave them effective power. This group included Humbert of Silva Candida and Hildebrand, who was to become Pope Gregory VII. Leo travelled through Europe holding local synods to combat evil in the church – an entirely new style of papal government – and although his rule ended unfortunately in 1053 when he was defeated in battle and captured by the Normans in southern Italy, his pontificate set in train the much needed reform and reappraisal of the western church.

On 1049 Pope Leo held a council at Reims in France. Anselm, a monk of Reims who attended it wrote down a list of its canons. Amongst these it was decreed that:

no one should be advanced to the rule of a church without election by clergy and people . . . that no one should buy or sell sacred orders, or ecclesiastical office or churches . . . that no one should injure poor men by thefts or frauds.[52]

Leo condemned such abuses as simony, the nomination of bishops by lay lords, the levying of military service on ecclesiastical lands, and probably clerical marriage. Certain abbots and bishops were named as guilty of particularly scandalous conduct and were excommunicated and deposed. Under Leo's successor, Victor II, the attempt to wipe out ecclesiastical abuses continued. In 1056 Hildebrand appeared as papal legate in France and had six bishops removed from their sees. As the political aspects of papal reform, which appeared as an attempt to centralise the church under the papal monarchy, emerged more clearly, there was a growing body of opposition to this in France. This was not only ecclesiastical resistance, for William duke of Normandy and Geoffrey Martel count of Anjou refused to obey certain papal commands.

Henry I of France, accused of simony (the buying and selling of ecclesiastical offices) and of tyranny by Cardinal Humbert in 1058, continued to sell off bishoprics and abbacies and ignored papal fulminations altogether. Meanwhile he continued to favour certain religious houses. The most important group was the canons whose houses were small and under episcopal and seigneurial control rather than directly subject to the pope as were the Cluniac abbeys; there was, probably then, a political element in his monastic patronage. He gave a number of houses of canons charters of confirmation and protection, and donations to a few. In about 1060, well after the papal reform programme had been proclaimed in France and many Benedictine houses even in the Ile de France had been drawn into papal dependence, Henry refounded the ancient abbey of Saint-Martin-des-Champs, deserted since the Norman invasions, endowed it generously, and while keeping it firmly under royal control gave it valuable privileges. Significantly it was for canons regular and not for monks. Its customs were also extended to other royal houses of canons, including Saint-Vincent at Senlis, founded by Henry's wife Anne after his death and in his memory. The royal house thus became an important patron of this growing religious order.

The origins of canons stretch back to the early church. By the Carolingian period they had emerged as clerks living in a community such as that of Bishop

Chrodegang of Metz. They followed a rule, but unlike monks were able to hold private property. Often the estates of a house of canons, a college, were divided into prebends for its incumbents. In 816 at the council of Aix a rule based on patristic writings and on the customs of Metz was drawn up for them. Colleges of canons were founded as an alternative to monasteries, and this was the organisation adopted by most French and by many English cathedral chapters. In the eleventh century reformed canons emerged. They took on the monastic style of organisation, adopting personal poverty and holding their property in common. They were known as regular or Augustinian canons in that they followed the Rule of Saint Augustine, a short set of precepts drawn up by Saint Augustine of Hippo in the early fifth century, to which many customs were added. This differentiated them from monks in the eleventh century, most of whom followed the rule of Saint Benedict; and so too did a greater emphasis on pastoral work. In the twelfth century reformed orders of canons regular, such as the Premonstratensians, emerged. These were in practice virtually indistinguishable from the reformed orders of monks such as the Cistercians in their way of life (4.3.3). In the eleventh century, though, before the proliferation of the new orders, the distinction between monks and canons, whether secular or regular, was clearer. In France some of the first reformed houses of canons were Saint-Barthélémy at Beauvais, refounded in 1037, and Saint-Martin at Laon, refounded before 1049. These probably provided the models for Henry I's house of Saint-Martin-des-Champs.

During Philip I's reign as king of France the western church saw two striking developments. One was the first crusade, the earliest of the holy wars conducted on the grand scale by the western nobility in Palestine (although there had been crusades in Spain from the 1060s) with the aim of regaining and protecting the holy places from their infidel captors. Conducted with papal backing, they canalised the piety, pugnacity and greed of the western nobles and earned much prestige for their lay and ecclesiastical leaders. In response to an appeal from Pope Urban II at the Council of Clermont in 1095, and the inspired preaching of the papal legate, Bishop Adhémar of Le Puy, a considerable force from the west, consisting mainly of men from the various regions and states of France, embarked in 1096 for the Holy Land via Constantinople. By 1099, despite the deep dissensions between their leaders – the Norman Bohemond (a Hauteville from Sicily), Godfrey of Bouillon, Hugh of Vermandois and Raymond IV count of Toulouse, Robert Curthose duke of Normandy and Robert II count of Flanders – they had succeeded in capturing Antioch and Jerusalem, having routed their Seljuk and Fatimid adversaries, and they then established four Latin states in Outremer. This was a striking achievement, from which the papacy did not fail to profit.

The second dramatic development in ecclesiastical politics in the later eleventh century was the emergence of a deep hostility dividing the papacy and the emperors. The substance of their dispute later became centred on the technicalities of the lay investiture of bishops, whereby the new bishop was granted his office and powers by the emperor, king or count, and was invested with his ring and staff, symbolic of his office. The rights of the lay potentate to do this were disputed by the reforming clergy. But also involved were far wider issues which had begun to emerge under Leo IX, when attempts to introduce disciplinary reforms had been accompanied with a build-up in papal power. Under Pope Gregory VII, formerly Cardinal Hildebrand, the political claims of the pope to rule the whole church, and even to have the power to depose the emperor, giving his authority a secular dimension, were clearly seen in action. With lay investiture as the specific point at issue, Gregory VII and his successors were involved in bitter conflict with Emperor Henry IV of Germany, and this dispute was not to be settled until 1122. Even then the basic problem of the rival claims of both pope and emperor to dominate western society was left unresolved.

The revitalised and aggressive church took a generally unfriendly view of Philip I, whose marital scandals and self-indulgent way of life alone would have made him a target of attack. He was excommunicated in 1095 as a result of his marriage to Bertrada de Montfort, but the impact of the papal anathemas was reduced to a great extent by the support from the king which came from a group of French bishops, some such as Walter of Meaux and John of Orléans, appointed by him, but all anxious about the encroachment of papal authority in the French church. The noted canonist Ivo of Chartres, whom the king imprisoned on this matter in 1093 (3.2.4), later played an important conciliatory role in the disputes of the king and the papacy. But this reformer also found much to criticise in Philip's attitude towards the church in France. The French king appears to have shared the conviction of his contemporary, William Rufus of England, that this organisation was there to be exploited.

Contemporary writers, ecclesiastics, made much of his behaviour, and they may well exaggerate considerably, but their accounts indicate that Philip I took a hard line against the church's attempts to diminish his control over it. He exercised his regalian rights to the full, sold offices when he could; and a number of sources suggest that he was capable of considerable depredations. In 1092–93 he did substantial damage to the estates of the bishopric of Chartres on the grounds that Ivo disapproved of his liaison with Bertrada. Early in his reign he is said to have fallen out with Guy bishop of Beauvais, whom he sent into exile for a year. In his absence the church lands and goods were pillaged and the plate sold. Renaud bishop of Langres was imprisoned by the king at Noyon, while in 1082 Philip removed Raoul, archbishop of Tours, from office. In 1080 when Manasses, archbishop of Reims, had been deposed, Gregory VII wrote to the king asking for a free election for the community – perhaps a measure of Philip's power. But opposition may well have hardened his attitude. In 1100 only a minority of the Beauvais chapter elected Stephen de Garlande, the king's chancellor, but the king supported his candidature and vowed that he would never let his rival, Galon, take his place; so novel did this seem to Ivo of Chartres that he wrote to Pope Paschal II denouncing it as sacrilege. A letter from Philip to Anselm, the exiled archbishop of Canterbury, written 1103–05, in which he offers him help because he has suffered unjustly at the hands of Henry I of England, reads somewhat ironically in this context.[53]

Philip was involved with a number of direct clashes with the papacy, not only over his personal life and his uncompromising attitude to ecclesiastical reform but also, as with the emperor, over the specific issues of simony and lay investiture. In 1075 Gregory prohibited lay investiture altogether, and gradually began to involve himself in French episcopal elections, particularly disputed or simoniacal ones as at Chartres and Orléans in 1077. In the next few years the papal legate Hugh of Die managed to effect the deposition of Manasses archbishop of Reims in the teeth of opposition from the king. The pope also suppressed the title of the archbishop of Sens as primate of Gaul, giving this instead to the archbishop of Lyon, a city in the empire (1079), much to Philip's anger.

But Gregory VII was not nearly as intransigent with Philip I as with Henry IV of Germany; at times he made political overtures to the French king which Philip resolutely ignored. With Pope Urban II Philip was at first on good terms. In about 1095 the sees of Arras and Cambrai were separated by their mutual agreement. But at the end of this pontificate the pope and Philip fell out over the issues of Philip's marriage and over the legitimacy of the elections of Daimbert archbishop of Sens, whom Philip had invested, and Sancho, bishop of Orléans. The rift was not deep. The king wanted his marriage accepted by the whole church and allowed some free elections to take place. Under the moderate influence of Ivo of Chartres, the king, the pope and the French bishops gradually arrived at a consensus: the king should not invest bishops with the ring and staff, symbols of their spiritual office, but they owed the temporalities of their sees to the king and should pay homage for them.

Elections were still a problem however. Pope Paschal II quarrelled with the king over the election to Beauvais and again over his divorce, but after 1104 their relations improved considerably. This was again probably on papal initiative, but this time the king was more ready to compromise. In 1107 Philip, his son Louis and the pope proclaimed at the council of Troyes their agreement over the investiture dispute, and promulgated further disciplinary reforms of the church in France. This rapport was a new development but a fruitful one. The French king and the papacy were to remain on generally good terms for almost two centuries.

If Philip tried to be a firm master of the French church and was often an unjust one, he showed some interest in a number of monasteries and made some moderately generous grants to them. In 1094 he placed Saint-Magloire in Paris under Cluniac tutelage for the purpose of reform, and when in 1106 he granted the college of Saint-Martin-les-Vielles at Etampes-les-Vielles to Morigny, he regulated the organisation of the prebends at Saint-Martin and spelt out the nature of its connections with Morigny. The Cluniacs found considerable favour with him. To Cluny itself he granted lands, and in 1079 he refounded Saint-Martin-des-Champs for monks and granted it to Cluny as a priory, reversing the decision of his father. To Saint-Benoit-sur-Loire he was not particularly generous, though he did grant it a church at Etampes and gave some help towards the building work. However, on his deathbed, Suger recounted, he suddenly decided to be buried here rather than in Saint-Denis with the rest of his family, for he proclaimed himself unworthy to lie so near to so great a martyr and commended himself to the mercy of Saint Benedict, the father of monks.[54] This story, if true, reveals a great deal about Philip's attitude to religious affairs. On the one hand, he was prepared to stand up for what he saw as his rights to exploit the lands and offices of the church, on the other he feared God's wrath enough to prepare with care for prayers for his soul, not with his relations in the royal pantheon, but on his own in a religious house where personalised intercession could be given to him.

NOTES AND FURTHER READING

Asterisked titles are recommended for further reading, and additional titles are suggested below. Place of publication London unless otherwise indicated.

Notes

1. *PL*, cxxxix, 477.
2. F. Behrends, ed., *The Letters and Poems of Fulbert of Chartres* (Oxford, 1976).
3. A. W. Lewis, *'Anticipatory association of the heir in early Capetian France', American Historical Review*, lxxxiii (1978), 906–27.
4. Werner, 'Kingdom and principality . . .' (*op. cit.* Ch. 2), 245 and n. 10.
5. I am grateful to Dr Janet Nelson for this information.
6. *PL*, cxxxix, 478
7. Lot, *Études . . .* (*op.cit.* Ch.2, n.12).
8. G. Duby, *Medieval Marriage: two models from twelfth-century France*, trans. E. Forster (Baltimore/London, 1978), 46.
9. Helgaud of Fleury, *Vie de Robert le Pieux,* ed. and trans. R. H. Bautier and G. Labory (Paris, 1965), 97; Adhémar of Chabannes, *Chronique*, ed. J. Chavanon (Paris, 1897), 154-5; Prou, ed., *Raoul Glaber* (*op. cit.* Ch. 2, n. 12), 27.
10. Prou, ed., *op. cit.*, 26.
11. Duby, *op. cit.*, 45–54.
12. Behrends, *op. cit.,* 19.
13. Here Bachrach 'Towards a reappraisal of William the Great' (*op. cit.* Ch. 2), 19, is undoubtedly right to stress Robert's vigour.
14. J. Dhondt, 'Quelques aspects du règne d'Henri Ier roi de France', in *Mélanges . . . Louis Halphen* (Paris, 1951), 199–208, esp. 199; J. F. Lemarignier, *Le Gouvernement royal aux premiers temps Capétiens* (Paris, 1965).
15. *RHF*, xi, 481.
16. Dhondt, *op. cit.*
17. Guibert of Nogent, *De vita sua,* ed. and trans. J. F. Benton as *Self and Society in Medieval France* (New York, 1970), 147; *PL*, clvi, 616.
18. Orderic Vitalis, *Ecclesiastical History*, ed. and trans. M. Chibnall, v (Oxford, 1975), 214–15.
19. Yves de Chartres, *Correspondance*, ed. J. Leclerq, i (Paris, 1949), 62–3.
20. Duby, *Medieval Marriage*, 29–45.
21. A. Longnon, *Atlas historique de la France, i, Atlas* (Paris, 1885–89); W. M. Newman, *Le Domaine royale sous les premiers Capétiens (987–1180)* (Paris, 1937).
22. G. Duby, 'The evolution of judicial institutions', in *The Chivalrous Society*, trans. C. Postan (1977), 15–58.

23. Lot, *op. cit.*; C. Pfister, *Études sur le règne de Robert le Pieux (996–1031)* (Paris, 1885).
24. Newman, *op. cit.*, introduction.
25. M. de la Motte Collas, 'Les possessions territoriales de l'abbaye de Saint-German-des-Prés du début du IXe siècle au début du XIIe siècle', in *Mémorial du XIVe centenaire de l'abbaye de Saint-Germain-des-Prés* (Paris, Bibliothèque de la société d'histoire ecclésiastique de la France, 1959), 49–80.
26. F. *Capetian Kings*, 108.
27. P. Lauer, ed., *Les Annales de Flodoard* (Paris, 1905), 139.
28. J. F. Lemarignier, 'De l'immunité à la seigneurie ecclésiastique', in *Études dediés à G. le Bras* (Paris, 1965), i, 619–30.
29. Suger, *Vie de Louis VI le Gros*, ed. H. Waquet (Paris, 1929), 38; F. *Capetian Kings*, 17.
30. Lemarignier, *Le Gouvernement royal*; see also M. Chibnall, 'Charter and Chronicle: the use of archive sources by Norman historians', in *Church and Government in the Middle Ages*, ed. C. N. L. Brooke, D. E. Luscombe, G. H. Martin and D. Owen (Cambridge, 1976), 1–17.
31. C. R. Brühl, *Fodrum, Gistum, Servitium Regis . . . ,* 2 vols (Cologne/Graz, 1968), ii, maps.
32. *PL*, cxxxix, 410.
33. F., *Capetian Kings*, 60–1; F. Lot, *Fidèles ou vassaux? Essai sur la nature juridique du lien qui unissait les grands vassaux à la royauté depuis le milieu du IXe jusqu'à la fin du XIIe siècle* Paris, 1904.
34. F., *Capetian Kings*, 60–1.
35. G. Duby, 'The nobility in eleventh- and twelfth-century Mâconnais', in Cheyette, ed. (*op. cit.* Ch. 2), 137–55.
36. J. F. Lemarignier, *Recherches sur l'hommage en marche et les frontières féodales* (Lille, 1945).
37. J. F. Lemarignier, *'Political and monastic structures in France at the end of the tenth and beginning of the eleventh century', in Cheyette, ed., *op. cit.*, 108.
38. *Ibid., passim.*
39. *RHF*, x, 501–2.
40. Guillaume de Poitiers, *Gesta Guillelmi ducis Normannorum et Regis Anglorum*, ed. R. Foreville (Paris, 1952), 66–8.
41. J. Boussard, 'Services féodaux, milices et mercenaires dans les armées en France, aux Xe et XIe siècles', *Settimane di studio del Centro Italiano sull'alto medioevo*, xv (Spoleto, 1968), 131–68.
42. Lemarignier, *Recherches sur l'hommage en marche . . . ,* 90.
43. Richer, *Histoire de France, 888–995*, ed. R. Latouche, ii (Paris, 1937), 180–1.
44. Coulson, 'Rendability and castellation . . . ' (*op. cit.* Ch. 2), 59–67.
45. A. Dumas, 'L'église de Reims au temps des luttes entre Capétiens et Carolingiens', *Revue d'histoire de l'église de France*, xxx (1944), 5–38.
46. E. F. Henderson, trans., *Select Historical Documents of the Middle Ages* (1892), 329–33.
47. C. N. L. Brooke and W. Swaan, *The Monastic World, 1000–1300* (1974), 51–9.
48. J. F. Lemarignier, 'Aspects politiques des fondations de collégiales dans le royaume de France au XIe siècle', in *La Vita Comune del clero nei secoli XI & XII, La Mendola 1959* (Milan, 1962), i, 19–40.
49. Behrends, ed., *op. cit.*, 50–1.
50. *Ibid.*, 52–3.
51. *Ibid.*, 102–5.

52. B. Tierney, *The Crisis of Church and State (1050–1300)* (New York, 1964), 31–2.

53. M. Prou, *Recueil des actes de Philippe Ier, roi de France* . . . (Paris, 1908), 380–2.

54. Suger, *op. cit.*, 84–5.

Additional title

M. Bloch, *The Royal Touch: sacred monarchy and scrofula in England and France*, trans. E. Forster (Baltimore/London, 1978).

See also Notes and further reading, Chapters 1 and 2.

CHAPTER FOUR

The Revival of Royal Power, 1108–1226

4.1 INTRODUCTION

4.1.1 The Capetian revival: an inevitable development?

In 1108 the new French king, Louis VI, was the master only of a small and ill-disciplined principality centred on Paris and Orléans. He could claim royal powers over the church and over the princes and other great nobles of France which in theory could not be denied, but which were in practice often ignored. He was little more powerful than his predecessors. But in 1226 when Louis VIII, his great-grandson, died, the royal lands included a now organised royal principality, the duchy of Normandy, the counties of Maine and Anjou and most of Poitou, and substantial holdings, if not outright domination in the Languedoc. The king's legal suzerainty was acknowledged and generally obeyed, and his power over the French church considerable. It is true that this power lacked deep foundations, and was to be challenged in the minority of Louis IX; but by the end of his reign (1270) it was firmly consolidated. The achievements of Philip Augustus and Louis VIII were remarkable, and because they gained so much power it is easy to imagine that this was bound to be the outcome, and that the early Capetians were not as weak as they may appear.

Professor Fawtier wrote from such a perspective in his *Capetian Kings*. Thus he thought that the early Capetians were 'powerful lords. To regard them as the *petits seigneurs* of the Ile de France is to perpetuate a myth.'[1] He emphasised the wealth of their domain, their powers over and alliance with the church and their legal rights over the nobility, the great princes, which were never lost sight of. He proposed, indeed, that they have been rather underestimated. The work of Professor Lemarignier, Professor Duby and other historians has, however, amply confirmed the views of another school of thought about the first four Capetians (987–1108), and has suggested that in reality they had only weak and localised power (3.3.4–5). Other work on the resources of the French monarchy also implies that Fawtier may have overestimated the wealth of the domain (4.4.4). But to accept the weakness of Hugh Capet, Robert the Pious, Henry I and Philip I makes the vast increase of power under Philip Augustus all the more remarkable, and all the more difficult to account for.

How can this expansion be explained? One factor which undoubtedly helped the kings in their rise to power was the social and economic changes taking place. This was a complex and long-term process, which manifested itself in population growth, land clearance, the spread of markets, fairs and commerce, an increasing prosperity and an economy more dependant on coinage than had been the case a century earlier. The nobility as a group, and particularly the castellans, appear to have suffered economically, and the division of their lands between heirs in many regions of France and the conspicuous consumption of luxury goods seem also to have taken their toll. The princes and the king, who did not divide their estates, on the other hand, did rather better, and by dint of constant warfare and an insistence on feudal duties managed to subjugate the more turbulent nobles in many principalities, to introduce their own administrations and to gain the support of the towns and the church. Thus throughout France principalities were gradually brought under the closer control of their rulers and patterns of power became clearer. The royal principality was subjugated later than Normandy but earlier than most of the other principalities, and the resources of the royal domain could now be fully exploited. Under Louis VII these were still not sufficient to allow the king to wage warfare on the grand scale, and only by finding new sources of revenue was Philip Augustus able to fight the wealthy Angevins, whose power extended over more than half his kingdom.

In 1199 Philip Augustus had a relatively well organised and quite thoroughly taxed principality as a power base. In addition, the feudal and sacral powers which went with his royal office were beginning to have some considerable practical meaning. The royal court had an increased competence, the princes were becoming more habitually his vassals, acknowledging his suzerainty. But Richard I of England still held all his lands firmly, and was making gains at Philip's expense. When Richard died, Philip was able to use all the weapons in his arsenal, both new and old, against Richard's brother John. He could not have proceeded without them, without the build-up in his acknowledged role in France, but against Richard they had no impact; John was less well armed. This matter of character is a fundamental one in the French conquest of the Angevin lands (4.4.8).

For Philip, seizing Normandy, greater Anjou, Poitou and Brittany was a matter of a well fought campaign backed up by faithful allies, and although Poitou was lost for a while and Brittany granted away, Normandy and greater Anjou proved easy to hold because of the political power already built up there by the Norman dukes and Angevin counts. But even after Philip's important victory at Bouvines, where the count of Flanders and the emperor, John's allies, were defeated, the English did not relinquish their claim to Normandy. Some of its links with England continued after 1204; but here the French king was more secure in 1226 than in the Languedoc, where the royal forces were half way through reducing the county of Toulouse where Louis VIII died. The rebellions during the minority of Louis IX showed that royal power was still far from being deeply entrenched throughout the kingdom; nevertheless Louis IX was able to consolidate what his father and grandfather had taken by force. Much could have been lost at this point, as much had been gained by Philip and Louis VIII. Looked at in this perspective, the rise of the Capetians looks far from

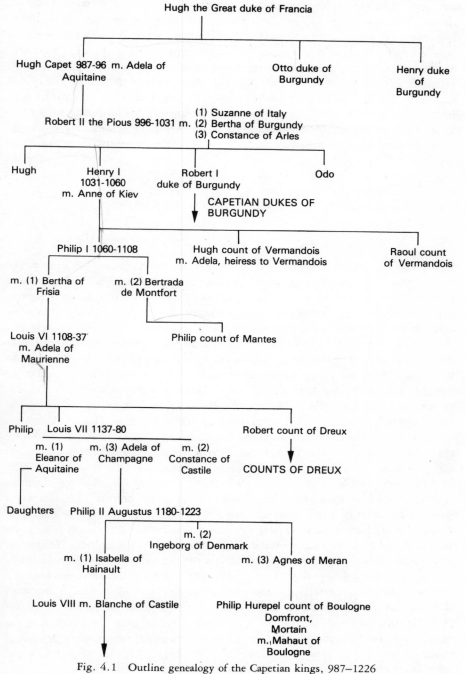

Fig. 4.1 Outline genealogy of the Capetian kings, 987–1226

inevitable, but rather appears as being made possible by underlying developments, which were only important because the king was able to turn them to good account. The significance of Philip Augustus's reign was very great; in the dramatic decade 1194–1204, Philip first lost his early gains to Richard, but then took them back from John and finally went on to seize the heartlands of John's French lands. These events reveal the significance of the characters and abilities of the chief protagonists in the struggle, the outcome of which was vitally important in the rise of the Capetians. Richard was a match for Philip and more, but Philip was a better soldier and politician than John, who overplayed his hand, and then left the game before it was finished. Yet Philip Augustus was a king of ability who profited from events, rather than a character acting out a role sketched out for him by a providence which decreed that the Capetians must rise.

4.2 THE KINGS AND THEIR REIGNS

4.2.1 Louis VI, 1108—1137

In his *Life of Louis VI*, Abbot Suger of Saint-Denis wrote that the king never relinquished the good habits formed in his youth, that he defended churches, protected the needy and the poor and worked ceaselessly for peace and for the defence of his realm. Suger's portrayal of Louis is an idealised one, written to emphasise his view of monarchy and to glorify his abbey, whose patron saint was the special protector of the king and kingdom (4.4.6). Louis VI was clearly in many ways unpromising material for such a role.[2] Except perhaps by contrast with Philip I his 'saintly' qualities were few, and his interests were directed more towards the battlefield than the cloister. Though vigorous and active in his youth, his tendency towards obesity and gluttony made him so fat that by the time he was forty-six years old he was no longer able to get on a horse. Although his marriage to Lucienne of Rochefort, from a castellan family, was dissolved by the pope in 1107 as not fitting to the royal dignity, Louis did not marry again until he was thirty-five. But Adela of Maurienne, his second wife, brought him six sons and a daughter, in addition to the nine illegitimate children produced by his many liaisons. His eldest son Philip was born in 1116, crowned in 1129 but died in 1131, after which his second son, Louis, became his heir.

Guibert of Nogent accuses Louis VI of a sordid cupidity, and this appears to be substantiated to some extent by the king's money-raising methods. He left his jewels and regalia in pawn for a period of over ten years. But he also seems to have had many good qualities. Both Suger and Ivo of Chartres portray him as a man of a simple, open nature, rarely perfidious, often kindly. And while quarrelling with the church on a number of occasions he was also a generous patron of monks (4.5.1). This vigorous warrior's achievements were of great importance to his royal office, for he managed effectively to tame the royal principality by dint of constant warfare against the castellans; he helped to develop the royal administration there and to set the monarchy on a firm footing.

In the first part of his reign Louis was dominated by Stephen de Garlande, archdeacon of Nôtre-Dame at Paris, from 1120 both royal seneschal and chancellor, and a noted pluralist, and his family (4.4.2). But Stephen's loyalty could waver, and in 1127 Louis, who had supported him against the enmity of the queen and numerous French churchmen, found him too overbearing and had him removed from office. Stephen rebelled, and in 1132 he was reinstated as chancellor. He had lost some of his influence, although the king was prepared to shield him from papal wrath after the murder of two reforming ecclesiastics, Archambaud, sub-dean of Saint-Croix at Orléans, by the retainers of Stephen's clerk John, and Thomas, prior of Saint-Victor at Paris, by Stephen's vassals. These events, which took place in 1133, brought the king into bad odour with Pope Innocent II.

From 1127 onwards the king's principal adviser was Suger, abbot of Saint-Denis, a man of humble birth who made his career in the church and the king's service. Later in Louis VI's reign Bernard, abbot of Clairvaux, who was largely responsible for the great popularity and influence of the Cistercian order, became involved in the politics of Louis's court as well. Severe and ascetic, his views on the role of the king in the French church and on the decoration of ecclesiastical buildings were antipathetic to those of Suger. The latter, however, was to achieve more for Louis VI and for Louis VII, by acting as a counsellor and an administrator and by stressing the inherent importance of the royal dignity both in his writings and his actions (4.4.6). Although qualified in a royal charter as a close and faithful counsellor to the king, Suger had no official title in royal government. Nevertheless he played a major part in the politics of the last decade of Louis VI's reign and then reappeared as the counsellor of his son from 1143 until his death in 1151. Professor Aubert suggests that

his excellent memory, his understanding of men and things, his grasp of affairs, his diligence, the power of his expression, his natural moderation, his love of conciliation, his absolute disinterestedness made him the ideal counsellor of the king.[3]

This is a roseate picture, but the abbot was clearly a man of qualities.

The king's principal preoccupation for most of his reign was the domination of the castellan families of the Ile de France. Their powers in the areas they controlled were often substantial and some appear to have behaved with considerable savagery, although the accounts of ecclesiastics such as Guibert of Nogent are obviously coloured by their outlook. Guibert says of Thomas of Marle:

So unheard of in our times was his cruelty that men who are considered cruel seem more humane in killing cattle than he in killing men. For he did not merely kill them outright with the sword and for definite offences, as is usual, but by butchery after horrible tortures. . . . No one can tell how many expired in his dungeons and chains from starvation, disease and torture.[4]

This bears all the hallmarks of exaggeration, but Thomas of Marle does seem to have displayed considerable anarchical and bellicose tendencies which made him a threat to the stability of the Laon area. He engaged in constant warfare with his father Enguerrand de Coucy; he cut the throat of a relative, Gautier, archdeacon of

Laon. When in 1112 the townsfolk of Laon murdered their bishop he gave protection to the ringleaders. He also occupied two properties of the abbey of Saint-Jean-de-Laon. In 1114 Thomas was excommunicated by a council held by the papal legate Conan of Palestrina, and declared unfit to bear arms. The king with the backing of the church waged war against him. Thomas's castles at Crécy and Nouvion fell to Louis, heading an army of men levied by the church parish by parish. The king razed these fortresses, and Thomas, surrounded at Marle, was forced to submit and offer indemnity to both king and church. But Louis, whose chivalrous instincts often overrode his common sense, mistakenly pardoned him, and he seems to have returned to his evil ways, now made more powerful by inheriting the castles of Coucy and Boves. At last in 1130 Raoul count of Vermandois, Thomas's personal enemy and the king's close adviser, joined with a group of bishops and persuaded Louis VI to organise another punitive expedition. At Coucy Thomas was wounded, and he fled to Laon where he was captured. Eventually he died in captivity.

A similar threat to law and order in the area of the Beauce and round Chartres was posed by Hugh du Puiset. Suger describes him as a man who devoured church lands and mocked excommunications.[5] In 1111 the king was holding court at Melun when Theobald, count of Blois, the archbishop of Sens, the bishops of Chartres and Orléans and various abbots laid such strong charges against him that the king ordered him to appear before the royal court. Hugh refused to do so, and the king declared his lands forfeit, besieged and took Le Puiset and captured Hugh. But he released him in 1112, and Hugh, like Thomas of Marle, again began to terrorise the neighbourhood. For some time he was supported by the Count of Blois, but in 1118 Louis managed to defeat him once more. Hugh killed in the fighting Anseau de Garlande, the royal seneschal, but he died himself soon after this on a pilgrimage to the Holy Land.

These two struggles of Louis against unruly castellans have become notorious, but they were paralleled with many others which are not so fully described by the chroniclers. Before his accession the king had fought the lords of Montmorency and Beaumont and Ebles de Roucy. In 1109 he reduced Péronne and granted it to the house of Vermandois, and in 1117 took the county of Amiens from local castellans and gave it to Enguerrand de Coucy. Not until 1130 when Thomas de Marle fell were the lands north of Paris really secure. To the south of Paris the powerful castellans who often aligned themselves with the counts of Blois and the dukes of Normandy against the king, such as Peter of Maule and Guy the Red and his son Hugh de Crécy, had many of their castles destroyed and confiscated. The removal of the Montlhéry family made the Paris area safer, that of the Puisets secured the Beauce. The defeat of other castellans such as Humbert of Saint-Sévère in 1107 opened up the way to the Loire.

Though Louis's work was not completed in 1137, it made the Capetian principality safer and augmented the ability of the crown to make use of its own resources. Furthermore, by summoning vassals to his court and then, if they did not appear, mounting campaigns against them, and often confiscating their lands, Louis emphasised his power as overlord and tightened the ties of vassalage. This was a first step in the formation of a 'feudo-vassalic' pyramid in the Ile de

France. The greater security, the increased royal power, and the confiscated resources were all of vital importance; so too were the new royal castles which Louis constructed at important strategic points. A chronicler lists these as Montchauvet, Lorrez-le-Bocage, Grez, Corbeil and la Ferté-Alais.[6]

Louis VI's office of king was also given a stronger emphasis, both in Suger's writings, which improved the royal image (4.4.6), and in the king's widening intervention inside other principalities. This change was in large measure the result of his activities in the Ile de France, where he showed himself both an effective soldier and a chivalrous adversary, protecting church lands and crushing the castellans. Hence nobles and ecclesiastics from further afield appealed to him for help, and the more he intervened effectively to help them, the greater his prestige, and the more others would be likely to turn to him. His often aggressive expeditions to regions previously outside the royal influence are clear signs of a slowly widening royal power in the kingdom. In 1108–09, for example, Louis made an expedition into the Bourbonnais, in Berry. Aimon II Vaire-Vache had seized the lordship of Bourbon on the death of his brother Archambaud, a royal vassal. The lawful heir was Archambaud's son, and the new husband of Archambaud's widow appealed on his behalf to the royal court. The king called Aimon to his court, and when he failed to appear, took an army to Berry and besieged his castle at Germigny. Aimon submitted and the lands went to the rightful heir. Suger commented that kings had long arms.

In 1122 a similar incident occurred. Amaury, bishop of Clermont, was cast out of his see by William VI, count of Auvergne, and appealed to Louis for help. William was summoned to appear before the king and when he failed to do so Louis called together an army, including the counts of Anjou, Brittany and Nevers, and descending on the Auvergne seized the castle of Pont-du-Château and drove the count out of Clermont. In 1126 he returned with a larger army and burnt Montferrand; and although William IX of Aquitaine intervened on behalf of the count of Auvergne, he forced the latter to appear before the royal court at Orléans and to make peace.

The duchy of Normandy posed the greatest problem to Louis outside the royal lands. In 1106 Henry I of England, William the Conqueror's youngest son, captured Normandy from the relatively ineffectual Robert Curthose his brother. At first Henry agreed with Louis VI that the important castle of Gisors should be held by a neutral castellan, but Henry soon occupied it and Louis called on him to account for his actions. Henry refused, and war broke out. Initially Louis, with the support of the count of Anjou and Theobald count of Blois, was successful. In 1109 he overran part of the Norman Vexin. But Theobald of Blois switched his support to Henry, and the English king also had the support of castellans, including Guy of Rochefort and Hugh du Puiset, together with Hugh count of Troyes. Louis defeated the castellans in the field but was pushed back by Henry I. In 1113 peace was signed, in which Louis recognised Henry's suzerainty over Maine and Brittany.

Another period of hostilities occurred between 1116 and 1120. Louis encouraged the rebellious Norman nobles and supported William Clito, Robert's son, as counterclaimant to Normandy. A long series of sieges and sporadic fighting ended in 1119 when Louis's army was crushed by Henry I's forces in pitched battle at Brémule. Louis was angry and humiliated but laid his case before Pope Calixtus II, conveniently holding a council at Reims. Orderic Vitalis describes the proceedings of the council, and gives Louis's speech in which he accuses Henry of violent aggression and lawless behaviour. Henry too appeared before Calixtus at a later date, and the pope did little more than persuade the two sides to negotiate. In 1120 Louis agreed to receive the homage of William, Henry's heir, and to cede Gisors to Henry. These were bad terms, but Henry was to lose a great deal in his turn by the death of his son William, drowned in 1120. This left the English king with no direct male heir to succeed him, and he was to leave his inheritance to his daughter Matilda, widow of the Emperor Henry V, whom in 1127–28 he married to Geoffrey 'le Bel', made count of Anjou in 1129 when his father Fulk went to the Holy Land (2.3.2).

In 1123 Louis managed to gather the support of Fulk of Anjou and the treacherous Galeran, count of Meulan, together with other Norman nobles, for another attempt to replace Henry I with William Clito. This was not successful. Louis did however enjoy a triumph over the Emperor Henry V, who in 1124 moved towards France from the east in support of his father-in-law and in the hope of building up his lands in Lorraine. Louis VI called on all his vassals, and their response was a measure of the greatly increased prestige of the king. Even Theobald II of Blois, like many other great nobles, sent troops to Reims, where a vast army gathered. Louis, carrying the *oriflamme*, the standard of the Vexin which was firmly believed to have belonged to Charlemagne, made, according to Suger, fervent and patriotic speeches (4.4.6). The emperor fell back before the great army. Later in his reign Louis continued to fight sporadically against Henry I, who caused considerable problems in Flanders and who kept up his policy of alliance with Theobald of Blois and the disaffected nobles of the royal principality.

In 1127 the king intervened in Flanders as well. The chronicler Galbert of Bruges gives a graphic account of events in this and successive years. The Flemish count Charles the Good, Louis's kinsman and friend, was murdered in the church of Saint-Donatien at Bruges while at mass. Louis immediately rushed to Flanders, to punish the wrongdoers, to try to seize his treasure, and possibly even in the hope of being elected count himself. In none of these objectives was he initially successful, but Flanders was in a state of complete confusion and he managed effectively to assert his authority for a short time at least. Charles had left no direct heir and there were many claimants to his office, but the king arranged for William Clito, a great-grandson of Baldwin of Lille, to be elected. Louis and William Clito together fought several other claimants, captured the murderers and had them killed, and subjugated Flanders. Here Louis had seemingly imposed his will inside a principality, but, as when Philip I had interfered with the Flemish succession in 1071 (3.2.4), his success was not longlived. Fighting soon flared up again as a growing number of Flemish, including the important towns, declared themselves in favour of Thierry of Alsace. When Louis attempted to settle the dispute himself he was accused of improper interference with the comital election. In 1128 he was occupied with other problems as well, and he managed little more than a show of arms joined with an excommunication for Thierry. But William Clito was wounded and died, and the king then decided to accept Thierry as the new count, receiving homage from him for his lands. Although Louis had exercised considerable influence in Flanders for a while, the concerted force of the towns and some of the nobility compelled him in the end to accept a candidate he did not want as count.

With Theobald of Blois, his intractable enemy, Louis VI was less firm. The chronicler of Morigny blamed Theobald for the constant warfare in France, and certainly the count was involved in most of the hostile coalitions against the king.[7] So angry was Louis after his defeat by the English king in 1119 with Theobald's support, that he ordered Chartres to be burned, and only the pleas of the chapter of Nôtre-Dame saved it. Louis never effectively brought Theobald to book, and in 1125, when the count joined Champagne to Blois, the king's difficulties with him increased.

Louis was able to summon a far wider group of vassals for aid than his father, and, more important, they tended to obey his orders. In his own lands Louis VI was still the territorial prince fighting for control, striving to establish his ascendancy. In the rest of France he was increasingly exercising his royal powers, defending the church, calling vassals to his court, intervening outside his own direct sphere of influence as a response to appeals made to him. And while his presence was still not felt in many parts of France, still his prestige, and the prestige of the monarchy was growing.

Good prop. + battle sense = prosper.

4.2.2 Louis VII, 1137–1180

Stephen of Paris wrote of Louis VII:

He was so pious, so just, so catholic and benign, that if you were to see his simplicity of behaviour and dress, you would think, unless you already knew him, that he was not a king, but a man of religion. He was a lover of justice, a defender of the weak.[8]

Odo of Deuil, abbot of Saint-Denis after Suger's death, who had accompanied Louis on crusade, said that his faith shone out from him, while a monastic annalist describes him as father of the church. Born the second son of Louis VI in 1120–21, he was educated at the cathedral school in Paris, probably to fit him for an ecclesiastical career. The death of his brother Philip in 1131 made him heir to the throne, to which he succeeded as a youth in 1137. All our sources suggest that, besides being a man of piety, he was very just, with simple tastes, but with a high view of monarchy. Walter Map, a harsh and satirical critic of kings and clerics, nevertheless found much to praise in Louis. He emphasised his love of justice, which was so strong that, when he found that the buildings of his palace at Fontainebleau encroached on the lands of a poor peasant, he ordered them to be pulled down. Count Theobald of Champagne found him asleep in a wood, attended by only two knights, and reproached him for this recklessness. Louis, says Map, answered:

'I may sleep alone quite safely, for no one bears me any ill-will.' It was a simple matter, the utterance of pure conscience. What other king can claim so much for himself?

When Map was staying with the king in Paris, Louis talked about the wealth of rulers:

'Your lord, the king of England, who wants for nothing, has men, horses, gold, silk, jewels, fruits, game and everything else. We in France have nothing but bread and wine and gaiety.'[9]

Contemporaries found much to praise in Louis VII, historians have been less enthusiastic about him. He has often been portrayed as a colourless nonentity, under the influence first of Eleanor of Aquitaine, then of Abbot Suger, then of Bernard of Clairvaux, formulating his policies and waging his wars at their behest, and by allowing the formation of the Angevin 'empire', committing a gross and dangerous political error. There is an element of fairness in this verdict, as there is also an element of fairness in Professor Pacaut's view, expressed in his monograph on Louis published in 1964, that this king's positive achievements were more important than his failures, that his building up of royal prestige and his consolidation of the royal domain paved the way for the eventual triumphs of his son Philip Augustus.

His misfortune – and a great misfortune it was – stems perhaps from the fact that he lived a century too early, when the Capetian dynasty had not yet attained the great level of prestige which it enjoyed after Philip Augustus, that there was no Joinville in his entourage, that he did not die on the road to Jerusalem.[10]

But could Louis VII ever have attained a reputation of the kind enjoyed by his great-grandson Louis IX? Certainly he shared some of his personal and political qualities, his piety yet firmness with the church, his simplicity of dress and behaviour, his love of justice. But he was perhaps more easily influenced than Louis IX, and he was capable both of deeds of impetuous rashness and of periods of lassitude and indecisive inactivity. He consolidated the domain and he continued to widen royal popularity and royal influence in France, but this was accomplished in the shadow of Angevin power, for to the lands inherited or captured by his father, Geoffrey 'Le Bel' of Anjou, and his mother, the Empress Matilda, Henry II added Aquitaine, by marrying Louis's ex-wife, Eleanor in 1152. Louis is often accused of having allowed this to happen – he was suzerain of the duchy – and this has seemed to many historians an act of utter folly. But in fact he lacked the power to prevent it.

∴ Lucky for L 7.

It is true that Henry II was in the short term more intent on consolidating his power in his heterogeneous collection of lands in France, on seizing castles and counties, than in trying to take the crown of France. He paid homage to Louis for his French lands and respected his rights as suzerain, but the Capetians themselves had come to power in France in part through the failure of the Carolingian line, in part through their powerful position as territorial princes. Could not the Angevins have done the same? When in the later 1150s Louis's daughter by his second marriage was betrothed to Henry's eldest son by Eleanor of Aquitaine, the young king, Louis had no sons. Eleanor had given him two daughters; his nearest male relation was a brother, Robert count of Dreux. Philip Augustus was born to his third wife, Adela of Champagne, whom he married in 1160, but before then, a succession crisis would have been on the cards if he had died. Even crowns, as Stephen of Blois had shown, might be won by the most active and forceful claimant. Henry had managed to displace Stephen in England, and his son might conceivably have at least tried to do the same in France, basing his claim on marriage rather than inheritance. Events did not turn out that way. The French king had a son who was eventually able to turn the dissensions within the Angevin family to account, and to take advantage of weakness when it appeared. Louis, too, had begun to do this at the end of his reign.

Louis came to the throne in 1137 with glittering prospects. The great rivals of the French kings, the counts of Blois-Champagne and the Anglo-Norman royal house, posed little immediate threat. Theobald of Blois-Champagne had perhaps hoped to gain the English crown, and when his brother Stephen seized it, had turned more towards the king than to his own momentarily successful brother. Furthermore hostilities were developing between Stephen and Geoffrey 'le Bel' of Anjou and his wife the Empress Matilda, daughter of Henry I of England and Henry's designated heir, over the title to the kingdom of England and the duchy of Normandy. Louis himself was thus in a strong position. Furthermore, William duke of Aquitaine, on his deathbed had left his daughter and heiress Eleanor to Louis VI's custody; and she was married to the future Louis VII in 1137. A woman of strong personality, vigorous and vivid, she seems to have exercised a strong influence over the king during the first part of his reign, to have involved him in schemes to further the interests of Aquitaine rather than of the whole kingdom or of the royal principality. At this time Angevin power began to build up in the north.

Professor Pacaut has suggested that in the first part of his reign, Louis indulged in politics of grandeur and illusion. Certainly the king managed to alienate many of his great vassals with remarkable rapidity. By investing Eustace of Blois, Stephen's son, with Normandy, Louis angered the Empress Matilda and Geoffrey of Anjou, while Theobald of Blois, who refused to give the king aid to crush a rebellion in Poitou in 1138, showed a mounting hostility. In 1141 the king intervened in Toulouse, to which Eleanor had a claim, but the results were indecisive. Events finally became out of hand when the king involved himself in the election to the archbishopric of Bourges. He was anxious to extend his influence in Berry, and wanted Cadurc who had replaced Stephen of Garlande as royal chancellor to be elected. When the cathedral chapter chose Pierre de la Châtre, the papal candidate, Louis vowed Pierre would never enter Bourges. Theobald of Blois-Champagne, however, received Pierre in his lands. The rift between Theobald and Louis was also widened by the marital problems of Raoul, count of Vermandois, Louis's seneschal. He repudiated his wife, Eleanor of Champagne, Theobald's niece, for Petronilla of Aquitaine, sister of Eleanor of Aquitaine, and managed to find bishops to marry them. Eleanor of Champagne and her uncle Theobald appealed to Pope Innocent II, whose legate excommunicated Raoul and suspended from office the bishops who had performed the marriage.

Louis now entered the conflict against Theobald on behalf of Raoul, his cousin. In 1142–43 he burned and ravaged parts of Champagne with extreme ferocity, according to William of Saint-Thierry. The campaign culminated with the burning of the church at Vitry, with 1,500 people caught in the flames, an event which apparently greatly horrified the king. Nevertheless it cost Bernard of Clairvaux and Suger a considerable effort to persuade Louis VII and Theobald to negotiate. Eventually Louis left Champagne on the understanding that Raoul's excommunication would be lifted. Now Raoul refused to give up Petronilla so his excommunication was renewed, and the interdict on the royal lands remained in force. Louis occupied part of Champagne again, and forbade any appointments to be made in episcopal sees. In 1144 the next pope, Celestine II, together with Suger and Bernard, managed to bring the king to make peace. Louis removed his troops from Champagne and gave in over the Bourges election. Raoul and Petronilla stayed together. Louis had gained nothing, and while he had been occupied with Champagne, Geoffrey 'le Bel' had overrun Normandy. Louis was compelled to recognise this as a *fait accompli*, although he managed to extract control of the important strategic town of Gisors in return.

Professor Petit-Dutaillis has suggested that the burning of Vitry was a shock which transformed the king, and brought him under the influence of Bernard of Clairvaux and Suger instead of Eleanor of Aquitaine. Professor Pacaut by contrast saw the break in the reign as coming after Louis's crusade, which was an attempt by the king to regain his lost reputation, to assuage his thirst for glory, as much as to manifest his increasing piety.[11] Odo of Deuil who accompanied Louis on crusade explained that the French king was full of zeal for the Christian faith and longed to save the Holy Places. Perhaps too his political humiliations at home needed redeeming. Certainly it was the first time that any king had been involved directly in a crusade, and when at Bourges on Christmas Day 1145 Louis initially announced his intention of going, he was greeted by both nobles and ecclesiastics with very little enthusiasm.

There was a clear need for an army from the west to go and relieve the kingdom of Jerusalem. In 1144 Edessa had fallen to the Atabeg Turks under Zengi and his son Nur-ed-Din, who were moving down from the north, and Mélisande, queen regent of Jerusalem, wrote to Pope Eugenius III asking for help. Eugenius directed an appeal to Louis VII, who responded with enthusiasm. He called together an assembly at Vézelay for Easter 1146, and here Bernard of Clairvaux, encouraged by Eugenius, also a Cistercian monk, preached the second crusade with dramatic success. The Emperor Conrad III was prevailed upon to join the western forces. *∴ Popularity.*

The crusaders set off for the Holy Land in 1147. The expedition proved a *débâcle*. The emperor at Constantinople, Manuel, was hostile, and the French and the German forces were unable to agree between themselves. Both suffered separate defeats, the French near Laodicea and the Germans at Dorylaeum. They met at Jerusalem, and were defeated again outside Damascus in 1148. Conrad III now went back to Germany, many others also departed, but Louis VII stayed in Palestine making pilgrimages to the holy places. Abbot Suger, left as regent, had much to contend with. Robert of Dreux, Louis's brother, had returned to France from the east and was plotting with a group of dissident nobles to take over the throne. Suger called an assembly at Soissons in 1149 and reminded the French nobility of their duty to the absent king, whose lands and goods were protected by his crusading vow, and the threat of rebellion died down. Suger had also managed to pay for the crusade, in part from the monetary reserves accumulated by Louis VI. But Louis's continued absence caused Suger considerable problems, and at Easter 1149 he called on the king to return to France. Louis at last did so. When the abbot died in 1151 Louis was to lose a valued administrator and loyal counsellor, and these he needed.

Suger and Raoul of Vermandois were replaced by a new group of advisers, headed by the king's brother, Henry, archbishop of Reims, and later William aux Blanches Mains. William was the brother of the count of Champagne and had been a *protégé* of Saint Bernard and a monk of Clairvaux; from 1168 to 1176 he was bishop of Chartres and archbishop of Sens; and in 1176 he moved to the archbishopric of Reims. Philip of Alsace, count of Flanders, was also a close associate of the king later in his reign, and a useful ally against the Angevins.

When Louis returned from the east it is clear that he recognised the size of the threat posed by the build up of Angevin power in Normandy. Geoffrey had handed over the duchy to Henry his son in 1150, but Louis again put forward Eustace, Stephen's son, and waged war vigorously on his behalf. In 1151 peace was made with Geoffrey and Henry, and Louis gained the Norman Vexin, including Gisors. There now followed a personal and political disaster for the king. When he had been on crusade there had been clear signs of a growing rift between him and his wife Eleanor of Aquitaine, who was accused by contemporary chroniclers of lewd and improper behaviour and of showing an unnatural attraction to her uncle, Raymond of Antioch. In 1149 Pope Eugenius III had reconciled Louis and Eleanor, but by 1151 the king had had enough of her; he withdrew his own servants from her duchy and in 1152 the council of Beaugency declared the marriage null and void on the grounds of consanguinity. A few months later, Henry Plantagenet, now count of Anjou after his father's death (1151), married Eleanor.[12] Louis again invaded Normandy in alliance with Stephen of England, but then Eustace, Stephen's son, died and Henry was accepted as the English king's heir. Louis's resistance crumbled, and in 1154 Henry became king of England as well as the greatest single landholder in France. His vast conglomeration of lands stretching from Durham to Dax entirely overshadowed those of his suzerain the French king.

In the face of this territorial prince extraordinary Louis lost much of the courage and vigour which had underlain many of his exploits early in the reign. This was perhaps in part because of the strong influence of the Cistercians and other ecclesiastics upon him. The contrasts between the two parts of his reign, though in many ways striking, should not be overstressed. In his first years as king, Louis VII had never been as effective in military terms as his father Louis VI, and later in his reign he continued to wage war sporadically, and not entirely fruitlessly, for the most part against Henry II. He had not the resources effectively to combat the power of the English king (4.4.4), and, as Henry showed no signs of wishing to seize the French crown from him, he had no need to fight for personal survival; he had rather to prevent himself from being overshadowed inside France. This precaution he did not pursue singlemindedly; he often allowed concessions to the Angevins, and would negotiate as often as fight. At the end of the reign the possibilities of diminishing Henry's power began to emerge and Louis took a firmer approach.

In the late 1150s Angevin power continued to expand and Louis appeared at his weakest. Geoffrey, Henry's brother, became lord of Nantes in Brittany in 1156, and when he died childless in 1158, Henry claimed the overlordship of Brittany and overran it. Louis put up no resistance to this, and when Henry

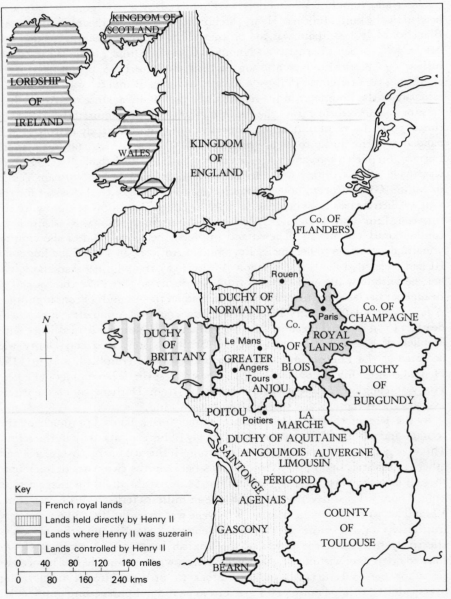

Map 4.1   The lands of Henry II and Louis VII in the 1170s

appeared to be on the verge of trying the same tactics in Toulouse, basing his claim here on those of Eleanor's family Louis nevertheless tried to remain on peaceful terms with him. He allowed his daughter Margaret who had issued from his second marriage to Constance of Castile to be betrothed to Henry's son and heir, the young Henry, and to be given into Henry's custody; both were infants at the time, but Louis had no son. Not until Henry set off for Toulouse in 1159 did Louis take firm action. Raymond V appealed to him and he managed to save the city by occupying it himself; the English king, unwilling to besiege his suzerain, fell back with his army. This was a significant event (4.4.5) but Henry's respect for an overlord only went so far. In 1162 the English king had celebrated the marriage of the young Henry and Margaret, and he seized the Norman Vexin, her dowry, for herself. The rupture with Louis now emerged openly.

In the 1160s the French king began to build up supporters against this rival. His marriage to Adela of Champagne in 1160 brought him the alliance of Henry the Liberal, count of Champagne, and was to produce him a male heir in 1165. Odo II and Hugh III of Burgundy were favourably inclined towards Louis VII; he also collected a following of nobles both in Burgundy and the Languedoc (4.4.5). Frederick Barbarossa, elected emperor in 1152, negotiated with Henry and Louis in turn. Matters were complicated when in 1159 another papal schism erupted (4.5.1): Frederick recognised Victor IV; Henry II and Louis VII accepted Alexander III in 1160. In 1162 Alexander was driven out of Italy by Frederick and took refuge in France.

When Alexander gave his sanction to Henry II for the marriage of the young king and Margaret, Louis negotiated with the emperor, but Henry of Champagne and Frederick Barbarossa arranged a meeting of both kings and both popes at Saint-Jean-de-Losne. The incident is an obscure one; Alexander refused to appear, and the apparent discourtesy of the emperor and his adviser Rainald of Dassel to the French king (Rainald called Louis *regulus*) drove Louis back to the support of Alexander. The pope now put himself under Louis's protection and took up residence at Sens; in 1163 he sent him a 'golden rose' to mark the help he had given to the vicar of Christ.[13]

In 1164 Louis VII gained another useful, though also rather embarrassing, ecclesiastical refugee in his lands. Archbishop Thomas Becket fled to France from the wrath of Henry II and stayed first at Pontigny, then at Sens. John of Salisbury canonised the phrase *rex Christianissimus*, most Christian king, for Louis, and in these years the French king was marked out as an ally of the church and his opposition to Henry was given a moral dimension. The king even fought Henry sporadically for several years, but here Alexander III gave him no backing, as he needed to keep the friendship of this powerful man. Later Alexander III's position became more secure, for in 1167 Frederick was forced out of Italy, and the pope then returned to Rome. Furthermore at the peace of Montmirail in 1169 Henry's sons did homage to Louis for the lands their father had parcelled out to them, and Louis was later able to make use of this connection. Then in 1170 Becket was murdered and Henry was blamed by all Christendom. Louis, who had protected the martyr, gained great general approval. He went into the last decade of his reign in a much strengthened moral position, and his opposition to Henry and his sons also became more effective, although the royal principality was still overshadowed by the Plantagenet lands.

Louis VII now began to foment discord between Henry II and his family, and probably played an important part in bringing about the major rebellion of the young king and his brothers in 1173–74 which posed a dangerous threat to Henry's power. Louis also campaigned against Henry, but did not lend full and wholehearted support to the rebels, and he helped the young king Henry, Richard and Geoffrey to arrange the peace which followed Henry's victory in 1174. This was a missed opportunity, and despite his continuing problems with his sons, Henry's power again began to increase. He bought the overlordship of the strategically important county of La Marche in 1177, and in the same year he threatened Louis with a strong army in support of his right to the French Vexin, which he claimed as Margaret's dowry, and to Bourges and its region, which he said was to be the dowry of Alice, Margaret's sister, betrothed to Richard. Neither claim was well founded. Louis did not want to fight, but his ally, the church, served him well. Alexander III, who in 1177 had finally concluded peace with Frederick Barbarossa, threatened Henry with an interdict, and the English king fell back.

The last years of Louis's reign were more peaceful. In 1179 the king, whose health was now deteriorating, held a great assembly of lay and ecclesiastical magnates in Paris, and his son Philip was elected, anointed and crowned as his successor; and in 1180 Louis VII died. Where he had just managed to contain Angevin power, Philip, by a combination of good fortune and skill, was to achieve vastly more.

4.2.3 Philip II 'Augustus' 1180–1223

Philip, called Dieudonné or God-given at his birth in 1165, came to the throne as a young man like his father before him, but unlike Louis VII he manifested qualities of intelligence, prudence and cunning from quite early on in his reign. His achievements as king were remarkable, and while he owed much of his success to luck, he had the ability to use fortuitous circumstances for his own ends, to exploit weaknesses and divisions amongst his enemies, to earn the title 'Augustus' given to him by his chaplain William the Breton by expanding his royal power into Picardy, into Normandy, Anjou and Maine, and into the Languedoc.

His first wife was Isabella of Hainault, who gave him a son and heir, Louis, and died in 1189. In 1193 he took as his second wife Ingeborg of Denmark, but developed a violent antipathy towards her on his wedding day. He cast her aside on grounds of affinity and in 1196 found complaisant bishops to marry him to Agnes of Méran. She produced a daughter and a son, Philip Hurepel, before her death in 1201, and they were to be legitimised by the pope. While Agnes was alive, Philip, like Robert the Pious and Philip I, aroused strong hostility from Pope Innocent III, with its concomitant excommunication. Later in his reign he despaired of obtaining a divorce from the pope and he took back Ingeborg in 1213, shortly after the birth of a son to his heir, Prince Louis.[14]

Philip, despite his cruelty, treachery and authoritarian behaviour, attested to by a number of chroniclers, remains a popular character with French historians. Likewise his official historians, Rigord and William the Breton, justify his bad deeds and describe him as a paragon of all virtues; the latter declares that it is uncertain whether he was loved more by his subjects than he loved them. The author of the *Chronicle of Tours*, Payen Gâtineau, a canon of Tours, presents a more balanced but still generally favourable view. Philip he said, loved wine, women and good cheer, and money. He was an attractive man, quick to judge, harsh with rebels and a fomenter of discord against his enemies, but he never let an enemy die in prison, and he helped the poor and needy and protected the church. Giles of Paris in his *Karolinus* wrote that Philip had augmented the kingdom but he was an evil man who showed intolerance and covetousness, and brought disgrace on France by his repudiation of Ingeborg. Anglo-Norman chroniclers, too, dwelt on his bad points. Bertran de Born described him as inert and cowardly. The epithet Augustus which was given by Rigord — because he was august, because he augmented the crown's possessions, and because he was born in August — has only become a part of his title in the recent past: in the Middle Ages he was known as Philip the Conqueror, an apt title. Other writers called him the prudent or the wise.[15]

All the descriptions so far quoted describe Philip in later life. In his youth he is supposed to have been pale, sickly and timid. On his return from the third crusade he had lost his shock of hair and developed extreme nervousness. Nevertheless, his political acumen was consistently strong, and if in many ways an unattractive figure, his achievements were remarkable; he also seems to have nurtured strong ambitions from early in his reign. Gerald of Wales has a pleasing, if probably apocryphal tale of Philip declaring to a group of barons that he had been daydreaming about whether God would grant him the glory of restoring the French kingdom to the extent and greatness which it had had at the time of Charlemagne.[16]

Philip was crowned king in 1179 when Louis VII's strength was failing fast. Shortly before this he had caught a chill when out hunting and Louis, fearing his only heir would die, went to Canterbury on pilgrimage to Becket's shrine. Philip recovered, and it was soon his father's turn first to retire to his monastery at Barbeaux, then to die. Philip's marriage to Isabella of Hainault, daughter of Baldwin V, count of Hainault and niece of Philip of Alsace, count of Flanders, brought him Artois as the queen's dowry, and was to give him a vital claim to the family's other lands. This alliance and Louis VII's death left the young king under the tutelage of Philip of Alsace, but this he would not tolerate for long.

By making an alliance with Henry II at Gisors, the young Philip alienated both the counts of Flanders and Champagne, who formed a hostile coalition with Stephen of Sancerre in 1182; there was sporadic fighting between the two sides until 1185. In 1182 countess Isabella of Hainault, Philip of Hainault's wife, died. She was in her own right heiress to Vermandois, Amiénois and Valois, and although her husband claimed these lands, they passed initially to her sister, Eleanor, countess of Beaumont. The king also intervened on Eleanor's behalf but claimed some lands himself on the basis of both blood and marriage ties. In 1185 he defeated Philip of Hainault in battle, and a settlement was reached at Amiens in 1186. The king was to retain Artois, his wife's dowry, and when Louis (VIII) was born in 1187 this looked as though it would be a permanent gain. Eleanor countess of Beaumont kept Valois, and Vermandois was divided. Philip of Alsace took the counties of Péronne and Saint-Quentin and the town of Ham, and the king the important city and county of Amiens and sixty-five castles, the county of Montdidier and the reversion of Philip of Alsace's share of Vermandois. This was something of a triumph, and in the same year the king made another successful expedition into Burgundy, and brought the duke, who was plotting with the emperor, to heel.

Henry II had given Philip Augustus his support in the early 1180s and relations between the two kings seemed good. But in 1186–87 this harmony broke down, perhaps because the deaths of both the young Henry and of Geoffrey of Brittany. The first had offered Philip the prospect of a congenial successor to Henry II, the second had been a valued fellow conspirator and friend.[17] Richard, Henry's eldest surviving son was a ruthless and dangerous rival, and when he failed to fulfil his promises to marry Alice, Philip's sister, Philip demanded that both she and the Norman Vexin, her dowry, should be returned to him. Further problems emerged over the overlordship of Brittany and Toulouse and Philip decided to make war on Henry. He marched into Berry, and besieged Châteauroux. A truce was made shortly afterwards largely on Richard's initiative and in 1188 both kings agreed to go on crusade.

Richard and Philip now became close allies and when Henry appeared to be favouring his youngest son John above Richard, Philip, following the example of his father, was able to turn this family quarrel to good account. Richard paid Philip homage for Henry II's continental lands, and they joined forces against the elderly and sick English king, overrunning Normandy, Maine and Touraine. In July 1189 Henry met Richard and Philip near Tours and conceded on all points: Richard was to be his successor, and although the Angevins were to keep the Norman Vexin, Philip was to retain his conquests in Berry and to be recognised as suzerain of the Auvergne. Philip had made his first gains at the expense of the Angevins; and two days later, Henry II, hearing that even John had rebelled against him, died.

Richard became king of England and Philip's vassal for Normandy, Maine, Anjou, Touraine, Poitou and Aquitaine.[18] His military prowess was formidable, and Philip, intent on reducing his great power in the French kingdom, would clearly need to use other weapons against him. Meanwhile the French and the English monarchs were both committed to a major crusading venture, and in 1190 Philip and Richard set off for Palestine together. Philip left his mother Adela of Champagne and his uncle the archbishop of Reims as regents, as his wife had died shortly before.

The two kings sailed first for Sicily, where their friendship soon broke down. Richard again refused to marry Philip's sister Alice, and instead made Berengaria of Navarre his wife. This was a shrewd alliance, probably aimed to protect Aquitaine and Gascony from the hostility of the count of Toulouse, whose power in southern France was considerable. Richard, it was said, refused to marry Alice because she had been his father's mistress, and he gained the alliance of Tancred of Sicily and Philip count of Flanders. The French king was now compelled to revise his agreement with Richard. By the Treaty of Messina in 1191 Richard paid Philip 10,000 marks and agreed to restore Alice and the town of Gisors to him, but the Norman Vexin was to remain in Norman hands unless he had no heirs. If Richard had two sons his lands were to be divided between them, and both were to hold lands in France directly from the French king. In the long term, Philip hoped to divide the Plantagenet lands as did probably Richard too (4.4.7); in the short term he was ready to exploit the rivalry of Richard and John for his own ends.

The crusaders arrived at Acre, their first objective, in 1191, Richard having captured Cyprus on the way. The town fell in July and the booty was divided; Philip then returned to France leaving Richard with his mind fixed on Jerusalem. Philip of Alsace, count of Flanders, had died on crusade, and Philip's regents had occupied Artois in the name of Prince Louis; Péronne and Saint-Quentin, the parts of Vermandois which Philip of Alsace had been allowed in 1186, also passed into the king's hands. Philip reached a new agreement with Eleanor, countess of Beaumont, when he arrived home. She renounced all claims to the Amiénois and a large portion of Vermandois; the rest, including the county of Saint-Quentin, she was to hold as a fief from the king to whom it would pass on her death. This agreement was to be opposed by Baldwin VIII of Flanders, the new count, nephew of Philip of Hainault, but Philip's gradual build-up of lands and rights in northern France was continuing.

On his way home from the east Philip probably met Emperor Henry VI at Milan. Henry VI was the counterclaimant to Sicily, and, angry at Richard's treaty with his rival Tancred of Lecce, agreed to support Philip against the English king. When Richard on his way home, fell into the hands of an enemy, Duke Leopold of Austria, Philip may have been instrumental in arranging for him to be handed over to Henry VI, who held him prisoner until early in 1194. Philip profited from his rival's absence. He overran the Vexin, seized Gisors and allied with John, planning it seems to invade Normandy and England in defiance of his agreement with Richard, violating both feudal and canon law. By the time that Richard returned he had captured Evreux. Richard mobilised all the resources of the duchy and Philip was soon driven back; when in 1196 a truce was made almost all his conquests were lost. Despite attempts on his part to secure the support of Count Baldwin IX of Flanders and Renaud of Dammartin, count of Boulogne, they were won over to Richard. In 1197 they attacked Philip's lands in northern France and the king invaded Flanders in retaliation, but nothing was settled. Richard overran the Norman Vexin, and eventually a truce was arranged in 1197. During this, the English king strengthened his lines of defence, building as the *pièce de résistance* Château Gaillard, modelled on crusader castles and virtually impregnable.

When war started again in 1198 Philip was driven out of the French Vexin as well. He was now in a most unfavourable position, and matters were made worse by his attempts to repudiate Ingeborg and the resulting disputes with the papacy. In 1199 a truce was arranged between the two kings, but Richard while involved in curbing the revolt of the viscount of Limoges, who had the French king's backing, was unexpectedly killed.[19] The new rival of the French king, John, when at his most effective was as determined and ruthless a man as his brother, but at other times he was petty, tyrannical and indecisive; though capable of waging brilliant campaigns, he often threw away success by inaction, and his vindictiveness meant that he often found it hard to win mens' loyalties.[20] Philip exploited his weakness and now turned the tables on his Angevin rivals. Luck had at last come to the aid of the Capetians.

Richard's sudden death left his various possessions in a state of some confusion. The aged Eleanor of Aquitaine rallied her duchy on behalf of John, and the English and Norman nobility, thanks in part to the counsels of William Marshall, accepted him as king and duke and had him crowned. But Arthur, count of Brittany, son of John's elder brother Geoffrey, was favoured in Anjou, Maine and Touraine. Philip lent Arthur support and invested him with Normandy, Brittany, Anjou, Maine and Touraine, and taking advantage of the confusion, he invaded Normandy and Maine. But William des Roches, seneschal of Anjou, defected from Arthur to John. Philip Augustus retreated, and peace was concluded at Le Goulet in 1200. By this treaty John was to hold all Richard's former fiefs from Philip, but was to pay 20,000 marks as a relief for them. Blanche of Castile, John's niece, was to marry the future Louis VIII and was given Graçay and Issoudun as a dowry. Philip was ceded the county of Evreux, a sizable portion of Normandy, and a valuable concession (4.4.8).

The person who suffered as a result of the Treaty of Le Goulet was Arthur of Brittany, who was now to hold his much reduced lands from John. By abandoning the Breton prince, Philip had gained valuable rights of suzerainty over John and important lands, at a time when his continuing efforts to put aside Ingeborg had brought excommunication on his head and an interdict on his lands from Innocent III. In the same year, Baldwin IX of Flanders relinquished all his rights over the Amiénois, Artois, and the counties of Saint-Quentin and Péronne to Philip. By the end of 1200 the French royal lands had grown considerably in size.

The events of the next four years were to bring unprecedented advantages to the French king, who again profited from the mistakes of his adversaries. In 1200 John married Isabella, heiress to Angoulême, which was of vital strategic importance in Aquitaine, particularly after the French king had overrun much of Berry. This was in itself a prudent move, and was probably dictated more by politics than passion. Isabella had previously been betrothed to Hugh of Lusignan, count of La Marche, who was legally entitled to a generous reparation from the English king, and John neglected to pay this: the Lusignans waited until 1201 and then declared war on him. John overran La Marche and threatened their Poitevin possessions; and they appealed to their suzerain Philip, who summoned John to his court in 1202. John failed to appear, and it is probable that Philip and his barons judged that he should forfeit all his lands as a penalty. Philip was legally entitled to seize the fiefs of a rebellious vassal, and this John had become. The king decided, it seems, to take Normandy for himself and to invest Arthur of Brittany, who had married his daughter Mary, with the other Plantagenet lands.

Philip and Arthur began hostilities against John in 1202, but Arthur was defeated by his uncle at Mirebeau, imprisoned, and disappeared, almost certainly murdered by John in 1203. This is an obscure incident, and some historians have suggested that John was tried a second time in the French court for Arthur's murder and condemned in 1204. It is more likely, however, that Philip did not learn for sure of Arthur's murder until 1210, when William de Briouze fled from John's court to France.[21] Rumours of Arthur's death were rife by 1203, and both then and later it was to provide excellent propaganda for the French king. John was gradually losing ground through his indecisiveness, and having been deserted by many of his followers he relied heavily on mercenary troops.

Meanwhile Philip continued to make progress in Normandy, buying the support of the nobility, the towns and the church with well-placed concessions. He was helped too by the departure of the frequently hostile Baldwin of Flanders on the fourth crusade. The nobility who stayed behind, including the duke of Burgundy and Renaud of Dammartin, count of Boulogne, tended to favour Philip and the field was at last clear for him to strike. The French king now staged an impressive and successful military campaign against his rival. By July 1204 he had overrun Normandy, taken Château Gaillard by storm and seized Rouen; for a while he contemplated the invasion of England, but this was not feasible. However, Maine, Touraine, Anjou and Brittany also fell to him, and he held Poitou from 1205 to 1206, until Amaury of Thouars, whom he made seneschal, went over to John. Although he also brought the Auvergne under royal suzerainty, Philip, after some attempts to reconquer Poitou, then left most of this county together with the duchy of Aquitaine in English hands. Poitou was a valuable holding, and Louis VIII was again to overrun it. Aquitaine and Gascony were a less appealing prospect, since the nobles here were unruly and difficult to dominate and the feudal and administrative structures remained weak. By taking the richest and best governed parts of the Angevin holdings, Philip had cut direct communications between England and the remains of its French lands and had gained immense advantages for the French crown in land, wealth and manpower. The balance between the king and the princes had tipped dramatically towards the king, but Philip was now faced with consolidating these advantages.

Meanwhile events were moving fast in the empire, and the continuing struggle of the English and French kings became part of this wider conflict. In 1198 the Emperor Henry VI died, leaving as his heir the infant Frederick II. A succession dispute immediately broke out in Germany, between Philip of Swabia, Henry VI's brother, and Otto of Brunswick, Henry the Lion's son and also the nephew of John of England. Alliances were made and broken rapidly in the next few years. At first, Pope Innocent III favoured Otto and excommunicated Philip of Swabia, who allied himself with Philip Augustus. While Philip Augustus was conquering John's lands, Philip of Swabia made progress in Germany, and seemed about to carry the day, but the French king feared a strong German monarchy and changed sides, making a truce with Otto.

In 1208 Philip of Swabia was assassinated, leaving the field clear for Otto, and the French king now again turned against him as well and put forward his own candidate, Henry of Brabant. Both Innocent III and John were favourably disposed towards Otto for a time, but he soon thoroughly alienated the pope by invading Italy. By this stage Philip Augustus had become the pope's favourite, while both John and Otto were his excommunicate enemies. When in 1212 Innocent III put forward the fourth candidate, Frederick II, Philip was ready to support him.

John remained the ally of Otto of Brunswick, and he also joined forces with Boulogne and Flanders, whose counts, Renaud of Dammartin and Ferrand of Portugal were alarmed by French royal expansion. Philip stayed closely aligned with the pope. He gave refuge to Stephen Langton, archbishop of Canterbury, while Pope Innocent III, who had selected Langton against John's wishes, laid England under an interdict (1208) and excommunicated John (1209). Philip's projected invasion of England in 1213 had papal backing, but John by submitting to the pope and making his kingdom a papal fief, replaced the French king as Innocent's favoured son, and the campaign was cancelled. The French king now turned against Flanders instead, but although by the spring of 1214 much damage had been done there, little had been achieved. Philip's forces were pushed back and he was left only with Douai and Cassel.

The slight success in Flanders emboldened John, and leaving his allies Ferrand and Otto of Germany to tackle Philip Augustus from the north, he set off for Aquitaine, hoping to advance from the south-west with his army. In this campaign he showed considerable military skill, but on 2 July he was defeated by Prince Louis and a much smaller force who moved in from Chinon and fell on John's army at La Roche-au-Moine. John fled rapidly to La Rochelle, putting up no further resistance, apart from trying to consolidate his position in Poitou. Prince Louis rapidly brought Anjou under control, and effectively secured Philip's rear against the English king. The French king had now to face the count of Flanders and Otto of Brunswick, supported by the count of Boulogne and an English force, who were threatening to march on Paris from the north. The battle between them which took place at Bouvines on 27 July 1214, was the major and resounding victory which Philip needed to secure his massive territorial gains, and it rapidly became the symbol of the revived royal power (4.4.6).[22]

Bouvines was an event of major importance in the politics of western Europe. Philip's enemies suffered a humiliating defeat. Otto was put to flight by the French, and Renaud of Boulogne and Ferrand of Portugal, count of Flanders, captured. Ferrand was kept imprisoned in Paris, leaving Joan, his wife, to rule Flanders. Renaud's daughter was married to Philip Hurepel, Philip Augustus's second son, who was granted his fiefs; and Renaud too was kept in custody until his death in 1219. This was an important gain for the French royal house, and the king consolidated it by siezing Ponthieu in 1221. The major ringleaders suffered badly in 1214, but to other rebellious French barons, Philip was more generous. Hervé de Donzi and Philip de Courtenai retained their lands. Otto returned to Brunswick and died in 1218, leaving Germany to Frederick II Hohenstaufen who had defeated him. John, supported by the pope, made a truce with Philip and Louis, and went back to England. Philip had thus consolidated his conquests of the Angevin lands, and his acquisitions of the northern french lands; he had defeated the emperor and the English king despite their papal backing, and had established his own pre-eminence in France. Bouvines was vitally important in the rise of the French monarchy.

In 1215 the French king was offered an even greater conquest than those he had already made: the crown of England for his son Louis. A great number of the English nobility, angered by John's financial demands and his ever-encroaching administration, unwilling to serve in France but angered by his defeat, rose against him and forced him to agree to the major concessions embodied in Magna Carta. John showed no sign of adhering to its conditions, and Innocent III declared it null and void. Both John and his adversaries negotiated for the support of the French king, but John's barons had more to offer Prince Louis: the English throne. Innocent III excommunicated the barons, but Louis still invaded England in 1216. 1216

Philip's attitude is not clear. William the Breton declared that he was not in favour of the expedition, and while the French king would not concede that England was, as a papal fief, immune from attack, he still appears to have made moves to confiscate Louis's lands. On the other hand, he allowed Louis to gather together 12,000 knights for the expedition and he paid him a substantial sum of money. Philip may have feigned reluctance, as he was unwilling to alienate the pope any further, and William the Breton, writing some years later, may have exaggerated this into genuine hostility to improve the look of subsequent events. In 1216 John died, leaving a very young son, Henry III, as his heir, who was favoured by the English nobility in a way his father never had been, and Innocent III's successor as pope, Honorius III, lent him considerable support. Louis appeared in an invidious light. Instead of opposing a detested king, he was fighting a child, chosen by his barons as king, and a papal protégé. Losing support, and defeated at the battle of Lincoln, he came to terms in 1217 at Lambeth. The French claims to England were thus relinquished, but their hold on most of the former holdings of the English kings in France was increasingly secure. Nevertheless, the legal possession of these lands was not settled until 1259 (5.2.2).

Prince Louis soon found another outlet for his ambition in the Albigensian 5TH crusade. The intervention of the French monarchy in this war was to bring further CRUSADE. gains to the French crown. The Languedoc contained many Cathar heretics, and preaching campaigns, organised by the papacy and conducted by the Cistercians and the followers of Dominic, failed to make any substantial impact on the heresy. Raymond VI, count of Toulouse, seemed to support the heretics; many of his nobility certainly did so (2.4.1–2). In 1208 Innocent III's legate, Peter of Castelnau, was murdered, but Philip Augustus held aloof, for it was clear that a crusade against the count was not justified unless Raymond himself had been proved a heretic. Nevertheless, a great force of French nobles and clergy, many from the north, descended on the Languedoc in 1209. They included the archbishops of Sens, Reims and Rouen, the duke of Burgundy and the counts of Saint-Pol and Nevers, and they were under the leadership of Simon de Montfort. After bloody campaigns against Raymond VI and Peter II of Aragon and Barcelona, the northern French army won an important victory in 1213 at the battle of Muret. At the Lateran council in 1215 Raymond VI was disinherited, and only a small part of his lands was left for his son Raymond VII. Simon de Montfort became count of Toulouse, and Philip Augustus was ready to receive his homage.

The king's attitude changed further in 1218 when Simon was killed at Toulouse and his young son Amaury was threatened by the rival count of Toulouse and his son, who organised a rising in the Languedoc. Louis had made a brief journey south in 1215, but now his father seems to have encouraged his closer involvement with the crusade, providing money and men. Louis remained in the south until 1219 but the success of the crusaders was not great. Raymond VI and Raymond VII, who had wide popular backing, offered considerable

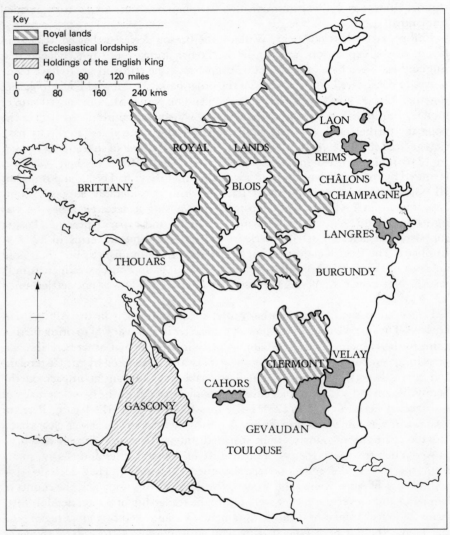

Map 4.2   The royal lands in 1223

resistance, and by the time of Raymond VI's death in 1221 he and his son had almost driven the northern forces out of the Languedoc. Louis's intervention as king was again to reverse events, however (4.2.4.; 4.4.9).

In 1222 Philip Augustus fell seriously ill, and in 1223 he died, apparently in a far more pious way than he had lived. His reign had seen spectacular changes in the fortune of the French monarchy. Though he had made considerable progress against Richard in the early 1190s, by 1199 he had suffered substantial reverses. Four years later he had utterly triumphed over the English king, and his great victory at Bouvines over the count of Flanders and the emperor gave him a pre-eminent position in France (Map 4.2) and in Europe. The extent of the opposition to his grandson Louis IX during his minority (1226–35) (5.2.1) was a testimony to the increase of royal power achieved by Philip.

∴ Good soldiering + luck (Richards death) led to land gains + prosperity.

4.2.4 Louis VIII, 1223–26

Louis VIII reigned only from 1223 until 1226, but in these three years he did much to complete his father's work and his own.[23] Matthew Paris declared that he was very unlike his father, and certainly he is said to have been small, pale and chaste, ruthless but with an almost saintlike personal reputation, a contrast with Philip Augustus, who in later life was an enthusiast for wine, women and good company. He was nevertheless an ambitious, able and effective soldier, described by Nicholas de Brai as Louis the Lion. He was a lover of learning and Rigord dedicated his *Deeds of Philip Augustus* to him, William the Breton his *Philippide*. Giles of Paris wrote the *Karolinus* for him, a poem in which he was exhorted to follow the example of Charlemagne, for Louis was believed to be a descendant of the great emperor, not only through his father via Adela of Champagne but also through his mother Isabella of Hainault. She was reputed to have been descended from Ermengarde, a fictitious, but by the thirteenth century a widely accepted daughter of Charles of Lorraine.

The figure of Charlemagne was of great importance to the French crown. Even though Frederick Barbarossa had had him canonised and used him to glorify the German monarchy a strong tradition connected him too with the French, and he had become the centre of many poems and legends in the twelfth century (4.4.6). Where in the eleventh century the replacement of the Carolingians by the Capetians had not needed justification, by 1150 it was necessary to show that the two dynasties were closely linked in order to make the Capetian pedigree more respectable. Louis VIII's descent from the line of Charlemagne on both sides set all to rights; the French chroniclers could rejoice because both houses were represented in their king. Louis was also the first Capetian heir to the throne not crowned in his father's lifetime.

Louis had taken an active part in the campaigns and politics in the later part of his father's reign, and perhaps for this reason there was a great continuity in interest and approach over the whole period from about 1210 until 1226. In 1224 the truce with England came to an end, and Louis decided to invade Poitou. The area around Poitiers was in general pro-French, but Niort and Saint-Jean-d'Angély by 1224 supported the English, while La Rochelle had done so continuously. Louis first made a treaty with the powerful Hugh le Brun of Lusignan, who had married John's widow, Isabella of Angoulême, and who was count of La Marche and Angoulême. He also made truces with other nobles including Amaury, viscount of Thouars. The king then moved into Poitou and subjugated Niort, Saint-Jean-d'Angély and La Rochelle, and he bought the support of the nobles with pensions and that of the towns and the church with privileges.

This policy was initially quite successful, but Louis then tried to win over Gascony, sending an army headed by Hugh of Lusignan there. Henry III's advisers built up a defensive force and rallied against him, trying both to reconquer Poitou and to negotiate at the same time. Pope Honorius III lent them his support, and warned Louis that he too, like Otto of Brunswick, might fall from power. Louis contented himself with his conquest of Poitou, and after consolidating his gains with further grants and privileges, returned to Paris. But already Hugh of Lusignan was moving back towards support of the English, and it was not until the reign of Louis IX that firm French control was finally established in Poitou (5.5.3).

The king now turned again to the Languedoc; by 1226 he had gained full papal backing and the title of count, ceded to him by Amaury de Montfort (4.4.9). Louis gathered together an unusually large army – Roger of Wendover put their number at 50,000 though this is doubtless an exaggeration – and swept down into the Languedoc. Avignon fell to him, and despite the defection from the king of Theobald, count of Champagne, and Peter Mauclerc, count of Brittany, two nobles who were to cause great problems in Louis IX's minority, the rest of the south submitted with very little resistance. Louis by now seemed invincible. He was careful to cultivate the communes and the church in the Midi, building up support in the devastated and conquered region, and establishing royal administration on the basis of Simon de Montfort's arrangements made by the statutes of Pamiers in 1212. At another assembly in Pamiers in 1226 Louis laid down that all fiefs confiscated from heretics belonged to the king. But he did not have time fully to reduce the area to order. When he died on his way back to Paris in 1226, he left the Languedoc temporarily subjugated, but not settled, and Raymond VII was to cause Louis's widow, Blanche of Castile, regent for the young Louis IX, considerable problems (5.2.1).

Louis VIII left a number of problems still to be solved before Normandy, Anjou, Maine, Touraine, Poitou and the Languedoc could be held firmly and freely by the Capetians. But compared with the position of the French kings in France in the reigns of Louis VI and Louis VII, Louis VIII's power showed vast gains. By a mixture of marriage, the exploitation of feudal law, and force, Philip Augustus and his son had delivered the French throne from the Angevin threat and brought it into a dominant position in the kingdom.

4.3 FRENCH SOCIETY, 1108–1226

4.3.1 *Social and economic changes*

The revival of Capetian power took place in a period of economic expansion and social changes, and the kings were able to profit considerably from many of the developments which took place. Professor Bloch, and with him many other historians, characterised the period 1050–1250 as the 'second feudal age', a time when an economic revolution took place. The changes which this brought with it 'affected in their turn, from the twelfth century onwards, the whole fabric of human relations'.[24]

How can such changes be measured? Some of the sources for this period give us much valuable information about rural life. The abbey of Cluny for example has, like many other religious houses, left us with a magnificent cartulary, providing all kinds of information about land, fairs and markets, tolls and mills. There is also an account dating from the 1150s, produced probably under the influence of Henry, bishop of Winchester, who stayed at the abbey and helped to reorganise its finances, by that time in a parlous state, as is shown by letters of the abbot, Peter the Venerable. Another important source is Abbot Suger's treatise about his administration of the abbey of Saint-Denis and its estates. But these and similar sources give us information only about ecclesiastical lands, and even here in the majority of cases the basic source material is charters, useful in many ways but limited by their nature and not suitable for making statistical surveys. The Cluniac account is the only one extant for the twelfth century in France; not until the middle of the thirteenth century do these become widespread. Thus much of our evidence for changes which took place must be sought on the land itself, in traces of new settlements and land clearance, in the appearance of new villages. Here too place names can help. Many of the settlements called 'Villeneuve' date from this period. But to reach the level of the individual peasant is more difficult still. Some idea of rural life emerges from the pages of illuminated manuscripts and the carved capitals of churches, but the lifestyle and aspirations of the agricultural labourer and his family do not. Most of the canvas has to be painted with broad sweeps of the brush, and only occasionally can the details be filled in.

Despite these problems, overall patterns of social and economic developments seem to emerge quite clearly. From the middle of the tenth century in some areas of France a growth in prosperity, a quickening in the economic life can be discerned, which became widespread in the second half of the eleventh century and the whole of the twelfth (1.2.1). Its manifestations varied from region to region, and time scales were widely different, but overall it is clear that by the time of Philip I's reign land clearance was increasing, villages and monastic communities expanding, long-distance trade growing as the demand for luxury goods gradually increased, local markets multiplying and coinage circulating widely in much of France. The population expanded as the birth rate grew and life expectancy increased, and this brought about a pressure on uncleared land and an increased mobility among the rural population. Patterns of landholding and farming changed; serfs as a group declined in numbers, parts of the lords' domain lands were frequently split into peasant holdings and then divided between heirs. Money was used more and more at a lower level of society and dues often replaced labour services.

How can the changes outlined above be explained? One important factor was probably improved climatic conditions, bringing drier and warmer weather and increasing agricultural production. Cereal cultivation in particular was expanded, barley and rye giving way to wheat in many areas. The growing crop yields appear to have resulted mainly from improvements in ploughing techniques. Heavy ploughs, reinforced with iron, replaced the lighter ones, and oxen gave way to horses as draught animals. This was a change which came about only gradually, but by the later years of the twelfth century in the Ile de France and Picardy, the wealthiest regions of France, horse-drawn ploughs were probably quite widespread. The heavier and stronger horse produced more work than the ox; it was also more expensive, and its arrival tended to widen the gap between the rich peasants and their poorer counterparts. But more food was available to feed the growing population, and surpluses could be sold, stimulating the growth of rural trade and provisioning the growing urban population as well.

The pressures of an expanding population and the stimulus of better agricultural techniques now caused land to be cleared and reclaimed from the forests for farming. Colonisers were encouraged to settle by landlords, many of whom stood to profit from such ventures. From the later eleventh century new settlements, villages and religious communities began to appear in clearings hacked from the forests. New patterns of peasant landholding emerged as a result, the newly reclaimed land being let out for rent or for a fixed proportion of the produce (the *champart*). Some rural communities were granted franchises and privileges or even in some cases a commune (4.3.2) which gave the peasants a considerably improved status. The changes of the twelfth century thus seem to have benefited many of the peasants, bringing better economic conditions and an improved social standing.

The Carolingian style of estate disappeared in France, but the bannal lordship remained the basic social agrarian unit. The powers of the lord over the peasants were considerable, involving rights of justice and the ability to levy taxes, tallage and tolls, which tapped the income of the more prosperous villagers. Many lords clearly also made considerable profits from their domains by selling surplus produce.

There were changes in the way in which their lands were worked, as in northern France the quite heavy labour services of the peasants began to be commuted in return for rents. This provided the lord with money to hire casual day labourers, although often the peasants were still obliged to provide the ploughs and draught animals to perform the work. Nevertheless those families paying fixed rents in lieu of services did well during the course of the twelfth century as inflation reduced the value of their rents, and the lords suffered proportionately. By 1100 many of the major landowners were running into debt as a result of conspicuous expenditure. By 1200 the same problems were affecting numerous minor bannal lords.

The great profits made from land from the middle of the eleventh century encouraged conspicuous expenditure. For the nobility, long-distance pilgrimages and crusades, the foundation of religious houses, lavish almsgiving, expensive clothing and entertaining on an extravagant scale all became expected. But as Professor Duby shows, chivalry

exemplified as the sole outlook worthy of the perfect man characteristic forms of behaviour with regard to wealth; not to produce but to destroy; to live in lordly fashion from the ownership of land and authority over people, the only sources of income not held ignoble, and to spend on entertainment without thought for the cost.[25]

The result was an ever-increasing burden of debt. The same was true for the great religious communities which spent immense sums on large new churches, on almsgiving, on a vast body of servants to care for their members, but which failed to administer their lands efficiently, often farming them out to unscrupulous agents who took much of the profits. Abbot Peter the Venerable of Cluny tried in the mid-twelfth century to remedy such problems, which were exacerbated by the falling-off of offerings from the faithful, previously a vitally important source of income for the abbey, but he was unable to do so, and had to resort to borrowing money from Jewish and Christian merchants and even to pawning jewels and plate.

The urban communities were becoming increasingly important in the twelfth century, their tradesmen, merchants and craftsmen all aware of the importance of profit and living from the rewards of flourishing trade, both local and long-distance. By the end of the twelfth century they seem, indeed, to have overtaken the countryside in their economic vitality and importance. From about 1180 a great quickening of the economic life of France occurred. It was about now that all the agricultural improvements reached their culmination, with cereal cultivation reaching a peak and mills for grinding corn and heavy ploughs becoming widespread; but the growing pressure on land was soon to lead to land-hunger. Corn began to rise in price, exchange built up and there was an economic boom. Towns expanded rapidly, and many of the greater nobles, the territorial princes and the king began to exploit their lands directly and to manage them better, using urban techniques of trading for rural estate management and encouraging commerce, the growth of towns and the passage of merchants through their lands. The counts of Flanders and Champagne and Philip Augustus all adopted deliberate economic policies, and their ability to tap the wealth of the towns gave them a great financial advantage over the nobles in their lands and helped political centralisation to take place. Some of the other great nobles also did well from the changes, but the middling and lesser bannal lords who were unable and unwilling to change their social and economic outlook suffered considerably (5.3.1; 6.3.1).

4.3.2 Urban and rural communities: the growth of Paris

As both long-distance and local trade grew, and professional merchants emerged in increasingly large numbers, the towns and villages which housed them grew in size and prosperity. Such communities began to require and demand freedom from the ties, economic, social and judicial, which bound them to their overlords. Privileges or franchises were won by force from, or granted by, many lords to both urban and rural communities during the course of the twelfth century. Such franchises were of various kinds, economic and fiscal, bringing exemptions from tolls and dues, often in return for a fixed payment or rights to clear land or hold fairs; and political, allowing a varying amount of administrative and judicial independence. Some associations achieved the status of a commune. They were often those towns and villages whose franchises were particularly favourable, but this was not always the case, for many communities described as communes enjoyed fewer privileges than other merely enfranchised settlements.

What, then, was a commune? Clearly it had a strong political element in it, in that it regulated its own affairs. Professor Petit-Dutaillis has defined it as being in the late eleventh and early twelfth centuries an association of burgesses or villagers bound by oath. This gave them their status and their solidarity and they often fought their overlord to defend the privileges felt to be due to the group. By the end of the twelfth century a change had taken place. A commune now depended on the charter granted to it by its lord which gave it legal validity. Such charters had been given throughout the century, but where earlier they confirmed a commune which already existed, now they created it.[26]

The emancipation of towns and villages by concessions of franchises occurred very sporadically from the late tenth century and through the eleventh. Communities, including Orléans, La Chapelle-Aude, Etampes and Souvigny, were given limited privileges. Towns in areas of expanding prosperity, such as Normandy, Flanders and other parts of northern France, began to seek franchises on a wider scale during the early twelfth century. Rural franchises also began to spread rapidly at the same time. There were many parts of France where there were great tracts of uncultivated land, and where a growing population put pressure on the lands already farmed. Thus often new villages were created or new colonisers allowed to move into existing settlements in order to clear neighbouring land.

The customs of Lorris in the Gâtinais, given by Louis VI to this village and confirmed by Louis VII in 1155, proved to be a blueprint for similar rural settlements made later on.[27] The grant gave the inhabitants of the village the status of freemen and all the colonisers a licence to assart. Serfs from other settlements who remained in the village for a year and a day also earned their freedom. Each man could sell his own produce and the community was exempted from service with the royal army, from paying tallage, aid and a variety of other dues; an exception was made in the case of carrying wine, corn and wood for the king, which had to be performed once a year. In return the king was owed six pence for each house and parcel of land paid annually, and the community was subject to royal justice.

Complete judicial and political independence, a full commune, was given to some rural communities, although often, as in the case of the urban communes, only as a result of forceful action. This was the case for Gamaches, a village belonging to the abbey of Corbie which during the reign of Philip Augustus declared its independence from its overlord, the abbot, who was chased out of the village when he tried to intervene; so he took other councils. In 1219 the commune was dissolved by judicial process. At about the same time a commune at Chablis, property of Saint Martin's abbey at Tours, was quashed by the count of Champagne. Indeed, in some cases villages formed confederations in order to seek full communal privileges, and these were quite numerous in Ponthieu and Laonnois. Among the successful, one of the most powerful was known as Marquenterre, centred on the village of Quend-le-Vieux.

Guibert of Nogent, when recounting the events which took place in Laon from 1108 onwards, gives a definition of a commune, which he evidently regarded as a newfangled and unpleasant invention. It is, he says

a new and evil name for an arrangement for all (the citizens) to pay a customary head tax, which they owe their lords as a servile due, in a lump sum once a year, and if anyone commits a crime, he shall pay a fine set by law, and all other financial exactions which are customarily imposed on serfs are completely abolished. . . . [It is] a sworn association of mutual aid amongst the clergy, nobles and people.[28]

At Laon the citizens attempted to escape from the control of Waldric[29] their bishop by forming a commune. The bishop agreed to this and granted a charter, but not long afterwards he revoked it. The scenes which followed were violent, as the bishop and his supporters engaged in pitched battles with groups of burghers. Waldric and a number of nobles were killed, and the commune called on the notorious castellan Thomas of Marle for support. Guibert commented that 'the conduct of the people of Laon surpasses all the provinces of France in its abomination'.[30] Eventually, however, in 1128 a commune was constituted officially in the city and confirmed by the king.

The events at Laon were by no means isolated, for the citizens of a large number of towns both in northern France and the Midi (2.4.1) strove against the power of their lords to achieve a recognition of their communal status. Most of the savage struggles took place in towns where a bishop or major abbot was the overlord, and this might seem to mark a stronger degree of hostility towards communal institutions from ecclesiastical lords than from their lay counterparts. The impression is confirmed by pronouncements from Ivo of Chartres and others on communes as contravening canon law and the rights of the fathers. In 1139 Pope Innocent II anathematised the putative commune at Reims and urged Louis VII to suppress it. Nevertheless much of this hostility is explicable. Since the church held most of the major towns in large areas of northern France whose prosperity was increasing in this period and whose inhabitants began to seek to control their own affairs, it had more to lose than the lesser nobles who tended to control only smaller centres. And opposition from the church was by no means universal. In 1108 the bishop of Noyon founded a commune in his episcopal city of his own volition. The townsfolk of Beauvais managed to retain a commune throughout the Middle Ages, and those at Corbie and Laon lasted to the early fourteenth century. Often such successes were gained intially by an appeal to the king for support.

The attitude of lay lords to communes also varied considerably. In Flanders some of the castellans were as powerful in major centres as the bishops further south, and equally savage struggles with the townsfolk took place. At Amiens the castellan stopped the bishop from setting up a commune. At Senlis and Abbeville, by contrast, the castellans agreed to the communes and allowed their own rights to be bought out. The territorial princes and the king profited from the communal movement as far as they could. The counts of Flanders and Champagne gradually took control of it, founded communes, conceded franchises and created new settlements to encourage trade, from which they gained considerable advantages. The dukes of Burgundy granted privileges to some towns but tried to maintain their own direct control where possible; by contrast their vassals the counts of Nevers espoused the communal cause with enthusiasm, exciting the burgesses of Vézelay against their abbot. Henry II and his sons organised the Norman communes to defend the duchy, and Philip Augustus likewise used the towns for his own ends, political, military and financial (4.4.3).

The grants of franchises and the spread of the communes are documented in charters and chronicles, but they are only one part of the urban development in the twelfth century. The expansion of towns can often be best understood by the study of their surviving buildings and through using archaeological skills, and this has recently become an expanding field of interest. Laon and Paris in the twelfth century, both important cities in northern France, provide a great contrast for the urban archaeologist. At Laon the pattern of medieval development is clearly chronicled in its surviving buildings, in Paris this must for the most part be excavated and pieced together from documentary sources.

Laon occupies an important strategic position on two hills which dominate the surrounding area. One contains the more ancient settlement, a pre-Roman and Roman fortified town, a Carolingian capital, with the cathedral, episcopal palace, and ancient royal palace; parts of the surviving city walls date back to the tenth century. Within the ramparts were the ancient abbey of Saint-Jean and a considerable number of churches as well as the ecclesiastical buildings round the cathedral. This was the city which saw the communal uprising in 1112. Following it a number of changes took place: the cathedral was entirely reconstructed in the new gothic style, royal chapels were endowed and built by Louis VII and his successors, and a fine round church was built by the Knights Templar. Later the walls were reconstructed by Philip Augustus, and the thirteenth-century gateways and ramparts which survive emphasise the continuing strategic importance of the city. Philip Augustus also fortified the bourg, the second hill of Laon, where a settlement grew up around the college of canons, which was refounded by Norbert of Xanten in 1124 for Premonstratensian canons. This, Saint-Martin's abbey, was also rebuilt during the twelfth century and the fine church still survives. Laon flourished in the twelfth century as an important royal strong point, and its prosperity in this period is still attested by its buildings.

Paris[31] was in the years 1108–1226 a settlement in the process of growth and expansion. By the end of the twelfth century it was clearly the capital city of

France and had outstripped in size and prosperity all its rivals in the northern part of the kingdom. The process began in earnest under Louis VI and Louis VII. At its heart the Ile de la Cité, previously semi-rural in aspect, was built over and work was done to embellish the old cathedral. Then in 1163 a complete rebuilding was begun under the auspices of Bishop Maurice of Sully which was to make Nôtre-Dame a masterpiece of early gothic architecture and art. To the south of the cathedral lay the episcopal palace, and at the other end of the island the royal palace, also extended in this period. There were a considerable number of churches and chapels in this area, many of them of twelfth-century foundation.

On the right bank the bourgs of Saint-Gervais and Saint-Germain-l'Auxerrois were expanding, as was the Grêve area, reflecting a growing commercial life. The merchant corporation of the *marchands de l'eau* was increasingly important and profited from royal patronage (4.4.1); in 1170 Louis VII confirmed the customs they had enjoyed in his own and his father's reigns. There were other trade guilds too, for butchers, fishmongers and bakers, and shops and money changers began to proliferate. To cater for the spiritual need of this growing population parish churches were founded in considerable numbers, an example being Saint-Jacques-de-la-Boucherie, a chapel belonging to Saint-Martin-des-Champs, which was probably rebuilt and given parochial status in the middle of the twelfth century. A substantial proportion of the parish churches of central Paris, indeed, date from this period. Beyond the bourgs of Saint-Gervais and Saint-Martin-l'Auxerrois other peripheral settlements grew up around the religious houses of Saint-Martin-des-Champs and the Temple.

Similarly on the left bank of the Seine, the bourgs of Sainte-Geneviève and Saint-Germain-des-Prés expanded; the latter was an independent lordship, later bisected by the city walls. The bourg Saint-Marcel also became larger. But the growth of the left bank did not depend only on commerce, for this was the centre of the schools of Nôtre-Dame, of Saint-Victor, founded by Louis VI for canons regular, and Sainte-Geneviève, an ancient royal monastery brought into the Victorine congregation before 1150. Masters such as William of Champeaux, Peter Lombard, Peter Abelard, Robert of Melun and William of Conches attracted students in large numbers, adding to the population of the area. Around Paris, too, more outlying settlements such as Saint-Lazare and Montmartre were showing signs of vigour, as were too the bourgs of Saint-Maur-des-Fossés and Saint-Denis, the latter stimulated by the profits of the fair of Lendit.

Under Philip Augustus Paris began to show signs of becoming a large urban conglomeration rather than the series of settlements it had been before, and much of this it owed to the king himself. He showed a considerable interest in the commercial life of the city. The Champeaux, later Les Halles, became an important centre for markets which were transferred here from elsewhere in Paris. In 1181 the fair of Saint-Lazare was brought here, for example; in 1182 houses belonging to Jews in the district were demolished to make more room for the site, and in 1183 the king ordered large buildings to be erected here for a covered market. This soon became an important commercial centre. The Parisian burgesses began to play an important role in royal administration; in 1190 when the king went on crusade they were given financial responsibilities and involved in the council of regency. Trade in salt and wine was increasing rapidly and the *marchands de l'eau* did well under royal protection, becoming the virtual monopolists of river traffic.

In 1186 the king decided to have the streets of Paris paved and in 1189–90 to build a wall round the expanded city. The earlier walls encircling the Ile de la Cité, Roman in origin, enclosed only 25 acres, while Philip's walls contained 625. They had over seventy towers along their length, one of which may still be seen in the Rue Étienne Marcel. The king also had the Louvre castle constructed; excavations in the nineteenth century revealed this as a rectangular building, commanding the roads to Clichy and Chaillot. These major works gave the city powerful defences and greatly increased its security. The king's archives and his principal residence, too, were here.

In the reign of Philip Augustus the university of Paris emerged from the schools. Gradually the teachers and students formed into corporations or guilds

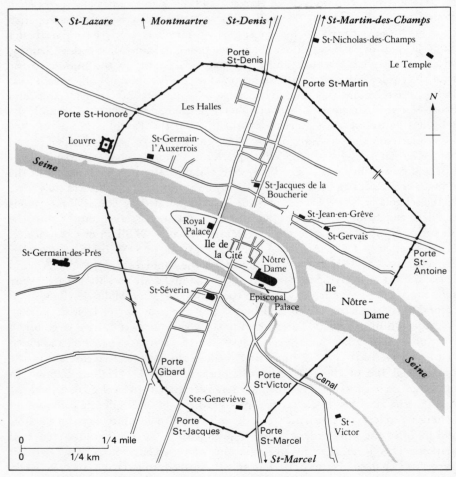

Map 4.3   Paris in the reign of Philip Augustus

which were to form the basis of the institution. It had built up a considerable reputation from about 1100, long before it was fully organised. The first college, the Dix-Huit, was founded in 1180, and in 1205 Baldwin of Flanders, emperor of Constantinople, begged Innocent III to persuade the masters and scholars of Paris to go to his lands and reform the study of letters there. Although Pope Innocent III wrote to the university in 1205, and William the Breton used the terms 'university' and 'faculty' in about 1212, these did not appear in an official record until 1221 when the faculties of theology, law, arts and medicine were constituted. At the same time the university was given its own seal.

The rapid increase of masters and scholars brought problems with it. In the 1190s Stephen of Tournai wrote to the pope complaining that 'the study of sacred letters among us are fallen into the workshop of confusion, while both disciples applaud novelty alone and masters watch out for glory rather than learning.'[32] In 1207 Pope Innocent III limited the number of theology professors to eight because

just as we believe it expedient that at the city of Paris to which there is a celebrated recourse of theologians for the study of the sacred page, there should be plenty of masters . . . so also is it becoming that their numbers be limited lest perchance . . . either their function be cheapened or less satisfactorily executed, since God made all things in number, measure and weight.[33]

In 1210 Innocent gave the university a bull recognising it as a legal corporation. The masters gradually formed a tightly knit fraternity and fought the chancellor over awarding licences to teach. The conflicts which arose were bitter and long lasting. In 1215 Robert de Courson, papal legate and a cardinal, attempted to remedy some of the problems by issuing rules regulating the length of time the students must study for and insisting that each be attached to a recognised master, prescribing a syllabus for lectures in arts and forbidding the study of Aristotle.

Following these statutes the students began to organise themselves into 'nations' for mutual protection. The king did much to encourage and protect them. In 1200 there was a violent riot when a group of German students fought the *prévôt* of Paris; several students died and the masters called on the king for redress, threatening to withdraw from the city. Philip flung the *prévôt* and his associates into prison and ruled that from henceforth the students were to be subject only to ecclesiastical justice (they were clerks). Anyone infringing their privileges would be tried by the court of the new *prévôt*, and the burgesses of Paris were enjoined to respect and protect the scholars. This generous grant did little to reduce the university to order, however, for disturbances continued well into the thirteenth century (5.3.2).

4.3.3 Orthodox and heretical religious movements

The turmoil and ferment of late eleventh- and twelfth-century French society contained within it a strong tide of monastic reform, which brought with it many new orders. The canons regular (3.4.2) had been the precursors of the movement in the eleventh century and were linked with the new spirit of renewal which was abroad. The church reforms and to some degree the new learning (4.3.4) encouraged a searching for fundamentals, a return to the *vita apostolica* (apostolic life) of the Bible and the early church, or to the *Rule of Saint Benedict* unadorned with the Aniane customs (3.4.1). Hermits fled from the world to deserted places in forests and mountains and imitating the desert fathers lived singly or in groups. Some in their enthusiasm strayed over the borders of orthodoxy into heresy, but all intended to return to the original precepts of the religious life.

By 1100 the great Benedictine monasteries appeared to many critics, both internal and external, to have become too closely bound by their elaborate liturgical rounds to concentrate fully on their spiritual life, and despite their emphasis on running their great estates, another source of distraction, many were heavily in debt. The new orders sought to avoid the traps of wordly splendour and an over-elaborate routine, and this was done in a number of different ways. The origins of almost all of the quite numerous French ones however, were similar, in offshoots from two groups of hermits living in deserted places, one in Colan in Burgundy, a second at Craon on the Maine-Brittany borders.[34]

The abbey of Molesme, an offshoot of the Colan community, led by Robert, formerly abbot of Saint-Michel at Tonnerre, attracted a number of celebrated men anxious to escape from the world. One was Bruno of Reims, who later founded the Carthusian order. Two others, Alberic and Stephen Harding became the leaders of the monastery at Cîteaux, another offshoot from Molesme founded by Robert of Molesme in 1098. Robert then returned to the parent community, leaving a small group of monks to follow the aims of poverty, seclusion and the observance of Saint Benedict's Rule to the letter. Manual labour became an important part of the daily round, and contact with laymen, including patrons and benefactors, was kept to a minimum.

In all likelihood the establishment would have remained small and obscure had not Bernard with a group of companions arrived in 1112 or 1113. Most scholars believe that his ability and enthusiasm was largely responsible for the spread of the Cistercian ideal and the expansion of the order. Men from many different walks of life, some of great eminence, were attracted to Cistercian communities which offered plain living and high thinking, a disciplined, ascetic and isolated existence far from the society for which they were interceding. In 1118 there were seven abbeys, amongst them Clairvaux, where Bernard himself was the first abbot; in 1152 there were 328 abbeys, many outside France and further expansion was forbidden. This slowed down rather than halted the growth. In 1200 there were 525 abbeys and this had increased to 694 by 1300. Bernard of Clairvaux, as the prophet and populariser of the order, came to hold an important place in the religious life of both France and western Europe. He preached the second crusade, he disputed and made friends with eminent scholars such as Peter Abelard, with Benedictine abbots such as Suger and with Peter the Venerable of Cluny, he intervened in episcopal elections against Louis VI of France and other rulers. The Cistercian success was remarkable. There was a Cistercian pope, Eugenius III, and a great number of patrons, including the French king and many of the princes, who were able and willing to provide the large tracts of land and buildings demanded by the order for new monasteries (4.5.1).

In returning to the Rule of Saint Benedict the Cistercians created a style of monasticism and organisation which was entirely new. Like many of the new orders they rejected all luxury and wealth, insisting on the utmost simplicity in food, dress and in their surroundings. Their early churches and buildings were stark and unadorned. As endowments they would accept only large tracts of land, preferably uncultivated, and finance only for building the monastery. In principle, they refused the churches, tithes, manorial dues and rights which formed an important part of the Benedictine income. Their patrons and the local bishops were to have no control over them; they were subject to Cîteaux and the pope alone, and their lands were held in free alms. Elections of the abbots were to be free. The houses were organised from the centre. Every year a general chapter of all the abbots was held to run the affairs of the whole order, and every year, too, each monastery was visited by members of its mother house. Thus uniformity and discipline were assured, and the churches and buildings which survive from this early period, such as Fontenay, illustrate this clearly. They also in their layout reveal other differences between the Cistercians and their Benedictine counterparts.

Most striking is the extra range of buildings in Cistercian monasteries for the lay brothers or *conversi*. These men were an important feature of the order for a number of reasons. Drawn from the uneducated peasantry, they carried out the bulk of the agricultural labouring necessary to sustain each community. Such an ascetic, organised existence appealed to and drew on a sector of society previously largely uncatered for in the religious life, and it responded with enthusiasm. This system also proved highly effective in economic terms, and many Cistercian abbeys became wealthy by the end of the twelfth century, provoking considerable criticism from such men as Walter Map.

Some of the precepts of the order were beginning to be relaxed by 1200 as well. At Pontigny a fine and elaborate *chevet* or apse was built at the east end of the church, though it was little ornamented; at the royal house of Barbeaux Louis VII was interred in the church in an elaborate and magnificent tomb. Soon the Cistercians were to accept parish churches, tithes and manorial dues in moderation. Nevertheless, despite some amelioration of the harshness of the Cistercian way of life, it was to retain its general characteristics of austerity, discipline and isolation throughout the middle ages.

From the hermit colony at Craon there arose other reformed congregations of religious houses. In 1109 Bernard, formerly a monk of Saint Cyprian's abbey at Poitiers, left his companions Robert of Arbrissel and Vitalis, to found the abbey of Tiron, which became the centre of a reformed Benedictine congregation not unlike Cîteaux, though lacking lay brothers. Another larger group of houses sprang from Savigny, founded in about 1112 by Vitalis and later incorporated into the Cistercian order. A third, rather different kind of community was founded by Robert of Arbrissel at the end of the eleventh century at Fontevrault. It was a monastery for lay brothers and priests who served a group of Benedictine nuns, and this was by the middle of the twelfth century a wealthy, select and aristocratic community under an ascetic rule, with a number of daughter houses. Fontevrault itself had valuable patronage from Eleanor of Aquitaine and it became the Angevin burial-house. It was, however, a double monastery, an unusual institution.

Apart from Fontevrault and the abbey of the Paraclete, founded for Heloise by Peter Abelard, and its dependent houses, there were relatively few opportunities outside a few ancient Benedictine nunneries for women in the religious life in the eleventh and twelfth centuries. Marcigny, the Cluniac nunnery founded in 1055, was created by abbot Hugh to house his mother and sister only with difficulty, and although a quite considerable number of small nunneries claiming to be Cistercian were founded in France in the early twelfth century, the Cistercian general chapter never even gave them official mention until 1191.[35] The Premonstratensian order at first contained a considerable number of nuns, but by the end of the century refused to accept women at all. In the thirteenth century opportunities began to widen further with the Béguines and minoresses (5.3.2).

The Augustinian canons (3.4.1) broke away from the Benedictine framework altogether, and their establishments were adaptable and flexible: 'they could live on comparatively little, and yet expand into affluence without disgrace.'[36] Like the monks they laid considerable stress on prayer for society, but they had a closer involvement with that society as well. They acted as parish priests, they cared for the sick — hospitals staffed by Augustinian canons were increasingly popular during the twelfth century — and they studied and taught. This adaptibility made them popular with lay patrons, especially the lesser nobility and townsfolk who could not afford to endow a major Cistercian house.

Under the general umbrella of the Augustinian rule a number of congregations formed. One was centred on Saint-Victor and had the support of the French kings and a considerable reputation for learning. Another was dependent on the house of Prémontré, founded by Norbert of Xanten, a friend of Bernard of Clairvaux, in 1120. This was on the encouragement of Pope Calixtus. Except that they began as a mixed order, the Premonstratensians were a halfway house between the Augustinians and the Cistercians. They had a harsh rule with a considerable emphasis on manual labour, but they were also encouraged to do pastoral work and to preach. By 1150 the white canons, as they were known, had become a very prestigious order.

The Carthusians were hermits living in community, their needs served by lay brothers, their way of life exceedingly harsh. Guibert of Nogent described it as follows:

They all have their own separate cells in which they work, sleep and eat. On Sunday the cellarer supplies their food, that is, bread and vegetables; the latter, which is all they eat with their bread, is cooked by each in his cell. They have water . . . from a conduit, which goes around all their cells and flows into each through interior holes in the walls. They have fish and cheese on Sundays and the chief festivals. . . . They are governed by a prior; the bishop of Grenoble, a very religious man, acts in place of an abbot or director. Although they subject themselves to complete poverty, they are accumulating a very rich library.[37]

This was the only such order to spread north of the Alps, although there were others in Italy. The mother-house, La Grande-Chartreuse which Guibert refers to, was founded in the mid 1080s by Bruno of Reims, one of the former Colan recluses and a respected scholar. The fifth prior Guigo I, an associate of both Saint Bernard and Peter the Venerable, wrote down the customs of the house, attracted a number of recruits and founded new communities, giving the order a wider recognition. Its popularity was limited by its extreme asceticism, but it was an order which kept to its ideals throughout the Middle Ages.

The same cannot be said for the religious houses dependent on Grandmont, founded by Stephen of Muret on a bare hillside near Limoges in about 1110. So extreme was the poverty and asceticism adopted by these monks that within half a century they had to modify their customs to keep their communities together. Initially the order rejected not only tithes and churches but also livestock, except for bees, and land apart from the very small estates on which each daughter house or cell stood. The choir monks lived in a community in very harsh conditions and their affairs were almost entirely in the hands of the lay brothers. The heroic reputation of the Grandmontines brought them much lay support – both the English and the French kings were major patrons of the order, and by the 1170s they were beginning to accept larger endowments. The control of the *conversi* over each community was reduced after a major revolt had been settled, and the Grandmontines moved nearer to the mainstream of the reformed monasticism of the twelfth century.[38]

Apart from the Augustinians, most of these communities fled from society in order the better to intercede for it. But in the wake of the crusades and the growth of the cult of chivalry two orders appeared which were dedicated to fighting the infidel – the Templars and the Hospitallers. They became the crack fighting troops of the crusading armies, living under a severe quasimonastic discipline, and spread widely in France during the twelfth century. The Templars were founded in Jerusalem specifically for the crusading armies. Ten years later in 1128 they adopted many Cistercian customs. The knights, who were aristocratic lay brothers, took vows of poverty, chastity and obedience. The small houses where they lived when not on campaign were served by priests and domestics. The Knights Hospitaller began as very similar to Augustinian canons but adopted many features of the Templars' organisation and became increasingly orientated towards warfare. By 1200 both orders had amassed considerable wealth, and the Templars were the bankers of both the French and the English kings.

How well did contemporaries distinguish between this multiplicity of orders? A monk or a canon (more probably the latter) from north-eastern France or the low countries wrote a treatise in the mid-twelfth century entitled *Of the different orders and professions in the church*, an explanation of 'how such servants of God differ and what the purposes of the different forms of callings are'.[39] Monks and canons cannot agree which of them is the more important, he says, but he is discussing the religious orders without pronouncing on this problem. First he looks at hermits, fewest in numbers, who live alone or in small groups imitating the life of the early church. He then discusses the monks and canons, each order of which he divides:

monks who live close to men, such as the Cluniacs . . . monks who remove themselves far from men, such as the Cistercians . . . monks who are called seculars, who take no vows . . . canons who establish themselves far from men, such as the Premonstratensians . . . canons who have their houses near the activities of men, such as the canons of Saint-Quentin (at Beauvais) . . . and of Saint-Victor . . . canons who live among men of the world and are called seculars.[40]

Although the differences between the orders are stressed, so too is the degree of removal from or closeness to the world, and the similarities between the Cistercian monks and Premonstratensian canons, for example, emerge clearly. The book is intended to clarify the confusion which has arisen since 'many kinds of callings have come into being and particularly, institutions of monks and canons differing in habit and worship are increasing',[41] clearly a necessary task. Matters were complicated further with the emergence of the friars in the thirteenth century (5.3.2).

It was possible, then, to confuse religious orders during the twelfth century, but the heretical sects became distinctive as outcasts from society. Saint Thomas Aquinas wrote that:

Heresy is a sin which merits not only excommunication but also death, for it is worse to corrupt the faith which is the life of the soul than to issue counterfeit coins which minister to the secular life. Since counterfeiters are justly killed by princes as enemies to the common good, so heretics also deserve the same punishment.[42]

The penalties which they met were often extreme and savage. In the early eleventh century isolated groups of heretics had appeared in France, especially in the decade of 1018 to 1028. A group at Orléans for example, denied Christ's human form, the validity of the sacraments, penance and marriage, and Robert the Pious intervened to crush it. The council of Charroux in 1028 condemned heresy and in the later part of the century the sources are silent on it. In the twelfth century it began to revive again in France, and heretical sects were created.

Some of the heretical movements of the early twelfth century began very much like their orthodox counterparts, groups of hermits and wandering preachers who espoused poverty and reacted against the wealth of the church and a burgeoning economic life in the towns. Robert of Arbrissel, Vitalis and Norbert of Xanten founded movements which were drawn into the framework of the traditional church; others began by criticising its wealth and moved away from its doctrines, finding themselves outside society. Henry the Monk (or Henry of Lausanne) an apostate from the religious life, began his career as a 'wild radical preacher'[43] whose extreme anticlericalism in the end brought him into heresy. He rejected the functions of the priesthood altogether, he denied original sin and prayers for the dead. His ideal of a poor wandering clergy with no sacramental functions but a preaching role he spread in northern France, in Aquitaine and Toulouse, and it was in the rich lands of the Midi that he met Peter of Bruis, another itinerant heretical preacher, some time after 1135.

Peter had begun his career as a parish priest in the Hautes-Alpes region but had rejected the authority of the Old Testament, the Fathers and the traditions of the church, denying the validity of the mass and infant baptism. He and his followers in the Alps and the Midi saw the church as a 'spiritual unity of the congregation of the faithful',[44] but at times they put forward their views through violent demonstrations. They forced monks out of their cloisters and compelled them to marry, they ate meat on fast days, they burnt crucifixes. Peter met his end at Saint-Gilles when he was thrown on his own bonfire by his opponents, but not before he had had a long and effective career as a preacher. He founded a sect known as the Petrobrusians, against whom Peter the Venerable, abbot of Cluny, wrote a powerful tract.

Peter of Bruis and Henry the Monk were the two most celebrated French heretical preachers of the earlier twelfth century, but there were others too. Odo of L'Etoile, probably a Breton nobleman, held that he was the son of God and addressed his peasant followers as angels, apostles and prophets. He died in prison after being condemned and ridiculed by the council of Reims in 1148. At Bucy-le-Long, not far from Soissons, two peasants who were eventually to be lynched brutally by a mob, began in about 1114 to preach a heresy akin to Bogomilism. This was a dualist belief which had originated in Bulgaria in the early tenth century and spread west. Its followers held that rather than one God there were two beings: God who had power in the future but none in the world, and Satan, who had created the visible world and held sway over it. Thus Christ the son of God had no human body and did not suffer. Many of the Bogomil tenets had cropped up in the heresies of the earlier twelfth century but Catharism, which began to emerge in southern France around 1150 drew more heavily from them.

A monastic letter writer from Périgord writing probably in the 1160s was the first to announce the existence of heretics in this area who followed the apostolic life, ate no meat and refused to bow before the cross. The Cathar heresy had originated in Cologne, and spread through the Rhineland, France and northern Italy, gradually developing into an organised church. Its progress in the Midi was rapid, and by 1170 the region had been divided into Cathar bishoprics; the Catholic hierarchy was as a result becoming heavily preoccupied with the problem of combating it, and major preaching campaigns were mounted by the Cistercians. But in the tolerant society of southern France, as in Northern Italy, its hold became strong (2.4.1). The small élite group in the Cathar church were the *perfecti*, both men and women, admitted by the ritual taking of the *consolamentum* to a life of strict asceticism and abstinence matching that of the harshest religious order. But they were not cut off from society, even though they had their own houses. The *perfecti* moved among the believers – the more heavily involved of their followers – and their adherents, who would attend sermons or the breaking of bread. These followers were from the higher as well as the lower ranks of society, and some nobles were important patrons of the movement. But whereas in the twelfth century there had been a considerable stress on the evangelical life, in the thirteenth dualist beliefs took an increasingly important place, and the hierarchy and organisation of the Cathar church was stressed at the expense of morality. This change, joined with the violent repression following the Albigensian crusade and later the introduction of the inquisition, contributed towards the decline of the heresy (5.3.2).

151

Meanwhile in the last years of the twelfth century another movement which, though not diverging doctrinally from the established church was regarded as heretical, had put down strong foundations in the Languedoc, the Waldenses. The founder was Waldo, a rich merchant of Lyon who gave up his fortune and his place in society to become an itinerant preacher and to spread the message of apostolic poverty. Some years later Francis of Assisi was to do the same and to be accepted and used by the church, but Pope Alexander III, after the examination of Waldo and his followers at the third Lateran council in 1179, refused them permission to preach unless welcomed by the local clergy – a very unlikely state of affairs. This Waldo's adherents refused to accept, and after clashes with local priests they were driven from the lands of the archbishop of Lyon, scattering into the Languedoc and northern Italy. The breach with the church became wider when they were named as heretics in 1184 in the papal bull *Ad abolendam*. This also removed all exemptions from episcopal authority in matters of heresy and laid down that each bishop or his representative should visit any parish where heresy was suspected at least once a year, and also that the secular authorities must cooperate in the extirpation of heresy. In the Midi, however, little was done against the Waldenses, who were well established in centres such as Albi, Limoux, Carcassonne and Montpellier by the time of the Albigensian crusade. In 1205 the French and Italian wings split, and some of the French Waldenses, such as Durand of Huesca and Bernard Prim and their followers, even rejoined the Catholic church. The rest, the preachers and their 'friends' who supported them in their austere existence, though they suffered heavy persecution in the first part of the thirteenth century, came through and were still found in small groups here in the early 1300s. Waldensianism was, indeed, probably the only twelfth century heresy to survive through from its foundation to the reformation.

4.3.4 Learning, literature and the schools in France

The twelfth century witnessed not only profound economic, social and political changes in western Europe, but also a burgeoning of artistic, literary and intellectual activity. The word 'renaissance' is often used to describe this movement, although, as with many such labels, care must be taken with it. The literal meaning of 'renaissance' is of rebirth, and here the drawback is that learning and literature were far from defunct in the eleventh century. Its usual definition at the present time is a revival of art and letters under the influence of classical models. This well sums up much of what happened in the twelfth century. Contemporaries were well aware of the influence of antiquity upon them. Bernard of Chartres, for example, declared that the men of his day were like dwarfs standing on the shoulders of the giants of antiquity; although smaller in stature, they could see further if they stayed aloft. The seeing further is important, for the writers and scholars of the twelfth century built on their classical legacy and went beyond it in many fields. If their movement was a renaissance, it was also more besides. The 'sublime meaninglessness' of the term may thus be a valuable quality.[45]

France, and particularly the Paris region, played a central and vitally important part in this movement. It was the home of a new artistic style, the Gothic (4.4.6), of important literary developments, and of a flourishing monasticism, inventive in rules and vocations and strong in spiritual fervour (4.3.3). The revival of learning took place in its schools, the monastic ones such as Bec in Normandy and Saint-Germain-des-Prés and Saint-Victor; and the cathedral schools at Paris, Reims, Laon, Orléans, and to a lesser extent, Chartres. Major libraries were built up by many ecclesiastical communities as texts, all copied by hand, were disseminated widely.

The schools of northern France concentrated on classical and scholastic disciplines and were at the centre of the revival. What were their contributions to the 'renaissance'?

Paris and the other schools of northern France were the focus of the study and development of the traditional classical disciplines: in particular the *trivium* (grammar, rhetoric and logic) and to a lesser degree the *quadrivium* (arithmetic, music, astronomy and geometry). There was a revival of interest in the teaching of logic, in which Anselm of Bec and Bernard of Chartres were major figures, and stemming from this exercises in the resolution of conflicting authorities, the development of the dialectical method, and the application of logic to other fields of study. Peter Abelard made an important contribution to the growth of scholasticism with his *Sic et Non*, a theological treatise where propositions such as that to God all things are possible and *contra* are discussed. Scholasticism reached full development with the *Summa Theologica* of Thomas Aquinas in the mid-thirteenth century. The rediscovery of Aristotle's *New Logic* and other texts increased a growing interest in logic at the expense of grammar, rhetoric and literature, and later the arrival of the works of Averroës, the twelfth-century Muslim philosopher, caused the church considerable concern over the upholding of orthodoxy. The study of theology was closely linked with that of logic; Abelard had moved theology away from the traditional glosses on the bible or the fathers. Peter Lombard's *Sentences* written in Paris around 1150 were to carry this a stage further and remained a vitally important textbook of theology for centuries.

Interest in ancient Rome was particularly strong in the early twelfth century, and had a number of different manifestations. The former monk of Cluny, Henry of Blois, bishop of Winchester, was a noted collector of antique Roman statues. The architect at Autun cathedral imitated the Roman city gate of the town in the elevation of the church. Classical Latin writings too were copied and widely studied. Many ecclesiastics regarded prose writers such as Cicero as far more suitable than Ovid or Horace; Guibert of Nogent declared that he regretted the profane poets he read in his youth. The renewed interest in classical authors went hand in hand with the study of Latin grammar, the works of Priscian and Donatus, and there was a serious interest in Latin literature. The fables of Avianus and the Carolingian Theodulus were widely studied, and writers such as the English Walter Map used collections of *exempla* or stories from their own day to considerable effect. Then there was the study of rhetoric which gradually moved away from its original basis of the study of Latin texts towards the practical art of the composition of letters, the *ars dictaminis*. The school of Orléans was noted for this skill, the fruits of which appear both in private letters and in charters. Latin poetry was also written in great profusion; some was on Christian themes such as the collection of poems and hymns by Baudri, abbot of Bourgueil and later bishop of Dol; other writers directly imitated classical models and subjects. There was also the Goliardic poem, a Latin lyric, often in a markedly satirical strain, by authors such as Hugh of Orléans. John of Salisbury, an Englishman much at home in France, who studied at Paris and perhaps at Chartres is an example of the learning of the earlier 'renaissance' at its best. Well versed in Cicero, the only twelfth-century scholar to cite Petronius, at the same time familiar with the Bible and the fathers but not averse to quoting from bogus sources, he was a historian, letter writer, political commentator and administrator of considerable ability. His letters have 'the mark of a genuine human situation, and thus they share with Heloise's an exceptional capacity to carry us into the heart of their world'.[46] This quality of 'humanism' is another aspect of the twelfth-century revival.

England rather than northern France was the leader in developments in the literature of government, but by the end of the twelfth century the French royal court was developing more sophisticated administrative records. Written instruments, charters and deeds, were becoming increasingly important as evidence, and the twelfth century saw, as well as an improvement in the style and form of the charter, flourishing schools of forgers who resolved gaps or ambiguities in their title deeds by filling them themselves. Some, such as the Saint-Denis monks were moderately skilful (4.4.6); others were less so, such as members of the order of Grandmont who were to be brought before Louis IX for their activities. The writing of history showed a marked improvement during the twelfth century, and there was a more critical approach to source materials and a better sense of chronology. The Anglo-Norman chroniclers were leaders here but other parts of northern France were quick to follow. The chronicle of Robert of Torigny, abbot of Mont-Saint-Michel, dating from later in the twelfth century is of a general European, not just a local interest, and shows a wide knowledge of current events doubtless culled from visitors to the abbey. The monks of Saint-Denis gradually emerged as the official royal historians (4.4.6). Biographies, too, improved, as is shown by examples such as Suger's *Life of Louis VI* and the work of Lambert of Ardres on the counts of Guînes. New forms appear, such as Abbot Suger's *De Administratione* and Peter Abelard's *History of my Calamities*, both in their own ways remarkable accounts. Works in the vernacular began to be written; Wace's Anglo-Norman poems and the *History of William the Marshall* prefigure works such as Joinville's prose *History of Saint Louis*.

In vernacular literature the south of France exercised a strong influence over the north. The troubadours, and the *trouvères*, their northern equivalents, were of great importance in the composition and the dissemination of the *chansons de geste*, vernacular epic poems such as the *Chanson de Roland*, recounting heroic exploits on the battlefields. At the end of the eleventh century there appeared in the south of France lyric poems, written about courtly love in the main, and also in the vernacular (2.4.1); these had spread to the north by the middle of the century. Some poets here, such as Theobald of Chartres, also wrote about courtly love. Chrétien de Troyes and Marie de France among others concentrated exclusively on the Arthurian cycle of stories, which were partly inspired by the fictional

History of the Kings of Britain by Geoffrey of Monmouth written earlier in the twelfth century. In these poems, though ideas and traditions of courtly love play their part it is not idealised blindly; human problems and human solutions also appear. Other poets such as Rutebeuf of Paris wrote in a genre known as bourgeois literature about subjects such as love and spring, or their own problems, often treating them in a satirical manner.

The schools in the south of France were closely bound up with intellectual developments in northern Italy, the focus of the revival south of the Alps. As well as making a contribution to these studies, they disseminated some of them to the north. An example is Roman law, centred at Bologna, where Justinian's great summary, the *Corpus Iuris Civilis*, was recovered in full, extensively analysed and commented on. A school of civil law was set up at Montpellier around 1160, which later became a university, and from here the study of Roman law filtered north to Orléans, Paris and the royal court, where trained civil lawyers, laymen not clerics, were to prove loyal and useful servants of the king. Under the influence of the southern French written law, the customary law of the north was codified. Again, canon law studies were centred at Bologna, where Gratian performed the same service for canon law as Peter Lombard had for theology in the *Sentences*, issued in about 1140. In this, imaginary cases are discussed with citations from various legal authorities. The study of canon law spread to the north as the growth of papal government brought with it an increase in case law, and papal decretals were collected in the northern as well as the southern centres. Likewise developments in the study of science, medicine and philosophy spread, stimulated by the recovery and translation of classical and Muslim texts, by Euclid, Galen, Hippocrates, Aristotle and Averroës, and by many others.

The south of France made an important contribution to the revival of learning, art and literature in its fine troubadour poetry, its distinctive styles of architecture (2.4.1) and its development and dissemination of legal and scientific studies; Burgundy was the centre of a monastic revival and flourishing ecclesiastical art (2.2.1). Other regions of France, too, made distinctive contributions, but at the centre of the movement was Paris and its surrounding regions. The schools here were renowned for the pursuit of classical and scholastic disciplines, abbeys such as Saint-Denis for historical writing (4.4.6). Poetry, both Latin and vernacular, flourished, and the new Gothic style of art and architecture grew up. As a result of all this activity, France became a popular land, and the Ile de France was thought of as 'sweet France', *la douce France*, by the cosmopolitan society of western Europe.[47] The French kings were popular rulers, if relatively poor, with administrators seemingly more interested in intellectual problems, life, death and eternity than the practical difficulties of government. This is certainly the impression given by the writings of Hugh of Champfleury, royal chancellor from 1150 until 1172. The ruthless efficiency of Henry II's administration was undoubtedly more effective, but had to be less personal. The Capetians, on the other hand, were able to benefit from the twelfth-century revival.

4.4 THE RISE OF THE FRENCH MONARCHY, 1108–1226

4.4.1 *The consolidation of Capetian power: the royal principality and the domain to c. 1200*

The reigns of Philip Augustus from 1200 and of his son Louis VIII constitute the critical period in the rise of the king to power in France, when political chances were seized and great conquests were made. In 1200 it was very far from inevitable that the Capetians would come to a dominant position in the kingdom in the next three decades, for royal power was still in reality a relatively localised affair. It is true that it had made some headway during the twelfth century, and this had been accompanied by the growth of royal prestige and by an increasing emphasis on the legal suzerainty of the king. But still the French king was overshadowed by the Angevins, and had no effective means of controlling a hostile coalition of princes apart from relying on his rights as overlord – and these might confine princely activities, but could not curb them. Nevertheless the gains made by Louis VI and Louis VII, although limited, were of great importance in giving the French kings an effective power-base from which to operate, and in spreading the idea of kingship more widely in the French kingdom.

Louis VI was largely responsible for the subjugation and consolidation of the royal principality, a considerable task. The greatest threat to the king's power in this area had come in the 1030s (3.3.3), but during the rest of the eleventh century the king's authority made only slow headway against the castellans of the Ile de France. Not until Prince Louis, later Louis VI, began systematically to attempt to reduce the more powerful amongst them did royal authority show real signs of recovery (3.2.4; 3.3.3). Louis continued this work as king, and as a result of his campaigns against Hugh du Puiset, Thomas of Marle and other nobles, which both Guibert of Nogent and Suger greatly praised (4.2.1), law and order were gradually brought to the principality. The local hegemony of many castellan families was broken, and the judicial and feudal authority of the king considerably augmented. The political domination of the Montlhéry-Rochefort and the Garlande families in the household was also broken. Thus Louis VI, like many of the territorial princes, fought his way back to power in his own lands, and no reversal to the king's position occurred under Louis VII.

The kings were greatly helped in this recovery by social developments in the principality, for the fortunes of many of the castellans in the area were beginning to decline. Many noble estates were divided on the deaths of their holders, the heirs taking them in *parage*, a custom of the area. The eldest son retained the most substantial portion and overall lordship, the younger sons were given smaller portions. In 1209 this 'custom' of France was abolished by the king, and gave way in most cases to outright division (although the lords of Montmorency continued to use *parage*), but both processes resulted in the disintegration of some noble holdings. But from the mid-twelfth century parts of fiefs were often sold off to meet cash crises, further weakening some nobles against the newly aggressive monarchy. And the castellans were gradually brought into closer feudal dependence on the king as chains of vassals began to form in the area, culminating in the sovereign.[48]

Similarly the counts of Champagne, Anjou and Flanders, and the dukes of Burgundy, amongst other princes, built up their authority in their own lands, and backed up conquest and growing overlordship with a developing administration. Louis VI extended the system of *prévôtés* which had appeared in his father's reign. Under him these administrative units were found at Montlhéry and Châteauneuf, Moret, Samois and Yèvre-le-Châtel, bringing the total to thirty or so. Under Louis VII more *prévôtés* emerged in the Gâtinais and also in outlying areas of domain rights such as Berry, the Mâconnais, around Nevers and Châlons-sur-Marne. In some important centres the king associated two or more of these officials; in 1154 he had three in Paris, the *prévôté* which reverted to him from the Riche family; and two at Bourges, Étampes, Sens and Orléans. In Senlis and Compiègne, however, these officials were suspended in favour of the communes.

Under Philip Augustus more *prévôtés* again appeared, bringing the total number to between forty and fifty in the period before the conquest of Normandy. Some already existed in lands acquired by the king, such as Issoudun, Graçay and Meulan. But by the end of the twelfth century a new kind of royal administrator had also begun to appear, the *bailli*. Philip first used them as early as 1184.[49] At first these were itinerant officials with judicial and financial functions sent out in groups of three or four by the king on temporary missions, to hold inquests and assizes. They had many similarities with, and were probably based on Henry II of England's itinerant justices. By the end of Philip Augustus's reign they held authority in given areas, and this probably developed from their financial functions. They supervised groups of *prévôtés*, heard appeals from their courts, and took over many of their sources of revenues, and in addition to this levied regalian rights, tallage, scutage and forest dues on the king's behalf *Baillis*, with specific areas of jurisdiction, *bailliages*, already existed in Normandy before Philip's conquest, and the king extended their local powers when he suppressed the office of seneschal in the duchy; indeed their introduction on a large scale into the royal principality had taken place in the 1190s when the royal seneschal's office was suppressed. The seneschals of the Languedoc were not, however, replaced.

But what of the royal domain, the resources of the monarchy? Louis VI increased this to some extent, and his major gains were summed up by the continuator of Aimon. 'From Fulk, viscount of Gâtinais, he bought Moret and Le-Châtelet-en-Brie, Boësses, Yèvre-le-Châtel and Chambon. And he also acquired Montlhéry and Châteaufort.'[50] Furthermore he took Chevreuse and Corbeil, and to the south, Meung-sur-Loire, Châteaurenard, and Saint-Brisson. Louis VII by contrast made fewer gains and some losses. By virtue of his marriage to Eleanor of Aquitaine he held the duchy from 1137 until 1152, although he rather unnecessarily styled himself as duke of Aquitaine, and these lands were never viewed as forming part of the royal lands. He gave away the Norman Vexin to his daughter Margaret as a dowry when she married the young king, Henry II's son, in 1160, and he granted Dreux to his own brother Robert. On a smaller scale he gave a castle at Saint-Clair-sur-Epte, built on the lands of the abbey of Saint-Denis back to the monks, though probably all he lost in effect was the burden of its upkeep. He made other alienations early in his reign, but later on he gained much more in small parcels. The latter included parts of Le Moulinet, Lorrez-le-Bocage and Préaux and a number of vills, some held in *parage*, as were also the great estates of Bichereaux and Flagy. A number of other important pieces of land, for example at Le Châtelet-en-Brie and Saint-Germain-des-Bois, first appear as part of the domain in Louis' reign, although this may be a reflection of improved documentation rather than acquisition.

Nevertheless, unlike in the reign of Louis VI, the geographical extent of the recorded domain under Louis VII widened – in Burgundy, with the gains of Saint-Pierre-le-Moutier, Tournus and other land following the royal campaigns in the area; in the Sens, Bourges and Orléans areas; and to the north with the acquisition of lands between Chaumont-en-Vexin and Mantes. The ecclesiastical domain also increased somewhat; Louis VI gained control of the bishopric of Arras and Louis VII of Autun, Mende and Agde. The number of royal monasteries also grew.[51]

In the first twenty years of his reign Philip Augustus also made a number of important gains. In 1183 he intervened in the Flemish succession and in 1185 by the Treaty of Boves took the counties of Amiens and Montdidier, the castellanies of Roye, Choisy-au-Bac and Thourotte, and rights of inheritance to Vermandois and Valois, which in fact came to him in 1213. In 1191 Philip of Alsace, count of Flanders died in the Holy Land and the king took Artois with the *mouvance* of the Boulonnois and Ternois on behalf of Louis, his own infant son, whose mother, Isabella of Hainault, had been an heiress of the Flemish count. These areas did not become part of the royal lands until 1223 when Louis VIII became king; meanwhile Philip kept firm control over them. He also acquired other towns and counties for himself, as when after 1184 he was granted Montargis by Pierre de Courtenai, and when in 1187 he took over the county of Tournai from the bishop. He also confiscated the county of Meulan from Robert IV, ally of the Plantagenets. From the last, too, he gained some castles and lands. He took Gisors in 1193, and in 1196 was acknowledged as holding Vernon, Gaillon, Paçy-sur-Eure, Ivry and Nonancourt. Nevertheless by 1198 he was prepared to relinquish all these save Gisors, and he was also facing problems with his gains in Berry and Flanders. Richard I's death in 1199 allowed him to keep his former conquests, and in 1200 he took Evreux and Issoudun. These important lands were sacrificed by John as the price of Philip's support, and this enabled him also to consolidate his gains in northern France. This increase in power was as nothing compared with the conquests after 1204 which radically altered the whole balance of power in the French kingdom (4.4.7–8).

There is a valuable list of towns and castles in the king's domain in the first register of Philip Augustus.[52] This was drawn up in about 1204–06 and it gives a clear idea of the geographical extent of the major centres held by the king and the nature of his rights in each. Philip had domainial rights in thirty-two towns and well over a hundred castles. In the list of towns it is clearly specified whether the king had the right of procuration, military service or regalia, or two, or all three of these. The list of the archbishops and bishops of the whole kingdom which follows shows that the king controlled a substantial proportion of these. In addition twenty-nine royal abbots, plus those of all the black monk (Benedictine) houses of Normandy are mentioned. These lists, and the great catalogue of royal vassals which follows, give a precise idea of royal rights following the collapse of the power of the English king in France, and show the extent to which they had been augmented by Philip's conquests. Philip was further to expand his power in Vermandois, Valois, Clermont-en-Beauvaisis, Beaumont-sur-Oise, Alençon and Nogent, and Louis VIII, in Poitou, at Saint-Riquier and Doullens, Perche, at Beaucaire and Carcassonne. ∴ *Royal domain = much stronger power base, helps monarchy of C12th to flourish.*

4.4.2 The royal household and royal administration

For most of Louis VI's reign the royal household changed very little in its composition from Philip I's time. Royal charters tended to be witnessed by local men, often of a moderate social standing, and by the great royal officials.[53] But as royal power grew, the great men of the kingdom were attracted back to court to act as royal counsellors and endorse royal decisions. Count Raoul of Vermandois, a relative of Louis VI who occupied the office of seneschal in his reign, was the sole layman of any consequence in attendance on this king. He was succeeded under Louis VII by Theobald, count of Blois, a relative of his third wife Adela of Champagne. Louis also raised several relatives of his own and of Adela to leading ecclesiastical positions (4.5.1). Furthermore after about 1150 there were a number of occasions when a large gathering of leading nobles and ecclesiastics assembled at the royal court (4.4.5). The routine work of administration was meanwhile being taken over by officials of more humble origins, who gradually replaced the dynasties of overmighty castellan and knightly families from the royal principality in their places at court.

The great officials who were pre-eminent in the household from about 1080 until 1127 were drawn from the castellan families of the Ile de France. The Montlhéry-Rochefort family which monopolised the office of seneschal until the end of Philip I's reign was descended from nobles who in the late tenth and early eleventh centuries had carved out bannal lordships based both on allodial holdings and benefices. By the late eleventh century they were well established with powerful connections both inside and outside the Ile-de-France. But after Louis VI's divorce from Lucienne de Rochefort in 1107 they were replaced by the Garlande family, Anseau, Stephen, William and Gilbert, who appropriated most of the great offices from 1107 until 1127. Stephen, chancellor in 1107, became seneschal as well in 1120, in succession to Anseau and William; and from 1112 Gilbert was butler. There was also the Senlis or de la Tour family. Guy of Senlis was royal butler from 1108–12, before Gilbert of Garlande.

These families originated not as castellans but as knights from the *milites* of the great cities and castles, who in the later eleventh century built up very considerable wealth through the royal service, but who had no allodial holdings at all. But these *nouveaux riches* officials started, like their predecessors, to dominate the household, and tried to consolidate their place in the entourage, until in 1127 Louis VI dislodged the Garlande family, and then began to undermine the practical importance of these offices. This was done first by refusing to recognise them as hereditary and then by giving them an honorific ceremonial significance. After this some of them were filled by the territorial princes. The success of this is attested to by the treatise of Hugh de Clers on the seneschalship of France, written in about 1158 to put forward the claims of Henry II of England, all bogus, to the office and insisting that he be given the highest honours at the French court. This is a far cry from the domination of the court by the Garlande family forty years before. The office of seneschal was actually held by Raoul, count of Vermandois, and then Theobald, count of Blois, in the later years of Louis VII, but was suppressed in 1191. The chancellor's office was left vacant from 1172 to 1179 and 1185 to 1223, and then filled in 1223–27 by Warin, bishop of Senlis, before being quashed again. The great officials were replaced at court by their lesser counterparts, the constable, butler and chamberlain, drawn on the whole from the lesser nobility of the Ile de France; some made their offices hereditary but were unable quickly to reach the dominant position or noble rank of their predecessors in the early twelfth century. They did, however, benefit in the longer term from their royal service; Walter the Chamberlain's family profited from a valuable marriage to the heiress of Nemours, and was endowed with substantial pensions; later three of his sons became bishops.

As the great officials declined in power the kings drew more and more on men of low birth to carry out routine administrative tasks. These were normally clerks who made their way in the royal service, and were known as *curiales*, court officials. The household knights, paid by fief-rents rather than lands, were their secular equivalent and played an important part in fighting the castellans under Louis VI. The royal clerks served in the royal chancery as notaries and scribes and had access to livings in the royal gift; they formed the core of the royal bureaucracy. Many were attached to the royal chapels which the Capetians founded or refounded in abundance during the twelfth and thirteenth centuries. Under Philip Augustus their importance increased and one family from this background, the la Chapelle, became the king's close advisers; by the late twelfth century burgesses also began to appear as counsellors to the king.

Early in the century, Guibert of Nogent described such new royal administrators as *viles personae*, and Aubri of Trois-Fontaines found Walter, chamberlain at the end of Louis VII's reign, more noble in deeds than birth. Abbot Suger, righthand man of both Louis VI and Louis VII, was of humble stock. But such men, usually clerics, raised by the king and usually holding no specific or specialised offices, did not pose the same kind of challenge to royal independence as had the great castellans or the newly but lavishly enriched knightly families. They were part of a new and slowly expanding royal administration.

In the early years of the reign of Philip Augustus the young king was under the influence of Count Philip of Flanders and then Count Henry of Champagne; later such territorial princes had less direct importance. In 1200 Giles of Paris complained that the king was inclined only to take counsel from the few men he tolerated in his court, but while there were only limited and varying opportunities for a few princes to act as close advisers of the king, the great dukes, counts and bishops continued to return to court regularly on important occasions to act as the king's councillors in the more formal sense (4.4.5). The work of administration was left as before to the royal clerks and chamberlains, and by 1213 a group of administrators, Walter the Younger, the chamberlain, whose family was of humble origins; Bartholomew of Roye and Henry Clément, both royal knights; and Warin, a king's clerk and knight hospitaller, and bishop of Senlis from 1213, had emerged as the king's close counsellors. The last remained constantly by the king's side and was his principal adviser in the later part of the reign.

Considerable strides forward in the development of royal administrative machinery seem to have been made by these men. From Philip's reign comes the first surviving royal account; the first full lists of royal domain rights and military service; the setting up of a central royal archive; the compilation of registers of royal documents: all these are signs of a growing bureaucracy. The charter, the basic instrument of government, shows a far greater degree of sophistication and uniformity, perhaps under English influence. Some of the underlying developments, such as the evolution of the system of royal accounting, may have taken place over a long period of time, but even allowing for the possibilities of distortion caused by the first appearance of several new kinds of records in the first half of Philip's reign, still this emerges as a period of great progress, which has been compared by Professor Hollister and Professor Baldwin with the reign of Henry I of England in its innovative importance.[54]

4.4.3 Communal privileges and royal defence

The establishment of order in the royal principality and the extension of the royal domain seem to have increased considerably the resources of the crown. The Ile-de-France and the surrounding areas were probably the wealthiest in France, and they provided a valuable financial as well as political base for the French king. But he was faced by almost continuous and increasingly expensive warfare, and sought for means to harness this wealth, to increase it, and to use it against his enemies. A number of new ways of exploiting it were found, many of which also had useful political and military consequences, or valuable economic repercussions. One such scheme was the encouragement of land clearance and the foundation of rural franchises and communes.[55] The customs of Lorris granted by Louis VI were the blueprint for the enfranchisement of villages, giving the peasants considerable autonomy but reserving justice for the king and allowing him profit (4.3.2).

In Louis VI's reign the customs were granted to La Chapelle-la-Reine and Moulinet as well as Lorris, while under Louis VII they went to a considerable number of new and existing communities. Between 1150 and 1180 as the forests of Othe and Orléans were cleared, they went to about forty villages in the Gâtinais including Sceaux-en-Gâtinais and Bois-Girard. New settlements were created south of the Loire and in the forests of Compiègne and Cuise and around both Saint-Germain-en-Laye and Laon. A number of agricultural serfs in existing villages and towns were freed; in 1180 for example, Orléans was given an important charter to this effect. Other villages were exempted from paying taxes and dues which were a burden on their inhabitants but difficult to collect. Some few villages achieved the status of a full commune, but these were rare. In 1174 Louis VII granted this privilege to a group of villages round Anizy-le-Château near Laon, but though this was during an episcopal vacancy and intended to counterbalance the bishop's powers, several such communes did emerge in the area. Philip Augustus was also generous to rural communities in the first part of his reign.

Louis VI and Louis VII were, it seems, cautious about granting full communal liberties, but they were also, like the counts of Flanders and Champagne, anxious to stimulate commerce in the towns as well as in the countryside. Thus they made many grants of the right to hold fairs and markets. Louis VII allowed these to take place in Poissy, Senlis, Meulan and other centres. The kings, and particularly Philip Augustus, who founded the market at Les Halles in 1183, encouraged the development of Parisian trade and commerce. They gave important privileges to the trade guild of the *marchands de l'eau*, which was allowed to supervise the river traffic on the Seine and to levy heavy tolls. In 1214 Philip Augustus allowed money to be exacted from boats carrying certain produce, including wine, salt and grain, to pay for extending port facilities in Paris. He also regulated the sale of wine and salt, and after his conquest of Normandy confirmed the pact drawn up between the merchants of Rouen and Paris. He gave the Parisian burgesses some political power as well, involving a group of them in the running of the kingdom while he was on crusade. Other towns besides Paris profited from exemptions from certain dues and tolls to attract trade, in return for a fixed payment, as at Compiègne in 1179. Individual burgesses could be brought into these franchises at the king's will; the earliest surviving example of this is for 1153, when Louis VII admitted Ernoul Perel into the enfranchised community at Orléans.

Key towns in the royal principality, such as Paris and Orléans, were allowed franchises but not the full political independence of a commune. In the lands under royal influence Louis VI allowed a commune at Dreux and Louis VII at Senlis only. However, outside these areas the kings encouraged a number of communal movements, often against bishops or abbots, as with Louis VI at Laon, Soissons, Noyon and Corbie and Louis VII at Mantes, Beauvais and Compiègne. Philip continued and expanded this policy. In the royal lands Etampes lost its charter but Chaumont, Pontoise, Poissy and Montreuil gained them; the king also granted the citizens of Sens a commune. Outside this area he confirmed many of the communes founded by the counts of Amiens and Ponthieu, and by the Angevins. He created new communes in the Vexin, in Normandy at Les Andelys and Nonancourt, and in Picardy at Crépy-en-Valois, Hesdin, Bapaume, Filièvre, Montdidier, Athies, Cappi, Péronne. It was important to gain the loyalty of the burgesses in all these areas. In Normandy he had merely to confirm and extend liberties on the pattern of the *Établissements de Rouen*, a set of privileges granted by the Plantagenets. In Artois, Vermandois and Valois he took the initiative.

The grants of communal privileges and franchises had a wider significance than the building of political support, for financially they could be of considerable value to the king; many of Philip's charters granting privileges stipulate that a substantial rent be paid to the king in return. Some towns acquired important military functions; a number of fortified towns on the borders of the royal lands with Normandy and Flanders were given full communal privileges, a recognition of their strategic importance, and were expected to give military service in return. While he was willing to accept monetary aid instead of contingents of troops from many towns, Philip was careful to maintain the urban militia in areas where it was needed. In 1188 the communal troops of Mantes held out bravely against Henry II, an illustration of the sense in this policy.

Bands of mercenary soldiers had been used on a large scale by Henry II and his sons against Louis VII, and Philip Augustus began soon after his accession to build up specialist mercenary corps which soon became a vitally important part of the French army. The king followed the Plantagenets in employing not only individual stipendiary soldiers, but also whole companies of mercenaries. These normally came either from outside the French kingdom, from Navarre or Germany, or most frequently from the Flanders, Hainault and Brabant area, on account of which they were often called Brabançons, and they enjoyed a fearsome reputation for their skill on the battlefield and their violent plundering and burning off it. Some of their captains, like Richard I's Mercadier, built up positions of considerable power. Cadoc, for example, was a mercenary leader both trusted and rewarded by Philip Augustus; he defended Gaillon against Richard I in 1195 and subsequently became its castellan, holding in addition the Norman fief of Tosny. Later he became *bailli* of Pont-Audemer.[56] Mercenaries were expensive and so too were castles. Philip constructed nothing on the scale of Richard's Château Gaillard on the Seine, but he spent a great deal on defending the Vexin forts, as the remains of the fortifications he had built at the castle of Gisors still testify.

Besides using mercenaries Philip continued to rely heavily on feudal contingents and dues for his armies. In 1194 he had drawn up for him a full list of military service due to him from the *prévôtés*, towns, villages, communes and abbeys of the royal domain, a document known as the *prisée des sergéants*.[57] The service is assessed in terms of soldiers and baggage carts. The former add up to over 5,000, and in addition the totals for the Flemish areas belonging to Prince Louis are listed; these may have been added around 1200 when the *prisée* was copied into Philip's registers. Not all the communities had to pay service in men: two towns, Arras and Beauvais, were allowed the alternatives of furnishing a contingent or paying a subsidy; others, including Orléans, Étampes, Paris and Bourges were assessed just for the subsidy. The money thus due totalled about £12,000 *parisis*. By 1202–03, a year for which the first surviving royal account is extant, these subsidies had been extended further. The going rate appears to have been £3 for a soldier and about £13.10s for each wagon per quarter. The account also reveals considerable expenditure by the king on stipendiary troops, on heavy knights, mounted sergeants who formed a light cavalry force, mounted archers and footsoldiers, as well as the troops of mercenaries. Many of these soldiers were on long contracts, and they were paid by the local royal *bailli* or *prévôt*.

4.4.4 Royal resources

The French kings needed to find new ways to tap the wealth of the principality and the kingdom, and during the twelfth century began to resort to various novel taxes. Feudal aids began to emerge as an important source of revenue; the first recorded one was levied in 1137 to cover the expenses of the future Louis VII when he went to Aquitaine to marry Eleanor. Louis VII levied another in 1147 to help to pay for his crusade, and this marks an extension of the incidents under which the tax could be raised. Philip Augustus did likewise in 1184–88, and Louis IX was to use the crusading aid to supplement the revenues conceded to him by the papacy. These latter were of considerable importance to the royal budget, and mark the cooperation of pope and king in the extraction of wealth from the French church.

In 1188 Philip Augustus levied the Saladin tithe to finance his crusade, but met with so marked an opposition from the clergy that he was forced to stop. In both 1211 and 1218, however, he levied twentieths to finance the 'crusade' in the Languedoc with less opposition. Another tithe was raised in 1226 for Louis VIII's campaign in the south. But these could only be used to fight wars sanctioned by the church, and to meet the costs of other campaigns different expedients were needed. Fighting the Angevins was an expensive business and in the 1180s and 1190s Philip's need for funds became acute. The Jews suffered persecution and heavy mulcting, even though in 1206 the king was to regulate their financial operations and canalise their revenues into the royal purse. A thousand marks was extracted by Philip from Saint-Denis in 1186, and in 1194 the king plundered the churches under Richard I's protection and raised considerable sums as well as marked hostility. Even in accounts as favourable to the king as Rigord's, the opposition to Philip's mulcting activities in the royal principality emerges clearly. But these were as necessary to him as similar measures were to the Angevins. Gerald of Wales declared:

One may therefore ask how King Henry II and his sons, in spite of their many wars, possessed so much treasure. The reason is that as their fixed returns yielded less they took care to make up the total by extraordinary levies, relying more on these than on the ordinary sources of revenue.[58]

The same holds true of the French monarchy. The bulk of the domain revenues were fixed, and although it is quite clear that the receipts from the principality increased in Philip's reign, as royal resources expanded and became better organised, still they were not sufficient to meet the king's needs. Nor did he find as many ways of expanding his revenues as Richard I. The point is worth emphasising since it has been customary to contrast the wealth of the Capetians in the 1190s with the overstrained resources of the Plantagenets; in fact both turned to the same expedients to raise extra money and both met with a considerable degree of opposition.

All discussion of royal resources under Louis VII and Philip Augustus are based on information from the royal account roll for 1202–03. The original document was lost in the course of the eighteenth century, but not before Brussel had produced an edition of it in 1725.[59] The text is interesting not only for its early date, but also because the accounts for all three financial terms of the year, Purification, Ascension and All Saints, have survived, whereas the quite numerous fragments from the later thirteenth century often only cover isolated terms. It also demonstrates that the royal finances were operating by a well-established system; indeed some of the pensions allowed to monasteries go back into the mid-twelfth century. In 1170 Louis VII gave the Hôtel-Dieu at Senlis a grant of £10 *per annum* in perpetuity and this was still being paid in 1202–03.[60]

We know something of how the accounts were rendered from the ordinance drawn up by Philip Augustus when he was preparing to go on crusade in 1190. This details the arrangements for the administration of the kingdom. It specifies that Adam, one of the royal clerks, shall receive all the money due to the king three times a year at the Paris Temple. This shall be done in the presence of six burgesses from Paris, and, probably, also a member of the royal household. Adam shall keep written accounts of the treasure, which shall be stored in large chests. The Templars and the king's regents shall keep the keys.[61] Royal accounts continued to be presented at the Paris Temple until the early fourteenth century, and even in 1190 this may not have been a new custom. The accounts detail both receipts and expenditure, and come under the broad headings of *prévôtés*, *bailliages*, sergeants-at-arms and marches (the revenues of and expenditure on the Vexin forts of John occupied by Philip). The first two represent the normal receipts of the French kings, while the two last give a clear indication of scale of expenditure on the war against the Plantagenets. Overall the receipts from the *bailliages* and *prévôtés*, the editors of the account estimated, amounted to over £106,000 *parisis*. About £26,000 was raised for the sergeants-at-arms, an extraordinary revenue, and incidentally a total very similar to that of the *prisée des sergéants* (4.4.3). In addition, amongst other receipts a sum of £68,000 or so was raised to finance the war effort and appears under the marches accounts,[62] bringing the overall total receipts to £198,000 *parisis* or so. Professors Lot and Fawtier thought that if the extra war revenues were discounted, the ordinary revenues of the king still amounted to more than the Plantagenets could raise, and the French domain yielded more than all the Angevin lands put together. Philip's victory over John in 1204 was, they believed, due to sound finances.[63]

This is, however, a rash assumption. Precise calculations about the size of royal incomes in the Middle Ages are impossible to make. Most of the evidence is missing, and what there is can only present a partial impression. For the English kingdom a full series of royal accounts, the pipe rolls, survive for the year 1129–30 and then in almost continuous sequence from 1155 onwards. But attempts to compute the annual revenues of the kings from this source have proved hazardous and controversial, since it is by no means clear how much of this money passed straight through the royal chamber rather than through the exchequer where the accounts were drawn up, thus going unrecorded.[64] How much more difficult it is to speculate about the finances of a monarchy for which the first isolated account does not appear until the early thirteenth century. These problems have not deterred historians, however, and this is perhaps understandable, for the problem is a crucial and central one in our interpretation of the rise of the Capetian monarchy.

Later in the thirteenth century Conan, provost of Lausanne, recorded the substance of certain conversations he had had with royal officials when he had been studying in Paris during the 1220s. They had told him that Philip Augustus

had enriched the kingdom and increased it beyond what can be believed; since although King Louis, his father, did not leave him an income, as the officials of the kingdom used to relate, except for 19,000 *livres*, he left to Louis, his son, a revenue of 1,200 *livres parisis* a day, and (as the said Conan, provost of Lausanne, who was present at the interment heard from intimates of the king and from common report), the said King Philip left in his will from the money he had collected for the aid of the land of Jerusalem, 700,000 marks for the defence of the kingdom of France and for the maintenance of his son, Louis.[65]

This statement, allowing for a degree of exaggeration in the figures, seems not unreasonable. For while in 1202–03 Philip's ordinary revenues were perhaps £100,000 *parisis*,[66] in the years after this the king made important conquests and levied aids and tithes on an unprecedented level. His difficulties in the 1180s and 1190s, which led to various exactions, also suggest that the domain revenues left to him by his father were not sufficient for his needs. By taking Normandy and Anjou, both wealthy provinces, from the English kings, it seems very likely that he tipped the financial as well as the political balance of power.

This is not a widely accepted view. A number of historians have maintained that Louis VII and in particular Philip before 1204 were wealthier than the Plantagenets, whose resources were becoming overstrained.[67] It is clear that both kings resorted to extraordinary means of raising money, but it still seems very unlikely that Richard, who held England (long famed for its silver), the well administered duchy of Normandy, an increasingly centralised Anjou and the duchy of Aquitaine, which the chronicler Ralph of Diceto found to overflow 'with riches of many kinds',[68] was overshadowed financially by someone whose wealth was based on the French royal principality alone. The thirteenth-century chronicler of Béthune recognised that Richard was far wealthier than Philip, and more recently Professor Powicke suggested that 'in Richard's hands, [his] military and financial forces . . . were potent weapons in checking Philip'. Professor Petit-Dutaillis, too, stated that 'Richard maintained a superiority in resources which would have given him the opportunity, had he lived, to crush his rival'.[69]

The idea of the great wealth of the Capetians before 1204 was based in large measure on a misreading of Conan's text. For Professor Waitz, when transcribing the text, instead of 'except 19,000 livres', (*nisi 19 milia librarum*) wrote '19,000 livres a month' (*mense 19 milia librarum*).[70] This error, pointed out by Professor Benton, implies that Louis VII had an annual income of £228,000 a year. The rest of the passage says that Philip Augustus increased Louis's income to £438,000 a year. This is an enormous sum, but it is possible that it is not far from the truth for 1223, for in 1286–87, the next year for which a full account survives, royal receipts from this source alone total about £605,000 (Table 6.1). The totals for individual terms earlier in the century are also quite high: £56,000 for Candlemas 1226, £101,000 for Ascension 1238. And besides the money collected at the Temple the king had other receipts, the rents collected in kind, a list of which first appear in 1227, and the revenues which went straight into the royal household.[71] By the 1280s the expenses of this body amounted to between £150,000 and £200,000 *parisis* a year (Table 6.2), though it is not clear how much came in directly. Nevertheless we are talking about large sums of money; and in these terms the £228,000 a year attributed to Louis VII, albeit based on a misreading, might not at first sight look too ridiculous. Thus many accounts of French royal finances such as that of Professor Pacaut have suggested that Louis VII's income was somewhere around this mark.[72] Professor Fawtier, who also accepted this figure, further asserted that the revenues from the royal domain remained virtually unchanged from the time of Hugh Capet to that of Louis VII.[73]

If both these propositions are accepted then the political weakness of the early Capetians is almost incomprehensible. If Conan's estimate of Louis VII's annual income of £19,000 *parisis* is also taken into consideration (though this is probably an underestimate), but the second proposition, that of broadly unchanged domainial receipts is accepted, then the need of Louis and Philip Augustus to raise extra taxes for crusades and warfare is more readily understood. But how can we explain Conan's figure for Louis VII's income? In the 1202–03 royal account, Philip Augustus's total recorded receipts are far greater than £19,000, amounting to almost £200,000, and although they were inflated by military expenditure and to a lesser extent by the conquests he had already made, still the discrepancy with Conan's account is too great. But Professor Pacaut has calculated that Louis VII made about £20,000 a year from the regular income of the domain,[74] and in the early fourteenth century Philip IV was attributed with £18,000 from the same source. It is possible that the provost of Lausanne left out Louis VII's extraordinary revenues but added those of Philip Augustus, which were enormous, further to heighten the contrast.

While any estimate of Louis VII's income must remain tentative, all the evidence seems to point to a fairly low figure, perhaps between £30,000 and £60,000 a year. This level of income would mean that 'the Ile-de-France was producing more than most if not all the feudal principalities of the kingdom, though less than the combined estates of Henry Plantagenet', a not unreasonable assumption since documentary evidence shows that Henry II took very approximately £25,000 sterling (worth about twice the parisian pound) from England alone each year, that in 1204 Normandy yielded about £20,000 Angevin, and that in 1187 Flanders produced about £10,000.[75] This interpretation explains Conan's statement that Philip enriched the kingdom almost beyond what could be believed. His total estimate of Philip's income may well be an exaggeration, but the great increase which clearly did take place enabled the Capetians to maintain their military superiority. This picture also seems to fit in with what we know of the kings' own attitudes to their wealth. Louis VII's declaration to Walter Map that the king of England lacked for nothing, but that in France they only had bread, wine and good cheer is well known, and Map himself said it was true (4.2.2). According to Rigord, Philip

Augustus was convinced that his predecessors had lost lands because of their poverty, which prevented them from raising a strong army in time of need. He was not himself willing to accept this, and found new ways to tax and mulct his lands and vassals. This enabled him to fight back, and by the end of Louis VIII's reign the crown had gained by conquest sufficient resources to give it financial superiority within the French kingdom.

4.4.5 The king in the kingdom

The years 1108–1226 saw two political developments in France which are at first sight contradictory; the expansion of royal power in the kingdom, slowly up to about 1200, then rapidly, and the political consolidation of the principalities. It might seem that the latter would hamper the former, and it is true that in order to increase their own lands and resources in any major way the Capetians had actually to conquer other principalities; but factors such as the achievement by many princes of feudal superiority in their lands, the growth of feudal bonds and the development of hierarchies, also brought the princes into a closer dependence on the monarchy. For most of the twelfth century this restricted their real activities very little, but Philip Augustus was able considerably to profit from it. Furthermore, when he captured Normandy and Anjou, the degree of ducal and comital control already built up there allowed him to take them over more easily.

Like the royal lands, many of the great principalities were gradually subjugated during the twelfth century as the princes imposed law and order and introduced or strengthened their administrations. Feudal hierarchies began to form. Some states, like Normandy and Flanders were already relatively well organised; in others, Champagne, Blois, Anjou, Toulouse, Aquitaine and Burgundy, this process took place with a varying degree of speed. The collection of principalities built up by Henry II and his sons blurred the distinctions between Normandy, Anjou and Maine and Aquitaine to some minor extent, but it is clear that these states, like the others in France, were in the process of developing their own distinctive customs and laws. The princes promulgated ordinances in their lands, as when Charles the Good instituted the public peace in Flanders between 1119 and 1127; when in about 1178 Philip of Alsace, count of Flanders regulated the *bailliages* in his lands by ordinance; and when in 1185 Count Geoffrey laid down the rules for noble inheritance in Brittany. Feudal assemblies, which may be seen as the forerunners of the provincial estates of the fourteenth century, met to sanction princely decisions, and princely courts such as the exchequer in Normandy or later the *Grands Jours* in Champagne had a growing competence to decide feudal and other matters. The princely households like the royal household contained lesser functionaries, often of humble birth, as well as nobles who from time to time counselled the prince. Princely finances were organised and developed, and here again Flanders and Normandy were precocious, as the Flemish accounts for 1187 and the Norman exchequer rolls show clearly. Here too was the basis for the future provincial financial bureaux. In many cases the princes continued to control the church in their lands, although in this the powerful prince-bishops of Brittany, or the many independent monastic houses and the limited regalian powers of the dukes of Burgundy, formed a contrast to the Norman prelates, strongly controlled by the dukes.[76]

The relationship of the king and the princes was, as in the eleventh century, crucial to royal power in the kingdom, and the changes served to strengthen the king's authority as suzerain.* In his *De administratione*, Abbot Suger emphasised that the king could do homage to no one. Louis VI, he said, would have become the vassal of the abbey of Saint-Denis for the French Vexin, had he not been the sovereign lord.[77] Likewise, in 1108, Henry I of England refused to do homage to Louis for Normandy (3.3.5). In 1185, when Philip Augustus was taking possession of the county of Amiens he denied homage to the bishop, even though it was owed for the land. Thus the principle emerged that the king could be a lord but not a vassal. The obligations of his vassals towards him likewise became increasingly well defined. Peace homage or border homage signifying the relative equality of the contracting parties had given way to homage for land, later for all the holdings of the prince in the kingdom, with clearly defined obligations attached (3.3.5). By the end of the twelfth century the idea that the king was liege lord, who was owed liege homage, superior to all other forms of homage, by the princes for all their lands, was becoming widely accepted.

These theoretical changes were to be of the greatest importance in tipping the balance between the king and the princes in the thirteenth century, but in the reigns of Louis VI and Louis VII, while they were taking place, they had few practical effects, for the power of the counts of Flanders and Champagne was considerable, while that of the Anglo-Norman and Angevin kings of England eclipsed that of the French crown; and despite the legal developments, in real terms almost exactly the same kind of relationship between king and princes obtained as had done in the later eleventh century (3.3.5). The king continued to make and break alliances with his neighbours, to receive homage and service from his allies and not his enemies. Not until the reign of Philip Augustus was the king fully able to realise the potential of the changes which had happened. A brief survey of the links between the king and some of the princes will clearly illustrate this point.

In the early twelfth century the counts of Flanders had fairly close ties with the French monarchy.[78] Robert II is said by Suger to have sent 4,000 knights to serve the king in 1109, and both he and Baldwin VII were killed while fighting for Louis VI. Both seem to have paid homage for Flanders. Charles the Good also campaigned with Louis. It has frequently been claimed that the king's intervention in the county after Charles's assassination in 1127 was a new departure, a sign of new royal aggression inside a principality, and it is true that Louis VI did not have to be called on to interfere with the succession. Still, Philip I had also meddled with the Flemish succession in 1070–71, having been summoned by both parties, and he had had an equal lack of success in imposing his own candidate.

Our sources suggest that Thierry and Philip of Alsace, the next counts, were vassals of the French king, and Baldwin VIII, who after a succession dispute followed Philip as count in 1192, was obliged to pay the king, his liege lord, 5,000 silver marks as a relief and to contribute a large force for the siege of Rouen

* feudal overlord.

in 1193. Baldwin IX went further. In 1196 he promised to submit to the judgement of the royal court if a disagreement arose between him and the king. But all these ties did not prevent him from allying with Richard I against Philip in the next few years and from invading his lands, just as having paid homage to Philip Augustus did not stop Ferrand, his successor, from allying with John and the emperor and from fighting the king at Bouvines. But the legal ties between the French kings and the Flemish courts were clearly understood throughout the twelfth century, even if they were often meaningless in practice. When allying with the English kings against the French, as in 1109 and 1163, the counts of Flanders still reserved their ultimate allegiance for the Capetians.

Like Flanders, both Burgundy and Champagne were drawn into a closer feudal dependence on the monarchy, but it was one which was firmly resisted on occasions. One source suggests that Hugh II, duke of Burgundy, refused homage to Louis VI in 1108; but in the following year he certainly fought Henry I of England alongside the king. Burgundy sent further contingents to the royal army in 1119 and 1124, and Duke Odo II was judged and condemned by the royal court for his depredations of the estates of the bishopric of Langres in 1153. Although his son Hugh III recognised the king as his liege lord, he still fought the Capetians in alliance with the emperor. In 1186 Philip Augustus mounted a punitive expedition against him, using as an excuse the complaints made by the lord of Vergy, one of the duke's most recalcitrant vassals; and he brought the duke to heel. After this the rulers of the duchy were more closely aligned with and obedient to the king.

The counts of Blois and Champagne maintained an independent line against the king early in the twelfth century. Stephen-Henry had been imprisoned by Philip I and compelled to pay homage. Theobald II was a constant foe of the French kings, and although he sent a contingent against the emperor in 1124, after this his hostility remained unabated until the 1140s. Later better relations were established. Louis VII married Theobald II's sister, Adela, and Count Henry the Liberal and Theobald his brother married the two daughters of Louis and Eleanor of Aquitaine.

In 1152 Henry the Liberal joined an expedition against Henry Plantagenet, and he also recognised the competence of the royal court. His sons were less faithful vassals; in 1198, for example, Theobald III supported Richard I against Philip Augustus. But in the same year he did Philip liege homage for all his lands and from now on the two became more closely connected. The early death of Theobald III, the regency of Blanche of Navarre and the minority of Theobald IV greatly weakened the independence of Champagne vis-à-vis the French crown.

The principalities of southern France had weaker connections with the French crown than their northern counterparts, but here too, a gradual extension of royal authority was visible. The exception was Barcelona, which although claimed by the Capetians until 1258, had by the middle of the twelfth century drifted off into the orbit of the kingdom of Aragon. William IX of Aquitaine was fairly hostile to the French crown, and in 1124 he failed to send a contingent to fight the emperor. However, he would not do battle with Louis VI when the king intervened in the Auvergne in 1126, because the king was his overlord; and

170

although the count of Clermont was his vassal and not the king's, and Louis was technically in the wrong, still he agreed that the count should be presented to the king for the judgement of the royal court. Later on, however, both he and his son William X fought Louis openly, observing no such restraint at all.

Richard the Lionheart as duke of Aquitaine paid homage to the French king for his lands, but also fought him. Indeed with the Angevins' most southerly lands the Capetians made far less progress in extending their rights than in other principalities, until by the Treaty of Le Goulet in 1200 John paid a vast relief to the king and recognised him as his overlord. It is interesting that although William IX had conceded that he held the duchy from the French king, when Louis VII controlled Aquitaine as Eleanor's husband he styled himself duke of Aquitaine as well as king of France. This may seem a pointless duplication of titles, but it is also a possible argument for the ambivalent status of the duchy in the kingdom, for Gascony, an important part of the duchy, was later claimed to be an allodial holding and was not brought into feudal dependence on the king until 1259 (5.5.7). The dukes of Aquitaine also claimed suzerainty over the county of Toulouse. Although Raymond V of Toulouse married Constance, Louis VII's sister and recognised the king as his lord, in 1173 he switched his allegiance to the Angevins. Later in his rule he vacillated again, and lent spasmodic support to Philip. Raymond VI, who continued with this policy became a more permanent vassal of Philip Augustus after the defeat of King John in 1204.

The Norman and Angevin kings of England and dukes of Normandy remained the foes of the French king throughout the twelfth century, and generally conceded as little as possible. Henry Plantagenet was ordered before the French court in 1152 after he had married Eleanor of Aquitaine without Louis's permission – as John was to be later on – but he ignored the summons altogether and Louis could do nothing about it. On the other hand Henry was well aware of what was due to his suzerain. In 1159 he was trying to make good the claims of the dukes of Aquitaine over Toulouse, and to impose his own suzerainty, but Louis VII decided to oppose him, gathered an army and defended the city. When Henry arrived there to find him in occupation he fell back, not willing, as contemporary chroniclers recorded, to attack his overlord. A recent biographer of Henry II, Professor Warren, suggests that the English king had a far clearer idea of feudal duties and obligations than the French, as he only took up arms when he had already been attacked.[79] It is interesting in this context that Henry II was the first crowned ruler of Normandy to do homage for it. Henry I and Stephen had allowed their heirs, William and Eustace, to become vassals of the French king for the duchy but neither ever became its duke. In 1144 Geoffrey 'le Bel' seized Normandy and did homage to Louis VII to legalise his conquest, and Henry his son did the same in 1151, but he repeated the homage for all his French lands in 1156, probably to gain the alliance of Louis VII and his support for Henry retaining Anjou and Maine (4.4.7), and this was, though an acceptance of a dangerous situation, a very important gain for the Capetians in the long term.

For the rest of the twelfth century, homage to the Capetians tended to be used by the Angevins as a weapon against one another in their internecine strife, and by encouraging and accepting it the Capetians established their suzerainty over

171

Normandy. This was to stand them in good stead in 1202. Henry did homage for Normandy again in 1169 and 1183, the young king in 1160, Richard in 1188 and 1189, Arthur of Brittany in 1199 and John in 1200. In practical terms these acts meant very little at the time, and most of them were performed on the borders, but taken together, they were important in the build-up of Capetian suzerainty. Of course, force was still essential in realising their potential, and Philip Augustus could never have hoped to confiscate lands from Richard I. But thanks to these developments, he had legal backing for his conquest of Normandy and Anjou.

obeyance
of princes
= prosper.

Not only did the princes gradually acknowledge the king's role as suzerain and its implications, they also began to fulfil their obligations to him more fully. The practice of giving military service, often without homage, was becoming more common in the later eleventh century (3.3.5), and it continued to revive in the twelfth. A crucial moment here was the German invasion of 1124, when contingents from Blois and Champagne, from Nevers and Vermandois and Flanders, and from various sees including Reims, Châlons, Laon, Soissons and Orléans, from Paris and Saint-Denis, all rallied in support of the king.

Other duties of the princes to the king were also more frequently recognised and performed. The leading lay and ecclesiastical magnates began to sit with the king and make judgements as peers of the realm. The first full list of these, made by the chronicler Matthew Paris in the mid-thirteenth century, included the counts of Flanders, Champagne and Toulouse, the dukes of Normandy, Burgundy and Aquitaine, the archbishop of Reims and the bishops of Beauvais, Noyon, Châlons, Laon and Langres. The title of *pair* dated from much earlier than this; in the *Song of Roland* it was used to describe Charlemagne's companions, but its regular appearance in the language of administration did not occur until Philip Augustus's reign when the most important princes were probably acting as the king's formal counsellors on a regular basis. Later the title became a mark of great distinction, and its functions became largely honorific.

The princes also began to attend royal councils more frequently during the twelfth century.[80] In the early twelfth century this was still rare. Under Louis VI and in the first part of Louis VII's reign some royal assemblies were called for crown wearings, others had the characteristics of Carolingian style *placita* or feudal councils, the king taking advice from a number of important men, described as his leading men (*proceres*), faithful men (*fideles*) or courtiers (*palatini*). Some councils were used for important political decisions to be made, as when in 1111 the opponents of Hugh du Puiset gathered at Melun, when in 1128 the disputed election in Flanders was discussed, and when in 1130 the choice between Anacletus II and Innocent II as pope was made. But except for the military gathering in 1124 the number of princes who attended such meetings was limited.

Following another major council in 1146, however, princes and great nobles appeared far more frequently at court, as in 1152 at Beaugency when Louis VII divorced Eleanor of Aquitaine, in 1155 at Soissons, in 1173 at Paris and in 1178 at Reims for the coronation of the young Philip Augustus. The princes who attended and endorsed royal decisions were described in royal charters as *barones*, a word which had begun life in the eleventh century as the rough equivalent of vassal, but in the twelfth became increasingly exclusive to the great men of the realm in its implications. In addition royal counsellors drawn from the major nobility as opposed to the royal household began to appear. These are signs of the formation of a royal council, probably under the influence of Roman law, and perhaps modelled on the idea of Charlemagne's court. By the end of Philip Augustus's reign it was meeting on a regular basis'.

One important function of the royal court was to render justice to all the king's vassals. Territorial princes appeared before the king on a number of occasions, and so too did the king's lesser vassals, both from the Ile de France and from more widely scattered areas throughout the kingdom; Louis VII, for example, had followers in Burgundy, Auvergne, Saintonge, Flanders and Toulouse. Under Louis VI, Aimon and Archambaud, disputing the lordship of Bourbon, came before the court, while in 1150 the quarrel of William, count of Nevers, and Geoffrey de Donzy over Geoffrey's fief ended in a judicial duel in front of the king. Abbeys, priories and cathedral chapters from an increasingly wide area of France also tended to turn to the Capetians for protection against the encroachment of local lords. In 1153 the bishop of Langres appealed against the refusal of Odo II, duke of Burgundy, to pay him homage. Other bishops sought redress against the activities of the communes which had formed in their cities. The abbot of Corbie appealed against the activities of the lord of Encre, and the abbot of Vézelay against the count of Nevers. The king showed himself ready to intervene in an increasingly wide area of France in response to such requests.

As well as extending the competence of royal justice, the twelfth-century French kings began to issue ordinances for the whole kingdom, not just for the principality. Probably the first was Louis VII's instructions of 1144 banishing relapsed Jews, and this was followed in 1155 by the constitutions of Soissons which established the peace of God throughout the kingdom for ten years. Philip Augustus issued an ordinance for the government of the kingdom in 1190 and one on succession to fiefs in 1209–10, though the latter only concerned the royal lands. In 1223 another ordinance concerning the Jews was issued. These examples mark the early revival of the king's right to legislate throughout the kingdom (5.5.1).

The royal charters issued by these four kings also witness the spread of royal influence and authority in the kingdom. Their beneficiaries came from an ever wider area, but there was an even greater spread of demands for royal confirmations and safeguards, particularly from churches. Louis VII was giving charters over a far wider area than Henry I had done a hundred years earlier, even discounting those he gave as duke of Aquitaine. The same holds true of the royal itinerary. Where Henry I hardly ventured outside the royal principality, Louis VII travelled extensively inside France and went outside it on a number of occasions. This, too, both his successors were to do. Although royal power in the twelfth century remained limited in terms of land and resources, the reputation of the king as overlord, lawgiver and protector was beginning to revive quite widely, well before the great conquests of the early thirteenth century. So too was the image of the French king as the holder of sacral powers and as the defender of the kingdom.

4.4.6 *The image of monarchy*

The revival of royal power was reflected in a growing tide of biographical and historiographical writing which gradually refurbished the royal image and rescued it from the battered and tarnished state into which it had fallen in the mid- and late-eleventh century. The contribution of the abbey of Saint-Denis, and of Abbot Suger in particular, to the revival was considerable. The picture of Louis VI and Louis VII which emanated from the royal monastery far outstripped the real power of these kings and clearly was intended to contribute towards the reputation of the abbey, its patron saint and its relics as well as to that of the king; indeed the second consideration was probably more important than the first. Hence it is misleading to give these writings too strong an emphasis – they were after all for the most part aimed only at a narrow audience, the literate clergy. Under Philip Augustus the claims made by such writers began to have a stronger basis in reality – although they became correspondingly greater so that even as his power grew they still outstripped his recognisable authority.

The works of Suger were nevertheless to make a seminal contribution to royalist theory at the highest level. He emphasised the links of the kings of France with his abbey and its patron saint and glorified the two together; he created certain links for the Capetians with Charlemagne, which were further to be emphasised in the reign of Philip Augustus. He contributed to the development of ideas about sacral kingship and France as a kingdom. All these notions were to fuse in writings concerned with a vitally important event in the rise of the Capetians – the battle of Bouvines.

Suger, administrator, builder and writer had been raised in the abbey of Saint-Denis. He and the future King Louis VI had attended the abbey school together, and Suger became Louis's closest counsellor and adviser after the fall of Stephen of Garlande in 1127. The abbot was a man of humble origins but grandiose ideas, and both as a builder and a writer he sought to increase the prestige of his abbey. His remarkable treatise, the *De administratione*, describes the reconstruction of the abbey church,

because of that inadequacy which we often saw and felt on feast days [when relics were venerated in the church] . . . for the narrowness of the place forced the women to run towards the altar upon the heads of the men as upon a pavement with much much anguish and confusion.[81]

Suger drew on donations as well as the ample revenues of the abbey, and in about 1135 began to have the west porch rebuilt to relieve the congestion at the entrance; this was followed by the reconstruction of the chevet at the east end in the form of a double ambulatory, which broke new ground architecturally. It was in the new Gothic style, with a complex vaulting system and pointed arches, which set it apart from other contemporary ecclesiastical buildings and reflected Suger's fascination with aesthetics. By using light, stained glass, and rich decoration he sought to create a beauty in the church which would transport the worshipper from the material to the non-material, and bring him closer to God. This is summed up in a verse which, Suger says, was inscribed on the great gilded doors at the west end of the church.

Whoever thou art, if thou seekest to extol the glory of these doors,
Marvel not at the gold and the expense but at the craftsmanship of the work,
Bright is the noble work; but being nobly bright, the work
Should brighten the minds, so that they may travel, through the true lights,
To the True Light where Christ is the true door . . .
The dull mind rises to truth through that which is material.[82]

These ideas were based on the writings, and particularly the *Celestial Hierarchy*, of the pseudo-Dionysius the Areopagite. He was probably in reality an important Syrian theologian who lived around A.D. 500, but Suger and his monks identified him with Saint Denis, apostle of the Gauls. A copy of the Greek texts of the Areopagite's works had been given to the abbey by Louis the Pious and had caused much interest; now Suger seemed to be realising the precepts of the patron saint of his abbey. He also used the pseudo-Dionysian writings in arguments against Saint Bernard, whose regular and scathing criticisms of the abbey in the 1120s had brought about its partial reform in 1127, but who, although he was from this time more favourably disposed to Suger himself, remained a bitter critic of ornamentation and decoration in ecclesiastical buildings.

In glorifying his abbey, Suger glorified the king; indeed as Louis VI's friend from childhood, his principal adviser for much of the reign, and his biographer, he and Louis were closely linked. Saint-Denis had been founded in the Merovingian period, supposedly by Dagobert I, who does seem to have given extravagant presents and to have granted the profits of a fair (in October – the later fair of Lendit was in June) which enabled the abbey to expand rapidly. Many kings were buried there, and their bones were held in veneration alongside the relics of Saint Denis and his legendary companions Eleutherius and Rusticus. These kings included Dagobert, Clovis II, Charles Martel and Pippin; some of the later Carolingians including Odo; and the Robertines, Robert, Hugh the Great and Hugh Capet, followed by Robert the Pious and Henry I. Philip I was, however, buried at Fleury, and Suger found the need to explain this away; Philip, he said, expressed on his deathbed the wish for personal intercession. In Saint-Denis he would have been lost amongst all the other kings.[83] In 1120 Louis VI made some amend for this. He presented his father's crown to the abbey and declared that the royal insignia should by right be in the keeping of the holy martyr as the protector of the kingdom. He was to be buried at Saint-Denis himself.

In his biography Suger describes the gathering which took place at Saint-Denis in 1124 before Louis VI and his army went out and defeated the emperor (4.2.1). His account of the ceremony which took place is of some interest in the history of the royal revival. Louis VI, he says, in the presence of certain great councillors, took from the altar the *oriflamme*, the standard of the French Vexin, to which he had the right as count of the Vexin, land held from the abbey.[84] In fact the ecclesiastical claims of the archbishop of Rouen over this crucially important province between the royal principality and Normandy were far better founded than those of Saint-Denis. But by acting as though the king was the lay advocate of the French Vexin on behalf of Saint-Denis Suger and the king brought the land and its nobles under French domination. The abbey was later to reap the profits in dues from the Vexin.[85]

The ceremony at Saint-Denis symbolised the special ties between king and community, and these were given immediate emphasis by the gifts made by Louis to the monks of rights of justice in the vill of Saint-Denis, and of revenues from the fair of Lendit, created in 1108 for the veneration of certain holy relics of the Passion in Paris. Indeed, Suger suggests that the king had from repeated experience as well as from hearsay discovered that Saint Denis was the special patron and protector of the realm after God;[86] and the cult of the saint and his connections with the king were further developed by the monks in the twelfth century by the production of forged charters and of historiographical works. One was a diploma purporting to come from Charlemagne but in fact probably forged in the mid-twelfth century under Suger's successor, Abbot Odo of Deuil. It makes Charlemagne give the monastery the status of the metropolitan church in France in gratitude for the aid the saint had given him in protecting the realm from its enemies. He also declares that he holds France in fief from God and the holy martyr and that he and his successors shall in recognition of this spiritual servitude henceforth place four besants on the altar of the abbey each year, and this the French kings, at least from Philip Augustus onwards, actually performed. In chronicles and lives of the saint produced at the abbey, too, the theme of the ties of the king and the saint is a constantly recurring one. An example is the *Life and Acts of Saint Denis*, written in about 1223, which places the life of the saint in the context of French history and shows that Saint Denis protected all the kings of France from Dagobert to Philip Augustus. This was followed by other works in the same vein later in the thirteenth century, and Louis IX was strongly to emphasise the connections of the crown and Saint-Denis.[87]

The ceremony at Saint-Denis in 1124 and the forged charter also expressed the links of the king with another increasingly important tradition of the abbey, the cult of Charlemagne, which the community was vigorously propagating. According to the *Song of Roland*, and the *New Deeds of the Franks*, composed in the abbey in the early twelfth century, the *oriflamme* was supposed to have been Charlemagne's standard. The story went that it had been presented to him by Pope Leo and was later deposited at the abbey by Hugh Capet, but it gradually lost its ecclesiastical connotations and took on the character of the royal banner, linking the Capetians and the Carolingians. The monks were meanwhile producing various literary exercises to further the cult. The most celebrated, and one which reached a wider audience than the pieces in Latin, was the vernacular *chanson de geste* entitled *How Charlemagne brought the cross and crown of the Lord from Constantinople to Aachen and how Charles the Bald brought them to Saint-Denis*. The title summarises the plot; but incidentally Charles the Bald is supposed, quite erroneously, to have brought the fair of Lendit from Aachen, where Charlemagne had established it, to Saint-Denis.

This *chanson* drew on a story, the journey of Charlemagne to Constantinople and his return with the relics, which was popular at the time, but biased it in favour of Saint-Denis. One motive must have been publicity, but another was far more mercenary, for in 1108 the bishop of Paris had been sent a fragment of the true cross from Jerusalem, and it was he who had set up the fair of Lendit to celebrate it — an event which rapidly became of major ceremonial and financial importance. His lands bordered on those of Saint-Denis, and suddenly, too, the abbey possessed relics of the true cross and the crown of thorns; the *chanson* was composed in about 1110 to explain and justify its relics. When they were given the profits of the fair in 1124 they had effectively taken over the relic cult as well as the Charlemagne cult, and not surprisingly they composed other *chansons* such as the *Pilgrimage of Charlemagne* and later the *Song of Fierabras* to celebrate and popularise their fair.[88]

By the mid-twelfth century the Capetians were becoming more closely identified with Charlemagne's cult than earlier but nevertheless some writers emphasised this more than others. The chronicle of Morigny, for example, recognised the emperors as his successors rather than the Capetians, and Frederick Barbarossa realised the potential importance of such an association. In the face of the links of Charlemagne and France in the *chansons de geste*, of the occasional use of imperial titles by the French king and of the hailing of Adela of Champagne, Louis VII's wife from 1160 onwards, as a direct descendant of the great emperor, Frederick attempted to divert the cult to Germany instead. He had Charlemagne canonised in 1165, and thus his burial place at Aachen became a very important shrine. The monks of Westminster Abbey, with the help of Henry II, had Edward the Confessor canonised in 1161; the Capetians however lacked a tutelary dynastic saint until Louis IX achieved this distinction in 1298.

Perhaps because of the ambiguities now surrounding Charlemagne, the writings about the emperor which circulated in Philip Augustus's court in the earlier part of his reign are rather inconsistent in their treatment of the Carolingian-Capetian links. In the works of Giles of Paris, a poem, the *Karolinus*, and a genealogy of the French kings, written for Prince Louis around 1200, these connections are not stressed unduly, even though the mothers of both Philip Augustus and Louis VIII were widely hailed as being of Carolingian stock.[89] Philip himself seems to have been obsessed with the idea of Charlemagne, however. He named a bastard son Peter Carlot in 1209, and Gerald of Wales describes his dreams of returning the French kingdom to its former glories. It may have been his interest which ensured the triumph of the tradition of the return of the kingdom to the race of Charlemagne (the *reditus*), which appeared in the *History of the French Kings*, where Adela of Champagne's ancestry was traced back to the Carolingians, and in the works of William the Breton who saw Philip as a new Karolid, in whom Charlemagne's virtue was revived. It was fully written up by Vincent of Beauvais in the 1240s. By contrast there was little attempt to glorify the early Capetians at all.[90]

Ideas about sacral kingship also developed during the twelfth century. Suger wrote:

The hand of kings is very strong; and by virtue of a consecrated right of their office [kings] repress the audacity of tyrants whenever they see them provoking wars and taking pleasure in endless pillaging, in persecuting the poor and in destroying churches. Kings intervene to prevent these excesses which, if not opposed, enflame tyrants still more madly.

Here is a clear harking back to Carolingian and early Capetian traditions of kingship, an emphasis on the royal duty of protecting the people. The abbot also wrote of the events of 1124:

Whether one considers our modern times or looks back to ancient times, France never accomplished a more remarkable exploit than this, nor, uniting the forces of its members, ever more gloriously deployed its powers than when at the same time, it triumphed over the Holy Roman Emperor and the English King.[91]

The idea of France as a kingdom and a community, even if not yet a territorial entity, is stressed. The word Francia had a number of meanings in the eleventh century, one of which and perhaps the most common was that of the royal lands, and although the whole French kingdom might also on occasions be described as Francia, it was quite often given instead a name such as 'all the land of the king of France' (tota terra regis Franciae) or 'the whole kingdom' (universum regnum). During the course of the twelfth century such alternatives began to give way to the simpler France or Francia again, as royal power in the kingdom revived.[92]

At the same time, the idea of the king as defender of the realm from internal threats and external enemies was developed. Louis VI was said by Suger to have enjoined his son to guard and defend the church, the poor and orphans and maintain the rights of all his subjects, and Rigord returned to this theme in the late twelfth century, in his justification of Philip Augustus's persecution of the Jews, which was in reality quite clearly more economic than religious in motivation. Rigord, however, suggested that this, like the persecution of heretics and of those who attacked churches, was God's work. He also justified both the subsidies raised by Philip in 1194, and Philip's attack on the churches controlled by Richard I, as necessary for the defence of the realm. These two linked ideas were to have a great future in French royal propaganda,[93] and they were both invoked by chroniclers describing the most dramatic event of Philip's reign, the battle of Bouvines in 1214.

Most of the ideas already outlined had an impact only in a limited circle of clerics and courtiers, and even here the royal attributes, often idealised, must have been recognised as vastly outstripping the real abilities and achievements of Louis VI and Louis VII. Nevertheless the glorification of the king and his realm at the highest level is also echoed in a different form at a more popular level, as in the chansons de geste, some produced at Saint-Denis, which retold the heroic exploits of the French and their kings and linked them with Charlemagne – and from these the Capetians clearly benefited. Louis VI and Louis VII also seem to have been popular kings; as Sir Richard Southern has it, they governed without a sense of strain.[94]

The victory of Philip Augustus in 1214 had a powerful effect on the image of the French monarchy, both at the intellectual and the popular levels. A small but well organised French force defeated an army thrice its own size (4.2.3), and this was heroic stuff, which could also be seen as an indication that God had favoured the French. The battle, provoked by Philip's enemies, had taken place on a Sunday, breaking the peace of God, and the French king's principal adversaries, John and Otto, had both in their time been at the receiving end of innumerable papal anathemas (as had indeed, Philip himself). 'Thus by the victory which God had given, the Capetian monarchy found itself . . . truly consecrated.' [95] Philip had gained a great treasure, noble captives and a prestige which enabled him to deal with the princes of France, with other kings and the emperor from a position of great strength. The French king made much of the event, and his one and only monastic foundation, a house of Victorine canons, was built near to Senlis and named La Victoire after the battle. As with William the Conqueror's foundation of Battle Abbey on the site of the battle of Hastings, the monastery was intended both as a celebration and a thank-offering to God for a great victory. There is no evidence that Philip performed a penance for victory as William did, however, nor did he pay very much of the cost of the foundation, which was left to Warin, bishop of Senlis, who had played an important role in the battle.

As with William the Conqueror, clerical historiographers made much of Philip's victory. The *Philippidos*, a vast work composed by William the Breton (1214–24) has as its high point the battle of Bouvines; the king's victory is given a mythical quality and symbolises a number of different kinds of triumphs – that of good defeating evil in a holy crusade against God's enemies, that of the triumph of the just man in the judicial duel, that of a national victory of God's champion. Unanimous rejoicing, William says, broke out throughout France as Philip, like Pompey, Caesar, Vespasian or Titus celebrated his great triumph. In later accounts, such as Philip Mousket's verses composed around 1240, and the writings of the Minstrel of Reims, dating from about 1260, Bouvines entered into the realm of legend and was linked with the flourishing cult of sacral kingship. With it went many of the earlier ideas. Mousket emphasised the role of Saint Denis and Charlemagne's *oriflamme*, and the Minstrel, the idea of the rebirth of the monarchy and the legitimacy of Capetian rule. In 120 years the Capetians had come a long way. From kings too powerless and too obscure even to find biographers, there had sprung a hero-king, whose grandson was to become a saint.

4.4.7 The Plantagenet lands, 1150–99

It is all too easy with the benefit of hindsight to see Philip Augustus's conquests at the expense of the English kings and the consequent collapse of the so-called Angevin empire as an inevitable process, the result of long-term underlying factors, social, economic and political, which were inexorably leading towards the capture of these lands by the French kings. But all our evidence suggests that while Philip's power had increased to some degree by 1199 there was no clear indication at all that the power of the English king was on the verge of total breakdown. If anything the contrary was true, for by 1199 Philip Augustus had lost many of his earlier gains in Normandy and Picardy. That he managed to reverse these setbacks in such a dramatic way seems to stem from the death of Richard I and the weakness of John of England, easily exploited by the Capetian king.

It is commonly said of the Angevin lands in the late twelfth century that they were an empire in decline, divided by the treachery of Henry II's sons and held together only with difficulty by Richard I and John; and that the attempt to hold them together gravely overstrained their resources and undermined their power from within, making their survival as a unit quite impossible. Thus Philip's conquest becomes unavoidable, and John's responsibility is greatly diminished. Closer investigation suggests that several of these assumptions are unfounded. One is that the Angevin lands formed an empire in any sense of the word. Professor Boussard saw them as forming a conceptual, administrative and geographical whole.[96] Indeed, the last perspective is perhaps the most striking: on the map, the lands of Henry II and Richard I appear as an elegant geographical bloc stretching from Northumberland to the Pyrenees, focused around important towns, great rivers and the English channel, bordered by natural defences such as ranges of hills and inaccessible tracts of undeveloped lands or with heavily fortified strongholds, although with a number of weak points, particularly Berry and the Vexin.

The administrative unity of these lands is less easy to find. Again Professor Boussard, its most enthusiastic proponent, who defined the 'empire' as a very strong state in a feudal framework, adduces as proof of its administrative coherence the measures promulgated by Henry II in several or all of its component parts. Examples are the Norman inquest of 1171, similar to the English Inquest of Sheriffs in 1170; the edict of 1177 dealing with debts which took effect in Normandy, Anjou, Aquitaine and Brittany; and the Assize of Arms of 1181 which appeared both in England and Henry's French lands. There are other rather less clearcut examples, but all-in-all, such measures were usually restricted to England and Normandy and were very much the exception rather than the rule. So too was the movement of officials from one area to another, as when Richard of Ilchester, an Englishman, overhauled the Norman exchequer in the 1170s; for although a number of royal officials from one region of the 'empire' took office at the highest level in another, this was in part a result of the operation of royal patronage, the rewarding of a *curialis* with whatever office was available at a given time, and in part, an attempt to use expertise from one part of the king's lands in another. Certainly there are no signs of plans for centralising the administration throughout the Angevin lands. Indeed most of the posts in each area were filled by local men.

As for the idea that the Angevin lands were seen as an empire, in the sense of a political unit, there is no substance for this usage in contemporary thought. Why do we need to use the term for all these states at all? Henry II and Richard I styled themselves as king of England, duke of Normandy and Aquitaine and count of Anjou. Richard I is credited with schemes of power and grandeur on a vast scale, of ambitions in the Near East and Italy, but no chronicler and no royal act ever described him as 'emperor'. Nor was the collection of lands gathered by Henry II seen as a unit to be kept together; on the contrary, he intended that they should be divided between his sons, as his father Geoffrey had intended and his son Richard was also to do. But on each occasion the sensible and natural principle of division between heirs was disregarded and one man took all the lands by force. This interference with the ordained course of events disguises the intentions of the rulers and imposes a retrospective unity on the lands. But the dispositions of each ruler, Geoffrey, Henry and Richard are a clear indication of their own view of their lands, a collection of holdings, a kingdom, two duchies, counties, lordships, an unwieldy and cumbersome collection which should naturally have been divided between their heirs.[97]

Geoffrey 'le Bel' reversed the normal inheritance pattern whereby the eldest son should take the patrimony and younger sons the acquisitions. In 1151 he laid down that Henry was to have his mother's land of Normandy, but that if once he had acquired England he should pass Maine and Anjou to his brother Geoffrey. Henry kept them because he had also gained Aquitaine in 1152, and Geoffrey who died in 1158 had to accept no more than the county of Nantes. But Henry II also envisaged a division of his lands. In 1169 he laid down that the young king was to inherit England and Normandy, Maine and Anjou, which had come to Henry from his parents. Richard was to get Aquitaine, and Geoffrey, Brittany by virtue of his marriage to Constance. Louis VII confirmed this arrangement, but in 1183 the young king died and Richard refused to relinquish Aquitaine to John. Thus he again took all his father's lands. In 1191, however, he made an agreement at Messina with Philip Augustus, that if he had two sons the second would take Normandy, or greater Anjou, or Aquitaine, and that he should hold it directly from the French king.[98] But he had no sons, and on his death there was a further problem: was John or Arthur of Brittany his rightful heir, and for which lands? Richard had named John as his heir on his deathbed, but both had strong claims. In the event the matter was settled by practical action. John managed to take England and Normandy, his mother held Aquitaine for him and Anjou and Maine followed suit. Arthur had to be content with Brittany for the time being.

It seems more surprising, in fact, that Henry II's lands were inherited in their entirety by two sons in succession, than that on a number of occasions it was intended that they should be divided. For they were a diverse collection of a kingdom and a number of French principalities, each with their own history, identity and customs. As Professor Warren says, 'so far as the "Empire" can be said to have any unity at all, it was a unity which rested solely in Henry's peripatetic court and household'.[99] And despite the links of family, landholding, feudal tenure and patronage between the component parts, which were strongest in the case of Normandy and England, each French principality continued to have its own identity under Plantagenet rule. Henry II reduced the nobles of Anjou to order while Richard made a considerable impact in Aquitaine, Geoffrey a lesser one in Brittany. The Norman administration was further developed. The component states, as they were brought under princely control, retained their own laws and customs, sentiments and loyalties and formed their own communities, to which the Capetian kings would have to concede in the thirteenth and early fourteenth centuries. By the later twelfth century indeed, despite Angevin attempts to levy service or scutage throughout their lands for any given campaign, it was beginning to be expected that this was due only inside each principality for its own defence; outside, expenses should be met by the prince.

By the 1180s and 1190s there were also signs of a growing rift between England and Normandy, the most closely connected components of the Angevin lands. This was manifested in an increasing differentiation between English and

Norman business on the exchequer rolls, and in diverging laws and inheritance customs. There was also a growing awareness of the differences between the 'English' and the 'French', of separate cultural traditions epitomised by the barbarous French spoken in England, mocked at by Walter Map as the French of Marlborough.[100] Henry II had had to use his authority over the succession of fees to prevent the English and the Norman parts of many cross-channel baronies from being split, and the closeness of the Anglo-Norman links under Henry I had not been re-established.

The differences between the various parts of the Angevin lands were thus arguably clearer at the end of the twelfth century than they had been in the middle, but this is still not sufficient to explain the collapse of Angevin rule in France between 1199 and 1204. The pacification and consolidation of Maine and Anjou and the measure of control imposed in Aquitaine perhaps made some of these principalities rather easier to govern than in 1150; certainly the centralised nature of the administration of Normandy and Anjou made it relatively easy for Philip Augustus to put himself in as ruler instead of John. Yet considerable force was needed to dislodge the English king. Nor is the idea of the greatly overstrained resources of the Plantagenet lands in the 1190s entirely convincing. It is true that Richard resorted to many different ways of raising money to finance his extremely expensive activities, but so too did Philip Augustus, and there seems little doubt that Richard was far richer than Philip (4.4.4). Why would John, on hearing of Richard's death, have made straight for Chinon, the treasury of Anjou, if it had been empty?[101]

In 1199, indeed, the position of the French king was not a favourable one. It is true that since 1180 his powers as the overlord of the Angevins had seemed to increase. In 1189, for example, he was able to insist that all those who had rebelled with Richard against Henry II need not return to the English king's allegiance until a month before Richard went on crusade, and that even Henry II's supporters were to swear to abandon him for Richard and Philip if he did not keep to the agreement. Again in 1198 the French king refused to negotiate with the count of Flanders and other supporters of Richard who were the French king's vassals, even though in 1194 at the truce of Tillières a number of defectors from Richard to Philip had been included in the discussions. But against this must be set the steady recovery of Richard's position between 1194 and 1199 (4.2.3). In 1199 Richard was killed when putting down the revolt of Philip's allies in Aquitaine. This was an enormous stroke of luck for the French king. William the Breton declared that in 1199 'God visited the kingdom of the French, for king Richard died'.[102] Had he lived longer, the events of the early thirteenth century would surely have been very different.

4.4.8 The conquest of Normandy, Anjou and Poitou

F. monarchy also prosp. cos. of problems of Eng. monarchy.

Richard's death in 1199 removed a powerful and charismatic figure, more than a match for Philip Augustus, and replaced him with one whose abilities as a warrior and a politician have sometimes been much overestimated. Where Richard was ruthless, ready to fight for his rights, John, once he had gained control of his brother's inheritance, preferred to hold on to it by concession, conciliation and diplomacy, and even when pushed into war seemed incapable of consistent effort. These characteristics were easily exploited by Philip. To secure his lands against the claims of Arthur of Brittany, John made enormous allowances to Philip in the Treaty of Le Goulet in 1200, which neither Richard nor Henry II would ever have considered. He rendered homage to the French king, he paid him an enormous relief, thus acknowledging Philip's right to decide the succession, and he agreed that though Arthur of Brittany was his vassal, Arthur's rights would never be diminished except by judgement of the French court. He arranged to receive back into homage the troublesome count of Angoulême and the viscount of Limoges, but acknowledged that the counts of Flanders and Boulogne ought to be Philip's vassals, and not his own. These substantial feudal gains for Philip were paralleled with material gains as well – the Evreçin and Evreux, the Norman Vexin and a greatly strengthened frontier with Normandy. Furthermore John's niece, Blanche of Castile, was betrothed to the young prince Louis, later Louis VIII, and John gave her as a dowry lands in Berry, Issoudun, Graçay and the Chauvigny estates, to be held by Philip until the marriage was consummated – and the two protagonists were still children.

Soon Philip was able to back up his new advantages with force, for John seemed to play into his hands. It was undoubtedly a wise move by the English king to marry the heiress Isabella of Angoulême, for this area was one of longstanding turbulence. Richard had waged regular warfare against the counts of Angoulême and the viscounts of Limoges since the 1170s. It was very foolish of John, however, not to compensate Hugh IX of Lusignan, count of La Marche, to whom Isabella had previously been betrothed. Fighting broke out, John sent his officials *— result of fighting = massive loss of land by John in France.* into La Marche to administer it directly and the Lusignans appealed to Philip Augustus, accusing John of unfairly attacking and plundering them. John agreed to give the Lusignans a fair trial but then failed to do so, and in 1202 Philip summoned him as his vassal to the royal court to answer for his misdeeds. John did not appear, as Henry II had ignored a similar summons in 1152; but now Philip and his council probably declared John's lands forfeit. It is not clear whether Normandy was included, for John had refused to appear as duke of Normandy in Paris, insisting that any meeting should take place on the border. This duchy still had a slightly different status from the other Angevin lands in France, then, and perhaps Philip Augustus intended to keep it for himself if he could capture it, for he invested Arthur of Brittany with all John's other French lands. And he was ready to fight John to back up his authority and dispossess him of his lands.

At first luck favoured the English king. At the battle of Mirebeau he defeated and captured Arthur of Brittany and the Poitevin barons including Hugh of Lusignan. At this stage it looked as though Philip was going to have to fight long and hard. But John then rapidly put himself at a disadvantage. By high-handedness he alienated William des Roches, seneschal of Anjou by hereditary right since 1199, and he caused or allowed Arthur mysteriously to disappear, which was to arouse Breton suspicions. Finally he made peace with the Lusignan camp and let them go; but soon they turned against him. Thus his enemies were gathered in Brittany, Anjou, Poitou and the Île de France, while potential allies such as the count of Flanders and a number of German princes had gone off on the fourth crusade. John put up some resistance at first but by 1203 seems to have lost the will to fight. He annoyed the Norman nobility more and more by frequent mulctings and by his reliance upon often ill-disciplined mercenary troops. He did nothing to rally the duchy and at the end of 1203 he fled to England.

Meanwhile Philip had been building up support in Normandy, making grants of privileges to towns and monasteries in areas as he captured them, attracting the Norman nobility as his vassals and the church as an ally. Following the capture of Château Gaillard he went north and then skirted Rouen, by way of Argentan, Falaise and Caen. The Breton forces came in through the Avranchin and Cotentin and Rouen, capital of Normandy, admitted Philip in 1204. William des Roches held Maine and Anjou, Brittany conceded to the French king in 1206; and in 1205–06 he held Poitou as well. John, however, managed to take it back again, helped by the fickleness of the great nobles of the region. The English king held it until in 1224 Louis VIII overran it again. It was not ceded formally to the French crown until 1259. Meanwhile in 1206 England, left only with part of the duchy of Aquitaine and the Channel Islands, was threatened with invasion by the French king. This did not materialise immediately, and when it again became a threat in 1213, John averted it by becoming the vassal of Pope Innocent III.

In the space of five years the balance of power in France had been radically altered. Philip Augustus had gained land, wealth and a considerable reputation, and this he was further to augment at the battle of Bouvines in 1214 when he defeated John's ally, the Emperor Otto of Brunswick, John himself having earlier been routed by Prince Louis further west at La Roche-au-Moine. These events greatly strengthened French control over the new conquests.   *Prosp.*

The transition from Angevin to Capetian rule in most of the lands confiscated from John went remarkably smoothly. In Anjou Philip relied heavily on William des Roches, the seneschal, whose powers had been granted to him and his heirs by Arthur in 1199, and who had widespread authority and support. The links of Anjou and England had never been strong, and Philip was the beneficiary of the work of Henry II. In Brittany the position was less clearcut. In 1203 Duke Arthur's whereabouts was not known, though he was suspected dead. His sister Eleanor was the next in line, but she was held captive by John, who claimed wardship over her. Her claims were set aside and her half-sister Alice, daughter of Constance of Brittany and her third husband, Guy of Thouars, was declared countess by an assembly of Breton nobles and clergy. But Guy was involved in intrigues with John and in 1206 Philip took over Brittany himself. He married Alice to Peter of Dreux or Peter Mauclerc, great-grandson of Louis VI, and in 1213 Peter did liege homage to him. Brittany was thus used to enrich a member of the royal house, as by Louis VIII's will Anjou and Poitou were also to be used (5.5.2). An exception was made in the case of Normandy which remained in royal hands for the rest of the Capetian period.

Normandy was a rich prize and Philip was careful to consolidate his power there as thoroughly and as speedily as possible. He had conquered it legitimately in his own view and he would continue to rule lawfully. The Norman clerics, advised by the pope to decide for themselves which king they preferred, wisely chose Philip, and he accepted the homage and fealty of the lay and ecclesiastical magnates. But until the treaty of Paris in 1259 the English kings continued to claim Normandy, and made some tentative attempts to recapture it. They were hampered by their need to concentrate on holding and defending Gascony and by the increasing unwillingness of their barons to fight overseas. What chances did John and Henry III stand of regaining Normandy? How did the ties created during well over a century of close association between Normandy and England stand up to the French conquest, and how long did they last?

Normandy had become discontented with John, and Philip Augustus had managed to capture it. But in 1204 the ties between the two states, the duchy and England were strong.[103] To consolidate his hold on Normandy, Philip had to break the most important, those of landholding. As a result of the French conquest the political affiliations of the holders of the cross-channel estates were called into question and in at least eight families of tenants-in-chief, brothers chose different allegiances. In 1204 Philip threatened those Norman landholders who did not make peace with him with confiscation of their lands, and John seized the English estates of the barons who remained in Normandy – lands which were to be of considerable importance to the English crown. He also banned the export of payments being sent by English priories to their Norman mother-houses.

Some of the Anglo-Norman barons came to an arrangement with Philip Augustus. William Marshall, for example, agreed to pay homage to him for his Norman lands after a year and a day if Philip would leave his estates unmolested. Other nobles, including several widows, were in the course of time regranted their Norman estates as a special favour. Alice, the countess of Eu in her own right was allowed to recover her inheritance in 1219 after the death of her husband Ralph of Exoudun, who had defected from Philip to John in 1214. She had to pay heavily for the privilege. A few English heirs to Norman lands whose claims had been created after 1204 were also allowed to inherit. In the 1220s, for example, Nicholas Malesmains was given part of the honour of Tillières. But Philip was more sparing in this kind of grant than John, who was anxious to re-establish his position in the duchy, and made a number of gifts in the period 1215–16. On the other hand, the French king did not wish to provoke undue hostility, and did not pursue John's followers with the utmost ruthlessness. Rather than granting the Norman barons who had lost their English possessions extra estates in compensation, he added most of the lands confiscated from John's supporters to the ducal, now the royal domain. These included the lands of the earls of Warenne, Leicester, Arundel and Clare, the holdings of Norman knights in England and a number of important towns and fortresses. By not granting these out he kept open the options of important former landholders. Other key castles he gave out only under strict safeguards. Robert de Courtenai who held Conches and Nonancourt had to promise not to sell, grant or mortgage them. Again, the French king allowed fairly strong lordships to form along the Breton border, but acquired other strategically important sites such as Mortemer or Langeais in Touraine. Still he was careful not to make his measures too draconian, and there are examples of several families with double allegiance up to and beyond 1259 (5.5.3). The king also made a thorough investigation of ducal castles, rights and customary revenues, and having abolished the post of seneschal split his functions between a number of *baillis* with territorial jurisdictions, his own men, who were answerable to the Norman exchequer.

The tenurial crisis and the shift in the patterns of landholding by the nobility in Normandy was one of the most striking changes which came about after 1204. The effects of 1204 on the Norman monasteries, many of which held important estates in England, were not so dramatic. After the confiscation of the revenues from England by John from 1204–07 and 1208–12 these began to cross the channel again, as did the pensions due from England, recorded on the pipe rolls. There was also some interchange of personnel. Nevertheless even before 1204 some Norman houses had had difficulty in collecting their English tithes, and after the French conquest their problems were exacerbated.[104] Many quitclaimed their tithes, rents and pensions in return for a down payment. The ties of English dependencies and their Norman mother houses were already much weakened by 1259, although they were to linger on until 1414.

Philip Augustus seems to have tried to build up support among the Norman monasteries both before and during the conquest. He built up an alliance with Raoul d'Argences, abbot of Fécamp, and, although his generosity can be overstated, he was careful to show himself a moderate donor to and protector of some houses in areas which he captured. Saint-Taurin at Evreux had almost been destroyed by fire by his army in 1194, but he granted it an annual rent of eleven measures of corn in 1201, and a church in 1207. And a comparison of the Norman exchequer roll for 1198 and the French accounts for 1202–03 has shown that in the Evreçin Philip allowed £143 *parisis* to monasteries, where Richard had allowed the equivalent of £105 *parisis*.[105] Some few important gifts and privileges went to the Norman religious houses after the conquest. On the other hand Philip also appears to have mulcted some monasteries after the conquest to reward his followers, or so an anonymous chronicler complained.

In his attempts to gain the alliance of the Norman towns he was more generous. He confirmed almost all the communes which John had created in 1199–1203 as an attempt to build up support and gain extra funds, probably for the same reasons. Five towns including Alençon and Barfleur lost their privileges, while Les Andelys and Nonancourt were given communes. He allowed certain trading links with England to continue and gave Caen, Falaise and Rouen special concessions. But Rouen lost most of the revenues from its cross-channel trade, and there is evidence that the charter of privileges granted to it in 1207 was an attempt to quell its dissatisfaction with the new régime. Louis VIII was to extract loans from the Norman towns, but overall they probably suffered less than the nobility and the church did from the conquest.

With the Norman episcopate Philip at first created a favourable impression. John had interfered in the Sées election in 1202–03 and had been threatened by excommunication if he did not accept the chapter's choice. Philip by contrast promised to observe the rights of the church. He called for an inquest into the powers enjoyed by the English kings over the Norman church and a full statement of custom, and this he promised to follow, often interpreting disputed points in a way favourable to the church. He also promised free elections; indeed no sooner had he taken Evreux in 1200 than he issued a charter to this effect, which was confirmed by Pope Innocent III. None of the episcopal elections after 1204 seem to bear the marks of his interference, and the same was probably true for the monasteries. But there are signs of a growing strain; in 1218 Archbishop Robert conceded a number of points at issue to the king, in particular yielding over the right of excommunication of royal officials. Under Louis VIII relations between crown and clergy became more difficult. In 1224 three Norman bishops refused to pay Louis military service outside the duchy, and the king had to extract a promise from the archbishop of Rouen that he would observe the rights and customs of Normandy.

The French king consolidated his hold on Normandy by a mixture of firmness and conciliation. Meanwhile John was finding its recapture an increasingly lost cause. It is true that in 1217 Prince Louis seems to have undertaken to try to persuade his father to restore Henry III his French lands, and the English king tried to win them back on a number of occasions. His attempts were far from baseless, for a certain amount of friction between the king of France's men and the Normans developed in the course of the thirteenth century. Rigord said that although Philip Augustus allowed the Normans to enjoy their own customs freely, many were unhappy with his rule. Under Louis VIII and Louis IX the rift opened further, as Normans found it increasingly difficult to get high office in the church and government of the duchy. But this was not enough to enable Henry III to take it back. By breaking many of the important tenurial links which had counted towards uniting England and Normandy in 1100–06 and 1152–54, and by gaining the support of the Norman episcopate, Philip had begun to sever Normandy from England where it really mattered. Commercial and monastic links continued, but these alone were not enough to restore Normandy to the English.

Poitou was a different matter. Amaury of Thouars was recognised by the French king as seneschal, as with William des Roches in Anjou, but by 1206 Philip had lost control of most of the region apart from Poitiers, which remained in royal hands and was given a commune in 1222. Neither Philip nor John was able fully to dominate the region, for the independent nobility and in particular the four leading families, the lords of Lusignan, Thouars, Mauléon and Parthenay, were ready and able to play off one against the other, and by doing so built up powerful regional lordships. In 1214 John won them over temporarily by offering them money and land, but they were not reliable allies.[106] The central administrative structures and law and order in Poitou both seem to have suffered. At the end of his reign Philip Augustus planned to invade Poitou, and Louis VIII did so in 1224. Hugh of Lusignan and other Poitevin nobles offered him homage in return for substantial concessions, and Louis was ready to negotiate. He arrived in Poitou with a substantial army, took Niort and La Rochelle and sent Hugh of Lusignan into Gascony. Hugh captured castles and towns as far south as the

Garonne but Bordeaux stood by the English king. The French king's gains were still substantial and he tried to consolidate them by making the promised grants to the nobles and allowing communes to the towns. Savary of Mauléon, seneschal of Poitou, who had defended La Rochelle against the king, now agreed to follow Louis rather then Henry III. The English king was again to invade in 1230, and not until after Louis IX's brother Alfonso became count, was Poitou to be fully subjugated (5.5.4).

4.4.9 The Capetians and the Languedoc

Philip Augustus expanded his power against the Angevins by using force, but here, as with the acquisitions in northern France which were made through creating or exploiting ties of marriage and inheritance, there was some legal justification as well. John, as a disobedient vassal, lost his lands. The implantation of royal power in the Languedoc came about in a rather different way, for there the king was called in by the pope to take over lands of which he was the suzerain, but where the church rather than the king was leading the drive to dispossess the counts for heresy. The king was active as suzerain until 1226 when he was ceded the comital powers as well, but he was also the secular arm of the papacy. Philip was unwilling to commit himself in the Languedoc, in part perhaps because of this lack of a legal title, in part because royal resources were not sufficient for an all-out war against the count of Toulouse as well as the king of England; the two could in combination have proved a dangerous coalition. Louis VIII, once he was king, was not ready to enter the fray until he was assured of the financial support of the church, and of making substantial gains which he would be able to grant out at will. This was, then, a conflict of an entirely different kind from the wars with the Angevins.

Pope Innocent III tried to involve Philip Augustus in the south of France on a number of occasions. In 1204 he wrote to him requesting him to move against the Cathars, adding that lands confiscated from all the heretics and their supporters would go to the king. Philip was clearly tempted but was too heavily committed against John. Then in 1208 the murder of the papal legate Peter of Castelnau, supposedly by a follower of the already excommunicate Raymond VI count of Toulouse, turned the pope's request for a crusade into a demand. Still the king was reluctant to get involved. He reserved his rights as suzerain in the eventuality of Raymond VI's dispossession by the church, and he allowed up to 500 French knights to take the cross; but he left the overall organisation and the control of the crusade to the pope. A considerable number of nobles from northern and central France, including the duke of Burgundy and the counts of Saint-Pol and Nevers, were involved, and Arnold Amaury, abbot of Cîteaux, and Simon de Montfort became their leaders in the field.

Raymond VI, realising the dangers he faced, submitted to the pope, thus removing the major grounds for the crusade; but by this time it was too late to stop the crusaders. Their conquests were rapid and it was to the pope, not the king, that Simon de Montfort went for recognition of his rights. In 1211 he paid homage to Peter II of Aragon for the Trencavel lands; but by 1212 King Peter realised that Simon posed a considerable threat to his own position in the Languedoc. He allied with the count of Toulouse but Simon roundly beat the two of them at the battle of Muret in 1213. In the same year Philip Augustus forbade Prince Louis to join the crusade, and when he did eventually arrive for a brief stay in the Languedoc in 1215 it was to find Simon in a position of great strength. The Lateran council of the same year declared that Raymond VI had forfeited his lands and that these should go to Simon de Montfort, and Simon quickly went north to do homage for Toulouse to Philip Augustus. Meanwhile Raymond VI and his son were building up support to mount a counter offensive, and Simon's death in 1218 was greatly to help them.

Pope Honorius III and Amaury, Simon's son, next began to try to involve the French king again. Philip Augustus remained unenthusiastic until the papal legate offered the leadership of the expedition to Theobald IV of Champagne, also heir to the kingdom of Navarre and a young and ambitious man. To prevent him from becoming too powerful the French king now put Prince Louis in his place, but his campaign in 1219 was brief, if violent, and achieved little. Raymond VI (who died in 1222) and his son Raymond VII continued to gain ground. In 1221 Honorius again appealed to Philip Augustus, offering him a large tax on ecclesiastical wealth and a full plenary indulgence as well as the lands remaining to Amaury de Montfort, if he would invade the Languedoc and annex it to the royal lands. Philip again refused. By 1224 Raymond VII was in almost full possession of the county of Toulouse and the pope seemed utterly stymied.

Louis, who succeeded his father in 1223 was, however, once he had conquered Poitou, more receptive towards the gains which he stood to make in the Languedoc, and ready to throw all his resources into it. In 1224 he offered to lead a crusade in person, but his price, which included enormous financial support from the church, was too high, and the pope, to his surprise and anger, turned his proposals down. A year later Honorius changed his mind and agreed to terms equally favourable to the French king. At the ecclesiastical council of Bourges in 1225 Raymond VII was declared excommunicate and his lands forfeit. Amaury de Montfort was recognised as the legal count, but in 1226 he ceded his rights to the king. This gave the king the princely as well as the royal authority in the region. Louis now gathered a vast army and marched south. Raymond VII aligned himself with Henry III of England who had recently lost Poitou and La Rochelle to Louis, but the royal army proved irresistible and once the resistance of Avignon had been overcome, the southern nobility was anxious to submit. The death of the king in 1226 however slowed up the seemingly inexorable progress of the royal forces. In 1229 Raymond VII was to acquire far more favourable terms from Louis IX and his mother Blanche of Castile, than he would have done from Louis VIII. The king took the Trencavel lands and the eastern provinces of the county of Toulouse; the remainder was to be retained by Raymond during his lifetime but was then to pass to his daughter Joan and her husband-to-be, Alfonso, Louis IX's brother.

As a result of these conquests the French monarchy gained a large and powerful foothold in the lands of the south. But the unwillingness of Philip II and Louis VIII to move into the area until their position *vis-à-vis* the Angevins had been made relatively secure, and their refusal directly to fight the counts of Toulouse and drive them into alliance with the English kings until the position of the latter had been greatly weakened, was a realistic policy. Philip only intervened in 1219 to prevent the expansion of another great principality, Champagne, at his own expense. The capture of Poitou and La Rochelle, the most populous and the wealthiest area held by Henry III, in 1224, greatly strengthened Louis VIII's hand; furthermore the willingness of the pope, after some prevarication, to allow him full financial support but the freedom to dispose of his own gains, made the invasion of the Languedoc a worthwhile proposition. But before this Philip, despite the conquests of 1204–05, and the great victory of 1214, was still potentially in a vulnerable position; and in 1226, despite the great gains made by the crown which brought it to a dominant position in France, it still had to secure its position; this Louis IX, the most celebrated Capetian king, was to do.

Philip Augustus and Louis VIII, then, captured an immense amount of land within their kingdom, and made the French crown the one dominant power. They greatly enriched royal resources. Nevertheless, they thought it neither necessary nor desirable to keep all their conquests in the king's hands, but like their contemporaries, they used some acquisitions to enrich members of the royal house. Thus Philip Augustus gave Brittany to Peter Mauclerc, grandson of Louis VI, and the county of Boulogne to his own son Philip Hurepel. Another son, Peter Carlot, entered the religious life. Louis VIII's grants were on a larger scale, rivalling only the presentation of Burgundy by Henry I to his brother in 1032, and they marked the beginning of the regular granting of apanages (5.5.2). In Louis VIII's will his second son, Robert, was to have the lands that Louis had inherited from his mother, Isabella of Hainault; the third, John, was to be count of Anjou and Maine; the fourth, Alfonso, count of Poitou and lord of Auvergne. The next two sons, both destined for an ecclesiastical career, were not longlived, but the seventh, Charles, was later to take John's place as count of Anjou. This left the king with the royal lands, Normandy, and lands and castles in the Languedoc and elsewhere in France. This, and his newly augmented powers of suzerainty, still left him very much the most powerful landholder in his kingdom.

4.5 THE KINGS AND THE CHURCH

4.5.1 Louis VI, Louis VII and the church

In 1108 when Louis VI became king, the tensions between the claims of the ecclesiastical reformers and the customary rights of kings, princes and nobles had not been resolved, despite the 1107 compromise over investitures (3.4.2); as a result Louis, who was anxious to preserve his regalian rights, was drawn into a number of disputes over elections and investitures in France. Nevertheless he was ready to protect religious communities which appealed to him for protection against local laymen, and he was a very generous patron of the monastic orders. Furthermore, he remained on good terms with the papacy, which sought the alliance of the French king to counterbalance the hostility of the emperors.

Louis VI was far more generous to the monastic orders than his father had been. He favoured the established Benedictine houses and was an important patron of the new orders. Foremost of the houses of the former group was Saint-Denis, to which the king gave the profits of the fair of Lendit in 1124 as an acknowledgement of the special place of its patron saint as defender of the realm (4.4.6). In about 1133 the king founded a Benedictine nunnery at Montmartre which was given substantial estates, made an abbey in 1134 and put directly under papal jurisdiction. When in 1136 a major consecration of the church took place, Pope Eugenius III, Saint Bernard of Clairvaux and Abbot Peter the Venerable of Cluny were all there, a measure of the importance of the event. Queen Adela, the joint founder, was buried here after her death in 1154, and she founded another Benedictine nunnery, Saint-Jean-aux-Bois near Compiègne.

The king was also responsible for another important monastic foundation in Paris, the abbey of Saint-Victor, on the Mont-Sainte-Geneviève. This was founded for canons regular in about 1113 and dedicated in 1114 by Pope Paschal II. It became the centre of a congregation of Augustinian houses and may have acted as a royal chancery under Louis VII; and the Victorine canons became celebrated for their learning. William of Champeaux, the celebrated theologian is, indeed, supposed to have given the king the idea of founding the house. Louis also, despite his disagreements with Saint Bernard, gave the Cistercian order important privileges, and in 1136 he refounded a Benedictine priory as a Cistercian abbey, Châalis, in memory of Charles the Good, count of Flanders. He gave land, possibly the site, to the Premonstratensian abbey of Dilo, founded by Henry archbishop of Sens, and made donations to Prémontré, the mother house, probably influenced by Bartholomew de Vir, bishop of Laon, a close associate of both the king and of the order's founder, Norbert of Xanten. And he helped to found three priories for the mixed order of Fontevrault at Orléans, Hautes-Bruyères and Chaumontois; he was generous to several small hospitals and founded perpetual chapels in the royal palaces at Paris and Senlis where chaplains would intercede for his soul. These institutions were to be very popular with his successors; as well as providing the king with the service of prayer they provided livings for chaplains from the royal household (4.4.2).[107]

Louis's powers as king enabled him to act as a reformer of monastic houses as well. According to the Tounai chronicler he used force to compel the monks of Saint-Médard at Soissons to accept the Cluniac customs. In 1128 he replaced what was reputedly a depraved community of nuns at Nôtre-Dame and Saint-Jean at Laon with monks. This extended his influence and also gave him credit with the church. He frequently intervened in the internal affairs of ecclesiastical establishments. In 1120 the cathedral chapter at Sens had to ask his permission to make alterations to their cloister. But his authority over royal bishoprics and abbeys was not always directed into channels regarded as worthwhile by the church. When his third son Henry was five he was already abbot of Saint-Mellon at Pontoise and Nôtre-Dame at Poissy, and to these he was to add four other abbacies and the dignity of treasurer of Saint-Martin's abbey at Tours.

Louis VI has often been portrayed as a protector of defenceless clerics against the ravages of lay lords. There is an element of truth in this view, for the king responded to a number of appeals from ecclesiastics such as the bishop of Clermont, thereby also building up influence in areas outside the royal principality (4.2.1). But he was also firm with bishops or abbots who had taken rights from laymen and ignored the law. In 1113 he instructed Arnaud, abbot of Saint-Pierre-le-Vif at Sens, to give back to a royal vassal the lands he had usurped from him. When in 1110 Waldric bishop of Laon was an accomplice in the murder of Gerard of Quierzy, he was tried before the king and exiled from his lands. Some ecclesiastical cases were heard first in the church courts and then came before the king, a pattern widely accepted by the French clergy, which was to prove of considerable benefit to the king.

He did not sell bishoprics or abbacies, but he supervised elections, insisted on his consent being obtained, and maintained his regalian rights where he could. Not all his interventions were malign; he wrote the following letter in about 1131:

Louis, by the grace of God king of the French, to all the clergy and people of Arras, greetings. We rejoice and we give thanks for your goodwill, that you have elected as your bishop the worthy Alvisus abbot of Anchin. We know him to be an honest and suitable person, whose irreproachable life and behaviour has much pleased us in the past and continues to do so. Therefore we desire and approve of his election . . . farewell.[108]

The incoming bishops and abbots, while they were not invested by the king, were expected to pay him homage for their lands. Such royal controls did not meet with much opposition; indeed in 1119 William of Champeaux, bishop-elect of Châlons, held Louis VI up as an example to the Emperor Henry V. He declared that he had received nothing from the king's hands, but still he owed him aid, military service and counsel. But Louis fell out with the church over some elections to bishoprics. Before he became king he supported his father against admitting Ivo of Chartres to the see of Beauvais, and in 1106 he quarrelled with Pope Paschal II over the archbishopric of Reims, in dispute between Gervais of Rethel and Raoul le Vert, provost of Reims, the candidate of the reformers. In 1108 both cases were resolved, the king accepting the candidates of the reformers but extracting oaths of homage and obedience.

He continued to stand up for royal rights in elections later in the reign. In 1112, according to Guibert of Nogent, following the murder of Waldric, bishop of Laon, he nominated his successor, Hugh, dean of Saint-Croix at Orléans. When in 1122 the monks of Saint-Denis informed him of Suger's election to Saint-Denis he imprisoned some of them in a tower for failing to ask his permission; and this despite the favourable outcome for him. Louis also quarrelled with Ivo bishop of Chartres, and drove Hildebert de Lavardin, archbishop of Tours from his see after he refused to put king's men into two offices he controlled. In 1128 Stephen of Senlis, bishop of Paris, attempted to introduce Victorine canons into the cathedral chapter with the support of Bernard of Clairvaux, and although the king was founder and patron of the order he refused to allow this, because his own powers over the see would have been reduced. He drove Stephen out of Paris and another disciple of Bernard, Henry le Sanglier, archbishop of Sens, was also dislodged at the same time, although the reasons are obscure. Bernard of Clairvaux described the king as a new Herod, the destroyer of his own kingdom and an enemy of his crown, and, the abbot's biographer relates, prophesied that his eldest son would die. Such breaches were not long-lasting, but they show that Louis was always ready to maintain his own position even while supporting disciplinary reforms of the church, the new orders and the new learning.

Compared with the emperors, Louis VI was not an intransigent foe of the papacy, and the king and the popes remained on generally amicable terms. In 1107 Pope Paschal II arrived in France to seek support against the Emperor Henry V, and obligingly annulled Louis's marriage with Lucienne de Rochefort. After the pope's imprisonment by the emperor in 1111 and subsequent humiliations he was anxious to gain French royal backing. The papal legate Conan visited the royal lands in 1114–15 and hurled anathemas against the troublesome castellans of the region, while in 1112 the pope supported the cause of the independence of the bishopric of Arras created by Urban II from the bishopric of Cambrai which was under German authority. Paschal II's successor, Gelasius II, was driven out of Rome by the nobility and fled to France where he died at Cluny. In 1119 Guy, archbishop of Vienne, was elected as the next pope and took the name of Calixtus II. In 1120 he held a general synod of the church at Reims, where reforming measures were promulgated and where Louis VI spoke out against Henry I of England. Henry V of Germany was again excommunicated, but the pope was not as hostile to the English king as Louis was. Indeed, he arranged a rather unfavourable peace for the French king with England shortly afterwards. He allowed the young Simon of Vermandois, a relative of the king, to be elected to the bishopric of Tournai, however, and he was opposed by the archbishop of Reims over this.

In 1122 the pope and the emperor sealed the concordat of Worms and Paschal could now afford to oppose the Capetian king. Louis was already angry with Daimbert, archbishop of Sens, who had relinquished his claims to be primate of France to the archbishop of Lyon, part of whose province lay in the empire. The pope delayed in finding a solution after the first great Lateran council in 1123, and remained aloof from the war between the French king and the emperor in 1124. Honorius II, his successor, never came to France, and appears to have played Louis VI off against his sometimes over-zealous reforming clergy, although without alienating the French king completely.

In 1130 a schism divided the western church. Pope Anacletus II was elected by the Pierleoni family, and Innocent II by the Frangipani. Louis seemed at first to be moving towards the support of Anacletus, but Innocent II, exiled from Italy, gained the powerful backing of Bernard of Clairvaux and the Cistercians. An ecclesiastical council for France met at Etampes and found for him in the king's presence. When Philip, Louis's eldest son died, Innocent crowned the future Louis VII as the next heir. In 1132–33 this pope, with the support of the Emperor Lothar III and Henry I of England as well as Louis VI, returned to Rome in triumph.

From 1133 Innocent II's relations with the French king became cooler. The pope blamed the archbishops of Sens and Reims as well as Louis himself for not avenging the murder of the prior of Saint-Victor and the subdean of Orléans. When in 1135 the pope called a council at Pisa, the king was unwilling to let the French bishops go, and this caused Bernard of Clairvaux to rain abuse and threats on him. Relations warmed up a little at the end of Louis's reign, and Innocent II gave the monastery at Montmartre important privileges.

Louis VII, while less ready to act violently, was as determined as his father to maintain his rights and powers over the French church; and he soon disagreed with the pope as a result.[109] In 1138 he refused a licence to elect their archbishop to the canons of Reims, for on the death of Archbishop Renaud the king had taken over the estates as was customary, and granted a commune to the townspeople. The pope's insistence that this be disbanded and that Louis should take his advice on the election infuriated the king. In 1140 he was angry because the canons of Poitiers elected a bishop without his consent, and he cited their choice, Grimoard, before the royal court. This dispute was only resolved by Grimoard's death in 1141, but Innocent II had meanwhile come down heavily on the side of the electors.

The most dramatic dispute came about over the Bourges election. Louis VII wanted his royal chancellor Cadurc elected, and forbade the canons to choose the papal candidate Pierre de la Châtre, but they ignored his instructions and elected Pierre. Louis refused to confirm him in office. The pope fulminated against the king and Louis vowed that Pierre would never hold the office. The conflict was widened to include the marital problems of Raoul de Vermandois and Petronilla of Aquitaine and the war in Champagne (4.2.2), but following the burning of the church at Vitry by the king, a papal excommunication and interdict, and the intervention of Suger and Bernard of Clairvaux, Louis was eventually persuaded to come to terms with Pope Celestine II in 1144.

For the rest of his reign Louis was far more conciliatory towards the papacy and less ready for disputes over episcopal elections, but he did not relax his control over royal churches. The Cistercian pope Eugenius III was anxious to gain his alliance. In 1147 he took refuge in France from problems in Rome for a short while, and he helped to launch the second crusade. His two successors, Anastasius IV and Adrian IV, were more closely aligned with the emperor than with Louis VII, but in 1159 there was another disputed papal election. Frederick supported Victor IV, and Henry II of England and Louis VII came out behind Alexander III in 1160. Louis tried to negotiate with Frederick I, but this was a failure (4.2.2) and in 1162 he became the firm supporter and protector of Alexander III. The two cooperated in a number of ecclesiastical matters, as when Alexander on behalf of the prior of Châteaufort asked the king to protect the abbey of Bourgueil against the inroads of a local lord. After Alexander's return to Rome in 1165 he remained on good terms with Louis, advising him in 1172 to have his son Philip crowned, and trying to mediate in the struggle of the Capetian king against the Angevins.

Louis VII had a reputation for considerable piety, and for being a protector and defender of the church. This was not undeserved, but it also benefited the king

194

frequently. He made considerable capital from his help to Thomas Becket, and became an adherent of the archbishop's cult (4.2.2). He extended the number of royal bishoprics, and supported the abbey of Vézelay against the count of Nevers, churches in the Auvergne against the count, and churches in the Mâconnais against local lords, spreading royal influence as well as helping the communities. He raised funds for the rebuilding of the cathedrals at Senlis and Paris, and he supported the canonisation of Peter of Tarentaise in 1175, although not that of Bernard of Clairvaux. He helped to reform some religious communities, including Sainte-Geneviève in Paris and Saint-Corneille at Compiègne; in the latter case a certain amount of force was needed to replace secular canons with Benedictine monks. He brought under royal control the abbeys of Manglieu, Saint-Gilles and Cusset, and the important Cluniac priory of La Charité-sur-Loire. Early in his reign he was an important patron of the Cistercian order. He gave Clairvaux an annual rent of £30 a year and he stepped in to become founder and patron at La Bénisson-Dieu in the 1140s with the encouragement of Saint Bernard. His brother Philip founded another Cistercian abbey at Fontaine-Jean, but again Louis took the credit. He also founded and generously endowed one major Cistercian abbey himself. This was at Barbeaux, where a community the king had founded in 1146–47 was moved in 1156. The king and queen were to be buried here in what was, according to Rigord, the most magnificent tomb conceived since the days of Solomon. It is probable that the king was so munificent that the Cistercians modified their statutes which forbade lay people to be interred in their churches in his favour; and in 1183 they allowed a special anniversary mass to be said for him, another relaxation of the normal rule that patrons were only to be remembered on four set occasions during the year.[110]

Louis VII did not give away nearly as much land to the church as his father had, particularly in the period after the crusade. He refounded Saint-Vincent at Senlis for Victorines in 1139–40, and the house of secular canons at Châteaulandon for the same congregation in 1151. He was generous to Saint-Victor but insisted on supervising its elections. In 1170 he refounded the priory of Saint John the Baptist at Nemours, founded earlier by the king's chamberlain Gautier. He built a small hospital in Senlis and two modest houses for the ascetic order of Grandmont at Vincennes, in the royal forest, and at Louye on land given by local men. He created small perpetual chapels in the palaces at Paris, Fontainebleau and Senlis, and gave the Templars the site for a commandery at Savigny near Melun, together with important rents and privileges. Thus he favoured the small monastic institutions which were becoming increasingly popular rather than orders which required substantial and expensive endowments. Only to his foundation of Barbeaux did he make substantial grants of land.

In such ways Louis VII gained and retained the support and alliance of the church in northern France, which was to serve his successors in good stead. Electors to royal bishoprics often chose incumbents from the royal entourage or from families who supported the king. Manasses, bishop of Orléans from 1146–85 was a Garlande; Hugh of Champfleury the royal chancellor became bishop of Soissons. The Châtillon-sur-Marne and Noyers family provided an archbishop of Sens, Guy; they were allied to the Capetians since Robert of Dreux's daughter had married the lord of Châtillon. In 1183 Hugh of Châtillon became bishop of Auxerre. The king's own family, and the relations of his third wife, Adela of Champagne, provided him with several bishops; his brother Henry became archbishop of Reims in 1162; his brother-in-law, William aux Blanches-Mains, held the same see from 1176. This dynastic policy was a contrast to that of Louis VI. There were some exceptions; the perfect regularity of John of Salisbury's election to the bishopric of Chartres in 1176 astonished the abbot of Reims, and many elections served to promote archdeacons and other officials already serving in the diocese, or regular clergy.[111] But by keeping a watchful eye on the selection of bishops, the king gained an episcopate which supported royal policy. He further extended royal influence into the sees of Autun, Mâcon and Mende. His was a piety with valuable political consequences.

4.5.2 Philip Augustus, Louis VIII and the church

Philip Augustus, said Joinville, declared on his deathbed that he would rather forfeit royal rights than quarrel with God's priests. William the Breton describes the king as an admirer and a defender of the clergy. His actions suggest that he was rather less accommodating than these eulogies imply, however, and when he did allow the church to enjoy rights and privileges, there were usually good political reasons, as in Normandy (4.4.8). He went on crusade, but he left the siege of Acre in 1191 to return to France in order to settle his claims in Artois and Vermandois, as well as to undermine Richard I's position in his French lands. Nor does he seem to have matched the personal piety shown by his father in the second part of his reign. The close links which Louis VII had built up with the papacy came under some strain. But the French church generally tended to support the king against the pope, particularly against the centralising and authoritarian Innocent III.

Philip's first quarrel with the pope came about in 1196 when he repudiated Ingeborg of Denmark and was married to Agnes of Méran with the backing of several French bishops. Pope Celestine III responded to an appeal from Ingeborg's brother, Cnut VI of Denmark, and sent papal bulls and papal legates to France, declaring that the divorce of Philip and Ingeborg was invalid. This had little effect, but Innocent III, who took office in 1198, was of sterner stuff. He instructed his legates to try the bishops who had supported the king and to order Philip and Agnes to separate, and threatened king and kingdom with excommunication. Significantly, when the interdict was pronounced by Peter of Capua in 1198 many French bishops refused to observe it. These included the archbishop of Reims and the bishops of Chartres, Orléans and Beauvais. The bishops of Senlis and Paris obeyed the pope, and Philip ravaged their lands. In 1200 Philip agreed to a reconciliation with Ingeborg and to submit the case to be heard by an ecclesiastical assembly. This took place at Soissons in 1201 but nothing concrete emerged. In the same year, however, Agnes died, and her children by Philip were legitimised by the pope. Still, Ingeborg was kept imprisoned by Philip until 1213, during which period negotiations between the king and the pope continued. In this year he took her back, perhaps to gain the alliance and support of both Denmark and the papacy, and she remained the recognised queen of France until her death in 1223. The disputed imperial throne was a further cause of friction between the king and the pope, but from 1210 Philip and Innocent both backed Frederick II. Philip also supported Innocent III against John of England (4.2.3).

Innocent played an important if rather controversial role in the wars of the early thirteenth century, and in examining his achievements it is too easy to overlook his important reforming activities which culminated in the Lateran council of 1215. He also encouraged Francis of Assisi and brought him and his order under the protection of the Roman see. But it was the temporal political side of his activities which concerned the sovereigns of western Europe most closely, and here his aims and intentions have proved controversial. Was he a forerunner of popes later in the thirteenth century who claimed temporal power, or did he only intervene in a spiritual capacity? Some of the claims of the pope over the sovereigns of western Europe were undoubtedly very grandiose; and they were also effective at times, particularly in the case of England. Recently a consensus of opinion has emerged which suggests that Innocent in his glorification of the papal office extended to some degree the claims of his predecessors to intervene in secular affairs. He did not claim world domination, but he suggested that since spiritual power was superior to temporal power, in some instances the pope might need to intervene in secular matters.[112]

Philip Augustus was not prepared to allow any extension of papal pretensions in France. In 1203 Innocent ordered him to make peace with John, but Philip, with the backing of his council, declared that the matter was a feudal one and not the concern of the pope; nor did the pope have a say in disputes between kings. Innocent disclaimed all interest in feudal matters, but, he said, this was a matter of sin. John had complained that Philip had acted wrongfully against him, and so he was bound to intervene. The pope wrote to the French bishops:

Let no one suppose that we wish to diminish or disturb the jurisdiction and power of the French king when he ought not to impede or restrict our jurisdiction and power; for we do not intend to judge concerning a fief, judgement on which belongs to him . . . but to decide concerning a sin, of which the judgement undoubtedly belongs to us, and we can and should exercise it against anyone.[113]

This approach to the French king and his bishops in 1204 was well chosen. A further instance of realism on the part of Innocent was his reply to the Norman clergy when they asked him whether they should follow John or Philip, and he instructed them to make their own decision.

The pope was far more closely involved in the early stages of the crusade against the Albigensians than was the French king. Prince Louis was allowed to go south by his father in 1215 when the position of the count of Toulouse, against whom the crusade was largely directed, was weak. But Raymond VI and Raymond VII subsequently made a comeback against the crusaders and Pope Honorius III had to give Louis VIII very generous terms in 1225 to persuade him to join the armies of the pope. It was the French crown which ultimately benefited the most (4.4.9).

Philip Augustus generally allowed free elections to take place in bishoprics, particularly in conquered lands, although his consent was required before the victorious candidate could be installed. In longstanding royal bishoprics the king's men were often elected, as with Warin, the king's principal adviser, made bishop of Senlis in 1213 (4.4.2). The king also enjoyed his regalian rights, and was ready to compel loyalty from the episcopate if necessary. In 1201, according to William the Breton, the clergy of Reims refused to give him aid in the war against John, and the king in his turn delayed taking action against the count of Rethel and Roger of Rozoy who were oppressing the church's lands, until they had changed their minds. In 1200 he confiscated the estates of the bishops of Orléans and Auxerre when they refused him military service. Philip, then, remained a firm master of the French episcopate.

He also maintained a strong control over the abbeys in his lands. He allowed 'free elections' but frequently expected his own candidates to be chosen. In the 1190s he mulcted religious houses to pay for his wars against Richard I. Even to Saint-Denis, which William the Breton emphasised as the most prestigious royal monastery, he gave very little apart from a few important relics from Constantinople in 1205, and to other monastic establishments he generally issued only standard confirmation charters. In general he seems to have kept any charitable instincts firmly subordinated to political reality, making only a few grants, sufficient to secure the wellbeing of his soul. Rigord says that in the 1190s Philip gave money to feed the poor at a time of famine, and instructed his bishops and abbots to do the same. He also endowed perpetual chapels at Choisy-au-Bac in 1181, at Bléron in 1189–90, at Eu in 1219, and in several other places, and gave modest grants to a number of small hospitals which would have been of considerable importance to them, as when the leper hospital at Chartres was allowed the profits of an annual fair in 1186.

These were broadly the same kind of grants made by King John in England, and reflect a general shift of interest towards small monasteries and hospitals. But even here Philip was not generous, and his 'foundations' of larger abbeys suggest that in this area of patronage at least, he was getting intercession on the cheap. In 1201 he refounded the priory of Saint-Corentin at Mantes as an abbey, and Agnes of Méran was buried here. William the Breton suggests that this was a new foundation, but this was clearly a mistake, for the establishment had existed during the twelfth century. After the battle of Bouvines the king founded a house for Victorine canons at La Victoire. But the archives of this establishment suggest that the king gave almost nothing. The site came from Warin of Senlis, and Louis VIII was to endow the establishment and give it a confirmation charter on its consecration in 1225.

Yet Philip, it seems, was only generous to the church in his testaments. In the first, drawn up in 1190 before he went on crusade, he left half his treasure to the poor and to churches in reparation for the damage done by war and the burden of his taxation. In a later will drawn up in 1222, he left La Victoire an annual pension of £240 *parisis* and £2,000 *parisis* immediately to build the church and monastery. He laid down that the Templars and Hospitallers should have substantial sums, 3,000 and 2,000 silver marks respectively, and a further

£21,000 was set aside for the poor and sick. Saint-Denis, where he chose to be buried, was given all his gold and jewels to endow a perpetual service of prayer for him. The king was far more generous to the church after his death than during his life.[114]   *: Poss done to save soul. is not so bothered about chch. Supp*

Louis VIII during his short reign was rather more openhanded to the church *Probably* than his father had been. About a quarter of his total surviving charters went to monasteries, although clearly the proportion is an inflated one, since most of the *cos by* standard confirmation charters were issued at the beginning of any reign, and *that time* later dropped in frequency. He was generous to the Cistercians, as his son Louis IX was to be, probably through the influence of Blanche of Castile. Louis VIII *he was* gave Cîteaux a £200 rent each year from Béziers and Carcassonne, for example. *powerful* He also issued his officials with instructions not to interpret too strictly the rights *enough* of the crown against certain religious houses. In 1225 he put Saint-Mesmin at *though* Orléans under his protection against the inroads of his own *baillis* and *prévôts*. As *other* with his father there was also a strong political element in his monastic *methods* patronage, for he was careful to give confirmations and to make some grants to important ecclesiastical establishments in the Languedoc. In the south of France the clergy played a very important role in securing the king's position.

In northern France Louis VIII maintained his rights over the clergy, as his father had done. The only strong opposition he encountered from the episcopate came in Normandy. When the king was invading Poitou three Norman bishops left the royal army between Tours and Poitiers, refusing the king service outside the duchy, and Louis, after taking counsel, had an enquiry made into their customary obligations. They were found to owe him service and had to pay a fine. Otherwise, however, the king received close cooperation from the bishops, many of whom attended royal councils and advised him.

On Louis VIII's death much of the French church was closely controlled by the king, and a number of important patterns of cooperation had been established. The king was prepared to allow canonical elections and customary rights to be observed, but he expected royal servants to be provided with important benefices. Military service from the major ecclesiastical establishments was insisted on, as was the king's right to administer the lands of royal churches in vacancies. Full political obedience was expected, and tithes and other taxes could be levied to finance royal crusades with the agreement of the papacy. But already the loyalty of the French church was given to the king above the pope, and this was to be of momentous consequence in the later Capetian period.

NOTES AND FURTHER READING

Asterisked titles are recommended for further reading, and additional titles are suggested below. Place of publication London unless otherwise indicated.

Notes

1. F., *Capetian Kings*, 108.
2. Louis VI's reign is discussed in A. Luchaire, *Louis VI le Gros, annales de sa vie et de son règne (1081–1137)* (Paris, 1890).

3. M. Aubert, *Suger* (Saint-Wandrille, 1950), 108.
4. J. F. Benton, ed., *Self and Society in Medieval France* (i.e. Guibert of Nogent, *De vita sua*, English translation) (New York, 1972), 184–5.
5. Suger, *Vie de Louis VI le Gros* (*op. cit.* Ch. 3), 62.
6. *RHF*, xii, 123.
7. Bur, *La Formation du comté de Champagne* [*op. cit.* Ch. 2] discusses Theobald's career.
8. *RHF*, xii, 89.
9. Walter Map, *De nugis curialium*, trans. M. R. James (1923), 249–50.
10. M. Pacaut, *Louis VII et son royaume* (Paris, 1967), 222–3.
11. *Ibid.*, 47–59; C. Petit-Dutaillis, *The Feudal Monarchy in France and England from the tenth to the thirteenth century*, trans. E. D. Hunt (1936), 95.
12. Duby, *Medieval Marriage* (*op. cit.* Ch. 3), 54–65.
13. M. Pacaut, 'Louis VII et Alexandre III', *Revue d'histoire de l'église de France*, xxxix (1953), 5–45.
14. Duby, *Medieval Marriage*, 74–80.
15. Philip's reign is covered in great detail in A. Cartellieri, *Philipp August König von Frankreich*, 4 vols (Leipzig, 1899–1922).
16. Gerald of Wales, *Opera*, viii, ed. G. F. Warner, *RS* (1891), 294.
17. W. L. Warren, *Henry II* (1973), 610–11.
18. On Philip's relations with Richard, and the political background, see J. Gillingham, *Richard the Lionheart* (1978).
19. J. Gillingham, 'The unromantic death of Richard I', *Speculum*, liv (1979), 18–41.
20. W. L. Warren, *King John* (1961), 15–31 *et passim*.
21. *Ibid.*, 97–100.
22. G. Duby, *Le Dimanche de Bouvines* (Paris, 1973).
23. C. Petit-Dutaillis, *Étude sur la vie et le règne de Louis VIII* (Paris, 1894).
24. Bloch, *Feudal Society* (*op. cit.* Ch. 1), 71.
25. Duby, *The Early Growth of the European Economy* (*op. cit.* Ch. 1), 287.
26. C. Petit-Dutaillis, *The French Communes in the Middle Ages*, trans. J. Vickers (Amsterdam/New York/Oxford, 1978).
27. The customs of Lorris as confirmed by Louis VII are in A. Luchaire, *Études sur les actes de Louis VII* (Paris, 1885), 212–13.
28. Benton, ed., *Self and Society*, 167.
29. Or Gaudri, formerly the chancellor of the English king, Henry I.
30. Benton, ed., *Self and Society*, 208.
31. J. Boussard, *Nouvelle histoire de Paris de . . . 885–86 à la mort de Philippe Auguste* (Paris, 1976), *passim*; see also J. W. Baldwin, *Masters, Princes and Merchants . . .*, 2 vols (Princeton, 1970).
32. L. Thorndike, *University Records and Life in the Middle Ages* (New York, 1944), 23.
33. *Ibid.*, 23–4.
34. Among a host of works covering twelfth-century monasticism, see C. N. L. Brooke and W. Swaan, *The Monastic World 1000–1300* (1974); R. W. Southern, *Western Society and the Church in the Middle Ages* (Penguin, 1970); and M. D. Knowles, *Christian Monasticism* (1969).
35. S. Thompson, 'The problem of the Cistercian nuns in the twelfth and early thirteenth centuries', in *Medieval Women*, ed. D. Baker (Oxford, 1978), 227–52.
36. Southern, *op. cit.*, 246.
37. Benton, ed., *Self and Society*, 60–1.
38. E. M. Hallam, 'Henry II, Richard I and the order of Grandmont', *JMH*, i (1975), 165–85.

39. G. Constable and B. Smith, eds, *Libellus de diversis ordinibus . . . qui sunt in ecclesia* (Oxford, 1972), 2–3.
40. *Ibid.*, 18–19, 44–5, 54–5, 56–7, 72–3, 96–7.
41. *Ibid.*, 2–3.
42. Southern, *op. cit.*, 17.
43. M. Lambert, *Medieval Heresy* (1977), 50, and R. I. Moore, *The Origins of European Dissent* (1977), 82–114.
44. Lambert, *op. cit.*, 53 *et passim*.
45. R. W. Southern, 'The place of England in the twelfth century renaissance', *History*, xlv (1960), 201–16, esp. p. 201; C. N. L. Brooke, **The Twelfth Century Renaissance* (1969).
46. Brooke, *op. cit.*, 63.
47. Southern, *op. cit.*
48. G. Fourquin, *Les Campagnes de la région parisienne à la fin du moyen age* (Paris, 1964); M. Mollat, *Histoire de l'Ile de France et de Paris* (Toulouse, 1971).
49. C. W. Hollister and J. W. Baldwin, **'The rise of administrative kingship: Henry I and Philip Augustus', *American Historical Review*, lxxxviii (1978), 867–905.
50. *RHF*, xii, 137; F., *Capetian Kings,* 106.
51. On Louis VII's domain see Pacaut, *op. cit.*, 119–60.
52. On Philip's first register see Hollister and Baldwin, *op. cit.*, 895–6 and notes. The list is reproduced in *RHF*, xviii, 681–6.
53. On the royal household and entourage see E. Bournazel, *Le Gouvernement Capétien au XIIe siècle, 1108–1180 . . .* (Limoges, 1975).
54. Hollister and Baldwin, *op. cit.*
55. Petit-Dutaillis, *op. cit.*
56. J. Boussard, 'Les mercenaires au XIIe siècle . . .', *Bibl. EC*, cvi, (1945–46), 189–224.
57. Edited in E. Audouin, *Essai sur l'armée royale au temps de Philippe Auguste* (Paris, 1913), 123–40, and discussed, *ibid.*, 7–34.
58. Gerald of Wales, *op. cit.*, 316.
59. F. Lot and R. Fawtier, eds, *Le Premier budget de la monarchie française* (Paris, 1932).
60. *Ibid.*, 98; A. Luchaire, *Études sur les actes de Louis VII* (Paris, 1885), 287 (no. 594).
61. F. Delaborde, ed., *Receuil des actes de Philippe Auguste*, i (Paris, 1916), 416–20 (no. 345).
62. Lot and Fawtier, *op. cit.*, 49–51.
63. Lot and Fawtier, *op. cit.*, 51, 133–9.
64. The calculations of Sir J. Ramsay, *A History of the Revenues of the Kings of England*, 2 vols (Oxford, 1925), have been widely used but also widely criticised.
65. J. F. Benton, **'The revenue of Louis VII', *Speculum*, xlii (1967), 84–91, esp. p. 90.
66. *Ibid.*, 87.
67. For example, Pacaut, *Louis VII et son royaume*, 150–60, and 'Conon de Lausanne et les revenus de Louis VII', *Revue Historique*, ccxxxix (1968), 29–32; Lot and Fawtier, *op. cit.*, 135–9. c.f. J. C. Holt, **'The end of the Anglo-Norman realm', *Proceedings of the British Academy*, lxi (1975), 223–65, for the suggestion that the balance was tipped in the 1190s.
68. Ralph of Diceto, *Opera*, ed. W. Stubbs, *RS*, i (1876), 293; Gillingham, *op. cit.*, 46. Mr Gillingham argues this point cogently, *ibid.*, 303–4.
69. See *ibid.*, 304; F. M. Powicke, *The Loss of Normandy*, 2nd edn (Manchester, 1961), 249; and Petit-Dutaillis, *Feudal Monarchy*, 191.
70. Benton, 'The revenue . . .', 89–90.

71. B. Lyon and A. Verhulst, *Medieval Finance, a comparison of financial institutions in north-western Europe* (Bruges, 1967), 41–52.

72. See n. 67 above. In his article Pacaut brings down the suggested total for Louis VII to £110,000–£120,000 *parisis* a year.

73. F., *Capetian Kings,* 107.

74. Pacaut, *Louis VII et son royaume*, 155–7; Benton, 'The revenue . . .', 86.

75. Benton, 'The revenue . . .' 85, 91.

76. A. Luchaire, *Manuel des institutions françaises, période des Capétiens directs* (Paris, 1892), 253; *RHF*, xiii, 349.

77. A. Lecoy de la Marche, ed., *Oeuvres complètes de Suger* (Paris, 1867), 161–2.

78. F. Lot, *Fidèles ou vassaux? Essai sur la nature juridique du lien qui unissait les grandes vassaux à la royauté depuis le milieu du IXe jusqu'à la fin du XIIe siècle* (Paris, 1904), *passim* on the material covered in this and the next paragraph.

79. Warren, *Henry II*, 87.

80. Bournazel, *op. cit.*, 129–73.

81. E. Panofsky, **Abbot Suger and the Abbey Church of Saint-Denis* (Princeton, 1946), 42–3.

82. *Ibid.*, 46–9.

83. A. Erlande-Brandenburg, *Le Roi est mort* . . . (Geneva, 1975), 68–75, Suger, *Vie de Louis VI le Gros (op. cit.* Ch. 3), 84–5.

84. Suger, *ibid.*, 220–1.

85. R. Barroux, 'L'abbé Suger et la vassalité du Vexin en 1124', *Le Moyen Age*, lxiv (1958), 1–26.

86. Suger, *op. cit.*, 220–1.

87. C. van de Kieft, 'Deux diplômes faux de Charlemagne pour Saint-Denis, du XIIe siècle', *Le Moyen Age*, lxiv (1958), 401–31; G. M. Spiegel, **The cult of Saint-Denis and the Capetian kings', *JMH*, i (1975), 43–70 for much of what follows.

88. J. Bédier, *Les Légendes épiques: recherches sur la formation des chansons de geste*, 2nd edn (Paris 1914–21), iv, 121–75.

89. A. W. Lewis, 'Dynastic structures and Capetian throne-rights: the views of Giles of Paris', *Traditio*, xxx (1977), 225–52.

90. R. Folz, *Le Souvenir et la légende de Charlemagne dans l'empire germanique médiéval*, (Paris, 1950); B. Guenée, 'La fierté d'être Capétien, en France, au moyenage', *Annales*, xxx (1978), 450–74.

91. Suger, *op. cit.*, 172–4, 230–1; G. M. Spiegel, 'The *reditus regni ad stirpem Caroli Magni*: a new look', *French Historical Studies*, vii (1971), 145–74.

92. B. Guenée, 'État et nation en France au moyen âge', *Revue Historique*, ccxxxviii (1967), 17–30.

93. G. M. Spiegel, ' "Defense of the realm": evolution of a Capetian propaganda slogan', *JMH*, iii (1977), 115–45.

94. R. W. Southern, 'England's first entry into Europe', in *Medieval Humanism and other studies* (Oxford, 1970), 153–4.

95. Duby, *Le Dimanche de Bouvines*, 180.

96. J. Boussard, *Le Gouvernement d'Henri II Plantagenêt* (Paris, 1956), 527–32.

97. T. K. Keefe, 'Geoffrey Plantagenet's will and the Angevin succession', *Albion*, vi (1974), 266–74; and C. W. Hollister and T. K. Keefe, 'The making of the Angevin empire', *Journal of British Studies*, xii (1973), 1–25. But compare Warren, *Henry II*, 46–7.

98. Delaborde, *op. cit.*, 204.

99. Warren, *Henry II*, 229.

100.J. C. Holt, *op. cit.*, discusses all these matters. An example of the limitation of service for Anjou and Maine is found in a charter of William des Roches dating from shortly after 1204, in C. J. Beautemps-Beaupré, *Coutûmes et institutions de l'Anjou et de Maine* . . ., i (3) (Paris, 1879), pp. cx-cxi.

101.Gillingham, *Richard the Lionheart*, makes this point.

102.H. F. Delaborde, ed., *Oeuvres de Rigord et de Guillaume le Breton*, i (Paris, 1882), 204.

103.On this see Powicke, *op. cit.*, *passim*, and the important discussion in W. B. Stevenson, 'England and Normandy, 1204–1259' (unpublished Ph.D. thesis, Leeds University, 1974), on which much of the following paragraph is based: see in particular, i, 204, 390–3, ii, 474–5.

104.E. Mason, 'The English tithe income of Norman religious houses', *Bulletin of the Institute of Historical Research*, cxvii (1975), 91–4.

105.J. W. Baldwin, 'Philip Augustus and the Norman Church', *French Historical Studies*, vi (1969), 1–30.

106.R. Hajdu, 'Castles, castellans and the structure of politics in Poitou, 1152–1271', *JMH*, iv (1978), 27–53.

107.On Louis's monastic patronage, see E. M. Hallam, 'Aspects of the monastic patronage of the English and French royal houses, *c.* 1130–1270' (unpublished Ph.D. thesis, University of London, 1976), 167–79.

108.*RHF*, xv, 345.

109.On episcopal elections see P. Imbart de la Tour, *Les Elections episcopales dans l'église de France du IXe au XIIe siècle* (Paris, 1891), esp. 438–52, and M. Pacaut, *Louis VII et les élections episcopales dans le royaume de France* (Paris, 1957). On the origins of the bishops, B. Guillemain, 'Les origines des evêques en France aux XIe et XIIe siècles', *Le Istituzioni ecclesiastiche della "Societas Christiana" dei secoli XI–XII, La Mendola, 1971* (Milan, 1974), 374–407.

110.On Louis VII's monastic patronage, Hallam, 'Monastic patronage'; the modification of their statutes by the Cistercians is discussed on 192.

111.Pacaut, *Louis VII et les élections episcopales*, 105.

112.Recent work on Innocent III is well explained in K. Pennington, 'Pope Innocent III's views on church and state . . .', in *Law, Church and Society, essays in honour of S. Kuttner*, ed. K. Pennington and R. Somerville (University of Pennsylvania, 1977), 49–67.

113.Tierney, *The Crisis of Church and State* (*op. cit.* Ch. 3), 134–5.

114.On Philip's monastic patronage, see Hallam, 'Monastic patronage', 195–214.

Additional titles for further reading

Galbert of Bruges, *The Murder of Charles the Good*, ed. J. B. Ross (New York, 1960).
Radice, B., trans. *The Letters of Abelard and Heloise* (Penguin, 1974).
J. Sumption, *The Albigensian Crusade* (London, 1978).

CHAPTER FIVE

Louis IX: The Consolidation of Royal Power, 1226–70

5.1 INTRODUCTION

5.1.1 Louis IX: holy kingship and political power

Most of the surviving narrative accounts of Louis IX written by near-contemporaries portray him as a one-dimensional figure, a saint in a stained glass window. This image has proved so compelling that almost all modern assessments of the king have been coloured by it, and cloak Louis with a solemn and reverend aura. Louis was clearly a man of strong piety (5.4.1), but he was also far more besides. Quite another impression of him emerges from the administrative, financial and legal records of the reign: a strong ruler, a constructive and innovative lawgiver, an administrator with a concern for those governed and with a powerful grasp of the workings of the royal bureaucracy (5.5.1). Both qualities, piety and administrative ability, helped to raise the French kingship as exercised by Louis to a peak of power and prestige in France and in Europe; and this in its turn created the legend of the golden age of Saint Louis, which developed rapidly after the king's death in 1270, and permeated so many accounts of his life and his reign written in the next forty years. But the legend concealed much about the nature of royal power. Louis IX was far from being a 'perfect' king. His unsuccessful crusades, his excessive reliance on the friars, his expanding administration all aroused strong opposition. His judgements and arbitrations were not always practical and sometimes created difficulties. Many of the developments of his reign were to have unhappy consequences in the late Capetian period (5.5.8). It is not feasible to attempt a balanced assessment of the man and his reign without bearing these considerations in mind, without removing Louis from his pedestal. But taking the problems and the limitations of his kingship into account, the desanctified Louis is still far more impressive than the glittering figure of legend.

What kind of a person was Louis? The Italian chronicler Salimbene describes him as 'thin, slender, lean and tall; he had an angelic countenance and a gracious person'.[1] Salimbene also found him gentle and charming, with a well-developed sense of humour. An amusing incident is retold in a newsletter sent from Paris in about 1262, which adds credence to descriptions of Louis's wit. It is concerned with the contests in piety between Louis IX and Henry III when Henry was attending the parlement in Paris. Proceedings were greatly delayed because each time the English king met a priest while on the way to the assembly, he stopped to hear mass, and he arrived very late indeed; so Louis on the next occasion removed all priests from the vicinity of his route, and Henry arrived puzzled and on time. He enquired whether there was an interdict on the French king's lands. Louis explained his ruse and asked Henry why he liked to hear so many masses. Henry riposted by enquiring why Louis was so fond of sermons. Louis replied that he liked to hear about his creator as often as he could, but Henry declared it was far better to experience and to see him. The two kings now became so intent on disrupting each others' devotions that parlement was allowed to continue without them.[2]

In his *Life of Saint Louis*, John, lord of Joinville, portrays a charming and likeable figure in a series of vivid anecdotes. Louis's concern with the good government of his kingdom is strongly emphasised.

In summer, after hearing mass, the king often went to the wood of Vincennes, where he would sit down with his back against an oak, and make us all sit round him. Those who had any suit to present could come to speak to him without hindrance from an usher or any other person. The king would address them directly and ask: 'Is there anyone here who has a case to be settled?' Those who had one would stand up. Then he would say: 'Keep silent, all of you, and you shall be heard in turn, one after the other.' . . . I have sometimes seen him, in summer, go to administer justice to his people in the public gardens in Paris, dressed in a plain woollen tunic, a sleeveless surcoat . . ., and only a hat of white peacock's feathers on his head.[3]

The reforming ordinances issued by the king confirm his preoccupation with just government (5.5.1). Louis's lack of ostentation in dress was paralleled in a temperate appetite and a moderation in his speech; Joinville says that he never heard him speaking evil of any man. This modest behaviour was not a sign of weakness, for the king often made decisions for himself, without the advice of his councillors. When the French bishops asked him to command his officials to enforce sentences of excommunication for them, he refused, unless he had first judged whether the sentences were justified, 'for it would be against God and contrary to right and justice if he compelled any man to seek absolution when the clergy were doing him wrong'.[4] Above all, Joinville emphasises Louis's piety, his regular hearing of masses and sermons, his generosity to the poor, but unlike many of the king's hagiographers, he succeeds in making the king seem human. For example, on one occasion Louis enquired of Joinville:

Which would you prefer: to be a leper or to have committed some mortal sin? And I, who had never lied to him, replied that I would rather have committed thirty mortal sins than become a leper. The next day . . . he called me to him, and making me sit at his feet said to me: 'Why did you say that yesterday?' I told him I would still say it. 'You spoke without thinking, and like a fool,' he said. 'You ought to know there is no leprosy so foul as being in a state of mortal sin.'[5]

Such is Joinville's Louis, but how fair a picture does he give of the king, and how much does he add to an understanding of the reign? Here his own history is of some importance. He came from a cadet family of the counts of Joigny, which possessed considerable estates and the hereditary title of seneschals of Champagne. Joinville was born in about 1222 and after a period of service with the count of Champagne, he went on crusade with the king in 1248. With him went a troupe of nine knights and 700 men, but to finance them he had to mortgage a large part of his lands. He became a close companion to the king, who rescued him from his financial problems by taking him into his own service. After his return to France he was regularly at court and remained a royal counsellor. He did not go to Tunis with the king in 1270, but he continued as a trusted servant of Louis's successors. Philip III put him in charge of the administration of the county of Champagne during the minority of Joan, later wife of Philip IV; and it was this queen who in 1305 asked the aged seneschal to write his *Life of Saint Louis*. For this, John used his own memoirs, compiled over a long period of time, and he also drew heavily on what he describes as 'a certain book, written in French',[6] almost certainly one of the Saint-Denis chronicles, in its turn related to the *Life* by Geoffrey of Beaulieu. His text was completed in 1309 and dedicated to Prince Louis (X), but Joinville lived on until 1317 or 1319.

Joinville's account was written long after Louis IX's death, in the roseate glow of his canonisation. It dwells in great detail on the king's piety and good works, and in this it draws heavily on and has much in common with the roughly contemporary accounts of Geoffrey of Beaulieu, William of Saint-Pathus, and other hagiographers. Joinville's vivid anecdotal style brings the king to life, where most of the other *Lives* of Louis are rather one-dimensional works, but how much more valuable than their accounts is his? Despite his admiration for the king, Joinville brings out some of the flaws in his character. He shows that Louis could be impulsive, stubborn, and impatient, as quickly roused to anger as to laughter.[7] He often acted without heeding the advice of his councillors, and sometimes infuriated them as a result, as over the treaty of Paris with Henry III (5.2.2). The king's pious activities also aroused criticism.

There were times when some of those who were most in his confidence found fault with the king for spending so lavishly on what seemed to them over-generous benefactions. On such occasions he would answer: 'I would rather have such excessive sums as I spend devoted to almsgiving for the love of God than used in empty ostentation and the vanities of this world.'[8]

His plain dress and modest behaviour were also, Joinville hints, regarded as unsuitable in a king.[9] Of course, the seneschal uses these criticisms, which he demonstrates were mistaken, to strengthen the reader's admiration for his subject; but that they are there at all gives Louis a greater degree of credibility. On the other hand, there is no sign of the sermons and strong criticisms of the king voiced by Rutebeuf, William of Saint-Amour and their followers (5.5.6).

In his account of Louis's reign Joinville provides a great deal of valuable information. He emphasises the influence of Louis's mother, Blanche of Castile, in his early years, her hatred for Louis's wife, Margaret of Provence and her importance in the politics of the period 1226–44. He gives a long and interesting description of Louis's first crusade, based on his own recollection of events. This presents the king in a favourable light, but makes no attempt to conceal his reliance on the councils of his brother, Robert of Artois, and the foolish and dangerous mistakes made by the French as a result. Emphasis on the king's piety and the importance he attached to good government and justice are well substantiated by surviving administrative records, but Joinville's anecdotes bring the king to life in a way that such records never could. Although the *Life of Saint Louis* is strongly coloured by its author's deep admiration for and warm recollections of the king, and presents a limited range of information, little of which is unfavourable to Louis, it seems on the whole a remarkably reliable account of the man and his reign. It is also arguably the liveliest and best royal biography of the Middle Ages.

5.2 THE REIGN OF LOUIS IX

5.2.1 Blanche of Castile and the early years of Louis's reign, 1226-1244

The decade 1226 to 1236 was crucial in determining whether the gains made by Philip Augustus and Louis VIII would last.[10] Louis IX was twelve years old when his father died leaving him under the tutelage of his mother, Blanche of Castile. Her powers were those of a regent, although this title was not actually used in France until 1316. The archbishop of Sens and the bishops of Beauvais and Chartres were at Louis VIII's deathbed and committed the king's dispositions to writing. At first it seemed as though the nobility would accept Blanche's rule, but it was not long before a number of them began to test their strength against the queen, in the attempt to increase their own powers at the expense of royal authority. The English king, Henry III, was anxious to regain the lost Angevin lands in France and from England and from his Gascon lands played a leading part in the hostile coalitions. His position as a papal vassal strengthened his hand to some minor extent. Two Capetian princes, Philip Hurepel count of Boulogne, son of Philip Augustus and Agnes of Méran, and Peter Mauclerc count of Brittany, a descendant of Louis VII's brother Robert of Dreux, put forward counterclaims to the throne; and supported spasmodically by other princes such as Theobald IV, count of Champagne, and regional lords such as Hugh of Lusignan, they tried to forward their own interests and to exercise a greater influence over the young king.

These shifting patterns of alliances proved a grave threat to royal power. Not since 1031-32 had there been such a challenge to the king, and now far more hung in the balance. In the event Blanche managed to hold her own, a remarkable achievement for a foreigner and woman in a land where politics were dominated by men. She had some advantages. She could count on a group of loyal castellan families from the royal lands for support, the Montmorency, Montfort, Beaumont, Milly and others. From their number came Gautier Cornut, archbishop of Sens, Matthew of Montmorency, royal constable, and John Clément, the royal marshal. Likewise the towns and villages of the royal lands seem to have supported the young king wholeheartedly and put their militias at the queen's disposal. She had the advice of experienced counsellors, Warin, bishop of Senlis (until his death in 1227), and the venerable Bartholomew of Roye, chamberlain to both Philip Augustus and Louis VIII. And she was a woman of remarkable character and determination.

The chronicle sources for Louis IX's reign all portray Blanche as a woman of strength and of piety. She had all the spirit of her grandmother Eleanor of Aquitaine and her great-grandmother the Empress Matilda. She was not afraid to take decisions nor to act on them and she proved herself an able and forceful politician. Some of her actions appeared imperious, but she could be merciful, and her piety was widely attested. She gave generously to the poor, supported the religious orders and founded several monasteries (5.4.1),but she always maintained the powers and dignity of the crown against the church and was firm with erring ecclesiastics (5.4.2). Her influence over Louis IX was profound, lasting until her own death in 1252 although weakening somewhat after 1244, when the king became obsessed with the idea of the crusade. God, says Joinville, kept Louis's soul from harm

through the good instruction he received from his mother who taught him both to believe in God and to love Him, and brought her son up in the company of religious-minded people. . . . He would always remember how she would sometimes tell him that she would rather he were dead than guilty of committing a mortal sin.

The king's sound and fair judgements and actions were made 'on the advice of the good mother at his side whose counsels he always followed'.[11] During Louis's minority Blanche aroused considerable opposition from the French princes and nobles and from the university of Paris. She was much derided and ridiculed, but historians have rightly assigned her a key role in the consolidation of royal power in the thirteenth century.

The coronation of the new king was attended by many important French magnates, but Peter Mauclerc and the Poitevin adherents of Henry III were missing. Blanche released Ferrand of Portugal, count of Flanders, from prison and thereby gained an adherent. Renaud of Dammartin, formerly count of Boulogne, remained incarcerated, and further to encourage the loyalty of his successor, Philip Hurepel, Blanche gave him the castles of Mortain and Lillebonne and the lordship of Saint-Pol. But Peter Mauclerc, Henry III's Poitevin and Gascon supporters and his brother Richard, earl of Cornwall, gathered an army at Thouars. For a while Theobald IV, count of Champagne, who had deserted Louis VIII in the Languedoc, joined the coalition. Blanche collected a large army, and with the counts of Boulogne and Dreux and the papal legate Cardinal Romano Frangipani marched south. Theobald of Champagne fell out with his allies and joined the queen's camp. This volatile and stout troubadour was reputed to have developed a strong affection for the queen and wrote many fine poems to her, and his enemies did not fail to comment on this. Peter Mauclerc and Hugh of Lusignan were now in an unfavourable position and in March 1227 they submitted to the queen. A treaty was drawn up at Vendôme and marriage alliances between Blanche's children and the Lusignans and

Mauclercs arranged. A truce was also made with Henry III.

Still Peter's hostility remained unabated. He and his allies captured the young Louis IX at Montlhéry, perhaps hoping to rule through him. But the militias of Paris and the Ile de France rescued Louis and he was fêted all the way back to Paris, an incident which Joinville suggests had a profound effect on him. It is not clear whether Philip Hurepel was amongst the conspirators, but in 1227 Renaud of Dammartin committed suicide in prison, leaving Philip with an undisputed claim to Boulogne, and he now gradually turned against Blanche. He joined a new alliance, with the English and Poitevins, Peter Mauclerc and Enguerrand III of Coucy, descended from Louis VI through his mother Alice of Dreux and another distant claimant to the French throne. Blanche took oaths of obedience from the northern French communes and summoned Peter Mauclerc before the royal court in December 1228. He failed to appear so she again called up her troops and with the support of Theobald of Champagne she and Louis marched to Bellême, an important stronghold of Peter Mauclerc, in January 1229. After a short siege this fell to the royal army. Peter's resistance died down again for a while, but he soon crossed to England to try to raise the active support of Henry III.

Meanwhile the royal army had been continuing Louis VIII's campaign in the Languedoc, under the leadership of the soldier Humbert of Beaujeu and with the support of Cardinal Romano Frangipani. By the end of 1228 the count of Toulouse had made some headway, but nothing decisive had been achieved by either side and the Languedoc was war-weary and devastated. The church, headed from 1227 by Pope Gregory IX, was increasingly interested in peace. In the spring of 1229 Raymond VII submitted to the papal legate and he concluded the treaty of Paris with the French crown, which was far more favourable to the southern prince than might have been expected in 1226. Raymond was to retain many of his lands for life, and his heiress Joan was to marry a Capetian prince – in the event Alfonso, Louis IX's brother. If they did not produce an heir then the city and diocese of Toulouse were to revert to the crown. The French king also took the sénéchausées of Beaucaire and Carcassonne, the conquests of Simon and Amaury of Montfort, and he was ceded a number of important fortresses in the Languedoc for a while. A new university was to be founded at Toulouse, and heresy was to be extirpated from the region. Later, in 1229, the count of Foix and Nevers also submitted to the king, but it was to take almost twenty years before the Midi settled down under the rule of northern France (5.5.3).

The northern barons were meanwhile unable to agree amongst themselves and take concerted action against Blanche and Louis. Theobald IV of Champagne became the target of attack because of his support for the queen. He was under the protection of the papal legate, but this availed him not at all in his disputes with Hugh, duke of Burgundy, and Guy, count of Foix and Nevers. Hugh of Burgundy had violated a treaty he had made with Theobald; and in reprisal the count of Champagne kidnapped Hugh's former tutor the archbishop of Lyon who had been responsible for ensuring the treaty was observed. Hugh was furious, but the count of Bar managed to rescue the archbishop. Hugh and Guy then ravaged Champagne with the support of many other nobles, including Philip Hurepel;

hostilities were interrupted, however, by the arrival of Henry III of England in France. Many from both sides were summoned to join the royal army.

Peter Mauclerc had gained the backing of Henry III, who was unable to bring an army across the channel in 1229, but in 1230 landed at Saint-Malo with a large force. Peter Mauclerc, his vassal for Brittany, gave him support, as did also the count of Bar and a number of Breton and Norman nobles (5.5.3). Blanche had the backing of the counts of Champagne, Flanders, Nevers, Blois and Vendôme, despite their mutual hostilities, and perhaps even of Philip Hurepel. The royal court declared Peter Mauclerc's land forfeit and the royal army captured land and towns from him, Ancenis, Oudon and Champtoceaux. As a result of this show of strength, some of Peter's allies moved to the royal camp, including his brother-in-law, André of Vitré, and the Poitevin lords Hugh of Lusignan count of La Marche, and Raymond and Guy of Thouars. But then the forty days of service to the crown expired and many of the barons returned to their own strife, still leaving the crown in a greatly strengthened position. Henry III was not much in evidence. Avoiding the French armies, and perhaps waiting for them to disperse, he had taken his own forces on an extended tour of Poitou; this may have been intended to consolidate his position there but was largely ineffective. Theobald of Champagne's lands were invaded by his enemies, but Theobald gained the support both of the duke of Lorraine, and of Blanche, who marched to Troyes. The barons besieging it fell back. Ferrand of Flanders attacked Boulogne, Philip Hurepel's lands, at the same time. The hostile coalition gradually collapsed as the barons were reluctant openly to fight the king, and by the end of 1230 peace had returned to north-eastern France. Louis IX's ordinance of 1230 against Jews and usurers was attested by Theobald of Champagne, Philip Hurepel, Hugh of Burgundy, the count of Bar and others. In 1231, furthermore, a three-year truce between the French and English kings was made, followed by the submission of Peter Mauclerc, who agreed to stay out of France for three years. The king was to keep the lands he had conquered including Bellême and Angers.

Theobald of Champagne was not however an unswerving ally of Blanche, and, being widowed, he had suddenly decided in 1232 to marry Peter Mauclerc's daughter Yolande of Dreux. Blanche managed to prevent this and instead he married Margaret, daughter of Archambaud of Bourbon. Meanwhile Alice, queen of Cyprus, a counterclaimant to Champagne, appeared in France, probably at the instigation of Philip Hurepel, and there was another war in the county before she could be induced to relinquish her claims. In 1233–34 Ferrand of Flanders, Robert of Dreux and Philip Hurepel died, and in 1234 Theobald of Champagne became king of Navarre on the death of his uncle. This cleared the decks to some extent, but it still left Peter Mauclerc and Henry III as a problem for the queen. The two had been negotiating and preparing for fresh hostilities as soon as the truce expired. Blanche acted even more quickly, sending three armies from Anjou, Poitou and Normandy into Brittany. Henry III was unprepared and Peter Mauclerc again submitted to the crown in 1234. He gave up certain key fortresses and promised fidelity to the king, and was allowed to retain control of Brittany until his son came of age. Henry III was angry and confiscated Peter's English lands, but after another bout of desultory hostilities with the French he concluded another truce in 1235.

During Louis IX's minority the queen became the butt of many popular songs. She was accused of undue hauteur, of improper relations with the papal legate, and also with Theobald of Champagne who was blamed for Louis VIII's untimely death. She squandered royal treasure, it was said, she surrounded her son with ecclesiastics, lesser men and Spaniards, denying the barons their proper place. Much opposition also came from the university of Paris. In 1229 a group of Picard students rioting at Saint-Marcel was crushed severely, supposedly on Blanche's orders (5.3.2). Appeals to Blanche and the papal legate went unanswered and the university actually dispersed, not to resume again until 1231 when all its privileges were renewed by the king and the papal legate. The rhymesters meanwhile knew Blanche as Dame Hersent, the she-wolf in the currently popular story of Reynard the Fox. But the queen's contribution to the way in which the crown was regarded in France was a vitally important one. Her piety found visual expression in the building works at the great abbeys of Royaumont and Saint-Denis, and later in the bringing of the relics of the passion from Constantinople and their housing in the Sainte-Chapelle (5.4.1).

More important, royal authority had been not only safeguarded but extended in the early years of Louis's reign. Blanche of Castile carried on the work of Philip Augustus and Louis VIII, in overcoming baronial reaction and safeguarding their conquests, and Louis IX was to complete this process. The young king married Margaret, daughter of Count Raymond-Berengar of Provence in 1234, and seems to have come of age at about the same time, but he remained closely under his mother's domination for the next decade. This was both personal – Blanche regarded the young queen Margaret as a rival for his affections and tried to keep them apart – and political. Contemporary accounts suggest that the king always wanted her presence in council and valued her advice; and in many instances her opinion was decisive. She continued to play a central part in the negotiations of the king and the barons.

In 1234 Blanche and Louis had made peace between Theobald of Champagne and Alice of Cyprus. The king paid a lump sum of £40,000 tournois to Alice who relinquished her claims to Cyprus. Theobald gave Louis suzerainty over Blois, Chartres, Sancerre and the viscounty of Châteaudun, thus breaking the feudal links of Blois and Champagne, and departed for his new kingdom of Navarre. But in 1235 he was back, and he made an alliance with Peter Mauclerc and Hugh of La Marche. Without asking the king's permission he arranged the marriage of his daughter Blanche of Navarre to John the Red, son and heir of Peter Mauclerc. As both he and Peter had taken the cross, they relied on the papacy to get them out of their difficulties. The king was not deterred by this. He gathered a large army at Vincennes and the conspirators' resistance soon collapsed. Louis made Theobald promise to stay out of France for seven years; he also made him renounce suzerainty over Blois and the other lands, and took several important castles as a pledge of good faith. In 1237 John, Peter's son, came of age and took control of Brittany, recognising Louis IX as his suzerain. Peter Mauclerc and Theobald of Champagne, both poets and warriors, then set off for the Holy Land in 1239. With them went Amaury of Montfort, John count of Mâcon, who sold his lands to the king, Hugh IV of Burgundy and Henry count of Bar, Guy of Nevers and Foix, and many of their followers. In 1237 Robert, Louis's brother, attained his majority and was invested with his apanage of Artois. His marriage to Mahaut of Brabant brought him more lands in the vicinity of his own. Other marriages of northern heiresses to Blanche's relatives were arranged by the queen – Joan of Ponthieu to Ferdinand III of Castile, and Mahaut of Boulogne to Alfonso, son of Urraca of Portugal, Blanche's sister. Both were to prove loyal to Louis IX. The king's position *vis-à-vis* the barons was thus increasingly strengthened.

But there were still a number of problems to be dealt with. The Languedoc was not settling well under royal control. The inquisition and the royal administrators stirred up considerable tensions (5.5.3). Raymond VII of Toulouse was trying to rebuild his power and independence and to regain the right to pass his inheritance to his own family in contravention of the terms of the treaty of Paris (1229). In 1237 his daughter Joan married Alfonso of Poitiers, but Raymond hoped for other heirs to the county of Toulouse. He had been invested with the marquisate of Provence by Gregory IX in 1234 which made him a vassal of the emperor as well as of the French king. In 1240 war broke out between him and Raymond-Berengar of Provence – the last manifestation of the ancient rivalry of their houses (2.4.2) – and royal troops were used to put this down. In the same year the dispossessed Raymond Trencavel of Carcassonne invaded the Midi from Aragon, where he had been sheltering, and tried to reclaim his lands. He had the backing of the Aragonese king who had interests in the area, and also the support of the nobles and towns of the Languedoc. Raymond Trencavel took back much of the Languedoc, and posed a grave threat to royal authority in the area. But the royal army under the constable John of Beaumont defeated him, taking Carcassonne and Limoux and committing horrible atrocities in the area. Trencavel fled back to Aragon and harsh reprisals were carried out against the nobles and towns who had supported him. The inquisition in the area was strengthened. But the royal victory did not solve the problems of the Languedoc, which remained ready to erupt.

In 1241 Alfonso of Poitiers attained his majority and was knighted and invested as count of Poitou. He went with his brother the king to Poitiers where the local lords paid him homage. But Hugh of Lusignan, count of La Marche, probably at the instigation of Isabella his wife, widow of John of England, soon organised a formidable coalition against Alfonso. According to an intelligence report which reached the queen they felt that 'the French have always hated us Poitevins, and they wish to seize from us all our goods . . . and they would treat us worse than the Normans and the men of the Albigeois'.[12] They were supported by Henry III of England from 1242, by Raymond VII of Toulouse, the Emperor Frederick II, by Aragon and Castile, and by a large concourse of regional lords. At Christmas 1241 Hugh of Lusignan retracted his homage to Alfonso; and the royal court declared his lands forfeit. The king gathered a large force at Chinon – Matthew Paris declared that there were 4,000 knights and 20,000 foot soldiers, no doubt an exaggerated figure – and besieged the castles belonging to Hugh and his allies. The viscount of Thouars and his brother gave in at once and in May and June 1242 Frontenay and Vouvant were taken by the royal army. In May

Henry III arrived at Royan with a small force, thus breaking his truce with the French. The French army advanced and took Taillebourg. They faced the English forces across the river Charente but Henry III fell back on Saintes, and then retreated to Blaye. The Poitevin lords now deserted Henry and made peace with Louis. Hugh of Lusignan was allowed to retain most of his lands although he lost a number of key castles and had to do homage to Louis IX for lands in Angoulême and to Alfonso for Lusignan and La Marche. Isabella was so angry at this humiliation, said a number of chroniclers, that she tried to poison Louis and Alfonso. This failed, and she tried to kill herself, but being frustrated in this too she fell ill from fury. Small wonder, perhaps, that the French and Poitevins saw her as 'rather Jezebel than Isabel'.[13] She ended her days as a nun at Fontevrault.

The French king had won a decisive advantage, but was forced to retreat to Tours as the result of a severe bout of dysentery which affected his army. Henry III then fell back on Bordeaux. This left Raymond VII to be dealt with. He went to Bordeaux and then on to besiege Penne d'Agenais, but finding that his allies were gradually submitting to the king he capitulated as well. In January 1243 peace was made at Lorris. Louis's great wrath against Raymond was moderated by Blanche of Castile, and again Raymond's terms were not as humiliating as they might have been. He promised to observe the terms of the treaty of Paris of 1229, to root out heresy from his lands, and to cede more castles in the Agenais to the king for a period of five years. Other nobles of the Languedoc who had supported Raymond, including Amaury of Narbonne and Olivier de Termes followed suit. Raymond himself now crushed most of the defiant heretics. The stronghold of Montségur capitulated to him 1244, although Quéribus was to hold out until 1255 (5.5.3). Louis IX and Henry III, after another bout of hostilities, made a further five year truce in 1243. Louis was to retain all the lands he had conquered and, according to Matthew Paris, Henry was also to pay him £5,000. This was by no means a favourable outcome for the English king, and no more English military expeditions crossed to France under Henry III.

By the early 1240s Louis IX had reached the dominant position in the kingdom anticipated by the conquests of Philip Augustus and Louis VIII but almost lost during his minority. His political and military superiority had been established and the princes brought into a state of quiescence. The religious role of the monarchy was visibly demonstrated in great prestige projects by which France was glorified and sanctified, and with it, Louis IX (5.5.5).

5.2.2 Louis IX, the crusader king, 1244–1270

In 1244 Louis IX fell seriously ill.

[He] came so near to dying that one of the two ladies who were tending him wanted to draw the sheet over his face . . . [but] our Lord worked within him, and quickly brought him back to such a state of health that although up till then he had not been able to utter a word he now recovered his speech. As soon as he was able to speak he asked for the cross to be given to him, and this was promptly done. When the queen mother heard that the power of speech had come back to him she was as full of joy as it is possible to be. But on learning he had taken the cross — which she heard from his own lips — she mourned as much as if she had seen him lying dead.[14]

By taking the cross the king had committed himself to go on crusade. Other monarchs found reasons not to go and were given absolution from their vows and penances by the pope, but not so Louis. For the rest of his reign his primary objective was the recapture of the holy places for Christendom. For this he tried to bring about peace in Europe, and went on crusade twice. After the failure of his first expedition he lived in extreme simplicity, attributing the disaster in part to his own sins. But his determination did not flag, and in the end he died in the pursuit of his ideal. The later part of the reign is a marked contrast with the earlier, both in its politics and in the behaviour of the king. The young Louis was a regal figure, the older an austere and single-minded man. The years 1244–48 when preparations were being made for the crusade form a transition between the two.

The 1240s was a decade of change in other ways too. After the defeat of the Poitevins, Henry III of England and Raymond VII of Toulouse, relations between these lords and the king stabilised. The English king became markedly less hostile, and in Poitou Alfonso of Poitiers began to centralise and to build up an administration, developing skills he was later to use in the Languedoc. But Louis's relations with the Emperor Frederick II deteriorated somewhat. In the 1230s Frederick had quarrelled bitterly with Pope Gregory IX and Louis had stood aloof. According to Matthew Paris, Gregory declared that Frederick should be deposed and replaced with Robert of Artois, Louis's brother, but he is the only source for this story. In 1241 matters had reached such a pass that when Gregory called a council of the church in Rome Frederick announced he would capture any prelates travelling there by land or sea; and furthermore he carried out his threat. Among the captured ecclesiastics were certain French bishops and abbots who were ill-treated along with the rest. Louis was furious and wrote two letters demanding that his subjects be released, for royal rights had been infringed. This Frederick did, but before a truce could be arranged between king and emperor the pope died. He was replaced first by Celestine IV and then after a long vacancy by Innocent IV, who proved an uncompromising proponent of papal power in secular affairs. He and Frederick continued to fight and in 1243 Innocent IV was driven out of Rome. The pope asked Louis IX to grant him refuge in France; Louis agreed only if his barons were to support the idea. This was a clever way of refusing the pope, since the French barons were extremely anti-papal. Both in 1235 and 1246 they formed leagues against the encroaching power of the pontiff. So instead the pope went to Lyon and called another general council of the church (1245). This gathering, as well as announcing a crusade, excommunicated Frederick and declared him deposed. Although no lay rulers supported this sentence, bitter fighting between the emperor and the pope continued until Frederick's death in 1250. In the meantime, Frederick declared himself ready to submit to the arbitration of the French king, but Louis never took this up: he was busy preparing to go on crusade, and he remained as aloof as possible from the disputes of Frederick and Innocent.

The king met the pope at Cluny at the end of 1245 and doubtless discussed a number of important issues: the crusade, the English king, the empire, and the fate of Provence. This had become an important problem since

Raymond-Berengar of Provence and Raymond VII of Toulouse were planning the marriage of Raymond himself and Beatrice, youngest daughter of Raymond-Berengar and to be made heiress to Provence and Forcalquier. Raymond-Berengar died shortly after this and Louis IX stepped in to prevent the union of the two southern families; Beatrice was married instead to his youngest brother Charles in January 1246. Just after this Charles was knighted and given his apanage of Anjou and Maine.

Louis continued to prepare for his crusade, but in November 1246 a group of French barons strongly encouraged by Frederick II formed a league against the clergy and particularly against the papacy. Their leaders were the ever active Peter Mauclerc; the duke of Burgundy; Hugh, count of Angoulême, and the count of Saint-Pol. They issued a manifesto complaining about the encroachment on secular jurisdiction by the ecclesiastical courts, and other related matters. Innocent IV reacted quickly. In January 1247 he ordered the papal legate Odo of Chateauroux to excommunicate all the members of the league and anyone else even remotely connected with it. The king discussed these issues with his nobles at a council in Lent, and despite his cooperation with the papacy over the crusade he found many of the protests, which were supported by the French church, quite justified. Two embassies went to Lyon in 1247. The first represented the French king, his barons, prelates, the chapters and the universities. Complaints were made about papal provisions (the gift of French benefices to outsiders by the pope), the too frequent use of and abuse of excommunication, the incursions of ecclesiastical courts on secular jurisdiction, the inordinately heavy financial demands made by the pope and his tax-collectors on the French church. Innocent promised to stop future provisions, and to prevent the further expansion of ecclesiastical jurisdiction. In June 1247 the same points were reiterated by another embassy. Louis's envoys furthermore claimed that the temporalities of the French church should belong to the king for his own needs and those of the realm, and that the king could use ecclesiastical property in cases of necessity. This may well have gone beyond the king's own views (5.4.2); nevertheless it is clear that Louis took an independent line *vis-à-vis* the papacy and was as careful as his predecessors to keep a check on the power of the church in France, even while preparing to fight the Muslims.

By 1248 the position of the Christians in the east seemed precarious in the extreme. The pattern of power was changing rapidly and in 1244 Jerusalem was taken from the Christians by Persian and Egyptian forces, who were retreating in their turn from the advance of the Mongol hordes from Asia. The confused politics, the weaknesses and divisions of the Muslims in Palestine, in fact made it a suitable time for the Christians to invade the area. The French king's crusade was the best armed, the best equipped and best supplied one ever to set off for the east. It was also popular in the kingdom. It was preached by the friars and praised by the poets. Most of the army which eventually set off came from the royal lands, but there were also contingents from Flanders, Champagne, Burgundy and England. The royal accounts which survive for this period put its total cost at over one million pounds tournois; of this the French clergy paid almost two-thirds, raised from them by a papal twentieth (5.5.1).[15] The French towns also contributed handsomely and many of the nobles who went, like Joinville, paid for themselves. The king, too, had to find a great deal of money. In addition to his annual receipts which must have been in excess of £200,000, he borrowed substantial sums from Italian bankers. Ships were hired from Genoa and Marseille and vast supplies purchased in advance. The army assembled at Aigues Mortes, the seaport on the Mediterranean built on land purchased by Louis from the abbey of Psalmodi, and given special privileges to aid its development. In August 1248 the expedition set out.

The king had made preparations for the administration of France in his absence. The truce with England was renewed, and the pope forbade Henry III to attack France during Louis's absence. Problems over the Flemish succession were also settled in 1246. Margaret, countess of Flanders, had married twice. Her first husband Bouchard of Avesnes, a knight, was generally considered to have been ordained sub-deacon, and after having two sons by him she left him on this excuse and was married again, this time to William of Dampierre by whom she had a second family. Not surprisingly the two branches of her family disputed her lands – the Avesnes were the older but also arguably illegitimate. Louis IX was called in to arbitrate and he gave the succession of Hainault to the Avesnes sons, and Flanders to the Dampierre sons of Margaret. This equitable settlement was not however to be the end of this troublesome issue. In 1247–48 royal officials known as *enquêteurs* (this is translated as inquisitor, but that term is here reserved for the ecclesiastical *enquêteurs* or inquisitors who acted against heretics) were sent round the royal lands to seek out and remedy where possible any injuries and exactions made by *baillis*, *prévôts* and other royal administrators, whose corruption, particularly in the Languedoc, had caused many problems. This was an important part of Louis's attempts to keep a check on his administrators and to improve the standards of their conduct (5.5.1). He left the kingdom under the care of his mother Blanche of Castile, assisted by Alfonso of Poitiers who only joined the crusade for a brief period in Egypt before returning home.

The crusaders wintered at Limassol in Cyprus and then went to Egypt in an attempt to take Damietta. It was not imprudent of Louis to go south rather than east. Egypt was of major political importance and its armies clearly needed to be reduced; but as Cairo was the ultimate target it might have been wiser to take Alexandria rather than Damietta from which the route to Cairo crossed the Nile (Map 5.1). The Egyptian forces were in a state of confusion owing to internal political problems and Damietta soon fell to the crusaders. A body of opinion in the army favoured moving on to Alexandria, but Robert of Artois counselled a march on Cairo; and Louis took his advice. At first the crusaders advanced rapidly, their opponents being further weakened by the death of the sultan. They had some difficulty in crossing a canalised branch of the Nile since every time they built a causeway the Muslims flooded it; but eventually they crossed by a secret route, and part of the crusading force led by Robert of Artois swept into Mansourah.

The invasion of Mansourah was an ill-considered step and the French had to fall back, losing many troops, including Robert himself, in the process. Instead of going straight back to Damietta they stopped near Mansourah, where their

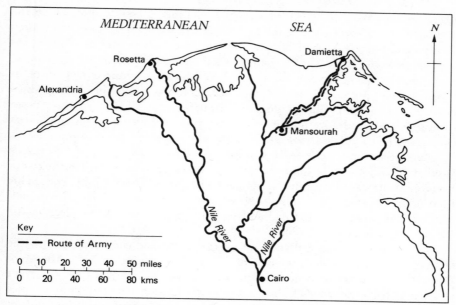

Map 5.1   Louis IX's first crusade, 1249–50

supply lines were blocked and sickness took a heavy toll. Eventually they withdrew; but the retreat went badly awry, and it left the king who was himself very ill, and a substantial part of his army, in the hands of the enemy. The queen, Margaret, held Damietta with some difficulty, promising substantial sums of money to the Genoese and Pisans to persuade them to stay. She also gave birth to a son, John Tristan, at this time. Louis IX was meanwhile negotiating the ransom of himself and his army; a million bezants, about £167,000 tournois was the price agreed, and a truce was made with Egypt for ten years. The murder of the new sultan by a group of Mamelukes did nothing to alter the terms of the truce, which was not ungenerous to the French, largely because the queen had rallied Damietta. The Egyptians were rather slow to fulfill all its terms, however, and it was not until the king with a much reduced army had sailed to Acre that he was able to get all his men freed, in return for supporting the Mamelukes against the sultan of Aleppo whose kinsman had been the victim of the Mamelukes. He also entered inconclusive negotiations with the Assassins, but essentially he held aloof from the struggles in the Middle East. He spent a year in Damascus and had the walls rebuilt, and then did the same at Jaffa, moving on to Sidon shortly after a terrible massacre of Christians there by the troops of the sultan of Aleppo, who by now had made peace with Egypt. The king helped to bury the much decayed bodies of the victims at Sidon himself, and this city was also refortified.

In 1253 news arrived that Blanche of Castile had died, and the king set off for France early in 1254. After a hazardous journey he disembarked at Hyères in Provence and returned to his kingdom overland. He had achieved some temporary gains in Palestine, but the *débâcle* in Egypt, his own humiliating capture and the loss of so much of his fine army had a profound impact on Louis.

According to Matthew Paris he declared: 'If only I could suffer alone the opprobrium and adversity, and my sins should not recoil on the universal church then I could bear it with equanimity. But woe is me, by me all Christendom has been covered with confusion'.[16] The king's self blame was manifested in the life of strong personal asceticism he adopted (5.4.1), which was admired by many of his subjects and immortalised by the hagiographers, and in an increased determination to unite Christendom in order to fight the Muslims, to bring peace to Europe and good government to his own people. But many contemporaries considered Louis's plain living and his close reliance on the friars unsuitable in a king and he was much criticised (5.5.6). Furthermore the failure of the crusade swelled the tide of disillusionment with the crusading movement. For the rest of his reign Louis was clearly out of alignment with many of his subjects, both in his lifestyle and his preoccupations; although these were traits which were to gain him his canonisation in the end and to assure him a permanent place in the affections of the French people.

During Louis's absence Blanche of Castile had coped competently with the affairs of the kingdom with the help of a council of bishops. In 1250 Alfonso of Poitiers and Charles of Anjou returned to France from Egypt. Alfonso went straight to Toulouse, which he had just inherited, and then on to Poitou. Charles of Anjou also had his own interests in mind. He had problems in his lands of Provence, Marseille and Avignon, and he hoped to gain papal support. Innocent IV was far too busy rejoicing over the death of Frederick II and preparing for war with his son and successor Conrad to give Charles much help, and despite appeals from Blanche the pope did very little to raise support for Louis in Outremer. The queen was so angry with the pope that she had confiscated the lands and goods of all those who joined the war against Conrad. Then at Easter, in the wake of the dismay at Louis's defeat, a popular movement, the *pastoureaux*, started in Picardy, where a preacher known as the Master of Hungary claimed that the Virgin Mary had appeared to him and had told him to lead all the shepherds to the Holy Land to rescue the king. A great armed mob under his leadership appeared at Paris and then moved on to Orléans, but their fervour was soon directed against the clergy and they began to attack priests, monks and friars. Now Blanche ordered that the mob be excommunicated and dispersed and this was done. In addition she extracted oaths from the university and the burgesses of Paris that everything possible should be done to maintain law and order. At about the same time, however, she fell foul of the chapter of Nôtre-Dame-de-Paris. This body had decided to raise a heavy tallage from its serfs at Paris and the queen intervened on their behalf. She attempted to bring the case into the royal court following an appeal from them, and threatened the chapter with men-at-arms. The affair went to arbitration and shortly after the queen's death it was decided that she had overstepped her rights, for matters affecting the chapter and its serfs did not properly come under royal justice. But in November 1252 the queen fell seriously ill, retired to her abbey of Maubuisson and died there, leaving the kingdom under the guardianship of Alfonso of Poitiers and Charles of Anjou.

Before the king returned the Flemish succession again became a problem. John of Avesnes had married Alice of Holland in 1246 and in 1251 he was given an official declaration of his legitimacy. But he was angry because although William of Dampierre had been invested with Flanders he had not himself officially been made count of Hainault. William died in a tournament in 1251 and Guy his brother was next in line, but John urged William of Holland, his brother-in-law and king of the Romans (i.e. emperor-elect) to seize all the lands of Margaret of Flanders which were in the empire and to invest John with them. Margaret raised an army in self defence but Hainault rose against her, and in 1253 she and her Dampierre sons were defeated in the battle of Walcheren by John of Avesnes and his supporters. The Dampierres were imprisoned, and Margaret called on Charles of Anjou for help, offering him Hainault if he would crush the Avesnes. Charles was a greedy man and he rapidly occupied much of Hainault. When Louis IX returned from the east he again settled the matter by arbitration. By the Dit de Péronne of 1256 John was allowed to keep most of Hainault, although he had to do homage to Charles of Anjou for it. He lost Crèvecoeur, Arleux and other lands to Flanders, and Margaret had to pay Charles a substantial indemnity.

There was still the problem of the lands of the English king in France to be settled. In 1254 Henry III visited Louis in Paris and good relations between the two kings were cemented. Negotiations continued for the next few years and in 1259 the treaty of Paris was made between France and England (5.5.7). Louis's own council was not happy with the terms; Joinville tells how they asked him why he was restoring to Henry III lands of which the English king had been justly dispossessed. Louis agreed that he held the lands by right of conquest, but he was hoping to establish a bond between his children and Henry's by the grant. He was also bringing Gascony into feudal dependence on the French crown.[17] Both were good reasons, but they did little to diminish the resentment against the treaty in France.

Opposition to the treaty was also strong in England and merged with a general discontent with and hostility towards the king. In 1257 Henry had been refused the help of his barons in the pursuit of the crown of Sicily for his son Edmund, which brought with it the obligation to fund the pope in his war against Manfred of Hohenstaufen, Frederick II's heir. As an attempt to improve the quality of royal government the English barons imposed the Provisions of Oxford on the king, which put Henry under the control of a council of twenty-four barons (1258). The arrangements proved difficult to work and open hostility erupted, but after negotiations, both sides eventually agreed to submit to the mediation of Louis IX in 1263. The French king came out almost entirely on Henry III's side. In the Mise of Amiens of 1264 he declared that the Provisions were null and void. The English king was to enjoy full powers in his kingdom except that this should not derogate from existing privileges, charters, liberties and praiseworthy customs of England. He could have whoever he chose as his advisers, and he could remove officials at any level. Why did Louis take this view? Doubtless the condemnation of the Provisions by two popes weighed with him, as did the influence of his wife Margaret, sister of Henry III's wife Eleanor. But above all the Mise seems to reflect the king's own view of his office (5.5.5). His sentence was eminently acceptable to Henry III, but far less so to his barons and war soon broke out again. In 1264 Henry III was defeated at Lewes, and Simon de Montfort, leader of the barons, ruled England for a brief period. The king's forces triumphed at Evesham in 1265, however, and Simon de Montfort was killed. Again Louis intervened to try to ameliorate Henry's vengeful treatment of the defeated barons. He supported the claims of Henry's sister Eleanor, widow of Simon, and her son Amaury to her lands and dower in England, and he gave her shelter. But although he had been called on by both sides to give a sentence, he achieved very little in practical terms. However, it is doubtful whether the tensions in England could have been resolved in any way other than war.

Another settlement of claims to lands in France was made with James of

Map 5.2 France in 1259

220

Aragon. By the treaty of Corbeil in 1258 the Aragonese king, who had intervened in the Languedoc on a number of occasions, gave up his claims to Carcassonne, Nîmes, Millau and Toulouse. Louis in his turn renounced any rights to Roussillon, Barcelona and Urgel, the old Spanish march conquered by Charlemagne, but which had effectively formed part of Aragon for the previous century. James's daughter Isabella was to marry Philip, Louis's son. But tensions soon emerged between Aragon and France when James decided to marry his son to the Hohenstaufen princess, Constance of Sicily. Louis IX and the new pope, Urban IV, a Frenchman elected in 1261, both tried to prevent this marriage, and the French king refused to allow the marriage of Philip, his heir, and Isabella to take place until James had promised not to help Manfred and not to foment problems in the Languedoc. James agreed and the marriage was solemnised in 1262; but the Aragonese king did not keep his promise and continued to interfere with the French Midi.

Sicily was now becoming a major political problem. In 1254 Conrad had died and his half-brother Manfred had usurped power at the expense of the legitimate heir, Conradin, a child. Alexander IV offered the crown to Henry III's son but withdrew his offer in 1258; his successor Urban IV tried to confer it on Charles of Anjou in 1263. The same suggestion had been turned down by Charles in 1252 on Louis's insistence; but this time the king's scruples were overcome and Charles accepted. By 1264 when Urban died this arrogant prince had forced terms highly favourable to himself from the pope. The next pontiff, Clement IV, renewed the arrangements with Charles of Anjou. Louis's brother now campaigned in northern Italy in 1265 and then attacked Sicily in 1266. He had the full support of Louis for this war against another Christian ruler. A crusade was preached in France, a tenth levied from the clergy, and the king allowed hundreds of his men to join his brother's army. In February 1266 Charles and Manfred met in battle at Viterbo and in March the victorious Charles and his wife Beatrice were crowned as king and queen of Sicily. Conradin continued to pose a problem, but in 1268 he was defeated at the battle of Tagliacozzo and Charles had him executed. Charles's ambitions were, indeed, as great as his ruthlessness: he hoped to move on to conquer Byzantium, and by the Treaty of Viterbo in 1267 he took over all the rights of Baldwin the deposed Latin emperor; he may also have hoped to profit from Louis IX's proposed second crusade, announced in 1267.

In 1260 the Egyptians, who were strongly anti-Christian, had defeated the Mongols. The western states in Outremer were further weakened when in 1261 the Latin emperor of Constantinople was deposed by a Byzantine claimant, Michael Paleologus. During the 1260s Baibars, sultan of Egypt, gradually overthrew Christian strongholds in Palestine: Caesarea and Arsuf (1265), Safad (1266), Jaffa and Antioch (1268). In 1267 Louis IX called a council of barons and announced his intentions of returning to the east. The decision was not a popular one; anti-crusading sentiment was strong, as the songs of the jongleurs show clearly, and many French nobles including Joinville himself were unwilling to go. The financing of the expedition was again a problem, but the pope granted Louis another tenth from the French church for three years from 1268. The king also asked Charles of Anjou to pay back the very substantial sum – about £49,000 –

that he owed him. Edward, son of Henry III of England, was to accompany Louis, and he too had to be funded.

Before Louis left on crusade he appointed as regents Matthew of Vendôme, abbot of Saint-Denis, and Simon of Nesle, a royal knight. The queen was left no responsibility, and she was also bequeathed only a meagre sum in Louis's will. Otherwise it was full of pious bequests to the poor, the sick and the mendicants. That these totalled little more than the bequests of Louis VIII is probably a measure of Louis IX's financial problems. He was by this time in very poor health and doubtless expected to die in the east. Louis VIII had provided handsomely for his family; Louis IX was less generous, leaving only small apanages to his younger sons Peter, John and Robert. Some good marriages had been arranged for his children however: Isabella to King Theobald of Navarre in 1255, Philip to Isabella of Aragon in 1262, John Tristan to Yolande of Nevers and Bourbon in 1266, Blanche to Ferdinand of Castile in 1269, Margaret to John duke of Brabant in 1270, leaving Agnes, the youngest, with £10,000 as her marriage portion.

Louis's last journey appears in retrospect to have been ill-fated from the beginning. The king's weakness made the progress of his army to Aigues-Mortes a slow one and meant that the expedition did not set off until the summer of 1270 – not a good season for campaigning in the east. Different groups within the army awaiting him began to fight between themselves, and when the king did embark, instead of going straight to help the beleaguered Christians of Palestine, his force sailed across to Tunis, where after a brief campaign the king waited for his brother Charles of Anjou to arrive. In the blazing heat disease spread rapidly through the army, and many died, among them the king himself, whose already feeble body could not survive these further rigours.

Why did Louis go to Tunisia instead of to Palestine? This is a question which has long vexed historians. Geoffrey of Beaulieu suggests that the sultan of Tunis was contemplating becoming a Christian, and that Louis wanted to encourage him, and to see his faith flourishing again in the land of Saint Augustine. Primat points out that an expedition to Tunis, which was far nearer to France than was the Holy Land, would still bring the same spiritual reward of a full indulgence. Possibly this consideration weighed with the sick king, and overcame his concern for the stricken Outremer. Other chroniclers made other suggestions. Peter Coral, a Limousin writer, said that

on the suggestion of Charles, king of Sicily, they all went to Tunis, because the emir of Tunis did not wish to pay Charles a tribute as had been the custom under Frederick and Manfred . . . and on account of this Charles prevailed upon his brother the French king, who with his whole army diverted to Tunis.[18]

M. Wallon, writing in the last century, heaped blame upon Charles of Anjou for influencing malignly his saintly brother and for bringing about his death.[19] A large body of more modern opinion follows him. Charles was, it is clear, a violent and ambitious man with his sights set on Byzantium, and the emir of Tunis had proved extremely troublesome. It is interesting too, that one of Rutebeuf's poems is concerned with a wily fox, and is quite probably intended to refer to Charles's attempts to exploit the stubborn piety of his brother for his own ends. But the point is not proved, for Charles seems to have joined the crusade only with some reluctance. Did he agree to go only if Tunisia was the first target? Recently Jean Longnon has shown that he was negotiating with the emir shortly before the crusade set off, and suggests that the attack on Tunisia was not immediately in his own interests.[20] Perhaps by this stage it was too late to stop it.

Certainly it was Charles who profited most from the crusade. He arrived just after Louis's death and he and Philip III made peace with the emir on terms quite favourable to Charles at least. Edward of England arrived just as the French were preparing to go home, and he sailed on to the Holy Land alone, earning himself a reputation for steadfast piety which contrasted well with the behaviour of his Gallic relatives. Having lost Louis IX and many others, the French, greatly weakened and demoralised, returned home via Italy, losing more of their number on the way, including Philip III's queen, Isabella of Aragon, Theobald of Navarre, Alfonso of Poitiers and his wife Joan of Toulouse. They took with them the bones of Louis IX (Charles of Anjou had buried his entrails at Monreale) which were finally laid to rest at Saint-Denis in 1271. On them was focused a growing cult, which reached a peak after the king's canonisation in 1297 (6.5.2).

Louis was survived many years by his wife Margaret of Provence,[21] whose influence over him had never matched that of his mother and brothers. During her early years as queen of France she was eclipsed by Blanche of Castile: according to Joinville, Blanche was consumed with jealousy for the young woman and she and the king, who were very fond of one another, had to meet in secret; and Blanche tried to drag Louis away from the bedside of Margaret when it was feared the young queen would die in childbirth. Margaret was, however, a woman of spirit whose actions at Damietta greatly improved the position of the crusaders. She played an important part in the relations of Louis and Henry III (her sister Eleanor was Henry's wife), but Louis unlike Henry refused to allow his wife's family and interests to dominate him. After Blanche's death Margaret gained a new and bitter foe in Charles of Anjou. One reason was the question of her inheritance. She was the eldest daughter of Raymond-Berengar of Provence, and Beatrice, the youngest, Charles's wife, had inherited all their father's lands. Charles seems to have been reluctant to allow Margaret any of the money due to her from her father's inheritance. The queen's hatred for him emerges in the oath she forced her son Philip, the future Philip III, to swear. He would remain under her tutelage until he was thirty, he would never take counsellors hostile to her, or make any pact or alliance with Charles, he would report to his mother any rumours hostile to her, and he would say nothing of his oath. The last he did not keep, since Pope Urban IV released him from it by a papal bull in July 1263. Furthermore when Charles was offered Sicily, one condition was reconciliation with the queen. After Louis's death, Margaret contemplated invading Provence, but this proved utterly abortive. In the last years of her life the dowager queen calmed down somewhat. She was given a substantial dowry, including Beaufort and Baugé, and later, ironically, Anjou itself. These lands she governed well and effectively until her own death in 1295, shortly before the canonisation of her husband.

5.3 FRENCH SOCIETY IN THE THIRTEENTH CENTURY

5.3.1 French society 1226–1270: the example of Paris and the Ile de France

The increasingly stable conditions of French society during Louis IX's reign undoubtedly helped its prosperity to increase; and the estate accounts and surveys which were produced and have survived in greater numbers from this period help with a better understanding of rural life. Such documents reflect the wider use of money throughout society, and better techniques of estate management and accounting. They also reveal and highlight the great diversity of social and economic conditions throughout France, as throughout Europe. However, they suggest one fairly accurate generalisation can be made, that the financial positions of bannal lords, both lay and ecclesiastical, had shown no overall improvement since the twelfth century. As a group they remained heavily in debt, and although many attempted to set their affairs in order by selling off parcels of land to *nouveaux riches* burgesses or leasing them to wealthier peasants, only a few managed to escape the problems of heavy debts. Undoubtedly, too, their levying of tallage and other dues at a higher rate and with greater frequency was a response to such financial problems. Nevertheless, there is no clear pattern of the decline of the lords and the improvement of the peasant's lot in France. Social and economic conditions varied greatly from one region to another; and a good illustration of this is the legal status of the peasants.

In certain areas the enfranchisement of communities and the growing trend towards freeing individual serfs meant that serfdom gradually disappeared during the thirteenth century, as in the Ile de France, the Beauce and Normandy. In other parts of France, such as Champagne, Franche-Comté and Vermandois, a group of privileged peasants was created in such ways, but the rest, still subject to services and charges, fell in wealth, rank and independence. The gulf between rich and poor peasants was in many regions a growing one, and wealth increasingly affected the legal status of the individual. Then there was the problem of the availability of land for cultivation; in some heavily populated regions a scarcity of farm land brought many problems, such as poverty and hunger, with it; in others, where colonisation was still taking place, peasant farmers could gain many valuable privileges and a good living.

Urban prosperity also continued to grow (4.3.2), but urban liberties suffered a reverse. Territorial princes such as Alfonso of Poitiers and Robert II of Burgundy, and the king himself, all interfered more frequently in the internal affairs of their towns, and royal or princely officials began to erode their independence. This happened in both the north and the Languedoc. In 1256 the king laid down that towns in the royal lands should present their accounts at Paris for auditing by royal officials each year, and gradually the idea spread that the king had an overall authority over the towns, just as he exercised a general protection over religious houses. Nevertheless, urban prosperity increased as much as rural prosperity.

The social and economic developments which took place in Louis's reign in Paris and the Ile de France provide a useful case study for one area of France. This is a region where growth was greatly helped by the size and economic importance of the capital city, with a resulting wealth in the surrounding countryside which supplied it. Thus it developed rather differently from other regions of France, but its political importance gives it an added interest.[22]

In the Ile de France agricultural expansion proceeded apace, as techniques improved and profits grew, and during Louis IX's reign there was an almost complete disappearance of serfdom and the semi-free status in the region, and the granting of privileges and franchises to many communities. The movement of manumission really got under way in 1246 when the king freed his serfs at Villeneuve-le-Roi and the canons of Sainte-Geneviève did the same for theirs at Rosny-sous-Bois. Saint-Denis, Saint-Germain-des-Prés and other major bannal lordships in the region followed suit, and by the 1260s grants of privileges were becoming widespread, further improving the lot of many of the peasants. Often both manumission and franchises had to be paid for with substantial sums of money, but cash was widespread at the peasant level, as the numerous parcels of rented land show clearly. The *cens* tenure, equivalent to villeinage, was widespread, but the *champart*, which gave the peasant greater rights over the land, became increasingly popular in the thirteenth century. The rights of the bannal lords became more and more limited. Clearly the proximity of Paris, the wealth of the area and the influence of the king all aided the peasants. The nobility and large religious houses on the other hand fared badly as their debts piled up; and there were also other problems affecting them. Only baronies and a few other fiefs could be handed down intact, and once *parage* had been abolished for most of the Ile de France in 1209 and the customs of the area had become clearcut, fiefs began to disintegrate more and more quickly. As a result many of the lesser nobles and knights began to sell off their lands, and often married into wealthy burgess families and took service with the king. The flourishing bourgeoisie moved into the land market and profited from the plight of the lesser nobles by buying fiefs, as did too some of the greatest lords, many of whom were ecclesiastics. The earliest surviving general account for the abbey of Saint-Denis dates from 1229-30. This shows that in this year money receipts were £13,321 parisis and expenses, £14,984. When some of the excess grain was taken into account the overall deficit was about £1,457.[23] The wealth of the abbey is clear from this document, and it was sufficient to support 150 monks and 50 servants in considerable style. Later in the century it began to face greater economic difficulties, however.

As the economic vitality and wealth of Paris grew (4.3.2) so its domination of the surrounding region increased. The city was administered through the *prévôté-vicomté*[24] which was sometimes referred to as a *bailliage* in the thirteenth century, a function of its importance. From about 1230 to 1260 the *prévôté* was farmed out, normally to burgesses such as Odo Popin and Simon Barbette who held this office in 1241. In about 1260 the king suppressed the farm and separated the supervision of the commercial life of the city, the *prévôté de la marchandise*, from the *prévôté* proper. The latter he gave to a knight, Stephen Boileau, who supervised the compilation of the code known as the *livre des métiers*; this regulated industry and trade, and also the financial, judicial and military responsibilities of the trade guilds towards the crown. Gradually the customs of the *prévôté* and *vicomté* of Paris developed, their influence reaching into the areas surrounding the city which came under its jurisdiction. In Louis IX's reign, the city's wealth and importance as the royal capital was demonstrated in the extension of the royal palace where parlement sat, the construction of the Sainte-Chapelle, the rebuilding of the cathedral of Nôtre-Dame. Matthew Paris describes Henry III's visit there in 1254 and how he admired the French capital, with its large and magnificent buildings, its elegant houses, its crowded streets, its fame and reputation.[25] Clearly this made it a fitting setting for a king who was admired and respected throughout Europe.

5.3.2 Religion and learning: the friars, the universities and the inquisition

By the end of the twelfth century new monastic orders such as the Cistercians, Premonstratensians, and the Carthusians (4.3.3) had lost momentum in their growth and expansion. But the tide of religious renewal which had brought them into being was still flowing strongly and was swelling to include laymen and women who had previously had few opportunities in the religious life. It found expression in France in the spread of the Béguine movement, and in the development of the mendicant orders. These new movements had in common a rejection of the claustral life as epitomised by the great Cluniac and Cistercian monasteries. Rather than shunning the world that they might serve it better, the new religious of the thirteenth century were very much caught up with society, and particularly with the citizens of the expanding towns; in their outlook and aims they showed many similarities to certain of the heretical movements of the twelfth century and in particular to the Waldensians (4.3.3). Yet the various orders of friars worked within the framework of the church,[26] where the Waldensians had been outside it, and as a result they had to make a number of compromises with it, as the Cistercians and most of the other new orders of the twelfth century had done.

The Franciscan order was created in Italy by Francis of Assisi, who rejected the affluence of his life as the son of a wealthy merchant, gave away all his goods and followed the apostolic life, repairing churches and preaching to the poor. He and his small group of followers had their modest rule approved by Pope Innocent III in 1210, and soon their way of life became remarkably popular. By Francis's death in 1226 he was already at the head of an order with its own centralised organisation. In his testament Francis left firm instructions that his followers should adopt absolute poverty, should seek no papal privileges or concessions, should obey their superiors, should uphold orthodoxy. Within two years he had been canonised and, as a sign of things to come, a magnificent church was rapidly built as his burial place in Assisi. In the succeeding decades some of his principles were not compromised, but on others, both opinion and practice in the order was divided. A substantial proportion of the friars, the conventuals, were in favour of the amelioration of the rule, while a smaller group, the spirituals, were anxious to follow the instructions of their founder. Nevertheless, when the Franciscans spread through France early in their history their appeal was in rejecting worldly goods, in living by begging, in making the poor their brothers and preaching and ministering to them; they were also missionaries with a strong interest in Palestine, and this commended them to the king (5.4.1). The success of their ideal is shown in the rapid appearance of Franciscan friaries all over Europe. By 1275, 423 mendicant houses had been founded in France, of which 195 were Franciscan. The majority of Franciscan establishments were concentrated in the Midi, where the Toulouse house was established in about 1222. The community in Paris was firmly settled by 1230.[27]

The other main mendicant order had an entirely different origin. It sprang from the attempts of the papacy and the ecclesiastical hierarchy in the Languedoc to contain the Cathar and Waldensian heresies in the region. In 1206 an Augustinian canon, Dominic, began to mount preaching campaigns like those carried out earlier by the Cistercians. The convent of Prouille was founded in 1207, and this became his base. Throughout the first phase of the Albigensian crusade, Dominic and his followers continued their activities with the support of Simon de Montfort and the bishops of Toulouse. A full order was constituted in 1216–17, which, because of the moratorium on new orders by the fourth Lateran council of 1215, was formed as a congregation of Austin canons. Their principal activity was to be preaching. Later in the same year Dominic dispersed his followers to Paris, to Spain, to Italy, throughout the Languedoc; their principal centres became Paris and Bologna. They were primarily priests and educated men, who were to make a great impact through using their learning to save men's souls.

Perhaps early in 1217 Dominic and Francis met, and it seems no coincidence that Dominic now adopted absolute poverty for his followers, forbidding them to own property, to carry money or to ride on horseback; and he sent them away from the Languedoc to concentrate on preaching to other groups apart from heretics. The influences were not all one way, for the Franciscans, predominantly laymen at this time, began to take holy orders in larger numbers and to follow the Dominican emphasis on education for their own members. It was thus that two orders with highly diverse origins were already growing close together soon after their foundation; yet Dominic, who died in 1221 and was later canonised, never became the centre of a cult such as that of Francis. Fewer Dominican houses were founded in France than Franciscan ones; by 1275 they had 87 monasteries, under half the Franciscan total: these included one at Toulouse, founded c. 1215, and one at Paris, c. 1217.

The mendicant way of life was followed by a number of other orders. The Carmelites originated in Palestine, the Austin friars in Italy (c. 1256), and both spread in France in the middle years of Louis's reign. In later medieval Europe these orders were next to the Franciscans and Dominicans in size and importance. In France the pattern of foundations was not typical, since the Carmelites and Austin friars were outnumbered by more local groups. These were the Trinitarian friars, founded near Meaux in about 1198 to rescue the Christians from the infidel; and the Friars of the Sack, founded in Provence just before 1250. Like other smaller orders such as the Pied Friars, the Trinitarians and Sack Friars were forbidden to take in new members by the Council of Lyon of 1274, and eventually their organisations were wound up. The king was an important patron of the mendicants, with whom he shared many ideals, and he supported the lesser orders as well as the Franciscans and Dominicans (5.4.1).

The twelfth-century monastic orders had on the whole found the desire of women to join them an unwanted embarrassment; the Cistercians, perhaps more anti-female than all the others, resisted the houses of nuns who sought to be accepted into their order until the early thirteenth century, and thereafter remained highly unaccommodating towards them; the Franciscan women, the Clares, named after Francis's first female follower, became a strictly cloistered order of nuns. There still remained many pious women who did not wish to withdraw entirely from the world but who had aspirations towards some kind of religious life. Their needs and wishes were served by the Béguine movement, which began in the Rhineland and Flanders in the early thirteenth century and spread rapidly throughout Europe. The Béguines were not a religious order in the formal sense, since the members had no rule, no organisation, no hierarchy, but took vows of celibacy and tried to live the apostolic life. They established themselves singly or in small groups in property they had inherited; they had no patrons and no formal connections with the ecclesiastical hierarchy. They were entirely independent from men. At first they were treated with contempt – the word béguine means a heretic – but by the middle of the thirteenth century they had won praise and admiration from characters as diverse as Matthew Paris, and the Franciscan bishop of Lincoln Robert Grosseteste. The latter thought that they represented the highest form of religious life.[28]

The mendicant orders and the Béguines had many aspirations in common, but by 1270 both the observant Franciscans and the Dominicans had modified many of their early precepts, including absolute poverty. Both orders became heavily involved with academic studies, and attracted and produced a number of brilliant scholars, including Alexander of Hales, Thomas Aquinas and Bonaventura. The Dominicans created a system of schools in which advanced theological study flourished, and the Franciscans later imitated these. By the 1250s the mendicant schools in Paris were well developed and effective, and had built up a strong and important influence which rivalled that of the secular masters. The university was a volatile body and disliked these developments; its powers of resistance had been shown when in 1228–29 Blanche of Castile had put down a riot and the whole university dispersed, not to reconvene until 1231, when it was given important privileges. Both the bishop and particularly the chancellor of Paris had their powers limited, the latter losing his criminal jurisdiction over the scholars almost entirely. The abbot of Sainte-Geneviève was allowed to share his right to issue licences to teach.

Meanwhile the Dominican and Franciscan schools were emerging as the intellectual leaders in the field of theology. Although Aristotelian writings had been prohibited in 1217, by 1250 they were accepted as part of the curriculum, and the attempt at the reconciliation of Christian theology and Aristotelianism by Alexander of Hales, who became a Franciscan, was a work of great importance. Albertus Magnus and Thomas Aquinas, both Dominicans, carried this further. Aquinas was an Italian by birth, but cosmopolitan by virtue of his training and his order; yet his great work, the *Summa Theologica*, places him firmly in the world of Paris.

A community of scholarship in Paris did not produce common interests between the mendicant and secular masters, however. In 1229 and 1230 the friars had not dispersed with the rest of the university, but stayed and opened up their theological schools, and to the resentment caused by this was added the anger of the secular masters when one of their number, such as Alexander of Hales, joined the mendicants. In 1251–52 the secular masters of theology forbade the admission of anyone who did not belong to a college as a master of the university, thus excluding the mendicants, and in 1252–53 there was another violent riot, suppressed in a way to contravene the privileges of the university. Again the friars, in defiance of their secular colleagues, continued to teach, and an oath of obedience to the statutes of the university was demanded of them: this they could not give, so they were expelled from the university. Innocent IV tried to mediate, but in 1255 Alexander IV found for the friars, probably with the support of Louis IX, who had turned against the secular masters after one, William of Saint-Amour, had criticised him outspokenly in a sermon. The secular masters who refused to obey the pope were excommunicated, and they then dissolved the university, their corporation, in retaliation. Polemical tracts were written by both sides. Eventually by 1256 all the seculars had given in, apart from William of Saint-Amour, who was first exiled to Anagni, and then to his native Franche-Comté. The victory of the friars was complete, but they became even more unpopular as a result of these events. The next pope, Urban IV, himself formerly a Parisian canonist, reduced the independence of the mendicant doctors by limiting their numbers in the university, and excluding them from the faculty of arts and from teaching secular students. The friars' privileges continued to be eroded, and by 1318 they were giving oaths of obedience to the university. Their unpopularity at the end of Louis IX's reign did much to increase that of the king, who was their major patron and protector (5.4.1).

The Dominican order assumed another important role in thirteenth-century France, shared to a much lesser extent by the Franciscans – that of inquisitors. The word inquisitor, or in French *enquêteur*, was used by the royal government as well as by the church for men who travelled round holding investigations and acting upon them. In the case of the papal inquisition, directed against heretics, the term has taken on sinister connotations. But the inquisition developed as an attempt by the papacy to set up a different kind of machinery for dealing with heretics from that which existed already, which was run often halfheartedly by each bishop in his own diocese. In the Languedoc the Cathar heresy proved difficult to crush (5.5.3), and the preaching campaigns of the Cistercians and later the Dominicans under commission from the pope had from the middle of the twelfth century begun to suggest the potential value of a different approach. The culmination of these developments was in 1233–34 when the Dominicans were given full powers to seek out and punish heretics; so successful were they that this was to become the standard method of combating heresy throughout Europe. By the 1250s the Dominicans had evolved a full inquisitorial method. They built up codes of practice and kept full accounts of their activities for future reference. The earliest manual for inquisitors was compiled in 1248–49 by Bernard of Caux and

John of Saint-Pierre. This instructs inquisitors first to find a centre of operations and preach a sermon about the inquisition there, then to summon all suspected heretics and to pardon anyone else who within a fixed period came forward to give evidence. All those thus confessing were required to swear an oath abjuring heresy, and were thoroughly questioned about whether they had seen or had dealings with heretics. Those summoned were permitted to defend themselves, but if convicted they were given heavy penances and absolution before being handed over to the secular arm for punishment, and having their goods confiscated.[29]

Some of the problems inherent in the use of zealous men under vows to find heretics, and in giving them unrestrained powers, emerged in the early days of the inquisition. Conrad of Marburg wreaked havoc by his misapplied zeal in Germany in the early 1230s, and another Dominican and an appointee of Gregory IX, Robert le Bougre, so-called because he was himself a converted heretic, carried out devastating purges in northern France, in the Nevers area and in Champagne, in 1233–34. So great was the hostility he aroused that he was told to cease his activities by the pope in 1234, but from 1235 he travelled round northern France as a general inquisitor, carrying out persecutions on a wide, often indiscriminate, scale. In 1239 at Mont-Aimé in Champagne he crowned his career with what seems to have been a veritable holocaust of Cathars. Contemporary chroniclers, not necessarily in sympathy with the heretics but horrified by his methods, portrayed him as a hypocrite and a sorcerer. The king, orthodox to the core, supported the inquisition in his lands, paying for keeping heretics imprisoned and for an armed guard for Robert. He was clearly an extreme case, and when Alexander IV (1254–61) reorganised the inquisition in northern France, putting it under the control of the provincial prior of Paris, a closer watch could be kept on the inquisitors. But although methods became more sophisticated and there was less scope for confused, indiscriminate persecution, the proceedings remained secret, so that 'the preservation of justice rested to a large extent on the integrity of the individual who conducted a case. There was scope for greed, political bias, the malice of neighbours, bullying and sadism',[30] and oversophisticated proceedings could give highly misleading results. Furthermore, the sphere of the inquisition was to be widened beyond the heretics proper, and the French king, Philip IV, was to find it an invaluable weapon against the Templars (6.5.4).

5.4 LOUIS IX AND THE CHURCH

5.4.1 The piety of Louis IX

On Louis IX's deep and sincere piety all sources are agreed. Most adulatory of all are the accounts of William of Saint-Pathus, Geoffrey of Beaulieu and William of Nangis: where Joinville (5.1.1) gives us an impression of a pious but human king they paint a picture of a saint; William of Saint-Pathus declared that Louis's life was exemplary. He liked to hear all the canonical hours and the mass each day and utterly shunned the songs of the world. The fervour of his piety was increased by his sufferings on crusade. He loved to hear sermons regularly, and to attend monastic chapters; and he was greatly devoted to holy relics. Much of his time was spent in prayer and in the study of the Bible. He was always kind and generous to his family and his entourage and exhorted them to follow God's ways. He was a generous benefactor to the poor and sick, to the friars, Cistercians and other orders. So great was his humility that he would kiss the hands of lepers he met in the streets, and his dress was always plain in the extreme – in fact his clothes were too poor in quality to be given to the needy after he had finished with them. He was an example to many priests. He died as he had lived and performed many miracles afterwards.

These works are hagiographical, and they give a very one-dimensional, uncritical and adulatory view of the king. Nevertheless, many of the details they provide about Louis's pious activities are amply confirmed in other sources. Joinville covers much of the same material – the king's humility, his generosity to the poor and the sick, his devotion to God – and he retells in a lively fashion many of the king's pious sayings.

At another time King Louis asked me if I washed the feet of the poor on Maundy Thursday. 'Your Majesty,' I exclaimed, 'what a terrible idea. I will never wash the feet of such low fellows.' 'Really,' said he, 'that is a very wrong thing to say, for you should never scorn to do what our Lord Himself did as an example to us. So I beg you, first for the love of God, and then for love of me, to accustom yourself to washing the feet of the poor.'[13]

Furthermore, there is a valuable source for the king's own views of his life and his office: his instructions to his son Philip, dictated on his deathbed. The original text is lost, but the most accurate version of those to survive is probably the version in the *Noster* manuscript of the chambre des comptes.[32] Louis lays out the moral precepts which he has followed in his life. He urges Philip to love God with all his heart and strength, not to commit mortal sin, to suffer sickness with good grace and not to become arrogant if God sends him good fortune. He should confess his sins frequently, revere the Host, serve the church and not speak vain words. He should give help to the poor and needy and be liberal in almsgiving. Good, wise and pious counsellors should surround him, both priests and laymen, and he should eschew the company of evil men. He should recognise the bounty and honour given to him by God and make himself worthy of the unction with which the French kings are blessed. He should uphold justice, the poor against the rich, and he should protect the clergy above all. He should take care of churchmen and give benefices to suitable men, and he should love and honour his mother and care for his brothers. He should try not to make war on other Christians but rather he should negotiate for peace. His *baillis* and *prévôts* should be picked with care, as, too, should his household. He should show due reverence for the Roman church and avoid and combat swearing, games of dice, visiting taverns and other sinful activities. His coinage should be good and sound. Finally Louis asks his son to have prayers said for his soul, gives him a father's blessing and commends him to God. The overwhelmingly religious tone of this document is a clear reflection of the king's principal preoccupation, God's service, which was the mainspring of his actions.

Many aspects of Louis's actual behaviour are reflected in this document. He made peace with his neighbours in order the better to fight the infidel, he legislated in the celebrated ordinance of 1254 both to reform his own officials, and on a wider basis against usury, blasphemy and prostitution, games of chance and the frequenting of inns meant for travellers, throughout the kingdom (5.5.1). He spent regularly and lavishly on religious patronage, as the royal accounts confirm; and this facet of his pious behaviour is well worth a more detailed examination.

William of Saint-Pathus estimated that the king spent about £7,000 each year in alms to monks and friars and that he gave extra in clothing and food.[33] Each year he also distributed 60,000 herrings amongst the religious orders. The sum total that he spent on all the hospitals and friaries he built amounted to more than £200,000 tournois, and when his counsellors reproached him for this excessive expenditure he replied that God had given him what he had, and what was handed out in this way was put to the best use.

A careful analysis of the surviving royal accounts suggests that far more money was going to certain religious orders in regular payments and alms than under Philip Augustus. Between a quarter and a third of the expenses in Ascension term 1248 went in religious patronage, while in 1202–03 the proportion was about one fifteenth.[34] Table 5.1 accounts for Louis's almsgiving during the summer of 1256, and illustrates the size of the sums spent.

During the early years of the reign much royal patronage and favour went towards the Cistercians. Matthew Paris called Louis 'supporter and protector of the Cistercian order'.[35] Blanche was probably largely responsible for this interest, for the king never founded a Cistercian house himself, despite several attributed to him, and later in his reign turned to other orders. In Louis's early years he and his mother gave generously to Le Trésor in Normandy, Saint-Antoine-des-Champs, Cîteaux and other houses, and had a special place in the prayers of the order. Blanche had been enjoined to found a Victorine house in memory of Louis VIII but she decided it should be Cistercian instead, and she and the young king devoted much care and attention to the establishment and building of the abbey of Royaumont from 1228. Its style was by Cistercian standards magnificent, as befitted the burial house of several members of Louis's family, and it may have been intended as Louis's own pantheon for a time. William of Nangis praised its decoration, but in 1253 the general chapter of the order instructed its abbot to alter the reredos to fit better with the general humility and simplicity of the Cistercian way of life. Such could be the problems of having royal patrons. Blanche herself later founded two Cistercian nunneries, Maubuisson in about 1236 and Le Lys in about 1241, and it was in the former that she was buried. Other members of the royal family were also patrons of the white monks. Alfonso of Poitiers became the founder of a college of Bernardines in Paris in 1253 and Charles of Anjou celebrated his victories over the Hohenstaufen at Benevento and Tagliacozzo with the foundation of Realvalle and Vittoria in his southern lands.

Other monastic houses received generous treatment from the king. He gave

Table 5.1   The almsgiving of Louis IX, 2nd June–15th August 1256 (in livres parisis)

Recipients (abbreviated)	£	s	d
To the Béguines of Cambrai	10	0	0
Pittances of bread and wine	39	16	6
Guernot the stableman injured by a horse		60	0
Alms at Maubuisson on 17th July		100	0
Gautier de Vendure sent on a mission		40	0
Alms at Corbeil on 23 July		100	0
Nuns of Beaulieu, Paris by the hand of brother Geoffrey de Beaulieu	20	0	0
Alms at Paris on 31 July		100	0
Three poor women		70	0
Alms at Paris on 4 August		100	0
Pittances of bread and wine for 14 days	38	17	8
Five books of divinity	55	0	0
A priest who has come from overseas		40	0
Alms at Poissy on 9 August	20	0	0
Alms at Poissy on 12 August		100	0
Demoiselle Richeut de Longchamp		20	0
Brother Stephen de Greftine		100	0
Brother Stephen de Greftine		20	0
Pittances from the kitchen for 18 days	33	2	6
Alms for 200 poor at Le Mans on 14 August	20	0	0
Total	£280	6	8

Source: RHF, xxi, 356 s 207

Saint-Denis a number of valuable privileges and financed its major rebuilding (5.5.5). He founded a Carthusian priory at Vauvert in about 1259 and was openhanded to, although he did not found, the Victorine Sainte-Catherine-de-la-Couture. Later in his reign began the flow of hospitals, friaries and royal chapels; in 1256 he began the refoundation of the hospital at Pontoise, and in about 1260 he refounded the Hôtel-Dieu at Compiègne at an estimated cost of more than £12,000. More expensive than these was the complete rebuilding of the Hôtel-Dieu at Vernon: Saint-Pathus said that it cost more than £30,000 because it was in the best part of the town, and the king provided the sisters here with all their needs down to the cooking pots.[36] The foundation of the Filles-Dieu in Paris, a house for former prostitutes, was widely though mistakenly attributed to him, although he did establish the Quinze-Vingts, a hospital for the blind, and also a convent for the Béguines; and he gave generously to the Hôtel-Dieu in Paris. Joinville emphasises the reverence shown by the king for the poor and sick. He fed thirteen poor at his table on Thursdays, Fridays and Saturdays during Lent and Advent and each Friday at other times of the year. He served them and ate with them himself, according to Saint-Pathus, and each Saturday he washed the feet of three particularly poor people and gave them donations. Sometimes he fed the poor in larger numbers, and he held substantial almsgivings at least twice a year.[37]

The influence of the friars over Louis was judged strong by both his admirers and his detractors. William of Saint-Pathus suggests that had the queen died before him Louis might have become a mendicant himself. But it would have been difficult for him to choose between the Franciscans and the Dominicans, for he was equally attached to both orders. He was also the major patron of several other orders of friars, and used friars as confessors and advisers. His enthusiasm for the hearing of the sermons and the emphasis he placed on them is very much a mendicant practice, and Saint Bonaventura, minister-general of the Franciscans, preached frequently before Louis and his family. Hugh of Digne, a forerunner of the spiritual Franciscans from Provence, was also a friend and close associate of the king. Joinville describes his advice to Louis on his return from the crusade: the king, he said, should administer justice well and wisely, so that he may rule his kingdom in peace for the rest of his days. Louis, declares Joinville, never forgot this advice.[38]

The Dominicans were closely involved in the extirpation of heresy and the king supported their work in the inquisition in France, giving Robert le Bougre and other friars funds and at times an armed guard (5.3.2). He refounded the black friars' houses in Compiègne and Rouen and he gave substantially to those in Carcassonne, Mâcon, Paris and elsewhere. Many other Dominican friaries claimed him as their founder. He was only marginally less generous to the Franciscans: he gave lavishly to their community known as the Cordeliers in Paris, and helped the house of minoresses at Longchamp founded by his sister Isabella. Other members of his family, including Queen Margaret and Alfonso of Poitiers, founded or refounded several Franciscan houses. The king established the Friars of the Sack in Paris in about 1261, and was reckoned the founder of the Pied Friars' establishment here too. He was also generous to the Trinitarian friars of Paris and he built them a house at Fontainebleau.

This support of the mendicants was bitterly criticised, especially in connection with the controversy in the university of Paris between the secular masters under William of Saint-Amour and the mendicant masters. At first the king stood aloof, but he was drawn into the contest by the intransigence of William, who preached a sermon criticising the king on grounds of hypocrisy and subservience to the friars. On Louis's recommendation the pope sent him into exile in 1256. The poets Rutebeuf and John of Meung echoed William in their castigations of Louis. Eventually the dispute was settled in favour of the mendicants, which added to their unpopularity in many quarters. The king was not opposed to the university, however; he showed much generosity towards the collège of the Sorbonne founded by the royal clerk and counsellor, Robert de Sorbon.

Like his predecessors Louis IX founded or refounded a number of small intercessory chapels and priories. Some of these were also to house relics, such as Saint-Maurice at Senlis (c. 1261–62), where a group of Augustinian canons took care of the bones of the Holy Theban Legion and prayed for the king. Royal chapels which the king favoured or refounded included Saint-Germain-en-Laye (c. 1238), Saint-Vaast at Pontoise (c. 1254) and above all the Sainte-Chapelle. This was conceived of as a massive shrine for the relics of the passion – the crown of thorns, acquired from Constantinople in 1239, and part of the true cross and other items, some of dubious authenticity, purchased in 1241. Such prestigious relics required a fitting setting, and William of Saint-Pathus estimated that the chapel cost more than £40,000 to build. It was served by chaplains and very generously endowed, and it was completed and finally dedicated with great ceremony in 1248. When Henry III visited Paris in 1254 he was much impressed with it, and contemporary rhymesters suggested that he would have liked to take it home with him. As a pattern for the court style of architecture and as a symbol of Louis's veneration for the relics of the passion it was of major importance. It also became an affirmation of the special sanctification of the French king (5.5.5).

The king and his court were regularly involved in magnificent religious events, such as the consecrations of major royal foundations. Relics were one of his major interests and he embellished a number of churches which possessed particularly efficacious ones. He also attended a number of translation ceremonies, as when, for example, in 1247, Edmund, formerly archbishop of Canterbury, recently canonised by the pope, was given a magnificent tomb at Pontigny, or in 1262 when some relics of the Holy Theban Legion were taken ceremonially to Senlis. The most festive occasions of all were for the relics of the passion at the Sainte-Chapelle.

The king's generosity and reputation for piety made many orders look to him for patronage. Monks from the order of Grandmont went as far as forging charters from him and in 1259 some were thrown into prison for their pains. Many other religious houses sought his protection and obtained safeguards from the king by virtue of his special royal powers of protection, and in many cases this was an attempt to escape their own patrons. The abbot of Saint-Pierre of Ghent tried to represent himself at court as the neighbour rather than the subject of the count of Flanders for example, but often the royal justices upheld the interests of the patrons rather than the wishes of the house when such matters came before them. Overall, however, the number of monasteries under royal protection increased. Many of the additions were in the Languedoc, and this was clearly a useful way of extending royal influence.

For those orders and houses which the king favoured, Louis's reign was a golden age. For the others, patterns of royal patronage such as the standard issuing of charters of confirmation continued in the same way as in earlier reigns. The king was as firm a master of the French church as Philip Augustus had been, exercising his regalian rights to the full, nominating bishops and abbots, and taxing the church heavily with papal consent. His piety made him all the more difficult to resist.

5.4.2 Louis IX, the French church and the papacy

The papacy in the thirteenth century was a very different kind of institution from the papacy in the early Middle Ages. Since the papal reforms of the eleventh century the popes had, like other monarchs, developed a substantial administration and bureaucracy, which reflected a wider involvement in and expansion of ecclesiastical affairs. Papal finances, papal justice, papal government and diplomacy were now major concerns, and the bishop of Rome was, despite his spiritual, supranational role, coming to resemble a secular monarch more and more closely. The thirteenth-century canonists, while following the same general lines of thought as their predecessors, emphasised the papal prerogative to intervene in secular affairs when the ruler had failed to give justice to his people; and the papal plentitude of power was seen as exercised in a political as much as a spiritual sense.[39] Here theory reflected reality, for papal intervention in secular affairs became far more frequent, and spiritual weapons, such as the crusade, excommunications and interdicts were over-used and debased.

As papal government and papal activities extended in their scope, the influence of Rome increased at a provincial and diocesan level, often causing great local resentment as it did so. In their need to extend their resources of patronage to find rewards and financial support for their vast bureaucracy, successive popes began to present their own men, usually Italians, to valuable benefices outside the papal lands, overriding the rights of the patrons and causing much opposition. The first formal statement of papal rights in this matter was in 1265, when Clement IV reserved the right to present to all benefices falling vacant at Rome, and this was subsequently extended. Provisions were justified by the general notion that all churches and ecclesiastical benefices were in the power of the pope, which also allowed for the future reservation of a benefice after the death of the incumbent. As a result they were disliked by kings, nobles, archbishops, bishops and clergy alike, as they could weaken the spiritual life of a diocese and cause a financial drain. Archbishops and bishops also found many of their spiritual and judicial powers being eroded by the papacy and their independence challenged, but by a power whose moral and spiritual authority was in decline. As a result many of them supported secular monarchs who might extend their liberties. Louis IX took an anti-papal line in many issues, he stood up for his own people, the French, and he took his role as God's anointed very seriously. The French church, with its strong traditions of independence against the pope, thus tended not to defy the king over most issues. But he extended and consolidated his own powers over it as a result, and in some matters, particularly in the field of taxation, he and the papacy cooperated in firmly controlling and exploiting the French church.

The complexity of the interactions between Louis IX, the papacy and the French church is well illustrated in the French protests to the pope in 1247 and their lack of results. In this year two delegations representing the king, the French barons, whose protests set the whole thing in motion, and the French clergy went to Pope Innocent IV and complained about the burden of papal taxation, the spread of papal jursidiction at the expense of that of the bishops, and the frequency of papal provisions. The pope promised remedies (5.2.2), but Matthew Paris, who gives a text of the second protest,[40] comments that it had little effect. Certainly nothing seems to have been done to lessen provisions, which became a point at issue between Louis and Pope Urban IV in the 1260s. Taxation of the French church grew heavier rather than lighter, but this benefited the king and he supported it. So great did opposition from the church become to the subsidies to finance Charles of Anjou's crusade, that in 1262 the archbishop of Tours refused to contribute. In 1268 the provinces of Reims, Sens and Tours all refused to pay towards Louis's second crusade, and Louis called in Pope Clement

IV, who hurled threats and anathemas against the erring ecclesiastics. The money was in these cases being raised for holy wars, whether generally considered legitimate or not. But from the position expressed by the royal envoys, perhaps rather extremely as far as Louis went, in Matthew Paris's text for 1247 — that since the king's ancestors founded and enriched the churches of the realm, all their temporalities belonged to the king — it proved only a short step actually to extend the king's right to tax the French clergy in times of need without papal permission. The papacy proved powerless to resist Louis's successors (6.5.3).

In another area of complaints, that of jurisdiction, Louis, following the example of his mother, resisted both papal and episcopal claims and upheld royal justice with great firmness. In the early 1230s, for example, he and Blanche intervened in a dispute between the burgesses and people of Beauvais. They meted out justice in the episcopal city, occupying the bishop's palace and demanding heavy payments of *gîte*. Bishop Milo, who had been a close associate of Louis VIII, felt that his rights had been infringed and he imposed an interdict on the see. A papal legate was sent, and then Milo set off for Rome but died on the way. Eventually a successor of his submitted to the king. In this case Blanche defended an unsatisfactory position with some success, although in another case involving Nôtre-Dame-de-Paris and its serfs she was not to do as well (1252, 5.2.2). Her dispute with the archbishop of Rouen at the beginning of the reign was more justifiable and illustrates the importance she attached to the superior competence of royal justice to ecclesiastical justice in secular matters. This was occasioned when Archbishop Theobald ordered some wood to be gathered from Vaudreuil for his own use. He was entitled to do this, but he had then had it transported for use in Rouen, which infringed royal rights. The royal *bailli* therefore seized the wood; but the archbishop excommunicated the *bailli* without royal permission, and was in his turn cited before the royal court in conformity with an exchequer decree of 1205. The archbishop refused to submit to royal justice and his temporalities were seized; he then laid the archdiocese of Rouen under interdict and appealed to the pope. His lands were restored but a stalemate was reached which was only to end with his death in 1231. His successor Maurice fell foul of the queen by asking her to back up an excommunication of the monks of Saint-Wandrille, and by interfering in the election of the abbess of Montivilliers, and in 1232 his lands were seized again. Taking on Theobald's mantle, he refused to go before the royal court and he excommunicated royal officials and chaplains in his archdiocese. In the next year both sides backed down. The incident resolved nothing but revealed the tensions between the two kinds of jurisdiction, lay and ecclesiastical.

Another problem was also illustrated in the Rouen clash: the extent of the king's obligations in acting as the secular arm in excommunication. In the 1229 ordinance for the Languedoc, *Cupientes*, Blanche laid down that the crown could seize the goods of convicted excommunicated heretics after a year and a day. The church tried to extend such royal support into other cases, and later the crown insisted on deciding whether an excommunication was justified. In 1235, for example, the burgesses of Reims quarrelled with their archbishop over financial matters, and the archbishop excommunicated some and asked the king for his support. Louis refused, since a secular court had not reviewed the case, and the archbishop appealed to the pope, and then with the backing of a provincial church council complained to the king. The king with baronial support protested to the pope at the refusal of the archbishop to appear in the royal court. The province, Reims, was then laid under interdict by the provincial council and the pope complained that it was an innovation to cite clergy before the secular courts in temporal affairs. But he did not press the matter too strongly since he needed Louis's support against Frederick II. In 1236 Louis settled the Reims dispute himself, and in 1237 he gained from the pope exemption from excommunication for himself and his family, which greatly strengthened his hand. Later in the reign the bishops stopped calling upon the king to enforce most sentences of excommunication. As late as about 1263, according to Joinville, Louis reiterated to a group of prelates that he would not seize the goods of excommunicates without certain proof of guilt. In 1270 he threatened to seize the temporalities of the see of Clermont because the bishop was issuing false coinage and excommunicating protesters. The king was not only deciding whether excommunication was justified in this case, but, having done so, he was threatening constraints to back up his decision.

The bishop's counterfeit coins arguably laid him open to such treatment, but it still illustrates the hard line taken by the king against erring churchmen throughout his reign. All ecclesiastics were made subject to the laws of the land in secular matters. Certainly, however, the king did not put forward the right to legislate for the whole French church, as was long thought. The Pragmatic Sanction, an ordinance supposedly issued by the king in 1269, and forbidding collations, simony and excessive taxes going from the French church to Rome, was in fact forged in the fifteenth century, probably in support of the claims of Charles VII over the church. In the seventeenth and eighteenth centuries it was regarded as one of the chief planks of Gallican liberties, but it has no value as evidence for thirteenth century conditions.

In general political dealings the king managed to remain on good terms with a papacy which could not deny his personal piety, but which he only supported when it suited his own ends: good order in the French church, the upholding of his royal power and the recapture of the Holy Land from the infidel. Louis remained uncommitted in the early years of the struggle between Frederick II and the papacy; not until Frederick imprisoned a number of French clergy did Louis protest strongly and then the emperor, fearing to alienate the king, let them go. Innocent IV, elected in 1243, tried to take refuge from his political problems in France; but the king tried without success to reconcile Innocent and Frederick. On his return home from crusade, Louis continued uncommitted in the struggle caused by the pope's attempts to wipe out the Hohenstaufen, and he refused Innocent's offer of the crown of Sicily for his brother Charles of Anjou in 1252, which was withdrawn by Alexander IV in 1258. This more pacific pope cooperated with Louis in settling the quarrel of the secular and mendicant masters in the university of Paris in 1256 (5.3.2). Alexander was succeeded by an aggressive Frenchman, Urban IV, who renewed the offer of Sicily to Charles of Anjou, and this time Louis was persuaded to throw all his weight behind the papal cause. It was thus that Charles became king of Sicily and papal champion (5.2.2).

Louis's ecclesiastical policy was a highly successful one. He carried to considerable lengths the attempts of his predecessors to dominate and control the French church. He kept his own clergy firmly in line, he supervised elections and excommunications, he checked the spread of ecclesiastical jurisdiction. With papal support he mulcted the French church to pay for his crusades. His personal piety and yet his strength of purpose where his own interests were concerned made him impossible to resist. He maintained an independent line against the papacy, using the hostility of the French people to the growth of papal government to check its spread in his kingdom, even while pursuing a higher aim and living an ascetic life which put many clerics to shame. Doubtless he would have been horrified at the outcome of many of his policies, of the misuse and extension of royal power over the church by his grandson Philip IV (6.5.3; 6.5.4). Nevertheless the actions of the saint-king made such later developments possible.

5.5 THE CONSOLIDATION OF ROYAL POWER

5.5.1 Royal government and administration

In Louis IX's reign the lands conquered by the French crown, Normandy and part of the Languedoc, were brought firmly under royal control. To these gains were added the county of Mâcon, purchased in 1239 for £10,000 tournois from its childless count. The king was now altogether the most substantial landholder in his kingdom (Map 5.2), and his administration was developed and expanded to cope with the changes.

In all the royal lands *baillis* (or seneschals in the south) were set over groups of *prévôts* and exercised both judicial and financial functions. Appeals from the *prévôts'* courts came to them in the first instance and from 1234 they were responsible for the profits of justice and other payments such as commutations of the *gîte*, subsidies from communes, regalian dues, fees for the use of the royal seal and payments raised from the royal forests. The *prévôts* brought their accounts to the *baillis* who presented them at the Temple in Paris for audit. They were also responsible for out-payments, which from the 1238 accounts onwards were divided under three broad heads: gifts, alms and pensions; the king's works; wages of officials such as castellans and judges. The *baillis* had an important military role, as they were responsible for overseeing the castles in their *bailliages* and levying troops for the royal armies. They were normally laymen, often of bourgeois or lesser knightly rather than noble families.

In his celebrated codification of the customs of the Beauvaisis, Philip de Beaumanoir sets out the ideal characteristics of a *bailli*: he should be wise, god-fearing, gentle, brave, generous, obedient to his lord, shrewd, and he should uphold the law. Such advice was not always followed and was difficult to enforce.

Following strong complaints about the conduct of his officials, Louis IX sent round *enquêteurs* from 1247 onwards, travelling agents of the king, usually friars, who would collect complaints about them and remedy these where possible. Their records suggest that while the *baillis* and *prévôts* generally followed acceptable lines of conduct many of the lesser officials were very corrupt. In his ordinance of 1254 the king tried to counteract such problems, but although his moral legislation had some impact, there were always difficulties in a system where many offices were farmed out; and since royal rights were viewed in terms of profit, they were constantly extended. Nevertheless the accounts were thoroughly audited; and the power of the *baillis* should not be exaggerated. In almost every *bailliage* there were independent nobles with administrative and judicial rights of their own, whose men could only be dealt with by royal officials through them. Though their rights were in many cases eaten away by agents of the king, they remained a stumbling block to the full extension of royal power. This was also the case in the *apanages* of Charles of Anjou and Alfonso of Poitiers (5.5.4) where these princes had their own administrations not unlike that of the king.

The great expansion in royal lands made the king by far the wealthiest man in the kingdom. The fire at the chambre des comptes in 1737 and the French Revolution destroyed the great bulk of the medieval financial records of the French crown. Those which survive are only a small part of what was a rich and copious archive, and the losses of Louis IX's records are greater than those of his successors. Nevertheless some idea of royal finances can be gleaned from the surviving accounts for the Candlemas term of 1226, at the end of Louis VIII's reign, and for the Ascension term of 1238,[41] summarised in Table 5.2. These set out both receipts and expenditure. There is also a fuller account of the *baillis* and *prévôts* for the Ascension term of 1248, which is compared with the 1238 account in Table 5.3.[42]

These accounts are by no means comprehensive statements of annual expenditure, however. The total receipts £53,730. 8s 0d parisis for Candlemas 1226, and £101,279.17s 5d parisis for Ascension 1238, represent the totals for one term only out of the three. The totals for the *bailliages* and *prévôtés* for 1238 and 1248 of £235,286. 7s 0d and £178,530. 12s 9d are estimates based on only part of the receipts. As a comparison two years for which complete accounts survive are 1202–03 (4.4.4) and 1286–87 (6.4.1): in 1202–03 receipts were £197,042.12s 0d and expenses, £95,445; in 1286–87, receipts were £604,942 and expenses £530,573. The general upward trend is clear and thus Louis IX's fixed annual revenue was probably by the time of his first crusade between £200,000 and £250,000 parisis. Not only did the profits of justice increase, together with the profits of the domain and feudal dues handled by the *baillis* and *prévôts*, so too did other sources of income such as regalian rights, and payments for amortisation (see p. 310), and the commutation of *gîte*; the latter alone raised £12,500 in the years 1254–69.[43]

Clearly in normal circumstances the king could easily balance his budget. Extraordinary expenditure called for extraordinary taxation, however. According to surviving accounts Louis's first crusade cost more than one million pounds

Table 5.2   Summary of the receipts and expenses of Louis VIII and Louis IX: Candlemas 1226 and Ascension 1238 (*expressed in* livres parisis unless otherwise indicated)

Candlemas 1226

Receipts	£	s	d	Expenses	£	s	d
Baillis	23,233	11	8	Household	11,074	9	0
	3,357	12	0	Gifts and			
Prévôts	18,456	13	4	equipment	7,756	7	0
Jews	8,682	11	0	Horses	1,182	14	0
				Soldiers	1,688	18	0
				Count of			
				Champagne	4,000	0	0
				Borders, new			
				castles	4,904	13	0
				Foresters	241	16	0
				Prévôts and			
				baillis	3,978	9	6
				Queen	1,852	13	3
				Count of			
				Boulogne	1,000	0	0
Total	£53,730	8	0	*Total*	£37,479	19	9

The treasurer owes the king. . .£16,250 8 3

Ascension 1238

Receipts	£	s	d	Expenses	£	s	d
Baillis	25,211	7	3	Household	12,187	5	4
Prévôts	15,672	8	8	Gifts and			
				equipment	17,301	11	3
Relief for the				Robes	382	6	0
county of				Horses	824	16	0
Flanders	15,000	0	0	Soldiers	1,046	16	8
Receipts in				Young queen and			
£ tournois	45,396	1	6	princes	1,210	9	7
				Fees and alms	15,930	2	5
				Wages	11,827	2	10
				Works	2,770	12	7
				Loans	6,800	0	0
				Miscellaneous	350	0	0
				War	2,207	5	0
Total	£101,279	17	5	Total	£72,638	7	8

The *baillis* owe the king £1,647 17s 8d apart from what is owed by Adam Panetarius
Total expenses are thus £75,286 5s 4d

The treasurer owes the king £25,993 12s 1d

Source: RHF, xxi, 251–60; *RHF, Docs. Fin.*, ii, xlv–xlvii.

Table 5.3   Estimated receipts from the *bailliages* and *prévôtés* for the years 1238 and 1248 based on the accounts for the Ascension terms (*in* livres parisis)

	1238			1248		
	£	s	d	£	s	d
Prévôte of Paris	11,502	17	7	5,467	19	3
Bailliage of Amiens	966	3	3	606	2	6
Bailliage of Bourges	1,747	14	9	1,402	0	9
Bailliage of Vermandois	21,576	4	9	12,907	3	0
Bailliage of Gisors	3,760	3	9	8,899	13	9
Bailliage of Sens	13,540	6	6	3,051	16	6
Bailliage of Orléans	1,696	19	0	7,292	7	3
Temple, *regalia* etc.	10,074	1	0	3,034	11	3
Prévôtés	47,017	6	0	46,397	2	0
Other receipts	2,895	13	0	228	0	0
Total of *bailliages* in northern France	£114,797	9	6	£89,286	16	3
Bailliage of Tours	7,213	13	3	1,420	16	0
Bailliages of Normandy	110,920	7	9	86,271	6	0
Bailliage of Poitou	2,354	16	6	–	–	–
Bailliage of Mâcon	–	–	–	1,551	14	6
General total	£235,286	7	0	£178,530	12	9

Source: RHF, xxi, p. lxxvi.

tournois,[44] most of this being culled from the French church with papal permission. Other similar subsidies were raised to finance Charles of Anjou's wars in Sicily and Louis's last crusade. The king also levied crusading aids from his subjects on both occasions, and another aid in 1267 for the knighting of his eldest son Philip. The towns were required to contribute substantial sums as well, even when they had charters of exemption. Far less was raised from the persecution of Jewish and Lombard moneylenders, which seems to have been moral rather than financial in motivation; despite this the king borrowed large sums from them in 1248–54.

Louis's reign saw a stabilisation and centralisation in the monetary system of France which was greatly to benefit trade and was considered one of the greatest achievements of his reign in the later Middle Ages. The striking of coinage was a royal and baronial prerogative and brought with it the power to fix the value and exchange rate of money. The scope for making profits was considerable and complaints about the debasement of coinage were frequent in the twelfth century. Louis IX introduced a new standardised gold and silver coinage, fixed in value, and ordered that it should circulate throughout the kingdom. In an ordinance of 1263 given with the assent of the burgesses of Paris, Orléans, Laon and other towns, he decreed that this coinage alone was to be valid in the royal lands but that outside them it was to be accepted alongside seigneurial money, which had to differ in appearance from it. It was forbidden to melt down or to counterfeit royal money. These provisions evidently caused some problems, since in 1265 the king modified them and allowed some outside coinages to circulate in the royal lands. Nevertheless they marked the beginning of a move towards a centralised monetary system, and the triumph of the royal pounds tournois and parisis (value approximately 5:4) over baronial money.

Some of the growth in royal receipts came from the great expansion in royal justice during Louis's reign. This was a profitable affair, a consideration which clearly weighed with officials in the localities. But it also reflected changes in the climate of opinion about the nature and legislative powers of the royal office. In the later Capetian period the king was seen to make laws not only for his domain but also for the whole kingdom. For the revival of Roman law coupled with the growth of real royal power extended royal rights with it. Thus Thomas Aquinas wrote that the power to make law belongs to the person who represents the multitude, and in the *Livre des Hommages* of 1256 John of Blanot emphasised the king of France as the first, the *princeps*, in his whole kingdom. The doctrine of what pleases the prince has the power of law was known to Philip de Beaumanoir. He declared that just as each baron was sovereign in his barony so the king was sovereign in his kingdom and could make whatever laws he pleased. In times of peace he had the right to legislate for his kingdom provided that the ordinances were made with reasonable cause, for the common good, and with the counsel of the great men, and that they did not contravene good customs or the Christian religion. The French king could with such provisos make new laws. His ordinances were not automatically binding on the nobility, but were created with baronial support and consent which made them applicable in some cases beyond the royal lands. Nevertheless baronial cooperation in enforcing them was expected. In 1230 an ordinance states that 'if any of our barons shall refuse to accept this *établissement*, we shall constrain them to do so, and our other barons shall be bound to help us constrain them with all their power and in good faith'.[45]

One of the most striking illustrations of the extension of matters dealt with by the king is Louis's reforming ordinance of 1254.[46] In its earliest form it was intended to bring about the improvement of the royal administration. The royal officials were given a series of oaths to swear, promising their good conduct, and they were forbidden to behave in dishonest ways. Lesser agents could appeal against *baillis* if their conduct was wanting in this respect. The king reserved the right to amend and alter the *ordonnance* and this he did, it seems, almost immediately, adding instructions on public morality, against usury, blasphemy and prostitution, games of chance and the frequenting of inns meant for travellers. This greatly widened the effects of the ordinance: rather than relating merely to the conduct of royal officials it now applied to society in general. Further similar additions were later made, one again forbidding usury, another regulating the requisition of horses for royal business. The ordinance reached this state by the end of 1254 and after some rearrangement of its clauses was promulgated in the royal lands both in the north and the Languedoc. It was much admired by contemporaries, and Joinville gives a text of it, with the comment that it greatly benefited the kingdom as a whole. In its attempts to improve the quality of administration it was paralleled in Louis's system of *enquêteurs*; in its general moral precepts it was reflected in other royal ordinances against blasphemy and usury. The latter was forbidden in 1230, 1243 and 1254; and in 1249, 1257 and 1268 the Jews had their goods confiscated and were expelled from France. The Lombard moneylenders too were expelled in 1268.

The texts of many royal ordinances have survived; others have been lost and their existence may only be deduced from writs to *baillis* enacting their provisions in practice. Clearly not all new legislation was promulgated as a solemn *établissement* applicable to the whole kingdom. These were rare under Louis IX though commoner under his successors. Most ordinances were intended for all or part of the royal lands. Many were issued as instructions to local officials, as for example the attempts in 1257–61 to stop trials by battle, which applied only to the royal domain: this measure was greatly disliked by the nobility and not fully accepted by the jurists; furthermore it seems to have been linked with an attempt to prevent private wars.

By forbidding trial by battle the king was drawing many cases into the royal court. It does not seem that this was the main aim of the exercise, which was again part of Louis's moral legislation, but it did greatly extend royal justice. This process was in any case well under way by the middle of the reign. All matters which directly touched the king were supposed to come before his court. These 'royal cases' included crimes of *lèse-majesté*, and certain disputes about royal land and rights, false money and forged royal *acta*, the illegal carrying of arms, the breaking of safeguards and the like. There is little evidence for a concerted drive to extend these cases against independent jursisdictions on the part of the king's officials in Louis's reign at least, although sometimes they pre-empted other courts. Appeals to the king also increased in numbers during Louis's reign. In his ordinance of 1190 for the administration of the realm, Philip Augustus had laid down that three times a year judicial sessions of the royal court should be held for appeals – *clamores* (lat.) or *requêtes* (fr.) – from the kingdom. These were cases passed on from the *baillis'* assize courts or brought straight before the king. No regular minutes of the court of appeal appeared until the series known as the *Olim* began in 1254, and then the cases were not numerous. Appeals to the king increased more rapidly in the later part of Louis's reign, however; many were heard by the *baillis* and *prévôts* and some went on to the parlement, causing considerable resentment in the royal lands.

The king's determination to make the nobles subject to the laws of the land was equally disliked, as is well illustrated in the trial of Enguerrand of Coucy. In about 1259 Enguerrand hanged three noble Flemish boys who trespassed on his lands and infringed his hunting rights. They were in the care of the abbot of neighbouring Saint-Nicholas-des-Bois, who complained to the king. Louis ordered Enguerrand to appear at his court and when he refused, claiming the right to trial by his peers, the king threw him into prison. When he appeared before the royal court he was supported by most of the French barons, but the king forbade him the right of trial by battle, convicted him, and punished him harshly. Likewise when a knight who had lost a case in Charles of Anjou's court appealed to the king and Charles had him flung into prison, Louis insisted that the case come before the royal court, and gave the knight help with legal representation; in the end Charles lost the case.

The royal court of justice, the parlement, gradually emerged from *curia regis*, reaching its maturity in the first half of the fourteenth century (6.4.1). In Louis IX's reign the royal court and its committees remained fluid and flexible in their business and operation and the word parlement had no one precise meaning. In 1248 the judicial sessions of the king's inner council ceased to be itinerant and were fixed in Paris. Committees of the council, composed mainly of royal knights and clerks sat and made judgements on behalf of the whole *curia regis*. This prefigured the separate parlement, but the committees' links with the royal court remained close and the justices were still known as counsellors or *consiliarii*. Furthermore meetings of the whole *curia regis*, sometimes very large and ceremonial in character, were often described as parlements. Some resembled their English counterpart, the parliament, quite closely. For example, ordinances on the coinage were issued by a full parlement in 1265 and in 1259 Enguerrand de Coucy was tried before a substantial assembly. In 1258 the Norman bishops petitioned about encroachments on their dignity and their jurisdiction at the parlement. But full assemblies became increasingly rare, meeting only to ratify treaties, declarations of war, crusades and major administrative decisions, and specialised committees of the royal council sat with a greater frequency to audit the accounts of the *baillis* and to hear royal cases. Often days were set aside for assemblies of representatives from one particular region of France to meet in Paris and consider local issues. Burgesses not only from Paris but from the regions also became involved. From 1259 to 1260 representatives of the towns were required to appear each November for a financial audit, and they also sent representatives at other times. They participated in the issue of an ordinance on coinage in 1262. From the fluid *curia regis* of Louis IX's reign was to emerge the states general, the chambre des comptes (financial bureau) and the parlement (the royal court of justice) (6.4.1).

The barons, the peers of the realm, came to have less real power and an increasingly ceremonial role in government, but their independence from the crown was at the same time eroded by the changes outlined above. The king valued the advice of his own family, his mother Blanche of Castile, his brothers Alfonso of Poitiers and Charles of Anjou, but otherwise his counsellors were very much in the pattern of previous reigns. They were ecclesiastics, nobles and knights from the royal lands and Champagne, such as Peter of Villebéon, the king's secretary, Master Robert of Sorbon, and John, lord of Joinville. There were also numerous friars such as Odo Rigaud who became archbishop of Rouen. Many royal counsellors apart from Odo achieved important ecclesiastical offices; examples are Matthew of Vendôme, abbot of Saint-Denis, William of Auvergne, bishop of Paris, Robert of Sorbon and Guy Foulquoi, later Pope Clement IV. The royal offices of seneschal and chancellor were left vacant and that of the chamberlain became purely honorific. The functions of the chancellor were taken over by a household official, the guardian of the seal, a royal clerk. He was in charge of the royal chancery, the king's writing office. This continued to produce royal *acta* which, although still developing in their form, were gradually dividing into clearcut categories. Diplomas, the most formal instruments, were becoming rare in Louis's reign. Letters patent, a more streamlined and flexible form of act lacking the royal monogram and the signs of the royal officials found on the diploma, were the normal instrument of government. They fell into three types ranging from the informal to the formal: *mandements* or writs for instructions to royal officials; an intermediate group of semi-formal writs; and occasionally, letters close for political and confidential correspondence.

The guardian of the seal also superintended the royal archives, kept close to the Sainte-Chapelle in the later part of the reign. Royal registers were drawn up but these were not systematic, as they were probably intended to safeguard royal rights rather than record all the royal *acta*. It is possible that the arrival of all of the administrative correspondence of Alfonso of Poiters, which was highly organised, at the archives in 1271 stimulated the royal chancery to register more royal acts, although there was no comprehensive system of registration until 1304. In this, the Capetian chancery was far behind that of the English kings which had been enrolling the bulk of their *acta* at least since 1199. In the French royal archives, loose documents were kept in chests or *layettes*; they covered a great variety of matters such as treaties and diplomatic affairs, correspondence with the king, requests and petitions. They were subdivided into eighteen categories after 1220, including fiefs, towns, castles, dukes, counts, soldiers, alms, and then into forty groups from 1264. After 1269 the whole collection was sorted into two main parts: documents relating to Normandy and the royal domain in the north, and documents concerning the Languedoc.

A royal ordinance of 1261 regulating the royal household and a few household accounts which have survived enable the organisation and the development of this body under Louis IX to be charted quite fully. Its departments, which catered for the day-to-day needs of the king, were the pantry, the buttery, the kitchen, the stores, and the victualling department. The king's chaplains and huntsmen never formed part of the household organisation. Each household department had its own officials appointed by the king and responsible to the two masters of the household, and the queen and princes also had their own establishments. The expenses of the royal household appear in the royal accounts under the heading *itinera* or journeys, reflecting the peripatetic nature of that body. Fortunately other more detailed accounts of its receipts and expenditure have also survived. In the period from Candlemas to Ascension in 1234, £23,504. 14*s* parisis was received from the Paris Temple and from other miscellaneous sources including regalia and the seal; the last brought in £421. 11*s* 4*d*, the whole of the receipts amounting to £24,717. 0*s* 7*d*. The money was spent on the household departments (*itinera*); on gifts and wages and equipment, including substantial payments in alms; on robes, horses, troops, and the queen's coronation at Sens. Other very detailed accounts of daily expenditure drawn up by a household accountant, John Sarrazin, survive for the period Candlemas 1256 until All Saints 1257, and are a valuable source of royal expenditure. The amounts spent on charitable donations are substantial (Table 5.1). Other members of the royal entourage also emerge in the records: the guards, the huntsmen, the royal physicians; and it was clearly a substantial body, handling large sums of money. The expenses for the knighting of Philip (III) in 1268 alone amounted to £13,758. 4*s* 10*d* parisis.[47]

By Louis IX's reign the obligations of the barons to do him military service were never denied, but this proved increasingly difficult to raise. First, many lords would not levy service from their own men but would turn up themselves with the smallest contingents possible. Then they would disappear as soon as their forty days' service was up, often in the middle of a campaign, as happened in 1230 (5.2.1). Armies remained small, however, and the king depended mainly on stipendiary troops, supplementing these with feudal levies, with the urban militias (in 1233 nineteen communes sent armies to put down the rising at Beauvais) and with troops raised by the *arrière-ban*. Often all these forces were allowed to commute their military obligations for money payments, but the royal right to military service was strongly upheld and extended and was to become an important source of revenues (6.4.1). The martial arts were far from dead, however; tournaments and jousts remained very popular, although the stylised fighting these demanded was little practical help in battle. The king did not found a navy for his crusades, he hired ships from Venice and Genoa; but he created a mediterranean port, Aigues-Mortes. This was fortified heavily by Louis IX and his successors and given important privileges, but it never became a commercial centre, remaining rather as the main embarkation point for pilgrims and crusaders bound for the holy land.

During Louis's reign the king's feudal powers were extended to the full, and he exercised all the rights of suzerainty. Royal government and administration became fully developed in the royal lands and became more widely applicable outside them. The extension of traditional royal powers, both ecclesiastical and feudal, began to modify the nature of royal authority to transform the king from suzerain into sovereign (5.5.5). The effects of such changes did not emerge fully until the later Capetian period. But the developments in the years 1226 to 1270 made them possible.

5.5.2 The royal domain and the apanages to 1328

During the thirteenth century, a change took place in the meaning of the term domain. Where earlier it had implied a collection of lands and rights held by the king or a noble, by the reign of Philip IV the expression royal domain meant the royal lands, a territorial unit. When did this shift in meaning take place? In Philip Augustus's first register dating from the first decade of the thirteenth century the term 'in domain' was still applied to the castles, lands, towns and rights held directly by the king, as had been the case throughout the early Capetian period. During Louis IX's reign, however, royal administration and royal justice penetrated deeply into the principalities held directly by the king, and gradually into the others. In the wake of a growing administration in the royal principality and the capture of Normandy and Languedoc the term royal domain began to take on a wider territorial sense.

Another royal institution which changed in its nature and implications during the thirteenth century was the apanage grant, the endowment of younger sons of the king with major holdings, to pass to their male heirs after their deaths. The term apanage was not used until the early fourteenth century, but the first really large-scale grants of this kind were made by Louis VIII in his will; and because there has been a tendency to regard the apanage as a largely static institution, the provisions he made have often puzzled historians. For example, one account suggests that 'With one stroke Louis VIII alienated about one third of the royal domain that he and his father had so patiently accumulated. . . . The loss to the domain and to the monarchy seems appalling.' But, the author argues, the effects were not as disastrous as they might have been, since the apanages were intended to strengthen royal powers in recently conquered lands which had never known them, and to provide the king with viceregents, but not permanently to alienate the lands from the crown, because of the clauses which stipulated that all apanages must return to the king in default of direct male heirs. The apanage system, he suggests, 'prepared the way for complete and easy annexation of these lands by the king at such time as each apanage reverted to the crown'.[48]

Was there really such a system? Although by Philip IV's reign a reversion clause was implicit in all apanage grants, earlier on it was not stipulated in all cases, and probably not intended in all cases. Even if it had been, but if each prince had produced a series of male heirs, as happened in the case of Clermont-en-Beauvaisis which came back to the domain only in 1589 with Henry IV, then the idea of using the royal family as viceregents would have failed. If this was the intended scheme, its success depended on the early death of each king's brothers without heirs.

A more plausible explanation of the apanage grants of the thirteenth century is that the Capetian kings, rather than acting with any abstract notions of sovereignty or schemes for administering a unitary kingdom in mind, were doing what many contemporary nobles were doing – using their acquisitions to enrich younger sons while keeping the patrimony intact.[49] It is striking that in some cases contemporary noble grants provided for reversion if there was no male heir, but in other cases made no such rule; and a similar variation appears in the grants made by the Capetian kings. Thus Louis VIII's will, made in June 1225, stipulates that all the land held by his father Philip Augustus should go to his successor, Louis IX, except that his second son should have Artois and all the lands which Louis VIII had inherited from his mother; if this son died without heirs the land would revert to the king. The third son would get Anjou and Maine, the fourth Poitou and the Auvergne, and the rest were to take holy orders (Fig. 5.1). The division was made, the king stated, to prevent discord from arising between his sons. Reversion was not stipulated in the Anjou and Poitou inheritances – lands which Philip Augustus and Louis VIII had conquered – but it was in the case of Louis's maternal inheritance and also for the lands already held by Philip Hurepel, the king's half-brother, the count of Boulogne. In 1284 the parlement was retrospectively to impose reversion on Anjou and Poitou, but there is no reason to suppose that Louis VIII intended this at first.

Louis IX allowed his brothers to take over their apanages as they came of age: Artois went to Robert, Poitou and Auvergne to Alfonso and Anjou and Maine not to John, who had died, but to Louis VIII's seventh son Charles, in 1246. Louis gave only acquisitions to his own cadets: Alençon and Perche to Peter, Valois to John Tristan, and Clermont-en-Beauvaisis to Robert; only the last founded a

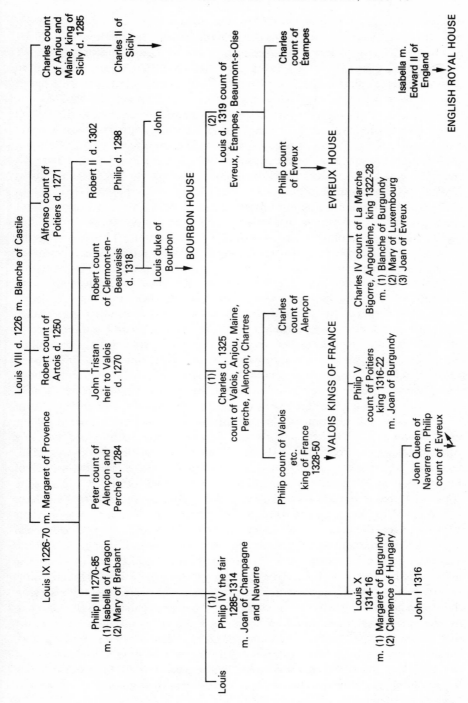

Fig. 5.1 Outline genealogy of the Capetian kings, 1226–1328

dynasty (the house of Bourbon) and the other lands reverted back to the crown in default of male heirs, according to the provisions made by the king. Philip III regranted Valois to Charles, his second son, and to Louis, the third, he gave Beaumont-en-Oise. Philip IV later gave Alençon, Perche and Chartres to Charles, and Evreux to Louis, as they reverted to the crown. Furthermore Charles was married to a daughter of Charles II of Anjou and Sicily, a descendant of Louis IX's brother, and she brought with her both Anjou and Maine. But Philip IV had less to spare for his own younger sons, both of whom in the event became kings after Louis X. One, Philip, was given a much circumscribed county of Poitiers, another, Charles, La Marche and Angoulême. Charles's and Louis of Evreux's apanages were both added to by Philip V, and Charles, when he became king as Charles IV, gave Louis of Bourbon, son of Robert of Clermont, La Marche in exchange for Clermont. The high mortality rate of royal princes brought their apanages back to the crown, and in 1328 the accession of Philip VI of Valois united his great holdings with the royal domain as well. This left only the Bourbon, Artois and Evreux apanages, and not until the later fourteenth century were similar grants of any size to be made again.

At the time of Louis IX's successors there was a gradual shift which eventually was to make all apanage grants conditional. Before then, the Capetians were doing what nobles of their own time such as Guichard of Beaujeu were doing, what the twelfth-century English kings, Henry II and Richard I had intended to do, and what their own ancestors had done. They were preserving the patrimony for the eldest son, and giving lands gained by marriage, inheritance or conquest to younger brothers; they were to hold their lands as fiefs from the principal heir, who preserved the overall authority. But such grants depended on the availability of lands and the resources of the father. Thus in 1034 Robert, younger brother of Henry I, was given Burgundy, an acquisition of his father Robert the Pious (3.2.3), and in 1137 Robert son of Louis VI was given the county of Dreux at a time when his brother, Louis VII, was about to marry Eleanor of Aquitaine. Other cadets were provided with good marriages, as when Hugh, brother of Philip I, gained Vermandois or when Philip Hurepel, son of Philip Augustus by Agnes of Méran, gained Boulogne. Again, Philip Augustus gave Peter Mauclerc, the son of Peter of Dreux the hand of Alice, heiress to Brittany. Similarly, in 1236–37 Joan, the heiress of Raymond VII of Toulouse, was married to Alfonso of Poitiers, brother of Louis IX. As it happened they died without heirs, and the great southern principality came into royal hands in 1271, but this was not foreseeable in the 1230s. Indeed the grants made initially by Louis IX and Philip III to cadets were small – a measure of the importance they attached to conserving the crown lands; but the reversion of most of the major apanages to the king one by one meant that these could be regranted again as acquisitions. As a result throughout the later Capetian period the king's brothers and sons formed a close family group whose members were close in blood to the king and who acted in effect as viceregents. But this was caused by the early death of most of the major holders of apanages rather than an apanage 'system' being constructed around rules of reversion.

Under Philip III and Philip IV increased stress was laid on the reversion of royal apanages, at the same time as current ideas about the nature of royal power changed and developed. When Alfonso of Poitiers died in 1271 Charles of Anjou claimed that his lands should go to him as the next heir. But in 1284 parlement found against this, saying that the royal grants had been made as gifts, not as inheritance, and that they must revert to the king. As there had been no reversion clause for Poitou in Louis VIII's will as it survives, this would seem to have overridden its provisions, and to be a step towards the transformation of the apanage grants, using royal power to change the stipulations of a testament made much earlier and with different intentions in mind. Gradually after this all apanage grants came to be seen as having reversion clauses implicit in them. At the same time two ostensibly contradictory ideas emerged: that the apanages formed part of a fixed territorial royal domain, but that the king's children could lay claim to any recently acquired part of this domain. For example, in 1317 Charles, brother of Louis X, was to demand a share in all the acquisitions made by the French kings since Louis IX, and Edward II of England did the same by virtue of the claims of his wife Isabella, daughter of Philip IV. But Isabella's claims were not perhaps as good as those of her brothers since in 1314 Philip IV had forbidden females the right to inherit the apanage of his son Philip of Poitiers. This was far from a universal restriction, and Louis X revoked the Poitiers provision, but it was a foretaste of the events which in this and following years were to deny women succession rights to the throne of France (6.2.3). Royal and baronial inheritance practices as exemplified in apanage grants had thus diverged considerably at the end of the Capetian period.

For most of the thirteenth century, however, the kings of France granted out land to their heirs in the same way that the nobility did, looking on them as family estates, not, as later, as a unitary holding distinct in character from those of other important families. For as Professor Fawtier wrote: 'No modern ideas of territorial unification lay behind their enrichment of the crown of France. They never sought to become the owners of all of France, to remove the great fiefs, to dismantle the feudal structure of the kingdom.'[50] This structure, rather, was tightened by Louis IX, at the same time as royal power and royal prestige also increased dramatically. Bur the apanages were not intended to encourage such developments, to introduce royal justice and administration into areas which had never known it: they were to enrich royal cadets. That they had the former effect as well was quite fortuitous.

5.5.3 Royal power in Normandy and the Languedoc

By 1226 Normandy had been thoroughly subjugated by Philip Augustus and Louis VIII, and many of its ties with England had been cut. The Languedoc on the other hand was still being overrun by the royal army, and it was to take until the late 1240s before it was brought firmly under royal control. Normandy passed to the French crown with a strong identity and traditions and a well-established administration of its own. The king became its duke, and although he did not use the title, Normandy remained a duchy, separate from the older royal lands, although coming increasingly under the influence of the royal government in Paris. The Languedoc was on the other hand divided between the king and first Raymond VII count of Toulouse, then Alfonso of Poitiers, Louis's brother (5.5.4). In both provinces the central institutions had to be substantially reconstructed and the nobility and towns subjugated; by 1270 this had been done with great effectiveness. Friction between the crown and the inhabitants was far greater in the Languedoc than in Normandy, although in the latter it is easy to overstate the degree of harmony achieved. The Normans were far from satisfied with being ruled from Paris.

The administrative system in Normandy was changed after the conquest.[51] By 1224 the previously quite substantial number of small *bailliages* had been consolidated into seven larger *bailliages*, reduced to six under Louis IX. These were subdivided into viscounties, and there were also peace keeping units known as sergeanties, smaller still. Then there were a number of *prévôtés*, some to govern towns, others as set up by Philip Augustus on the border, which were accountable to Paris. The other officials, nearly all royal administrators, were responsible in the first instance to the Norman exchequer, both financially and judicially. The king kept a firm eye on Norman finances, and the accounts were presented at the royal court after audit by the Norman exchequer. Lists of royal rights were kept and so too were checklists of the revenues to be collected from each administrative district. Some, like the list of the royal domain in the *bailliage* of Rouen (*c.* 1261–66) were very detailed, and the complaints of the Normans to the royal *enquêteurs* for 1247, the *Querimoniae Normannorum*, contain many instances of royal rights being extended too far. The *baillis* were responsible for drawing up the accounts and presenting them at Rouen and in Paris. By 1230 these documents had become well organised and summaried under headings, a contrast with the less clearly set out state of the preconquest exchequer rolls. This change took place earlier than in the French *bailliages* and may reflect a more advanced financial system which influenced the rest of the royal administration.

The accounts covered the main royal sources of revenue: the domain, much of which was farmed out to collectors who paid a fixed sum for gathering the money themselves; the forests, which had their own administration; and various rights of lordship such as regalia, hearth-tax, money from the Jews and the like. Extraordinary taxation was collected separately. Normandy was a wealthy province: at Michaelmas 1230 it brought in nearly £32,000 parisis and at Ascension 1238 nearly £39,000, over a third of the takings from all the royal *bailliages* put together. Its wealth and the sophistication of its administration, as well as its proximity to the royal lands surely explain its retention by the French kings; the lands granted out as apanages were a far less straightforward proposition.

The judicial side of the Norman administration was interfered with less by the French officials than its financial machinery. By 1230 Norman law was well developed. The customs of the duchy had probably crystallised in the late eleventh century, and they were codified early too. The first part of the *Très Ancien Coutûmier* dates from *c.* 1200, the second from around 1220. Between 1235 and 1260 the *Summa de legibus Normanniae* (summary of Norman laws) was composed, a far clearer and more systematic account than the *Summa* for Maine and Anjou (about 1245) and reflecting the precocity of Norman legal development. It sets out the principle that existing legal procedure could be modified only when this would define existing rights more clearly, and Louis IX's administrators seem to have respected both this and more detailed aspects of Norman customs. Louis IX's ordinances for the province, dealing with matters such as amortisation, the abolition of trial by battle and the conduct of royal officials, also followed Norman procedures. Nevertheless there were some changes. Certain cases, involving royal rights, and complaints against royal administrators and the higher nobility went to the parlement at Paris. The parlement also acted as a court of appeal from the exchequer, and although in all the cases which went there were few in numbers they caused some resentment. At times, too, the royal *enquêteurs* interfered with the course of justice at a lower level. Nevertheless Norman law retained its own defined character throughout the thirteenth century.

The king was generous to some Norman religious houses, but his gifts seem to have had little political significance. The Norman church retained its links with England, though these were constantly weakening. Early in the reign, disputes between the queen and the archbishop of Rouen caused considerably tensions (5.4.2), and royal officials appear gradually to have eroded ecclesiastical rights. The high posts went to men from the Ile de France; indeed, despite Philip Augustus's promises of free elections, royal influence was brought heavily to bear, particularly from the 1240s onwards; and often royal clerks and administrators were chosen, such as Odo, a royal chaplain, elected bishop of Bayeux in 1263. This occasioned some resentment, but there were many good appointments, such as Odo Rigaud, archbishop of Rouen from 1248 until his death on crusade in 1270. He was a close friend and counsellor of the king, a Franciscan friar and highly trained theologian. He kept a full register of his work in Normandy which is an unusually personal account, and reveals Odo as an able administrator and a just yet compassionate man. In 1251 he went to the priory of Saint-Martin-la-Garenne where he found that there were four monks, all priests.

There used to be five. Two of them, that is to say, William the sacristan and Richard the bell-ringer are topers and are light headed. They (the monks) do not confess each month as the statutes of Pope Gregory required, they eat meat at times when there is no need. Item, although they are often present in the choir, some of them do not sing when the hours are being sung. Item, they go off to the Seine without getting permission from the prior. They owe about eighty pounds.[52]

Most of the problems he has to deal with are relatively minor ones, but what he had to contend with generally was above all, 'passive unspirituality',[53] a lack of enthusiasm for the religious life, and this may well sum up the condition of the church as a whole in the province. But when in 1247 the Norman bishops were asked who should hold Normandy, Henry III or Louis IX, they found for Louis; their resistance was far weaker than that of the nobility.[54]

Military service was levied from the duchy on many occasions during Louis's reign, the king retaining the right to take scutage instead if he chose. The quotas of knights remained unchanged from the time of Henry II in many cases, as a list drawn up for a campaign against the count of Foix in 1272 illustrates. There seems to have been little friction in this area, but the issues of royal taxation of communes and communal privileges caused considerable problems. Disputes between towns and *baillis* over tallage and communal rights were frequent; although many of the towns prospered it was more the result of the peaceful conditions and an expanding economy than royal favour. The tensions between royal officials and urban communities were to increase under Philip III and Philip IV, and the days of the independence of the towns were numbered.

Right up to the signing of the treaty of Paris in 1259 the English still claimed Normandy and some links between the duchy and the kingdom continued. The Normans probably did not settle down under the French king as peacefully as has sometimes been suggested. Tenurial ties between England and Normandy continued up to 1259 and beyond; in 1241 the widowed Agatha Trussebut, living in England recovered her dower in Normandy, and in 1242 Robert Malet, living in Normandy, was given back his English lands by Henry III as a reward for his support of the English king. The Estouteville family had lands on both sides of the Channel into the fourteenth century, although this was a rare exception. But a number of Norman noble houses were ready to sell their support to Henry III up to the 1240s.[55] In 1230 when Henry III was in Brittany he was asked by Fulk Paynel to recapture the duchy, and when he refused, Fulk requested two hundred knights for a rising against Louis IX. His dislike of French rule was not isolated, and in 1244, according to Matthew Paris, Louis IX seized the Norman lands of several English lords, although still leaving a few families with dual allegiance.[56]

There were other links too, for in the 1230s and 1240s the Norman towns were still trading with England, and the connections of the English and Norman churches were strong. All this generated a feeling of mistrust between the French and English kings, while the Normans, as their complaints showed, resented the soldiers of Philip Augustus and the administrators of Louis IX who held high office in the duchy, and disliked the increasing influence of Paris in their affairs. But this hostility did not erupt into open revolt as in the south, where tensions were far greater. As Louis's reign wore on local men, too, began occasionally to receive higher offices, and they had always held the lesser ones. Furthermore Norman nobles, knights and citizens had continued to be heavily involved in making judgements in the courts, which probably limited the scope for corruption of the royal officials. Particularly after 1259 Normandy began to settle down under French domination, a prosperous and relatively well ruled province. But it kept its own identity, and in the early fourteenth century it regained some of its autonomy (6.4.5).

The tensions between the king and the Normans were certainly mild in comparison with the disturbances and hostilities in the Languedoc. By the treaty of Paris of 1229 the Midi was divided into two parts (5.2.1). Raymond VII was given a truncated county of Toulouse; the Capetians took the whole of its eastern part and various possessions of Raymond including Nîmes, Beaucaire and Saint-Gilles, and the former estates of the Trencavel family. The Venaissin went to the church for a while, although in 1234 Raymond VII had it back from Pope

Gregory IX. Under the terms of the treaty Raymond was to restore land and possessions to the church, to found a university in Toulouse and to extirpate heresy from his lands. His daughter Joan was to marry a French prince, in the event Louis's brother Alfonso of Poitiers, and the two of them were to inherit Toulouse jointly after Raymond's death, notwithstanding the claims of any male heirs of his. The settlement, although better than might have been expected in 1226, was still humiliating to Raymond and he spent more than a decade trying to reverse its terms.

In the persecution of heresy Raymond showed little enthusiasm. Together he and Cardinal Romano Frangipani published a set of constitutions making the bishops responsible for crushing the Cathars. Even the moderate attempts of the episcopate caused resistance and in 1233 an official attempting to enforce the constitutions was murdered. These efforts were also largely ineffective. The well-known noble patron of Cathars, Bernard-Oth de Niort, remained free even though he was accused of numerous crimes against the church. Gregory IX intervened and Raymond had the heretic taken into custody, but at the same time the pope ordered an inquisition in the Languedoc. It was composed not of bishops but of Dominican friars acting on behalf of the papacy. The first inquisitors were zealous in the extreme. In 1233–36 they convicted many heretics, both living and dead. Many of the living were burnt, and some who were dead and buried were disinterred. This provoked violent reaction. There was bloodshed in Narbonne in 1233–35, and in 1235 the citizens of Toulouse were so angry with the activities of the inquisitors and the infringement of their own privileges that they stormed the Dominican friary in the city, and ejected not only all the friars but the bishop as well. Raymond VII protested on the citizens' behalf; Gregory IX first asked the inquisitors to moderate their zeal and then suspended them for three years (1237–40).

The inquisition caused problems throughout the Languedoc, but in the lands ceded to the king there were other tensions too. In 1212 Simon de Montfort had promulgated the statutes of Pamiers in which he decreed that the customs of Paris be followed in the Languedoc. This in effect introduced feudal tenures and laws and they were harshly upheld. Simon's own men were given substantial holdings in the area, and although in Toulouse these grants, and the customs of Paris, were rescinded in 1229, many were confirmed in the lands kept by the king. It is true that many of the ancient nobility of the region were given some compensation, and some of their lands back, but two major fiefs were firmly established for Guy de Lévis, marshall of Simon de Montfort, at Mirepoix, and for Philip de Montfort, Simon's nephew, south of Albi. Other lesser fiefs were created as well, and these also followed northern customs. The result was considerable tension between the inhabitants of the lands and their new overlords. In the 1270s Guy III de Mirepoix was to try to uphold his rights to take the lands of his tenants who were leaving his estates; the peasants insisted on their ancient rights to sell or alienate their own lands. By the end of the fourteenth century the older written law generally overruled these customs in most important matters; in the thirteenth century they still caused resentment.

Further problems were caused by the conduct of the royal officials in the *sénéchaussées* of Beaucaire and Carcassonne. They seem to have succeeded in mulcting churchmen and laity alike; their corruption was such that Gregory IX requested Louis IX to take remedial action. He did do so, but not before violence had erupted in the area. Raymond Trencavel invaded from Spain (5.2.1) and with widespread local support seized western Languedoc and Carcassonne. Royal power in the region was threatened, but the royal army headed by John of Beaumont crushed the rising with extreme brutality. Raymond VII had not been involved, but in 1242 he too rebelled. In 1241 he had tried to marry Sancia of Provence and had even divorced his wife in preparation, but there was a papal vacancy and thus he could not get a dispensation to enable the nuptials to take place, and Sancia was married to Richard of Cornwall instead. Raymond lacked a male heir and he joined Henry III's coalition with the Poitevin nobility against the French king. This rising too was crushed and Louis IX was only prevented from harsh action against Raymond by Blanche of Castile. But the count of Toulouse's attempts to carry on his dynasty beyond Joan his daughter did not end here. In 1245 he again negotiated with Raymond-Berengar of Provence for the hand of his youngest daughter and heiress Beatrice. But Raymond-Berengar died, and the heiress and her lands went to Charles of Anjou.

The risings in the Languedoc were crushed harshly and were followed by severe reprisals. There was a strong feeling that the heretics had played a major part in them and the inquisition was brought back with redoubled powers and enthusiasm. By the Treaty of Lorris in 1243 Raymond VII promised the king to obtain oaths of obedience from his subjects and to support the king and the inquisition. This in effect reiterated the terms of the 1229 treaty; but now he realised at last that it would be prudent to take firm action. He decided to crush the Cathars by force, and the important Albigensian stronghold of Montségur fell to his troops in 1244. Although the heretics continued to defy the French and the church at Quéribus until 1255, the events of the mid-1240s dealt them a death-blow. The old nobles of the region, many of whom had been important patrons of the Cathar church, were again dispossessed of their lands and many became the victims of the inquisition, their estates going to the crown. Only the ancient noble houses of Lautrec, Narbonne and Foix survived. Many of the former Languedocian leaders went to the Holy Land as crusaders and men such as Olivier de Termes ended their lives there. The towns, too, where heresy had flourished, had harsh treatment meted out to them. The royal armies, the inquisition, and the efforts of Raymond in support of the king brought the Languedoc to heel, and Alfonso of Poitiers who succeeded Raymond in Toulouse in 1249 was to continue the work of subjugating these lands (5.5.4).

How did the Languedoc fare under the domination of Louis IX and Alfonso of Poitiers? In the royal lands in the Languedoc the king made an attempt to improve the conduct of his officials, dissatisfaction with which had contributed towards the unrest of the early 1240s. He sent round *enquêteurs* in 1247 and 1255, he strove to be scrupulously fair in his judgements in the region, and in 1254 he promulgated his ordinance for the better conduct of the royal officials. In the same year he issued ordinances for the reform of the cities of Beaucaire and Nîmes. But in general there was a marked loss of liberty in the region; for example, the governing consuls of Beaucaire were replaced by royal men while the numbers of those at Nîmes were cut by half, and they were nominated by the king. Royal officials eroded other urban privileges of minting, charging tolls, protecting merchants. Similar changes occurred in the county of Toulouse (5.5.4). Nevertheless prosperity returned rapidly to the Languedoc; as trade revived new towns such as Pavie and Bologne were founded. Some local assemblies were allowed to meet to resolve economic questions. The new Gothic style of the Ile de France which appeared at the rebuilt cathedrals at Albi and Carcassonne perhaps symbolises the domination of the north but is also a mark of this wealth. Troubadour poetry from the region declined in its quality but it is arguable that this trend was under way before the Albigensian crusade. Nor were the influences all one way. The written law of the south based on Roman law exercised a marked impression on the customary law of the north, and its practitioners, jurists such as William de Nogaret and Pierre Flotte, were to play an important role at the royal court (6.4.2).

In the twelfth century the Languedoc had been a wealthy region with weak political institutions, a flourishing culture and a considerable number of heretics. The Albigensian crusade and its aftermath crushed the heretics and introduced strong administration, but the price of this was the dominance of men from the north and a loss of liberty, as well as the dispossession of many nobles of the region. But it is by no means clear that the wars alone destroyed the culture of the region, and nor did they affect its prosperity in more than the short term. Economically the Languedoc was to suffer far more from the crises of the later Middle Ages than from the Albigensian crusade.

5.5.4 Louis IX and Alfonso of Poitiers

Blanche of Castile had a considerable influence on Louis IX in his younger years and played an important part in the government and administration of the kingdom. Alfonso of Poitiers, Louis's brother, was a close confidant and counsellor of the king, particularly after Blanche's death. The role he played, however, was different from Blanche's, and although it has frequently been suggested that he acted as a kind of viceregent for his lands of Poitou and the Languedoc which were to revert to the crown on his death, this pattern of inheritance was by no means a foregone conclusion. In the event Alfonso had no male heirs to inherit his lands; had he had some he would have passed these lands to a cadet dynasty of the Capetian house. His administrative and political achievements, which were considerable, were not in his early years made with the French crown in mind. Nor were his acts as a ruler as similar to those of Louis IX as M. Boutaric in his classic study, *Saint Louis et Alphonse de Poitiers*, suggested;[57] although the general outlines were similar, Alfonso's government had a style and an impact of its own.

Alfonso was assigned Poitou as an apanage by Louis VIII's will, and he was invested with it in 1241. This was a difficult land to deal with. He and Louis had to crush the regional lords of the area, and in 1245 he took a substantial amount of land from Hugh of Lusignan, making himself the possessor of Poitou, the overlordship of La Marche, Aunis and Saintonge. The lands of the regional lords were redistributed in smaller parcels. He also claimed lordship of Clermont but this was judged by parlement in 1255 to belong to the crown. Alfonso's settlement in 1248 with Archambaud, lord of Bourbon, regularised his authority here. His important Poitevin holdings were further augmented when in 1249 his wife's father Raymond VII, count of Toulouse died. Louis already held lower Languedoc, and Alfonso now inherited the other part of the region, the county of Toulouse, the northern Albigeois, Rouergue, Venaissin, part of Quercy and the Agenais – the last two claimed by Henry III. Since the 1229 treaty Raymond VII had increased the comital domains in the region which gave the count a more solid power-base. Alfonso was on crusade when Raymond died, and there was resistance to his succession. Many of the towns refused oaths of obedience, but Blanche of Castile as regent took a firm line with them which secured Toulouse for the Capetian prince. Raymond had left his lands to Joan, Alfonso's wife, in his will, but Alfonso insisted that this was invalid. The lands were his by virtue of the treaty of 1229. He found jurists to disallow the will, and this also allowed him to disregard several generous bequests to religious houses by Raymond. He did well from the treaty of Corbeil made by Louis with Aragon in 1258 when the Aragonese king renounced his claims to part of Rouergue, but the treaty of Paris with England gave Henry III the reversion of several lands after Alfonso's death (5.5.7).

After the demise of both Alfonso and Joan on the way home from the crusade in 1271 the problem of the Toulouse succession emerged again: but in the end their lands all went to the French crown. Joan, like her father had made a will, leaving most of the Languedoc to her cousin Philippa, who was, however, disallowed it by parlement in 1274; she also bequeathed the Venaissin to Charles of Anjou but this was equally disregarded. Charles of Anjou tried to claim that all Alfonso's lands including Poitou should be divided between his family, but in 1283 parlement found that when the male line of an apanage holder had died out his apanage should return to the crown. Alfonso's lands proved a valuable gain for Philip III (6.2.1).

Alfonso had his own household, his own chancery, and a court; and he kept careful records of his official activities. In his correspondence he emerges as a rather cold figure, a thorough administrator who could delegate only with difficulty, but who was often greedy and rapacious. His main aims appear to have been the upholding and consolidating of his own rights and the gaining of maximum profits from them; but he also gave his lands moderately fair government. In Poitou he found a rather weak three-tiered system of administration composed of a seneschal controlling *bailliages*, in their turn divided into *prévôtés*. He abolished the *bailliages* and made the *prévôts* responsible to two seneschals. The Auvergne was put under a *bailli*. In the Languedoc Alfonso inherited an administration divided into six *sénéchaussées* (the equivalent of *bailliages* in the north) subdivided into *baylies*. He reduced their number to four. To survey the conduct of his officials he sent round *enquêteurs*, friars and government administrators; these were appointed in Poitou in about 1249, and in the Languedoc by Blanche shortly afterwards. They were sent round regularly after 1251, but unlike Louis's *enquêteurs* they had an administrative function, collecting taxes such as the crusading aids and acting in a wider judicial capacity as a check on the local officials. They could, for example, give licences to assart comital woodlands and settle the status of fiefs held by peasants. They dealt with some legal cases themselves; others they sent to the count's court, as their substantial surviving records show clearly. Some were given special commissions to deal with important individual suits. In 1258–59 however they were instructed to deal with official abuses, and Alfonso issued an ordinance for the good conduct of his officials *c.* 1254 which closely echoed that of Louis IX in its tone and content. Another was issued in 1270, probably in response to complaints about exactions of his officials when levying the crusading aid.

Alfonso, like Louis, introduced a centralised uniform coinage in his lands without forbidding local ones; this greatly benefited commerce as well as administration. He also systematised the financial organisation of Poitou in the 1240s, as a register for the years 1243–48 clearly shows. In this, the early accounts are confused, but by 1245 the receipts and expenses are tabulated and listed under headings as in the royal accounts. Furthermore each seneschal or his equivalent drew up a survey of royal rights that he was responsible for, and these survive for Poitou, Albigeois, Auvergne, Agenais, Quercy, Rouergue and Venaissin. Alfonso clearly profited from the careful consolidation of his domain: M. Boutaric has estimated that in the year 1258 his fixed revenues alone amounted to £31,468. 2*s* 6*d*; these were augmented by less regular but substantial sums raised by aids, the *cens*, the hearthtax, tallage. In 1263–65 the hearthtax in Quercy and Agenais alone amounted to £26,088.[58] According to M. Boutaric's figures, the total receipts for the three terms of 1258 came to £71,879. 5*s* 5*d*, and those for 1268, £102,730. 18*s* 1*d*. These are very substantial sums, amounting to about a third of Louis's income (5.5.1), and it is clear that in normal circumstances the count's revenues were quite sufficient for his needs.

In all these records and in his administrative correspondence covering the years 1267–70 Alfonso emerges as a firm master of his lands and a remarkably thorough administrator. He was strongly opposed to major representative institutions, and where in the Midi assemblies met to ratify matters such as extraordinary taxation these were on a very local level, a contrast with the days of Raymond VII when large feudal assemblies had met regularly. Alfonso's men encroached gradually but firmly on the independence of the nobles and the towns, eroding the liberties of Toulouse, yet there was relatively little concerted resistance, perhaps because of the competence of Alfonso's administrators and because although he was Louis IX's brother he was also the husband of Joan of Toulouse. The Languedoc had furthermore been exhausted by the Albigensian crusade, and by the activities of the royal armies and the papal inquisitors. There were some eruptions, however – in 1255 in Toulouse over its liberties, and over the government of Montpellier and Albi. But Alfonso seems to have been resented more in his apanage than in the Languedoc; in Poitou, where until 1242 the local nobility had held sway, Alfonso's insistence on the rendability of many castles, his limiting of the carrying of weapons and judicial duels was very unpopular. *Enquêtes* or appeals in the count's court were encouraged as an alternative to the last, and such actions elicited protests from the Poitevin nobles that the customs of Poitou were being overturned. The much circumscribed descendants of the regional lords looked back to the days of the rule of the English kings, when their fathers had been the true lords of the land, with nostalgia. This is a measure of Alfonso's achievements. Not only did he crush the turbulent barons of Poitou and bring them under comital control, he also became an only moderately unpopular ruler in the Languedoc, a land strongly opposed to the encroachments of the French crown.

5.5.5 *The image of monarchy and changing views of the kingdom*

In Louis IX's reign the prestige of the French crown reached great heights, in part as a response to vastly increased royal power and wealth, but also in part as a reflection of Louis's reputation as a pious and just monarch. In his later years, he adopted a frugal and ascetic lifestyle and elicited criticism from those who thought this unsuitable in a king (5.5.6). But this is only one part of the picture. Early in the reign Blanche of Castile and Louis gave visual expression both to the sacral characteristics of the royal office and to their own personal piety in a series of magnificent church buildings and ceremonial occasions. These assumed political as well as religious and artistic dimensions, and so splendid was the image created that it survived the more restrained period after 1254 and merged into the growing legend of Saint Louis after the king's death.

What part did Louis and Blanche play in creating the new styles of architecture and illumination which emerged during the reign and were closely associated with the court? Blanche herself was clearly an active patron with a love for the splendid and magnificent; recently it has been suggested that she rather than her son was the principal patron of the illuminators who produced works such as the Sainte-Chapelle evangeliary for the royal library.[59] Louis himself was not a connoisseur of books such as was John, duke of Berry, but he needed texts for his devotions. His involvement with the design of the new work at Saint-Denis and with the Sainte-Chapelle seems to have been greater, although his interest in magnificent buildings waned somewhat after Blanche's death. Nevertheless by this time the royal court was seen as a major artistic centre and the French 'court style' was widely copied. At last the reputation of the French for learning and culture, the idea of *la douce France* (4.3.4) seems to have been fully enmeshed with the image of the French monarchy.[60]

Early in the reign the Cistercians, strongly favoured by Blanche as by her father King Alfonso VIII of Castile, had an important influence on royal taste (5.4.1). In 1228 the great abbey of Royaumont was founded in memory of Louis VIII near Paris, and in 1236 it was dedicated with magnificent ceremony. Intended initially as a royal burial house like Las Huelgas at Burgos, it was executed in a simplified version of the local style but on a magnificent scale. In *c*. 1237 work began at Saint-Denis, which was to progress rapidly in a decade and to be completed by about 1254, and showed a splendour of style more in keeping with royal taste. The architect, whose work showed the influence of the Reims School, destroyed the remains of the Romanesque church and built on Abbot Suger's work to create the effect of a glass wall, with slim, light piers and a great deal of stained glass. The success of the design was considerable, and the same man also worked at the royal chapel at Saint-Germain-en-Laye on the king's instructions. Louis was clearly concerned that Saint-Denis should be rebuilt as befitted the royal necropolis, once such a role for Royaumont had been abandoned. According to William of Nangis Louis decided the layout the tombs of his ancestors should take in the crossing of the new church, placing the Merovingian Clovis II, and Carolingian monarchs, including Charles Martel and Carloman, to the south of the main altar, and the Robertines and Capetians to the north; Philip Augustus and Louis VIII were left to the east of the altar between the others, perhaps symbolising the unity of the two races. All had magnificent new tombs, into which they were translated in 1263. Later the pattern of tombs was disturbed by additions, but for the rest of the Middle Ages only members of the royal dynasty were buried in the royal necropolis.[61]

It is doubtful whether Louis contributed as much in financial terms to this reconstruction as was once thought, but the connections of the king and abbey were as strong as in the days of Abbot Suger. Royal coats of arms adorned the church, much of the regalia was kept there, and the abbey was allowed major privileges, including freedom from tolls throughout France and freedom from the *gîte* in 1259. When the king fell ill in 1244, declared William of Nangis, a monk of the house, the bones of Saints Denis, Eleutherius and Rusticus displayed in the abbey alone could cure him. Such a step, he suggested, could be taken only when king or kingdom were at risk, for the patron saint of the house was the special defender of France and the Gallic people. Another link of the king and the abbey through Charlemagne was stressed in the literary works of the monks (4.4.3). The transfer of the kingdom to Charlemagne's race was portrayed as finding its full expression in the brilliant reign of Louis. The king, like Philip Augustus before him, followed the idea set out in Charlemagne's false donation and placed four gold besants on the altar each year (4.4.6); and before he went on crusade in 1248 and 1270 he went to Saint-Denis and received from the abbot the *oriflamme*, supposedly Charlemagne's standard (4.4.6). The links with the king and Saint-Denis remained strong throughout the reign and the monks were to be eulogists of the king in death as in life.

As an example of the royal taste the great abbey was rapidly superseded. In the early 1240s a master from Amiens rather than Reims built the Sainte-Chapelle to house the relics of the passion acquired from Constantinople. This was a seminal building in the spread and development of the court style, as much from its function as its design, although the latter was magnificent enough. It was built as 'a reliquary of monumental size',[62] a stone screen finely wrought like metalwork supporting superb carvings and stained glass, richly encrusted with gold and jewels, frescoes and enamels. It was a national shrine, and one which reflected the glory of both king and kingdom. Archbishop Gautier Cornut of Sens declared that France had been singled out for the veneration of the relics of the passion, and that the crown of thorns was the special glory of the whole kingdom. In a bull of 1244 Pope Innocent IV stated that Christ had crowned Louis with his own crown.

This religious lustre was added to the already bright prestige of the culture and language of France, the reputation of Paris for learning and art, and it was centred in the king. Louis's crusade of 1248 epitomised his role as the holy Christian king.

The architectural styles of northern France were widely imitated throughout Europe, and they were an important influence on the design of Westminster abbey as rebuilt by Henry III from the mid-1240s. The Norman church of Edward the Confessor, the English coronation church, was replaced by a vast shrine whose proportions and decoration drew heavily on northern French models, particularly Amiens and Reims. But it was more a screen for political weakness than a manifestation of strength. Matthew Paris, the Saint Albans chronicler who was no admirer either of his own king or of the French people, recognised the contrast: he called Louis 'king of terrestrial kings, both because of his heavenly unction and because of his power and military eminence'.[63] It was the chrism which gave the French kings their special power, he thought, and it is clear that they were regarded as the first in western Europe.

After Louis's return from crusade in 1254 his tastes were far plainer and he built a considerable number of unadorned churches for the mendicant orders and hospitals. But there were still some great ceremonies, as with the translation of the king's ancestors at Saint-Denis in 1263. The royal chapel at Senlis, built 1261–64, which was destroyed at the French Revolution, was compared with the Sainte-Chapelle in its splendour. By the 1260s the court style had become fixed into a pattern which was to be followed in France for the next century. Drawings of another lost church, Saint-Louis at Poissy, built by Philip IV and dedicated to his canonised grandfather, suggest that this was a fine example of the style and a suitable memorial to Louis IX (6.5.2).

What were Louis's own views on the nature of his office? The protests to the pope in 1247 made by the king's envoys and the Mise of Amiens of 1264 (5.2.2) reflect a far more elevated view of royal power than Louis's actual behaviour might suggest. The second protest to the pope contained the suggestion that the goods of the church were the king's to use in time of need, and may have gone beyond his own views (5.4.2); the actual text of the sentence he gave at Amiens was based on the pleadings of Henry III's lawyers, but its general tenor must reflect the king's own opinions on royal authority. Louis allowed that Henry III should have full power and unrestricted rule saving only that this should not derogate from existing customs, a strongly authoritarian view of royal as against baronial power, and perhaps a product of the king's experiences during his minority (5.2.1). Contemporary evidence seems to suggest that the king gave judgement as Henry's overlord rather than as an arbiter finding according to natural law; and this would imply that Louis believed that Henry's act of performing liege homage had created a French jurisdiction even in those cases where Henry was acting solely as king of England.[64]

Certainly during Louis's reign the idea of the sovereignty of the king in France was growing rapidly in the wake of the realisation of his powers as suzerain. The king's power was extended first to all the vassals of his vassals and then beyond to burgesses and peasants.[65] It gradually spread in all kinds of spheres – political, religious, financial, military. The king replaced the church as the guardian of the peace for the whole realm and from 1258 attempted to abolish private wars. Then, as Beaumanoir showed, he exercised a special guardianship over all the churches in the kingdom, over and above baronial advocacy, which enabled him to draw them under his own influence. He legislated in some cases for the kingdom, not just the domain, he extended royal coinage throughout the realm, he levied military service from the principalities. All these powers stemmed from ancient royal prerogatives or from feudal suzerainty, but Louis IX was able to extend them as his real authority increased so that in many spheres the French king was no longer ruling in his kingdom only by delegation through baronial consent. For the first time in the Capetian period, the king's power was felt throughout the realm.

These changes were paralleled in changing ideas about the French kingdom. The expression 'Francia' when used in the context of France and not in its more general senses, came increasingly to describe the whole kingdom and was less often applied just to the royal principality. The idea of the 'French people' was similarly widened as the notion that the kingdom of France consisted of the lands under the king's protection, tutelage and suzerainty, gave way to a territorial conception of the French realm. For as knowledge of Roman law spread through northern France, the idea of the *communis patria*, the community of the fatherland, was adopted to fit the French kingdom, with the king as its embodiment. Thus in 1270 Jacques de Revigny, a jurist of Orléans, wrote that: 'Just as Rome is the common fatherland of the Romans, the crown of the kingdom is the common fatherland of the kingdom because it is the head.'[66] References to the common good and public necessity also increase, reflecting the idea of a community of the realm, and with them goes the concept of a *naturalis*, a citizen of the kingdom as opposed to a foreigner or alien. In 1274 Primat, when translating Suger's Life of Louis VI for the *Grandes Chroniques*, added to the description of the 1124 campaign against the emperor, that Theobald of Champagne and Henry I of England and Normandy supported Louis, with whom they were at war, 'for the needs of the kingdom against foreign nations.'[67] French royal power was making great strides forward; the full implications of this were to be realised in the reign of Louis's grandson, Philip IV (6.4.3).

5.5.6 Criticisms of the king

Louis's achievements in government and administration were very considerable (5.5.1). The extension of royal power throughout the kingdom, however, provoked considerable reaction, which, though glossed over by Joinville, William of Saint-Pathus and other writers, should not be ignored by historians. One poet wrote bitterly of the king's attempts to limit private wars and to forbid trial by battle, both highly valued prerogatives of the nobility. The men of France, says the writer, are no longer free. They have been deprived of their franchises because they are judged by *enquête*. France is no longer *la douce France*, it is a land of slaves.[68] The value of these rights to the nobility is amply demonstrated in the vehemence with which they claimed them in the unrest of

1314–15 (6.4.5). The king's insistence that the nobility be subject to the laws of the land also provoked anger (5.5.1).

Joinville shows that certain of the king's policies were disliked by his council, and he also suggests that his personal asceticism and pious lifestyle were not accepted well by all his court (5.1.1). But there are no hints of the polemics against Louis's close involvement with the friars, his crusading fervour and his way of life. These provoked a spate of hostile poems, and even a hostile sermon, preached by William of Saint-Amour in 1256 (5.3.2); this clearly though indirectly accused Louis of being a hypocrite. He imitated the poor, yet he mulcted the kingdom to pay for wars in which Christians were killed. Nothing in the scriptures suggests that kings should dress humbly; Jerome says that they should use their wealth for their kingdom; and maintaining royal dignity in magnificence and state is an important part of this. The king should render justice and he should not be surrounded and counselled by selfrighteous vagrants who should be out begging their own bread. Nor does canon law suggest that a king should be a vagabond.[69] This open criticism of the king and his reliance on the friars also found expression in the poems of Rutebeuf, a supporter of William, who accused the mendicants of heresy, hypocrisy, greed, tyranny over the church, menacing the laws of Christ. Their original state of poverty was contrasted with their present wealth and power. Other religious orders favoured by the king also came in for criticism, and Louis was revealed as at best misguided and gullible; his crusades were criticised as ill-judged, influenced by others, and his need for money was seen as a rapaciousness which was bad for the kingdom. In this enthusiasm the king was cutting down the expenses of the royal household and denying many nobles their proper place.[70] Other similar points were made by John of Meung in the second part of the *Roman de la Rose*. The forces of hypocrisy had driven William of Saint-Amour into exile, and the friars were tricking the king.

True, these are very much partisan accounts, biased heavily towards William of Saint-Amour and his cause, and violently against the friars, but there does seem to have been a strong reaction against crusading in France after the *débâcle* of 1248–54, and an antipathy towards the king's ascetic way of life seems also to have been widespread, contrasting as it did with the magnificence of state ceremonies earlier in his reign. A revealing story appears in an early fourteenth-century Franciscan collection of *exempla* for sermons. A knight in Louis's entourage criticised the king for continuing to behave like a friar despite all the criticisms levelled against him. Louis replied:

Pay no attention to what fools say; let me tell you what happens when sometimes I am alone in my private apartments. I hear cries of '*Frater Ludovicus*' and curses against me, thought to be beyond my hearing. Then I wonder in my own mind whether I should have them slain, but then I realise that this takes place for my benefit, if only I bear it safely for God's sake.[71]

The king was, if the tale is true, well aware of the criticisms against him but was not willing to relinquish his way of life. He retained a very high view of the office of kingship in the latter part of his reign, but he remained firmly committed to the idea of the crusade and to the ideals of the mendicants.

5.5.7 *The king and the principalities: the problem of Gascony*

During Louis IX's reign the French principalities retained their own identities, laws and customs. Some, such as Normandy, Poitou and Toulouse, came heavily under the influence of the Capetians and many changes resulted from this (5.5.3; 5.5.4). In general the trend was towards a firmer ducal or comital power, a growing administration, the closer dependence of the nobility on their overlords, and this was the case as much in the royal lands and the apanages as in the other principalities, Brittany, Champagne, Burgundy, Aquitaine. The different regions of northern France retained their own customs (Map 5.3), and the influence of Roman law and the developments in legal processes resulted in the codification of many of these including the customs of Normandy, Beauvaisis, Anjou, Champagne. The customs of the Orléannais form the basis of the *Livre de Jostice et de Plet* (*c*. 1260s), an attempt to synthesise Roman, canon and customary

Map 5.3   Legal customs in northern France in the thirteenth century

law. The so-called *Établissements de Saint Louis*, compiled before 1273 and widely and mistakenly attributed to the king, are based largely on the customs of Anjou. The work is an attempt to use Roman law for commentaries upon French law, and as such was highly influential. The most successful legal treatise of this period is the *Coutûmes de Beauvaisis* (the Customs of the Beauvaisis) by Philip de Beaumanoir, a poet and royal *bailli*; written before 1283, it is a valuable analysis of contemporary legal practice.

During Louis's reign royal suzerainty in the kingdom was strengthened to a considerable extent and the idea of royal sovereignty, too, became firmer (5.5.5). This reflected a real shift in political balance. In the early years of the reign royal power had been threatened by a strong and hostile coalition of barons, overcome only with difficulty by Louis and Blanche of Castile (5.2.1). After about 1235 the princes as a group began to go into eclipse; many went on crusade, others became loyal vassals and those who continued to resist the king, such as the count of Toulouse and the kings of Aragon and England, were gradually brought into line by a mixture of warfare and diplomacy. Feudal relations within the French kingdom became clearly laid out and well defined.

The French king also controlled a slowly growing number of principalities directly or through closely related apanaged princes; these grants were handed out by Louis IX and his successors only in small blocs, a contrast to the massive endowments by Louis VIII. The reserve of crown land was substantially increased by the large number of reversions of apanage and of other land to the king, which could not have been foreseen; but the retention of much of this land, such as Toulouse, and the attempts made to extend it, as with the marriage of the future Philip IV and Joan of Champagne, suggest that the expansion of the domain was a conscious policy. Where Philip Augustus and Louis VIII could not cope with large amounts of royal land, Philip IV was well able to manage (5.5.2; 6.4.1). Thus many principalities came into royal hands, and the princes – the barons, the peers of France – occupied a place of diminishing importance in the affairs of the kingdom. Royal justice and administration centred on Paris gradually gained ground in the royal domain and in the other principalities; this eventually resulted in 1314–15 in strong local reaction and the concession by the crown of charters of liberties to the different principalities of the kingdom, after which the power of the princes began to grow again (6.4.5). Thus under Louis IX and his successors the idea and the reality of the French kingdom revived dramatically, but it was not powerful enough to break down the regional communities, the principalities within the realm.

The relationship between the king and one territorial prince, the king of England and duke of Gascony, was a particularly difficult problem until the peace of 1259; but even after 1259 the disagreements of the two sides were never fully resolved.[72] Until the treaty Henry III still held Gascony and parts of Poitou, and he claimed Normandy and greater Anjou, which Philip Augustus had taken from John (4.4.8). Campaigns were fought with the French king spasmodically until 1248 when Louis went on crusade (5.2.1; 5.2.2) and Henry, on papal encouragement, agreed not to attack his lands in his absence. Meanwhile English resources and effort had been thrown into warfare rather than the administration of Gascony, which remained a difficult region to control. In 1248 Henry III gave Simon de Montfort overall authority here, and his harsh attempts to dominate the Gascons brought about a violent reaction, endangering English authority; a revolt broke out and in 1253 Henry III was forced to travel to the duchy to quash it. He waged an effective campaign and Gaston of Béarn and the other insurgents gradually gave in. He also made peace with Alfonso X king of Castile who had supported the rebels, and arranged that his young son, Edward, later Edward I of England, should marry Eleanor of Castile. Edward was given control of Gascony, and he succeeded in further pacifying the Gascons. In one charter he was styled as prince and lord, ruling in Gascony, *regnans in Vasconia sicut princeps et dominus*,[73] but he found himself in disagreement with his father over how and by whom Gascony should be controlled. Edward's administrators set up an exchequer at Bordeaux, levied hearth taxes, and made a survey of his lands and rights, but in 1258 the prince fell out with his seneschal Stephen Longuéspée, whom he tried to replace with his uncles Geoffrey and Guy of Lusignan. Henry III prevented this and Dreu de Barentin became seneschal instead. Edward was angry, but he disagreed with his father even more fundamentally over the treaty of Paris of 1259.

The treaty,[74] the terms of which would have been almost unthinkable to Philip Augustus and John, was made by Louis as a regularisation of the anomalous position of Henry of England in France — just as in 1258 Louis had made a settlement with James of Aragon — and as part of Louis's European peace programme. Henry for his part was intent on gaining the crown of Sicily for his son and on dealing with his barons. Both kings conceded a great deal, and both were bitterly criticised by their baronage as a result. Henry III did homage to Louis IX for Bordeaux, Bayonne and Gascony, which lost their allodial status, and he became a peer of France. As a result Gascony was opened up for the first time to the final appellate jurisdiction of the French royal court, and lawsuits between Gascons and the subjects of Louis which had previously been settled on the borders of Gascony, on matters such as the inheritance of Turenne, now went to Paris for resolution. Gradually too the rights of the French king to levy service inside the duchy were strengthened, overriding local custom. Henry III had sworn to protect the liberties of Gascony, but Edward and his barons found this an empty promise. Worse, Henry also finally relinquished his claims to Normandy, Anjou, Maine, Touraine and Poitou, concessions which greatly angered his son Edward and his associates. On his side Louis gave Henry substantial sums of money — to be of great value in his wars with the barons — and promised the reversion of Agenais, Quercy and Saintonge, held by Alfonso of Poitiers, after Alfonso's death. In the meantime a rent was to be paid for these lands. Although Alfonso died in 1271, the Agenais was not ceded to the English until 1279 and Saintonge until 1286, and at this time the claim to Quercy was given up by the French king in exchange for an annual rent of £3,000 tournois to the English king.

Another bone of contention was the lands and rights in the dioceses of Périgueux, Limoges and Cahors which Louis had in theory ceded to Henry straight away. On 16 December 1259 he issued this letter:

Louis, by the grace of God king of France to his beloved prelates, ecclesiastical chapters, barons, knights, vassals and towns, and to all others in the cities and dioceses of Périgueux, Limoges and Cahors to whom these letters pertain, greetings. Since by the peace treaty concluded recently between us and our beloved kinsman and faithful man Henry, king of England, lord of Ireland and duke of Aquitaine, we have assigned him all the rights which we have and hold in the aforesaid cities and dioceses of Limoges, Périgueux and Cahors, for which he has done liege homage – saving only the homage of our brothers for anything which they hold from us, and those rights which we cannot grant away because of letters given by us and our ancestors – we command, order and require you to obey this king as your lord and to observe his mandate from now on, faithfully and devotedly, in all rights given and conceded by us to him in the aforementioned peace treaty; so that we and he will be able most justly to commend your fidelity and devotion. Given at Pontoise . . .[75]

This grant caused strong ill-feeling in the area and a hostility to Louis so deeprooted that in 1297 the inhabitants of these areas would not celebrate his canonisation. More immediately many of the nobles refused homage to Henry III, who in 1263 asked Louis to allow him unrestricted rights. Louis offered to negotiate, but nothing was settled until 1279 when Edward I relinquished the English claims. This local hostility to both the English and the French kings made it difficult to enforce such a grant. Nevertheless in the long term the French crown seems to have done better than the English from the treaty. As a recent account suggests, 'despite his protestations of affection towards Henry III of England, Saint Louis, in concluding the treaty of 1259, had done nothing but continue the politics of expansion of his two predecessors.'[76] His financial support was to help Henry in the baronial wars, however, and by the Mise of Amiens he firmly supported his rights as king (5.2.2). In the event Henry had to fight his way back to power in his own kingdom, and the events which followed the 1259 treaty left behind a troubled legacy of Anglo-French relations (6.4.3).

5.5.8 The achievements of Louis IX

Louis IX was clearly a man of remarkable qualities and abilities, who seems to overshadow contemporary rulers in both his character and his achievements. It is true that Henry III shared many of his pious interests; and there was a strong element of rivalry between the two kings in their religious devotions and their benefactions. It was Louis who was canonised in the end, however. The French king was also far more successful politically than Henry III; he and his mother overcame the French baronage where Henry fought the English, and the criticisms of Louis from contemporary writers were mild in comparison with the hostility shown to Henry from many English chroniclers. It is also true that Frederick II was an infinitely more successful crusader than Louis. He gained by negotiation what Louis failed to do in two expeditions which cost dear in lives and capital. But his achievements have often been overestimated by historians,[77] and his dynasty was soon supplanted in Sicily by Louis's own, which had acted more conventionally and had not alienated the papacy.

Louis had personal failings and suffered political disasters, and these should not be ignored. He could be and was influenced strongly by others, by his mother, his brothers and his confessors, and where the influence of his mother had stood him in very good stead, Charles of Anjou's persuasions had dangerous and farreaching consequences. Louis's judgements did not always prove effective, as events in Flanders and England showed. His obsession with the crusade proved fruitless and cost his kingdom dear; his asceticism in later life lessened his popularity with his people. He was brutal to Jews and blasphemers, as were so many others in his age. But in his character and achievements he still outstripped his contemporaries by a very long way.

Louis's reign was not a golden age; it was a time of failure as well as of success. It marked the culmination of many of the developments in royal power which had taken place in the twelfth and early thirteenth centuries. The royal lands, the king's power-base in the kingdom, were finally consolidated and the conquests from the Angevins and the house of Toulouse legitimised. The king's feudal superiority was reinforced, his role as sovereign began to emerge, and his image and reputation as lawgiver and God's anointed given great lustre. Royal administration, both central and local, royal finance and justice all made great strides during his reign, and although they had their defects, still they were strongly influenced by the king's own ideals of fair and honest government. This was an authoritarian régime, as the French church found, but to resist such a good Christian and firm ruler as Louis IX was difficult. As a result the French king became pre-eminent not only in France, but also in western Europe.

From the achievements of Louis's reign stemmed other trends, the culminations and consequences of which were to be worked out in later reigns. Like his predecessors Louis was firm with the French church, and because of his moral and religious reputation he was not widely criticised for the build up of royal authority over it and for his heavy taxation of it in conjunction with the pope. This was to stand his successors in great stead and to enable them to exercise an unprecedented power over the church for blatantly political reasons (6.5.3). Then Louis's support of the conquests of Charles of Anjou, made in furtherance of papal policy, were to give the French crown a close involvement with the political aims of the papacy and also a stake in Italy; both developments were to have dramatic consequences. Louis's settlement with Henry III in 1259, although broadly speaking a wise move to regularise an anomalous situation, provoked great opposition immediately and created many more problems and contentious issues in the long term. Neither warfare nor negotiation had worked these out by the end of the Capetian period and they were to erupt into the Hundred Years' War (see Ch. 7). The spread of royal justice and royal administration into the principalities gathered momentum in Louis's reign as well, as more came under royal influence – a development which was to provoke a strong reaction in the early fourteenth century (6.4.5).

Louis's reign was in many ways a watershed, a time when the French king stopped concentrating on internal politics, on wars with the princes, and appeared as the leading protagonist on the European stage. The nature of his power inside and outside the kingdom changed, just as ideas about the nature of the French and other kingdoms modified and developed.

NOTES AND FURTHER READING

Asterisked titles are recommended for further reading. Place of publication London unless otherwise indicated.

Notes

1. Salimbene, *Chronica*, ed. F. Bernini, i (Bari, 1942), 317; *Cambridge Medieval History*, vii (1932), 331.
2. M. Champollion-Figeac, *Lettres des rois, reines et autres personnages des cours de France et d'Angleterre*, i (Paris, 1839), 140–2. The exchange between Henry and Louis also appears in William Rishanger, *Chronica et Annales*, ed. T. R. Riley, *RS* (1865), 75.
3. Jean, sire de Joinville, *Vie de Saint Louis*, ed. and trans. N. de Wailly (Paris, 1874); the most readable English version is by M. R. B. Shaw, as **Life of Saint Louis*, in *Chronicles of the Crusades* (Penguin, 1963), 164–353. Quoted from Shaw, 177.
4. *Ibid.*, 167–8, 178.
5. *Ibid.*, 169.
6. *Ibid.*, 352.
7. These traits are well brought out by E. R. Labande, 'Quelques traits de caractère du roi Saint Louis', *Revue d'histoire de la spiritualité*, i (1974), 135–46.
8. Joinville, trans. Shaw, 343.
9. *Ibid.*, 170–1.
10. On the politics of this period and on Blanche, see R. Pernoud, **Blanche of Castile*, trans. H. Noel (1975). Louis's reign is covered by M. W. Labarge, **Saint Louis: a life of Louis IX of France* (1968), but the most detailed monograph of the reign remains J. le Nain de Tillement, *Vie de Saint Louis*, ed. J. de Gaule, 6 vols (Paris, 1849), written in the late seventeenth century.
11. Joinville, trans. Shaw, 181–2, 190.
12. L. Delisle, 'Mémoire sur une lettre inédite adressée à la reine Blanche', *Bibl. E.C.*, xvii (1856) 526; trans. Labarge, *op. cit.*, 73–4.
13. *RHF*, xxi, 77.
14. Joinville, trans. Shaw, *op. cit.*, 191.
15. J. R. Strayer, 'The crusades of Saint Louis', in *A History of the Crusades, ii. The Later Crusades*, ed. R. L. Woolff and H. W. Hazard (University of Pennsylvania, 1962), 491.
16. Matthew Paris, *Chronica Maiora et Liber Addimentorum*, ii–vi, ed. H. R. Luard, *RS* (1876–82); v, 465–6; Labarge, *op. cit.*, 145.
17. Joinville, trans. Shaw, *op. cit.*, 334.
18. *RHF*, xxi, 77.
19. H. Wallon, *Saint Louis et son temps* (Paris, 1876), 482–3.
20. J. Longnon, 'Les vues de Charles d'Anjou pour la deuxième croisade de Saint Louis', in *Septième Centenaire de la mort de Saint Louis* (Paris, 1976), 183–95.
21. E. Boutaric, 'Marguerite de Provence . . ., son caractère, son rôle politique', *Revue des questions historiques*, iii (1867), 417–58.
22. Fourquin, *Les campagnes de la région parisienne . . . (op. cit.* Ch. 4).
23. *Ibid.*, 144–5.
24. R. Cazelles, *Nouvelle histoire de Paris de la fin du règne de Philippe Auguste à la mort de Charles V, 1223–1380* (Paris, 1972), *passim*.
25. Matthew Paris, *op.cit.*, v, 478–82.

26. R. B. Brooke, *The Coming of the Friars* (London/New York, 1975); J. Moorman, *A History of the Franciscan Order from its origins to the year 1517* (Oxford, 1968).
27. R. W. Emery, *The Friars in Medieval France* (New York/London, 1962), 4 *et passim*.
28. Southern, *Western Society and the Church in the Middle Ages* (*op. cit.* Ch. 4), 320–1; B. M. Bolton, 'Mulieres Sanctae', *Studies in Church History*, x (1973), 77–95.
29. W. L. Wakefield,*Heresy, Crusade and Inquisition in Southern France, 1100–1250* (1974), 320–1.
30. M. Lambert, *Medieval Heresy* (1977), 170.
31. Joinville, trans. Shaw, 169.
32. D. O'Connell, *The Teachings of Saint Louis: a critical text* (Chapel Hill, 1972).
33. Guillaume de Saint-Pathus, *La Vie et les Miracles de Monseigneur Saint Louis, Roi de France*, ed. M. C. d'Espagne (Paris, 1971), 60; Hallam, 'Monastic patronage' (*op. cit.* Ch. 4), 220–83 for a fuller account of Louis's monastic patronage.
34. *RHF*, xxi, 661; Lot and Fawtier, eds, *Le Premier budget de la monarchie française* (*op. cit.* Ch. 4), 129.
35. Matthew Paris, *op. cit.*, v, 596.
36. Guillaume de Saint-Pathus, *op. cit.*, 62.
37. *Ibid.*, 52; Joinville, trans. Shaw, 58.
38. R. B. Brooke, *Early Franciscan Government* (Cambridge, 1959), 221–3, *et passim;* Joinville, trans. Shaw, 176, 328–9. I am grateful to Dr Brooke for drawing Hugh's importance to my attention. For Louis's connections with the friars, see L. K. Little, *'Saint Louis's involvement with the friars', *Church History*, xxxiii (1964), 125–48.
39. J. Watt, 'The theory of papal monarchy in the thirteenth century', *Traditio*, xx (1964), 179–317, *passim*.
40. Matthew Paris, *op. cit.*, vi, 99–112.
41. *RHF*, xxi, 251–60; *RHF, Docs. Fin.* ii (Paris, 1930), pp. xlv–xlvi.
42. *RHF*, xxi, 260–84 and p. lxxvi; see also above, n. 15; M. de Wailly, 'Dissertation sur les recettes et les dépenses ordinaires de Saint Louis', *RHF*, xxi, Introduction.
43. *RHF*, xxi, 398–403.
44. *RHF*, xxi, 404, 512–15.
45. A. Teulet, ed., *Layettes du trésor des chartes*, ii (Paris, 1866), 16, no. 1615; F., *Capetian Kings*, 193.
46. L. Carolus-Barré, 'La grande ordonnance de 1254 . . .', in *Septième centenaire . . .*, *op. cit.*, 85–96.
47. For this paragraph see *RHF*, xxi, 226–51, 284–329, 381–97.
48. C. T. Wood, *The French Apanages and the Capetian Monarchy, 1224–1378*, Harvard Historical Monographs, lxi (Cambridge, Mass., 1966), 12, 150.
49. A. W. Lewis, *'The Capetian apanages and the nature of the French Kingdom', *JMH*, ii (1976), 119–34.
50. F., *Capetian Kings*, 167–8.
51. J. R. Strayer, *The Administration of Normandy under Saint Louis* (Cambridge, Mass., 1932).
52. J. O'Sullivan, ed., *The Register of Eudes of Rouen*, (Columbia University Press, 1964), 148.
53. C. R. Cheney, *Episcopal Visitations of Monasteries in the Thirteenth Century* (Manchester, 1931), 165.
54. Matthew Paris, *op. cit.*, iv, 646.
55. Stevenson, 'England and Normandy . . .' (*op. cit.*, Ch. 4), i, 199–237; cf. Powicke, *Loss of Normandy* (*op. cit.*, Ch. 4) on double land-tenures in Normandy after 1204.
56. Matthew Paris, *op. cit.*, iv, 288.

57. E. Boutaric, *Saint Louis et Alphonse de Poitiers* (Paris, 1870).

58. *Ibid.*, 275, 374.

59. R. Branner, 'Saint Louis et l'enluminure parisienne au XIIIe siècle', in *Septième centenaire . . ., op. cit.*, 69–84.

60. R. Branner, **Saint Louis and the Court Style in Gothic Architecture* (1965).

61. Erlande-Brandenburg, *Le Roi est mort (op. cit.*, Ch. 4), 81–3; Guillaume de Nangis, *Chronique latine . . .*, ed. H. Géraud (Paris, 1843), 233–4.

62. Branner, *Saint Louis and the Court Style . . .*, 57.
(Oxford, 1948), 223–39.

63. Matthew Paris, *op. cit.*, v, 430, 606.

64. C. T. Wood, 'The mise of Amiens and Saint Louis's theory of kingship', *French Historical Studies*, vi (1970), 300–10; compare R. F. Treharne, 'The mise of Amiens, 23 January 1264', in *Studies . . . presented to F. M. Powicke*, ed. R. W. Hunt, *et al*. (Oxford, 1948), 223–39.

65. J. F. Lemarignier, *La France Médiévale* (Paris, 1970), 260–3.

66. B. Guenée, 'État et nation en France au moyen âge', *Revue Historique*, ccxxxvii (1967), 17–30, esp. 24–5.

67. *Les Grandes chroniques de France*, ed. J. Viard, v (Paris, 1928), 241; and see Guenée, *op. cit.*, 21.

68. Le Roux de Lincy, 'Chansons historiques des XIIIe, XIVe et XVe siècles', *Bibl. E.C.*, i (1839), esp. 370–4.

69. The text is given by Little, *op. cit.*, 147–8.

70. E. B. Ham, *Rutebeuf and Louis IX* (Chapel Hill, 1962).

71. Little, *op. cit.*, 145.

72. J. P. Trabut-Cussac, *L'Administration anglaise en Gascogne sous Henri III et Edouard III, de 1254 à 1307* (Geneva, 1972); P. Chaplais, 'Le traité de Paris de 1259 et l'inféodation de la Gascogne allodiale', *Le Moyen Age*, lxi (1955), 121–37.

73. T. Rymer and R. Sanderson, *Fœdora, Conventiones, Littera . . .*, i (1) (1816), 310.

74. P. Chaplais, ed., *Diplomatic Documents preserved in the Public Record Office*, i, *1101–1272* (1964), 212–15, no. 305.

75. *Ibid.*, 217–18, no. 308 (4).

76. P. Chaplais, 'Le duché-pairie de Guyenne', *Annales du Midi*, lxix (1957), 5–38, esp. p. 5.

77. See J. Gillingham's review of T. van Cleve's *Frederick II of Hohenstaufen*, *Immutator Mundi* (Oxford, 1972), in *English Historical Review*, xci (1976), 358–63.

CHAPTER SIX

The Last Capetians, 1270–1328: The Apogee of Royal Power

6.1 INTRODUCTION

6.1.1 *Royal power under the last Capetians*

The extent of the royal lands in 1259 had given Louis IX a predominant position in the French kingdom in terms of resources, and he was able to hold and consolidate the conquests of his predecessors and to build up royal power to formidable proportions (Map 5.1). By 1328 even more of the kingdom was held directly by the king and administered by his servants, and much of the rest had been granted out as apanages to members of the royal house.

Furthermore, most of the remaining independent principalities had been brought closely under royal influence, and those rulers such as the count of Flanders and the English king, also duke of Gascony, who put up strong resistance to Capetian authority, had had to fight long and hard for their independence. Under the last Capetians, French royal power reached its medieval apogee.

This expansion is reflected not only in the extension of the royal domain, but also in the widening competence of the king himself in all his roles. Like Robert the Pious in A.D. 1000 Philip IV was in 1300 responsible for meting out justice, for defending his realm as sovereign and as suzerain and for the protection and support of the church as God's anointed. Where Robert and his itinerant court had settled a limited range of judicial matters largely concerning the men of the royal principality and surrounding areas, under Philip a great variety of cases came to the royal judicial court, the parlement at Paris, and were dealt with by professional justices. The king's judicial ordinances were in many cases effective throughout the kingdom. Robert the Pious had had some difficulty in defending the royal principality, but Philip IV could call on all his vassals and their vassals for military service, and on some occasions levied taxes throughout the French kingdom for its protection. His feudal and sovereign powers were, if sometimes opposed, denied only with impunity, where those of Robert the Pious had been largely theoretical. Similar coronation ceremonies had been used in 996 and in 1285, and both kings had a special sacral role, but in Robert's reign the French

Key

▨ Royal lands
▨ Lands of Edward III of England
☐ Valois apanage

0   50   100 miles
0   50 100 150 kms

N

KINGDOM OF ENGLAND

COUNTY OF FLANDERS

COUNTY OF ARTOIS

COUNTY OF PONTHIEU
COUNTY OF EU

Amiens

COUNTY OF
RETHEL

VERMANDOIS

COUNTY OF CLERMONT

Rouen

NORMANDY

COUNTY OF
EVREUX

Reims

COUNTY OF
VALOIS

BAR

COUNTY OF
MORTAIN

Paris

COUNTY
OF ALENÇON

CHAMPAGNE

LORRAINE

ILE DE
FRANCE

Troyes

DUCHY OF
BRITTANY

MAINE
ANJOU

COUNTY
OF BLOIS

COUNTY
OF
NEVERS

DUCHY
OF
BURGUNDY

FRANCHE
COMTÉ

BERRY

Poitiers

BOURBON

Mâcon

POITOU

LA
MARCHE

Lyon

COUNTY
OF
ANGOULÊME

Limoges

Bordeaux

COUNTY OF
FOREZ

COUNTY OF
VALENCE

Cahors

DUCHY
OF
GASCONY

Agen

Rodez

LANGUEDOC

Avignon

COUNTY OF
ARMAGNAC

Beaucaire

KINGDOM OF
NAVARRE

Toulouse

Carcassonne

COUNTY
OF BÉARN

COUNTY OF
FOIX

Map 6.1   France in 1328

church had in practice been forced to fend for itself, from which the peace and truce of God had grown, whereas Philip the Fair controlled it in an iron grip and was powerful enough to humble the papacy. Of course, Philip IV and his sons were very far from being omnicompetent; they provoked much opposition, and they were unable to carry out many of the policies which they wished to implement. Nevertheless, royal power was a vastly more impressive and sophisticated affair in 1300 than in 1000, and the French kingdom, long celebrated for its learning and culture, and now with a royal cult which was more than a match for Edward the Confessor in England, if not for Charlemagne in Germany, overshadowed the other states of western Europe.

6.2 THE KINGS AND THEIR REIGNS

6.2.1 Philip III, 1270–1285

Philip III[1] had the historical misfortune to rule France between two of its most celebrated kings, Louis IX and Philip IV, and posterity has not been kind to him. He did not share many of the qualities of his father, but he was not a nonentity either: the nickname 'Philip the Bold' was won perhaps during his lifetime, certainly before 1300, and was an acknowledgement of his prowess in Tunis and in Spain. In statues, coins and miniatures of his time he appears as a strong and handsome man;[2] the chroniclers relate that he had a love of hunting and tournaments, and a taste for luxury which Joinville found displeasing. This contrasted with the simplicity of Louis IX's later years. Philip shared his father's generosity in almsgiving; indeed there are some hints that he was utterly indiscriminate in his largesse. He was also firmly and conventionally pious, and led a quiet private life. Chroniclers reproach him for being a near-illiterate, however, and he was also easily dominated and influenced, as was demonstrated in the oath of obedience he took to his mother, the fiery Margaret of Provence, when a young man (5.2.2). Although strong and brave in action, he appears to have been less ready to act in government and administration, which he left largely to his advisers; in this, he was to be a considerable contrast with his son, Philip IV (6.2.2).

Because of Philip's political weakness, the French court soon became the centre of intrigues. At their centre was Pierre de la Broce, a man from the lesser nobility of Touraine who had risen in the royal service and had been a chamberlain to Louis IX. He was Philip III's favourite, and one chronicler asserts that he 'attended the royal council at any hour he chose, and when the barons had given the king their wise council, it was rejected if [he] disagreed with it'.[3] He became inordinately wealthy and proud, and was hated and feared by many of the court. In 1274, however, the king, whose first wife Isabella of Aragon had died, married again. The new queen, Mary of Brabant, a lively and attractive woman, soon began to influence him strongly, and she and her family and supporters formed a group at court which was opposed to the power of Pierre de la Broce. When Louis, Philip's eldest son (by Isabella of Aragon) and heir died in 1276, Pierre's followers made veiled allegations of foul play, pointing out that this death was in the Brabançon interest. Philip, it is said, was more inclined to put it down to sorcery. The queen's faction managed to repay Pierre early in 1277, when Robert of Artois, sent as an envoy to Castile, pretended he had seen some French secret information there, revealed by Pierre. The king entirely lost faith in his favourite as a result, and Pierre was arrested, tried rapidly and hanged in 1278.

Mary now dominated Philip for the rest of the reign, although faction fights between the many powerful personalities surrounding the king continued. Charles of Anjou, king of Sicily had exercised influence over Louis IX. Now, in alliance with Mary, he strove to maintain his power under the new regime. Louis IX's widow, Margaret of Provence was Charles's implacable enemy and plotted consistently against him (5.2.2). Then there was Philip's cousin, Robert of Artois, a rash adventurer and a supporter of Mary. The day-to-day administration seems to have been conducted by Matthew of Vendôme, abbot of Saint-Denis; a group of greater officials such as Pierre Barbet and Henry of Vézelay, guardians of the seal; and the lesser administrators from northern and central France such as the Villebéon, Chambly and Machaut families who had served Louis IX.

When Philip arrived back in Paris in 1271 he found a number of problems waiting for him. The most pressing was to determine who should take the lands of Alfonso of Poitiers and his wife, Joan of Toulouse, both of whom had died on their way home from the crusade leaving no heir. By the treaty of Paris of 1259, Henry III of England should now have taken Alfonso's lands of Quercy, Saintonge and Agenais (5.5.7), but Philip's envoys fobbed him off with excuses. Joan had made a will leaving her Toulouse lands to Charles of Anjou and to her cousin, Philippa of Lomagna. But these provinces, like Poitou, were seized by the royal officials, and they all put up surprisingly little resistance. The king's legal hold on Alfonso's and Joan's inheritance was finally secured in 1284 when the claims of Charles of Anjou and Philippa were disallowed, and Louis VIII's will was deemed to have had a reversion clause implicit in all the apanage grants. Edward I, on his way home from Palestine, did homage to Philip III in 1273 for his French lands which was only conditional on the observance of the treaty of Paris of 1259. A compromise on this vexed issue was found in 1279 at the treaty of Amiens, when Edward was granted the Agenais and his wife Eleanor of Castile was allowed to succeed to Ponthieu, the right to which she had just inherited. The question of Quercy and Saintonge was left unresolved.

In 1272 Richard of Cornwall, the claimant to the empire of longest standing, died, and Charles of Anjou put Philip III forward as a suitable candidate who would favour his schemes in Italy. Pope Gregory X evidently did not agree and Rudolf of Habsburg was elected as emperor. Nevertheless, in 1273–74 the French king handed over the Venaissin to the pope, a county to the north of Provence and east of Avignon, claimed by the papacy since the Albigensian crusade; in 1274 Philip met Gregory and confirmed the cession of the lands, as well as discussing the crusade which the pope proposed to lead. Nothing came of this, and in 1276 Gregory died.

A betrothal took place in 1275 which was to bring more lands under royal domination. In 1274 Henry III, king of Navarre and count of Champagne died, leaving his three-year-old daughter Joan as his heiress. She was already betrothed to one of the sons of Edward I of England, but since her mother and guardian Blanche of Artois put herself under the protection of her brother Robert, at the French court, Philip III was able to influence events. He betrothed Joan to his second son Philip, later Philip IV. By the treaty of Orléans (1275), Navarre was put under the control of Eustace de Beaumarchais, seneschal of Toulouse, who marched in at the head of an army, and began to reorganise the kingdom, much to the fury of its inhabitants. Champagne was administered by Blanche's second husband, Edmund, earl of Lancaster, until Joan married Philip in 1284, and its people put up little resistance to the change of authority. Navarre, on the other hand, broke out in open revolt in 1276, but a French army was at hand to crush this rising, since the king had gone to the defence of his Castillian relatives.

The son and heir of Alfonso X of Castile, Prince Ferdinand, died in 1275, leaving a widow, Blanche of France, Philip III's sister, and two sons later known as the *infantes* (children) of La Cerda. Alfonso passed the elder of these over as his heir, choosing instead Ferdinand's brother, Sancho. According to William of Nangis, Blanche was left destitute and sent back to France.[4] In 1276 Philip III sent an army to both Navarre and Castile, but the expedition proved disastrous. Part of the force reached Navarre and cruelly crushed the revolt; the rest only got as far as Sauveterre near Pau and was then sent home again by the king. This was a great humiliation, explained away by a Saint-Denis chronicler as a result of the treachery of the king's advisers. The *infantes* took refuge at Barcelona, but Alfonso X and his new heir Sancho soon quarrelled, reducing the problem for France from Castile.

Philip III next found himself hostile to Aragon. In 1282 the Sicilians rose against Charles of Anjou in the revolt known as the Sicilian Vespers, and they offered the throne of Sicily to Peter III of Aragon, husband of the Hohenstaufen heiress Constance. Charles, left in control of the kingdom of Naples, was given full support by Pope Martin IV, who as Cardinal Simon of Brie had been a friend of his. On Martin's election in 1281 a violent war had broken out in the papal states, which Philip III had helped to put down with men and money. Now the pope excommunicated the Aragonese king, and offered his crown to Philip for one of his sons. After much deliberation, Philip accepted it on behalf of Charles of Valois, but only on condition that the pope financed the war and had it preached as a crusade. Major preparations were made, and although the principal instigators of the policy, Charles of Anjou and Martin IV, both died in 1285, by this time it was too late to stop the campaign.[5]

The cost of the Aragonese crusade was immense – about £1,229,000 tournois – and it left the French monarchy heavily encumbered with debts which were to prove difficult to recoup. The expedition was an almost total failure. The great French army, having gained the support of Roussillon, crossed the Pyrenees and besieged and captured the town of Gerona, but it was stricken with sickness, and its supply lines were cut at the sea battle of Las Formiguas. The king, too, fell ill, and with a severely depleted force struggled back over the mountains, leaving a garrison at Gerona which was to capitulate before long. Philip III died at Perpignan, under a cloud of failure and defeat. The lesson of this campaign was not lost on his son, Philip IV, who turned away from expensive expeditions to the south in support of papal policy and began to concentrate on problems nearer at hand, and on the interests of the French monarchy. This approach was to undermine the position of the pope in Italy and also further to diminish the value of the crusade as an instrument of papal policy.

6.2.2 Philip IV 'the Fair', 1285–1314

During Philip IV's reign royal power in France arguably reached its medieval apogee.[6] Royal records were kept far more systematically than earlier on, and far more of them survive, as do also a great number of other different kinds of sources. Despite this evidence, Philip IV has remained an enigmatic and controversial king, both in terms of his character and in the extent to which he controlled and directed his administrators and their actions. This is in large measure the result of the king's own withdrawn and aloof behaviour, which left contemporaries to surmise what kind of man he was. Bernard Saisset, bishop of Pamiers declared, 'the king is like an owl, the most beautiful of birds, but worth nothing. He is the most handsome of men but he stares fixedly in silence. . . . He is neither man nor beast, he is a statue.'[7]

Hostile writers of the time pointed to Philip's silence as a sign of lack of interest in government and administration. Geoffrey of Paris blamed him for an obsession with hunting and for allowing himself to be duped by his counsellors who were in control of his affairs. Ivo of Saint-Denis, an eulogist of the king, by contrast, described him in terms which would not have put Louis IX to shame. He was very pious, and almost too gentle and modest.[8] William de Nogaret, his leading adviser from 1303 to 1313, portrayed Philip as 'full of grace, charity, piety and mercy, always following truth and justice, never a detraction in his mouth, fervent in the faith, religious in his life, building basilicas and engaging in works of piety'.[9]

The 'official' sources, the administrative documents, appear to confirm some elements of each view, by showing that early in his reign the king devoted much time to hunting, but that later on he engaged in large-scale works of piety.[10] These included the foundation of monasteries, and substantial charitable donations, and seem to reflect an increasing concern with the health of Philip's soul and with making amends for the wrongs he had done.[11] But should measures of this sort be taken as an index of piety? Philip was far more generous to the church and the poor in his testaments than Saint Louis had been in his, for example. There was also a considerable element of convention in matters such as charitable bequests and religious foundations; and although Philip showed more than conventional enthusiasm for such activities, this may in part have been an expression of his devotion to the cult of his grandfather, Saint Louis, to whom several of his monasteries were dedicated and who was a pattern for his donations. The king's motives in this may have been religious – we cannot tell, for we cannot open a window into his soul – but the cult was also of the greatest political importance. Saint Louis was the symbol of the French monarchy at its apogee, of holy kingship and royal power combined. Professor Fawtier saw Philip as a pious man, but also as a proud king with great faith in his dynasty, which enabled him to defeat and humble the pope and to suppress the Templars, claiming God as his guide.[12] It is arguable that Philip's belief in Capetian kingship far outstripped his faith in God, and that he made a cynical use of the cult and trappings of holy kingship to further his political ends.

Despite his reserved behaviour, and despite his other interests and preoccupations apart from government, there seems little doubt that Philip IV bore the ultimate responsibility for the policies carried out in his name, and that he controlled and directed his councillors.[13] Royal records demonstrate that the extent of his involvement with the processes of government fluctuated, and that while he was normally present when major decisions were made, he often left the details and the execution of policies to his principal advisers. But he was not dominated by one favourite, he chose and directed his own servants. His confidence in Flotte, Nogaret, Marigny (6.4.2) did not amount to an abdication of power, but to its delegation.[14] Perhaps the most convincing picture of the king is that of a cynical, cold and withdrawn politician, not often in the limelight, but still controlling the events of his reign.

In 1285 the lands of the crown overshadowed the remaining principalities and apanages. Philip's marriage to Joan of Navarre brought him the kingdom of Navarre and the counties of Champagne, Brie and Bar; the latter were eventually united to the royal domain (6.4.3). The reversion of several apanages also swelled the royal lands, and when new apanage grants were made to royal sons, these were far smaller than the earlier ones (5.5.2). The royal princes continued to play an important role at court and in supporting the king's policies. Charles of Valois, Philip's brother,[15] followed in the footsteps of Charles of Anjou, and indulged in schemes to build up his power in southern Europe and in intrigues at court. Other dominant figures around Philip were the queen, and the king's principal advisers, Pierre Flotte (c. 1295–1302), William de Nogaret (1302– c. 1313), and Enguerrand de Marigny (1313–14). With their assistance, the king broke away from many of the policies of his predecessors.

On his accession a pressing problem confronting the king was to settle the Aragonese affair. His mother, Philip III's first wife, had been an Aragonese princess, and the young king seems to have opposed his father's crusade. Certainly he was anxious to make peace with his cousin Alfonso as soon as possible, despite the claims of Charles of Valois to the throne of Aragon. Negotiations were complicated by the Sicilian problem and a settlement was not arrived at until 1291. Charles of Valois agreed to relinquish his claims to Aragon, but was given the hand of Margaret, daughter of Charles of Naples, the heir of Charles of Anjou; her dowry was to be Anjou and Maine, and Charles of Naples was to get Sicily back. But the rights of the actual holder of Sicily, James of Aragon, were ignored, and when soon after the arrangement had been made, Alfonso of Aragon died and he became king here too, he showed great indignation and hostility towards the French. In 1295 he was induced to give up Sicily, however, and the peace of Anagni was made. The Sicilians next refused to agree to this settlement, and chose Frederick of Aragon, James's brother, as their king. Philip IV took no further action here, and nor did he intervene in Castile on behalf of Blanche of France and the *infantes* of la Cerda. He needed to keep the goodwill of the Spanish kingdoms lest they should support the English in Gascony.

War broke out in Sicily when Charles of Naples tried to regain the throne from Frederick. Pope Boniface VIII was as hostile to the Aragonese as his predecessors, and he preached a crusade and called in the French, a traditional way of dealing with papal enemies in Italy. Philip IV refused to help, but Charles of Valois was ready to embark on southern adventures. His first wife died in 1299 and he soon remarried. His new consort, Catherine Courtenay, had strong claims to the eastern empire, and Charles evidently regarded southern Italy as a suitable staging-point for this. His expedition was not a success, and in 1302 his army was called back to France. Philip IV had him put forward as holy Roman emperor in 1308, and was to do the same for his son, Philip of Poitiers, in 1313, but neither attempt bore any fruit.

From the 1290s Philip IV's government was more heavily preoccupied with the subjugation of the two hostile principalities of Flanders and Gascony than with ambitious and expensive southern schemes. His wars north of the Alps were also to prove costly and were to necessitate a number of financial expedients on the part of the crown which had momentous long-term consequences.

Early in Philip's reign, France and England were at peace, and Edward I did homage for Gascony. The problems created by the treaty of Paris in 1259 had still not fully been resolved, and resentment bubbled under the surface. In 1293 the seamen of Bayonne, La Rochelle and the Cinque Ports were involved in a series of mutual raids and reprisals, and Philip summoned Edward I before the court of peers. The English king tried to be pacific. He sent his brother to negotiate and agreed to hand over certain castles in Gascony to the French for forty days while the whole question was investigated. This was a standard procedure, but Philip's men showed bad faith and refused to hand them back. In 1294 Edward withdrew his homage and prepared to fight.

The French army mounted a series of campaigns in Gascony led by Raoul de Nesle, constable of France, by Charles of Valois and by Robert of Artois. The French forces did well in Gascony, helped by the Scots who attacked Edward from the north in 1295 and became allies of the French king in the same year. Edward built up a coalition of princes of which the kingpin was Guy of Dampierre, count of Flanders. He had been angered by the attempts of Philip IV to levy financial aid from Flanders for the war against England and by Philip's currency manipulations and controls on the export of money, which threatened Flemish trade; the king had taken into his own hands five of the principal Flemish towns when Guy resisted. Furthermore the French king had forbidden the marriage of the young Philippa of Flanders and the future Edward II. This action, rather than subjugating Guy, made him more hostile. By the time Edward I arrived in Flanders in 1297, however, Guy had already been defeated by Robert of Artois at the battle of Furnes. Their Germany ally, Adolf of Nassau, did not materialise and taking refuge in Ghent, they made a truce with Philip IV.

A full peace between France and England was not made until 1303 after protracted negotiations; and it marked a return to the *status quo* of early 1294. In 1298–99, on the urging of Pope Boniface VIII, the marriages of Edward I to Margaret of France, Philip IV's sister, and the future Edward II to Isabella of France, Philip IV's daughter, were arranged. The latter, which took place in 1308, was to have momentous political consequences in England and in France. For the rest of Philip's reign the tensions between the two kingdoms remained unresolved, but war was not to break out again until 1324 (6.2.3).

The Flemish were quite a different matter. In 1300 Guy of Dampierre, deserted by all his allies, submitted to Philip and was put in prison. Flanders was administered by Jacques de Châtillon, the queen's uncle; the king toured the land and was well received by the population. Within a year, however, the turbulent and independent burgesses of many of the large towns had fallen out with their domineering French governors, and in May 1302 there was a massacre of the French at Bruges.

This rising, the so-called Matins of Bruges, is often compared with the Sicilian Vespers (6.2.1), and it certainly had equally important results. The whole of western Flanders was soon up in arms and the French royal army was sent to crush the rebels. This was considered the finest fighting force in Europe at the time, but it suffered total defeat by the Flemish urban militia at the battle of Courtrai in 1302. The Flemish withstood the French cavalry charges with massed pikes, and dug pits and used archers against them. They lost only a few hundred men, but the French lost one thousand knights, including Robert of Artois and Pierre Flotte. Their humiliation, too, was intense, and for the court, this was a grave political setback. Strong resistance to royal taxation emerged in France, and Edward I was able to get far better terms from Philip IV than he would have done earlier. The French attitude was that the flower of their chivalry had been defeated by a handful of unarmed rustics, and despite Philip V's military reorganisation in 1317 (6.4.1), the French continued to rely on cavalry charges in the opening stages of the Hundred Years War, while the English, who had learned their lesson in Scotland, used and profited from the newer tactics.

A truce was made between France and Flanders in 1303 and Guy of Dampierre, the count, was released from prison in an attempt to calm the uprising. This was not successful and in 1304 the French mounted another massive campaign by land and sea. They won a partial victory at Mons-en-Pévèle, and the Flemish were now induced to negotiate under the leadership of their new count, Robert of Béthune (since Guy of Dampierre had died). The terms seemed highly unsatisfactory to the Flemish: Robert was to succeed to his father's fief and to do homage to the French king, but was to pay a substantial war indemnity, levied from all those who had opposed the French; the king was to hold the castellanies of Lille, Douai, Béthune, Cassel and Courtrai; the city walls of Ghent, Bruges, Ypres, Lille and Douai were to be razed; and three thousand men from Bruges were to go on pilgrimage to expiate the sin of the Bruges Matins. The towns of Flanders refused to ratify the treaty and would only agree to do so in 1309 after considerable modifications had been made to it. Then the indemnity proved very difficult to collect, and resentment between the king, the count and the towns grew. In 1312 Count Robert was threatened by the king with the confiscation of his lands, but he managed to make peace, and handed over to the French permanently the castellanies of Lille, Douai and Béthune. Trouble boiled up again in 1314 and the French sent an army to Flanders, which achieved nothing. The subsidy demanded to finance it sparked off a number of disputes. The problem of Flanders, like that of England, was passed on to Philip's sons (6.2.3).

Philip and his advisers are perhaps best remembered for their dealings with the church, producing scandals which horrified their contemporaries and later commentators alike. In the name of the grandson of Louis IX the traditional alliance of the French king and the papacy was broken, the Roman pontiffs brought closely under French control, and a major religious order suppressed.

In 1296 Philip and his councillors fell out with Pope Boniface VIII over the issue of clerical taxation, and after a bitter quarrel the French king established his right to tax the French clergy (6.5.3). Another dispute broke out in 1301 when Boniface refused to remove from office Bernard Saisset, bishop of Pamiers, whom Philip accused of inciting the Languedoc to rebellion. Boniface issued bull after bull reiterating papal sovereignty, but the tables were entirely turned when in 1303 William de Nogaret and a group of his French followers broke into the papal palace at Anagni and sacked it. Boniface died soon afterwards (6.5.3), and the pontificate of Clement V (1305–14) marked the beginning of the papal residence at Avignon (6.5.5), and the domination of the papacy by the French king. The strength of royal power was demonstrated by the suppression of the Templars, forced on the pope by the French. The process began in 1308 when Nogaret began to carry out enquiries about the estates and the persons of the French Templars, and the pope was pressured into dissolving the whole order in 1312 (6.5.4). Such developments were only possible because Louis IX had built up and consolidated the already well-established alliance of the French king and the church, and an ironic prelude to them was his canonisation in 1297 (6.5.2). The activities of Philip IV's advisers, performed at his command, transformed the relations between the French king and the church, and arguably gave the papacy a shock from which it did not recover until the counter-reformation. It is hard to imagine that such developments represent an expression of piety on Philip's part, as is sometimes argued. A more probable explanation is that they were motivated by political and financial expediency.

Philip's reign ended in a number of troubles. The cost of the 1314 war with Flanders proved too great, and despite the consent to a subsidy given by an assembly at Paris, leagues were formed in the principalities to protest against royal taxation and administration (6.4.5). Philip agreed to cancel the Flemish subsidy shortly before his death, and Louis X settled most of the protests by issuing charters of liberty in 1315. Philip's last year also saw a scandal at court which was exaggerated and romanticised by Alexandre Dumas into the legend of the Tour de Nesle. We know that in 1314 Philip arrested Margaret of Burgundy, wife of the future Louis X, at that time king of Navarre; Blanche of Burgundy, wife of Charles, count of La Marche, later Charles IV; and Joan of Burgundy, the wife of Philip, count of Poitiers, later Philip V. Margaret and Blanche were accused of conducting adulterous liaisons with two brothers, Philip and Gautier d'Aunay, knights of the royal household. Joan knew about these, it was said, but her crime was that of silence. The two knights were executed and the three women imprisoned, and although Joan was later cleared, Margaret was to die in prison and Blanche in the abbey of Maubuisson. Who brought the charges against them? Several chroniclers had no doubt that it was Isabella of France, sister-in-law to all of them, and wife of Edward II of England. She was in France in 1314, she was a woman who was to have a spectacular career in English politics, and she had some kind of motive beyond pure jealousy: she had shortly before produced a son, the future Edward III of England, and any discrediting of the wives to the three heirs to the French throne might improve his chances of succession in France. Such suggestions may sound implausible, and should not be stressed too much, for it could not be foreseen that all Isabella's brothers would die without male heirs. Nevertheless, a strong element of doubt was attached to the legitimacy of Joan of Navarre, daughter of Louis X and Margaret of Burgundy, which may have been instrumental in denying her the throne.[16] Resulting developments in the succession law also, perhaps ironically, cut out Isabella's son. This sordid and quite probably trumped-up scandal provided a fitting end to an extraordinary reign.

According to Ivo of Saint Denis and William Baldrich, the king, deeply troubled by these events, died an extremely pious death, although their evidence is not unambiguous. On his deathbed Philip is supposed to have instructed his heir, Louis X, to show respect for the church, to govern in the traditions of Saint Louis, and not to be as avaricious as he himself had been. So lavish were the provisions of his will, including the grant of £4,000 tournois to the Celestine hermits, oppressed by Boniface VIII, and bequests of enormous sums to compensate for the wrongs he had done, that his successor was forced to disregard many of them. It is fitting irony that this was done in the name of needs of state.[17]

6.2.3 Louis X (1314–16), Philip V (1316–22) and Charles IV (1322–28)

Philip IV was succeeded by his three sons in turn. All of them were described by the chroniclers as tall, handsome, generous and pious, and all are shadowy figures. Louis X was given the nickname 'le Hutin', the stubborn, but it is difficult to see why, for he seems to have been a weak and ineffectual figure, heavily dominated by his uncle, Charles of Valois and the parlement party. They persuaded the king to have Enguerrand de Marigny tried for treason and condemned to death, and his execution came about not as a result of his dishonest deals, but because of the malice and hatred of Charles of Valois. Louis, indeed, felt some remorse, and remembered Enguerrand's wife and family in his will. Other advisers of Philip IV also suffered; Raoul de Presles was tortured and Pierre de Latilly imprisoned. These events did not come to pass as the result of pressure from the provincial leagues, although they doubtless helped the king in his dealings with them.

During the course of 1315 Louis X negotiated with the leagues and granted them charters of liberties. The lack of concerted general opposition to the crown from the kingdom as a whole, the strength of local interests, and the narrow objectives of the lesser nobles, leaders of the leagues, enabled general promises to be made without committing the crown's interests too far (6.4.5). By 1316 all the provinces save Artois had settled down again. The king was able to demand another subsidy for the next war against Flanders, indeed, as early as 1315. Count Robert had promised him homage but failed to do it, and the court of peers pronounced his lands confiscated. The campaign proved an unmitigated disaster, however: the summer in this year was exceptionally bad, with long periods of cold and torrential rain, and much of Flanders was flooded, while the rest became a quagmire which threatened to engulf the French forces and forced them to turn back.

Louis X died in June 1316. His second wife, Clémence of Hungary, was with child, and in November gave birth to a son, John I, who lived and reigned for five days. France had been ruled by a council of twenty-four barons, then by Philip of Poitiers as regent. On the death of the infant king, Philip set aside the rights of Joan, Louis X's daughter by Margaret of Burgundy, and took the throne for himself. Although her uncle, Odo IV of Burgundy, appealed to parlement on her behalf and tried to rally some of the leagues behind her, Philip gained the support of Charles of Valois and Mahaut of Artois, who were present at his coronation in 1317. Shortly afterwards, a general assembly of clergy, nobles, citizens and academics at Paris supported his accession and set out the general principle that a woman could not succeed to the French throne. This, buttressed by similar decisions in 1322 and 1328, was at the time of Charles V (1364–80) to be elaborated into the *lex Salica* or Salic law, supposedly based on the inheritance rules of the Salian Franks, and cutting women out of the succession. In 1316 Joan was compensated with a substantial pension and a promise that Champagne would revert to her if Philip V died without male heirs. She was to marry Philip of Evreux, and Odo IV of Burgundy took as his wife Philip V's daughter, also called Joan.

Philip V's great height gave him the nickname 'le Long', the Tall, although some chroniclers called him the Great. He appears to have been more peaceloving than Louis X but also a stronger and more effective ruler who restored many of his father's administrators to power. It is true that he made spasmodic interventions in Flanders, whose count still refused him homage, and in 1319 mounted another fruitless campaign there, but in 1320 he came to terms with Robert, who agreed that Louis of Crécy, eldest son of his heir, Louis of Nevers, should marry the king's daughter Margaret, and that he would do the king homage. Yet in 1321 Philip began to make further complaints about Robert's behaviour. The king refused to fight for the papal party in Italy, however, and he also managed to obtain homage from Edward II for Gascony, by proxy in 1319, in person in 1320. By a mixture of diplomacy and force he finally pacified the league in Artois, and came to terms with the troublesome Robert of Artois. He also made a number of administrative changes, organised a national militia and attempted to regulate weights and measures in the kingdom. His reign was a period of innovation in government and administration,[18] but his attempts to raise a subsidy in peacetime to finance reform in 1321 produced a strong reaction against his régime. Charles IV was to return to the policies and advisers of Louis X.

Charles IV (1322–28), formerly count of La Marche, succeeded Philip, again cutting out the claims of female relations. He had proved a turbulent and unruly subject of Philip V, and he was an aggressive king. The succession remained a problem, however, as he had no male heir, and in 1322 he was able to repudiate his first wife, Blanche of Burgundy, not on the grounds of the adultery for which she had been imprisoned, but for spiritual affinity, since Blanche's mother, Mahaut of Artois, was Charles's godmother. He then married Mary of Luxembourg, daughter of the late Emperor Henry VII. In 1324 Pope John XXII, who had quarrelled with the Emperor Louis IV of Bavaria and excommunicated him, offered Charles the empire, in return for substantial sums of money. Nothing was to come of this.

In 1322 Louis of Nevers succeeded to the county of Flanders, and was immediately confronted with an uprising of the burgesses of Bruges and its surrounding districts. Charles went to his rescue in 1325, but could do very little, and matters were only patched up at the peace of Arques in 1326, but not finally resolved. Philip VI (1328-50) inherited the problem of subduing what a contemporary described as a rude and brutal nation.[19] Nor was any final settlement made with England over Gascony. In 1324 war broke out over the judicial rights to the *bastide* of Saint-Sardos, Gascony was again declared forfeit, and Charles of Valois invaded the duchy. Isabella, queen of England, was instrumental in making peace in 1325, and had her young son Edward invested as duke of Gascony and count of Ponthieu, although Charles of Valois (who died in 1325) refused to relinquish the Agenais which he had retained as an indemnity. The deposition of Edward II by Isabella and Mortimer, generally supposed her lover, left her and Edward III in a weak position; and this was reflected in the terms of the treaty of Paris of 1327. Philip of Valois kept many of the lands his father had taken, and the English were left with a very diminished Gascony. They also had to pay a substantial indemnity for the war. This was a triumph for Charles IV, but a humiliation the English were not to forget.

When Charles IV died in 1328 he left his wife with child, but this baby turned out to be a girl. In conformity with recently established precedents the throne passed to Philip VI of Valois, grandson of Philip III in the male line, and a cadet branch of the family replaced the direct Capetians as kings of France. It was not long before the English, in an attempt to consolidate their powers in Gascony, began to claim the French throne for their king (7.1.1).

6.3. THE FRENCH ECONOMY AND SOCIETY

6.3.1 *Economic and social conditions: the first signs of crisis*

Up to about 1300 French society remained settled and prosperous, but during the fourteenth century its stability was gradually undermined by a series of crises. Climatic changes resulted in cooler and wetter conditions which exacerbated the problems already created by over-population and the over-expansion of the land area under cultivation. The long and large-scale wars with England brought with them disproportionately heavy financial demands, devastation and economic disturbances which caused further problems. By 1350, famines, the disruptions of war and the Black Death had all taken a heavy toll, and had produced rural depopulation in many areas and a decrease in the amount of land farmed. Grain prices fluctuated wildly but fell in the long term, and while wages paid to unskilled labourers slowly increased, landowners living from the exploitation of their estates suffered considerably. This was a time of pronounced social and economic instability.[20]

The crises and changes did not gather momentum until the 1330s and 1340s, but in the first three decades of the fourteenth century there was a clear foretaste of the problems to come. In 1305 food was short in Paris; in 1309 there was general dearth of grain, and in 1314 another bad harvest afflicted the Ile de France.[21] Climatic conditions were intemperate in the extreme in 1315. There was a summer of freezing cold and torrential rain, which affected the whole of north-west Europe; but Flanders seems to have suffered more than anywhere else. Parts of the coastal area were under deep floods and the royal army, mounting its invasion (6.2.3), became completely bogged down in the mud and had to retreat. The harvest in most of France failed altogether, and there was a widespread famine which lasted until 1317, exacerbated by a hard winter. Prices for wheat reached unprecedented levels (a measure normally worth 10–15 shillings fetching sixty or as much as eighty shillings) and starvation was accompanied by disease, crime and even cannibalism. The church organised processions and prayers. A chronicler wrote that 'we saw a large number of people, gathered from near and far, barefoot, and many, apart from the women, entirely naked. They came with their priests in procession to the place of the holy martyr (Saint-Denis), devoutly carrying bodies of the saints and other relics to be adored.'[22]

In 1318 there was a recovery, but these events had a profound psychological impact. In 1320 a great band of *pastoureaux*, poor men and fanatics, roamed the land, and declaring themselves to be crusaders, released prisoners and massacred Jews. The pope hurled anathemas against them, but eventually hunger led them to disperse. The next year there was a massacre of lepers. A growing social instability was accompanied by fluctuating prices; for this much of the blame must be laid at the door of Philip the Fair's administration, for the currency manipulations disrupted economic conditions and raised living costs, while diminishing the value of fixed incomes. This also had considerable international repercussions, for the value of French debts owed to foreign bankers fell, causing great resentment, particularly in Italy. These measures made international trade less secure, as did also Philip's attempts to wage economic warfare against the papacy and the rulers of England and Flanders who retaliated in turn. In such conditions trade could be carried out in France only under royal licence, and the export of foodstuffs was forbidden in 1302, 1304–05 and 1314. It became difficult to provision Paris's great population and in 1307 the king regulated the price of corn here, and issued an ordinance temporarily to fix wages and conditions of trade in the capital. In an age of growing crisis, the idea of Louis IX's reign as a golden age became increasingly compelling.

6.3.2 The population of France in 1328: a problem in quantitative history

Shortly after the accession of Philip VI in 1328 royal *enquêteurs* carried out a survey of the parishes and hearths of the *bailliages* and *sénéchausées* in the royal domain. The original lists were made with considerable care, if one surviving for the *sénéchausée* of Rouergue is anything to go by. They were collected and correlated by officials at the chambre des comptes into a document which was then copied, not always entirely accurately, into royal registers and used for reference. This list was a full survey of royal rights in the levying of hearthtax. Some principalities and lordships – Brittany, Gascony, Flanders, Burgundy, Blois and Barrois – were omitted, as were the apanages of Artois, Alençon, Evreux, Bourbon, La Marche and Angoumois-Mortain. A few *seigneuries* within the areas covered by the *bailliages* also do not appear, but it is striking that the great majority do, implying that the crown was sufficiently strong to levy hearthtax from them. Ferdinand Lot, in his important study of the document, suggested that this indicates that 'the prestige of the monarchy in 1327–28 was strong enough to have important demographic exercises carried out in the whole kingdom, with the exception of four or five great fiefs and the apanages'.[23] The list, known as the *Etat des paroisses et des feux*, is useful as a survey of the domain. Historians have also drawn on it to provide statistical data on the population of France in 1328, and the diversity of estimates made on the basis of it is a clear indication that quantitative history, like qualitative, has its pitfalls and problems.[24]

One of the crucial questions is how medieval data of this type should be treated. This royal survey was intended as a checklist, not a census return, and it must be used as the latter only with great caution. Two basic pieces of information are given for each *bailliage* or its equivalent: the number of parishes, and the number of hearths in each. On the basis of this it is quite easy to calculate population densities for various regions once the additional information of their extent has been supplied. This gives some interesting results. Poitou, with a ground area of over 15,000 square kilometres, contained only about 112,000 hearths or households, but the Paris basin, a third of the size, had about 117,000 hearths, making it the most densely populated region of France.[25] The problem is then to find a suitable coefficient for converting numbers of hearths into numbers of people. What was a hearth, and if it was a household, how many people did each one contain? On such issues the debate continues, but figures as high as five or even more, and as low as 3.5 have been suggested. Lot chose the latter figure for use in his calculations. He also added an extra number of hearths to the totals in the survey to cover the missing areas, and he arrived at a grand total of between $17\frac{1}{2}$ and 19 million for the rural population of France, with an additional figure of between a tenth and a fifth added for the townspeople.[26] This is a lower overall figure than that arrived at by many other historians; Professor Perroy, however, suggested that it was far too high.[27] In a period when England's population was around 3 million, it was difficult to believe that France's was seven times as great: a more likely estimate would be 10 or 11 million, he thought. His figure was not based on the *État des paroisses* as Lot's was, and Lot's methods were careful and scrupulous. So how accurate is the document itself? Does it give what appears to be sound data, or are its figures suspect?

Here again we are in an area of controversy. It is clear that surviving copies of the *État des paroisses* contain a number of mistakes and copying errors. For example, the hearths enumerated for the *vicomté* of Paris actually add up to 113,786, even though the total given is 116,786;[28] again, Anjou is attributed with 61 parishes, a mistake for 701.[29] But does this mean that other figures it provides are suspect, and with them the grand totals estimated on the basis of the survey? Professor Dollinger believed that a similar error was made in the number of hearths given for the city of Paris. The total supplied is 61,089, but he suggests that the first figures, the 61,000 (LXI^m), should read 21,000 (XXI^m); and this would mean that after the normal multipliers had been applied the population in Paris added up to 80,000, not 210,000 people; this he believed fitted in with evidence about other European cities. In the 1350s Ghent, a substantial settlement, had only 56,000 inhabitants. Earlier in the century Florence was about the same size, and London had perhaps 35–40,000 people. Paris was clearly a sizeable city, but it was unlikely that it had a density of about 500 people in each hectare, while Reims had 52, and Toulouse about 138. Many historians disagree with this point of view. Professor Cazelles argued strongly for the higher figure.[30] He suggested Dollinger's figures for population density were based on an estimated ground area for the city which was much too small, and thus appeared far too high. Again, the estimates for the sizes of other cities used by Dollinger were probably too low; a recent figure proposed for Venice's population at this time is around 200,000 people. Paris was clearly strikingly bigger as well as being wealthier than Reims and Châlons, for where they were assessed by the royal tax-collectors for around £10,000 *parisis*, Paris had to pay ten times as much. Then there is an undated but roughly contemporary figure for the number of hearths in the French capital in the cartulary of Nôtre-Dame, which puts them at 50,000 or so. Paris was an exceptional city in size as in so much else, he ended. Any firm conclusions should not be drawn at the moment from this debate, but its moral is clear. In many cases statistics are a valuable tool for historical research, but care must be taken that they do not cloud the issues rather than elucidating them.

6.3.3 *Rural life: a village community: Montaillou*

From about 1300 onwards the details of rural life are far better documented than in earlier periods, and the studies of matters such as demographic trends and fluctuations in crop yields which have been made possible by the wider range of sources throw into relief the differences betwen the various parts of the French kingdom. Despite periods of crisis and economic regression, it is clear that at least from the fourteenth century until the eighteenth there was a strong economic contrast between the lowland areas of northern and central France and the more farflung and highland regions. In areas such as the Ile de France and Picardy, corn and wine-growing areas, methods of cultivation were relatively advanced, crop yields were high and society was comparatively affluent. By contrast subsistence farming and stock-raising were more commonly found in regions such as the Massif Central and the Languedoc, making peasant communities far less prosperous overall. This contrast was to be of great significance in the material and the political development of the French kingdom.

Estate records and accounts tell us a great deal about the material condition of the peasants and how their lives were organised. It has always been far more difficult to discern what they thought and believed, and because of this, the inquisition register for the Pyrenean village of Montaillou in the county of Foix, covering the years 1318 to 1325, is a particularly valuable document. It was drawn up by the bishop of Pamiers, Jacques Fournier, later Pope Benedict XII, and the Dominican inquisitors of Pamiers, during their attempts to extirpate Catharism from this village, which was the last stronghold of the heresy in the French kingdom. The register, which is one out of a series of three, gives a full record of the procedures and sentences against the heretics, whose depositions were translated from the Occitan tongue into Latin at a fairly late stage of its compilation. This question of translation is one problem in using the register, for we cannot know how carefully this was done. It may well be misleading to examine too precisely the way in which the peasants' evidence is expressed, and to draw too many conclusions from the nuances in what they said. Furthermore general theories about medieval peasant society cannot be extrapolated from Montaillou, which is atypical in many ways. The strength of the heresy in the community clearly coloured the outlook of its inhabitants to a marked degree. It was a small village, containing 200–250 inhabitants, almost all of them peasants; it was poor, isolated and very enclosed, and as such was probably unrepresentative even of Pyrenean mountain communities. Bearing these *caveats* in mind, however, the register provides remarkable evidence about the outlook and beliefs of the whole community; and the recent study of Montaillou by Professor le Roi Ladurie brings the village vividly to life.[31]

The people of Montaillou made their living from subsistence farming and sheep-raising. The landless peasants of the type who were often day-labourers in northern villages, generally tended to work as shepherds, and were constantly on the move in the mountains and returned home only at intervals; this was one way the community kept in contact with heretical groups across the Pyrenees. Although one peasant family, the Clergues, dominated the village – one brother was the parish priest, another the *bayle* – there was far less differentiation in personal wealth than would have been found in a village in the Paris basin, for example, or even in some larger Pyrenean villages. The *châtelaine* of Montaillou held little more land than any of the other families and was very much part of the community; the villagers' resentment seems to have been directed against the Catholic church, not against the nobility. Here again the large number of the villagers who were heretics was important, and the strength of their loyalty to their *domus*, the community of their home, strengthened the influence of the heresy. Wandering Cathar preachers also arrived at Montaillou from time to time, and were given a warm welcome in heretical households.

Ladurie's study presents us with a number of arresting analyses of the attitudes of the Montaillou villagers to sexuality, to marriage, to death, to religion and magic. Furthermore, several of the villagers come to life and their relationships and differing outlooks can clearly be seen. Some of the most interesting characters are Pierre Maury, the wandering shepherd with strong heretical beliefs but few possessions; the impoverished noble *châtelaine*, Béatrice de Planissoles, liberal with her favours throughout the village; and the Clergue family, wealthy peasants who had a very strong hold on the community. Bernard Clergue, the *bayle*, wielded considerable economic power; his brother Pierre Clergue, as parish priest, a committed heretic, and a great womaniser, had great influence of other kinds. There were several non-heretical households in the village, and religious as well as other rivalry between households was often intense. The peasants under questioning from the bishop revealed a great number of personal and intimate details about their lives, and they also described the fears and doubts they had about their own and others' faith in their heretical beliefs. William Bélibaste, a heretical preacher, told Pierre Maury that when he returned from the mountains: 'We felt both joy and fear. Joy, because it was a long time since we had seen you. Fear, because I was afraid lest the inquisition had captured you up there; if they had, they would have made you confess everything.'[32] This statement, made to the inquisitors themselves, now seems full of dramatic irony; nevertheless we have reason to be glad that the record of it survives.

6.3.4 The king and the social order

From Louis VI's reign onwards the crown had granted charters of enfranchisement, and Louis IX had given numerous serfs their freedom. The later Capetians granted many such licences, and in 1315 an ordinance freed all the serfs in the royal domain. This was an important step, and also perhaps an attempt to rally popular support at a time of crisis.

From about 1300 the problems of the communes in running their affairs became increasingly pronounced, and a number gave up their charters and submitted to the king. Financial difficulties were a major factor in this, and so too was the government of these towns and villages. A group of Corbie's citizens petitioned Louis X about the bad administration of the town by their mayor and officials, and Louis ordered an assembly to be summoned and a vote taken. A majority decided the commune should be abolished, and parlement pronounced its suppression in 1318. The commune of Compiègne and the village association of Bourbonne-Chantemerle were also wound up shortly afterwards, royal officials taking over their administration. The Hundred Years War was to speed up this process.[33]

The decline of the communes does not seem to reflect severe problems for the burgesses as a group. Some suffered badly from the financial expedients of Philip IV's reign, and became bankrupt; many others remained prosperous. The king had rights of *embourgeoisement*, the grant of burgess status; and these were used widely by the last Capetians, who often allowed the beneficiary to become a burgess of the king himself (*bourgeois du roi*) rather than being attached to a town. Thus he was under royal protection, and did not have to reside in a specific community. The towns often supported the king's financial and military policies, and only a few joined the leagues in 1314–15. The backing of the burgesses for the king was of some political importance.

The king also developed the right to ennoble men of non-noble birth. This was used only on a relatively small scale by the late Capetians, but was to be of great significance to their successors. By 1200 the nobility in many parts of France seems to have become a closed caste with a rigid set of rules and etiquette and defined legal privileges. By 1300 a substantial proportion of lesser nobles were suffering from economic decline, and many took service with the king in order to rebuild their fortunes. The noble ethos remained a powerful one despite the problems of many of its exponents, and a number of non-nobles in the royal administration sought a patent of nobility, so that they could be knighted and enjoy the status and privileges which went with this.

A recent analysis of these grants[34] has shown that the earliest such grant to survive is to Giles of Concevreux in 1285–90, the second to John of Taillefontaine in 1295. From 1307 to 1314, ten more were registered, but others may have been lost, as Nogaret's own patent was. Of the twelve surviving grants, three went to men from northern France, nine to southerners. The northerners were royal administrators whose status was ambiguous and needed definition, the rest were satellites of Nogaret and Plaisians who had helped to extend royal influence in the south. Louis X made six grants on similar lines, but Philip V gave forty-five, ten of which went to members of the household from the north, burgesses, merchants and bankers who had made an important contribution in the royal service. The northern grants overturned far more social barriers than those to the southerners, for social distinctions between nobles and burgesses were far less clear in the south. The royal service had thus become a way of breaching the barrier of noble status, and this power of ennoblement by the king was to be widely used in the future.

6.4 THE NATURE OF ROYAL POWER

6.4.1 Royal government and administration

A key consideration in the royal administration of the later Capetian period was finance, and many of the political events of the period were the result of the financial expedients used by the monarchy. Philip IV's experiments with taxation on a large scale and with currency manipulations are two particularly striking instances of attempts to raise money for the wars with England and Flanders, which provoked great and widespread hostility to the crown.

In the early Valois period a royal administrator, Robert Mignon, drew up an inventory of the royal accounts for the years before 1328. His list is long and full, and shows that what survives today is only a small part of what was extant then. It is still rather greater than the coverage of Louis IX's reign, however, and it consists of a number of different kinds of documents. There are some general accounts, such as the rolls of the *baillis* for the Ile de France, Normandy and Champagne, and of the seneschals for the Languedoc. There are also more detailed accounts for the domain and for lands temporarily in the king's hands. There are lists of the profits of regalia and amortisation; debts, gifts and loans; and extraordinary taxes. Expenditure on certain military campaigns is covered, as are the forest accounts, and there are a few fragments concerning the currency changes. The royal household, too, is quite well represented. From these scattered pieces of information it is possible to get an overall picture of patterns of expenditure, but the diversity of the accounts makes any detailed conclusions very tentative.

In the period 1270–95 royal finances functioned very much as earlier. A number of general accounts survive, which are summarised in Table 6.1. The annual incomings which they record average at about £656,000 and the outgoings, £652,000. The household expenses were around £191,720 (Table 6.2), and all these amounts were far greater than fifty years earlier. The system of auditing accounts continued as before, and the process was carried out in the chambre aux deniers, the bureau of the royal accountant. What these accounts do not show is that Philip III's Aragonese expedition cost the monarchy about £1,229,000 tournois – or so another account suggests[35] – and this proved impossible to recoup from the normal sources of royal income. If anything, these were falling in the long term, as some accounts from the early 1320s suggest (Table 6.4). The war with England in 1294 made this problem worse, and new sources of income had to be tapped.

Table 6.1 Summary of royal receipts and expenses, 1286–93 (*in* livres parisis)

Term		Receipts £ s d			Expenses £ s d		
I. By term							
1286	All Saints	209,321	5	4	159,362	6	2
1287	Candlemas	291,107	1	10	266,065	0	2
	Ascension	104,513	7	8	105,146	1	2
1288	Candlemas	149,910	11	7	157,643	18	0
1289	Candlemas	89,824	18	8	182,608	3	4
	Ascension	255,358	18	10	279,043	6	1
	All Saints	250,136	14	8	219,877	3	4
1290	Candlemas	256,060	14	9	355,772	2	1
	Ascension	238,708	10	5	224,558	1	4
	All Saints	378,916	16	1	349,804	12	4
1291	Candlemas	118,160	4	7	137,331	12	6
	Ascension	183,039	0	11	176,131	4	8
	All Saints	344,297	13	2	179,965	6	4
1292	Candlemas	72,517	19	10	125,286	1	0
	Ascension	121,806	18	3	111,073	9	3
	All Saints	178,745	17	4	164,606	14	10
1293	Candlemas	289,232	0	4	421,542	2	6

Term	Receipts	Expenses
II. By year		
1286–87	604,942	530,573
1289	759,982	844,695
1290	738,143	712,697
1291	587,205	486,483
1292	589,785	687,443
Average (approximate)	656,000	652,000

Source: HIFr., ii, 191.

Table 6.2. Household expenses of the king, 1286–92 (*in* livres parisis)

	£	s	d
1286–87	157,514	16	7
1289–90	209,674	7	10
1290–91	206,056	11	4
1291–92	193,633	14	9
Approximate average	191,720		

Source HIFr, ii, 191.

Table 6.3 Royal expenses, 1296–1301 (*in* livres parisis)

	Term	*Total*	*Daily average*
1296	All Saints	550,974	4,021
1298	Christmas	858,319	4,664
1299	Saint John	801,245	4,426
1299	Christmas	770,734	4,118
1301	Christmas	339,205	2,169

Source HIFr, ii, 231.

Table 6.4 Royal receipts and expenses, 1322–29 (*in* livres parisis)

	Receipts	*Expenses*
1322	477,366	457,482
1323	598,052	585,743
1324	538,382	552,021
1325	610,437	536,930
1329 (Saint John and Christmas only)	839,535	666,674

Source HIFr, ii, 232.

Philip IV pushed a number of royal rights to their limit and beyond in his attempts to raise money.[36] His feudal aids, levied in 1308 for the marriage of Isabella and in 1313 for the knighting of Louis (X), were extended to rear vassals and towns with charters of exemption. There was a heavy tallage on the Jews in 1284, 1292 and 1303, and in 1306 they were expelled from the kingdom and their goods seized; Louis X allowed them back, and Charles IV expelled them again. The Lombard and Florentine bankers had similar treatment from Philip III and Philip IV. Revenues began to be levied on imports and exports by Philip IV, and Charles IV set up a system for the regular collection of duties. Tenths were levied from the church in 1285 and 1288 for the Aragonese war, and in 1294 and 1296 for the war with England. The latter brought about the rupture with Boniface VIII, but Philip continued to raise these lucrative taxes, with or without papal consent, in 1297, 1299, 1301, 1303, 1304–06 (to restore the coinage), 1310 and 1312 (for a crusade). The last Capetians continued to levy them, and there were also occasional grants of annates, the first year's income from an ecclesiastical benefice by its new incumbent.

Extraordinary taxation was raised from the church on the basis of the needs of state and the defence of the realm in time of war, and the same justification was used for the taxation of the lay community. The emphasis placed on this was to make peacetime subsidies very difficult to levy; but such was the opposition even to war subsidies that a number of methods of raising them had to be tried before an effective way could be found. In 1291 a penny in the pound was levied on all sales and purchases, and this was repeated in 1296 and 1314. In 1295 a tax on all stock and merchandise was imposed which caused a great outcry, and was widely known as the *maltôte* (the bad tax), but it too, was repeated in 1327 and later. Clearly neither of these taxes was very successful in the 1290s, however, so Philip tried another approach, and in 1295 levied a hundredth on the value of lands, goods and revenues. Declarations were rather low, and so were yields, but a hundredth was reckoned by a contemporary to raise in the order of £315,000 tournois. In 1296 it was levied at the rate of a fiftieth, and in order to raise it from outside the domain, the king allowed the great barons to keep one half, ecclesiastical lords, one third, and certain other nobles, one quarter. A twenty-fifth was levied in 1297, and fiftieths in 1300 and 1302. These levies were based on the principle that the king could raise a general tax for the defence of the realm by declaring a state of emergency but not summoning the army.

This system caused considerable opposition and after the crisis of 1303 the king abandoned this approach and based later subsidies on his controversial right to military service in times of war. The *arrière-ban* was called, and was then extended to compel each person to pay a tax instead: for nobles this consisted of a fifth of their annual income, while non-nobles were subject to hearth-tax, that is for paying for a number of sergeants for every hundred hearths which varied according to the status of the contributors. Serfs were exempted in 1304. The consent of the regional and local communities was sought, and on some occasions they were allowed to share the profits, but this measure was hated as much as the others. There was some reaction to it in 1304–05, and a great deal in 1313 and 1314–15. In 1313 when the tax was already being raised for the war with Flanders, peace was made, and the subsidy was cancelled and returned, setting an important precedent. If the emergency ended, the king could no longer demand taxation. In 1314 Philip was forced to cancel the subsidy again because of the extent of opposition to it. Hostility to these taxes continued during the reigns of Philip's sons, and as an attempt to placate the contributors, varying methods of raising them were used from region to region. The non-nobles in the south would accept the hearthtax, the north preferred the *maltôte*, and the nobility, a straight subsidy.

How much money did these measures bring in? Isolated accounts show that sums from any one source varied greatly from year to year; in 1291 the Jews yielded up £80,000 parisis; in 1295 the Lombards produced £65,000 tournois, but in 1323, only £8,652. In the mid 1290s a three-year ecclesiastical tenth brought in about £800,000 in all – about £266,000 tournois a year; and in 1298–99, £225,000 was collected as a back-payment for the 1297 tenth. In 1313 the crusading tenth produced about £300,000 tournois. The 1295 subsidy brought in £350,000 parisis or so, and that of 1304, £565,170 tournois, while in

1329 only £149,265 parisis was raised. These sums must have more than doubled the royal incomings in years of war, but warfare was highly expensive and they did not bring in enough. Philip IV borrowed large sums of money, and often neglected to repay it for many years, if at all. In 1294 the towns gave him £630,000 and he was advanced £200,000 from the fairs of Champagne. In 1325 Charles IV borrowed £87,000.

These measures were still not enough to meet the scale of royal expenditure which amounted to over £4,000 a day in the late 1290s (Table 6.3), and from 1295 onwards the king began to manipulate the currency.[37] The process was a complex one, involving the modification of exchange rates between currencies fixed by weight, such as the silver mark (approximately 490 grammes) and the royal silver coinage. This latter was recalled, melted down and restruck at a lower weight but with the same face value, the king thus gaining by creating more coins from a given weight of metal, and retaining the surplus money. In the early stages there was no obvious debasement of the metal used, although this later became a much favoured expedient. The effects were dramatic, for the mark, which had exchanged for 54 shillings tournois in 1290 rose to 68 shillings by the end of 1296, and 104 shillings in 1303. The king made £1,200,000 in 1298–99, and £185,000 in 1301, but prices rose rapidly and there were considerable international repercussions, since trade was disrupted and money owed to foreign bankers was devalued. The import and export of bullion was banned in 1295, in part as a measure to protect the French economy, in part as a means of putting pressure on Pope Boniface VIII. It also had serious repercussions in Flanders, which depended heavily on trade with England, and in 1297 its count, Guy of Dampierre, broke with the king. The warfare which followed made necessary further manipulations of the currency.

By 1303 a crisis point had been reached, and strong demands were made throughout the kingdom for a return to the coinage of Saint Louis. In 1306, the king began to revalue the currency in response, and fixed the price of a silver mark at 55s 6d; but prices failed to come down and the reform did not last long. Royal coins struck after 1311 were debased in quality, and this created another financial crisis; many merchants were ruined, according to Geoffrey of Paris. Another return to good money was followed by further debasements under Charles IV, and the Valois kings used currency manipulations as a regular measure to finance their wars.

A system for levying customs duties was also developed in the late Capetian period. It seems to have been intended initially as much to protect the French economy and to derive political advantages as to raise revenues, but later it was to become a valuable source of income for the French king. Pierre de Chalon, a royal clerk, is associated with the establishment of the customs administration. From about 1305 he had the borders closed and manned so that tariffs could be collected on goods crossing them, and set up a central organisation to audit the books. In the 1320s he helped to establish the *droit de rève*, a fixed tax on the export of a large number of commodities.[38]

The committee of the royal court which had dealt with the king's financial affairs began to develop into a full institution in the late Capetian period. The king removed his treasury from the Temple to the Louvre palace in 1295, and by 1306 instructions were being given for accounts to be rendered up to the chambre des comptes. Enguerrand de Marigny reorganised this financial bureau and removed non-specialists, but after his fall, noble amateurs were again given a part to play. In 1320, however, the chambre des comptes was constituted by royal ordinances as the royal accounting department; it was put under the control of the royal chamber (*camera*), to which it was responsible for the auditing of the accounts, and it was allowed judicial powers. Its personnel became fixed and specialised, and under Philip VI it grew into a substantial department. While it administered the domain and audited the accounts, the money was collected in the king's treasury. In 1303 this body returned from the Louvre palace to the Temple, where it stayed until Philip V's reign, and then went back to the Louvre. In this period the royal treasurer had no part in financial policy; he kept safe the money, helped by clerks, but later he became more closely involved with the chambre des comptes.

The king's judicial machinery also increased in scope and scale in the period 1270 to 1328. The parlement, fixed in Paris from 1303, was becoming more exclusively a legal body with a permanent professional staff, composed in the main of lay and clerical judges in almost equal numbers. Many were *baillis* and *sénéchaux*, canons and archdeacons from quite humble backgrounds, well versed in the different branches of the law – Roman, canon and customary. The principal body within the parlement was the grande chambre, the royal court where the king sat. After about 1300 the peers of the realm also sat as a committee of this court, rather than as a court of their own, and the highest feudal court had thus been absorbed by the main royal court. The grande chambre handled all the royal cases and appeals from other royal courts, but two specialised bodies also grew up, the chambre des requêtes, numbering five justices in 1336, and the chambre des enquêtes, with fifty-one. The first handled requests, and later all civil cases; the second, appeals. A long and complex process developed for hearing such cases in parlement. The earliest surviving ordinance regulating procedures dates from 1278, and there were others in 1291 and *c.* 1296. By the 1330s the judicial system had become clearly delineated and firmly fixed, losing in the process some of its early flexibility. A large staff of advocates and notaries was employed, and series of registers of different kinds of cases built up in great bulk. In addition to the *Olim*, these recorded criminal cases from 1312, *jugés* or judgements from 1319, *accords* or concords from 1320.

Larger assemblies still continued to meet under the title of parlements, and to give judgements, as in 1317, 1318, 1326 and 1332, but these developments reflect a move towards an increased professionalisation in government and administration. The nobility and higher clergy still performed many of their traditional functions, but they were gradually becoming less influential in the affairs of state. The rudiments of a professional bureaucracy had emerged during the twelfth century, but in the early fourteenth it was expanded into a departmentalised civil service. At the same time, the range of affairs in which the king could intervene widened considerably.

Ordinances and *établissements* which applied to the whole realm, not just the royal domain, were issued in far greater numbers than in Louis IX's reign. These covered a variety of matters, such as the regulation of coinage and military service to the crown, which was extended to the rear vassals of the king. This was used as the basis for levying war subsidies, and in 1317 Philip V organised a national military force on this basis. Each town and castellany was to be responsible for providing soldiers and their arms, and military leaders and regional commanders were also appointed. Another area where the king's authority was extended was in the prohibition of private wars, the carrying of arms in peacetime, and judicial duels. These were matters which he managed to enforce in a number of principalities before 1314; after the crisis of 1314–15 they were rather harder to forbid, for they appear to have been privileges greatly valued by the nobility. The king exercised a general authority over taxation, amortisation (6.5.1), imports and exports; he was involved with the regulation of wages and prices in Paris and many other such matters. His sovereign powers were widely and frequently realised.

6.4.2 Factions and policy changes: the royal entourage

It has long been fashionable to see the administration of Philip IV and his sons as dominated by a group of career lawyers, many raised from humble origins, and many of whom made their way in the royal service. During the last two hundred years, the royal lawyers have been credited with many different achievements, such as strengthening royal power against that of the baronage and the church, creating the absolute monarchy of the *ancien régime*, embodying the triumph of the bourgeois class over the aristocracy. One recent tendency has been to view them as a defined and homogeneous group, the instruments of royal policy[39]. Many of these interpretations contain useful insights, but they need to be approached with care. For there were many lawyers in the royal entourage before Philip IV's reign, and although men with a legal training assumed a greater importance at this time than earlier on, they did not completely replace or eclipse other royal councillors drawn from the king's own family, his knights and clerks. What is more striking about the later years of Philip IV and the reigns of his sons is the clear emergence of two parties at court, whose conflicts played an important role in the politics of the late Capetian and early Valois periods.[40]

This is not to say that no parties existed before this at the royal court. The later years of Louis IX's reign witnessed struggles between the supporters of the queen, Margaret of Provence, and her English relatives, and Charles of Anjou, Louis's ambitious brother (5.2.2). These hostilities continued after the king's death and were further magnified, so that the court of Philip III became a centre of intrigue matched only by that of Robert the Pious (3.2.2). The king's favourite, Pierre de la Broce, and the queen, Mary of Brabant, and their followers engaged in a bitter dispute which terminated only in Pierre's fall and execution. After this, Mary and the ever-active Charles of Anjou persuaded the king to embark on the crusade against Aragon, with disastrous results (6.2.1).

Philip IV was, if elusive, a far stronger character than his father. He was prepared to listen to the advice of Queen Joan of Champagne, Charles of Valois, and Robert and Mahaut of Artois, but he relied principally on his *curiales* for the formulation and execution of his policies (6.2.2). They departed from the lines laid down by his predecessors in many different ways. But although they differed from one another in their backgrounds and training and in their approach to their tasks, not one was executed or disgraced by the king once he had lost a leading position at court. Philip IV was loyal to the men he chose to do his bidding.

In the first part of his reign Philip devoted more time to hunting than to ruling but he retained the overall direction of policy. From about 1290 the Florentine bankers, Albizzo (Biche) and Musciatto (Mouche) Franzesi, were given considerable responsibility in the field of royal finances. Although they were eclipsed by other advisers from the mid-1290s they remained in positions of trust until their deaths in 1307.

At first receivers-general, then treasurers of the king, they played an important part in the opening phases of the Anglo-French war, and raised considerable sums from loans and export taxes. In the later 1290s their influence declined as the royal court began to use financial policies which made cooperation from foreigners less practical.

It was now that a succession of royal advisers drawn from the royal administration emerged, and dominated royal policy. Many were lawyers by training, others were not, and they came from a variety of social backgrounds. By 1296 Pierre Flotte had become Philip's leading adviser, a position he maintained until his death at the battle of Courtrai. A southern lawyer of noble extraction, he masterminded the king's negotiations with Boniface VIII, the Colonna, the English and Flemings. He also played an important role in the momentous financial expedients of the time. He was assisted by Giles Aicelin, archbishop of Narbonne, his nephew, a lawyer and diplomat,[41] and Pierre de Mornay, bishop of Auxerre.

The *débâcle* at Courtrai, when Flotte was killed, however, left the king angry and humiliated, and he began to take a more active interest in the mechanics and details of government as well as its general direction in his attempt to avenge the honour of the crown. At this time William de Nogaret emerged in the forefront of events. He was of bourgeois origins, formerly a professor of law at the university of Montpellier in the south of France, and appears to have been an able and ruthless character. Like his master, he has proved a controversial figure. Whether he was determined to combat the evils he saw in the Roman church, or whether he was a fanatical supporter of French royal power, particularly *vis-à-vis* the papacy, he certainly played a central role in some of the most important incidents of the reign, the humbling of Pope Boniface VIII, and the suppression of the Templars, as well as working out various financial plans for the king. He and William de Plaisians, who had probably been a student of his, devised many sophisticated and vindictive expedients in the carrying out of their policies.

Nogaret died in 1313, and Enguerrand de Marigny, a Norman knight, and not a lawyer became the king's leading adviser.[42] He was Philip's finance minister; the controller of the treasury, the chambre aux deniers and the chambre des comptes; and the centre of a complex and corrupt web of patronage. The king entrusted him with rather more power than his predecessors, and he aroused great hatred and opposition; indeed, he was under investigation at the time of Philip IV's death. By 1314 he looked fair to be replaced by Pierre de Latilly, a lawyer from northern France, the king's chancellor and bishop of Châlons-sur-Marne, but the king then died.

Such men as these built up important followings and they also created a substantial degree of hostility. By the end of Philip IV's reign the two factions which were still dominant at court in the early years of Philip VI's reign can already be discerned.[43] One was the chambre des comptes party, the followers of Marigny and Miles de Noyers, noted for devising financial expedients. The other was the parlement party, headed by the Valois princes and Robert of Artois, conservative in approach, and associated with a return to the traditions of Saint Louis. This faction dominated Louis X, who was an ineffectual character, and engineered the fall and execution of Marigny. Stephen de Mornay, one of its leading lights, of noble origins, and formerly chancellor to Charles of Valois, became the king's chancellor. He was the nephew of Philip IV's adviser, Pierre de Mornay. The party's financial demands were moderate, as were any administrative changes it sought to make. Philip V, a stronger ruler than his brother, reversed his policies and restored the chambre des comptes party to power again. He reappointed to high positions Henry of Sully, Miles de Noyers, William Flotte and others who had risen under Philip IV. They began to demand heavy subsidies, and worked to bring about a streamlining of the administration. Ordinances were promulgated to regulate the parlement, household and finance bureaux, and attempts were made to extend the levying of taxes to times of peace, reforms being offered in return. This approach was unpopular, and Charles IV probably averted a crisis by a return to the more moderate policies and personnel of the parlement party. Stephen de Mornay was reinstated and traditional methods of raising money exploited to the full. On his accession Philip VI continued to favour this faction for a while; but in the 1330s the chambre des comptes party under Miles de Noyers, a Burgundian nobleman, was again recalled from political exile by the king, when he found himself unable to live from the ordinary revenues of the crown.

6.4.3 Land and rights: the extension of royal power

The royal domain expanded immensely during the later Capetian period. With the deaths of Alfonso of Poitiers and Joan of Toulouse all their lands came to Philip III, this being backed up in 1284 by the parlement's decision that a reversion clause had been implicit in Louis VIII's will of 1226. Philip IV's marriage brought him Navarre, Champagne and Brie. A number of other apanage holdings reverted to the crown, and were regranted as apanages only in smaller parcels, if at all. As a result, in 1328, after Philip of Valois's accession, only the Artois, Bourbon and Evreux holdings remained as apanages and the royal domain was greater by far than the other lands put together (Map 6.1). The apanage system had worked in the king's favour (5.5.2). Land was also acquired by the crown in smaller parcels; Philip III bought Guînes in 1281, and Philip IV purchased Chartres in 1286, Beaugency in 1291, Lomagne and Auvillars in

1302, while in 1306 he lent Hugh XIII of Lusignan, count of La Marche, considerable sums of money on the security of his lands, and in 1308 took them over after his death. The marriage of Joan of Burgundy and the future Philip V brought the county of Burgundy to the crown at considerable expense to Philip IV. These lands – Franche Comté – lay beyond the borders of France and in the empire, but Philip extended the French boundary *de facto* to include them. Similarly Valenciennes, Bar, Lyon and Viviers were brought into French suzerainty at the expense of the empire by a process of purchase or peaceful penetration, a highly effective way of enlarging the French kingdom.

As earlier, royal administration was extended into new acquisitions to the domain. While some parts of the royal lands were relatively peaceful, the last Capetians experienced considerable opposition from a number of provinces, which came to a head in 1314–15. The Languedoc and Normandy both grew turbulent after a period of relative quiescence. The Norman nobles became disgruntled with the number of cases going from the exchequer to parlement, and although the actual infringement of Norman rights was limited they reacted strongly against what appeared a strong drive from the central government to increase its power.[44] The Languedoc, too, reacted against a growing number of appeals going to Paris and against the increased powers of the royal *enquêteurs*. In 1271 it had passed peacefully to Philip III, but under Philip IV it began to show strong signs of disaffection. This hostility should not be exaggerated too much, however, for while certain officials, such as tax-collectors and sergeants, and some *baillis* and *sénéchaux* whose offices were farmed out to avaricious deputies, were much hated, others, such as the viscounts in Normandy and the *viguiers* in the Languedoc, carried out their routine tasks with very little opposition. Professor Strayer suggests that they provided the administration with 'some of the stability which was badly needed in the France of Philip the Fair.'[45]

Champagne came to Philip IV with his marriage to Joan of Navarre in 1284, and although on her death in 1305 it passed to Prince Louis (X), and was not officially united to the royal domain until 1361, it was actually closely under royal control from Philip IV's accession. Its own institutions were far weaker than those of Normandy, and whereas the Norman exchequer managed to resist the encroachment of royal power and to survive to the end of the Middle Ages, its equivalent in Champagne, the *Grands Jours*, was rapidly brought under the authority of the parlement and staffed by justices from Paris. By the beginning of the fifteenth century it had faded away altogether, and its business was conducted in the capital.[46]

In the apanages the king's rights were in theory the same as in the other great fiefs; general *établissements* were valid in them, appeals and royal cases went to parlement, and royal officials under the control of neighbouring *bailliages* administered royal rights. These rights were rarely opposed, and in return the apanaged princes were permitted to raise taxes and military service on the king's behalf. Although their status was the same as that of the other peers of the realm, in fact their close family ties to the king meant that generally they cooperated far more closely with royal measures than the other great nobles. Royal administrative measures tended to be copied in the apanages, perhaps in part because the princes, as councillors of the king, helped to frame them. The royal and apanage administrations were closely linked in their personnel too. In short, the apanagists' legal relationship with the crown was the same as that of the other peers of the realm, but their family ties with the king meant that there was a far greater measure of collaboration between them.[47]

The king's interest in extending his rights and powers into the other fiefs of the kingdom is often stressed, but it can easily be exaggerated overall. Burgundy's dukes were tied closely to the Capetians by marriage, and supported them fairly consistently in their political activities. It has recently been shown[48] that there was little jurisdictional tension between the king and the duke and that appeals went from the ducal courts (the *Grands Jours de Beaune)* and other courts to Paris, relatively automatically and unchallenged. So too did specifically royal cases. Furthermore royal legislation was not enforced in Burgundy unless the duke gave his consent, and frequently he was awarded substantial concessions for doing so. The duke granted licences of amortisation to his vassals, and although the king in theory exercised this power over the duke's rear vassals, the duke frequently ignored this and performed the function himself. Only a proportion of the Jews were expelled at ducal convenience, and the Templars were suppressed only in return for a grant of all the profits.

The king had more substantial, though still limited rights over the coinage of Burgundy, but when it came to taxation, although the duke gave his consent to the levying of subsidies on a number of occasions, this was frequently only on condition that he kept half, as in 1296; after 1298 he had the tax collected by his own officials. Nevertheless, the dukes gave Philip extra service in the years that followed Courtrai, and they were unable to prevent or control the collection of the hearth-tax, based on royal rights of military service, in 1303 and 1314. It was the latter which finally sparked off the formation of the noble leagues, and it was curious that no reference to unjust taxation appeared in the 1315 charter to the Burgundians. During the reigns of Philip IV's sons, ducal consent to taxation was given on a number of occasions, although there was more resistance in the early Valois period. Nevertheless, the frequently painted picture of an aggressive, centralising late Capetian monarchy is not an accurate one in the case of royal dealings with Burgundy.

In Brittany, royal justice and other royal rights became increasingly effective, and the king was here able to impose taxation fairly freely, and to appoint to several bishoprics, even when allowing the duke the theoretical power to do so.[49] But although these inroads built up long-term resentment they were not always pursued aggressively and again the duke tended to cooperate with the king.

The later Capetians were by contrast very militant in their dealings with Gascony. By the early 1300s the English royal lawyers were beginning to argue that Gascony was an allod, independent of the French crown, and all Philip IV's efforts in the duchy were aimed to show that it was, rather, an integral part of the French kingdom.[50] As in Burgundy the royal ordinance controlling amortisation had little effect, but this was because the king of England resisted it. Despite strong French protests Edward II refused to expel the Jews in 1308 and did not cast them out until 1310. The Gascon nobles refused to obey the French king's prohibition of bearing arms without royal permission, while the English king and the Gascon seneschal protested angrily against Philip IV's currency regulations in 1313. Even greater tensions were stirred up by the French king's attempts to extend his rights over justice in the duchy. Philip III intervened on several occasions to try to change its customs; and when Philip IV, against local custom, divided the lands of the dead viscount of Béarn between his daughters the local inhabitants petitioned Edward II, declaring that Gascon customs were being overturned. Appeals went to Paris, and were dealt with by the parlement, and there was strong resistance to this from the English kings, as there was, too, to French taxation of Gascony. Edward I and Edward II continued to exercise regalian rights such as legitimising bastards and giving licences for fairs and markets. They also did homage which was only conditional on the fulfilment of the obligations incurred in the treaties of 1259 and 1303 by the French kings.

Resistance from the Gascons to French sovereign rights was strongly combated by the French king in such circumstances, and the same was true of Flanders; hence the strong attempts of the last Capetians to bring it to heel. The policy of an expansion of royal power throughout the French kingdom was certainly followed, but it was not adhered to rigidly. In cases where a strong resistance to royal authority needed to be crushed, it was applied strongly; other parts of France, which were not so hostile, but might resist strongly if pressed too hard, were given certain concessions in return for their support. The concessions did not penalise the king very greatly, but enabled him to use all his energies in the pursuit of his major objectives, both inside and outside the kingdom.

6.4.4 General and regional assemblies

The assemblies summoned by Philip IV and his sons have sometimes been characterised as institutions which, while not as 'representative' as the English parliaments, still had a limiting function on the monarchy, since they were required to give consent to taxation and backing for royal policies, and to support and limit royal power as seemed necessary in return for concessions. It is true that later Capetian assemblies often made demands and sometimes refused their agreement to taxation, but their effectiveness in doing so can easily be overestimated. Most of these meetings were called primarily to give counsel, to show support for royal policies, rather than to consent to them; the latter course was only necessary when the king was attempting to infringe the rights of his subjects.[51] They were above all a vehicle for royal propaganda, and their great variations in composition and business are a clear sign that they were still, in 1328, very much in the experimental stage.[52] When they began to make demands, the king sometimes paid lip service to meeting them, but made almost no real concessions, even after the 1314–15 crisis.

The most celebrated assemblies of this period were those summoned by Philip IV to give backing to the French opposition to Boniface VIII (1303) and to support the dissolution of the Templars (1308). They were general assemblies drawn from many parts of the kingdom and from the three estates – nobles, clergy and burgesses – and on both occasions they gave the royal policies their full support. Other general assemblies considered matters such as the coinage, military service, and a proposed French crusade. A general meeting of burgesses gave the proposed subsidy of 1314 its approval but it proved impossible to collect in practice, and in 1321 two general assemblies at Paris and Poitiers did not show any enthusiasm for the idea of a peacetime subsidy to finance general reforms. The clergy agreed, the nobles remained indifferent, and the townsmen deferred their answer to another general assembly at Orléans. When this met, they gave a refusal, and apologised for giving 'so little counsel to the king'.[53] Furthermore this meeting rebounded as a propaganda exercise, as wild rumours about extortionate taxation began to circulate, and a gathering crisis was only averted by the death of Philip V. Such experiments demonstrated the ineffectiveness of using central assemblies to endorse taxation, and Charles IV returned to the policies of Philip IV and Louis X, who had used general assemblies only in a limited way, and carried out most of the effective negotiations with regional and local assemblies.

Regional assemblies had taken an important place in the political life of many parts of France in the later thirteenth century. In the Languedoc they had filled various functions, acting as courts, endorsing the regulation of imports and exports, and being consulted about military service and taxation.[54] Like regional assemblies in other parts of France, they laid great stress on their duties of giving counsel rather than their right to grant consent, and this attitude continued into Philip IV's reign, when they were used more systematically to endorse royal subsidies. But there also was a growing opposition to this royal taxation and demands were made for the redress of grievances in return for consent to subsidies.[55] In 1304, for example, many of the regional assemblies demanded the repayment of royal debts, freedom from further impositions for a year, and the recognition that this grant was a gift, not an obligation. In the same year, provincial assemblies of clergy, called to endorse the same taxes, almost all demanded the reform of the currency, free amortisation and exemption from military service for French prelates. Some of these conditions were agreed, and the subsidy given, but certain provinces resisted, and the archbishop of Rouen was imprisoned.

There was some hard bargaining with the regional assemblies, too, and the royal officials were compelled to reduce their demands to secure payment at all. In 1314 the regional assemblies refused to endorse the subsidy already consented to at a general assembly, and the strength of reaction to it compelled the king to cancel it. The leagues which then formed were in effect unofficial regional assemblies, flexing their political and military muscles, and their demands reflected many of those made earlier. They were put forward as a general programme but adapted to regional needs, and Louis X conceded in a limited way to many of their demands as his father had done earlier. On the whole the regional assemblies were a far more effective way of raising taxes than the general ones, however, and despite the strength of opposition to the king, consent was not actually refused until 1314. Under the Valois kings the regional assemblies continued as flourishing institutions while the general ones developed and then faded away. This was symptomatic of the importance of provincial loyalties and provincial institutions in later medieval France.

6.4.5 The crisis of 1314 and the charters of 1315

In the last twenty-five years of Capetian rule there were three periods of crisis when royal authority was resisted. The first was in 1303–05, when the French king was defeated at Courtrai, had his taxation demands strongly condemned, and was forced to reissue Louis IX's ordinance for the reform of the realm. He also granted a charter of liberties to the nobles of the Auvergne, and promised other general concessions, thus reducing the opposition. A third crisis was gathering in 1322 when Philip V died (6.4.4). But the reaction of 1314–15 was by far the most severe of the three. The king's demands for taxation were opposed openly, and hostile leagues, composed mainly of nobles, formed all over the areas directly under royal domination and in some of the principalities most closely under royal influence. Their demands reiterated many of those of the local assemblies, but this time they were ready to back them up with force.[56]

In 1314 the royal tax-collectors found the subsidy for the Flemish campaign difficult to collect, and the failure of the war exacerbated a general anger in the French provinces. Local assemblies met first in secret, then openly, to discuss their grievances, and groups of nobles from northern France complained to Philip IV that the taxation was unjust. All they got in return, said Geoffrey of Paris, who told the tale, were fine words,[57] and the king wrote to his *baillis* and *sénéchaux* ordering them to arrest local troublemakers. Meanwhile, provincial leagues had been forming.

The earliest, which may serve as an example, coalesced in Burgundy, at a massive assembly held in Dijon. It was headed by the important nobles of the region under John of Chalon, count of Auxerre, and also represented twenty-nine important religious houses and chapters, including Cîteaux and Flavigny, and eleven communes, including Autun and Avallon. The duke was not involved. The members of the league took a solemn oath to resist the subsidy and all other unreasonable royal activities. A small committee was deputed to organise the league's activities and to keep its records. Alliances were made by Burgundy with neighbouring leagues in Champagne, Forez, and later with Vermandois, Beauvaisis, Ponthieu and Artois. Charters were drawn up, expressing the aims of the allies, but retaining a tone of great respect of the king, by now on his deathbed. One of his last actions, indeed, was to cancel the subsidy, and he was prepared to reissue the 1303 reforming ordinance, but by the end of 1314 the leagues had become firmly entrenched, and were demanding a return to the customs of Saint Louis. The accession of the new king brought about a change of policy and personnel at court, and the fall of Marigny. This was not connected with the demands of the leagues, although it undoubtedly helped Louis X to negotiate with them.

Early in 1315 the new king granted charters to those parts of the domain which had raised their objections at court. The first to benefit was Normandy (19 March). Louis X agreed that he would provide good administration in the duchy, and promised that sound money would be established and maintained. Aids not prescribed by ancient custom would not be levied, and tallage would be raised only in cases of urgent necessity. In April another charter was given to the

Languedoc, limiting the powers of the parlement and the royal administrators. Some reimbursements for the subsidies already collected were also made, and the opposition, so strong that two of the consuls of Nîmes had been imprisoned for refusing to pay, gradually abated. Louis then began to agree to the demands of the leagues and to issue charters to them. A first batch was given at Easter, and after royal *enquêteurs* had made investigations in each region, a second series of charters was given embodying the results of their enquiries. Common to all was a promise that the activities of the royal officials would be carefully supervised and curtailed if necessary. The ancient right of the nobles to hold tournaments, wage private wars and have trial by battle would also be respected, and the king would not levy aid and military service from their vassals, but from them alone.

Although these general promises appeared in most of the charters, the other concessions made varied from region to region. The Norman charter affected non-nobles as well as nobles and was heavily biased towards legal procedure. The charters to the Burgundians, Champenois and men of Artois were aimed at redressing the grievances of the nobles who had organised and led the leagues. The charter to the Languedoc reflected clearly the importance of Roman law and popular liberties in this region. Another set of charters was issued to the French bishops, promising that their ancient customary rights would be observed.

There were many elements in these charters in common, and general charters of liberties based on the models of 1303 were issued both to the French church and the French people. But the differences between the leagues proved stronger than the similarities, and the real bargaining between the king and his disaffected subjects went on at a regional level, the charters which resulted reflecting the differences between the regions. In some there was hostility between the nobles and the townsfolk over the leagues, the townsfolk refusing to support the demands of the nobles so that the king made promises only to a limited section of society. This inability of the opposition to form a national, broadly based and coherent programme allowed Louis X to negotiate separately with each group, and greatly strengthened his hand. In this, the charters form a contrast with the great charter given to the English barons in 1215, which contained statements of general principle as well as the redressment of specific grievances. It may not be a coincidence that the Norman charter of 1315 reflected a wider range of interests than the others, and that it became as much a symbol of Norman liberties as Magna Carta was in England, being confirmed in 1339 by Philip VI, in 1380 by Charles VI, and later in 1423, 1458 and 1461.

The other provinces assigned less long-term importance to their charters and all settled down quite quickly after 1315, apart from Burgundy and Picardy which gave some trouble, and Artois. Here the revolt was complicated by being directed against the apanaged countess Mahaut as well as against the king — a contrast with Burgundy where ducal activities had occasioned far less resentment than royal ones. All the other apanaged princes at court supported Mahaut, and the king succeeded in getting them to put pressure and constraints upon her to secure her fair dealing with her baronage. After Louis X's death, however, the revolt entered a new phase as leadership of the barons of Artois was assumed by Robert, Mahaut's nephew and a rival claimant to the county. He gained some support from the duke of Burgundy and tried to mobilise the leagues in Burgundy and Picardy. But Mahaut was Philip V's mother-in-law, and supported his succession to the throne; furthermore, when Philip settled his differences with the duke of Burgundy, and when his own wife Joan became the recognised heiress to Mahaut for Artois in 1318, Robert's claims were overruled by the other princes and careful steps taken to conciliate Mahaut and the nobles of Artois. Thus a major dissension in the kingdom was finally put down, and the rebellious county submitted to the king's will.

6.4.6 *Kingdom and principalities in fourteenth-century France*

The baronial movement of 1314–15 is of a wider significance than that of a reaction of Capetian taxation and administrative centralisation, for the charters given by Louis X to the various leagues are a clear indication of the continuing regionalism in French society. France in 1314 was divided between the provinces which acknowledged and accepted a degree of royal control, such as Normandy, Languedoc, Champagne, and those which tried to deny it, Gascony and Flanders. The hostility towards the independence of the latter by Philip IV explains his constant attempts to bring them to heel by warfare and diplomacy; an effort which did not succeed in the way that Philip Augustus's military drive a century earlier had done. But many of the other provinces protested against royal control, and while this should not be overestimated (6.4.3), it is symptomatic of the regional cohesion found in many parts of France which later in the fourteenth century proved stronger than a general loyalty to the crown.

The issues involved in trying to see how kingdom and principality fit together in the later Capetian and Valois periods were well analysed by Professor Le Patourel.[58] He traced the consolidation of independent princely power in the fourteenth century, leading to princely domination of the monarchy in the fifteenth. In the struggle of the great nobles for royal patronage and revenues, and even for the crown, he suggested, French society looked remarkably like English society during the Wars of the Roses. While under the last Capetians, France appeared a remarkably centralised state, one hundred years later it seemed to be a loose confederation of principalities. During the fourteenth century the princes came to look upon their lands as 'political entities with interests which might not coincide with those of the kingdom as seen by the king'.[59] The early stages of the Hundred Years War were a French civil war as much as a war of succession, and once princely independence had been established institutions developed in each state. In the fifteenth century France passed through an age of principalities; 'unity under the king was not the only possible outcome. . . . But the monarchy eventually took over the princely governments as the basis of its provincial organisation.'[60]

The revival or formation of these principalities may be traced clearly in their institutional and political developments. Brittany's administration had been created by the Angevin kings and later by Peter Mauclerc; by 1297, when its ruler was given formal recognition as a duke and made a peer of France, it had its own parlement and financial institutions. By the 1340s the dukes, with English support, were claiming to rule by the grace of God over the Breton 'kingdom', and in the 1390s suggestions were made that Brittany, like Gascony, was no part of France. The dukes developed its power and administration sufficiently well to back up these claims. Flanders, a county whose institutions were well developed by 1200, began to break away from France in the 1290s on economic grounds, and by the 1360s had achieved almost total autonomy, again with English support, before it was submerged in the important Burgundian state (1384). Other smaller principalities also emerged, such as Forez, Beaujolais, Béarn, each with its own identity and institutions. The same tendencies were at work in certain of the royal provinces. Normandy kept its customs and its exchequer, and its charter became the symbol of its liberties. At the end of the fourteenth century it too was denying that it belonged to the French kingdom at all, even though its dukes were the French kings or their heirs. Languedoc kept its language and its law and developed its own representative institutions and its own parlement at Toulouse. From about 1337 it was also placed permanently under its own governor, who acted as a viceroy, and it remained relatively independent throughout the fourteenth century.

This picture of the build-up of princely power during the Hundred Years War appears at first sight to be very similar to developments in the eleventh century; in the reign of Henry I (1031–60) the princes seem to be wielding the same amount of authority and influence *vis-à-vis* the king as three hundred years later (2.1.1–2; 3.3.5). This raises a number of crucial and fundamental questions about French society. What happened in the intervening period? Were the events of the fourteenth century a repetition of those in the eleventh?

Clearly there was an acknowledged king of France with a recognised role both in the eleventh and the fourteenth centuries. Earlier his actual power was hardly worth fighting over but his office was much respected; later on, however, the struggle was focused upon it. Its potential powers and attributes had greatly increased during the later Capetian period. Nevertheless they had not swamped regional identities in the way that a concentration on royal administration alone might suggest. The principalities retained their own customs, and their leaders resisted the growth of royal justice as local communities, not just as individuals. The struggles of Philip IV with Gascony and Flanders might imply that their opposition was a narrow political one, but it is echoed to a lesser extent in Normandy, Champagne, Languedoc, communities who resented royal control not only *per se*, but because of its encroachment on their local liberties and privileges.

This is not to suggest that later Capetian government was a chimera. The power of the French kings was admired throughout Europe, and was based on an intricate and broadly based administrative, judicial and financial system. The principalities had something to react against. But successful kingship was an expensive business. The early Capetians were kings with limited resources; their successors, by contrast, were very wealthy and very powerful, but the Hundred Years War and social conditions in the fourteenth century exacerbated a difficulty which was already emerging in Philip IV's reign, that of funding an ambitious foreign policy. The resultant weakening of the Valois monarchy enabled the princes to rebuild their power at royal expense. The principalities, the regional communities, though seemingly submerged and certainly weakened under Louis IX and his successors, continued to exist throughout the thirteenth and early fourteenth centuries, and later in the fourteenth century were to re-emerge under their new leadership.

6.4.7 The image of monarchy and the reality of royal power

The last Capetian kings were, by most criteria, formidably powerful. To contemporary rulers, the France of Philip III and Philip IV was the dominant state in Europe, with wide political connections and great wealth. The king's subjects, too, were affected by the growth of sovereign authority inside the kingdom. The royal lands, rather than forming only a small fraction of France as in the eleventh century (Map 3.1), stretched from north to south, virtually engulfing the remaining independent fiefs (Map 6.1). The king's feudal suzerainty was widely obeyed, and resisted only by the most determined princes. He had a broadly based administrative system; and royal justice was effective throughout the kingdom. The royal system of tax collection was gradually extended, and the church in France was kept firmly under royal control. The papacy, too, increasingly appeared to be dominated by the French king, whose power seemed unmatched in Europe.

The later Capetian monarchy lost a great deal of the popularity built up by Louis IX and his predecessors, however. It is true that Saint Louis had had his critics, but under Philip IV his reign became an idealised golden age, a contrast with contemporary political life. The king's councillors generated widespread hostility. For example the character and career of Enguerrand de Marigny was satirised by a number of writers, including one of his own chaplains, Gervais du Bus, who wrote the *Roman de Fauvel*, a poem which took its final shape in c. 1314. Marigny appears as the beast Fauvel, a personification of all the vices, who marries vainglory thinking she is fortune, overturns the church, and subjugates the pope to the king. The standpoint of the poem is that of the parlement party, faithful to the traditions of Louis IX.[61] The king himself was criticised by Geoffrey of Paris for his indolence and for allowing evil councillors to dominate him, while Bernard Saisset, bishop of Pamiers, prophesied that Philip's reign, that of the tenth Capetian, would be the last; and a later writer looked back on it as a time when the Jews, Templars and Christians were all thrown to the lions. A hopeful poet addressed a piece to Louis X advising him to honour the church in the way his father had not done, but Philip IV's sons generated little more enthusiasm than he had. In the eleventh century the Capetians had been criticised for being ineffectual; now their vastly increased power produced considerable hostility.

Quite another picture emerges in the writings of the royal propagandists who used both Roman law and Christian concepts to justify the actions of the king and to glorify the kingdom. In pamphlets and speeches produced at court, Philip IV is portrayed as a righteous ruler. Stress was laid on his personal piety and on the holiness of the French nation. Nogaret, for example, called France 'the principal pillar supporting the Roman church and the Catholic faith.'[62] God had chosen and blessed it, and established it to last forever. William de Sanqueville, a Dominican writer, suggested that no kingdom was Frank or free except the kingdom of heaven (a pun on 'Francia'). The king was a type of Christ, and king and kingdom were glorified together.[63] As well as France's spiritual wholeness, its territorial unity was stressed, as was too its separation from and superiority over other nations. From about 1300, indeed, there was a strong vein of national sentiment in French, as in English writings. Boniface VIII was portrayed as violently anti-French by royal propagandists. He was said to have declared that no measures were too strong as long as he could destroy French power.[64]

The emergence of the idea of France as a state appeared to justify the frequently used argument that its king could call on its inhabitants to defend it. He could thus raise military service or taxation in time of war. The notion was also used to justify currency manipulations, the prohibition of private wars and judicial duels, and the control of imports and exports, but although it allowed heavy war subsidies to be levied it did not prove possible to extend it to cover the peacetime needs of France's rulers. Subsidies were cancelled when peace was made, and in 1321 Philip V met with strong opposition to his plans to use taxation to finance reform rather than fighting, and abandoned them. The idea of the needs of the defence of the realm was a valuable one, but was also limited in its long term applications.[65]

The provincial lawyer Pierre Dubois produced a different kind of propaganda, based on ideas which were widely current, and extreme in nature. His works contain a glorification of French royal power so striking that surely Philip IV could do little more than dream of the vistas of grandeur opened up for him. In Dubois's two principal treatises, *The Recovery of the Holy Land*, and the *Brief Summary*, he suggested that the whole of Europe should be made subject to the French king, since the French people were inherently superior to all other races. The pope should reside permanently in France as a first step, and the brothers and sons of Philip IV be given the kingdoms and principalities of the west to rule. The Byzantine empire could then be recaptured, and next the patrimony of the church handed over to the French king, so that peace would rule perpetually in Europe under French domination.[66] Pierre's ideas clearly interested the court, since some of his work was copied into a royal register, but they failed to get him the post in Paris which he sought, and it is a mistake to see them as official propaganda.

Such notions as these outstripped the actual extent of royal power as much as Abbot Suger's writings had done in the mid-twelfth century. Nevertheless, the real authority of Philip IV was very great in contemporary terms. He was bound by constraints such as the refusal of some of his subjects to cooperate over certain matters, but his will was frequently imposed against strong opposition. His successors made concessions, and limited their own authority in a minor way, but actually lost very little. They also did not succeed in lessening the tensions building up within French society, which were to weaken the monarchy again later in the fourteenth century. The later Capetian kings were not all-powerful rulers, for the opposition to them from the regions of France could not be fully contained. But they have a claim to being the nearest to absolute rulers that their time could produce.

6.5 THE KINGS AND THE CHURCH

6.5.1 The kings and the French church, 1270–1328

The French church was kept firmly in line by the successors of Saint Louis. In 1275 Philip III promulgated an important ordinance on the amortisation of land – that is, its granting to the church. For a long time lay lords had been extending their rights to control this process, and Louis IX had shown some interest in it. During the thirteenth century this authority had gradually been concentrated into the hands of the barons and the king, and Philip III gave the king overall control of the process, extending his authority into allods as well as fiefs. Selected peers were granted powers in their own rear-fiefs, and the notion of a licence to amortise was introduced. The licensor, the king or peer, collected one or more years' revenues from the land or rights being transferred to the church or could refuse permission for the gift to take place together.

Most of the French prelates supported Philip IV in his quarrel with Boniface VIII, and in his suppression of the Templars, one good reason being that many had been given their benefices by the king, and had risen in the royal service. The French church was taxed heavily and consistently by both the king and the pope. Boniface VIII's opposition to the levying of subsidies from it without papal permission was completely relinquished by his successors. The king's councillors considered it to be the duty of the church to pay these taxes, and when in 1305 the archbishop of Tours invoked Boniface VIII's rulings and refused to collect a double tenth until certain conditions had been met, Plaisians had his temporalities seized. The same treatment was given to those prelates who attended this pope's synod in Rome in 1302, and had the royal army not shortly before been defeated in Flanders, it is doubtful whether more than a handful of bishops would have dared to go at all (6.5.3).

The provincial assemblies of clergy, meeting to ratify the royal demands for taxation, forwarded their grievances to the royal administration with great regularity. These were discussed fully at the council of Vienne in 1311–12. Lay jurisdiction was constantly encroaching on ecclesiastical jurisdiction, and clerks were being tried and sentenced in lay courts. Clerks were being forced to pay tallage from which they were exempt; if they refused their goods were seized. Royal officials were persecuting ecclesiastics, preventing them from making excommunications, taking their land. The king's men declared, on the other hand, that ecclesiastics were invading royal privileges, and using benefit of clergy to get off scot-free from their crimes. There were major disputes between royal officials and the churches of Chartres, Poitiers and Lyon. The royal chancery issued many charters of safeguard and protection to individual churches, and charters of liberties to ecclesiastical assemblies, as in 1290, 1300 and 1303. In practical terms these were useless. The king held most of the French church in an iron grip, and only in the south was there any concerted resistance to him.

The opposition which came from the church in the Languedoc was in part a response to demands for subsidies, in part connected with a wider dissatisfaction in the region with northern French rule. There was also a great hatred of the inquisition run by the Dominicans, and in 1301 a Franciscan friar of Carcassonne, Bernard Délicieux, leader of the opposition to it, persuaded the king to revoke its privileges and to have it submitted to the episcopate and the Franciscans. This success was celebrated in an extreme and inflammatory way, and the Languedoc was soon in such turmoil that the king planned a visit to investigate (1303). Some of the inhabitants of Carcassonne treated him with rude familiarity, however.[67] Philip was greatly angered, and revoked his rulings over the inquisition. Délicieux, also furious, turned to Ferdinand of Majorca for help, but his treason was discovered and he was brought to Paris for trial. In the stirring events of the next few years he was forgotten, and released, to reappear a few years later, still fighting the inquisition; he was eventually accused of necromancy and poisoning Pope Benedict XI, convicted and degraded from his orders (1318).

Bernard Délicieux was perhaps fortunate in 1303 that the attention of the royal court was focused on Bernard Saisset, bishop of Pamiers, who was at the centre of the second dispute between the king and Boniface VIII (6.5.3). But like Saisset, other ecclesiastics became scapegoats for crimes and offences they clearly had not committed, and had lurid and preposterous accusations levelled against them. Boniface VIII and the Templars are obvious examples; the affair of Guichard, bishop of Troyes is another important instance, and indicative of the lengths to which the king's advisers would go.

Guichard, a brutal and violent man who attracted many enemies, had risen to prominence in the service of Queen Joan of Champagne, but after his elevation to the bishopric of Troyes he quarrelled bitterly with Joan and her son, the future Louis X. Louis attributed Joan's death in 1305 to sorcery at Guichard's behest and the *bailli* of Sens was charged with making a full enquiry. Then Nogaret took over the case, and presented Guichard to a group of papal commissioners as a sorcerer and a witch. These were probably baseless allegations which still seemed to be treated quite seriously by Guichard's judges, who had him imprisoned. But while he lost his place in court politics, he was fortunate enough to escape execution at the last minute, like Bernard Saisset and Bernard Délicieux. His fall seems to have been engineered by his enemies for purely political reasons, and many contemporary writers, including Geoffrey of Paris, and the author of the *Roman de Renart*, were convinced of his innocence. A number of similar vendettas were pursued in the reigns of Philip IV's sons, many against royal councillors, such as Marigny and Pierre de Latilli. Perhaps some of the most extreme and unlikely accusations of all were made against Boniface VIII's nephew, Francesco Gaetani, who hoped to become pope. He was denounced at Louis X's court and accused of directing curses and spells against the king, his brother and the Colonna. The deaths of Louis X and Philip V were also attributed to sorcery, a force whose potency was widely accepted at both the learned and popular levels. The denunciations of Boniface VIII and the Templars by Philip's councillors were very much an expression and a canalisation of contemporary fears and preoccupations.

6.5.2 The canonisation and the cult of Louis IX

In August 1297 Pope Boniface VIII canonised Louis IX and gave the French royal dynasty its own tutelary saint at last (4.4.6). This was of great moment to Philip IV and to the French people. All the imagery of holy kingship could be used by Philip IV's councillors in the struggle with the papacy to even greater effect than before, in the glorification and justification of his actions. The special relationship of the Capetians and the church had finally reached this high point, but at the moment when Philip was building up towards a bitter struggle with the vicar of Christ.

Louis IX's qualifications for canonisation were excellent, and miracles were reported at his tomb soon after his burial. Yet it was twenty-seven years before he was actually proclaimed a saint. Pope Gregory X made great efforts to this end by commissioning Cardinal Simon of Brie, an adviser to the late king, to take evidence, and by asking Louis's former confessor, Geoffrey of Beaulieu, to write a *Life* of the king. This was complete by 1275, when the archbishop of Reims and his clergy also sent a letter to the pope begging that Louis might be canonised as soon as possible. But in 1276 Gregory died, and although enquiries continued under his successors, no major step forward was made until 1280 when Simon of Brie became pope as Martin IV. In 1282 a public enquiry on Louis was held at Saint-Denis, which produced a vast amount of evidence. This was used by William of Saint-Pathus in his *Life*, written in 1302-03, and the list of the witnesses he gave in his preface shows that they were an august and ageing group; many had died long before the canonisation took place. Pope Martin's successors did nothing about the matter, until in 1297 Pope Boniface VIII agreed to reopen the case and to canonise Louis. This was a conciliatory gesture in the last stages of his first dispute with Philip IV, made under pressure from Pierre Flotte, and although the weight of evidence about the sanctity and miracles of the late king was overwhelming, the pope's motives in pronouncing him a saint seem to have been mainly political.

The already flourishing cult now expanded rapidly under royal leadership and patronage. Philip IV seems to have devoted much care and attention to the veneration of Saint Louis, which possessed great political and propaganda value. In 1298 a feast was held at Saint-Denis, where Saint Louis's relics were translated in great splendour. A magnificent reliquary was made for the skull, which was placed in the Sainte-Chapelle, and in 1308, numerous fragments of bone were distributed among the royal family and royal churches. Blanche, queen of Castile and Louis's daughter commissioned William of Saint-Pathus to write an account of the king, and John, lord of Joinville did the same at the behest of Joan of Champagne, Philip IV's wife.

Both accounts proved to be of great value, particularly Joinville's *Vie*. Interest in the cult from members of the royal family continued, for in about 1330, Joan, queen of Navarre, daughter of Louis X, had a Book of Hours made for her, containing first-rate illustrations of incidents in the life of Louis IX. Somewhat earlier, Joan of Evreux, wife of Charles IV, had had a similar volume made (c. 1325), and these are two fine examples of Parisian illumination of the period.

Philip IV had other ideas to celebrate his grandfather's cult. Among the several religious houses he founded, four monasteries were modelled on Saint Louis's.[68] One was Royallieu, a house of Victorine canons situated at Neuville-aux-Bois (*c.* 1303), all traces of which have now disappeared. A Carthusian priory, Mont-Saint-Louis, was founded near Noyon in about 1308, and a house of Clares, Franciscan nuns, at Moncel at the same time. Fourth and most lavish was Saint-Louis at Poissy, a well-endowed convent for Dominican nuns, begun in 1297. Philip had already spent £65,000 on the works by 1301, and engravings show it was a fine work in the best traditions of the court style, its plan based closely on that of Royaumont. Louis's heart was said to have been translated here, and after Philip's death, his own heart was buried in this shrine to holy French monarchy.

6.5.3 *Philip IV and Boniface VIII – a crisis in church–state relationships*

In 1293 western Christendom was given a remarkable pope in Benedict Gaetani, who took the name of Boniface VIII. He was a brilliant canon lawyer whose work on decretals was of great importance, an excellent administrator whose attempts to quell the disputes of the secular and mendicant clergy were highly practical, and a proud leader of the church, whose celebration of the Jubilee in 1300 was to epitomise the might of the papacy. But he was also a man of hot temper and unbounded arrogance, and this the French had experienced at first hand when he came to Paris on a mission in 1290, the only time when he met Philip IV face-to-face. His reign as pope had been preceded by that of an ancient, saintly and highly confused hermit, Peter Morrone, Pope Celestine V, who within a year had brought almost total chaos to his office and his administration, and who had eventually resigned. Boniface found it necessary to keep him in custody and to annul his acts, and when the unfortunate old man carried out a daring escape, was recaptured, and died in captivity, rumours of foul play began to circulate among the new pope's enemies. Among these were the Colonna family, one of the most powerful in the papal states, and formerly his enemies; they had given him their full support at the election conclave, but were soon alienated again by his failure to reward them. The spiritual Franciscans, bitterly upset at losing Celestine V, who had been their patron and protector, took a similar line. This opposition probably occasioned Boniface's retreat from his first struggle with Philip IV.

The first round of hostilities broke out over the issue of royal taxation of the French church. Louis IX and Philip III had collaborated with the pope in tapping this ready source of money to finance 'just' wars in defence of their realm, recognised as crusades by the pope. In 1296 both Edward I of England and Philip IV levied subsidies from the church for the war against each other, and without papal permission. Large sums of money were involved, for in France a clerical tenth yielded £240,000 tournois or so, not much less than a capital levy of a hundredth on property (£315,000). Boniface VIII would not stand for this, and he issued the bull *Clericis laicos*, addressed to all secular rulers. It began with a quotation from Gratian, with comments upon it. 'That laymen have been very hostile to the clergy, antiquity relates: and it is clearly proved by the experiences of the present time. For not content with what is their own the laity strive for what is forbidden.'[69] No specific references to the English and French kings were made, but they were clearly the target of the bull. The pope forbade any clerical subsidies to be levied without his permission, on pain of excommunication. It was also implied that papal consent would not be given readily. It has been suggested that this formed part of a general review of papal finances, but in its context it proved highly contentious, and was probably intended to be. The southern French clergy, meeting at Narbonne to consider Philip's latest demands, received a copy of the bull, and, less subservient than their northern brethren, refused outright to pay. But Philip, as well as making written protests, took the highly effective measure of forbidding the export of all bullion from France. This would hit the pope's finances badly, for not only did he rely on French money for much of his income, but he was dependent on highly complex international banking systems, which would be badly affected.

Boniface took the French king's move as a personal insult, and issued the bull *Ineffabilis amor*, which denounced Philip for allowing himself to be led astray by evil advisers. Various threats, including the king's excommunication, were added. The body of argument was a highly abstract defence of the power of the church. At the French court, hostile propaganda began to circulate, and opposition to Boniface was orchestrated in Italy. The two Colonna cardinals and an important spiritual Franciscan, Jacopone da Todi, issued manifestoes accusing Boniface of heresy, simony, trickery in his election, and the murder of Celestine V. They demanded a general council to discuss the whole question, and they also negotiated with Pierre Flotte who was on his way to the papal curia. Boniface was beginning a great struggle with the Colonna, and perhaps realised the danger of allowing them to combine with the French against him. Certainly when Flotte arrived at Boniface's court he found the pope ready to negotiate. Boniface showed himself prepared to rescind any excommunication of Philip, to canonise Louis IX (6.5.2), and in the bull *Etsi de statu* he conceded that kings might tax their national churches without papal consent in time of urgent necessity. The French king's victory had been won quite easily. In the next few years, however, the pope crushed the Colonna in Italy and built himself up a powerful position again. He was soon ready to fight Philip again.

In 1301 Boniface received a letter from Philip demanding that he should degrade from holy orders Bernard Saisset, bishop of Pamiers. This unruly and turbulent former protégé of Boniface had been tried by a French assembly and accused of trying to stir up the Languedoc against the king, and of speaking treasonably of Philip, his advisers and their policies. Lurid, scandalous and obscene charges, almost certainly concocted by Nogaret, were added, and Saisset was convicted as a heretic and a traitor. He would have to be degraded to the status of a layman before he could be punished. The pope, however, utterly denied the right of the king to try a bishop, for according to canon law this was a papal prerogative. He summoned Saisset to Rome, demanded that his temporalities, seized by the king, be restored, and called the French clergy to Italy for a synod to consider and reform the abuses committed by the French king and his councillors. In the bull *Ausculta fili* he accused the king of usurping papal power in the collation of benefices and of meting out justice over the church unlawfully. He also revoked all the privileges granted to Philip since 1297 and forbade taxes to be paid on church goods without his authorisation. This marked a return to the position of *Clericis laicos*. Philip gathered his forces for the struggle.

One sentence in *Ausculta fili* reads: 'Let no-one persuade you that you have no superior or that you are not subject to the head of the ecclesiastical hierarchy, for he is fool who so thinks.'[70] This was certainly inflammatory, but the action of Philip's advisers was even more so. The papal bull was burnt, and a shortened and garbled version circulated on Flotte's orders.

Boniface, bishop, servant of the servants of God to Philip king of the French. Fear God and keep his commandments. We want you to know that you are subject to us in spiritualities and temporalities. The collation of benefices and prebends does not belong to you at all.

Philip's supposed reply, circulated with it, was even more insulting.

Philip by the grace of God, king of the French, to Boniface who acts as though he were pope, little or no greeting. Let your great fatuity know that in temporalities we are subject to no-one; that the collation of vacant churches and prebends belongs to us by royal right. . . . All those who think otherwise we hold for fools and madmen.[71]

An estates general was summoned to Paris to discuss the matter, and Flotte delivered an impassioned speech on the theme that the French kingdom was held from God alone. The pope, he said, was trying to suggest that he held temporal as well as spiritual power in France and was summoning the French clergy to Rome in an attempt to realise it. But it was the king, not the pope who had cause to complain about the heavy taxation of the French church by the papacy and the placing of foreigners into French benefices.

So effective was Flotte's harangue that the nobles and the townmen both wrote to the college of cardinals denouncing the pope. The text of the nobles' missive survives and is highly vituperative in tone. The clergy hesitated, and then sent representatives to the pope himself, bearing letters which begged Boniface to excuse them from attending the council. The pope received them in full council, and made a fervent speech against Philip, complaining about his advisers, regretting that his own words had been misinterpreted and threatening to depose him. The cardinals' reply to the French nobles likewise utterly demolished the case which Flotte had constructed, and accused them of misrepresenting both the general tenor and the more detailed points of the papal bulls. But meanwhile the war in Flanders had reached a climax in Philip's defeat at the battle of Courtrai, at which Pierre Flotte was killed. This somewhat weakened the French king's position, and when Boniface's synod of French bishops met in Rome, thirty-six out of a possible seventy-eight – though none from the north – were there. The king confiscated their goods in revenge. The council condemned Flotte, but not his royal master, and nothing of any significance was achieved by it. Shortly afterwards, however, the pope issued the celebrated bull *Unam sanctam* (November 1302) which caused great anger at the French court. It begins: 'That there is one holy, Catholic and apostolic church, we are bound to believe and to hold, our faith urging us, and this we do firmly believe and simply confess; and that outside this church there is no salvation or remission of sins.' The text continues with an analysis of the relationships of the spiritual and the temporal power, with much use of the Gelasian metaphor of the two swords. The final sentence is the only place where there is doctrinal definition, and this is limited to spiritual affairs alone. 'Therefore we declare, state, define and pronounce that it is altogether necessary for salvation for every human creature to be subject to the Roman Pontiff.'[72]

The bull was a general statement about church unity and about the subordination of secular power to ecclesiastical authority, and it reiterated many of the ideas current amongst ecclesiastical theorists since the days of Gregory VII. Only the last sentence was arguably novel, and here the words were borrowed from a treatise of Saint Thomas Aquinas. Why, then, did *Unam sanctam* cause such a furore? One reason was that in its political context it was inflammatory. Another was that in many of its phrases and words it closely echoed the current writings of papal propagandists, known to the French court, and far more extreme than the bull itself. Giles of Rome, once Philip IV's tutor, had recently produced a work strongly upholding papal power, called the *De ecclesiastica potestate* (On ecclesiastical power).[73] *Unam sanctam* echoed many of its ideas. Despite his indignation Philip IV showed himself ready to negotiate with the pope at first, and this is perhaps a measure of the adverse psychological effects of Courtrai. But Boniface, forgetting his past record, tried not for compromise, but for his total submission, and this was going too far. The king's new chief adviser, William de Nogaret, seems to have advocated the adoption of a new policy, a violent and farreaching attack on Boniface, and action was taken accordingly.

First at a council of barons and bishops, and later at a larger assembly, Philip's councillors denounced the pope, and then circulated propaganda in full support of their claims. Boniface was a heretic, a simonist, and no true pope. He sought not to gain but to lose souls. Lurid, obscene and fantastic allegations were made, many of which were to reappear in the trial of the Templars. Boniface had a private demon as an adviser, and he had silver images of himself erected in churches. He was guilty of the crime of sodomy. He had said 'that he would rather be a dog or an ass or any brute animal than a Frenchman, which he would not have said if he believed that a Frenchman had an immortal soul'.[74] Demands were made for an assembly of the church to try to depose the pope and William de Nogaret travelled to Italy to threaten him. Boniface had meanwhile rallied all the support he could find in Italy, and retreated to Anagni. Here he was preparing to excommunicate Philip IV, when Nogaret and Sciarra Colonna arrived at the head of an armed band to settle the matter by force. They broke into the papal palace where the pope received them calmly; some accounts suggest that he was sitting on the papal throne, clad in full regalia, and holding a crucifix. Nogaret and Colonna insulted him and possibly laid violent hands on him, but having taken him prisoner, they could not agree on what course to adopt next, and the citizens of Anagni came to his rescue and drove them out. The shock proved too much for Boniface, however, and shortly afterwards he died. The incident greatly horrified many contemporaries, and Boniface was compared by an English chronicler with Saint Thomas Becket the martyr.

In fact the French king had defeated the papacy, and showed himself unrepentant. The next shortlived pope, Benedict XI, negotiated with the king while demanding punishment for Nogaret, but Clement V, his successor, capitulated completely. He restored all the privileges of the French king, he suppressed the Templars at his demand (6.5.4), and was even compelled to try Boniface posthumously. On this issue he did not concede complete defeat, since he refused to pass sentence, but he commended Philip the Fair on his zeal in bringing the charges, and he erased all the acts of Boniface deemed hostile to the French king from the papal registers. Still, he canonised Celestine V, but in his private capacity, not as pope, and Boniface was not removed from office posthumously. But this was a hollow victory for his successors, for although they were to rebuild much of the authority and the administrative machinery of the papacy, Boniface, in his over-confidence, and Clement V, in his weakness, had lost the papacy much prestige and moral authority.

6.5.4 The suppression of the Templars

The Templars were a large, exceedingly wealthy and influential group of religious, who had been involved closely in the politics and financial affairs of many western states. It is true that the collapse of the crusader states in the later thirteenth century, and in particular the fall of Acre in 1291, removed much of the justification for their existence; but this was equally true of the Hospitallers. They were clearly not as fervent in their observance as they had been; yet in the 1230s the Benedictines had been advised on reform and reorganisation by Pope Gregory IX to meet similar problems. The real reasons for suppressing the Templars seem to have been the needs of Philip IV and his advisers for money. Using their skills of intimidation and propaganda, they conjured up damning evidence against the order and forced Pope Clement V, a pliable figure, into its outright suppression.[75]

In September 1307, secret orders were sent to the royal *baillis* and *sénéchaux* ordering them to arrest all the members of the order throughout the kingdom. Their lands and goods were to be seized as well. It was stated that Philip had conferred with the pope and the chief inquisitor of France on the matter of the grave accusations levelled against the Templars, and because these were so horrifying, it had been decided to make a full investigation in defence of the faith. The arrests, which took place in October, had the full appearance of legality, but it seems that Pope Clement V was almost entirely ignorant of French plans, and was highly indignant at what had been done. Furthermore the papal inquisitor, the Dominican William of Paris, was the king's confessor and privy to his schemes.

The weakest part of the king's case was that the arrests were made only on 'vehement suspicion'. It was not long before this was remedied by 'evidence' extracted from the Templars by the use of torture, starvation and physical humiliation. The king's men began the interrogation, and then handed the Templars over to the inquisition, which recorded their 'confessions'. These were highly coloured in content. The order of the Temple was made to look like a heretical sect, indulging in blasphemous and obscene practices, such as spitting on the cross, idol worship, homosexual practices and rituals. Most of the rank-and-file tried to reduce their own supposed participation in the rites to that of observation alone, but almost all admitted to some evil practices. The Grand Master of the order, Jacques de Molay, and some of the other leaders, were forced to 'confess' in public, in front of an assembly of the university. This central showpiece of the investigation was probably carefully stage-managed by William de Nogaret. With such a weight of damning evidence, it looked as though the days of the order were numbered.

Was there any truth in these 'confessions'? Although they were for a long time accepted as well founded, many modern historians believe them to have been trumped-up by Philip's councillors, and entirely baseless. They were carefully calculated to stir up emotions of fear and hatred at a time when there was a growing belief in witches and demons, and they had many themes and ideas in common with the earlier attacks on Boniface VIII. Many of the Templars themselves were later to deny them, and to reveal that they had been extracted under torture. It is this that appears as the true testimony. Certainly the English and Aragonese kings both expressed surprise and incredulity when they heard of the charges. The pope reacted angrily, and wrote to Philip condemning his attacks and depredations on papal subjects, which showed an insulting contempt for the Holy See. It was this attitude on the king's part rather than the substance of the allegations which appeared to concern him, and although the imprisoned Templars hoped throughout the whole process that he would deliver them, his preoccupations appear to have been with power rather than with truth. He threatened to send cardinals to France to take over the custody of the persons and properties of the order, and he suspended the inquisition in France.

The response of Philip the Fair and his councillors was characteristic. Anonymous propaganda against the pope was circulated widely in the kingdom, and the masters of the university of Paris were called upon for their opinion. Their statement, although very cautious about the powers of the king in this matter, admitted that the Templars' confessions might justify their condemnation. A large estates general met at Tours and when the accusations were aired again by the king's councillors in strongly worded speeches, the Templars were declared guilty. As the next step a consistory of clergy and laity was summoned at Poitiers where the pope was now resident. Plaisians and other royal advisers made orations denouncing the order and threatening the pope. The motives of the king were painted as pure and white.

Despite this pressure the pope refused to agree with Philip's action, maintaining that churchmen should be tried and sentenced in church courts. So the king's advisers brought seventy-two Templars to Poitiers to confess before the pope. Doubtless they were handpicked for the task, but certainly Clement now showed himself ready to compromise with the king. It was agreed that the Templars themselves should be handed over to the church, but that the king should guard them, giving the pope's men free access. Their lands should be taken back by the church and put under administrators, who could, however, be nominated by the king. Ultimately their temporalities were to be spent on the defence of the holy land. Eight commissioners were appointed to enquire into the order as a whole throughout Europe. The inquisition was also reconstituted in France, and a general council of the church called. Clement's pacific line may be explained in part by the pressure put on him by Plaisians for Boniface VIII's posthumous trial, a matter potentially exceedingly damaging for the papacy.

Early in 1310 a movement to defend their order began amongst the imprisoned monks, which grew to formidable proportions. The papal commissioners allowed them to present evidence, much of which was highly critical of king and pope, and which denounced the methods used to extract confessions by the royal enquiry. Certain people from outside the order were also permitted to testify in its defence. The proceedings were slow and the king was increasingly displeased with their results, so in the summer of 1310 he ordered the new archbishop of Sens, Philip of Marigny (brother of Enguerrand) and his suffragans to act against the supporters of the order. The papal commissioners, whose president, Giles Aicelin, was a member of the royal council, now stood aside, and on the orders of the archbishop of Sens fifty-four Templars who had defended their order were burnt to death. The commissioners protested but the defence of the order collapsed, only a few brothers resisting the pressure from the king's men. In 1311 the council of Vienne met, but the French were unable to convince the other delegates of the guilt of the Templars. A vote against winding up the order without examining some of its members was won by five or six to one. So at a time when the council was temporarily adjourned, Clement V was browbeaten by Philip's men into suppressing the order. The spectre of the posthumous trial of Boniface VIII was probably decisive. In March 1312 he issued the bull *Vox in excelso*, which stated that the order of the Temple was being suppressed not as the result of a judicial sentence but because the accusations against it endangered the Christian life and Christian souls. The council, when it reassembled, was angry but impotent.

The ex-Templars were for the most part pensioned off, and sent to other religious houses to end their days. Their leaders, however, were sentenced to life imprisonment by the papal representatives. When in 1314 they appeared in Paris to hear their fate, two, Geoffrey de Charnay, Preceptor of Normandy, and Jacques de Molay, the Grand Master, openly declared their innocence, and that of the order. Their confessions had been wrung from them under torture, and the Templars had followed a holy and righteous rule. At Philip IV's orders they were immediately burnt at the stake, a sure indication of the royal attitude. Most of the Templars' property was transferred to the Hospitallers, but the beneficiaries were compelled to pay vast sums of money before the king would release it; £260,000 by 1314, more goods and quittances in 1315–16 and a final £50,000 in 1318. The chronicler Villani declared that the Hospitallers made a large net loss on the transaction, and his summary of this affair, one of the most percipient of contemporary comments, provides a fitting postcript.

(The king) was moved by his avarice, and made secret arrangements with the pope and caused him to promise to destroy the order of the Templars, laying to their charge many articles of heresy; but it is said that this was more in the hope of extracting great sums of money from them . . .[76]

6.5.5 *The Avignon papacy*

The settlement of the papacy at Avignon had an important influence on the development of the church in the later Middle Ages. It reflected the influence and the importance of the French king, but it was not a 'captivity' to the extent that its Italian critics suggested. Nor did it mark such a radical break with the past as is sometimes supposed. For from about 1240 until 1303 the popes had spent most of their time in Italy, but it was exceptional for them to reside in Rome; and both Innocent IV (1244–51) and Gregory X (1273–75) governed the church from Lyon. The settlement of the papacy in Avignon, a city adjoining the papal state of the Comtat Venaissin, just outside the French kingdom, was thus not an entirely unprecedented event, but it was still a clear symptom of the pull of France on the pope and the college of cardinals. The events which led up to Boniface VIII's death in 1303 revealed the amount of financial and political control the French king could exercise over the holy see, but the papacy had also become politically dependent on the French to maintain its position in Italy. In the late 1260s Charles of Anjou, Louis IX's brother, had set up a powerful kingdom in Naples and Sicily as the pope's champion. Successive popes were in effect his clients, and the number of French cardinals in the *curia* increased, producing factions and disputes. Although Angevin power in Sicily was destroyed in 1282, Charles and his successors continued to exercise a powerful influence over the papal states from their Neapolitan kingdom, and Pope Celestine V was virtually an Angevin puppet. Charles of Valois was another important papal supporter as a rival claimant to the crown of Aragon. Thus until the 1290s the French were vital allies of the papacy, ready to further its political schemes, and the *curia* had a strong French party in it. This gave an added bitterness to the disputes of Philip IV and Boniface VIII, and made it difficult for any pope to maintain himself in Italy without French support. Furthermore after 1303 the papal states were thown into confusion as the result of Boniface VIII's attacks on the Colonna, who after his death tried to re-establish themselves against Boniface's own family, the Gaetani. Papal authority in central Italy was weak in the extreme.

Nevertheless, the settlement of the papacy at Avignon took place initially as a temporary measure.[77] Clement V, a much respected canon lawyer and archbishop of Bordeaux, was elected pope in 1305 as a compromise candidate. He had taken an independent line in earlier Anglo-French disputes, and it was hoped that he would continue to do so. In fact, once pope, he proved singularly accommodating to the French king, whose business detained him north of the Alps for several years. His own ill-health and a strong affection for his native Gascony were other good reasons for staying, and after several years of wandering he made Avignon his centre. This city was in the empire and on the western edge of the Venaissin, the only land in the region held directly by the pope; Avignon itself was held by Charles of Naples and Provence, a papal vassal. Clement dealt with the suppression of the Templars and the council of Vienne, and was then ready to return to Italy, but political events in the peninsula made this impossible. Henry VII of Germany invaded Italy and threw the papal states into further confusion, and there was no French papal champion to help Clement to return. He therefore remained in the north until his death. His successor, Pope John XXII, elected in 1316, was a former bishop of Avignon, and it was quite natural for him to plan his return to Italy from here. He made strenuous efforts to involve himself in Italian politics, he tried to set up a client kingdom in Lombardy and planned to move the *curia* to Bologna, but these schemes merely fomented further discord, and he also remained in Avignon until his death in 1334. The next pope, Jacques Fournier, who took the name of Benedict XII, recognised the need of the *curia* to have a settled centre, even if this were not in Italy. In 1336 he began the construction of a great fortress-like papal palace at Avignon, and in 1339 the papal records were brought here from Assisi. Avignon was purchased from the Angevins in 1348 and was to continue as the papal residence almost continually until 1403.

Thus the papacy stayed at Avignon, and this period of its history was far from being a disaster. The popes were mainly men from the Languedoc, and although the Italians saw them all as puppets of the French king, only Clement V and Clement VI, former chancellor of Philip VI, appear fully to have justified this view. Most of them attempted to bring peace between France and England and to regain political power in Italy. The Rhône valley with its good communications was a highly convenient place to operate from. Under the Avignon popes the whole administrative system of the papal monarchy was highly organised and centralised. John XXII and his chamberlain Gasbert of Laval built up an efficient machinery for collecting, banking and disbursing papal revenues. Avignon became a major cultural centre, thriving on papal patronage. But while the western church was provided with a well-run government it was given very little spiritual leadership, and this neglect of its *raison d'être* was to prove a serious defect. Nevertheless this period of papal history was not an unmitigated failure, and nor was the pontiff as dependent on the French king as might have been anticipated at the time of Philip IV's defeat of Boniface VIII.

NOTES AND FURTHER READING

Asterisked titles are recommended for further reading. Place of publication London unless otherwise indicated.

Notes

1. C. V. Langlois, *Le règne de Philippe le Hardi* (Paris, 1887).
2. *Ibid.*, 6, n. 3.
3. *RHF*, xxi, 180; F., *Capetian Kings*, 43.
4. William of Nangis, *Chronique Latine* . . . , ed H. Géraud (Paris, 1843), 247.

5. J. R. Strayer, 'The crusade against Aragon', in *Medieval Statecraft and the Perspectives of History. Essays by J. R. Strayer*, ed. G. Post (Princeton, 1971), 107–22.
6. J. Favier, *Philippe le Bel* (Paris, 1978); E. Boutaric, *La France sous Philippe le Bel* (Paris, 1861).
7. See C. V. Langlois, *Saint Louis, Philippe le Bel, les derniers Capétiens directs* (Paris, 1901), 121.
8. *RHF*, xxi, 207–8.
9. P. Dupuy, *Histoire du differend d'entre le Pape Boniface VIII et Philippe le Bel* (Paris, 1665), 518; M. Barber, *The Trial of the Templars* (1978), 30.
10. R. H. Bautier, *'Diplomatique et histoire politique: ce que la critique diplomatique nous apprend sur la personnalité de Philippe le Bel', *Revue Historique*, cclix (1978), 3–27.
11. E. A. R. Brown, *'Royal salvation and needs of state in late Capetian France', in W. C. Jordan, B. McNab and T. Ruiz, eds, *Order and Innovation in the Middle Ages: essays in honour of J. R. Strayer* (Princeton, 1976), 365–79.
12. F., *Capetian Kings*, 38–40.
13. On this problem see Strayer, *'Philip the Fair –a "constitutional" king', in *Medieval Statecraft . . .*, *op.cit.*, 195–212; B. Lyon, 'What made a medieval king constitutional?', in T. A. Sandquist and M. R. Powicke, eds, *Essays . . . to B. Wilkinson* (Toronto, 1969), 157–75; and J. Favier, 'Les légistes et le gouvernement de Philippe le Bel', *Journal des Savants* (Avril–Juin, 1969), 92–108.
14. Favier, *Philippe le Bel*, *op. cit.*, 48; Bautier, *op. cit.*
15. J. Petit, *Charles de Valois, 1270–1325* (Paris, 1900).
16. C. T. Wood, 'Queens, queans and kingship; an enquiry into theories of royal legitimacy in France and England', in Jordan *et al.*, eds, *Order and Innovation*, *op. cit.*, 385–400.
17. Brown, *op. cit.*; C. Baudon de Mony, 'La mort et les funérailles de Philippe le Bel', *Bibl. EC*, lviii (1897), 1–14.
18. P. Lehugeur, *Philippe le Long. Le mécanisme du gouvernement* (Paris, 1931).
19. Langlois, *op.cit.*, 311.
20. G. Duby, *Rural Economy and Country Life in the Medieval West*, trans. C. Postan (1968), 289–357, 520–23; E. Perroy, 'Les crises du XIVe siècle', *Annales*, iv (1949), 167–82.
21. H. S. Lucas, 'The great European famine of 1315, 1316 and 1317', *Speculum*, v (1930), 343–77.
22. Nangis, *op. cit.*, 422.
23. F. Lot, 'L'état des paroisses et des feux de 1328', *Bibl. EC*, xc (1929), 51–107, 226–315, esp. 288.
24. R. Floud, *An Introduction to Quantitative Methods for Historians* (1973); E. le Roi Ladurie, *The Territory of the Historian*, trans. B. and S. Reynolds (1979), 3–31.
25. G. Duby, ed., *Histoire de la France rurale*, i (Paris, 1975), 554.
26. Lot, *op. cit.*, 303–4. On general problems of demographic studies see Ladurie, *op. cit.*, 88–94, *et passim*.
27. Perroy, *op. cit.*
28. R. C. van Caenegem and F. L. Ganshof, *Guide to the Sources of Medieval History* (Amsterdam/New York/Oxford, 1978), 101, n. 4.
29. P. Dollinger, 'Le chiffre de la population de Paris au XIVe siècle: 210,000 ou 80,000 habitants', *Revue Historique*, ccxvi (1956), 35–45, esp. 42.
30. Cazelles, *Nouvelle histoire de Paris . . .*, (*op. cit.* Ch. 5), 131–40.
31. E. le Roi Ladurie, *Montaillou, Catholics and Cathars in a French Village, 1294–1324*,

trans. B. Bray (1978). The text is in J. Duvernoy, ed., *Le Registre d'Inquisition de Jacques Fournier, évêque de Pamiers (1318–25)*, 3 vols (Toulouse, 1965).

32. Ladurie, *Montaillou . . ., op. cit.*, 130.
33. Petit-Dutaillis, *French Communes . . . (op. cit.* Ch. 4), 110–11.
34. J. Rozoginsky, 'Ennoblement by the crown and social stratification in France, 1285–1322 . . .', in Jordan *et al.*, eds, *Order and Innovation . . . op, cit.*
35. *RHF*, xxi, 315–17.
36. On what follows see *HIFr*, ii, and works there cited; also J. B. Henneman, **Royal Taxation in Fourteenth-century France: the development of war financing, 1322–56* (Princeton, 1971).
37. L. Borelli de Serres, 'Les variations monétaires sous Philippe le Bel . . .', *Gazette Numismatique Française* (1901–02), 245–425; A. Grunzweig, 'Les incidences internationales des mutations monétaires de Philippe le Bel', *Le Moyen Age*, i-ii (1953), 117–72.
38. Strayer, 'Pierre de Chalon and the origins of the French customs service', in *Medieval Statecraft . . ., op. cit.*, 232–8.
39. F. J. Pegues, *The Lawyers of the Last Capetians* (Princeton, 1962).
40. Favier, *Philippe le Bel, op. cit.*, and 'Les légistes . . .' *op. cit.*
41. J. MacNamara, *Gilles Aycelin, the servant of two masters* (New York, 1973).
42. J. Favier, **Un Conseiller de Philippe le Bel: Enguerrand de Marigny* (Paris, 1963).
43. R. Cazelles, *La Société politique et la crise de la royauté sous Philippe de Valois* (Paris, 1958), and Favier, 'Les légistes . . .', *op. cit.*
44. J. R. Strayer, 'Exchequer and parlement under Philip the Fair', *Droit Privé et institutions régionales. Etudes historiques offertes à Jean Yver* (Paris, 1976), 655–62.
45. Strayer, 'Viscounts and viguiers under Philip the Fair', in *Medieval Statecraft, op. cit.*, 213–31, esp. 229.
46. J. F. Benton, 'Philip the Fair and the "jours" of Troyes', *Studies in Medieval and Renaissance History*, vi (1969), 281–344.
47. Wood, *French Apanages and the Capetian Monarchy (op. cit.*, Ch. 5), *passim.*
48. C. M. Martin, 'The enforcement of the rights claimed by the kings of France in the duchy and county of Burgundy, 1285–1363' (unpublished B. Litt. thesis, Oxford, 1965).
49. B. Pocquet de Haut-Jussé, 'Le grand fief Breton', *HIFr.*, i, esp. 276–7.
50. P. Chaplais, ***Le souveraineté du roi de France et le pouvoir législatif en Guyenne au début du XIVe siècle', *Le Moyen Age*, lxix (1963), 449–66.
51. This important point is made by G. I. Langmuir, 'Counsel and Capetian assemblies', *Études présentées par la commission internationale pour l'histoire des assemblées d'états*, xviii (1958), 19–34.
52. P. S. Lewis, *Later Medieval France* (1968), 332.
53. C. H. Taylor, ***French assemblies and subsidy in 1321', *Speculum*, xiii (1968), 214–44.
54. T. N. Bisson, *Assemblies and Representation in the Languedoc in the Thirteenth Century* (Princeton, 1964).
55. J. R. Strayer and C. H. Taylor, *Studies in Early French Taxation* (Cambridge, Mass, 1939). See also Henneman, *op. cit.*, for a full bibliography of the numerous useful articles on royal taxation which have appeared recently.
56. The classic work on this period is A. Artonne, *Le Mouvement de 1314 et les chartes provinciales de 1315* (Paris, 1913).
57. *RHF*, xxii, 151–4.
58. J. le Patourel, 'The king and the princes in fourteenth-century France', in J. Hale,

R. Highfield and B. Smalley, eds, *Europe in the Late Middle Ages* (1965), 155–83.

59. *Ibid.*, 183.
60. *Ibid.*, 155.
61. Favier, *Un Conseiller . . ., op. cit.*, 198–9.
62. Dupuy, *op. cit.*, 241; Strayer, *'France: the Holy Land, the chosen people and the most Christian king', in *Medieval Statecraft . . ., op. cit.*, 300–14, esp. 309.
63. Strayer, *ibid.*, 311–12.
64. Strayer, 'The laicisation of French and English society in the thirteenth century', in *ibid.*, 251–65, esp. 263.
65. Strayer, 'Defense of the realm and royal power in France', in *ibid.*, 291–9.
66. Pierre Dubois, *The Recovery of the Holy Land*, ed. and trans. W. Brandt (New York, 1956).
67. Langlois, *op. cit.*, 204.
68. On these see P. Guynemer, *Cartulaire de Royallieu* (Compiègne, 1911); L. Meister, *L'Acquisition du Moncel par Philippe le Bel* (Beauvais, 1900); R. Fawtier, *Registres du Trésor des Chartes,* i (Paris, 1958), 220, no. 1170; A. Erlande-Brandenburg, 'La priorale Saint-Louis-de-Poissy', *Bulletin Monumental*, cxxix (1971), 85–112. See also Branner, *Saint Louis and the Court Style . . . (op. cit* Ch. 5) and Brown, *op. cit*.
69. H. Bettenson, *Documents of the Christian Church* (Oxford, 1943), 157.
70. G. Digard, *et al.*, eds, *Les Registres de Boniface VIII*, iii (Paris, 1921), 328–32; Tierney, *The Crisis of Church and State (op. cit.* Ch. 3), 186.
71. Dupuy, *op. cit.*; Tierney, *op. cit.*, 187.
72. E. Friedburg, ed., *Corpus Iuris Canonici*, ii (Leipzig, 1881), 1245–6; Tierney, *op. cit.*, 188–9.
73. T. S. R. Boase, *Boniface VIII* (1933).
74. Dupuy, *op. cit.*, 102–6; Tierney, *op. cit.*, 190.
75. This section draws heavily on Barber, *op. cit.*, who gives a full bibliography of the considerable material on the subject. See also N. Cohn, *Europe's Inner Demons* (1975), 75–98.
76. R. E. Selfe and P. H. Wicksteed, trans., *Selections from the first Nine Books of the Chroniche Fiorentine of Giovanni Villani* (1896), 378.
77. Y. Renouard, *The Avignon Papacy, 1305–1403*, trans. D. Bethell (1970).

CHAPTER SEVEN

Conclusion

7.1 THE SUCCESSION AND THE HUNDRED YEARS WAR

The death of Charles IV without male heirs produced a number of problems. He and his elder brothers had left numerous daughters, and although they could not inherit the crown of France they clearly had some rights over the royal lands. Joan, daughter of Louis X and Blanche of Burgundy, had been promised the reversion of Champagne should Philip V die without male heirs, as he did. Then there was the difficulty of the succession to Navarre. Should a daughter of Philip V or of Charles IV become its queen? If a daughter of Philip V was given it, this might suggest that Charles IV's accession as its king was not legitimate. Furthermore in 1318 Joan, daughter of Louis X, had promised that she would renounce it, but does not appear actually to have done so. Her husband, Philip of Evreux, claimed it on her behalf, and at a great council held in 1328 they were awarded the Pyrenean kingdom. Philip VI kept Champagne and Brie, and in 1336 the daughters of Philip V and Charles IV were given substantial financial compensation. The implications of these settlements were considerable. A grandson of Philip III had succeeded to the throne, chosen by the leaders of the people before the daughters of the last Capetians, but the rights of these daughters to the acquisitions by the crown, Navarre and Champagne, had been clearly recognised. In the case of a disputed succession, the leading men of France could still choose one of the claimants to rule.

There remained the problem of any possible claims by Edward III of England on the French throne. The French magnates elected Philip VI in preference, in part because of previous inheritance patterns, in part because of their hatred for Queen Isabella, Edward III's mother and regent. But she was Philip IV's daughter, and arguably had rights upon the French royal domain. She did not claim the throne itself, but Edward was to do so, on the grounds that he was Charles IV's nearest surviving male relative, as his nephew, whereas Philip VI was merely a cousin. But if Isabella, who never asserted that she was in line for the crown herself, could still transmit a right over it to her son, any sons of the daughters of the last Capetians would also have a claim. In 1332 Joan and Philip of Evreux produced a son, the future King Charles the Bad of Navarre, who was to argue that his claims to France were far better than those of Edward III. But the English king left his claims in abeyance, and did homage to Philip VI, until in 1337 the French king confiscated Gascony. Then Edward, hoping to get back his duchy intact, claimed the whole French kingdom. In 1339 the Hundred Years War broke out, which was to raise the relatively impoverished English king to great heights of power and influence, and to reduce the French king for a time to powerlessness. This was a dynastic conflict, but it was far more as well: a feudal struggle, and an attempt by the French principalities to gain their independence and to dominate or to take over the monarchy. The later fourteenth century was to be a second golden age for the French princes.

7.2 THE RISE OF THE CAPETIANS: SOME GENERAL PERSPECTIVES

Between 987 and 1328 the political power, administrative machinery and the resources of the Capetian kings changed and developed almost out of all recognition. The west Frankish ruler, struggling to maintain his position against a group of princes, gave way to a French king whose authority inside the kingdom was challenged only with impunity and who had a dominant place in European politics. Since this was the outcome, it is all too easy to imagine that it was an inevitable process, and that the careful policies of the early Capetians, the consolidation of the power they had, enabled their successors to adopt more aggressive tactics, and naturally produced the monarchy of Philip IV. If one simply traces their history as a series of themes – the royal domain, royal administration, relations with the nobles, relations with the church – this increases such an impression and not only disguises the fluctuations in royal power, but also distorts the effects of the changing political, social and economic conditions in France upon monarchical authority.

Royal power certainly did not increase gradually and ineluctably between 987 and 1328. The Capetians suffered a number of setbacks, and none more striking than the decline in their authority up to the 1040s. Hugh Capet and Robert the Pious adhered firmly to Carolingian traditions of monarchy to hide a contracting power, but the succession crisis in 1031 dealt royal control a great blow, and revealed its debility both inside the royal principality and in the kingdom at large. Political authority rested with the princes in some regions, with counts and castellans in others. The king, rescued by the duke of Normandy, came through the crisis of the 1030s, but his authority remained weak. From about 1050 until 1200 royal power increased gradually. This was in part the result of social and legal developments, as the community became more hierarchical and feudal obligations better defined and better observed. From c. 1100 to 1137 and c. 1170 to 1200 the kings themselves, Louis VI, Louis VII and Philip Augustus, made concerted efforts against the castellans in the royal lands, and against the princes; but in the later 1150s Louis VII, while having a stronger power-base round Paris than his predecessors, seemed eclipsed politically by Henry II, king of England and French territorial prince extraordinary. Of course this is not the whole story, for culturally Paris was the capital of western Europe, but in the mid-twelfth century there was little to show that it would become the political centre as well.

The years c. 1200–26 were crucial in the rise of the Capetians, and the events of 1204, when Philip Augustus took Normandy and Anjou from John, were the turning-point. Philip and Louis VIII confined English power to Gascony and tipped the balance between the king and the princes in the king's favour. They added Normandy and part of Languedoc to the royal lands, vastly increasing royal authority and royal resources, and giving the king power bases with outlets to the sea in the north and the south of the kingdom. These gains were strongly resisted by the princes during Louis IX's minority (1226–c. 1235) but in the face of the most dangerous challenge to royal power since 1031, Blanche of Castile, the regent, acted with firmness and determination and by c. 1235 has brought most of the rebels to heel. After this, Louis IX was able to consolidate the gains of his father and his grandfather, and while he was unable to drive the English from the kingdom altogether, his settlement with Henry III in 1259 was a serious attempt to curb and contain the Plantagenet menace.

From about 1240 until 1295 royal power in France as a whole expanded rapidly. The royal domain increased, helped by the reversion of apanage grants, and soon overshadowed the remaining principalites. Henry II had looked to be in a similar position a century before, but he had lacked the crucially important attributes of monarchy in France which enabled landed power to become something wider. The feudal suzerainty of the Capetians was fully developed and their sovereign powers extended throughout the kingdom. France was becoming a powerful and unified state, and as politics and statecraft in western Europe changed, and other states emerged, it moved away from its traditional position as a supporter and executor of papal policies in the east and became involved in ruinously expensive wars nearer home. These produced severe financial difficulties for the crown, and from 1295 onwards Philip IV's administrators developed new and wider forms of taxation. These appeared on one level to be a symptom of the further increase of royal authority, but they also generated strong resistance from the provinces.

The most serious seeming challenge came in 1314–15 with the formation of the provincial leagues, but this opposition foundered on its failure to put forward a general series of grievances and its concentration on local issues. The king, who now held the papacy almost in tutelage, was able to overcome it in the short term, but it was a first sign of the struggles between the kings and the regional communities to come. Thus from 1295 to 1314 royal authority and local resistance to it were both increasing, and from 1315 to 1328 royal power remained roughly stable, before declining again at the expense of the principalities in the middle of the fourteenth century.

Between 987 and 1328 the king had preserved his royal powers and attributes, sacral, feudal and sovereign, but their implications, both theoretical and practical, had altered out of all recognition. Where Philip I had been defeated by a castellan in the royal lands, and had been obliged to rely on the alliance and cooperation of neighbouring princes in order to wage an effective campaign, Philip IV could call on all the French people to defend their land against enemies and could levy vast sums of money to finance his wars. Where Hugh Capet had depended on the support of the northern French bishops for his accession as king, Philip IV held not only the French church, but the papacy itself in an iron grip. Henry I had engendered a profound indifference from chroniclers and contemporaries, but Louis IX was a popular king throughout France and Europe, a saint and a symbol of French aspirations. Yet these changes were far from being inevitable, for the rise of the Capetians must be attributed in large measure to the tenacity and ability of Philip Augustus.

7.3 THE FRENCH KINGDOM AND EUROPEAN SOCIETY

Seen from a purely political angle, the importance of the Capetian kingdom in western Europe was limited until the thirteenth century. But a different impression emerges when its contributions to the cultural, artistic and religious movements of the time are assessed. To scholars and to poets, to reforming churchmen and monks, to crusaders and to the designers of churches, France – and to many Paris – was the hub of their universe from the early twelfth century onwards. However insignificant its kings, *la douce France* drew men like a magnet. Its resplendent reputation was well deserved, for it is clear that the French people made a vitally important contribution to almost all of the most significant movements of the Capetian period, particularly in the twelfth and thirteenth centuries.

In religious affairs, the significance of the French contribution is indisputable. In the eleventh century France produced the peace and truce of God, an attempt by the church to curb the anarchy and brutality of society; and the cult of chivalry, which gave the knight, around whom military strategy revolved, a sanctified role, a code of conduct and a set of ideals to follow. The crusades, which provided for him the opportunity to wage a holy war against the infidel, were a logical development from this, and the French nobility, particularly from Normandy and the Languedoc, played a crucial part in the campaigns in the east. Later, Louis VII became the first crusading king and papal champion, a role which his successors were to continue with; and he was known as *rex christianissimus* (most Christian king), a title which symbolised and reflected his close ties with the papacy and the church. France was also a flourishing centre of the religious life, producing many of the great monastic orders of the Middle Ages: the Cluniacs, the Cistercians, the Premonstratensians, and later the Dominican friars. The culmination of this enthusiasm for ecclesiastical affairs was the reign, and later the canonisation of Louis IX; and it was ironic that Philip IV was to use this cult for his own ends while turning on the papacy and the Templars, and all the more so because of the long-lasting enthusiasm of his people for religious matters.

In cultural developments the French kingdom also exercised a powerful and long-lasting influence, as the monastic centres of learning of the eleventh century gave way to the cathedral schools and then to the universities. For legal and scientific studies the Midi was of considerable importance, but it was Paris, centre of the study of classical disciplines, of theological and scholastic learning, which dominated the intellectual world of the twelfth and thirteenth centuries. In vernacular poetry, the troubadours of the south and their northern equivalents, the *trouvères*, were strongly influential from the eleventh century onwards, and in the thirteenth and fourteenth centuries vernacular prose works of a high quality were produced. Artistically, too, the French kingdom was of great significance. Various regions, Burgundy, Normandy, western France, developed their own styles of church design and decoration, and from the Ile de France came the Gothic style of architecture and sculpture, which emerged in buildings from Suger's Saint-Denis to Louis IX's Sainte-Chapelle, became an identifiable court style, and continued to be used and copied throughout Europe up to the end of the Capetian period. In the production of stained glass, illuminated manuscripts and other such arts, French craftsmen showed themselves inventive and innovative.

In administrative and political developments France was far less precocious than many of her neighbours, and in particular, than the English kingdom. But to the cosmopolitan, educated man of the twelfth century, such as John of Salisbury, France was a civilised and desirable place to live in; and the relative political weakness of its king did nothing to diminish this impression, but may rather have increased his popularity. The people of Capetian France, then, had a wide and long-lasting importance in European society, and this was an influence which could only profit the Capetian kings.

APPENDIX I
Why the 'Capetians'?

Until 1790 the surname Capet was used only for Hugh, who became king in 987, and occasionally for his father Hugh the Great. But then Marat coined the term 'Capetian' for all the French kings from 987 to his own day – that is for the 'third race of France'. His contemporary Camille Desmoulins referred to Louis XVI as 'a citizen, Monsieur Capet the elder'. It was against the name in this kind of wide usage that de Barthelémy protested in 1873. The 'third race', he said, should be known as the 'house of France'. The name Capetian has however remained in use, although subsequently it has been applied only to Hugh Capet and his direct descendants to 1328, when a cadet line, the Valois, replaced them. This is still not entirely satisfactory, since the 'Capetians' were descended directly from the 'Robertines' (1.4.1). Yet it is invariably used by modern historians, as it is here, as a matter of convenience. But what are the origins of the name itself?[1]

In about 1160 a monk of Foigny wrote: 'King Robert was succeeded in his duchy but not in the kingdom by his son Hugh, who was called the Great and 'Cappatus', from the cap (*cappa*) of the Lord which it is said he brought over from the promised land.'[2] Here Hugh the Great not his son is called Capet, and many writers from Adhémar of Chabannes in the 1030s onwards refer to the duke as *Ugo Capetus* or *Ugo Capetius*. The annals of Saint-Germain-des-Prés, written in the 1060s, however, give the name to his son in some versions, and so too does William of Jumièges in his *Deeds of the Dukes of Normandy*, dating from 1070–72. By the end of the thirteenth century the son had outstripped the father as the holder of the name.

The name Capet is clearly associated with the Latin words *cappa* or *capa* meaning respectively a hat or a stole or cape. The term *chapet* refers to the wearer of a short cloak or coat, and surnames or nicknames incorporating such descriptions are not uncommon in the tenth and eleventh centuries, as with Geoffrey Greymantle, count of Anjou. The use of the name Capet for both Hugh the Great and his son is not unusual either; indeed there is some evidence that both were described as Hugh the Great as well. But by the twelfth century legends about the origins of the name were legion. A monk of the Limousin writing in the twelfth century suggests that Hugh was called 'the cap-wearer' because he did not want the crown.[3] No matter how scanty our sources might be, it would be very difficult to give any credence to this explanation. But the name Capet has remained with King Hugh, son of Hugh the Great, and more recently has been given to his dynasty.

NOTES

1. F. Lot, *Études sur le règne de Hugues Capet et la fin du Xe siècle* (Paris, 1903), 304–50.
2. *RHF*, xiv, 2.
3. *RHF*, x, 259.

A note on the sources for Capetian history

General

The best general account of the sources for Capetian history is A. Molinier, *Les Sources de l'histoire de France* . . . , ii–iii (Paris, 1902–03), which, though rather old, gives a wide and valuable coverage. Another helpful account is by R. C. van Caenegem and F. L. Ganshof, *Guide to the Sources of Medieval History* (Amsterdam/New York/Oxford, 1978). A useful analysis of the evidence for Capetian history is contained in Fawtier, *Capetian Kings*, 1–12, and is recommended introductory reading.

Manuscripts

The Archives Nationales and the Bibliothèque Nationale, both in Paris, contain important collections of manuscripts relating to the Capetian period; many of these have been edited, translated and calendared (see below, *printed sources*). Many of the local departmental archives (Archives Départementales) have useful material; and some relevant manuscripts may also be found in the collections at major foreign archives such as the Vatican archives and library at Rome and the British Library and Public Record Office in London.

Printed sources

Useful collections of chronicles, letters, etc, appear in *RHF*; in the *Monumenta Germaniae Historica* (Hanover, etc., 1826–); in *PL*; and in the *RS*. There is also the important series published by the Ministère de l'instruction publique: *Collection des documents inédits sur l'histoire de France* (Paris, 1835–). The acts of most of the Capetians have been edited, and are usefully listed in Fawtier, *Capetian Kings*, 7–9. See also A. Teulet and others, eds., *Layettes du Trésor des Chartes*, 5 vols (Paris, 1863–1909); R. Fawtier and J. Guérout, ed., *Registres du Trésor des Chartes*, 2 vols (Paris, 1954–66). A selection of financial records to 1328 appear in *RHF* and in vols i–iv of *RHF*, *Documents financières*, ed. C. V. Langlois, R. Fawtier and others (Paris, 1899–1961). See also Lot and Fawtier, *Premier Budget* (*op. cit.*, Chapter 4); E. Boutaric, ed., *Actes du parlement de Paris*, 2 vols

(Paris, 1863–67); *Ordonnances des roys de France de la troisième race*, 22 vols (Paris, 1723–1849).

The above list covers only a selection of the range of sources available. Many of the monographs cited in Appendix III contain comprehensive lists of printed and unprinted sources for individual topics.

Other sources

Buildings which have survived from the Capetian period are often important historical sources. On castles, see J. F. Fino, *Forteresses de la France médiévale* (Paris, 1967); on churches, see R. Huyghe, ed., *The Larousse Encyclopaedia of Byzantine and Medieval Art*, trans, D. Gilbert *et. al*. (London, 1963), and Brooke and Swaan, *Monastic World* (*op. cit.*, Ch. 4, p. 200); these are also valuable on sculpture, stained glass, tombs, *etc*. See also Branner (*op. cit.*, Ch. 5, p. 272); K. J. Conant, *Carolingian and Romanesque Architecture, 800–1200*, 3rd edn (Harmondsworth, 1973); and A. Erlande-Brandenburg, *Le Roi est mort . . .* (Geneva, 1975). On numismatics, P. Grierson, *Monnaies du Moyen Âge* (Fribourg, 1976), is essential.

Select Bibliography

General

A good historical atlas is a vital prerequisite for serious study of Capetian France. The classic work here is A. Longnon, *Atlas Historique de la France*, I, *Atlas* Paris, 1885–9); but R. F. Treharne and H. Fullard, ed., *Muir's Historical Atlas – Ancient, Medieval and Modern*, 9th edn (London, 1962) is more likely to be generally available.

Fawtier's *Capetian Kings* is still a useful introduction in English to this topic; see also the relevant volumes of the *Cambridge Medieval History*, and Petit-Dutaillis, *The Feudal Monarchy . . . (op. cit.*, Ch. 4). On the later Capetians, Fawtier's account in *L'Europe Occidentale de 1270 à 1380*, in G. Glotz, ed., *Histoire générale*, vi (i), (Paris, 1940) is useful. The old Lavisse, *Histoire de France* series remains a sound and often quite detailed general history, although it is not well documented. The relevant volumes are ii and iii (Paris 1901–03). A useful and recent account of medieval France with a good bibliography is J. F. Lemarignier, *La France médiévale, institutions et société* (Paris, 1970).

On institutions see *HIFr.;* A. Luchaire, *Histoire des institutions monarchiques de la France sous les premiers Capétiens (987–1180)*, 2nd edn, 2 vols (Paris, 1891), and *Manuel des institutions françaises; période des Capétiens directs* (Paris, 1892); L. L. Borelli de Serres, *Recherches sur divers services publics du treizième au dix-septième siècles*, 3 vols (Paris, 1895–1909); C. R. Brühl, *Fodrum, Gistum, Servitium Regis*, 2 vols (Koln-Graz, 1968).

On the church see the excellent introduction by R. W. Southern, *Western Society and the Church in the Middle Ages* (Penguin, 1970). The general series *Histoire de l'Église*, ed. A. Fliche and V. Martin, contains a number of relevant volumes, in particular, vii–xiii (Paris, 1945–64).

On French society, see G. Duby, *Histoire de la France rurale*, i (Paris, 1975), and his *Rural economy and country life in the medieval west*, trans. C. Postan (London, 1968); also G. Fourquin, *Histoire économique de l'occident médiévale* (Paris, 1969); and vols i–iii of the *Cambridge Economic History of Europe*, 2nd edn of vols i and iii (Cambridge, 1952–66).

The latest work on a variety of topics is covered in the *Bibliographie Annuelle de l'histoire de France*, published by the Centre National de la Recherche Scientifique (Paris, 1953–).

Chapter 1. French society in the early Capetian period

On the historical geography of France see W. G. East, *An Historical Geography of Europe*, 5th edn (1966). On the French economy, Pirenne *op. cit.*, n. 1 and Grierson, *op. cit.*, n. 3, are useful; and for good general introductions, Latouche, *op. cit.*, n. 2, and Duby, *op. cit.*, n. 4. On the invasions, L. Musset, *Les Invasions, le second assaut contre l'Europe chrétienne (VIᵉ–IXᵉ siècles)* (Paris, 1965); P. H. Sawyer, *The Age of the Vikings*, 2nd edn (1971); and compare J. M. Wallace-Hadrill, *The Vikings in Francia*, Stenton Lecture 1974 (University of Reading, 1975). On the development of towns, for Normandy, see J. Boussard, 'Hypothèses sur la formation des bourgs et des communes en Normandie', *Annales de Normandie*, viii (1958), 423–40, and for Flanders, J. Dhondt, 'Développement urbain et initiative comtale en Flandre au XIᵉ siècle', *Revue du Nord*, xxx (1948), 133–56. A useful summary of recent research on urban development is M. W. Barley ed., *European Towns, Their Archeology and Early History* (1977).

Recent work on the nobility is well and usefully summarised in Martindale (*op. cit.*, n. 11); Werner's article is important (*op. cit.* n. 8); see also G. Duby, 'The nobility in medieval France', in *The Chivalrous Society* (*op. cit.*, p. 25), 94–111. The volume of essays on the nobility translated by Reuter (*op. cit.*, n. 12), is also useful on the general issues and problems. Among the many accounts of rural lordship, see G. Duby, *Rural Economy and Country Life in the Medieval West*, trans. C. Postan (1968), and Fourquin, *op. cit.*, p. 25.

The classic study of the political disintegration of France is Dhondt, *op. cit.*, n. 13. See also Lemarignier, 'La dislocation du "pagus" . . .', *op. cit.*, p. 26, and 'Les fidèles du roi de France (936–987)', *Recueil . . . Clovis Brunel* (Paris, 1955), ii, 138–62; Werner, *op. cit.*, n. 12; and the papers of a colloquium which sets the French disintegration in a wider, European, context: *L'Europe aux IXᵉ–XIᵉ siècles, aux origines des états nationaux* (Warsaw, 1968). On castles, see Chapter 2, p. 63, for articles by Coulson and Yver.

Among the vast number of works on feudalism, those by Bloch, Ganshof, Fourquin and Brown cited in the 'Notes and further reading', are all useful, as is Strayer, *op. cit.*, n. 10. These studies give an idea of the range of opinions on this subject. J. F. Lemarignier, *Recherches sur l'hommage en marche et les frontières féodales* (Lille, 1945), and many of the monographs and articles cited in the Notes to Chapter 2 are also important. See in particular the work of Duby on the Mâconnais and the accounts by Magnou-Nortier and others on the Midi.

Cowdrey, *op. cit.*, n. 19, gives a useful account of the peace and truce of God. Lemarignier, *op. cit.*, n. 18, tackles the problem of the place of the church in the growth of ideas of social hierarchy; see also H. E. J. Cowdrey, *The Cluniacs and the Gregorian Reform* (Oxford, 1970). G. Duby, *L'An mil* (Paris, 1967) is an interesting account of popular fears connected with the year 1000.

On the change of dynasty, see F. Lot, *Les Derniers Carolingiens . . . (954—991)* (Paris, 1891) and *Études sur le règne de Hugues Capet et la fin du Xᵉ siècle*

(Paris, 1903). A. Dumas, 'L'église de Reims au temps des luttes entre Carolingiens et Capétiens', *Revue d'Histoire de l'Eglise de France*, xxx (1944), 5–38, is useful for the ecclesiastical dimension.

Chapter 2. Politics and society: A regional view

On some of the general problems raised in this chapter see the articles by C. L. H. Coulson, E. M. Hallam, K. F. Werner, T. N. Bisson and J. Yver cited in 'Notes and further reading'.

The standard works on Burgundy are M. Chaume, *Les origines du duché de Bourgogne*, i (Dijon, 1925); J. Richard, *Les ducs de Bourgogne et la formation du duché . . .* (Paris, 1954). Richard's article 'Châteaux, châtelains et vassaux en Bourgogne aux XIe et XIIe siècle', *Cahiers de Civilisation Médiévale*, iii (1960), 433–47, is also valuable.

Professor Duby's research on the Mâconnais is summarised in *Lordship and Community* (see n. 1): the original version is G. Duby, *La Société aux XIe et XIIe siècles dans la région Mâconnaise*, 2nd edn (Paris, 1971), which is highly recommended.

In addition to the works on Normandy by J. le Patourel, D. C. Douglas, R. W. Hollister and J. Yver, cited in 'Notes and further reading', see J. le Patourel, 'Norman kings or Norman "king-dukes"', *Droit privé et institutions régionales, études historiques offerts à J. Yver* (Paris, 1976), 469–79, and K. F. Werner, 'Quelques observations au sujet des débuts du "duché" de Normandie', *ibid.*, 691–709, for some recent research on the duchy.

L. Musset has produced numerous valuable articles; see, for example, 'Les destins de la propriété monastique . . . IXe–XIe siècle', *Jumièges* (Rouen, 1955), 49–55. See also M. de Bouard, 'De la neustrie Carolingienne à la Normandie féodale', *Bulletin of the Institute of Historical Research*, xxviii (1955), 1–14; R. A. Brown, *The Normans and the Norman Conquest* (1969); D. C. Douglas, *The Norman Achievement* (1969), among a host of useful works on the subject. The research of Dr Bates, shortly to be published, will make an important contribution.

A major and detailed piece of research on the county of Champagne is M. Bur, *La Formation du comté de Champagne, v. 950 – V. 1150* (Nancy, 1977). Other recent work on Blois-Champagne includes A. Chédeville, *Chartres et ses campagnes, XI–XIIIe siècles* (Paris, 1973), and T. Evergates, *Feudal Society in the Bailliage of Troyes under the Counts of Champagne, 1152–1284* (Baltimore, 1975); the last is heavily overburdened with statistics. A useful account of Odo II is L. Lex, 'Eudes comte de Blois (997–1037) et Thibaud son frère', *Mémoires de la société academique . . . de l'Aube*, 3rd ser., xxviii (1891), 197–383.

A useful account of the history of Flanders is F. L. Ganshof, *La Flandre sous les premiers comtes* (Brussels, 1949), while a detailed study by E. Warlop, *The Flemish Nobility before 1300,* 4 vols (Kortrijk, 1975) is also of value. An interesting administrative study is R. Monier, *Les Institutions centrales du comté de Flandre . . . à 1384* (Paris, 1943). R. Fossier, *La Terre et les hommes en Picardie jusqu'à la fin du XIIIe siècle*, 2 vols (Louvain, 1965), is a monumental work, of major importance. Early Brittany is usefully, though far less fully covered in J. Delumeau, *Histoire de la Bretagne* (Toulouse, 1969), 117–215.

On Anjou, see Southern, (n. 18), and the work by O. Guillot, *Le Comte d'Anjou et son entourage au XIᵉ siècle*, 2 vols (Paris, 1972), which supplants to some degree the older L. Halphen, *Le Comté d'Anjou au XIᵉ siècle* (Paris, 1902). The most useful account of Aquitaine is the unpublished Oxford D. Phil. thesis by J. Martindale, 'The Origins of the Duchy of Aquitaine and the Government of the Counts of Poitou (902–1137)', 1964, which should replace A. Richard, *Histoire des comtes de Poitou, 778–1204*, 2 vols (Paris, 1903). An important study of Berry has appeared by G. Devailly, *Le Berry du Xᵉ siècle jusqu' au milieu du XIIᵉ siècle* . . . (Paris, 1973), and on the castellans of Poitou, see Beech (*op. cit.*, p. 63) and R. Hajdu, 'Castles, castellans and the structure of politics in poitou, 1152–71', *JMH*, iv (1978), 27–53, and J. Gillingham, *op. cit.*, Ch. 4, n. 18–19.

A. R. Lewis's account of the Languedoc (*op. cit.*, p. 63) gives a good background to the political events of the period, discussed by d'Abadal i de Vinyals and Hignounet (*op. cit.*, n. 24). Three major monographs on southern society, all of great value, have recently appeared. They are by Magnou-Nortier on Toulouse (n. 21), J. P. Poly on Provence (n. 26) and P. Bonnassie on Catalonia (n. 27). W. L. Wakefield, *Heresy, Crusade and Inquisition in Southern France, 1100–1250* (1974) is also recommended.

It will be seen that there is still great scope for further research in French regional history. Many of the general works cited above contain useful, more detailed bibliographies.

Chapter 3. The early Capetians, 987–1108

On the similarities between the king and the princes see some of the works cited in the Notes and further reading for Chapter 2. On the cult of kingship see Bloch (*op. cit.*, p. 110), J. F. Lemarignier, *La France Médiévale* . . . (Paris, 1970), 191–96, and the useful account of coronations in C. N. L. Brooke, *The Saxon and Norman Kings* (1963), 32–8. F. Behrends, 'Kingship and feudalism according to Fulbert of Chartres', *Medieval Studies*, xxv (1963), 93–9, and Lewis (*op. cit.* n. 3) are also useful, and background is provided by Dumas (*op. cit.*, n. 45), and J. Dhondt, 'Élection et héredité sous les Carolingiens et premiers Capétiens', *Revue Belge de Philologie et d'Histoire*, xviii (1939), 913–53.

J. F. Lemarignier's study of royal government (*op. cit.*, n. 14), is essential reading; see also his 'Autour de la royauté française du IXᵉ au XIIIᵉ siècles', *Bibl. EC*, cxiii (1956), 5–36. W. M. Newman's *The Kings, the Court and the Royal Power in France in the Eleventh Century* (Toulouse, 1929), is a rather rare but quite interesting account of the kings, most of whom are also covered more fully in the monographs by Lot (*op. cit.*, n. 7), Pfister (*op. cit.*, n. 23) and A. Fliche, *Le Règne de Philippe Iᵉʳ roi de France (1060–1108)* (Paris, 1912). On Henry I see Dhondt (*op. cit.*, n. 14), and other articles by the same writer, including 'Une crise de pouvoir Capétien, 1032–34', in *Miscellanea* . . . *J. F. Niermayer* (Groningen, 1967), 137–48, and 'Henri Iᵉʳ, l'Église et l'Anjou', *Revue Belge de Philologie et d'Histoire*, xxv (1947), 87–109. Duby's *Medieval Marriage* (*op. cit.*, n. 20) is of great value for

Philip I's liaison with Bertrada.

On the royal domain, Newman (*op. cit.*, n. 21) is essential, and Brühl (*op. cit.*, n. 31) is very useful on royal resources. Duby's essay on judicial institutions (*op. cit.*, n. 22) is a useful introduction in English. See also *HIFr.*, ii, *passim.* On the royal principality in this period, there is a useful section in M. Mollat, ed., *Histoire de l'Ile de France et de Paris* (Toulouse, 1971). G. Fourquin, *Les Campagnes de la région parisienne à la fin du moyen age* (Paris, 1964), has a little on this as yet rather understudied region in the eleventh century. On the royal entourage Lemarignier's *Le Gouvernement royal* (*op. cit.*, n. 14), is essential, and see his 'Les fidèles' (*op. cit.*, Ch. 1 bibl. above), and F. L. Ganshof, 'L'entourage des premiers Capétiens', *Revue Historique de Droit Français et Étranger*, xliv (1968), 263–74. On the links of the king and the princes see Lemarignier (*op. cit.*, n. 36), and Lot (*op. cit.*, n. 33), and the bibliography to Chapter 2. Boussard (*op. cit.*, n. 41) is important on military service paid to the king.

On the political significance of royal patronage of monasteries, see Lemarignier (*op. cit.*, nn. 37 and 48). Motte-Collas's study (*op. cit.*, n. 25) is also very interesting. Among the host of books on the Cluniacs, N. Hunt, *Cluny under Saint Hugh, 1049–1109* (1967) is a good recent study. On canons regular, C. Dereine, 'Chanoines', *Dictionnaire d'Histoire et de Géographie Ecclésiastique*, xii (1953), 353–405 is a useful summary. For the background to the monastic orders see Brooke and Swaan (*op. cit.*, n. 47), and more generally, see R. W. Southern, *Western Society and the Church in the Middle Ages* (Penguin, 1970); Tierney (*op. cit.*, n. 52); and ed. K. M. Setton *et al.*, *A History of the Crusades*, i (Philadelphia, 1955), all with suggestions for further reading.

Chapter 4. The revival of royal power, 1108–1226

On the kings and their reigns see the monographs by Luchaire (n. 2), Pacaut (n. 10), Cartellieri (n. 15) and Petit-Dutaillis (n. 23). Cartellieri's account of the early years of Philip's reign has been translated into French as 'L'avènement de Philippe Auguste', *Le Moyen Âge*, lii (1946), 241–58; liii (1947), 261–79; liv (1948), 1–33. On the expansion of the royal lands, see C. Petit-Dutaillis, *Le Déshéritement de Jean-sans-terre* . . . (Paris, 1925) and L. L. Borrelli de Serres, *La réunion des provinces septentrionales à la Couronne* (Paris, 1899).

In addition to the general works on French society cited above, Petit-Dutaillis (n. 26) on the French communes, and Brooke and Swaan, Southern, and Knowles (all n. 34) on monasticism are all important. On heresy, see the works by Lambert and Moore (both n. 43) and M. Roquebert, *L'Épopée Cathare, 1198–1212: l'invasion* (Toulouse, 1970). On learning, see Brooke (*op. cit.*, n. 45), and the older classic, C. H. Haskins, *The Renaissance of the Twelfth Century* (repr. Cleveland/New York, 1957). On Paris, Boussard (*op. cit.*, n. 31) is useful and interesting.

For the royal principality and domain, see Mollat and Fourquin *ut supra*. *HIFr*, ii and Luchaire, *Manuel des Institutions* (*op. cit.*, n. 76) are essential works on the royal administration. Bournazel (*op. cit.*, n. 53) is a fairly useful continuation of Lemarignier's *Gouvernement royal* (*op. cit.*, Ch. 3, n. 14), and for Philip Augustus's administration, see Hollister and Baldwin (*op. cit.,* n. 49). G. Tessier, 'L'enregistrement à la chancellerie royale française . . .', *Le Moyen Âge*, lii (1956), 39–62, explains the use of royal registers. On the royal army, see the works by Boussard (n. 56) and Audouin (n. 57), and C. Stephenson, 'Les "aides" des villes françaises aux XIIᵉ et XIIIᵉ siècles', *Le Moyen Âge*, xxxiii (1922), 274–328. The main works on royal finances by Lot and Fawtier, Pacaut, Benton and Lyon and Verhulst are cited in the notes. On the king's feudal powers, see L. Halphen, 'La place de la royauté dans le système féodale', *Revue Historique*, clxxii (1933), 249–56, and Lot, *Fidèles ou Vassaux? (op. cit.*, Ch. 3). The article by Barroux (n. 85) is a useful case study, while a valuable recent survey is given by Bisson (*op. cit.*, Ch. 3).

Much important work on the 'image' of monarchy has been done by G. M. Spiegel (nn. 87, 91, 93). Panofsky's *Abbot Suger (op. cit.*, n. 81), Van de Kieft (n. 87), Bédier (n. 88) and Folz (n. 90) are all useful, while Duby's work on the impact of Bouvines (n. 22) is highly recommended. On the French kingdom, see Guenée (n. 92), and C. T. Wood, *"Regnum Francie'* . . . .', *Traditio*, xxiii (1967), 117–47.

The classic study of the collapse of the Plantagenet lands is Powicke (n. 69). Holt and Gillingham (n. 18, 67) both have useful and important things to say on this problematical issue. On the Angevin administration, see Boussard (n. 96) and Warren (n. 17). More generally, see Y. Rénouard, 'Le rôle de l'Empire Angevine dans la formation de la France', *Revue Historique*, cxcv (1945), 289–304, and J. le Patourel, 'The Norman conquest, 1066, 1106, 1154', *Proceedings of the Battle Conference on Anglo-Norman Studies, I, 1978*, ed. R. A. Brown (Ipswich, 1979), 103–20. On the aftermath of the conquest, see Stevenson (n. 103), and the works cited below on Normandy under Louis IX.

On the Albigensian crusade, P. Belperron, *La Croisade contre les Albigeois et l'union du Languedoc à la France* (Paris, 1942), is now rather oldfashioned. See Wakefield (*op. cit.*, Ch. 2), and in particular J. Sumption, *The Albigensian Crusade* (1978).

On the kings and the church, see *HIFr.*, iii and the relevant sections of the general monographs cited above. On episcopal elections, see Imbart de la Tour and Pacaut (n. 109), and on royal patronage of monasteries, Hallam (n. 107).

Chapter 5. Louis IX: The consolidation of royal power, 1226–70

The fullest monograph on the reign of Louis IX is still Le Nain de Tillemont (*op. cit.*, n. 10), which is not only wideranging, but drew on certain documentary evidence which has now been lost. See also Labarge's and Pernoud's studies of Louis and of Blanche of Castile (n. 10). Wallon (*op. cit.*, n. 19) is quite useful and so is Boutaric on Margaret of Provence (*op. cit.*, n. 21) and on Alfonso of Poitiers (*op. cit.*, n. 57). The colloquium published to celebrate Louis's seven-hundredth anniversary (*op. cit.*, n. 20), contains a number of useful essays, and Strayer's article on Louis IX's crusades (n. 15) is of considerable value. For a good outline of the activities of Charles of Anjou, see S. Runciman, *The Sicilian Vespers* (Cambridge, 1958).

On the social and economic background see Fourquin (*op cit.*, n. 22) and Cazelles (*op. cit.*, n. 24) for the Paris region. For the religious background see Southern (*op. cit.*, Ch. 4), while the Béguines are usefully discussed by Bolton (*op. cit.*, n. 28), and the friars by Brooke (n. 26), Moorman (n. 26) and Emery (n. 27), among a number of valuable works. On the inquisition see Wakefield (*op. cit.*, n. 29), Lambert (*op. cit.*, n. 30) and C. H. Haskins, 'Robert le Bougre and the beginnings of the inquisition in Northern France', *Studies in Medieval Culture* (New York, 1929).

On Louis IX's piety, see Labande (*op. cit.*, n. 7), and O'Connell (*op. cit.*, n. 32). On his monastic patronage, Hallam (*op. cit.*, n. 33), A. Dimier, *Saint Louis et Cîteaux* (Paris, 1954), and Little (*op. cit.*, n. 38). Branner's work on the court style is useful and interesting (*op. cit.*, n. 60). Louis's relations with the papacy are discussed in E. Berger, *Saint Louis et Innocent IV* (Paris, 1893), and see Watt (*op. cit.*, n. 39). G. J. Campbell, 'The attitude of the monarchy towards the use of ecclesiastical censures in the reign of Saint Louis', *Speculum*, xxxv (1960), 535–55 is also recommended.

On government and administration, see *HIFr.*, ii and de Wailly (*op. cit.*, n. 42). Strayer (*op. cit.*, n. 51) is useful on Norman administration, and Wood (n. 48) and Lewis (n. 49) are essential reading on the domain and the apanages. On Louis's rôle as an arbiter see the works by Wood and Treharne (n. 64), and on the annexation of Languedoc, P. Timbal, *Un Conflit d'annexation: l'application de la coutûme de Paris au pays d'Albigeois* (Toulouse, 1950). Much useful research has been done on Gascony, amongst which the works by Chaplais and Trabut-Cussac (n. 72) are of particular value. On the French kingdom, see Guenée (*op. cit.*, n. 66).

Chapter 6. The last Capetians, 1270–1328

The general political background for the later Capetians is well covered in Langlois (*op. cit.*, n. 7). On individual reigns see the works by Langlois (n. 1), Boutaric (n. 6) and Lehugeur (n. 18). A vast amount of research has been done on Philip IV, his reign and his councillors. The recent account of Philip by Favier (*op. cit.*, n. 6) makes an important contribution but unfortunately lacks documentation. Favier's work on Enguerrand de Marigny (n. 42) and his article on the lawyers (n. 13) are also important. On Philip and the problems of interpreting his character, see the articles by Strayer and Lyon (n. 13); H. Finke, 'Zur charakteristik Philipps des Schönen', *Mitteilungen des Instituts fur österreichische Geschichtsforschung*, xxvi (1904), 201–24; and most recently the useful article by Bautier (*op. cit.*, n. 10). Also see Brown (*op. cit.*, n. 11), and Baudon de Mony (*op. cit.*, n. 17). On the royal councillors Pegues (*op. cit.*, n. 39) is solid but somewhat limited. MacNamara (n. 41), R. Holzmann, *Wilhelm von Nogaret, Rat und Grossiegel bewahrer Philipps des Schönen von Frankreich* (Fribourg, 1898), and Petit 'n. 15) are useful on individual members of the royal council. The emergence of parties at court is covered in Cazelles (*op. cit.*, n. 43).

On social and economic developments, the works by Duby and Perroy (both n. 20) and Lucas (n. 21) are useful on the crises of the early fourteenth century.

On the problems of quantitative history, see works by Floud and Ladurie (*op. cit.*, n. 24); and on the population of France and of Paris, Lot (n. 23), Dollinger (n. 29) and Cazelles (n. 30) are all important. Le Roi Ladurie's study of Montaillou (n. 31) is an abridged version of the French edition, *Montaillou, village occitan de 1294 à 1324* (Paris, 1975) which is also recommended. Rozoginsky's study of ennoblement by the crown (n. 34) is a useful account.

On royal administration, see *HIFr.*, ii; the works by Strayer (nn. 44, 45), and the article by T. N. Bisson, 'Consultative functions in the king's parlements, 1250–1314', *Speculum*, xliv (1969), 353–73. Henneman (*op. cit.*, n. 36) is valuable on royal finances, and see also Taylor (*op. cit.*, n. 53), Strayer and Taylor (*op. cit.*, n. 55), and on the coinage, Borelli de Serres and Grunzweig (n. 37).

On royal authority in the apanages and the great fiefs, see the works cited in notes 46–49, and Chaplais (*op. cit.*, n. 50). On assemblies, see Langmuir's article (cited in n. 51), the monograph by Bisson (n. 54), and the works on royal finance cited above. On the reaction of 1314–15 see Artonne (*op. cit.*, n. 56). Wood (*op. cit.*, Ch. 5), covers the later stages of the reaction well. There are several articles by Strayer (nn. 62–65) on changing ideas about the French kingdom, and see also B. Guenée, 'État et nation en France au moyen âge', *Revue Historique*, ccxxxvii (1967), 17–30. Le Patourel (*op. cit.*, n. 58) is an important analysis of central and regional authority. There is a useful article on amortisation by G. Sautel, 'Note sur la formation du droit royal d'amortissement', *Études . . . G. le Bras* (Paris, 1965), 689–704. On Philip IV and the cult of Louis IX see the works cited in note 68 and also Bautier (*op. cit.*, n. 10). On Philip IV and Boniface VIII see Boase (*op. cit.*, n. 73); the classic work by Dupuy (n. 9); G. Digard, *Philippe le Bel et le Saint Siège de 1285 à 1304*, 2 vols (Paris, 1936); and ed. C. T. Wood, *Philip the Fair and Boniface VIII*, 2nd edn (New York, 1971). On the suppression of the Templars, Barber (*op. cit.*, n. 9), is a must, and see also Cohn (*op. cit.*, n. 75). Rénouard's account of the Avignon papacy (n. 77) is a useful one.

Chapter 7. Conclusion

On the succession, see E. Perroy, *The Hundred Years War*, trans. W. B. Wells (London, 1965); Cazelles (*op. cit.*, Ch. 6, n. 43); and Le Patourel (*op. cit.*, Ch. 6, n. 58); Wood's article (Ch. 6, n. 16), is also useful.

Index

Note: *People identified by a title are indexed in the alphabetical sequence of their titles, e.g.* : Eleanor [of England] countess of Leicester *before* Eleanor [of Champagne] countess of Vermandois; John, bishop of Orleans *before* John of Chalon, count of Auxerre.

Abbreviations used: abss, abbess; abt, abbot; arbp, archbishop; bp, bishop; ct, count; ctss, countess; d., duke; dss, duchess; k., king; ld, lord; p., pope; q., queen; vct, viscount.

Aachen, 176–7
Abbeville, 142
Abbo, abt of Fleury, 65, 94
Adalbero, arbp of Reims, 21–4, 68, 92, 99
Adalbero, bp of Laon, 67–70, 100, 102
Adela, ctss of Blois, 48
Adela [of France] ctss of Flanders, 50, 72, 82
Adela [of Champagne] q. of France, 50, 120, 125, 128, 135, 159, 170, 177, 196
Adela [of Maurienne] q. of France, 114, 191
Adhémar, bp of Le Puy, 105
Adhémar of Chabannes, 11, 19, 70
administration, royal, 85–6, 91–4, 154, 159–61, 239–47, 251–7, 291–7
   see also court, royal; entourage, royal; finances, royal; household, royal; justice, royal; records, royal
Adolf of Nassau, 280
Adrian IV, p., 194
Agapitus II, p., 21
Agatha Trussebut, 254
Agde, bishopric, 158
Agenais, 213, 258–9, 267, 276
Agnes [of Méran] q. of France, 126, 196, 198, 207, 250
Agnes [of France], 222
agriculture, 11–12, 137–9, 224–5
   improved techniques, 224, 285–6
   see also peasants

aids, feudal, 15–16, 164–5, 293
Aigues-Mortes, 216, 222, 247
Aimon II Vaire-Vache, ld of Bourbon, 117, 172
Alberic, abt of Cîteaux, 146
Albert, ct of Vermandois, 45
Albertus Magnus, 228
Albi and the Albigeois, 255, 257, 258–9
   bishop, 57, 152
Albigensian crusade, 54, 133–6, 151, 197, 227
   effects, 256–7
Albizzo Franzesi, 298
Albon, 33
Albret, 59
Alençon, 159, 186, 248, 250, 287
   count, *see* Peter
Alexander III, p., 125, 152, 194–5
Alexander IV, p., 229–30, 238
Alexander of Hales, 228–9
Alfonso, ct of Poitou and Toulouse, 54, 188–90, 209–10, 214, 218, 223, 232, 240, 246, 248–51, 255, 257–60, 276, 299
   administration and character, 257–60
Alfonso, ct of Provence, 62
Alfonso Jordan, ct of Toulouse, 60–1
Alfonso II, k. of Aragon, ct of Barcelona, 61–2

Alfonso VIII, k. of Castile, 260, 279
Alfonso X, k. of Castile, 267, 277
Alice, ctss of Britanny, 52, 184, 250
Alice, ctss of Eu, 185
Alice [of Holland] ctss of Hainault, 218–19
Alice, q. of Cyprus, 210
Alice of Dreux, 209
Alice of France, 126, 128–9
allods, 12, 55–6
Amaury, bp of Clermont, 117
Amaury [de Montfort] ct of Toulouse, 136, 189, 209, 211
Amaury [of Thouars] seneschal of Poitou, 131, 136, 187–8
Amaury, vct of Narbonne, 213
Amaury de Montfort, 220
Amboise, 52
Amiens, 51, 89, 142, 158, 162, 261
    bishopric, 86
    county, 116, 127–30
    mise, 219–20, 262, 268
    treaty, 276
amortisation, 297, 310
Ampurias-Roussillon, county, 54
Anacletus II, anti-p., 172, 193–4
Anagni, 282, 316
    peace, 279
Anastasius IV, p., 194
Ancenis, 210
André of Fleury, 68
André of Vitré, 210
Angers, 8, 210
    Saint-Serge, 102
Angevin 'empire', 120, 179–82
Anglo-Norman 'realm', 42
Anglo-Saxon chronicle, 40
Angoulême, 8, 53, 183, 287
    counts, see Charles; Hugh
    countess, see Isabella
Anizy-le-Château, 162
Anjou, county and counts, 10, 12–14, 17, 38, 52–3, 89, 94, 96, 117, 131, 157, 171, 180–7, 203, 223, 248, 250, 267; see also Charles; Fulk; Geoffrey; Henry; Richard
    countesses, see Beatrice; Bertrada; Margaret; Matilda
    early history, 52–3
Anne [of Kiev] q. of France, 72–3
Anseau de Garlande, 116, 159

Anselm [of Bec] arbp of Canterbury, 106, 153
Anselm of Reims, 104
apanages, 190, 247–51, 299–300
    see also domain
Aquitaine, duchy, 1, 6, 10, 13, 19, 23, 53–4, 94, 128, 130–1, 157, 164, 170–1, 180–2, 184–7, 265
    dukes, see Henry; John; Richard; William
    duchesses, see Brisca; Eleanor; Philippa
    early history, 53–4
    see also Gascony; Poitou
Aragon, kingdom, 258, 277
    kings, see Alfonso; James; Peter
    queen, see Constance
Archambaud, arbp of Tours, 71
Archambaud, ld of Bourbon, 117, 173
Archambaud, ld of Bourbon, 210, 258
Archambaud, sub-dean of Orleans, 115
architecture
    Cistercian, 147, 232, 260–1
    court style, 260–3, 312, 329
    Gothic, 144, 174–5, 226, 234–5, 257, 260–3, 313, 329
    Norman, 39
    northern French, 88, 260–3
    southern French, 57, 155, 257
Arcis-sur-Aube, 89
Argentan, 184
Argenteuil, 83
Argonne, 48
Aristotle, 145, 153, 155
Arles, 57, 71
Arleux, 219
armies, royal, 97–9, 161–3, 207–8, 247, 281
    see also communes; footsoldiers; knights; mercenary troops; military service
Arnaud, abt of Saint-Pierre-le-Vif at Sens, 192
Arnulf, arbp of Reims, 68–9, 99–100
Arnulf, bp of Orléans, 68, 100
Arnulf II, ct of Flanders, 71
Arnulf of Flanders, 50
Arques
    counts, 38, 74
    peace, 285
Arras, 49, 107, 163, 192–3
    bishopric, 158, 192
art, French, 143, 152–5, 257, 329
    Cistercian, 147, 232, 260–1

illuminated manuscripts, 88, 260, 313, 329
see also architecture
Arthur, ct of Brittany, 52, 130–1, 172
Artois, 127, 130, 158, 162, 248, 250, 283–4, 287
counts and countesses, *see* Mahaut; Robert
revolt in 1314–18, 304–6
assemblies, general and regional, 302–4
Assisi, 152, 197, 226–7, 321
Athies, 162
Attigny, 48, 88
Atuyer, 32
Aubri of Trois-Fontaines, 160
Augustine, saint, 105
Augustinian (Austin) canons, *see* canons
Aunis, 258
Ausculta fili, 315
Austin friars, 227
Autun, 30–2, 153, 196, 304
bishops, 32, 158
Saint-Symphorien, 93
Auvergne, counts and county, 13, 53, 94, 96, 128, 131, 170, 173, 194, 248, 258–9
see also William
Auvillars, 299
Auxerre, 30–1, 33, 72
bishopric and bishops, 86, 198; *see also* Hugh; Peter
count, *see* John
Saint-Germain, 70, 102
auxilium, *see* aid
Avallon, 31, 72, 304
Averroës, 153
Avignon, 57, 136, 189, 218
papal residence at, 282, 320–1
Avranches, 35, 184
Aymard, abt of Cluny, 101

baillis, bailliages, 150, 157, 239–40
Baldwin I, ct of Flanders, 50
Baldwin IV, ct of Flanders, 50, 71–3
Baldwin V, ct of Flanders, regent of France, 38, 50, 72, 76, 96, 118
Baldwin VI, ct of Flanders, 50, 76
Baldwin VII, ct of Flanders, 169
Baldwin VIII, ct of Flanders, 129, 169
Baldwin, ct of Hainault, 51
Baldwin V, ct of Hainault, 127

Baldwin IX, emperor of Constantinople, ct of Flanders, 129–31, 145, 170
bannal lordship, 12, 14–18, 138–9, 224
Bapaume, 162
Barbeaux, abbey, 127, 147, 195
Barcelona, county (Spanish March), 13, 54–62, 94, 170, 221
counts and countesses, *see* Alfonso; Berengar-Raymond; Borel; Peter; Petronilla; Raymond-Berengar
see also Aragon, kings
Barfleur, 186
barones, 172–3, 245
see also princes
Bar-sur-Aube, 48–9, 51, 279, 287, 300
Bartholomew [de Vir] bp of Laon, 191
Bartholomew of Roye, 161, 208
Basques, 4
Baudri [of Bourgueil] bp of Dol, 154
Baugé, 223
Bayeux
bishop, *see* Odo
tapestry, 40
Bayonne, 59, 267, 280
Béarn, principality, 59, 61, 302, 307
Beatrice, q. of Sicily, ctss of Provence and Anjou, 215, 223, 256
Beatrice de Planissoles, 289–90
Beaucaire, 159, 209, 254, 257
sénéchausée, 256
Beauce, 90
Beaufort, 223
Beaugency, 77, 123, 172, 299
Beaujeu, 34
Beaujolais, 307
Beaumont, 32
Beaumont-sur-Oise, 89–90, 116, 159, 207
Beaune, 31
Beauvais, 82, 89–90, 162–3, 172, 196, 304
bishopric and bishops, 86, 99, 106–7, 207, 237; *see also* Guy; Milo
count, *see* Hugh
Saint-Barthelémy, 105
Saint-Quentin, 150
Bec, abbey, 106, 153
Béguines, 226, 228
Bellême, 37, 89, 209–10
Benedict VIII, p., 102
Benedict XI, p., 311
Benedict XII, p., *see* Jacques Fournier

Benedictine monks, 87–8, 100, 105, 146, 158–9, 317
  royal rights over Benedictine abbeys, 87–8, 100
  see also Rule of Saint Benedict
benefices, see fiefs
Berengar, arbp of Narbonne, 58
Berengaria [of Navarre] q. of England, 128
Berengar-Raymond II, ct of Barcelona, 61
Berengar-Raymond, ct of Provence, 61
Bernard, abt of Clairvaux (Saint Bernard), 115, 121–3, 146–7, 149, 175, 191–5
Bernard, abt of Tiron, 147
Bernard Saisset, bp of Pamiers, 278, 282, 308, 311, 314–15
Bernard of Caux, 229
Bernard of Chartres, 153
Bernard Clergue, 289–90
Bernard Délicieux, 311
Bernard of Prim, 152
Bernard-Oth de Niort, 255
Berno of Baume, 101
Berry, 14, 27, 53, 86, 117, 128, 130, 157, 180, 183
  see also Bourges
Bertha, q. of France, ctss of Blois, 45, 69–71
Bertha [of Holland] q. of France, 76–7, 82
Bertha of Burgundy, 47
Bertrada de Montfort, q. of France, ctss of Anjou, 75–7, 84, 91, 106
Bertran de Born, 127
Bertrand, ct of Toulouse, 60
Bessin, 34, 37
Béthisy, 73
Béthune, 281
Beynes, 88
Béziers, 55, 199
Bichereaux, 158
Bigorre, 61
biographies, royal, see Helgaud of Fleury; John, ld of Joinville; Suger
bishops, French, 2–3, 64–7, 86–8, 92–3, 99–100, 102–3, 105–7, 141, 192–9, 236–9, 253, 310–12
  royal investiture of, 105–7, 190, 192–5
  see also church, French
Black Death, 285–6
Blaisy, 31
Blanche [of Burgundy] ctss of La Marche, 282, 284

Blanche [of France] q. of Castile, 222, 277, 312
Blanche [of Castile] q. of France, 130, 183, 199, 206–14, 217–18, 228, 237, 257, 260, 327
  character and achievements, 207–14
Blanche, q. of Navarre, ctss of Champagne, 50, 170
Blanche [of Artois] q. of Navarre, 276
Blaye, 213
Bléron, 198
Blois, county and counts, 13–14, 30, 43–50, 94–9, 170, 210–11, 287; see also Odo; Stephen-Henry; Theobald
  countesses, see Adela; Bertha; Matilda
  formation of county, 43–50
  see also Champagne; Troyes
Boësses, 157
Bogomilism, 151
Bohemond, prince of Antioch, 39, 105
Bois-de-Boulogne, 83
Bois-de-Vincennes, 83
Bois-Girard, 161
Bologna, 155, 321
Bologne, 257
Bonaventura, Saint, 228, 234
Boniface VIII, p., 279–80, 282, 298, 302, 309, 312–17
bordages, 12
Bordeaux, 8, 213, 267
Borel, ct of Barcelona, 68
Bouchard [the Venerable] ct of Vendôme, 90
Bouchard of Avesnes, 216
Bouchard of Montmorency, 99
Boulogne, 158, 183
  counts, see Philip; Renard
Bourbon, 89, 117, 173, 250, 287, 299
  lords, see Aimon; Archambaud
Bourbonne-Chantemerle, 290
Bourges, 126, 157–8, 163, 189, 194
  archbishopric and archbishops, 86, 122, 194; see also Gauzlin; Peter
  viscounty, 78, 82, 89; see also Odo
Bouvines, battle, 132–3, 135, 178–9, 198
Boves, 116
  treaty, 158
Brabant, 163
Brémule, 118
Breteuil, 89
Brie, county, 279, 299

Brisca [of Gascony] dss of Aquitaine, 53
Brittany, 4, 12–13, 23, 38, 52, 76, 94, 117,
    128, 131, 168–9, 180–3, 210, 265,
    287, 301, 306–7
    counts and dukes, *see* Arthur; Conan;
        Erispoé; Geoffrey; John; Nominoé;
        Peter
    countesses and duchesses, *see* Alice;
        Constance; Mary
    early history, 52
Broyes, 49
Bruges, 51, 118, 281, 285
    Matins, 281
    Saint-Donatien, 118
    see also Galbert
Bruno of Reims, 146, 149
Bucy-le-Long, 151
burgesses, 97–8, 140–2, 160, 224–5, 245
    grants of burgess status, 290
    see also communes
Burgundy, county (*Franche Comté*), 30, 229,
    300
Burgundy, duchy and dukes, 4, 6, 8, 12–14,
    19, 21, 29–33, 73, 82, 84–5, 131,
    133, 142, 155, 169–70, 173, 215,
    265, 287, 300, 304–5, 307, 329; *see
    also* Henry; Hugh; Odo; Odo-
    William; Richard; Robert
    disintegration, 30–3
    duchesses, *see* Joan; Mahaut
    league, 304–5
Burgundy, kingdom, 30, 47, 54
    kings, *see* Conrad; Rudolph
Byzantine empire, *see* Constantinople

Cadoc, 163
Cadurc, 121, 194
Caen, 8, 184, 186
Cahors, 267
Calixtus II, p., 118, 148, 193
Cambrai, 49, 107, 193
canons, secular and regular (Augustinian or
    Austin), 104–5, 148–9
    see also Prémontré; Saint-Victor
Capetian kings
    accession in 987, 20–4
    origins of name, 330–1
    see also France; Francia; monarchy, French;
        Robertines
Cappi, 162

Carcassonne, 57, 61, 152, 199, 209, 212,
    221, 234, 311
    counts, 59, 159; *see also* Raymond
    sénéchausée, 256
Carmelite friars, 227
Carolingian empire and emperors, 1–7, 18; *see
    also* Charlemagne; Louis the Pious
Carolingian kings, 4–5, 7, 10, 13, 15, 20–4,
    29, 54, 89, 91, 175, 261
Carolingian nobility, 10, 20–4
Carthusian order, 148–9, 226
    see also La Grande-Chartreuse
Cassel, 132, 281
    battle, 76
castellanies, castellans, 13–14, 32–4, 93
    see also bannal lordship; castles
Castile, kingdom, 277
    kings, *see* Alfonso; Sancho
    queens, *see* Blanche; Joan
Castillon, 59
castles, 163, 239
    control or rendability, 25–6, 28, 83,
        98–9
    design, 97
Catalonia, 54–62
Cathar heresy, 58–9, 133, 151, 227, 255–6,
    289–90
Catherine Courtenay, ctss of Valois, 280
Celestine II, p., 122, 194
Celestine III, p., 196
Celestine IV, p., 214
Celestine V, p., 313, 317
Celestine hermits, 283
cens, 83, 225
Châalis, abbey, 191
Chablis, 141
Chaillot, 144
Châlons-sur-Marne, 92, 99, 157, 172
    bishopric and bishops, 48, 86, 88; *see also*
        Peter; William
    Saint-Père, 73
Chalon-sur-Saône, 31
    bishopric, 86
Chambly, 90, 276
Chambon, 157
chambre aux deniers, 292, 299
chambre des comptes, 231, 240–2, 245, 287,
    295–6, 298
    party, 298–9
chambres des enquêtes, 296

chambre des requêtes, 296

Champagne, county and counts, 30, 43–50, 94–9, 121, 139, 142, 157, 162, 170, 189–90, 206, 209–10, 215, 230, 265, 276–7, 279, 299–300, 304, 325; see also Henry; Theobald
  countesses, see Blanche; Margaret
  formation of principality, 43–50
  see also Blois

champart, 83, 225

Champtoceaux, 210

Channel Islands, 184

Chanson de Roland, 154, 172, 176

Chansons de geste, 176–7

Chantilly-Hermenonville, forest, 83

Chappes, 48

Charlemagne, emperor, 4, 7, 86, 100, 118, 127, 135, 172
  cult, 66, 135, 174–9, 261, 275

Charles [the Good] ct of Flanders, 16, 51, 118–19, 168–9, 191

Charles, ct of Valois, Anjou and Maine, 250, 277, 279–80, 283–5, 297–8

Charles, d. of Lorraine, 22–4, 68–9, 100, 135

Charles [the Simple] k. of France, 8, 34

Charles IV, k. of France, ct of La Marche and Angoulême, 250, 282, 284–5, 325
  character and reign, 284–5

Charles V, k. of France, 284

Charles VI, k. of France, 305

Charles VII, k. of France, 238

Charles, k. of Naples, 279, 321

Charles [the Bad] k. of Navarre, 325–6

Charles [of Anjou] k. of Sicily, ct of Anjou and Provence, 190, 215, 218–19, 221–3, 236, 238–40, 242, 244, 248–51, 256, 269, 276–7, 297

Charles the Bald, 50

Charroux, 19, 150

charters, 154
  forged, 154
  granted to provincial leagues, 305–6
  royal, 91–4, 154
  see also records, royal

Chartres and the Chartrain, 10, 45, 102–3, 116, 119, 198, 211, 299, 310
  bishopric and bishops, 86, 103, 107, 116, 196, 207; see also Fulbert; Ivo; John
  canons, 99

Château Gaillard, 129, 131, 163, 184

Chateaudun, 45, 211
  viscount, see Geoffrey

Châteaufort, 157, 194

Châteaulandon, 195

Châteauneuf, 157

Châteaurenard, 157

Châteauroux, 128

Châtillon, 31

Châtillon-sur-Marne, 195–6

Châtrais, 88

Chaumont-en-Vexin, 82, 158, 162, 191

Chauvigny, 183

Chelles, synod, 69

Chevreuse, 157

Chinon, 132, 182, 212

chivalry, cult of, 139, 328

Choisy-au-Bac, 158, 198

Chrétien de Troyes, 154

chrism, 66

church, French, 2–3, 18–20, 64–6, 86–8, 99–108, 158–9, 190–9, 230–9, 281–3, 305, 310–21
  and French kings, 19, 99–108, 125–6, 190–9, 230–9, 281–3, 293, 310–21
  see also bishops; crusades; papacy; religious life

Cinque ports, 280

Cistercians, 32, 58–9, 115, 133, 146–8, 191, 195, 199, 226, 228, 232, 260–1, 328

Cîteaux, abbey, 146–7, 199, 232, 304
  abbot, see Alberic

Clairvaux, abbey, 146, 195
  abbot, see Bernard.

Clares, 228

classical Latin writings, 153

Clemence [of Hungary] q. of France, 284

Clement II, p., 103–4

Clement IV, p., 221, 236–7, 245

Clement V, p., 282, 317–20

Clement VI, p., 321

Clericis laicos, 314

Clermont, 171, 238, 258
  council, 77, 105

Clermont-en-Beauvaisis, 159, 248

Clichy, 144

Cluny, abbey and its congregation, 16, 18–19, 32–3, 48, 100–2, 104, 107,

137, 149, 191, 214, 328
abbots, *see* Aymard; Hugh; Maiolus;
  Odilo; Odo; Peter
Cnut VI, k. of Denmark, 196
coinage, *see* currency
Colan, 146
Colonna, 298, 313–14, 320
Combs, 88
Comminges, counts, 61–2
communes, urban and rural, 97–8, 140–2,
  161–3, 186, 253–4, 304–5
  communal armies, 97–8, 161–3, 247,
    281
Compiègne, 82, 88, 162, 234, 290
  assemblies at, 22–4
  forest, 161
  Hôtel-Dieu, 233
  Saint-Corneille, 70, 87, 99, 157, 195
Conan II, ct of Brittany, 38
Conan, provost of Lausanne, 166–7
Conan of Palestrina, 116, 193
Conches, 185
Conques, 57
Conrad II, holy Roman emperor, 47, 72–3
Conrad III, holy Roman emperor, 122
Conrad, k. of Burgundy, 68
Conrad [of Hohenstaufen] k. of Sicily, 218,
  221
Conrad of Marburg, 230
Conradin of Hohenstaufen, 221
counsel, *consilium*, 15–16, 91–4, 161,
  172–3, 245
  see also barons; court, royal
counts, counties, 13–14, 36
  counts palatine, 47
  see also bannal lordship; nobles
Constance [of France] ctss of Toulouse, 171
Constance, ctss of Troyes, 48
Constance, dss of Brittany, 52, 181, 184
Constance [of Sicily] q. of Aragon, 221, 277
Constance [of Arles] q. of France, 47, 71–3
Constance [of Castile] q. of France, 125
Constantinople and the Byzantine empire,
  7–8, 39, 122, 176–7, 198, 211,
  221–2, 234–5, 261–2
  Latin emperors, 221–2; *see also* Baldwin
    IX
convenientiae, agreements of, 55–6, 60
conversi, *see* lay brothers
Corbeil, 90, 117, 157

treaty, 221, 258
Corbie, 76, 98, 290
  abbey, 51, 98, 141, 162, 173
  lordship, 82
Corbonnais, 89
corvée, 83
Coucy, 116
Coulombs, 102
Coulommiers, 49
court, royal (*curia regis*), 160–1, 245, 295–7
  see also entourage, royal; justice, royal;
    parlement
courtly love, 57–8, 155
Courtrai, 281
  battle, 281, 298, 315
Coutances and the Cotentin, 34, 37, 184
coutûmes, *see* customs
Craon, 52, 146–7
Crécy, 116
Crépy-en-Valois, 89, 162
Crèvecoeur, 219
crusades and the crusader states, 17, 38–9,
  149, 164, 328
  first crusade, 20, 105
  second crusade, 122–3, 146
  third crusade, 128–9, 164–5
  fourth crusade, 131
  Louis IX's first crusade, 206, 213–18,
    240, 242
  Louis IX's second crusade, 206, 221–3
  political crusades, 221, 269, 277, 279,
    292
  see also Albigensian crusade; Constanti-
    nople; Jerusalem
Cuise, forest, 161
culture, French, 152–5, 174–9, 328–9
  southern, 57–8
  see also art; architecture; history; learning;
    literature; poetry; vernacular writ-
    ing
curiales, 160–1, 298
  see also administration, royal
currency
  gold coinage, royal, 242, 263
  manipulation by Philip IV, 280, 286, 294
  silver coinage, 7, 9, 12, 242–3
Cusset, 195
customs, *coutûmes*, 12, 54, 82, 92, 257,
  265–6
  codification, 265–6

Norman, 252–3
  regional, 265–6, 307
  see also Philip de Beaumanoir
Cyprus, kingdom, 129, 210
  queen, *see* Alice

Daimbert, arbp of Sens, 107, 193
Damasus II, p., 103–4
Damietta, 216–17
Dammartin, 73, 90
Dampierre, 48
Dax, viscounts, 59
Dijon and Dijonnais, 30–1, 72, 304
Dilo, 191
Dol, 76
  bishop, *see* Baudri
domain, royal
  changes in meaning of the term, 247–51
  ecclesiastical, 86–8, 99, 156–9
  secular, 78–88, 156–9, 247–51, 265,
    279
Domfront, 42
Dominicans, order, 58, 133, 226–30, 234,
    311, 313, 328
Douai, 132, 281
Douce, ctss of Provence, 61
Doullens, 159
Dreu de Barentin, 267
Dreux, 45, 79, 82, 88, 96, 162
  county and counts, 82; *see also* Robert
Dudo of Saint-Quentin, 37
Duesmois, 33
dukes, *duces*, 13–14, 30
  see also Aquitaine; Brittany; Burgundy;
    Francia; Gascony; Normandy
Durand of Huesca, 152
dux francorum, *see* Francia

Echauffour, 37
Edmund [of Pontigny] arbp of Canterbury,
    235
Edmund, earl of Lancaster, 277
Edward the Confessor, k. of England, 177,
    275
Edward I, k. of England, d. of Gascony,
    222–3, 267–8, 276, 280, 302, 313
Edward II, k. of England, d. of Gascony, 251,
    280, 284–5, 302
Edward III, k. of England, d. of Gascony,
    283, 285, 325–6

Egypt, 216–17
Eigenkirche, 56
Eleanor, ctss of Beaumont, 127–9
Eleanor [of England] ctss of Leicester, 220
Eleanor [of Champagne] ctss of Vermandois,
    121
Eleanor, q. of England and France, dss of
    Aquitaine, 50, 53, 120–3, 130, 148,
    157, 171, 208
Eleanor [of Castile] q. of England, 267, 276
Eleanor [of Provence] q. of England, 219, 223
Encre, ld of, 173
England, kingdom, 8, 16–17, 38, 131, 133,
    165–6, 181–2, 215, 266, 285
  kings, *see* Edward; Harold; Henry; John;
    Richard; Stephen; William
  Norman conquest of, 38
  queens, *see* Berengaria; Eleanor; Isabella;
    Margaret; Matilda
Enguerrand de Coucy, 115–16
Enguerrand III de Coucy, 209, 244–5
Enguerrand de Marigny, 278, 288–9, 304,
    308, 311
enquêteurs, 216, 240, 243, 300
entourage, royal, 91–4, 154–5, 159–61,
    195–6, 239–47, 295–9
  see also court, royal; household, royal
Epernay, 45, 48–9
Epernon, 90
Erispoé, prince of Brittany, 52
Ermengarde of Lorraine, 135
Ermentarius, 7–8
Ernoul Perel, 162
Estouteville, 254
établissements and *ordonnances* (ordinances),
    royal, 173, 243–4, 296–7
Etablissements de Saint Louis, 266
Etampes, 83, 88–9, 102, 140, 157, 162–3
  canons, 85, 102, 107
  count, *see* Louis
état des paroisses et des feux, 286–8
Etsi de statu, 314
Eu, 198
  countess, *see* Alice
Eugenius III, p., 122–3, 146, 191, 194
Eustace de Beaumarchais, 276
Eustace of England, 37, 121, 123
Evreux, city and county, 130, 158, 183,
    186–7, 287, 299
  counts, *see* Louis; Philip

countess, see Joan
Saint-Taurin, 186

Falaise, 184, 186
fealty, fidelity, 15–16, 94–9
Fécamp, abbey, 102, 186
Ferdinand of Castile, 277
Ferdinand of Majorca, 311
Ferrand [of Portugal] ct of Flanders, 132,
    170, 208–9
'feudalism', 9–18
    changes in implications of feudal ties, 95
    feudal obligations, see aid; fealty; homage,
        military service
    'two levels of feudalism', 11
    see also armies; castles; fiefs; hierarchy,
        social; knights; nobles; princes;
        suzerainty; vassalage
fideles, 14–18, 92, 172
    see also vassalage
fidelity, see fealty
fiefs, 14–18, 39–40
    introduction to Languedoc, 255
    see also vassalage
Filièvre, 162
finances, royal, see revenues, royal
Flagy, 158
Flanders, county and counts, 8, 13, 17, 20,
    42, 50–1, 72, 82, 118–19, 129, 132,
    139, 142, 157, 162–3, 167, 169–70,
    173, 183, 215–16, 280–1, 283–5,
    287, 302, 307; see also Arnulf;
    Baldwin; Charles; Ferrand; Fulk; Guy;
    Louis; Philip; Robert; Thierry; Wil-
    liam
    countesses, see Adela; Isabella; Joan;
        Judith; Margaret; Richilda
    formation of county, 50–1
Flavigny, 304
Fleury, abbey (Saint-Benoit-sur-Loire), 70,
    76, 86–7, 93, 100–1, 175
    abbots, see Abbo; Gauzlin
Flodoard, 36
Florentine bankers, 293, 298
Foix, county and counts, 62, 254–5, 287
    see also Guy
Fontainebleau, 119, 195, 234
Fontaine-Jean, abbey, 195
Fontevrault, abbey and order, 147, 191, 213
footsoldiers, 87–8, 163, 281

see also prisée des sergéants
Forez, 304, 307
Fouvent, 32
France
    kingdom, 1–6, 13–24, 64–7, 94–6,
        111–14, 169–72, 174–9, 260–3,
        265–8, 306–10, 325–9
    kings, see Henry; Hugh; John; Louis;
        Philip; Robert
    queens, see Adela; Agnes; Anne; Bertha;
        Bertrada; Blanche; Clemence; Con-
        stance; Ingeborg; Isabella; Joan;
        Margaret; Rozala
    regents, see Baldwin, Blanche
    regnum francorum, 1–5, 24
    see also Francia; monarchy, French
Francesco Gaetani, 311
franchises, 140–1, 161–3
Francia, 1–6, 13, 89, 174–9, 263, 309, 328
    dukes and duchy of, 6, 21–2, 44, 89; see
        also Hugh; Robert
    la douce France, 155, 261
    see also France
Francis of Assisi, 152, 197, 226–7
Franciscan friars, 226–30, 233–4, 313
    spirituals, 313–14
Franco, bp of Paris, 103
Franconia, 5
Frederick I Barbarossa, holy Roman emperor,
    50, 61, 125, 135, 194
Frederick II, holy Roman emperor, 131–2,
    197, 212–14, 218, 238
Frederick [of Aragon] k. of Sicily, 279
friars, 150, 263–4
    see also Austin friars; Dominicans; Carme-
        lites; Franciscans; Pied friars; Sack
        friars; Trinitarian friars
Frontenay, 212
Fulbert, bp of Chartres, 15, 27, 65, 71,
    102–3
Fulk, bp of Orléans, 102
Fulk Nerra, ct of Anjou, 28, 52, 69, 71, 73,
    98
Fulk Réchin, ct of Anjou, 52, 75
Fulk [the Good] ct of Flanders, 52
Fulk V, k. of Jerusalem, ct of Anjou and
    Maine, 52, 118
Fulk, vct of Gâtinais, 157
Fulk Paynel, 254
Furnes, battle, 280

Gaillon, 158, 163
Galbert of Bruges, 16, 51, 118–19
Galeran, ct of Meulan, 90, 118
Gallardon, 90–1
Gamaches, 140–1
Garlande, 91, 93, 156, 159–60
Garonne, 188
Gasbert of Laval, 321
Gascony, duchy, 13, 17, 23, 53–9, 94, 96,
    131, 136, 171, 185, 187–8, 219,
    266–8, 280–1, 284–5, 287, 301–2,
    307, 320, 326
  connections with England, 266–8, 301–2
  dukes, see Edward; Henry
  see also Aquitaine
Gaston de Béarn, 267
Gâtinais, 78, 82, 89, 140, 157, 161
  viscount, see Fulk
Gaul, Gauls, 1–4, 9, 23
Gautier Cornut, arbp of Sens, 207, 261
Gautier, archdeacon of Laon, 115–16
Gautier d'Aunay, 282
Gauzlin, arbp of Bourges, abt of Fleury, 70,
  102
Gelasius II, p., 193
Gendouin de Breteuil, 90
Geoffrey [the Bearded] ct of Anjou, 52
Geoffrey Greymantle, ct of Anjou, 52, 330
Geoffrey 'le Bel', ct of Anjou, 43, 49, 52,
  118, 120–3, 171, 181
Geoffrey Martel, ct of Anjou, 38, 74, 104
Geoffrey, ct of Nantes, 124, 181
Geoffrey, d. of Brittany, 52, 126, 168, 181
Geoffrey, vct of Chateaudun, 99
Geoffrey of Beaulieu, 206, 222, 230, 312
Geoffrey de Charnay, 319
Geoffrey de Donzi, 173
Geoffrey of Lusignan, 267
Geoffrey of Monmouth, 155
Geoffrey of Paris, 278, 295, 304, 308, 311
Gerald of Wales, 127, 164, 177
Gerard of Quierzy, 192
Gerbert of Aurillac, Pope Sylvester II, arbp of
  Reims, 20–4, 68–70, 100, 103
Germany, Germania, 4, 6, 7, 20–4, 177, 275
  see also holy Roman empire
Germigny, 117
Gerona, 277
Gervais du Bus, 308
Gervais de Rethel, 192

Gevaudan, 61–2
Ghent, 280–1, 288
  Saint-Pierre, 235
Gilbert de Garlande, 159
Giles Aicelin, arbp of Narbonne, 298, 319
Giles of Concevreux, 291
Giles of Paris, 127, 135, 160–1, 177
Giles of Rome, 316
Giovanni Salimbene, 204
Giovanni Villani, 319
Gisors, 118, 122–3, 129, 158, 163
gîte, 83, 240
Godfrey, d. of Lorraine, 74
Godfrey de Bouillon, 105
Gonesse, 83
Gothia, 23, 54, 59
Graçay, 130, 157, 183
grande chambre, 296
Grandes chroniques de France, 263
Grandmont, monastery and order, 149, 154,
  235
Gratian, 155, 315
Gregory V, p., 71
Gregory VII, Hildebrand, p., 57, 77, 104–7,
  316
Gregory IX, p., 209, 214, 230, 255–6, 317
Gregory X, p., 276, 312, 320
Grenoble, bp, 148
Grez, 117
Grimoard, bp-elect of Poitiers, 194
Gros Brief, 51
Guibert of Nogent, 75, 114–16, 141, 148,
  153, 160, 192
Guichard, bp of Troyes, 311
Guichard of Beaujeu, 250
Guigo I, prior of La Grande-Chartreuse, 149
Guînes, 299
  counts, 154
Guy, arbp of Sens, 195
Guy, bp of Beauvais, 106
Guy [of Dampierre] ct of Flanders, 219,
  280–1, 295
Guy, ct of Foix and Nevers, 209, 212
Guy [the Red] ld of Crécy, 116
Guy [de Levis] ld of Mirepoix, 255
Guy III, ld of Mirepoix, 255
Guy [Troussel] ld of Montlhéry, 82, 91
Guy, ld of Rochefort, 117
Guy, vct of Thouars, 52, 184, 210, 212
Guy Foulquoi, see Pope Clement IV

Guy of Lusignan, 267
Guy of Senlis, 159
Guy-Geoffrey, *see* William VIII, d. of Aquitaine

Hadewig, 25 n21
Hainault, 50, 163, 216
  counts, *see* Baldwin; John; Robert
  countess, *see* Alice
Halatte, forest, 83
Ham, 128
Hariulf of Saint-Riquier, 73
Harold, k. of England, 38
Hautes-Bruyères, 191
hearthtax, 287–8
Helgaud of Fleury, 67, 69–70
Heloise, abss of Paraclete, 148
Henry, arbp of Reims, 123, 128, 196
Henry, arbp of Sens, 191, 193
Henry [of Blois] bp of Winchester, 49, 137, 153
Henry, ct of Bar, 210, 212
Henry I [the Liberal] ct of Champagne, 49–50, 125, 170
Henry II, ct of Champagne, 50, 160
Henry, d. of Bavaria, 21
Henry I, d. of Burgundy, 30, 72
Henry II, holy Roman emperor, 45, 103
Henry III, holy Roman Emperor, 74, 93, 103–4
Henry IV, holy Roman emperor, 106–7
Henry V, holy Roman emperor, 43, 118, 192–3
Henry VI, holy Roman emperor, 129, 131
Henry VII, holy Roman emperor, 284, 321
Henry I, k. of England, d of Normandy, 37, 40–3, 49, 76–7, 96, 106, 117–18, 171, 263
Henry II Plantagenet, k. of England, d. of Normandy, and Aquitaine, ct of Anjou and Poitou, 37, 43, 52–3, 61, 120–6, 128, 160, 171–3, 177, 179–82, 250, 327
Henry III, k. of England, d. of Gascony, 133, 136, 183, 205–8, 212–14, 219–20, 235, 253–4, 256, 258, 262, 266–9, 276, 327
Henry 'the Young King' of England, 123, 126, 128, 157, 172
Henry I, k. of France, 30, 37–8, 65–6, 72–5,

82, 90, 96, 103–5, 175, 307, 328
  reign, 72–5
Henry III, k. of Navarre, ct of Champagne, 276
Henry of Brunswick, 131–2
Henry Clément, 161
Henry the Monk, 58, 150–1
Henry of Sully, 299
Henry of Vézelay, 276
Herbert, ct of Maine, 38
Herbert ['the Old'] ct of Vermandois, 21, 44–5
Herbert ['the Young'] ct of Vermandois, Meaux and Troyes, 45
Herbert II, ct of Vermandois, 21, 44–5
heretics, *see* Albigensians; Waldensians; inquisition
Hervé de Donzi, 132
Hesdin, 162
Hiémois, 35
hierarchy, social, 9–11, 18, 27–8, 95–6, 174, 290–1
Hildebert de Lavardin, arbp of Tours, 192
Hildebrand, *see* Gregory VII, p.
Hincmar of Reims, 66
history, writing of, 154, 174–9
  see also Saint-Denis; Suger
holy Roman empire and emperors, 21, 118, 177, 193, 214; *see also* Conrad; Frederick; Henry; Lothar; Louis; Otto; Rudolph
  conflicts with papacy, 105–6
  empress, *see* Theophano
  see also Germany
homage, 14–16, 66, 94–9, 168–73
  border homage (*hommage en marche*), 96–7
  liege homage, 17
  of dukes of Normandy to French kings, 37
Honorius III, p., 133, 136, 189, 197–8
Hospitallers, knights, order, 149, 198, 319–20
hospitals, 148, 198
hôtes, 12
household, royal, 159–61, 246, 297–9
  see also entourage, royal
Hugh, abt of Cluny, 101, 103, 148
Hugh [of Châtillon] bp of Auxerre, 58, 196
Hugh, bp of Laon, 192
Hugh [of Champfleury] bp of Soissons, 155, 195

Hugh ['le Brun' of Lusignan] ct of Angoulême and La Marche, 136, 207–8, 210–13, 215

Hugh, ct of Beauvais, 71

Hugh IX [of Lusignan] ct of La Marche, 130, 183

Hugh XIII [of Lusignan] ct of La Marche, 300

Hugh, ct of Troyes, 48, 117

Hugh, ct of Vermandois, 105, 250

Hugh I, d. of Burgundy, 31–2

Hugh II, d. of Burgundy, 170

Hugh III, d. of Burgundy, 33, 125, 170

Hugh IV, d. of Burgundy, 209, 212, 215

Hugh [the Great] d. of Francia, 21, 88–9, 175, 330–1

Hugh Capet, k. of France, d. of Francia, 20–4, 25 n21, 64–5, 67–70, 175, 326, 330–1
    accession, 20–4
    reign, 67–9

Hugh, ld of Crécy, 116

Hugh, ld of Le Puiset, 78, 91, 116–17, 156, 172

Hugh, ld of Lusignan, 16

Hugh de Clers, 160

Hugh of Die, 107

Hugh of Digne, 234

Hugh of France, 71

Hugh of Orléans, 154

'humanism', 154

Humbert of Beaujeu, 209

Humbert of Saint-Sévère, 116

Humbert of Silva Candida, 104

Hundred Years War, 269, 290, 306–7, 326

Hungarians, 7

Hyères, 217

Ile de France (Paris Basin), 8–9, 12, 73, 88, 94, 117, 156–9, 167, 209, 224–6, 286–7

Ineffabilis amor, 314

infantes of La Cerda, 277, 279

Ingeborg [of Denmark] q. of France, 126–7, 196

Innocent II, p., 115, 121–2, 141, 172, 193

Innocent III, p., 58, 126, 130–3, 145, 184, 188–9, 196–8, 226

Innocent IV, p., 214–15, 218, 229, 236, 261, 320

inquisition, 151, 212, 229–30, 255–6

Irminon, abt of Saint-Germain-des-Prés, 11, 88

Isabella [of Hainault] ctss of Flanders, 127

Isabella [of Angoulême] q. of England, ctss of Angoulême and La Marche, 130, 136, 183, 212–13

Isabella [of France] q. of England, 251, 280, 282–3, 325–6

Isabella [of Aragon] q. of France, 221, 223, 275

Isabella [of Hainault] q. of France, 126–8, 135, 158, 190

Isabella [of France] q. of Navarre, 222

Issoudun, 130, 157–8, 183

Italy, 7–9, 151, 153, 155, 216, 228, 269, 316, 320

Ivo, bp of Chartres, 77, 106–7, 114, 141, 192

Ivo of Saint-Denis, 278, 283

Ivry, 158

Jacopone da Todi, 314

Jacques Fournier, bp of Pamiers, Pope Benedict XII, 289–90, 321

Jacques de Molay, grand master of the Templars, 318–19

Jacques de Chatillon, 281

Jacques de Revigny, 263

James, k. of Aragon, 220–1

James [of Aragon] k. of Sicily, 279

Jaroslav, grand d. of Kiev, 73

Jerusalem, city and kingdom, 52, 120, 122–3, 129, 215, 217, 222, 317
    see also crusades

Jews, 84, 164, 173, 178, 210, 240, 244, 252, 269, 293

Joan, ctss of Flanders, 132

Joan [of Burgundy] ctss of Poitou, 282–3, 300

Joan, ctss of Toulouse, 189, 209, 223, 250, 255, 258, 276, 299

Joan [of France] dss of Burgundy, 284

Joan [of Ponthieu] q. of Castile, 212

Joan, q. of France and Navarre, ctss of Champagne, 50, 206, 276–7, 279, 297–8, 312

Joan, q. of Navarre, ctss of Evreux, 283–4, 313

John [of Salisbury] bp of Chartres, 125, 154, 196, 329

John, bp of Orléans, 106
John [of Chalon] ct of Auxerre, 304
John [of Avesnes] ct of Hainault, 218–19
John, ct of Mâcon, 211
John Tristan, ct of Valois, 217, 222, 248
John [the Red] d. of Brittany, 211
John, k. of England, d. of Normandy and
    Aquitaine, ct of Poitou and Mortain,
    29, 53, 113–14, 128, 130–3, 171–3,
    181–8, 197
John I, k. of France, 284
John, ld of Joinville, 120, 196, 204–9, 216,
    221, 230–5, 238, 243, 245, 263–4,
    275, 312
John XV, p., 68
John XVIII, p., 102
John XXII, p., 284–5, 321
John of Beaumont, 212, 256
John of Blanot, 243
John Clément, 207
John of France, 190
John of Meung, 234, 264
John of Saint-Pierre, 230
John Sarrazin, 246
John of Taillefontaine, 291
Joigny, 89, 206
Joinville, see John, lord of Joinville
Jonas, bp of Orléans, 65
judicial appeals, 244, 260
Judith, ctss of Flanders, 50
justice
    ecclesiastical, 215, 235–7, 310–11
    high and low, 12, 84–5
    royal, 84–6, 157, 173, 187, 216, 219,
        231, 236–40, 243–5, 254, 256,
        267, 295–7, 300–2, 307, 310–11,
        317–18, 327; see also court, royal;
        chambre des enquêtes; chambre des
        requêtes; établissements and ordon-
        nances; parlement
    see also bannal lordship

kingship, cult of, 64–7, 174–9, 260–3,
    308–10, 312–13
knights, 9–11, 55–6, 97–9, 139, 159
    see also chivalry, cult of

La Bénisson-Dieu, abbey, 195
La Chapelle, 160
La Chapelle-Aude, 140

La Chapelle-la-Reine, 161
La Charité-sur-Loire, 195
La Châtre, 89
La Ferté-Alais, 117
Lagny, 49
La Grande-Chartreuse, priory, 148–9
    prior, see Guigo
    see also Carthusians
Laigle, 37
La Marche, county, 53, 94, 126, 258, 287
    counts and countesses, see Blanche;
        Charles; Hugh; Isabella; Louis
Lambert of Ardres, 154
Landri, ct of Nevers, 30, 72
Langeais, 186
Langres, city and county, 30, 33
    bishopric and bishops, 33, 86, 170, 172;
        see also Lietri; Renaud
Languedoc, 19, 54–62, 93–4, 135–7, 157,
    164, 188–90, 199, 209, 212–13,
    221, 235, 246, 252, 254-7, 282, 300,
    303, 305, 307, 311
    culture, 57–8, 155, 257
    society, 54–6, 255–7
    see also Albigensian crusade; Barcelona;
        Gascony; heresy; Toulouse
Langue d'oc, 5–6
Langue d'oil, 6
Laon, city and county, 21, 68, 82, 88, 116,
    141–2, 153, 161–2, 172, 191, 242
    archdeacon, see Gautier
    bishops and bishopric, 86, 99; see also
        Adalbero; Bartholomew; Hugh;
        Waldric
    commune, 141
    Saint-Jean, 116, 142
    Saint-Martin, 105, 142
La Réole, abbey, 94
La Roche-au-Moine, 132, 184
La Rochelle, 132, 135–6, 187–90, 280
Las Formiguas, battle, 277
Las Huelgas, abbey, 260
Lateran councils
    first, 193
    third, 152
    fourth, 133, 197
Lautrec, 256
La Victoire, abbey, 179, 198
law
    canon, 105–6, 265

feudal, 14–17, 94–7, 168–9, 171, 182, 247, 253, 255, 263, 327
Roman, 12, 19, 55, 155, 173, 243, 257, 262–3, 265, 297–8
royal, 173, 195, 216, 219, 239–40, 243–5, 262–3, 295–7, 300–2, 309
study of, 145, 152–5
see also appeals; bannal lordship; customs; *établissements* and *ordonnances*; Salic law
lawyers of the last Capetians, 297–8
lay advocates of abbeys, 56
lay brothers or *conversi*, 147–9
leagues, provincial, 282–4, 304–6
see also principalities
learning, 144–5, 148, 152–5, 228–9, 328–9
see also schools, universities
Le Châtelet-en-Brie, 158
Le Goulet, treaty, 130, 183
Le Lys, abbey, 232
Le Mans, bishopric, 86
Le Moulinet, 158
Lendit, fair, 143, 176, 191
Leo IX, p., 74, 104, 106
Leopold, d. of Austria, 129
Le Puiset, 73, 116
Le Puy, bishops, 86; *see also* Adhémar council, 19
Les Andelys, 162, 186
Lesparre, 59
Le Trésor, abbey, 232
Lézat, 56–7
Lietri, bp of Langres, 30
Lille, 8, 281
Lillebonne, 39, 208
Limoges, Limousin, 8, 19, 53
bishopric, 267–8
viscount, 130, 183
Limoux, 152, 212
literature, Latin and vernacular, 152–5, 329
Lodève, viscounts, 55
logic, 153
Loire region, 10–11, 86
Lomagne, 299
Lombard moneylenders, 242, 244
Lombers, council, 58
Longchamp, 234
Lorraine, 21–4, 49, 75
dukes, 45, 210; *see also* Charles; Godfrey

Lorrez-le-Bocage, 117
Lorris
customs, 140, 161–2
peace, 213, 256
Lothar III, holy Roman emperor, 193
Lothar, k. of France, 20–4
Louis, ct of Evreux, Etampes and Beaumont-sur-Oise, 250
Louis [of Crécy] ct of Flanders, 284–5
Louis [of Nevers] ct of Flanders, 284–5
Louis, d. of Bourbon, ct of La Marche, 250
Louis the Pious, emperor, 7, 86, 100
Louis IV of Bavaria, holy Roman emperor, 285
Louis IV '*d'Outremer*', k. of France, 21
Louis V, k. of France, 20–4
Louis VI ['the Fat'] k. of France, 42, 49, 51, 64, 91, 111, 114–19, 158–60, 174–7, 190–4, 326
character, 114
reign, 114–19
Louis VII, k. of France, 37, 49–50, 53, 61, 65, 119–27, 158–60, 171, 173–9, 184–96, 327–8
character, 119–20
reign, 119–26
Louis VIII, k. of France, 111, 126, 130, 132–6, 158–9, 178–9, 187–90, 199, 207, 222, 248, 260–1
character, 135
reign, 135–6
Louis IX, k. of France (Saint Louis), 111, 120, 136, 176–9, 204–72, 304, 328–9
canonisation, 312
character and achievements, 204–7, 268–9
criticisms of, 263–4
crusades, 213–23
cult, 204, 260, 278, 308–9, 312–13
death, 222, 229–30
minority, 207–12
piety, 230–5
religious patronage, 232–5
Louis X, k. of France, 206, 282–8, 290–1, 303
character, 283
reign, 283–4
Louis of France, 275
Louye, 195

Lucienne de Rochefort, 159, 193
Lusignan, 52–3, 183, 187
    see also Guy; Hugh
Lyon, city and province, 1, 215, 300, 310,
    320
    archbishopric and archbishops, 107, 152,
        193, 209–10
    councils, 214, 227

Machaut, 276
Mâcon and Mâconnais, 10, 17, 29–30, 33–4,
    51–2, 89, 95, 157, 195–6, 234
    bishops, 86
    counts and county, 33–4, 211, 239; see
        also John; Odo-William
    Saint-Vincent, 33
Magna Carta, 133
Mahaut [of Brabant] ctss of Artois, 212, 298
Mahaut [of Artois] dss of Burgundy, 284,
    305–6
Mahaut of Boulogne, 212
Maine, county, 12–13, 38, 52, 74, 89, 128,
    131, 171, 203, 215, 248, 250, 267
    counts and countess, see Charles; Fulk;
        Herbert; Margaret
Maiolus, abt of Cluny, 101
maltôte, 294
Manasses, arbp of Reims, 106–7
Manasses [de Garlande] bp of Orléans, 195
Manasses, ct of Dammartin, 90
Manfred [of Hohenstaufen] k. of Sicily, 219,
    221
Manglieu, abbey, 195
manorial rights, 82–4
Mansourah, 216–17
Mantes, 76, 82–3, 158, 162–3, 198
    Saint-Corentin, 198
Marcigny, abbey, 148
Margaret [of Burgundy] ctss of Champagne,
    282, 284
Margaret, ctss of Flanders, 216–219
Margaret [of France] ctss of Flanders, 284
Margaret [of Naples] ctss of Valois, Anjou and
    Maine, 279
Margaret [of France] dss of Brabant, 222
Margaret [of France] q. of England, 280
Margaret [of France] q.-designate of England,
    125, 157
Margaret [of Provence] q. of France, 206,
    211, 217, 222–3, 275, 297

Margaret of Maine, 38
Marie de France, 50, 154
Marle, 115–16
Marmoutiers, abbey, 102
Marquenterre, 141
marriage, royal, 71, 77–8
Marseille, 218
Martin IV, p., 277, 312
Mary [of France] ctss of Brittany, 130
Mary [of Brabant] q. of France, 275, 297
Mary [of Luxembourg] q. of France, 284–5
Master [of Hungary] 218
Matilda, ctss of Blois, 45
Matilda ['the Empress'] dss of Normandy, ctss
    of Anjou, holy Roman empress, lady of
    England, 43, 49, 118, 120–1, 123,
    208
Matilda [of Flanders] q. of England, dss of
    Normandy, 38, 51, 76
Matilda, q. of France, 72
Matthew [of Vendôme] abt of Saint-Denis,
    222, 242, 276
Matthew, bp of Toul, 58
Matthew of Montmorency, 207
Matthew Paris, 135, 172, 212–14, 218, 226,
    228, 232, 236–7, 262
Maubuisson, abbey, 218, 232, 282
Maule, 88
Mauléon, lôrds, 54, 187
Maurice, arbp of Rouen, 237
Maurice of Sully, bp of Paris, 143
Meaux, 45, 47, 49, 227
    bishopric and bishops, 48, 86; see also
        Walter
    counts, see Herbert; Odo; Stephen;
        Stephen-Henry
medium plantum grants, 56
Melun, 69, 73, 88–90, 172
    canons, 102
    county, 82, 89
Mende, bishopric, 158, 196
medicants; see friars
Mercadier, 163
mercenary troops, 98–9, 163
Merovingians, 4, 6–7, 17
Messina, treaty, 129
Meulan, 90, 157–8, 162
    counts, see Galeran; Robert
Meung-sur-Loire, 157
midi see Languedoc

Miles de Noyers, 299
military service, by princes to French kings, 97–9, 169–72, 199, 247, 253–4, 263
Millau, 61–2, 221
Milly, lords, 207
Milo, bp of Beauvais, 237
Minstrel of Reims, 179
Mirebeau, 131, 183
Moissac, abbey, 57
monarchy, French
    image, 64–7, 174–9, 260–3, 308–10, 312–13
    power, 64–7, 78–99, 111–14, 156–90, 204–7, 239–70, 273–5, 291–310, 325–9
    see also administration, royal; Capetian kings; court, royal; domain, royal; entourage, royal; France, kingdom; household, royal; justice, royal; principalities, royal; revenues, royal; sacral kingship; sovereignty; suzerainty
monasteries, see religious life
Moncel, abbey, 313
monks, see Benedictine monks; Carthusian order; Cluny; Cistercians; Grandmont; Tiron; Savigny
Mons-en-Pévèle, battle, 281
Montaillou, 288–9
Mont-Aimé, 230
Montargis, 158
Montchauvet, 117
Mont-de-Marsan, 59
Montdidier, 51, 128, 158, 162
Montferrand, 117
Montfort, 90
    lords, 207; see also Amaury; Simon
Montivilliers, abbey, 237
Montlhéry, 90–1, 93, 157, 159, 209
Montmirail, 125
Montmorency, 90, 116, 156, 207
Montpellier, 57, 152, 155, 259
Mont-Saint-Louis, priory, 313
Mont-Saint-Michel, abbey, 154
Montségur, 213, 256
Montreuil-sur-Mer, 51, 71, 82, 92, 162
Moret, 157
Morigny, abbey, 107
    chronicler, 119, 176
Mortagne, 89

Mortain, 42, 208
Mortemer, 186
    battle, 38–9, 74
Mouliherne, 74
Moulinet, 161
Mouzon, 46
Muret, battle, 133, 189
Musciatto Franzesi, 298
Muslims, 7, 20, 39, 54, 68, 105, 122, 215–16, 221–2
    see also crusades

Namur, 10
Nantes, ct, see Geoffrey
Naples, kingdom, 38–9, 279, 321
Narbonne, city, 19, 55, 57, 59, 255–6, 314
    archbishopric and archbishops, 57; see also Berengar; Giles
    council, 20
    viscounts, 55, 60–2
Navarre, Kingdom, 210, 276–7, 299, 325
    kings, see Charles; Henry; Philip; Theobald
    queens, see Blanche; Isabella; Joan
Nemours, priory of Saint John the Baptist, 195
Neustria, 4, 13, 34
Neuville-au-Bois, 313
Nevers, 30, 117, 142, 157, 172–3, 195, 230
    counts and countesses, 133, 142, 210; see also Guy; Landri; William; Yolande
Nicholas de Brai, 135
Nicholas Malesmains, 185
Nicholas of Normandy, 36
Nîmes, 59, 221, 254, 256–7, 305
    bishop and chapter, 57
    viscounts, 55
Niort, 135–6, 187
nobles, nobility, 9–11
    grants of noble status by the king, 290–1
    see also dukes; counts; knights; princes
Nogent, 159
Nogent-le-Roi, 88, 90
Nominoé, prince of Brittany, 52
Nonancourt, 158, 162, 185–6
Norbert of Xanten, 148, 150, 191
Noirmoutier, 7
Normandy, duchy, 6, 8, 10, 12–14, 16–17, 20, 23, 29, 34–43, 94, 96–9,

117–18, 128, 130–1, 157, 162–3, 180–7, 245–6, 251–4, 262, 267, 300, 307, 329
administration, 39–40, 180, 185–7, 252–4
dukes and duchess, see Henry; John; Matilda; Richard; Robert; Rollo; Stephen; William
league and charter, 304–5
Nouvion, 116
Noyers, 195
Noyon, 106, 141, 162, 172–3
bishop, 86, 141
commune, 141
numismatics, see currency
nuns, see Béguines; Cistercians; Clares; Fontevrault; religious life

Odilo, abt of Cluny, 70, 101–3
Odo, abt of Cluny, 101–2
Odo [of Deuil] abt of Saint-Denis, 119, 122, 176
Odo Rigaud, arbp of Rouen, 245, 253
Odo, bp of Bayeux, 253
Odo I, ct of Blois, 45, 68–9
Odo II [the Great] ct of Blois, 28–9, 45–8, 71–2, 88, 90, 95–6, 98
character and achievements, 45–8
Odo III, ct of Blois, 48
Odo III, ct of Troyes and Meaux, 48
Odo IV, ct of Toyes, 48
Odo II, d. of Burgundy, 33, 125, 170, 173
Odo IV, d. of Burgundy, 284
Odo, k. of France, 21
Odo Arpin, vct of Bourges, 82
Odo of Chateauroux, 215
Odo of France, 47, 73–4
Odo of l'Etoile, 151
Odo Popin, 225
Odo of Saint-Maur, 90
Odoran of Sens, 68
Odo-William, d. of Burgundy, ct of Mâcon, 30–1, 72, 74
Olim, 244, 296
Olivier de Termes, 213, 256
Omois, 45
Orderic Vitalis, 118
ordinances, ordonnances, see établissements
oriflamme, 118, 175–6, 179, 261
Orléans, 6–7, 49, 79, 83–4, 86, 88–9, 92,

140, 150, 153, 155, 157–8, 162–3, 172, 191, 194, 218, 242
bishopric and bishops, 86, 101–2, 107, 116, 196, 198; see also Arnulf; Fulk; John; Jonas; Manasses; Sancho
forest, 161
Saint-Aignan, 86, 102
Saint-Croix, 115
Saint-Mesmin, 199
sub-dean, see Archambaud
treaty, 276–7
Othe, forest, 161
Otto I, holy Roman emperor, 21–2
Otto II, holy Roman emperor, 21
Otto III, holy Roman emperor, 21, 67–9, 71
Otto [of Brunswick] holy Roman emperor, 131–2, 184
Oudon, 210
Oulchy, 45

Paçy-sur-Eure, 158
pagi, 13–14, 36
pairs de France 172, 245
Palaiseau, 88
palatini, 172
Pamiers, 136
bishops, 289; see also Bernard; Jacques
statutes, 136, 255
papacy, 18, 56–7, 94, 133–4, 188–9, 190–1, 193–4, 196–7, 214, 226, 235–9, 269, 277, 282, 310, 312–21
baronial opposition to in France, 212, 236–7
papal provisions, 215, 236
papal schisms, 193–4
papal reforms, 40, 56–7, 75, 77, 86, 103–4, 106–7
Paraclete, abbey and order, 148
parage, division of lands in, 28, 45, 56, 61, 156, 158, 225
Paris, 6, 8, 49, 79, 82–3, 86, 88–92, 142–5, 152–7, 172, 204, 209, 218–19, 225–7, 261–2, 286–8, 303, 313
administration, 225–6
bishop, cathedral and chapter of Nôtre-Dame, 115, 143, 177, 195–6, 218, 226, 237; see also Franco; Maurice; Stephen; William
bourgs, 143

burgesses, 143–4, 165, 242, 245
Champeaux, Les Halles, 143, 162
Cordeliers, 234
county, 82
Filles-Dieu, 233
guilds, including *marchands de l'eau*,
   143–4
Hôtel-Dieu, 233
Montmartre, 191, 194
population in 1328, 287–8
prévôté and *vicomté*, 142–4, 225–6
Quinze-Vingts, 233
royal palace, 143, 195
Sainte-Chapelle, 211, 226, 234–5,
   260–3, 312, 321
Sainte-Geneviève, abbey, 143, 195, 225,
   228
Saint-Magloire, 107
schools and university, 144–5, 211,
   228–9, 234
Temple, 143, 165
treaty (1229), 209; (1259), 185, 213,
   219–20, 254, 266–7, 276
walls, 144
see also Saint-Denis; Saint-Germain-des-
   Prés; Saint-Martin-des-Champs;
   Saint-Victor
Paris basin, *see* Ile de France
parlement, 205, 245
   party, 283–5, 299
   see also court, royal
Parthenay, 53–4, 187
Paschal II, p., 77, 106–7, 191–3
pastoureaux, 218, 286
Pavie, 257
Payen Gatineau, 127
peace associations, 98
peace and truce of God, 11, 19–20, 32, 39,
   60–1, 98, 101, 103, 173, 274, 328
peasants, 11–12, 137–9, 288–90
   see also bannal lordship; serfdom
peers, *see pairs de France*
Penne d'Agenais, 213
Perche, 159, 248, 250
perfecti, *see* Cathar heresy
Périgueux and the Périgord, 8, 53, 267
   diocese, 267
Péronne, 116, 128–30, 162
   dit de, 219
Perpignan, 277

Perthois, 45, 49
Peter [the Venerable] abt of Cluny, 137, 139,
   146, 151, 191
Peter, ct of Alençon, 222
Peter Mauclerc, d. of Brittany, 52, 136, 184,
   190, 207–12, 215, 250, 306–7
Peter II, k. of Aragon, ct of Barcelona, 62,
   133, 188–9
Peter III, k. of Aragon, 277
Peter Abelard, 143, 146, 148, 153–4
Peter of Bruis, 58, 150–1
Peter Carlot, 177, 190
Peter of Capua, 196
Peter of Castelnau, 133, 188
Peter Coral, 222
Peter Lombard, 143–153
Peter of Maule, 116
Peter of Villebéon, 245
Peter of Tarentaise, 195
Petrobrusians, *see* Peter of Bruis
Petronilla of Aragon, ctss of Barcelona, 61
Petronilla of Aquitaine, 121, 194
Philip [of Marigny] arbp of Sens, 319
Philip Hurepel, ct of Boulogne, 126, 132,
   190, 207–8, 248, 250
Philip [of Alsace] ct of Flanders, 49, 51, 123,
   127–9, 158, 160, 168–70
Philip I, k. of France, 19, 40, 48, 50, 64–7,
   75–8, 82, 91, 93, 105–8, 175, 327
   character, 75–6
   reign, 75–7
Philip II Augustus, k. of France, 29, 33,
   53–4, 65, 111–14, 126–35, 139,
   157–61, 163–8, 176–9, 182–9,
   196–9, 207, 244, 261, 327–9
   character, 126–7
   events of reign, 126–35
   importance of reign, 135, 328
Philip III, k. of France, 206, 221–3, 231–2,
   246, 258, 275–7, 292, 297, 310
   character, 275
   reign, 275–7
Philip IV [the Fair] k. of France, 50, 206,
   230, 239, 250, 262, 273–4, 276–7,
   279–83, 291–8, 300–4, 308–9,
   312–19, 326–7
   character, 278–9
   councillors, control of, 279
   reign, 278–83
Philip V, k. of France, ct of Poitiers, 250–1,

280–3, 283–5, 303–4, 306, 325
character and reign, 284
Philip VI [of Valois] k. of France, 250, 285,
305, 325–6
Philip, k. of Navarre, ct of Evreux, 325
Philip d'Aunay, 282
Philip de Beaumanoir, 239, 243, 263, 266
Philip de Courtenai, 132
Philip of France, 114, 193
Philip de Montfort, 255
Philip Mousket, 179
Philip of Swabia, 131
Philippa of Toulouse, dss of Aquitaine, 53
Philippa of Flanders, 280
Philippa of Lomagna, 258, 276
Picardy, 12, 14, 17, 28, 51–2, 86, 162–3,
218
Pied friars, 227, 234
Pierre [de Mornay] bp of Auxerre, 298–9
Pierre [de Latilly] bp of Chartres, 283, 299,
311
Pierre Barbet, 276
Pierre de la Broce, 275–6, 297
Pierre de Chalon, 295
Pierre [de la Châtre] abp of Bourges, 121, 194
Pierre Clergue, 289–90
Pierre de Courtenai, 158
Pierre Dubois, 309
Pierre Flotte, 257, 279, 281, 298, 312, 315
Pierre Maury, 289–90
Pincerais, 88
Pippin, 66, 175
poetry, 154–5, 257, 329
epic, 154
troubadour, 57, 154–5
Poissy, 73, 79, 83, 162
canons, 70, 102
Nôtre-Dame, 191
Saint-Louis, 262, 313
Poitiers, 19, 135–6, 258, 303, 310, 318
bishop, see Grimoard
count, see Philip
Saint-Cyprien, 147
Poitou, 10, 12–13, 53–4, 89, 93, 131,
135–6, 159, 187–90, 199, 248, 250,
257–9, 265, 267, 276, 287
counts, see Alfonso; Henry
countess, see Joan
Pont-Audemer, 163
Pont-du-Château, 117

Ponthieu, 51, 89, 132, 141, 176, 285, 304
counts, 38, 162
Pontigny, abbey, 125, 147, 235
Pontoise, 162
Hôtel-Dieu, 233
Saint-Mellon, 191
Saint-Vaast, 234
population trends, 286–8
Porcien, 45
pounds parisis and tournois, value, 243
Pragmatic sanction, 238
Prémontré, abbey, and the Premonstratensian
order, 105, 148, 191, 226, 328
prévôts, royal, 50, 85–6, 94, 157, 239–40
primacy of Gaul, 107, 193
Primat, 222, 263
princes, territorial, 13–14, 28–30, 44, 64–7,
94–9, 168–73, 179–84, 265–8,
306–8, 326
see also hierarchy, social; principalities;
nobles
principalities
and the kingdom, 94–6, 168–73, 265–8,
306–8
development, 27–63, 265–8, 299–302
disintegration, 27–8
northern French, 30–54
origins, 13–14
revolt of (1314), 304–5
royal, 79–80, 88–91, 156–9
southern French, 54–62
see also Anjou; apanages; Aquitaine;
Barcelona; Blois; Brittany; Burgundy; Champagne; Flanders;
Gascony; Normandy; Languedoc;
Poitou; Toulouse
prisée des sergéants, 163
proceres, 172
Prouille, 227
Provence, 54, 212, 218
counts, see Alfonso; Berengar-Raymond;
Charles; Raymond-Berengar
countesses, see Beatrice; Douce
Provins, 45, 48–9
provisions of Oxford, 219
Psalmodi, abbey, 56, 216

quadrivium, 153
Quend-le-Vieux, 141

Quercy, 258–9, 267, 276
Queribus, 213, 256

Rainald of Dassel, 125
Ralph of Diceto, 166
Ralph of Exoudun, 185
Ramerupt, 89
Raoul [d'Argences] abt of Fécamp, 186
Raoul [le Vert] arbp of Reims, 192
Raoul, arbp of Tours, 106
Raoul IV [of Crépy] ct of Valois, 48, 51
Raoul, ct of Vermandois, 116, 121–3, 159–60, 194
Raoul, k. of France, 21, 34
Raoul Glaber, 9, 16, 22–3, 45, 67, 71, 73
Raoul de Nesle, 280
Raoul de Presles, 283
Raoul Tortaire, 76
Raymond Trencavel, ct of Carcassonne, 212
Raymond III, ct of Toulouse, 59
Raymond IV [of Saint-Gilles] ct of Toulouse, 60, 105
Raymond V, ct of Toulouse, 58, 61–2, 125, 171
Raymond VI, ct of Toulouse, 57, 62, 133–4, 136, 171, 188–90
Raymond VII, ct of Toulouse, 58, 134, 136, 188–90, 209, 212–14, 252, 254–6, 258
Raymond, prince of Antioch, 123
Raymond-Berengar I, ct of Barcelona, 61
Raymond-Berengar II, ct of Barcelona, 61
Raymond-Berengar III, ct of Barcelona, 61
Raymond-Berengar IV, ct of Barcelona, 61
Raymond-Berengar, ct of Provence, 211–12, 215, 223, 256
Razès, 61
records, royal, 91–4, 134, 163–8, 240, 245–6, 278, 291–6
see also charters; finances, royal
Reims, city and county, 20–4, 45, 49, 88, 99–100, 118, 141, 151, 153, 172, 198, 261, 288
archbishopric and archbishops, 48, 86, 92, 133, 192, 196, 236–8; see also Adalbero; Arnulf; Gerbert; Henry; Manasses; Raoul; Renaud; William
coronations at, 66
schools, 21–2

relics of the passion, 176–7, 211, 234–5, 261–2
religious life and religious orders, 87, 100–2, 145–50, 226–9, 328
new orders, 145–50
opportunities for women, 148
see also Benedictines; canons; Cluny; Cistercians; Fontevrault; friars; Grandmont; Hospitallers; Prémontré; Saint-Victor; Templars
Renaud, arbp of Reims, 194
Renaud, bp of Langres, 106
Renaud [of Dammartin] ct of Boulogne, 129, 131–2, 208–9
Renaud, ct of Sens, 82
Rethel, 45, 198
revenues, royal, 164–8, 215–16, 240–3, 252, 291–6, 307–8, 313–14
accounts, 164–8, 240–3, 291–2
Louis VII's resources, 164–8
taxation of kingdom, 164, 243, 293–4, 302–4
taxation of French church, 282, 293, 313–14
taxation and political crisis, 304–5
see also aids, feudal; currency
Richard [the Justiciar] d. of Burgundy, 30
Richard I, d. of Normandy, 21, 36
Richard II, d. of Normandy, 36, 45
Richard III, d. of Normandy, 36, 69
Richard, earl of Cornwall, 208, 256, 276
Richard I [the Lionheart] k. of England, d. of Normandy and Aquitaine, ct of Anjou, 53, 57, 59, 113–14, 126, 128–30, 164, 166, 171–2, 179–83, 250
Riche, 93, 157
Richer, 22–3, 67, 70
Richilda, ctss of Flanders, 50
Richmond, earldom, 52
rights and customs, royal, 82–6
Rigord, 126–7, 135, 164, 167–8, 178, 187
Robert [of Torigny] abt of Mont-Saint-Michel, 154
Robert, arbp of Rouen, 187
Robert [Grosseteste] bp of Lincoln, 228
Robert I, ct of Artois, 207, 212, 214, 216–17, 248
Robert II, ct of Artois, 275–6, 280–1, 298–9
Robert III, ct of Artois, 283–4, 306

Robert, ct of Clermont-en Beauvaisis, 248, 250
Robert, ct of Dreux, 120, 122, 157, 195–6, 207, 250
Robert I [the Frisian] ct of Flanders, 50–1, 76, 96
Robert II, ct of Flanders, 96, 105, 169
Robert [of Béthune] ct of Flanders, 281, 284–5
Robert [of France] ct of Hainault, 190
Robert IV, ct of Meulan, 158
Robert, ct of Rochefort-en-Yvelines, 90
Robert I, d. of Burgundy, 30–1, 47, 72–3, 250
Robert ['the Strong'] d. of Francia, 89
Robert Curthose, d. of Normandy, 39–42, 51, 76–7, 105, 117–18
Robert ['the Magnificent' or 'the Devil'] d. of Normandy, 36–7, 47, 52, 73
Robert I, k. of France, 21
Robert II ['the Pious'] k. of France, 30–1, 45, 47, 50, 64–7, 69–73, 75, 82, 92–3, 102–3, 150, 273–4, 326
    character, 69–70
    reign, 69–72
Robert of Arbrissel, 147, 150
Robert of Bellême, 42
Robert le Bougre, 230, 234
Robert de Courson, 145
Robert de Courtenai, 185
Robert of France, 222
Robert Malet, 254
Robert of Melun, 143
Robert Mignon, 291
Robert of Molesme, 146
Robert de Sorbon, 234, 245
Robert of Torigny, 37
Robertines, 6, 13, 20–4, 30, 89–90, 100, 175
Rochefort, 79, 159; see also Guy; Robert
Roger of Mortemer, 39
Roger Mortimer, 285
Roger of Rozoy, 198
Roger of Wendover, 136
Rollo, d. of Normandy, 34, 36
Roman de Fauvel, 308
Roman empire, 1, 3–4, 6, 65
Romano Frangipani, 208–9, 255
Rome, 103, 197, 235–6, 315
    see also Roman empire

Rosny-sous-Bois, 225
Roucy, 45, 49
Rouen, 36, 131, 169–70, 175, 184, 186, 234, 252–3
    archbishops, 36, 133, 237, 303; see also Maurice; Odo; Robert; Theobald
Rouergue, 55, 258–9, 286
Roussillon, 221, 277
Rouvray, forest, 83
Royallieu, abbey, 313
Royan, 213
Royaumont, abbey, 211, 260–1, 313
Roye, 158
Rozala (Suzanne), q. of France, 71
Rudolph, k. of Burgundy, 47
Rudolph [of Habsburg] holy Roman emperor, 276
Rule of Saint Augustine, 105
Rule of Saint Benedict, 100, 105, 146
Rutebeuf, 155, 206, 222, 234, 264

Sack friars, 227, 234
sacral kingship, 24, 64–7, 174–9, 260–3, 308–10, 312–13
Saint-Antoine-des-Champs, 232
Saint-Basle, council, 68–9
Saint-Benoit-sur-Loire, see Fleury
Saint-Brisson, 157
Saint-Clair-sur-Epte, 34, 158
Saint-Denis
    abbey, 70, 100, 102, 107–8, 154, 158, 164, 169, 173–9, 191–2, 198–9, 206, 211, 223, 225, 260–1, 286, 312; abbots, see Matthew; Odo; Suger
    town, 82, 85, 143
Sainte-Catherine-de-la-Couture, 233
Sainte-Chapelle, see Paris
Saintes, 213
Saint-Eutrope, 19
Saint-Florentin, 48
Saint-Germain-des-Bois, 158
Saint-Germain-des-Prés, abbey, 11, 70, 88, 100, 102, 143, 153, 225
    abbot, see Irminon
Saint-Germain-en-Laye, 161
    royal chapel, 234, 261
Saint-Gilles, 57, 151, 254
    abbey, 56, 195

Saint-Jean-au-Bois, abbey, 191
Saint-Jean-d'Angély, 135–6
Saint-Jean-de-Losne, 125
Saint-Malo, 210
Saint-Martin-des-Champs, abbey, 19, 73, 76, 84, 87, 104–5, 107, 143
Saint-Martin-la-Garenne, 253
Saint-Maur-des-Fossés, 90
Saint-Nicholas-des-Bois, 244
Saintonge, 12, 52–3, 173, 258, 267, 276
Saint-Pierre-le-Moutier, 158
Saint-Pol, 133, 208, 215
Saint-Pons-de-Thomières, 57
Saint-Quentin, 45, 49, 128–30
Saint-Riquier, 51, 86, 159
Saint-Sardos, 285
Saint-Victor, abbey and its congregation, 115, 143, 148, 153, 191, 194–5, 232, 260
Saint-Wandrille, 237
Saladin tithe, 164
Salic law, 284
Samois, 157
Sancerre, 50, 211
Sancho, bp of Orléans, 107
Sancho, k. of Castile, 277
Sancia of Provence, 256
Savary of Mauléon, 188
Savigny, 195
Savigny, abbey and order, 147, 150
Sceaux-en-Gâtinais, 161
schools, 57, 144–5, 152–5
  see also Paris; Orléans
Sciarra Colonna, 316
science, 155
Sées, 186
Senlis, 22, 73, 79, 82–3, 142, 157, 162, 195, 235
  assembly at, 22–3
  bishopric and bishops, 86, 196; see also Warin
  family, see de la Tour
  Hôtel-Dieu, 165
  royal chapel, 262
  Saint-Maurice, 234
Sens, 30, 47, 66, 72–3, 82, 89, 125, 157–8, 162, 191, 236, 246
  archbishopric and archbishops, 86, 107, 116, 133, 207; see also Daimbert; Gautier; Guy; Henry; Philip

county and counts, 82, 102; see also Renaud
Saint-Pierre-le-Vif; abbot, see Arnaud
Saint-Rémi, 83
Sentences, 153
Septimania, see Toulouse
serfdom, 11–12, 218, 224–5, 237, 290
Sergius IV, p., 71
servientes, see footsoldiers
Sic et non, 153
Sicily, kingdom, 8, 38–9, 128–9, 219, 221–2, 238, 277, 279
  kings and queens, see Beatrice; Charles; Conrad; Frederick; James; Manfred; Tancred
Sicilian Vespers, 277
Simon [of Vermandois] bp of Tournai, 193
Simon [de Montfort] ct of Toulouse, 133–4, 136, 188, 209, 255
Simon [of Crépy] ct of Valois and Vexin, 48, 51, 76
Simon [de Montfort] earl of Leicester, 219–20, 267
Simon Barbette, 225
Simon of Brie, see Pope Martin IV
Simon of Nesle, 222
simony, 104
social and economic developments, 6–20, 137–45, 224–6, 285–6
  regional, 27–62
Soissons, 51, 82, 89, 151, 162, 172–3, 196
  bishopric and bishops, 86; see also Hugh
Saint-Médard, 45, 73, 93, 103, 191
Souvigny, 140
sovereignty, 247, 262–3, 266, 297
Spanish March, see Barcelona
Stephen Langton, arbp of Canterbury, 132
Stephen [of Senlis] bp of Paris, 192–3
Stephen, ct of Sancerre, 50
Stephen, ct of Troyes, 45
Stephen I, ct of Troyes and Meaux, 48, 73
Stephen [of Blois] k. of England, d. of Normandy, 43, 49, 53, 121
Stephen Boileau, 225
Stephen of Garlande, 106, 115, 159
Stephen Harding, 146
Stephen Longuéspée, 267
Stephen de Mornay, 299
Stephen of Muret, 149
Stephen of Paris, 118–19

Stephen of Tournai, 145
Stephen-Henry, ct of Blois and Meaux, 48, 170
Suger, abt of Saint-Denis, 16, 49, 64, 67, 91, 95, 107–8, 114–23, 137, 146, 153, 160, 169, 174–9, 192, 261, 309, 329
    work as royal councillor, 115
Summa theologica, 153
suzerainty, 94–7, 247, 262–3
Sylvester II, p., *see* Gerbert of Aurillac

taille, tallage, 84
Tancred [of Lecce] k. of Sicily, 129
Templars, knights, order, 149, 165, 195, 198, 230, 328
    grand master, *see* Jacques de Molay
    suppression of, 278, 282, 302, 317–20
Ternois, 158
Theobald, arbp of Rouen, 237
Theobald [the Trickster] ct of Blois, 21, 45
Theobald I, ct of Blois, 48, 73–4
Theobald III, ct of Blois, 50, 160
Theobald II, ct of Blois and Champagne, 43, 48–9, 71, 116, 118–19, 121, 159–60, 170, 263
Theobald III, ct of Champagne, 50, 170
Theobald IV, k. of Navarre, ct of Champagne, 50, 136, 154, 170, 189, 207–11
theology, 153
Theophano, holy Roman empress, 22, 68
Thérouanne, bishopric, 86
Thierry [of Alsace] ct of Flanders, 49, 51, 118–19, 169
Thomas Becket, arbp of Canterbury, 125, 127, 195, 317
Thomas, prior of Saint-Victor, 115
Thomas Aquinas (saint), 150, 153, 228, 316
Thomas of Marle, 115–16, 141, 156
Thouars, 54, 187, 208
    viscount, *see* Guy
Thourotte, 158
Tillières, 45, 182, 185
Tinchebray, battle, 42, 76
Tiron, abbey and order, 147
    abbot, *see* Bernard
tithes, 84
Tonnerre, Saint-Michel, 146
Tosny, 163
Toulonges, council, 20

Toulouse, city and county, 8, 13, 17, 54–62, 121, 125, 128, 171, 173, 209, 221, 227, 254–7, 259, 265, 288
    counts, *see* Alfonso; Amaury; Bertrand; Raymond; Simon; William
    countesses, *see* Constance; Joan
    political development, 59–62, 257–60
    see also Languedoc
Touraine, 48, 52, 128, 131, 267
Tournai, bishops and bishopric, 86, 158; *see also* Simon
Tournus, 7, 33, 158
    Saint-Philibert, 7, 33
Tours, 8, 45, 82, 84, 92, 128, 213
    archbishops and archbishopric, 52, 86, 236, 310; *see also* Archambaud
    Saint-Martin, 141, 191
    towns and trade, 6–9, 40, 57, 139–44, 224–5, 257, 286
    see also communes
Trainel, 48
Trencavel, 60, 62, 254
trial by battle, 244, 259
Trinitarian friars, 227, 234
trivium, 153
troubadours, 53, 57, 154
Troyes, city and county, 31, 43–50, 210
    bishops and bishopric, 86; *see also* Grimoard
    council of, 107
    counts and countess, *see* Constance; Herbert; Hugh; Odo; Stephen
truce of God, *see* peace of God
Tunis, 206, 222–3, 275
Turenne, 267
twelfth-century 'renaissance', 152–5

Unam sanctam, 316
universities, 57, 145, 152–5, 228–9, 328–9
    see also Paris
    Urban II, p., 77, 105, 107
    Urban IV, p., 221, 223, 236, 238–9
    Urgel, 221

Valenciennes, 300
Val-ès-Dunes, battle, 74
Valois, 89, 127–8, 158–9, 162, 248, 250
counts, *see* Charles; John; Raoul; Simon
countesses, *see* Catherine; Margaret

Valois kings of France, 303–4, 308; *see also* Philip VI

Varaville, 38, 74

vassalage, 14–18, 32–4, 39–40, 94–7, 116–17, 156–7, 168–73

Vauvert, priory, 233

Venaissin, county, 255, 258–9, 276, 320–1

Vendôme, 45, 48, 52, 89–90, 208
count, 210; *see also* Bouchard

Verberie, 88

Verdun, 21, 68

Verdun-sur-le-Doubs, 19

Vergy, lords, 33, 170

Vermandois, county and counts, 10, 51, 89, 127–9, 158–9, 162, 172, 304
see also Albert; Herbert; Hugh; Raoul

vernacular writing, 5–6, 154–5, 329

Vernon, 158
Hôtel-Dieu, 233

Vexin, county and counts, 36, 38, 51, 76, 78, 82, 89–90, 117–18, 123, 125–6, 129–30, 157, 162, 165, 169, 171, 175–6, 180
see also Walter

Vézelay, 142
abbey, 101, 122, 142, 173, 195

vicars, *vicarii*, *viguiers*, 55, 82

Victor IV, anti-p., 125

Victor II, p., 104, 194

Victorine canons, *see* saint-Victor

Vienne, council, 310, 319, 321

Viking invasions and settlements, 7–9, 23, 34

Villebéon, 276

Villemeux, 88, 102

'Villeneuve', 137

Villeneuve-le-Roi, 225

Vimeu, 89

Vincennes, 211
forest, 195, 205

Vincent of Beauvais, 177

Visigoths, 4

Vitalis, abt of Savigny, 147, 150

Viterbo, treaty, 221

Vitry, 48, 122, 194

Viviers, 300

Vouvant, 212

Vox in excelso, 319

Wace, 154

Waldensian heresy, 58, 152, 226

Waldo of Lyon, 152

Waldric, bp of Lyon, 141, 192

Walter, bp of Meaux, 106

Walter, ct of Vexin, 38

Walter the Chamberlain, 160–1

Walter Map, 119–20, 147, 153, 167, 182

warfare
and 'feudalism', 14
see armies, royal; castles; communes; footsoldiers; knights; mercenary troops; military service

Warin, bp of Senlis, 160–1, 179, 198, 208

Westminster abbey, 177, 262

William [aux Blanches-Mains] arbp of Rouen, 123, 196

William [of Champeaux] bp of Châlons, 191–2

William [of Auvergne] bp of Paris, 245

William I, ct of Arles, 71

William, ct of Arques, 39

William VI, ct of Auvergne, 117

William [of Dampierre] ct of Flanders, 216, 219

William, ct of Mortain, 42

William, ct of Nevers, 172

William [Taillefer] ct of Toulouse, 60

William [Aigret] d. of Aquitaine, 74–5

William [the Great] d. of Aquitaine, 11, 15, 47, 53, 65, 72, 74

William VIII, d. of Aquitaine, 53

William IX [the Young] d. of Aquitaine, 17, 19, 53, 59, 117, 170–1

William X [the Toulousain] d. of Aquitaine, 53, 59, 61, 121, 171

William (Longsword) d. of Normandy, 36

William [the Bastard or the Conqueror] k. of England, d. of Normandy, 28, 34, 37–40, 42, 52, 74–6, 89, 93, 96, 104, 179
character and achievements, 37–40

William II [Rufus] k. of England, d. of Normandy, 39–42, 76–7, 106

William [of Holland] k. of the Romans, 219

William Aetheling or Adelin of England, 37, 43, 118

William Baldrich, 283

William Bélibaste, 290

William the Breton, 126–7, 133, 135, 145, 177, 179, 182, 196, 198

William de Briouze, 131
William of Champeaux, 143
William Clito of Normandy, 16, 42, 51, 117–19
William of Conches, 143
William Flotte, 299
William de Garlande, 159
William of Jumièges, 40
William Marshall, 130, 185
William of Nangis, 230, 232, 261, 277
William of Nogaret, 257, 278–9, 282–3, 291, 298–9, 309, 316–18
William de Plaisians, 291, 318–19
William of Poitiers, 40, 96
William des Roches, 130, 183–4, 203 n100

William of Saint-Amour, 206, 229, 264
William of Saint-Pathus, 206, 230–5, 263, 312
William of Saint-Thierry, 121
William de Sanqueville, 309
William of Volpiano, 88
William of Warenne, 39
wills, royal, 198–9, 222, 248, 283
Wipo, 47
witchcraft and sorcery, 311–12

Yèvre-le-Châtel, 157
Yolande, ctss of Nevers and Bourbon, 222
Yolande of Dreux, 210